URISM PRINCIPLES AND PRACTICE

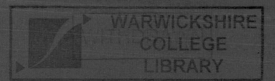
Visit the *Tourism: Principles and Practice*, **third edition**
Companion Website at **www.pearsoned.co.uk/cooper** to access
a rich resource of valuable learning materials for students, including:

- ■ Multiple choice questions for every chapter, with instant feedback
- ■ Annotated weblinks to relevant, specific Internet resources to facilitate in-depth independent research
- ■ Interactive online flashcards that allow the reader to check definitions against the key terms during revision
- ■ Searchable online glossary
- ■ A full compendium of part bibliographies for you to print out and take with you to the library

CHRIS COOPER

JOHN FLETCHER

ALAN FYALL

DAVID GILBERT

STEPHEN WANHILL

TOURISM
PRINCIPLES AND PRACTICE

THIRD EDITION

FT

Pearson Education Limited
Edinburgh Gate
Harlow
Essex CM20 2JE
England

and Associated Companies throughout the world

Visit us on the World Wide Web at:
www.pearsoned.co.uk

First published 1993
Second edition 1998
Third edition published 2005

Guided tour   xii
Case matrix   xiv
Authors and contributors   xviii
Preface   xx
Publisher's acknowledgements   xxiv
Abbreviations   xxvii

0   An Introduction to Tourism   2

Part One Tourism Demand   30

1   Managing Tourism Demand   34

2   Tourism Consumer Behaviour   50

3   Measuring Demand for Tourism   82

4   Tourism Demand Determinants and
    Forecasting   112

Part Two The Tourism Destination   146

5   The Economic Impact of Tourism   150

6   The Environmental Impact of
    Tourism   194

7   The Socio-cultural Impact of
    Tourism   224

8   Sustainable Tourism   258

9   Tourism and Development Planning   296

Part Three The Tourism Sector   338

10 Attractions   344

11 Accommodation   384

12 Intermediaries   420

13 Transportation   460

14 Public Sector and Policy   502

Part Four Marketing for Tourism   542

15 Marketing for Tourism – the
    Historical Roots   548

16 Managing Marketing for Tourism   572

17 Marketing Planning   606

18 Marketing Mix Applications   640

Part Five Developments in Tourism   696

19 Information Technology in Tourism   702

20 The Future of Tourism: Trends and
    Issues Beyond our Control   738

21 The Future of Tourism: Trends and
    Issues Within our Control   764

Glossary   790
Index   799

Guided tour   xii
Case matrix   xiv
Authors and contributors   xviii
Preface   xx
Publisher's acknowledgement   xxiv
Abbreviations   xxvii

0   An Introduction to Tourism   2
    Chris Cooper
    Introduction   3
    Learning outcomes   3
    Tourism – myths and realities   4
    The subject of tourism   6
    A tourism system   7
    Definitions of tourism   12
    Interrelationships and classifications   15
    Conclusion   22
    Self-check questions   23
    Essay questions   23
    Annotated further reading   23
    References cited   24

Part One Tourism Demand   30

1   Managing Tourism Demand   34
    Chris Cooper
    Introduction   35
    Learning outcomes   35
    Managing tourism demand   36
    Definitions of tourism demand   38
    Concepts of tourism demand   38
    Demand schedules   41
    Conclusion   43
    Self-check questions   44
    Essay questions   44
    Annotated further reading   44
    References cited   45

2   Tourism Consumer Behaviour   50
    Chris Cooper

    Introduction   51
    Learning outcomes   51
    The individual decision-making
       process   52
    The fundamentals of consumer
       behaviour and tourism   52
    Energisers and effectors of
       demand   54
    Roles and the decision-making
       process in tourism   60
    Models of consumer behaviour in
       tourism   64
    The buying decision process in
       tourism   65
    Conclusion   74
    Self-check questions   74
    Essay questions   74
    Annotated further reading   75
    References cited   75

3   Measuring Demand for Tourism   82
    Chris Cooper
    Introduction   83
    Learning outcomes   83
    Demand for international tourism   84
    Demand for domestic tourism   89
    Using tourism statistics   94
    Researching tourism markets: the
       value of research   95
    The research process   96
    Conclusion   104
    Self-check questions   105
    Essay questions   105
    Annotated further reading   105
    References cited   106

4   Tourism Demand Determinants
    and Forecasting   112
    Chris Cooper
    Introduction   113
    Learning outcomes   113

Determinants of demand for tourism 114
Suppressed demand for tourism 120
Macro determinants of tourism
  demand 120
STEP analysis 121
Forecasting tourism demand 127
Conclusion 136
Self-check questions 137
Essay questions 137
Annotated further reading 138
References cited 138

Part Two The Tourism Destination 146

5 The Economic Impact of Tourism 150
John Fletcher
Introduction 151
Learning outcomes 151
Overview 152
The generation of economic
  impacts by tourist spending 161
Leakages of expenditure out of the
  local economy 161
The measurement of economic
  impact 162
The multiplier concept 163
Types of multiplier 166
Methodological approaches 167
Weaknesses and limitations of
  multiplier models 174
The policy implications of multiplier
  analysis 180
Conclusion 183
Self-check questions 183
Essay questions 184
Annotated further reading 184
References cited and bibliography 185

6 The Environmental Impact of Tourism 194
John Fletcher
Introduction 195
Learning outcomes 195
Environmental impact 196

Environmental impact assessment 202
The EIA process 204
Environmental auditing 209
Environmental action programmes 210
Conclusion 218
Self-check questions 218
Essay questions 218
Annotated further reading 219
References cited and bibliography 220

7 The Socio-cultural Impact of Tourism 224
John Fletcher
Introduction 225
Learning outcomes 225
The nature of socio-cultural impacts
  of tourism 226
Approaches to the study of
  socio-cultural impacts of tourism 226
The tourism development process 229
The psychological basis of tourism
  development 230
The sociological basis of tourism
  development 231
Some general negative socio-
  cultural impacts of tourism 236
Some specific negative socio-
  cultural impacts of tourism 239
Some general positive socio-cultural
  impacts associated with tourism 246
Methods of measuring the
  socio-cultural impact of tourism 247
Conclusion 250
Self-check questions 251
Essay questions 251
Annotated further reading 252
References cited and bibliography 253

8 Sustainable Tourism 258
John Fletcher
Introduction 259
Learning outcomes 259
Historical background 260
Definitions of sustainability 261
Definitions of sustainable tourism 264

Sustainability of tourism 264
Sustainability as a strategy 284
Conclusion 286
Self-check questions 287
Essay questions 287
Annotated further reading 288
References cited and bibliography 289

9 Tourism and Development Planning 296
John Fletcher
Introduction 297
Learning outcomes 297
Tourism and economic development
  theories 298
Integrated planning and
  development 304
Development planning layers 314
The tourism development planning
  process 315
Tourism development planning:
  when it goes wrong 324
Conclusion 328
Self-check questions 329
Essay questions 329
Annotated further reading 329
References cited and bibliography 331

Part Three The Tourism Sector 338

10 Attractions 344
Alan Fyall and Stephen Wanhill
Introduction 345
Learning outcomes 345
The nature and purpose of
  attractions 346
Characteristics of attractions 347
Natural attractions 352
Man-made attractions 356
Developing attractions 357
Managing attractions 363
Conclusion 375
Self-check questions 375
Essay questions 376
Annotated further reading 376

References cited 377

11 Accommodation 384
Paul Barron
Introduction 385
Learning outcomes 385
Accommodation and the tourism
  product 386
Defining the accommodation sector 387
The distinctive nature of
  accommodation 397
The management of commercial
  accommodation 398
Sectoral overlap 399
Sector origins and influence of
  the United States 400
Quality issues and grading in the
  accommodation sector 402
The accommodation sector and
  environmental issues 408
Information technology and the
  accommodation sector 409
Human resources and the
  accommodation sector 410
Conclusion 411
Self-check questions 411
Essay questions 411
Annotated further reading 412
References cited 413

12 Intermediaries 420
Alan Fyall and Stephen Wanhill
Introduction 421
Learning outcomes 421
The nature of intermediation 422
The role of the retail agent 437
The role of the tour operator/
  wholesaler 441
Conclusion 453
Self-check questions 453
Essay questions 453
Annotated further reading 454
References cited 455

13 Transportation 460
John Westlake and Derek Robbins

Introduction 461
Learning outcomes 461
Transport as a component of the
  tourist product 462
Mode of transport 465
Components of the transport system 469
A competitive analysis 475
Political influences on transport for
  tourism 486
Regulation of competition 486
Future trends 489
Globalisation and integration 490
Conclusion 492
Self-check questions 492
Essay questions 493
Annotated further reading 493
References cited 494

14 Public Sector and Policy   502
Stephen Wanhill
Introduction 503
Learning outcomes 503
Public policy framework 504
Administrative framework 508
Impact of the public sector 514
Intervention policy 528
Conclusion 529
Self-check questions 530
Essay questions 530
Annotated further reading 530

**Part Four Marketing for
Tourism   542**

**15 Marketing for Tourism –
      the Historical Roots   548**
David Gilbert
Introduction 549
Learning outcomes 549
What is marketing? 550
The evolution of marketing 551
Definitions and concepts of
  marketing 553
The differences between marketing
  and selling 557

Different business philosophies 558
Marketing orientation 562
Conclusion 565
Self-check questions 565
Essay questions 566
Annotated further reading 567
References cited and bibliography 567

16 Managing Marketing for Tourism 572
David Gilbert
Introduction 573
Learning outcomes 573
The service product 574
Tourism products and risk 578
Planning the service encounter 579
Quality management 581
Management tasks 593
The adoption of a marketing
  orientation 594
Criticisms of the marketing concept 594
A societal marketing approach 598
Conclusion 599
Self-check questions 599
Essay questions 600
Annotated further reading 600
References cited and bibliography 601

17 Marketing Planning   606
David Gilbert
Introduction 607
Learning outcomes 607
What is marketing planning? 608
The marketing environment of the
  organisation 609
The purpose of the marketing plan 610
Successful planning 613
Structure of the marketing plan 615
Conclusion 634
Self-check questions 634
Essay questions 634
Annotated further reading 635
References cited and bibliography 636

18 Marketing Mix Applications   640
David Gilbert

Introduction   641
Learning outcomes   641
What is the marketing mix?   642
Product   644
Price   653
Promotion   662
Place (distribution)   671
The marketing mix revisited: are
    the four Ps sufficient?   680
Destination marketing   682
Conclusion   688
Self-check questions   688
Essay questions   688
Annotated further reading   689
References cited and bibliography   689

**Part Five Developments in
Tourism**   **696**

19   **Information Technology in
     Tourism**   **702**
     Dimitrios Buhalis
Introduction   703
Learning outcomes   703
Information communication
    technologies as a business tool   704
Tourism and information
    communication technologies   707
The utilisation of the Internet and
    ICTs by the tourism industry
    sectors   716
Conclusion – The contribution of
    ICTs to the future tourism industry   727
Self-check questions   728
Essay questions   728
Annotated further reading   728

References cited and bibliography   730

20   **The Future of Tourism: Trends
     and Issues Beyond our Control**   **738**
     Chris Cooper
Introduction   739
Learning outcomes   739
Approaching the future   740
The external environment for
    tourism: future drivers   742
Social drivers of change   743
Political drivers of change   744
Safety, security and risk   751
Climate change   755
Human resources for tourism   755
Conclusion   757
Self-check questions   758
Essay questions   758
Annotated further reading   758
References cited   759

21   **The Future of Tourism: Trends
     and Issues Within our Control**   **764**
     Chris Cooper
Introduction   765
Learning outcomes   765
Future drivers of the tourism system   766
Future tourism product markets   779
Conclusion   783
Self-check questions   783
Essay questions   784
Annotated further reading   784
References cited   785

Glossary   **790**
Index   **799**

xi

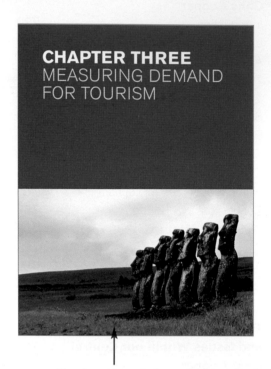

CHAPTER THREE
MEASURING DEMAND FOR TOURISM

The **Introduction** concisely describes the themes and issues explored in the chapter, so you can assess the importance of the chapter at this specific point in your study

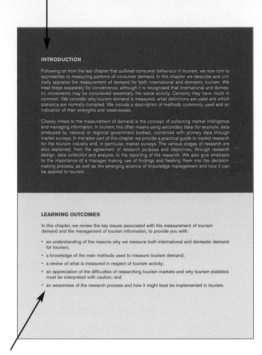

INTRODUCTION

Following on from the last chapter that outlined consumer behaviour in tourism, we now turn to approaches to measuring patterns of consumer demand. In this chapter we describe and critically appraise the measurement of demand for both international and domestic tourism. We treat these separately for convenience, although it is recognised that international and domestic movements may be considered essentially the same activity. Certainly they have much in common. We consider why tourism demand is measured, what definitions are used and which statistics are normally compiled. We include a description of methods commonly used and an indication of their strengths and weaknesses.

Closely linked to the measurement of demand is the concept of collecting market intelligence and managing information. In tourism, this often means using secondary data (for example, data produced by national or regional government bodies), combined with primary data through market surveys. In the latter part of this chapter we provide a practical guide to market research for the tourism industry and, in particular, market surveys. The various stages of research are also explained, from the agreement of research purpose and objectives, through research design, data collection and analysis, to the reporting of the research. We also give emphasis to the importance of a manager making use of findings and feeding them into the decision-making process, as well as the emerging science of knowledge management and how it can be applied to tourism.

LEARNING OUTCOMES

In this chapter, we review the key issues associated with the measurement of tourism demand and the management of tourism information, to provide you with:

- an understanding of the reasons why we measure both international and domestic demand for tourism;
- a knowledge of the main methods used to measure tourism demand;
- a review of what is measured in respect of tourism activity;
- an appreciation of the difficulties of researching tourism markets and why tourism statistics must be interpreted with caution; and
- an awareness of the research process and how it might best be implemented in tourism.

Stunning **colour photography** is used to theme each part around the key tourist destinations of a particular continent

Learning outcomes enable you to focus on what you should have achieved by the end of the chapter

CHAPTER FIVE THE ECONOMIC IMPACT OF TOURISM

MINI CASE STUDY 5.1
Tourism as a redistribution mechanism of wealth

Tourism has been lauded as an excellent vehicle for redistributing income from rich areas with abundant employment opportunities to poorer areas where employment opportunities are scarce. Consider domestic tourism in an economy such as France. The tendency is for people from the relatively affluent urbanised areas of, say, Paris to travel to less populated, poorer and more scenic rural areas. This results in a transfer of demand from the wealthier urban areas to the sparsely populated rural areas. Such transfers can stimulate investment and act as a catalyst for general economic development.

The same redistributive qualities of tourism have not been so apparent at the international level where the vast majority of tourism activity takes place between the wealthy industrialised economies. Tourism has done little to bridge the north–south divide. Indeed, it has been argued quite convincingly that tourism can exacerbate the income inequalities between rich countries such as the USA and less rich countries such as Kenya. The drive towards globalisation by some of the key elements of the tourism industry adds further substance to this belief.

The existence of economies of large-scale production, **comparative advantage** and the global nature of communications might suggest that any attempt to redress the imbalances will result in a misallocation of resources.

DISCUSSION QUESTIONS

1 Explain why tourism may act as an effective means of redistributing wealth at national level but often fails to do so at regional levels within an economy.

2 If the natural market forces are left to their own devices will tourism result in income redistribution that works in favour of the poorer segments of the population (nationally and internationally)?

3 What actions could be taken to encourage tourism to assist in redressing income inequalities without damaging the development of the industry?

In terms of the discussions in this chapter, the multiplier models are used to determine the economic impact of changes in tourist spending on the income, employment, government revenue and foreign exchange of any economy. They can also be used to identify opportunity costs by assessing the effects of comparable changes in other industries. TSAs, on the other hand, offer a way of improving the estimation of the significance of tourism to an economy.

The concept of tourism satellite accounts is based on the need for a framework that will provide consistency over time and between countries and comparability between industries when calculating the significance of tourism to an economy. Providing the extensive data needs can be met with timely and accurate data the accounts should do much to promote the importance of tourism globally and within countries. There have been some serious concerns however, that some tourism

Mini case studies concentrate on specific destinations or organisations to illustrate theories of tourism in practice

Key terms are highlighted throughout the text: definitions are listed within a full Glossary at the back of the book, creating a particularly useful revision tool

Each chapter ends with **Self-check questions** for you to test your understanding and track your progress

If you want to explore topics further, **Essay questions** encourage stimulating debates and class exercises

Each chapter is supported by an annotated **Further reading** section and a list of **References**, both of which direct your independent study to valuable printed and electronic sources

Longer, colourfully illustrated and up-to-date **Case studies** at the end of every chapter consolidate the major themes by encouraging you to apply what you have learnt to real-life tourism scenarios

Extensive **Multiple choice questions** with helpful feedback on incorrect answers, help develop your subject knowledge and improve your understanding. See **www.pearsoned.co.uk/cooper** for this and other useful resources

Mini	Major	Case No.	Case Title	Destination	Page
●		0.1	Characteristics of Elements of the Eco-tourism System		11
●		0.2	Tourism and Mobilities		14
	●	0.1	Tourism as an Agent of Poverty Alleviation	Asia	25
●		1.1	Contrasting Approaches to the Responsible Consumption of Tourism		37
●		1.2	The Gravity Model	Australia/Spain	40
	●	1.1	Indicators of Tourism Demand: Travel Propensity		46
●		2.1	Applying Plog's Theory of Travel Motivation	Blackpool, UK	58
●		2.2	Are Models of Consumer Behaviour in Tourism a Waste of Effort?		72
	●	2.1	The Impact of September 11, 2001 Terrorist Attacks on the USA on Tourism Consumer Behaviour	New York, USA	77
●		3.1	An Example of Household Surveys: The United Kingdom Tourism Survey	UK	92
●		3.2	Comparing Data Collection Procedures		100
	●	3.1	Managing Tourism Information	Singapore	107
●		4.1	Domestic Age and Tourism Demand		117
●		4.2	The Demographic Transition and Tourism		123
	●	4.1	World Patterns of Demand for Tourism		139
●		5.1	Tourism as a Redistribution Mechanism of Wealth	USA/Kenya	160

xiv

Mini	Major	Case No.	Case Title	Destination	Page
●		5.2	Tourism's Contribution to Global Prosperity		181
	●	5.1	Tourism and Day Visitors to Gibralter	Gibraltar	187
●		6.1	Tourism and the Environment: Enemies or Allies?	Kenya	200
●		6.2	Eco-tourism in Thailand: The Thin End of the Wedge?	Thailand	214
	●	6.1	Tourism Development in Fragile Environments: The Arctic	The Arctic	222
●		7.1	Income Inequality in Taman Negara National Park, Malaysia	Malaysia	238
●		7.2	The Trouble with TOURISM WITHOUT AIDS	Africa	240
	●	7.1	Udaipur as a Learning City	Rajasthan	254
●		8.1	Sustainable Development Networks (SDNs) for Grenada	Grenada	277
●		8.2	Sustainability and Accreditation Schemes in Costa Rica	Costa Rica	283
●		8.3	User-Friendly Interactive Planning Software – A Schematic Presentation of a Tourism Planning Tool Kit		286
	●	8.1	Encouraging Sustainable Tourism: Chanting the Eco-tourism Mantra in India	Sikkim, India	291
●		9.1	Can We Turn Back the Clocks in Benidorm?	Benidorm, Spain	305
●		9.2	How Do You Plan for the Unexpected? Turkey 1999	Turkey	322
	●	9.1	A Three-year Tourism Strategy for New Zealand, 2003–2006	New Zealand	332
●		10.1	Functional Zoning Applied by Parks Canada	Canada	348
●		10.2	Snoasis	Suffolk, UK	361
	●	10.1	Legoland	Billund, Denmark/ Windsor, UK	378

Mini	Major	Case No.	Case Title	Destination	Page
●		11.1	Le Meridien		390
●		11.2	Scotland's Commended Hotels	Scotland	404
	●	11.1	Shangri-La Hotels	Hong Kong	414
●		12.1	Thomas Cook AG	UK	424
●		12.2	Expedia		435
	●	12.1	My Travel Group plc		456
●		13.1	Differences in Travel Time and Modes of Travel – Thailand	Thailand	467
●		13.2	The Expansion of the Low-cost Concept in Airlines	Europe/Australasia	483
	●	13.1	The Cruise Ship Industry	Caribbean	495
●		14.1	The World Tourism Organization (WTO)		505
●		14.2	FONATUR: Mexico	Mexico	520
	●	14.1	Tourism Project Assistance from the European Union	Europe	532
●		15.1	The Risks of Tourism have Affected the Operation of Cruise Ships	Trinidad/Tobago	554
●		15.2	A New Departure for the easyJet Business Model		560
	●	15.1	Airline Strategies in Times of Adversity		569
●		16.1	The SAS Experience	Scandinavia	589
●		16.2	Pollution Problems of Aircraft	UK	596
	●	16.1	Scottish Tourism: Excerpts from the Progress Report 2003/4	Scotland	602
●		17.1	Tourism in a Postenchanted World		612
●		17.2	Targeting Different Segments	Manchester, UK	630
	●	17.1	Disneyland® Resort Paris	Disneyland® Resort Paris	637
●		18.1	An Assessment of Retail Travel Agents	China	678

Mini	Major	Case No.	Case Title	Destination	Page
●		18.2	Tourism: Culture Tool to Lift the Neglect	Bilbao, Spain/ Newcastle, UK	685
	●	18.1	Nisbet Plantation Hotel and Relationship Marketing	Nevis, Caribbean	691
●		19.1	Lastminute.com: from Reservation System to Lifestyle Portal		714
●		19.2	Hotel Property Management Systems: Fidelio		722
	●	19.1	Global Distribution System: Amadeus		733
●		20.1	Tourism SMEs Fight Back	Austria	748
●		20.2	Destination Recovery: The Bali Bombings	Bali	753
	●	20.1	The Effect of Climate Change on Australia's Great Barrier Reef	Australia	760
●		21.1	The Experience Economy		768
●		21.2	Visitor Management	China	773
	●	21.1	Space Adventures	Space	786

AUTHORS

Professor Chris Cooper is Foundation Professor and Head of the School of Tourism and Leisure Management at The University of Queensland, Australia. He has a PhD from University College London and worked in market planning and research for the tourism industry before entering higher education. He has authored a number of leading tourism texts and is co-editor of *Current Issues in Tourism*, with C. Michael Hall. Chris Cooper has worked closely with the World Tourism Organization helping to raise the profile and standards of tourism education globally. He has acted as a consultant and researcher in every region of the world.

Professor John Fletcher is Professor of Tourism and Head of Bournemouth University Graduate School, as well as Director of the International Centre for Tourism and Hospitality Research and Editor-in-Chief of the *International Journal of Tourism Research*. John has undertaken tourism development and impact studies throughout the Caribbean, the South Pacific, the Indian Ocean and across Europe on behalf of national governments, local authorities and international agencies. He has led research on projects funded by the EU, USAID, WTO, WTTC and international development banks. In his efforts to improve the accessibility of tourism impact research, he has pioneered the development of interactive economic and environmental impact models and has written more than 130 articles, official reports and book chapters on the topic of tourism impacts. He has also written on the place of tourism in national accounts and presented to the British Association for the Advancement of Science. John is a member of the International Academy for the Study of Tourism and a Fellow of the Tourism Society.

Dr David Gilbert is Professor of Marketing at the School of Management, Surrey University. He has 21 years' academic experience in higher education and over 8 years' operational marketing experience for the private sector, having worked as a Product Manager and as a Marketing Manager for Rank Leisure. He specialises in the teaching of marketing related to: relationship marketing, consumer behaviour, market research, research methods and the functions of marketing management and was the founder of the MSc in Tourism Marketing at Surrey. Alongside his academic duties, he has worked with several government and private organisations and consultancies on tourism project work. He was the Research Director of the Thomas Cook Research Centre at the University of Surrey and has in-depth knowledge of marketing in relation to the service industry.

Professor Stephen Wanhill is Professor of Tourism Research, School of Services Management at Bournemouth University. He is tourism consultant to a number of UK planning and management consulting firms and has undertaken a wide range of tourism development strategies, tourism impact assessments, project studies and lecture programmes, both in the UK and worldwide, covering some 45 countries. He has written extensively on public sector intervention in tourism, tourism impact methodology and project appraisal and development in academic journals and edited books. He acted as tourism policy advisor to the Select Committee on Welsh Affairs, House of Commons and has been a board member of the Wales Tourist Board with responsibilities for the development and research divisions. Stephen is Editor of *Tourism Economics* and Editorial Board Member of *The Service Industries Journal*, *Tourism Management*, *International Journal of Tourism Research* and *Journal of Travel Research*.

Alan Fyall is Reader in Tourism Management in the International Centre for Tourism and Hospitality Research at Bournemouth University. Alan has authored over 50 published articles in the fields of marketing and tourism and is Resource Editor for *Annals of Tourism Research* and Consulting Editor for the *International Journal of Tourism Research*.

He has also co-edited the book *Managing Visitor Attractions: New Directions* and co-authored the book *Tourism Marketing: A Collaborative Approach.* Alan has conducted teaching and research in many countries around the world including most member states of the EU, the United States, India, Malaysia, and Australia. In the UK, Alan has undertaken a large number of marketing and tourism projects with a variety of organisations, which include the Commonwealth Policy Studies Unit, London Development Agency and British Tourist Authority.

CONTRIBUTORS

Paul Barron is a Senior Lecturer in hospitality management in the School of Tourism and Leisure Management at The University of Queensland, Australia. Paul has extensive hospitality management experience and after completing his first qualification in hotel management worked for prestigious hotel companies such as Hilton. Paul commenced his academic career at Glasgow Caledonian University during which time he completed an MSc in Personnel Management at The University of Strathclyde. Paul has authored over 30 articles in the field of hospitality management education and is currently Executive Editor of *The Journal of Hospitality and Tourism Management.* Paul has recently been awarded his PhD which examined international students' educational experiences in Australian universities.

Dr Dimitrios Buhalis holds an MSc and PhD from the University of Surrey. He is currently Course Leader, MSc in eTourism, Director of the Centre for eTourism Research (CeTR) at the School of Management, University of Surrey, UK. Dimitrios is also Adjunct Professor at the MBA in Hospitality Management at the Institut de Management Hotelier International (Cornell University-Ecole Superieure des Sciences Economiques et Commerciales ESSEC) in Paris. He has written several books including *eTourism: Strategic Information Technology for Tourism*; *Distribution Channels of Tourism*; and *Managing Alliances in the Global Hospitality and Tourism Industry.* He served as Chairman of the Scientific Committee of the ENTER '98, '99, and 2000 conferences, as well as ENTER Destination Chair for 2002 and ENTER Overall Chair in 2003. He is the Vice President of the International Federation for Information Technology for Travel and Tourism (IFITT) and the Chairman of Events of the Tourism Society. He regularly works closely with the World Tourism Organization, the World Travel and Tourism Council and the European Commission on Tourism and Technology issues.

Derek Robbins trained as a transport planner and is currently Senior Lecturer in Transport and Tourism in the School of Services Management at Bournemouth University where he has held a variety of management posts. He has developed specialised undergraduate and postgraduate units in transport on tourism degrees and published widely on the relationship between transport and tourism. Specific research interests include cruise shipping, deregulation of the bus and coach industry, transport impacts of tourists in destination areas, cycle tourism and sustainable transport policies. He is an active member of the Institute of Logistics and Transport and has undertaken consultancy for a number of bodies including the EU and the Lulworth Estate.

John Westlake is Professor of Tourism Management in the School of Services Management at Bournemouth University, United Kingdom. He is involved in teaching of masters students and supervising doctoral students. He is active in undertaking research and publishing in academic journals and is on the Editorial Board of the journals *Tourism Economics* and the *International Journal of Tourism Research.* His interests are in the planning for tourism, transport for tourism and tourism and hospitality education where he has been active in publishing and undertaking project work in these areas. John has undertaken work for the World Tourism Organization and has been involved in European Union funded projects. He is widely travelled, especially in the Asia Pacific region and maintains close contact with institutions and academic practitioners in many parts of the world.

xix

Welcome to the third edition of *Tourism: Principles and Practice*. We have completely revised and substantially restructured this edition to provide the reader with far more practical applications by means of extensive case studies, discussion and essay questions, clear learning objectives and a more colourful and user-friendly format. This re-engineering of the text is in response to feedback from our readers and adopters, and is a reflection of the growing maturity of tourism as a subject area in higher education.

THE FEATURES OF THIS BOOK

These changes build upon the previous two editions, while at the same time this new edition retains many of the key philosophies that made the earlier editions so successful. In a changing and turbulent environment for tourism, we offer readers the fundamental and underlying principles with which to approach the study of tourism, contributing a complete framework that effectively integrates theory and practice, and which we feel, stands the test of changing times. Of course we have updated the text to take into account events such as September 11, 2001 and growing concerns for the safety and security of tourists.

While the basic structure of this book follows earlier editions, we have updated, refined and improved all subject areas, added substantial additional material and introduced some important features to enhance the use of the book in the classroom. These include:

- The introduction of **Chapter Learning Objectives** at the beginning of every chapter to orientate the reader and to focus his or her mind in respect of the key concepts that underpin each chapter in the book.

- The inclusion of **Self-check Questions and Essay Questions** at the end of each chapter. These are designed to help the reader consolidate their knowledge as they work through the book and to draw out key contemporary issues and apply the theoretical content of the chapter to industry practice.

- The use of a **Major Case Study** at the end of each chapter to allow the reader to link the theory of the chapter to contemporary issues and practice. Each of these case studies with accompanying questions has been specially selected for this book.

- The use of two **Mini Case Studies** embedded within the chapters, again to draw out examples of how the material relates to the real world and to current issues. Discussion questions are provided at the end of each case study.

- The identification of key texts and web-based material in a section of **Annotated Further Reading** at the end of each chapter. Here we have provided a short description of the key sources to guide the reader though the increasingly complex maze of tourism literature. In addition, each section of the book has a bibliography which will act as the first port of call for assignments and presentations and provides an opportunity for guided specialised investigation where core concepts are reviewed in more detail and from which the user may derive a deeper understanding.

- The introduction of **Photographs** to bring the material to life and the use of **Colour** in the presentation of the text to make the book more attractive and easier to use.

- The addition of a **Glossary of Key Terms** to guide the reader through the specialist terminology in the chapters.

THE STRUCTURE OF THIS BOOK

Leiper's model of the tourism system, presented in Chapter 0, entitled 'An Introduction to Tourism', provides the basic format for the book. In this first chapter we clearly define the elements of the system and our approach, and provide a case study analysing the issues surrounding one of the most important innovations in tourism – the use of tourism to alleviate poverty. The main body of the book is then structured around five key headings:

- Part One   Tourism Demand
- Part Two   The Tourism Destination
- Part Three   The Tourism Sector
- Part Four   Marketing for Tourism
- Part Five   Developments in Tourism

Part One

Part One of the book examines all aspects of tourism demand in detail. We review the various concepts of demand, examine models of consumer behaviour and the decision-making process as it relates to tourism, look at factors that will influence demand for tourism at individual and global levels and analyse the techniques and approaches used to measure and forecast demand. We have written major case studies for this section that include new ideas of knowledge management for tourism data, the impact of September 11, 2001 upon travel behaviour and an analysis of patterns of tourism demand across the globe.

Part Two

Part Two of the book is focused upon the destination and how tourism interacts with the economy, the environment and the people. The impacts of tourism are explored along with the various techniques that have been used to measure them. Case studies have been selected to illustrate the diverse issues relating to tourism and its development in a wide range of circumstances. Comparisons and contrasts are also made between the different impact tools available to tourism researchers. Having put down the foundations for the study of tourism's impacts, the concept of sustainability is examined in some detail concluding with a chapter that sets out the parameters of planning and development.

Part Three

It will be readily appreciated that tourism is not a single product but an amalgam of different goods and services offered by a variety of suppliers, made up largely of small independent operators from a diffuse range of industries as defined by common standard industrial classification systems that are used by national statistical offices around the world. This part explains, under broad headings, the characteristics of the various suppliers meeting the needs of the tourist and their mode of operation. Each chapter aims to show the principles governing the behaviour of the relevant suppliers and to provide examples of good practice that can be adopted elsewhere. Being fragmented in this way, tourism needs leadership and partnership in order to thrive, so that the product on offer matches the overall demand pattern expressed by the tourist. In most countries, the responsibility for carrying out this function falls upon the public sector, through the funding of a national tourist office to take on the role of both catalyst and a coordinator.

Part Four

Part Four offers an understanding of the process and application of marketing to the unique characteristics of tourism. In this part, we provide a comprehensive overview of the management of tourism marketing including the strategies and tools that may be applied to deliver the tourism product effectively and efficiently to satisfy the tourism consumer. The chapters will anchor the concepts of marketing in the historical roots of its development and establish why services' marketing is different. Tourism as a service process is covered with major exposure of services and quality concepts. Marketing planning has its own designated chapter with an expanded section on strategic aspects as well as tactical and strategic marketing planning procedures in respect of the tourism product. We review the benefits and purposes of marketing planning, consider the structure of a marketing plan and explore the implications of neglecting tourism marketing planning. The final chapter in this part relates to the marketing mix. This is a key strategic tool which is integral to achieving the marketing planning objectives. Thus, this revised Part Four presents a more complete approach to the marketing of tourism, together with a comprehensive review of key issues and considerations.

Part Five

Part Five highlights issues that will influence the future of tourism. This section comprises three chapters: information technology and the future of tourism; a chapter analysing the future drivers of the external environment within which tourism will operate; and a final chapter that examines future trends within the tourism sector. Part Five is instrumental in consolidating the strands and themes discussed throughout the book and presents them in a format that demonstrates the likely future development of all aspects of the tourism system. A wide range of influences are reviewed and assessed, together with an evaluation of impacts on both tourism products and tourists. In this section we have resisted the hype of futurologists and instead provide a disciplined framework with which to analyse tourism futures, including cases on IT applications in tourism, global warming and the realities of space tourism.

OVERVIEW

The philosophy behind this book remains the same as earlier editions: namely to provide a comprehensive text which can be used for both teaching and learning about tourism. We have many people to thank for the fact that this book has been produced. Alan Fyall has joined the author team to work on the tourism sector chapters; Paul Barron, Dimitrios Buhalis, Derek Robbins and John Westlake each contributed chapters reflecting his own expertise; and David Cox and Matthew Walker at Pearson Education have been professional and highly supportive editors. Also, Anita Atkinson, who has been an excellent editor, and Adam Renvoize, who is responsible for the amazing look and format of this new edition, have our thanks.

Chris Cooper, John Fletcher, Alan Fyall, David Gilbert and Stephen Wanhill

Companion Website and Instructor resources
Visit **www.pearsoned.co.uk/cooper** to find valuable online resources

For students

■ Learning objectives for each chapter

■ Multiple choice questions for every chapter, with instant feedback

■ Annotated weblinks to relevant, specific Internet resources to facilitate in-depth independent research

■ Interactive online flashcards that allow the reader to check definitions against the key terms during revision

■ Searchable online glossary

■ A full compendium of part bibliographies for you to print out and take with you to the library

For instructors

■ Customisable PowerPoint slides, including key figures and tables from the main text

■ A fully updated Instructor's Manual, including sample answers for all question material in the book

Also: The Companion Website provides the following features:

■ Search tool to help locate specific items of content

■ E-mail results and profile tools to send results of quizzes to instructors

■ Online help and support to assist with website usage and troubleshooting

For more information please contact your local Pearson Education sales representative or visit **www.pearsoned.co.uk/cooper**

We are grateful to the following for permission to reproduce copyright material:

Table 0.2 from *Recommendations on Tourism Statistics* (WTO/UNSTAT, 1994), Table 4.9 from *Tourism 2020 Vision: Global Forecast and Profiles of Market Segments* (WTO 2001), Table 4.10 based on WTO data, www.world-tourism.org, Tables 5.1 and 5.2 based on *Yearbook of Tourism Statistics* (WTO, 1988, 1992, 1997, 2003), Table 5.3 derived from Euromonitor, International Monetary Fund, International Financial Statistics, www.world-tourism.org, Table 5.4 derived from *WTO Tourism Highlights 2003*, www.world-tourism.org, Table 9.2 from www.world-tourism.org (WTO, 1980), Table 12.5 (adapted) and Figure 12.2 from *Tourism in the Age of Alliances, Mergers and Acquisitions* (WTO, 2002), Table 20.1 from *Climate Change and Tourism* (WTO, 2003), Figures 3.1 and 3.2 from *Data Collection and Analysis for Tourism Management, Marketing and Planning*, Madrid, World Tourism Organization (WTO, 2000), reproduced by permission of the World Tourism Organization, Madrid; Table 0.3 from *Tourism Analysis: A Handbook*, Harlow, Longman, (Smith, S. L. J. 1989), Tables 12.1, 12.2 and 12.3 based on *eTourism: Information Technology for Strategic Tourism Management*, Harlow, Pearson Education (Buhalis, D. 2003), Figures 2.8 and 2.9 from *Tourism: Economic, Physical and Social Impacts*, 2nd edition, London, Addison Wesley Longman, (Mathieson, A. and Wall, G. 1982), reproduced with permission of Pearson Education Limited; Table 2.1 adapted from *Consumer Behaviour*, 3rd edition, Englewood Cliffs, NJ, Prentice Hall (Solomon, M. R. 1996); Table 4.1 from 'The determinants of tourism demand: a theoretical perspective,' pp. 79–98 in D. Ioannides and K. Debbage (eds) *The Economic Geography of the Tourist Industry*, London, Routledge (Uysal, M. 1998); Table 4.2 adapted from *The Stages of Economic Growth*, Cambridge, Cambridge University Press (Rostow, W. W. 1959); Table 7.1 from *Hosts and Guests: The Anthropology of Tourism*, 2nd Edn, edited by Valerie Smith. Reprinted by permission of the University of Pennsylvania Press; Tables 13.3 and 13.5 from www.crusing.org, 2004, reprinted by permission of Cruise Lines International Association; Table 19.2 adapted from 'Where next for DDS?' *Airline Business*, March, pp. 34–43 (Field and O'Toole, 2004) and Table 19.5 from 'Value proposition,' *Airline Business*, March, pp. 44–5 (Clarke, 2004), reprinted from *Airline Business* magazine, www.airlinebusiness.com, with permission of Reed Business Information Limited; Table 19.4 adapted from 'Hilton Hotels Corporation announces record-breaking month in February 2004 for Hilton Family Brand website bookings,' Hilton Hotels Corporation News Release 13.4.04, http://www.coprorate-ir.net/ireye/ir_site.zhtml?ticker=HLT&script=412&layout=9&item_id=514223, reprinted with permission, Hilton Hospitality, Inc; Table 21.1 from *The Experience Economy*, Boston, MA, Harvard Business School Publishing, reprinted by permission of *Harvard Business School Publishing*, copyright 1999 by the Harvard Business School Publishing Corporation, all rights reserved (Pine, J. B. and Gilmore, J. H. 1999); Table for Mini Case Study 18.1 from 'D. Blastland – Managing Director of First Choice Holidays 'Can tour operators and travel agents survive,' January 2004, reproduced with permission of First Choice Holidays and Flights (CIMtIG, 2004); Figure 0.1 adapted and reprinted from *Annals of Tourism Research*, Vol. 8, No. 1, J. Jafari and J. Ritchie, 'Towards a framework for tourism education,' pp. 13–34, copyright 1981, Figure 0.4 reprinted from *The Geography of Travel and Tourism*, B Boniface and C Cooper, copyright 2001, Figures 2.4, 10.1 and Table 4.2 reprinted from *The Geography of Travel and Tourism*, B Boniface and C Cooper, copyright 1977, Figures 10.2, 10.5, 10.6 and 10.7 reprinted from *Managing Visitor Attractions: New Directions*, in A Fyall, B Garrod and A Leask (eds), The nature and purpose of visitor attractions, pp. 5–15, copyright 2003 (Leask, A 2003), Table 2.1 reprinted from *Consumer Behaviour in Tourism*, J. Swarbrooke and S. Horner, copyright 1999, with permission from Elsevier; Figure 0.1 adapted from *Tourism: Principles*,

Practices, Philosophies, New York, Wiley, copyright © 1990, this material is used by permission of John Wiley & Sons, Inc. (McIntosh, R. W. and Goeldner, C. R. 1990); Figures 0.2 and 0.3 from *Tourism Systems*, Massey University Department of Management Systems Occasional Paper 2, Auckland, Massey University, reproduced with permission of Professor Neil Leiper (Leiper, N. 1990); Figures 1.1 and 1.2 from 'Demand for accommodation,' pp. 23–44 in R. Kotas (ed.) *Managerial Economics for Hotel Operation*, Guildford, Surrey University Press, reproduced with permission of Professor S. Wanhill (Wanhill, S. R. C. and Airey, D. W. 1980); Figure 2.3 reproduced with permission of Professor David C. Gilbert from 'A study of factors of consumer behaviour related to overseas holidays from the UK,' Ph.D. thesis, University of Surrey, Guildford (Gilbert, D. C. 1992); Figure 2.10 first published by Henry Stewart Publications in *Journal of Vacation Marketing*, Vol. 2, No. 2, pp. 109–22 (Moscada, G., *et al.* 1996); Figure 3.4 from *Kennismanagement Inrichting en besturing Van Kennisintensieve Organisaties*, Schiedam, Scriptum (Weggeman, M. C. D. P. 1997); Figure 4.3 from 'Demand forecasting in tourism and recreation, pp. 4–32 in C. P. Cooper (ed.) *Progress in Tourism, Recreation and Hospitality Management*, Vol. 1, London, Belhaven (Witt, S. F. and Martin, C. A. 1989), Figure 9.2 from *Progress in Tourism, Recreation and Hospitality Management*, Chichester, Wiley (Cooper, C. 1991), copyright 1989, 1991, © John Wiley & Sons Limited, reproduced with permission; Figure 7.1 from 'Patterns of the development of tourism in mountain environments,' *Geojournal*, Vol. 27, No. 1, pp. 87–96, reproduced with permission of Springer and Dr Stanley C. Plog (Plog, S. C. 1977); Figure 12.4 from 'Travel retailing: 'switch selling' in the UK,' in D. Buhalis and E. Laws (eds) *Tourism Distribution Channels: Practices, Issues and Transformations*, London, Continuum, reproduced by permission of Thomson Publishing Services (Hudson, S. *et al.* 2001); Figure 13.1 adapted from *Business World Travel*, May 1997, reproduced with permission of Business Travel World; Figure 16.4 from *Strategic Management and Marketing in the Service Sector*, Helsinki, Swedish School of Economics and Business Administration, reproduced with permission of Dr Christian Grönroos (Grönroos, C. 1982); Figure 16.5 from 'A conceptual model of service quality and its implications for future research,' *Journal of Marketing*, Vol. 49, No. 4, pp. 41–50 (Parasuraman, A., *et al.*, 1985), Figure 18.14 from 'Marketing strategies and organization structures for service firms,' pp. 47–51 in J. Donnelly and W. R. George (eds) *Marketing of Services*, Chicago, IL: American Marketing Association (Booms, B. H. and Berry, L. L. 1981), reproduced with permission of the American Marketing Association; Figure 18.4 reprinted with permission of The Free Press, a Division of Simon & Schuster Adult Publishing Group, from *Managing Brand Equity: Capitalizing on the Value of a Brand Name* by David A. Aaker, copyright © 1991 by David A. Aaker, all rights reserved, Figures 17.3 and 18.12 adapted with the permission of The Free Press, a Division of Simon & Schuster Adult Publishing Group, from *Competitive Strategy: Techniques for Analyzing Industries and Competitors* by Michael E. Porter, copyright © 1980, 1998 by The Free Press, all rights reserved; Figure 19.1 reprinted with permission from 'Trends in European internet distribution or travel and tourism services,' www.crt.dk/trends, 6 September 2004, © Carl H. Marcussen and Centre for Regional and Tourism Research, Denmark; Figure 21.2 from *Tourism, Technology and Competitive Strategies*, Oxford, CABI Publishing (Poon, A. 1993); Major Case Study 11.1 based on www.shangri-la.com and Shangri-La Hotels and Resorts and Traders Hotels logos reproduced with permission of Shangri-La International Hotel Management Limited.

Photograph 1.2 Edward Webb/Rex Features; Photograph 2.2 Jeff Pappas/Rex Features; Photograph 3.1 © Reed Kaestner/CORBIS; Photograph 4.2 Jeremy Sutton Hibbert/Rex Features; Photograph 5.1 Travelex PLC; Photograph 6.1 Lehtikuva Oy/Rex Features; Photograph 7.2 Tim Rooke/Rex Features; Photograph 8.1 ECOCLUB.com – International Ecotourism Club; Photograph 9.1 © Owen Franken/CORBIS; Photograph 9.2 of Dinarobin Hotel Golf & Spa, courtesy of Beachcomber Hotels; Photograph p.344 © Jose Fuste Raga/CORBIS; Photograph 10.1 from Newscast; Photograph 10.2 from Grand Canyon National Park; Photograph 10.3 courtesy of LEGOLAND Windsor, The LEGO Company; Photograph 11.1 courtesy of Jumeirah International; Photograph 11.1 © Dave G. Houser/CORBIS; Photograph 12.1 Advertising Archive;

xxv

Photograph 12.2 courtesy of Expedia.co.uk; Photograph 13.1 Terminal 5/BAA/Artist's Impression courtesy of BAA; Photograph 13.2 courtesy of Cunard Line; Photograph 14.1 © In Visu/CORBIS; Photograph 14.2 courtesy of European Parliament. ASP: AEL, avenue des Courses 15 1050 Brussels; PHS: Association des architects du CIC, rue du Prince royal 19, 1050; Photograph 15.1 Advertising Archive; Photograph 15.2 courtesy of easyJet; Photograph 16.1 James Davis Photography/Alamy; Photograph 16.2 courtesy of Scream.co.uk; Photograph 17.1 (left) Richard Young/Rex Features; Photograph 17.1 (right) © JFPI Studios, Inc/CORBIS; Photograph 17.2 James Boardman/Rex Features; Photograph 18.2 © David Samuel Robbins/CORBIS; Photograph 19.1 screenshot of lastminute.com UK homepage, http://engb.lastminute.com, 6 September 2004, reproduced with permission of lastminute.com; Photograph 19.2 screenshot of homepage www.tiscover.co.za, 24 June 2004, reproduced with permission of Dr Karsten Kärcher, Tiscover AG.

Elsevier for adapted extracts from "Applications of the Delphi Technique in Tourism" by D H Green, C J Hunter and B Moore published in *Annals of Tourism Research* Vol 17 1990 and "Economic aspects of developing theme parks" by S Wanhill published in *Managing Visitor Attractions: New Directions*, edited by A Fyall, B Garrod and A Leask; VisitBritain for extracts adapted from *The UK Tourist: Statistics 2002* and "A layman's guide to market research for the tourist industry" by C P Cooper and J Latham published in *Insights* 1990; The Haworth Press Inc for an extract from "On-line Research Modes: Waiting for Leisure, Hospitality & Tourism Researchers" by A D A Tasci & B J Knutson PHD published in *Journal of Hospitality & Leisure Marketing* Vol 10 Issue 3/4 pp. 57–83; United Nations Environment Programme for *GRID Arendal* published as a News and Press Release February 1999; Shikshantar for an extract on tourism in Udaipur published at www.swaraj.org/shikshantar/ulc-tourism.htm; Centre for Science and Environment, New Delhi for an extract from "Ecotourism: scrambling for paradise" published in *Down to Earth July 31 2002*; New Zealand Tourism Board for an extract from *Tourism New Zealand 3-Year Strategic Plan 2003–2006*; Thomson Publishing for an extract from *Tourism: A Community Approach* by P E Murphy 1985; Le Meridien Hotels and Resorts Limited for an extract from their *Welcome Charter Manual*; Dr Alison J Morrison for the article "Scotland's Commended Hotels"; Shangri-La International Hotel Management Limited for extracts from their website www.shangri-la.com; Thomas Cook UK & Ireland for extracts from their website www.thomascook.Info; Guardian Newspapers for an extract adapted from "Make passengers pay for aircraft pollution says MP" by A Clark published in *The Guardian* 30th July 2003 © The Guardian; and Dr Peter Tarlow for an abridged version of *e-Review of Tourism Research (eRTR)* Vol 1, no. 2.

We are grateful to the Financial Times Limited for permission to reprint the following material:

Mini Case 15.2 A new departure for the easyJet business model, © *Financial Times*, 8 October 2003; Mini Case 16.2 Pollution problems of aircraft, © *Financial Times*, 8 November 2003; Mini Case 18.2 Tourism: culture tool to lift the neglect, © *Financial Times*, 27 May 2003.

In some instances we have been unable to trace the owners of the copyright material, and we would appreciate any information that would enable us to do so.

ABBREVIATIONS

AA Automobile Association
AAA American Automobile Association
ABTA Association of British Travel Agents
APC Annual physical capacity
APEX Advanced purchase excursion fare
APT Advanced Passenger Train
ARC Airlines Reporting Corporation
ASEAN Association of South East Asian Nations
ASP Application service provider
ASTA American Society of Travel Agents
ATC Air traffic control
ATMs Air traffic movements

B2B Business-to-business
B2C Business-to-consumer
BA British Airways
BCG Boston Consulting Group matrix
BTA British Tourist Authority
BWCA Boundary Waters Canoe Area

CAPI Computer-assisted personal interviewing
CPGI Country potential generation index
CRO Central reservations office
CRS Computerised reservation system
CSF Community support framework
CTO Caribbean Tourism Organisation
CVB Convention and visitor bureau

DAGMAR Defining Advertising Goods for Measured Advertising Results
DICIRMS Destination integrated computer information reservation management system
DMO Destination management/marketing organisation
DMS Destination management system

EAGGF European Agricultural Guidance and Guarantee Fund Guidance System
EAP East Asia and the Pacific
EC European Community
ECSC European Coal and Steel Community
EDI Electronic data exchange
EEA European Economic Area
EFTA European Free Trade Association
EIA Environmental impact assessment
EIB European Investment Bank
EPS model Extended problem-solving model
ERDF European Regional Development Fund
ESF European Social Fund
ETB English Tourist Board

ETC European Travel Commission
EU European Union

FBP Family brand performance
FFP Frequent flyer programme
FIFG Financial Instrument for Fisheries Guidance
FIT Fully-inclusive tour
FTE Full-time equivalent

GATS General Agreement of Trade in Services
GDP Gross domestic product
GDS Global distribution system
GNP Gross national product

HFS Hospitality franchise system

IATA International Airline Transport Association
ICAO International Civil Aviation Organisation
ICT Information communication technology
IDD International direct dial
ILG International Leisure Group
IMC Integrated marketing communications
IMF International Monetary Fund
IPEX Instant purchase fares
IPS International passenger survey
ISIC International Standard Industrial Classification
IT Information technology
ITN Internet Travel Network

KM Knowledge management

LAC Limits to acceptable change
LDC Less developed countries
LPS models Limited problem-solving models
LTV Lifetime value

MA Moving average
MIS Management information system

NAFTA North American Free Trade Association
NGO Non-governmental organisation
NITB Northern Ireland Tourist Board
NTO National tourist organisation
NZTS New Zealand Tourism Strategy

OAS Organization of American States
OECD Organization for Economic Co-operation and Development
OECS Organization of East Caribbean States
OPEC Organisation of Petroleum Exporting Countries

PATA Pacific Asia Travel Association
PBP Product brand performance
PMS Property management system
PNR Passenger name record
PR Public relations
PRC Peoples' Republic of China

RBD Recreational business district
RM Relationship marketing
RVs Recreational vehicles

SAS Scandinavian Airline System
SBU Strategic business unit
SCH Scotland's Commended Hotels
SDNs Sustainable development networks
SIC Standard industrial classification
SICTA Standard industrial classification of
activities
SIDS Small Island Developing States
SIS Strategic information system
SIT System of information technologies
SMART Specific, measurable, achievable, realistic,
time limits
SME Small and medium-sized enterprise
SPC Sustained physical capacity
SPD Single programming document
SRA Strategic Rail Authority
STB Scottish Tourist Board
STEP Social, technological, economic and political
factors
STSC Sustainable Tourism Stewardship Council
SWOT Strengths, weaknesses, opportunities and
threats

TALC Tourist area life cycle
TAT Tourist Authority of Thailand

TCSP Tourism Council for the South Pacific
TDC Tourist Development Corporation
TGV Train de Grande Vitesse
THISCO The Hotel Industry Switch Company
TIC Tourist information centre
TIP Tourist information point
TOMM Tourism optimum management model
TOP Thomson Open-Line programme
TPI Tourism Penetration Index
TQM Total quality management
TSA Tourism satellite account

UKTS United Kingdom Tourism Survey
UN United Nations
UNDP United Nations Development Programme
UNEP United Nations Environment Programme
UNSTAT United Nations Statistical Commission
USTTA United States Travel and Tourism
Association

VALS Values and lifestyles
VAT Value Added Tax
VFR Visiting friends and relatives
VOC Visitor orientation centre
VR Virtual reality

WestLB Westdeutsche Landesbank
WTB Wales Tourist Board
WTO World Tourism Organization
WTTC World Travel and Tourism Council
WWW World Wide Web

YHA Youth Hostel Association
YM/WCA Young Men's/Women's Christian
Association

AN INTRODUCTION
TO TOURISM

INTRODUCTION

In this chapter, we introduce the concept of a tourism system and outline its role in offering a way of thinking about tourism and providing a framework of knowledge for students approaching the subject of tourism. This framework is particularly important in the early years of the twenty-first century when the world is experiencing rapid and unexpected change. In addition, tourism has become a major economic sector in its own right and we use this chapter to demonstrate the scale and significance of tourism.

At the same time, we outline some of the commonly held myths that surround tourism and identify some of the issues that are inherent both in the subject area and in the study of tourism. In particular, we emphasise the variety and scope of tourism as an activity and highlight the fact that all elements of the tourism system are interlinked, despite the fact that they have to be artificially isolated for teaching and learning purposes. Finally, we consider the difficulties involved in attempting to define tourism and provide some ideas as to how definitions are evolving.

LEARNING OUTCOMES

In this chapter, we focus on the concepts, terminology and definitions that underpin the study of tourism to provide you with:

- a basic understanding of the nature of the tourism system and a knowledge of the myths that surround tourism today;

- a comprehension of the problems associated with the academic and practical study of tourism;

- an appreciation of the individual elements which, when combined, comprise the tourism system; and

- a knowledge of basic supply-side and demand-side definitions of tourism and the associated difficulties and issues.

TOURISM – MYTHS AND REALITIES

In a world of change, one constant in the last thirty years has been the sustained growth and resilience of tourism both as an activity and an economic sector. This has been demonstrated despite the 'shocks' of '911', the bombing of a major Asian tourism destination – Bali, SARS (severe acute respiratory syndrome) and the second Iraq war. Nonetheless, the events of '911' have accelerated changes in consumer behaviour; changes which are making an impact on travel patterns around the world. In 2003, the World Travel and Tourism Council (WTTC) demonstrated the tremendous scale of the world's tourism sector (WTTC, 2003):

Tourism directly and indirectly generates and supports 195 million jobs globally. This is equivalent to 7.6% of the world's workforce and is forecast to rise to over 250 million jobs in 2010.

At the same time around half of these jobs are in small or medium-sized enterprises (SMEs), the lifeblood of tourism.

- Tourism is responsible for over 10% of global gross domestic product (GDP).

- By 2020 international arrivals are forecast to exceed 1.5 billion.

It is clear that tourism is a major force in the economy of the world, an activity of global importance and significance. It is also a sector that has the capacity to impact negatively upon host environments and cultures, the raw materials of many tourism products. As a result, increased prominence has been given to tourism in the United Nation's world summits such as the 1992 'Rio Earth Summit' and the 'World Summit on Sustainable Development' in Johannesburg in 2003. A combination of the 'youth' of tourism as an activity – international mass tourism is at best only 35 years old – with the pace of growth in demand has given tourism a Cinderella-like existence we know it is important, but it is not taken seriously. This has created a variety of issues for the sector.

First, as well as demonstrating sustained growth, tourism has been remarkable in its resistance to adverse economic and political conditions. Events such as '911', the Bali bombings and SARS clearly demonstrate the sector's ability to regroup and place emphasis on a new vocabulary including words such as 'safety', 'security', 'risk management', 'crisis' and 'recovery'. Inevitably though, growth is slowing as the market matures and, as the nature of the tourist and his/her demands change, the sector will need to be creative in supplying products to satisfy the 'new tourist'.

Second, international organisations support tourism for its contribution to world peace, poverty alleviation, the benefits of the intermingling of peoples and cultures, the economic advantages that can ensue, and the fact that tourism is a relatively 'clean' industry. But an important issue is the stubbornly negative image of tourism as a despoiler of destinations, a harbinger of adverse social change and even the employment and monetary gains of tourism are seen to be illusory in many destinations. The International Labour Organization (ILO) clearly states that they are concerned with decent work, the goal is not just the creation of jobs but the creation of jobs of acceptable quality. A critical issue for the successful future of tourism will be for all involved to demonstrate that the sector is responsible and worthy of acceptance as a global activity. The WTTC has been an influential lobbyist in this regard. As the representative body of the major companies in the tourism sector, it has led an active campaign to promote the need for the industry to take responsibility for its actions.

Third, technology increasingly pervades the tourism sector. Tourism is ideally placed to take advantage of developments in information technology from the use of the Internet to book travel and seek information about destinations, through the use of mobile telephone technology to revolutionise the way that tourism information can be delivered direct to the user in situ at the destination, to the innovative role technology plays in interpreting and displaying destinations. But this has all come at the price of restructuring the distribution channel in tourism and in changing the nature of jobs in the sector.

Finally, in many respects general perceptions of tourism are misplaced. Tourism is surrounded by a number of myths which have contributed unrealistically to its glamorous image. These are demonstrated in Table 0.1.

TABLE 0.1	Tourism – myths and realities
Myth	The majority of tourism in the world is **international**.
Reality	Tourism in the world is predominantly domestic (people travelling in their own country). **Domestic tourism** accounts for about 80% of tourist trips.
Myth	Most tourism journeys in the world are by air as tourists jet-set from country to country.
Reality	The majority of trips are by surface transport (mainly the car).
Myth	Tourism is only about leisure holidays.
Reality	Tourism includes all types of purpose of visit including business, conference and education.
Myth	Employment in tourism means substantial travel and the chance to learn languages.
Reality	Most employment in tourism is in the hospitality sector and involves little travel.
Myth	Large multinational companies such as hotel chains and airlines dominate tourism.
Reality	The vast majority of tourism enterprises in every destination are SMEs.
Myth	Tourism is a straightforward sector demanding little research or planning.
Reality	Tourism is a complex multi-sectoral industry demanding high-level planning underpinned by research to succeed.

THE SUBJECT OF TOURISM

In historical terms, tourism activity is a relatively new development and only recently has it been considered worthy of serious business endeavour or academic study. However, the tourism industry is of sufficient economic importance and its impact upon economies, environments and societies is significant enough for the subject of tourism to deserve academic consideration. There is no doubt in our minds that tourism is a subject area or domain of study, but that at the moment it lacks the level of theoretical underpinning that would allow it to become a discipline. Nevertheless, the popularity of tourism as a subject, and the recognition of its importance by governments, has accelerated the study of tourism. Tourism as a subject is showing signs of maturity with a growing academic community, increasing numbers of both journals and textbooks which are becoming specialised rather than all-embracing, and a number of professional societies both internationally and within individual countries. All of these indicators point to the increasing professionalism of the tourism sector.

As an area of study, tourism is still relatively young and this creates a range of issues for all of us involved in teaching, researching and studying the subject:

- The subject area itself is bedevilled by conceptual weakness and fuzziness. We are therefore faced with many questions that would be taken as common ground in other subjects (such as finding a way through the maze of terminology related

| PHOTOGRAPH 0.1 | Tourism has become an increasingly important element of study for many students as the subject gains acceptability in the academic community |

to the type of tourism which is less destructive – green, alternative, responsible, sustainable, eco!). This results in a basic lack of rigour and focus leaving tourism as a subject area open to criticism by others. Franklin and Crang for example are unrelenting: 'The rapid growth of tourism has led researchers to simply record and document tourism in a series of case studies, examples and industry-sponsored projects' (2001, p. 6). This highlights the apparent conflict between 'academic' and 'applied' approaches which is also an unresolved issue.

- The subject encompasses a number of diverse industrial sectors and academic subjects, raising the question for those studying tourism as to whether or not tourism is, in fact, too diverse and chaotic to merit separate consideration as a subject or economic sector. According to Gilbert (1990) what makes tourism difficult to define is the very broad nature of both the concept as well as the need for so many service inputs. Tourism also envelops other sectors and industries (Gilbert, 1990, p. 7) and therefore has no clear boundary due to the expansive spread of activities it covers. We would argue, of course, that it should warrant a subject and sector in its own right, but that there is a need for a disciplined approach to help alleviate potential sources of confusion for students. It is therefore important in this respect to provide a framework within which to locate these subject approaches and industries. In reality the tourism industry consists of a mass of organisations operating in different sectors each of which supplies those activities which are termed tourism.

- As if these problems were not sufficient, tourism also suffers from a particularly weak set of data sources – in terms of both comparability and quality, although the World Tourism Organization (WTO) has made significant progress in this regard.

- Traditional approaches have tended to operationalise and reduce tourism to a set of activities or economic transactions while more recent authors have been critical of this 'reductionism', stressing instead post-modern frameworks which analyse the significance and meaning of tourism to individuals.

- Finally, tourism does suffer from an image problem in academic circles. Indeed, many are attracted to it as an exciting, vibrant subject and an applied area of economic activity – which we believe that it is. But to be successful, tourism demands very high standards of professionalism, knowledge and application from everyone involved. This is sometimes felt to be in contrast to the image of jet-setting, palm-fringed beaches and a leisure activity.

A TOURISM SYSTEM

In response to the issues identified above, we feel that is important at the outset to provide an organising framework for the study of tourism. There are many ways to do this. Individual disciplines, for example, view the activity of tourism as an application of their own ideas and concepts, and an approach from geography, economics or whatever could be adopted. An alternative is to take a multidisciplinary, or even an interdisciplinary, approach. Figure 0.1 shows one such attempt to integrate a variety of subjects and disciplines and to focus upon tourism.

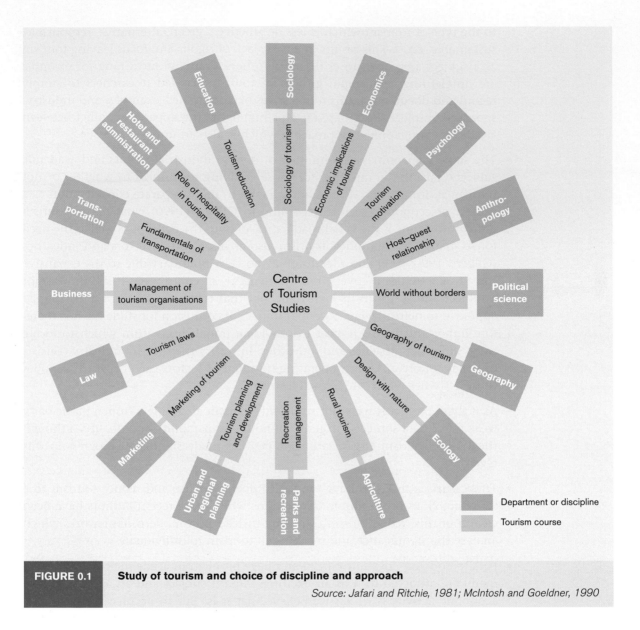

FIGURE 0.1 **Study of tourism and choice of discipline and approach**

Source: Jafari and Ritchie, 1981; McIntosh and Goeldner, 1990

However, in a book of this nature it is impossible to cover the complete range of approaches to tourism. Instead, as an organising framework, we have adopted the model suggested by Leiper in 1979 and updated in 1990 (Figure 0.2). As Figure 0.2 shows, Leiper's model neatly takes into account many of the issues identified above by considering the activity of tourists, allowing industry sectors to be located and providing the geographical element which is inherent to all travel. It also places tourism in the context of a range of external environments such as society, politics and economies.

There are three basic elements of Leiper's model:

1 **Tourists.** The tourist is the actor in this system. Tourism, after all, is a very human experience, enjoyed, anticipated and remembered by many as some of the most important times of their lives. Defining the tourist and attempting to produce classifications of tourists form the latter section of this chapter.

| FIGURE 0.2 | A basic tourism system | Source: Leiper, 1990 |

2 **Geographical elements**. Leiper outlines three geographical elements in his model:
1. traveller-generating region;
2. tourist destination region; and
3. transit route region.

The traveller-generating region represents the generating market for tourism and, in a sense, provides the 'push' to stimulate and motivate travel. It is from here that the tourist searches for information, makes the booking and departs.

In many respects, the tourist destination region represents the 'sharp end' of tourism. At the destination, the full impact of tourism is felt and planning and management strategies are implemented. The destination too is the *raison d'être* for tourism, with a range of special places distinguished from the everyday by their cultural, historic or natural significance (Rojek and Urry, 1997). The 'pull' to visit destinations energises the whole **tourism system** and creates demand for travel in the generating region. It is therefore at the destination where the innovations in tourism take place – new products are developed and 'experiences' delivered making the destination the place 'where the most noticeable and dramatic consequences of the system occur' (Leiper, 1990, p. 23).

The transit route region does not simply represent the short period of travel to reach the destination, but also includes the intermediate places which may be visited en route: 'There is always an interval in a trip when the traveller feels they have left their home region but have not yet arrived . . . [where] they choose to visit' (Leiper, 1990, p. 22).

3 **The tourism sector**. The third element of Leiper's model is the tourism sector, which we can think of as the range of businesses and organisations involved in delivering the tourism product. The model allows the location of the various industrial sectors to be identified. For example, travel agents and tour operators are mostly found in the traveller-generating region, attractions and the hospitality industry are found in the destination region, and the transport industry is largely represented in the transit route region.

TGR: Traveller-generating region
TR: Transit route
TDR: Tourist destination region

| FIGURE 0.3 | Geographical elements in a tourism system with two destinations |

Source: Leiper, 1990

Each of the elements of Leiper's tourism system interacts, not only to deliver the tourism product, but also in terms of transactions and impacts, and of course, the differing contexts within which tourism occurs (Figure 0.3). The fact that tourism is also a sector of contrasts is illustrated by examining two major elements of Leiper's model. Demand for tourism in the generating region is inherently volatile, seasonal and irrational. Yet this demand is satisfied by a destination region where supply is fragmented, and inflexible – surely a possible recipe for the financial instability of tourism!

The major advantages of Leiper's model are its general applicability and simplicity which provide a useful 'way of thinking' about tourism. Indeed, each of the alternative models that we have considered tend to reveal Leiper's basic elements when they are dissected. There are also other advantages of this approach:

- It has the ability to incorporate interdisciplinary approaches to tourism because it is not rooted in any particular subject or discipline but instead provides a framework within which disciplinary approaches can be located.

- It is possible to use the model at any scale or level of generalisation – from a local resort to the international industry.

- The model is infinitely flexible and allows the incorporation of different forms of tourism, while at the same time demonstrating their common elements. For example, heritage or eco-tourism can be analysed using the model (see Mini case study 0.1). Here, we can see that eco-tourism does not require a completely new approach, but simply an analysis of each of the particular characteristics of each of the elements of the eco-tourism system.

- Finally, the model demonstrates the highly important principle of tourism studies that all the elements of tourism are related and interact – in essence we are studying a system of customers and suppliers who demand and supply the tourism product and services. Naturally, in any textbook or course, the elements of tourism have to be separated and examined individually, but in reality all are linked and the realisation of their interrelationships provides a true understanding of tourism.

MINI CASE STUDY 0.1
Characteristics of elements of the eco-tourism system

GENERATING REGION

Demand for eco-tourism:

- is purposeful;
- is poorly documented;
- desires first-hand experience/contact with nature/culture;
- has the motive to study, admire and/or enjoy nature/culture;
- is tempered by the need to consume tourism responsibly;
- can be segmented in many ways including by level of commitment, level of physical effort, motives;
- comes from those who are more likely to be well educated, have a higher income and be slightly older than the average tourist.

DESTINATION REGION

Destinations for eco-tourism:

- are relatively natural areas which are undisturbed and/or uncontaminated;
- have attractions of scenery, flora, fauna and/or indigenous culture;
- allow eco-tourism to deliver economic and conservation benefits to the local people;
- develop eco-tourism with a view to conserving/enhancing/maintaining the natural/cultural system;
- apply integrated planning and management techniques;
- apply environmental impact and auditing procedures to all elements of the tourism destination (such as accommodation, facilities);
- encourage local ownership of facilities.

TRANSIT ZONE

Transport for eco-tourism:

- should be of low impact to the environment in terms of noise, emissions, congestion, fuel consumption and waste;
- should monitor emissions and environmental impacts;
- should promote the conservation ethic;
- should be used as a management tool;

- should encourage use of public transport;
- should encourage the use of locally owned transport companies;
- **but**, reaching a long-haul eco-tourism destination may consume large amounts of aircraft fuel and be more damaging to the environment than the tourist realises, and thus defeat the purpose of the trip itself.

DISCUSSION QUESTIONS

1 Do the principles of eco-tourism apply equally to each of the elements of the eco-tourism system?

2 Should eco-tourists be true to their beliefs and not use any from of powered transport?

3 There is a view that eco-tourism is used by developers as a 'soft' medium to access valued natural resources to 'pave the way' for more aggressive tourism development – do you agree with this view?

DEFINITIONS OF TOURISM

We can see from Leiper's model that tourism can be thought of as a whole range of individuals, businesses, organisations and places which combine in some way to deliver a travel experience. Tourism is a multidimensional, multifaceted activity, which touches many lives and many different economic activities. Not surprisingly tourism has therefore proved difficult to define – the word 'tourist' first appeared in the English language in the early 1800s, yet two centuries later we still cannot agree on a definition. In some senses, this is a reflection of the complexity of tourism, but it is also indicative of its youth as a field of study. It is difficult to find an underpinning coherence of approach in defining tourism, aside from the need to characterise the 'otherness' of tourism from similar activities such as migration. Indeed, geographers are increasingly of the belief that tourism is but one form of 'mobility' and does not need to be separated out. As might be expected, definitions have been created to cater for particular needs and situations. Yet, it is vital to attempt definitions of tourism, not only to provide a sense of credibility and ownership for those involved, but also for the practical considerations of both measurement and legislation.

Definitions of tourism can be thought of as either:

1 demand-side definitions; or

2 supply-side definitions.

Tourism definitions are unusual in that, until the 1990s, they were being driven more by demand-side than supply-side considerations. Some writers find this surprising: 'Defining tourism in terms of the motivations or other characteristics of travellers would be like trying to define the healthcare professions by describing a sick person' (Smith, 1989, p. 33). The 1990s saw considerable progress in the development and consensus of both demand and supply-side definitions. This was stimulated by two key initiatives:

1 **Demand-side definitions** – the World Tourism Organization's (WTO) 1991 International Conference on Travel and Tourism Statistics – a conference called to tidy up definitions, terminology and measurement issues. The recommendations of this conference were adopted by the United Nations Statistical Commission (UNSTAT) and published as *Recommendations on Tourism Statistics* (WTO and UNSTAT, 1994).

2 **Supply-side definitions** – in March 2000 the United Nations Statistical Commission approved the adoption of tourism satellite accounts as the method of measuring the economic sector of tourism.

Demand-side definitions of tourism

Demand-side definitions have evolved, first, by attempting to encapsulate the idea of tourism into 'conceptual' definitions and, second, through the development of 'technical' definitions for measurement and legal purposes.

From a conceptual point of view, we can think of tourism as: 'The activities of persons travelling to and staying in places outside their usual environment for not more than one consecutive year for leisure, business and other purposes' (WTO and UNSTAT, 1994). While this is not a strict technical definition, it does convey the essential nature of tourism, i.e.:

- Tourism arises out of a movement of people to, and their stay in, various places, or destinations.

- There are two elements in tourism – the journey to the destination and the stay (including activities) at the destination.

- The journey and stay take place outside the usual environment or normal place of residence and work so that tourism gives rise to activities that are distinct from the resident and working populations of the places through which they travel and stay.

- The movement to destinations is temporary and short term in character – the intention is to return within a few days, weeks or months.

- Destinations are visited for purposes other than taking up permanent residence or employment in the places visited.

From a 'technical' point of view, attempts to define tourism have been led by the need to isolate tourism trips from other forms of travel for statistical purposes. These 'technical' definitions demand that an activity has to pass certain 'tests' before it counts as tourism. Such tests include the following:

- Minimum length of stay – one night (visitors who do not stay overnight are termed **same-day visitors** or excursionists).

- Maximum length of stay – one year.

- Strict purpose of visit categories.

- A distance consideration is sometimes included on the grounds of delineating the term 'usual environment' – the WTO recommendation is 160 kilometres.

MINI CASE STUDY 0.2
Tourism and mobilities

A NEW WAY OF THINKING ABOUT TOURISM

The social sciences – in particular geography and sociology – are rediscovering tourism as an area for research, case studies and examples. The approach that these subject areas have adopted, however, is different from the more traditional approach taken by academics in the tourism area. In a new way of thinking about tourism, geographers and sociologists see it as one form of 'mobility', locating tourism within a spectrum ranging from permanent migration to daily shopping.

In other words geographers and sociologists see tourism as one dimension of our 'connections' with the world ranging across many different localities. The key message from the idea of tourism 'as a form of mobility' is that tourism is no longer treated as a distinct and special activity, but simply one that is a part of a range of other activities in society. The reason that this way of thinking has emerged is partly due to 'space–time compression' – the fact that with transport and communication technology it is possible to visit distant places for a day. In Europe, for example, it is perfectly possible to visit Paris for lunch from the UK.

This means that we can think of the idea of tourism being part of a 'leisure mobility spectrum' ranging from daily leisure around the home through to tourism where an overnight stay is taken. Here we can see that what may initially be a tourism-related mobility – travelling to and from a second home for example, may eventually become retirement migration. In this way, the concept of 'mobility does provide valuable insights into travel behaviour'.

THE ISSUE

The approach does create a major issue, however. Effectively, it blurs the distinction between home, work and tourist destinations; and between differing types of traveller – whether they are commuters, shoppers or migrants. This makes reconciling the 'mobilities' approach with the drawing up of 'definitions' of tourism problematic – particularly when we go back to the definitions of tourism designed by the World Tourism Organization. The WTO's definitions see tourism as a distinct activity, taking place away from home and for a period of more than twenty-four hours. Of course, the formal definitions do now recognise the day trip as an activity, but there is no recognition of the 'spectrum of mobilities' that tourism may embrace, and there is a rigid exclusion of certain types of mobile populations such as migrants, refugees and travellers.

DISCUSSION QUESTIONS

1 Is tourism still a 'special' activity or has it become part of everyday life and expectations?

2 Thinking of your own 'mobility' over the last week, how many trips could be seen as 'leisure related'?

3 Thinking of the world, and the idea of 'space–time compression' there are many places which are highly accessible due to improved transport access. Has this had any impact on your own travel patterns over the last few years?

Supply-side definitions of tourism

As with demand-side definitions there are two basic approaches to defining the tourism sector – the conceptual, or descriptive, and the technical. From a conceptual point of view, Leiper suggests: 'The tourist industry consists of all those firms, organisations and facilities which are intended to serve the specific needs and wants of tourists' (1979, p. 400).

A major problem concerning 'technical' supply-side definitions is the fact that there is a spectrum of tourism businesses and organisations, from those which are wholly serving tourists to those who also serve local residents and other markets. The tourism satellite account (TSA) is the agreed approach to defining the tourism sector as it measures the goods and services purchased by visitors to estimate the size of the tourism economic sector (WTO, 2001) (see also Table 0.2). The TSA:

- provides information on the economic impact of tourism including contribution to gross domestic product, investment, tax revenues, tourism consumption and the impact on a nation's balance of payments;

- provides information on tourism employment and its characteristics; and, importantly;

- allows tourism to be compared with other economic sectors.

It is clear from this section that the tourism sector has been late in recognising the importance of supply-side definitions. However, the benefits are clear, as the TSA allows tourism to be compared with other economic sectors, delivers important data for planning and policy, as well as providing an important conceptual framework for studying and researching tourism.

INTERRELATIONSHIPS AND CLASSIFICATIONS

Not only are the elements of tourism all interlinked, but also we can see that tourism has close relationships with other activities and concepts. It is therefore a mistake to consider tourism in isolation from these other related activities. For

TABLE 0.2	WTO supply-side definition of tourism (International Standard Industrial Classification, ISIC)	

ISIC divisions	Business activity[a]	Example
Construction	T	Hotels, recreational facilities, transport facilities, resort residence.
Wholesale and retail	P	Motor vehicles sales, sales of motor vehicle fuels, retail food sales, retail sales of textiles.
	T	Retail sales of travel accessories, souvenir sales, etc.
Hotels and restaurants	P	Fast food restaurants, food.
	T	Hotels, camping sites.
Transport, storage and communications	P	Transport via railways, chauffeured vehicles, inland water transport.
	T	Interurban rail, airlines, special rail tour service, long-distance bus services, cruise ships.
Financial intermediation	P	Exchange of currencies, life insurance, credit cards.
	T	Travel insurance.
Real estate, renting and business activities	P	Buying or selling of leased property, letting or owning of leased property.
	T	Rental of ski equipment, letting of owned tourism property.
Public administration	P	Translation services, customs administration, fishing regulation, foreign affairs, border guards.
	T	Tourism administration, information bureaux, visa issuance, regulation of private transport.
Education	P	Adult education, driving schools, flying schools, boating instruction.
	T	Hotel schools, tourism education programmes, recreation and park service schools, tourist instruction.
Other community	P	Swimming, scuba instruction, flying instruction, boating instruction, motion picture entertainment.
	T	Visitor bureaux, travel clubs, travel unions.
Extra-territorial organisations	P	OECD, World Bank, IMF, ASEAN.
	T	International tourism bodies.

[a] P = part involvement with tourism; T = totally dedicated to tourism.
Source: WTO and UNSTAT, 1994

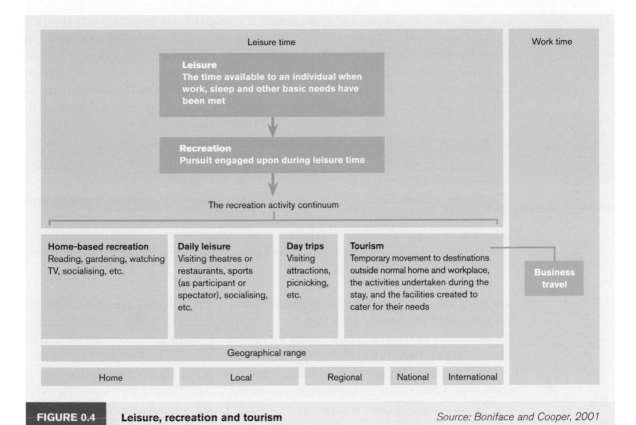

example, most tourism throughout the world is a leisure activity and it is important to locate tourism in the spectrum of leisure activities.

Although the Latin translation of leisure literally means 'to be free', defining leisure is, if anything, more problematic than defining tourism. In essence, leisure can be thought of as a combined measure of time and attitude of mind to create periods of time when other obligations are at a minimum. Recreation can be thought of as the pursuits engaged in during leisure time and an activity spectrum can be identified with, at one end of the scale, recreation around the home, through to tourism where an overnight stay is involved (Figure 0.4).

Although same-day visits or excursions are a common recreational activity, for tourism to occur, leisure time has to be blocked together to allow a stay away from home. Traditionally, these blocks of leisure time were taken as paid holiday entitlement, though innovations such as flexi-time and three-day weekends have also facilitated tourism.

Tourists

While all-embracing definitions of tourism and a tourist are desirable, in practice tourists represent a heterogeneous, not a homogeneous, group with different personalities, demographics and experiences. We can classify tourists in two basic ways which relate to the nature of their trip:

1 A basic distinction can be made between domestic and international tourists, although this distinction is blurring in many parts of the world (for example, in the European Union). Domestic tourism refers to travel by residents within their country of residence. There are rarely currency, language or visa implications, and domestic tourism is more difficult to measure than international tourism. As a consequence, domestic tourism has received little attention (see Chapter 3). In contrast, international tourism involves travel outside the country of residence and there may well be currency, language and visa implications.

2 Tourists can also be classified by 'purpose of visit category'. Conventionally, three categories are used:
   1. leisure and recreation – including holiday, sports and cultural tourism and visiting friends and relatives (VFR);
   2. other tourism purposes – including study and health tourism;
   3. business and professional – including meetings, conferences, missions, incentive and business tourism.

Not only are these categories used for statistical purposes, they are also useful for the marketing of tourism. Consider, for example, Figure 0.5 where we demonstrate the flexibility of travel for each of the categories from the point of view of airline fare pricing and validity.

There are many other ways to classify tourists. These range from simple demographic and trip classifications (see, for example, Table 0.3) through their lifestyles and personalities, to their perception of risk and familiarity and post-modern interpretations of consumers and commodities. However, one approach with increasing relevance to contemporary tourism is to classify tourists according to their level and type of interaction with the destination. Classifications of tourists that adopt this approach commonly place mass tourism at one extreme and some form of alternative, small-scale tourism at the other with a variety of classes in between. It is then argued that mass tourism has a major impact upon the destination because of the sheer scale of the industry and the nature of the consumer. On the other hand, small-scale, alternative types of tourism are said to have a much reduced

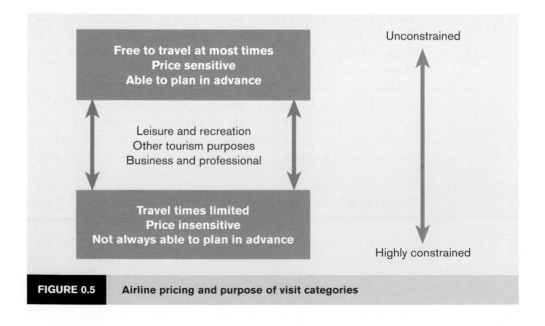

FIGURE 0.5   **Airline pricing and purpose of visit categories**

TABLE 0.3	Suggested socio-economic characteristics for tourism analysis
	Levels of measurement
Socio-economic variable 1 Age	Collect by single years. It may be convenient to summarise by age cohorts.
2 Sex	Male/female. Age–sex cohorts may also be useful.
3 Education	Given the diversity of educational systems in North America, a basic four-part classification may be most useful: elementary, secondary, post-secondary non-university and university. It may be useful in other circumstances to distinguish between completion of secondary or post-secondary programmes and partial work (drop-out before completion).
4 Occupational status	Categories can include employed full-time, employed part-time, retired (some reference to former occupation may be desired), homemaker, student, unemployed. If employed, refer the respondent to the next question, 'occupation'.
5 Occupation	This is best determined through an open-ended question. Responses can be summarised according to the *Occupation Classification Manual* or other comparable national statistical coding system such as the *Canadian Classification and Dictionary of Occupations*. These codes refer to the type of industry in which the traveller is employed.
6 Annual income	This is an especially sensitive subject; some of the concern over reporting income can be reduced by using income categories. The specific categories should be based on those used in the most recent national census. Household income is often the most relevant measure of income, although the respondent's income may be useful in special circumstances.

7 Family composition	This can be an especially important variable if the purpose of study includes some analysis of the effect of travel party composition on travel behaviour. One possible classification is:
	Single individual living alone
	Husband–wife family
	    No children under 18 years
	    No children at home or no children at all
	    Adult children or other adult relatives living at home
	    With children under 18 years
	    With no other adult relatives
	    With other relatives
	Single-parent families
	    Male head
	    Female head
	    All other families

TABLE 0.3	(continued)

	Levels of measurement
8 Party composition	This is closely related to the previous variable for many travelling parties. Levels include: 　One person alone 　One family with children 　Two families with children 　Organised group 　One couple 　Two or more couples 　Group of friends (unorganised group) 　Other
Trip variable 1 Season or trip period	Calendar quarters: 　January to March 　April to June 　July to September 　October to December If the trip overlaps two or more quarters, the following convention is often used: for household surveys, use the quarter in which the trip ends; for exits or re-entry surveys, use the date of the survey. It is sometimes desirable to distinguish weekend trips from other trips.
2 Trip duration	Both days and nights are used as the unit of measurement. The number of nights is usually one less than the number of days; a three-day weekend lasts 'two nights'. The actual number of days or nights up to one week is often collected. Periods longer than one week are often measured as ranges, e.g. 8–15 days (or 7–13 nights).
3 Trip distance	This should be based, in part, on the threshold distance required for definition of a trip. Narrow ranges for lowest levels are desirable to permit aggregating or exclusion of data so that comparisons can be made between surveys using different distance thresholds. A possible classification would be: 　25–49 miles 　50–99 miles 　100–499 miles 　500–999 miles 1 000–1 499 miles More than 1 500 miles (2 400 km) Metric conversion is usually necessary for international comparisons; however, international travel is normally not measured by distance.
4 Purpose of trip	Very simple classifications are used, such as business versus pleasure. This dichotomy is normally inadequate for analytical purposes and is too simplistic to represent the purposes of many trips. More precise classifications would include:

TABLE 0.3 *(continued)*

	Levels of measurement
	Conventions or other business meetings Buying, selling, installation, or other business Recreation/vacation Touring/sightseeing Attending cultural/sporting events Participating in cultural/sporting events Visiting friends or relatives Other family or personal matters Shopping Study tour Health/rest Many trips involve more than one purpose, so it may be useful to specify 'primary' purpose.
5 Mode of transportation	Private automobile Rental automobile Bus/motor coach Train Scheduled airline Chartered airline Private aeroplane Boat/ship (additional categories for ferries, cruise ships, private boats may be added as necessary) Some trips involve multiple modes, such as a combination of scheduled airline and rental car. These combinations may be specified or a primary mode may be requested.
6 Expenditures	Transportation (broken down by mode, if desired) Accommodation (including camping fees, but not park entrance fees) Food and beverages (restaurant meals may be separated from food purchased at a store) Convention or registration fees Admission fees and other entertainment, including park admissions, licence fees for hunting and fishing Souvenirs Other purchases
7 Type of accommodation	Hotels and inns Motels and motor inns Resorts Campgrounds Hostels Commercial cottages Institutional camps Private cottages

TABLE 0.3	*(continued)*
	Levels of measurement
	Bed and breakfast/tourist home Homes of friends or relatives Other Additional classifications could be based on size of accommodation, price, public versus private ownership, function (e.g. fishing camp, ski resort), type of location (e.g. airport strip; downtown), availability of liquor and so on.

Source: Tourism Research Planning Committee, 1975; and from Tourism Analysis: A Handbook, *Harlow, Longman with permission of Pearson Education Limited (Smith, S.L. 1989)*

impact upon the destination, not only because of the type of consumer involved but also because they will shun the travel trade and stay in local pensions or with families. In this case, it is argued, the impact of tourism is less disruptive than for mass tourism. Unfortunately:

> Some commentators have oversimplified the complex relationship between the consumption and development of tourism resources. This is particularly true of the so-called 'alternative' tourism movement which is lauded by some as a solution to the ills of mass tourism. Indeed, the tenor of much of the writing about alternative tourism is that any alternative tourism scheme is good whilst all mass tourism is bad. There is, of course, a case for alternative tourism, but only as another form of tourism in the spectrum. It can never be an alternative to mass tourism, nor can it solve all the problems of tourism. (Archer and Cooper, 1994)

These issues, and the fallacy of lauding 'alternative' tourism as a literal alternative to mass tourism, come into clear focus when examined against the frameworks of analysis developed in this book. For example, only by matching appropriate types of visitor to particular types of destination will truly sustainable development be achieved.

CONCLUSION

Mass tourism, as an activity, remains relatively youthful and while it has experienced unprecedented growth rates in the past four decades, the study of tourism inevitably lacks the maturity of other subject areas and disciplines. This lack of maturity is manifested in many ways, not least the lack of agreement as to what actually constitutes tourism activity on both the demand and supply side. Nevertheless, the economic importance of tourism has guaranteed increased governmental and international attention and accompanying this has not only been a growing recognition of the significance and importance of tourism and the need to be able to define and measure all aspects of it; but also a need for the sustainable development and management of tourism.

This introduction provides the basic underpinning framework for the remainder of this book, offering contemporary views on important tourism-related definitions, acquainting the reader with the fundamentals of the dynamics of the tourism system, and pointing out the impact of a changing world on the way that tourism does business.

Self-check questions

1 Identify five reasons why tourism can be a beneficial force in society.

2 Draft a checklist of the security threats posed by tourists when travelling internationally.

3 Review the major methods used to classify tourists – which one do you prefer?

4 Which of the following can be counted as tourists in the official definitions:
   - invading armies
   - space shuttle pilots
   - international conference delegates
   - travelling diplomats
   - nomads
   - immigrants

5 Review the major elements of the tourism system – how do they relate to each other?

Essay questions

1 Draft a justification for the introduction of a new tourism programme at your educational institution.

2 Identify the reasons why it has proved difficult to agree on supply-side definitions of tourism.

3 Summarise the impacts of the September 11, 2001 terrorist attacks on international tourism.

4 Evaluate the potential of tourism to be an agent of poverty alleviation.

5 Discuss the view that responsible tourism can never be a replacment for mass tourism.

Annotated further reading

Books

Goeldner, C.R. and Ritchie, B. (2003) *Tourism: Principles, Practices, Philosophies*, 9th edn, Wiley, New York.
A comprehensive textbook with a strong North American flavour.

Jafari, J. (2001) *The Encyclopedia of Tourism*, Routledge, London.
A comprehensive volume with definitive statements on every tourism term written by the leading expert in each field.

Urry, J. (2000) *Sociology Beyond Societies. Mobilities for the Twenty-First Century*, Routledge, London.
A refreshingly different approach, focusing on the concept of mobilities and tourism.

Web sites

http://www.world-tourism.org
An all-embracing web site providing the official United Nations' view on tourism issues such as **pro-poor tourism** and providing definitions, definitive statistics and approaches to tourism.

http://www.wttc.org
A comprehensive web site from the private sector's representative body for tourism with up-to-date statistics and reports on the tourism industry and its contribution to economies.

References cited

Archer, B.H. and Cooper, C.P. (1994) 'The positive and negative aspects of tourism', pp. 73–91 in Theobold, W.F. (ed.), *Global Tourism: The Next Decade*, Butterworth Heinemann, Oxford.

Boniface, B. and Cooper, C. (2001) *Worldwide Destinations: The Geography of Travel and Tourism*, Heinemann, London.

Franklin, A. and Crang, M. (2001) 'The trouble with tourism and travel theory', *Tourism Studies* **1**(1), 5–22.

Gilbert, D. (1990) 'Conceptual issues in the meaning of tourism', pp. 4–27 in Cooper, C. (ed.), *Progress in Tourism, Recreation and Hospitality Management*, Belhaven Press, London.

Jafari, J. and Ritchie, J.R.B. (1981) 'Towards a framework for tourism education', *Annals of Tourism Research* **8**(1), 13–34.

Leiper, N. (1979) 'The framework of tourism', *Annals of Tourism Research* **6**(4), 390–407.

Leiper, N. (1990) 'Tourism systems', Massey University Department of Management Systems Occasional Paper 2, Auckland.

McIntosh, R.W. and Goeldner, C.R. (1990) *Tourism: Principles, Practices, Philosophies*, Wiley, New York.

Rojek, C. and Urry, J. (1997) *Touring Cultures – Transformations of Travel Theory*, Routledge, London.

Smith, S.L.J. (1989) *Tourism Analysis: A Handbook*, Longman, Harlow.

Tourism Research Planning Committee (1975) *Standard Definitions and Classifications for Travel Survey*, Federal–Provincial Conference on Tourism, Ottawa.

WTO (2001) *Basic Concepts of the Tourism Satellite Account (TSA)*, WTO, Madrid.

WTO and UNSTAT (1994) *Recommendations on Tourism Statistics*, WTO, Madrid and United Nations, New York.

WTTC (2003) *Progress and Priorities 2003/2004*, World Travel and Tourism Council, Brussels.

MAJOR CASE STUDY 0.1
TOURISM AS AN AGENT OF POVERTY
ALLEVIATION

INTRODUCTION

The World Travel and Tourism Council's vision for a new tourism in the twenty-first century states:

> New Tourism is a force capable of dramatically improving economic and social well-being right across the globe, waiting to be unleashed. (WTTC, 2003, p. 5)

Indeed, one of the key issues in the twenty-first century will be the development of strategies to tackle poverty. Poverty is an unacceptable human situation. It is also a situation from which people want to escape and it is the aim of this case study to explore the potential of tourism to help reduce poverty in the world.

DEFINING POVERTY

The World Bank states that poverty is hunger, lack of shelter, sickness and above all power-lessness – in other words there are many dimensions to poverty. We can look at a range of ways to measure poverty including not only income measures, but also non-income dimensions of poverty such as health, education or housing. The most obvious approach to measuring poverty is by using income, in other words a person is considered to be poor, or 'below the poverty line', if their income falls below a level necessary to meet basic needs. Here, for example, the World Bank's definition of poverty is 'anyone living on less than one US dollar per day'. The World Bank estimates that in 1999 1.2 billion people came under this definition (23% of the population of the developing world).

REDUCING POVERTY

There have been two drivers of the poverty reduction agenda in the twenty-first century. First, the 2002 World Summit on Sustainable Development placed poverty reduction as a development imperative. Second, in 2000, the lead international agencies in the world distilled key development goals and targets from the previous decade into Millennium Development Goals (MDGs). The first MDG is to 'eradicate extreme poverty and hunger', calling for a halving of those living on less than one dollar per day by 2015.

Three key strategies to reduce poverty emerge from these initiatives:

1 Accelerate economic growth.

2 Improve the distribution of income and wealth.

3 Accelerate social development.

International agencies and charities around the world are working to this agenda, but tourism has been slow to recognise its potential to alleviate poverty. In part this is because it is difficult for tourism to operate in isolation. To be successful as a tool of poverty reduction, tourism must be seen as one dimension of a destination's economy and society. For broader based approaches such as changing systems of land tenure, planning procedures, training and education, and infrastructure improvements, tourism can play a role but has to work within national and regional policy frameworks.

THE PRO-POOR TOURISM AGENDA

The use of tourism to reduce poverty is sometimes termed '**pro-poor tourism**' (PPT). PPT has been embraced by the developing world and international agencies (including the World Tourism Organization (WTO), UNCTAD, the Asian Development Bank and the World Bank). The WTO has outlined an ambitious programme in this area known as 'sustainable tourism–eliminating poverty' (ST–EP) (WTO, 2002).

PPT can be defined as 'tourism that results in increased net benefits for poor people'. It is an approach to developing tourism focused on the key question:

How can tourism reduce poverty at the local level, and therefore what policies, strategies and plans can be put into place to enhance poverty alleviation?

But, as mentioned above, tourism is a newcomer to the arena of poverty reduction and while there is much potential and hope for the approach, there is little real experience of operating pro-poor tourism at tourism destinations. Nonetheless, tourism brings a number of benefits as a sector for pro-poor development:

- tourism is produced where it is consumed – the tourist has to visit the destination allowing opportunities for economic gain;

- tourism is labour intensive and employs a high percentage of women;

- tourism is naturally attracted to remote, peripheral areas where other economic options are limited; and

- tourism is significant and growing in the developing and least-developed countries (LDCs).

And of course, there are real benefits to the tourism sector in tackling the issue of poverty. For example:

- reducing poverty at the tourism destination will help to make that destination safer and reduce possible hostile attitudes from the local community;

- poverty reduction will also make the destination more attractive by reducing the numbers of shanty towns and beggars and enhancing the environmental quality of the destination; and

- tourism needs to find ways to enhance its own acceptability in the wider community and poverty reduction is one medium for doing this.

STRATEGIES FOR PRO-POOR TOURISM

One of the key lessons that tourism can learn from international agencies and charities involved in poverty reduction is the imperative to ensure that pro-poor tourism strategies can be implemented at the local level. Ashley, Boyd and Goodwin (2000) identify three types of pro-poor tourism strategies:

1 Strategies focused on economic benefits including:
   – job creation to deliver a measure of security in household income;
   – small business opportunities in the tourism market directly and indirectly supplying tourists with goods such as handicrafts and food;
   – local cooperative development; and
   – increasing the economic benefits for the whole community – by renting communal land for camping for example.

2 Strategies focused on improving living conditions:
   – strategies here include training and education, reducing the environmental impacts of tourism, reducing competition for natural resources, and improved access to services such as schooling, healthcare, communications and infrastructure improvements.

3 Strategies focused on participation and involvement:
   – here strategies are designed to change the policy and planning framework to allow participation by local communities in tourism, decision making and partnerships with the private sector.

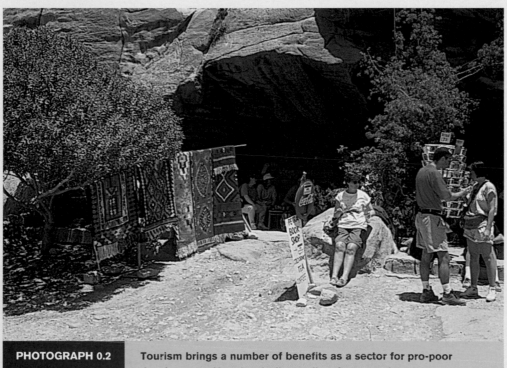

PHOTOGRAPH 0.2 Tourism brings a number of benefits as a sector for pro-poor development. Here local tribes sell crafts to tourists

The success of tourism as a tool of poverty reduction will then depend upon implementing the most appropriate of these strategies for particular situations and communities. The principles of pro-poor tourism are the same everywhere, but their implementation will vary according to the type of tourism product from say, small-scale eco-tourism to mass tourism. Destination-based strategies, for example, are appropriate for particular groups, encouraging economic linkages between tourism businesses and local community groups such as farmers. At the destination it is important to reduce leakage through imports, boost partnerships, develop local enterprises and increase community pride. In Asia a particular group that is being targeted for pro-poor tourism projects is the urban poor. In Asian cities tourism is labour intensive, has low barriers to entry for workers, and women can be major beneficiaries.

Already, pro-poor tourism initiatives around the world have come up with some valuable lessons for successful implementation. These include the importance of local ownership and control and the need to develop partnerships with the private sector on an equitable footing. Pro-poor tourism must also recognise the basic principles of tourism development and realise that it will only succeed if there is access to transport, accommodation and the wider range of support services and products.

Despite the growing momentum for the development of pro-poor tourism, there are some issues which make the concept controversial. For example, there is a perception by aid agencies that tourism is for the wealthy and they do not support the concept. In part this stems from a lack of education, training and understanding about pro-poor tourism. There are also some real practical barriers including:

- Significant economic leakages out of the local community reducing the net benefits of tourism.

- Lack of investment and low interest loans to allow local tourism enterprises to get under way.

- The fact that not all the poor will benefit equally and this can lead to conflict.

- A lack of infrastructure and basic services in very poor areas.

But, however difficult the practical adoption of pro-poor tourism may be, there is no doubt that the philosophy of tourism as a tool for poverty reduction must be embraced by the public and private sectors in tourism. Tourism has a real contribution to make in this area.

WEB SITES

http://www.adb.org/Documents/Policies/Poverty_Reducation/default.asp

http://www.propoortourism.org.uk

http://www.worldbank.org/poverty

REFERENCES

Ashley, C., Boyd, C. and Goodwin, H. (2000) Pro-poor tourism: putting poverty at the heart of the tourism agenda, *Natural Resource Perspectives* **51** (March) 1–12.

World Tourism Organization (2002) *Sustainable Tourism – Eliminating Poverty*, WTO, Madrid.

World Travel and Tourism Council (2003) *Blueprint for New Tourism*, WTTC, London.

DISCUSSION QUESTIONS

1 Can tourism be a real force for the alleviation of poverty or is the debate simply rhetoric?

2 Do you think that the role of tourism in poverty alleviation should be confined to governments and aid agencies, or is there a role for the tourist in this strategy? How can tourists 'do their bit' to alleviate poverty at the destination?

3 Should the future tourism development agenda also focus on alleviating other problems in society in addition to poverty?

PART ONE
TOURISM DEMAND

CHAPTER ONE
MANAGING TOURISM DEMAND   34

CHAPTER TWO
TOURISM CONSUMER BEHAVIOUR   50

CHAPTER THREE
MEASURING DEMAND FOR TOURISM   82

CHAPTER FOUR
TOURISM DEMAND DETERMINANTS AND
FORECASTING   112

INTRODUCTION

This part provides you with a comprehensive introduction to tourism demand. It aims to provide you with five key knowledge areas:

1 The concepts, definitions and indicators of tourism demand.

2 Tourism consumer behaviour.

3 How tourism demand is measured and reported.

4 The determinants of tourism demand.

5 Tourism demand forecasting.

The part is organised into four chapters, with each covering one or more of the key knowledge areas above. Each chapter explores the area of knowledge in depth and is structured to meet a set of learning outcomes which are provided at the beginning of the chapter. In addition we identify and annotate selected reading, not an easy task for tourism demand, which has not received the attention that it deserves. A range of case studies bring to life the concepts and theoretical issues in the chapters and a series of self-check, discussion and essay questions throughout the text allow you to review and test your understanding of the material.

In the introduction to this book we identified Leiper's tourism system as an effective organising concept for tourism. Tourism demand originating from Leiper's generating region is effectively the subject of this section of four chapters. In Chapter One – Managing Tourism Demand – we introduce the key approaches to tourism demand. There are two key themes running through this chapter. The first is the way that the views of tourism managers have changed as demand has grown since the Second World War. There is no doubt that managing tourism demand is one of the challenges for tourism in the twenty-first century as the volume of tourists grows. We chart how the perceptions of demand have changed over the years with early pronouncements such as the UN's Universal Declaration of Human Rights in 1948 encouraging everyone to travel as a 'right', to the present day when the tourist is urged to travel 'responsibly'. On this point we provide a mini case study demonstrating how different sectors of the tourism industry have approached the 'education' of tourists to behave 'responsibly'. The second theme of the chapter is the recognition that, in order to manage tourism demand, it is important to understand the nature of demand in terms of definitions, the various components of demand and simple indicators.

Chapter Two – Tourism Consumer Behaviour – probes more deeply into demand by providing an overview of the consumer decision-making process in tourism. The themes of this chapter focus around, first, understanding the components of the tourism consumer decision process, and, second, assessing models of the process. We show that there is a range of factors that influence travel decisions; factors such as motivation, attitudes, perceptions and images. The chapter provides you with a thorough overview of these ideas and the major literature debates. The second theme shows how these factors have been drawn together and structured in the form of models of consumer decision making. For tourism, these models have been adapted from more general approaches in the consumer marketing literature. Perhaps one of the key lessons from this chapter is to question whether these models are purely academic exercises or have a practical use for tourism managers. Finally, the chapter draws these threads together in a major case study showing how consumer decision making has changed since September 11, 2001.

In Chapter Three – Measuring Demand for Tourism – we turn to approaches to measuring patterns of consumer demand. This chapter has two distinct sections. First, we provide detail of the approaches used to measure demand for both international and domestic tourism and assess their effectiveness. We go on to consider why tourism demand is measured, what definitions are used and which statistics are normally compiled. Second, we describe in detail approaches to collecting market intelligence and managing information, ending the chapter with a major case study on the need for the tourism sector to develop a knowledge management approach. The key lesson from this chapter is the need to be cautious in interpreting and using tourism statistics.

In Chapter Four – Tourism Demand Determinants and Forecasting – we focus on two key areas of knowledge. First, we provide a detailed assessment of the major determinants of demand for tourism. We consider specific determinants of demand at the individual level and go on to demonstrate how they can be aggregated to explain patterns and rhythms of tourism demand globally. In this way we can show that those countries with a high level of economic development and a stable, urbanised population are major generators of tourism demand – the chapter ends with a major case study analysing global patterns of tourism demand. The second area of knowledge relates to tourism forecasting. We show that an understanding of demand determinants is fundamental to forecasting future demand. Accurate forecasts in tourism are essential to inform decision making in both governments and the industry and we examine the different approaches available to forecast tourism demand and the reasons why we should maintain forecasts. This is an important issue given that tourism is a perishable industry and its assets such as beds or aircraft seats cannot be stored. The lesson of this chapter is that, despite the fact that tourism is a volatile industry operating in a world of rapid and unexpected change, tourism forecasts are necessary for informed management decision making.

CHAPTER ONE
MANAGING TOURISM DEMAND

INTRODUCTION

In this chapter we introduce the key approaches to tourism demand that underpin its management. There is no doubt that managing tourism demand is one of the challenges for tourism in the twenty-first century as the volume of tourists grows and the remotest corners of the world are visited. In fact, we can chart how the perceptions of demand have changed over the years with early pronouncements such as the UN's Universal Declaration of Human Rights encouraging everyone to travel as a 'right', to the present day when the tourist is urged to travel 'responsibly'.

In order to manage tourism demand it is important to understand the nature of demand in terms of definitions, the various components of demand and simple indicators. In particular, we must recognise the fact that demand comprises much more than just those who are active as tourists. There are large sections of society who would like to travel but who experience barriers to travel. From a management and marketing point of view it is important to understand these barriers and to devise strategies to remove them. Finally, this chapter provides you with a number of techniques that allow you to estimate the demand for tourism, in particular, populations.

LEARNING OUTCOMES

In this chapter we focus on the basic concepts, definitions and indicators of tourism demand to provide you with:

- an awareness of how approaches to the management of demand have changed since 1945;

- a thorough understanding of the concept and definitions of tourism demand;

- an awareness of the components of tourism demand;

- a grasp of the importance of indicators of demand such as propensity to travel; and

- a comprehension of the purpose of demand schedules and an understanding of how to interpret them.

MANAGING TOURISM DEMAND

Considering Leiper's overall system for tourism that we described in the introductory chapter, demand for tourism is the result of activities and decisions made in the generating region (see Figure 0.2). As such, demand for tourism is a fundamental element in the tourism system. Yet, while the history of tourism may be traced back many thousands of years to the Ancient Greeks and Romans, it is only relatively recently, with the advent of demand for mass tourism, that international tourism activity has become so prevalent in the developed world. Indeed, the rapid expansion of leisure travel from the 1960s onwards continues to influence all aspects of the tourism system today. The level of demand for tourism is predicted to reach unprecedented levels during this century, providing the tourism industry and all those involved in its production and consumption with major challenges.

In this respect we can identify how perceptions and approaches to the management of tourism demand have changed as volumes have increased and the integrity of destinations been threatened. For example, just after the Second World War, the United Nations (UN) stated in its Universal Declaration of Human Rights that: 'everyone has the right to rest and leisure including . . . periodic holidays with pay' (1948). By 1980 the Manila Declaration on World Tourism declared the ultimate aim of tourism to be: 'the improvement of the quality of life and the creation of better living conditions for all peoples' (World Tourism Organization, 1980). With this statement we can see the emphasis changing from the earlier 'right' of everyone to demand tourism, to statements stressing the 'quality of demand' and the 'form' of demand and/or experience. This observation is further supported by declarations in the 1990s which state that if individuals demand tourism, they must take responsibility for the environment and host societies at the destination: 'tourists share responsibility for conservation of the environment and cultural heritage' (World Tourism Organization, 1994). This shift in thinking culminated in 1999 with the World Tourism Organization's 'Global Code of Ethics for Tourism'. In other words, as society increasingly demands travel, it is important to manage tourist behaviour through codes of ethics, visitor guidelines, and education about responsible conduct at destinations.

Clearly then there is pressure for the management of tourist behaviour through encouraging tourists to exercise their 'right' to travel in a responsible or ethical manner. Since the 1980s, this pressure has come from the media and consumer groups such as 'Tourism Concern', rather than from the tourism industry itself; indeed it could be argued that the industry entered the movement for responsible tourism rather later than might have been expected. Nonetheless, there is now considerable support for the responsible consumption of tourism with a number of guidebooks for the consumer (see, for example, Mann, 1999). The first mini case study in this chapter examines contrasting examples of initiatives for responsible travel from the public sector, pressure groups and the tourism industry itself and asks you to reflect on their relative effectiveness.

MINI CASE STUDY 1.1
Contrasting approaches to the responsible consumption of tourism

THE PUBLIC SECTOR

The most influential public sector initiative for the responsible consumption of tourism is the World Tourism Organization's 'Global Code of Ethics for Tourism'. This initiative sets the framework for the responsible and sustainable development of world tourism (www.worldtourism.org/projects/ethics). The code was developed between 1997 and 1999 and has 10 principles, a number of which relate to responsible tourism behaviour. However, the wording is both diplomatic and non-specific. For example, in article 1, tourism's contribution to mutual understanding and respect between peoples and societies, the code states:

> Tourists themselves should observe the social and cultural traditions and practices of all peoples … and tourism activities should be conducted in harmony with the attributes and traditions of the host regions and countries and in respect for their laws, practices and customs.

PRESSURE GROUPS AND CHARITIES

Pressure groups for responsible tourism issue consumer guidelines for behaviour at destinations, while charities such as Oxfam now offer tours to Asia, Cuba and Australia. These tours put the people, their culture and the environment of the destination first and introduce the tourist to the host communities (www.caa.org.au/travel). A San Francisco-based group – Partners in Sustainable Tourism – have put together a comprehensive code for travelling responsibly covering cultural understanding, social and environmental impacts (www2.pirt.org/travelcode.html). The code contrasts with the WTO's code of ethics in its specific and useful advice. For example:

> Support the local economy by using locally owned restaurants and hotels, buying local products, made by local people with renewable resources.

THE TOURISM INDUSTRY

The response of the tourism industry to the call for responsible consumption of tourism has been mixed. However, where the industry has embraced the concept, the results have been impressive. For example, the Dutch tour operator TUI has developed an environmental awareness campaign for its dive tourism operation in the Caribbean islands of the Netherlands Antilles (Tour Operators Initiative, 2001). The project began in 1999 and aims to 'provide customers with information on responsible travel and sustainable products at various stages of their holiday'. Their approach is also very practical providing actionable information and advice to customers, from the brochure through to their time on the islands:

- information on responsible travel is provided in the TUI brochure;

- information tips on environmentally sound practice is provided in a booklet with the client's tickets;

- a video on sustainable activities and excursions is shown on the flight;

- hostesses meet clients on arrival and brief them;

- the TUI resource book on sustainable excursions, activities and attractions is available in hotel lobbies; and

- partner companies, such as dive operators, who comply with the programme, are actively promoted to clients.

DISCUSSION QUESTIONS

1 Of the three approaches, discuss the relative effectiveness of the communication approaches used.

2 Why has the tourism industry been slow to adopt responsible tourism principles?

3 Considering the examples above, which do you feel will be the most effective in changing tourists' behaviour?

DEFINITIONS OF TOURISM DEMAND

Definitions of demand vary according to the subject perspective of the author. For example, economists consider demand to be the schedule of the amount of any product or service that people are willing and able to buy at each specific price in a set of possible prices during a specified period of time. In contrast, psychologists view demand from the perspective of motivation and behaviour. Geographers, on the other hand, define tourist demand as: 'the total number of persons who travel, or wish to travel, to use tourist facilities and services at places away from their places of work and residence' (Mathieson and Wall, 1982).

Each approach is useful. The economic approach introduces the idea of elasticity – which describes the relationship between demand and price, or other variables. The geographer's definition implies a wide range of influences, in addition to price, as determinants of demand and includes not only those who actually participate in tourism, but also those who wish to, but for some reason do not. On the other hand, the psychologist scratches underneath the skin of the tourist to examine the interaction of personality, environment and demand for tourism.

CONCEPTS OF TOURISM DEMAND

The notion that some individuals may harbour a demand for tourism but are unable to realise that demand suggests that demand for tourism consists of a number of components. We can identify three basic components that make up the total demand for tourism:

1 **Effective** or **actual demand** is the actual number of participants in tourism or those who are travelling, i.e. *de facto* tourists. This is the component of demand most commonly and easily measured and the bulk of tourism statistics refer to effective demand.

2 **Suppressed demand** is made up of that section of the population who do not travel for some reason. Despite burgeoning demand for tourism across the world, even in the twenty-first century it is still true that only a very small percentage of the world's total population engages in international tourism. Of course, a considerably greater number participate in domestic travel, but in many parts of the world tourism remains an unobtainable luxury.

   Two elements of suppressed demand can be distinguished. First, potential demand refers to those who will travel at some future date if they experience a change in their circumstances. For example, their purchasing power may increase, or they may receive more paid holiday entitlement, and they therefore have the potential to move into the effective demand category. Second, deferred demand is a demand postponed because of a problem in the supply environment, such as a lack of capacity in accommodation, weather conditions or, perhaps, terrorist activity. Again this implies that when the supply conditions are more favourable, those in the deferred demand category will convert to effective demand at some future date.

3 Finally, there will always be those who simply do not wish to travel or are unable to travel, constituting a category of **no demand**.

We can also consider other ways in which demand for tourism may be viewed and influenced. For example, substitution of demand refers to the case when demand for one activity (say a self-catering holiday) is substituted by another (staying in serviced accommodation). A similar concept is redirection of demand where the geographical location of demand is changed – say a trip to Spain is redirected to Greece because of over-booking of accommodation. Finally, the opening of new tourism supply – say a resort, attraction or accommodation – will:

- redirect demand from similar facilities in the area;

- substitute demand from other facilities; and

- generate new demand.

Economists refer to the first two of these as the 'displacement effect' – in other words, demand from other facilities is displaced to the new one and no extra demand is generated. This can be a problem in tourism and is an important consideration when appraising the worth of new tourism projects.

   Finally, given Leiper's model of tourism described in the introductory chapter, it is clear that tourism demand results in flows between the generating region and the destination region. One of the key considerations of tourism demand is understanding the flows of tourism between different generating markets and tourism destinations. These flows are complex and determined by a wide variety of factors including geographical proximity, historical trade and cultural ties, and, of course, the notion of contrasting environments, exemplified by the flow of tourists from northern Europe to the warmer countries of the Mediterranean. These factors can be thought of as either push factors (generally determined by the nature of the

MINI CASE STUDY 1.2
The gravity model

One approach to explaining the flow of tourism between generating markets and destinations is the gravity model. The gravity model is based upon Newton's law of gravitation and takes into account the push and pull factors that influence tourism demand. Effectively, the greater the 'mass' of the generating region or destination, the greater will be the flow of tourists. But the gravity model also adds a constraining factor, that of distance and intervening opportunities. The greater the time and cost involved in reaching a destination from an origin point, the smaller will be the flow.

In effect, the gravity model can be used as a crude tourism demand forecasting tool based upon the size of a generating market (mass or 'push'), the attractiveness of a destination ('pull'), and the distance between them. The difficulty in using the model in practice is finding surrogate measures for the key variables. For example, it is difficult to measure 'attractiveness'; population is often supplemented by using other indicators such car ownership, education or gross domestic product; while physical distance may be supplemented by time or cost of travel. Finally, it is also possible to construct resorts to act as 'an intervening opportunity' and divert flows from a key market – Cancun in Mexico, for example, was created to capture North Americans travelling.

The following examples show the effectiveness of the gravity model approach:

- As a destination, Australia has a strong 'pull' factor with stunning destinations, exotic wildlife and a climate suited to tourism. Yet the other variables of the gravity model conspire to mean that international demand for Australia's tourism will never be on the scale of say Spain or the Caribbean. This is due to the constraining factor of the 'tyranny of distance' of Australia from the world's generating markets; and the fact that there are no significant tourism-generating countries to provide the 'push' nearby Australia.

- Spain's tourism has benefited from its proximity to the large generating markets of Western Europe, providing both the 'push' of the market and minimising the friction of distance. While the 'pull' of Spain is strong – particularly in terms of climate and lifestyle – criticism of some of the early coastal development is easily outweighed by the other two variables.

DISCUSSION QUESTIONS

1 Make a list of the quantifiable elements of a destination that might be used as a surrogate measure of attractiveness.

2 Identify six countries in the world that might be expected to receive a large volume of tourists according to the gravity model.

3 Identify a list of 'intervening opportunities' in tourism – either resorts or countries.

generating regions – such as affluence) or pull factors (destination features such as attractiveness, accessibility and relative price). We look at one approach to explaining these flows in the second mini case study.

A second approach to understanding tourism flows is through the concept of **travel propensity**. In order to manage tourism demand we need to be able to measure and estimate the demand behaviour of different groups in society. One of the most useful indicators of effective demand in any particular population is travel propensity. This measure simply considers the penetration of tourism trips in a population. Once we know the levels of travel propensity of a population, we can then begin to explain the reasons why different groups in society have different levels of travel propensity. This is considered in detail in the major case study later in this chapter.

DEMAND SCHEDULES

In economic terms, a demand schedule refers to the quantities of a product that an individual wishes to purchase at different prices at a given point in time. Generally, the form of this relationship between price and quantity purchased is an inverse one, i.e. the higher the price of the product, the lower is the demand; the lower the price, the greater is the demand. This is shown in Figure 1.1.

It is normal to characterise the demand curve DD in Figure 1.1 by an appropriate measure which expresses the responsiveness of quantity to changes in price. Such a measure is termed the 'elasticity of demand' for product X with respect to its own price P_x. The own price elasticity of demand (ei) measures the ratio of the percentage change in quantity to the percentage change in price, i.e.:

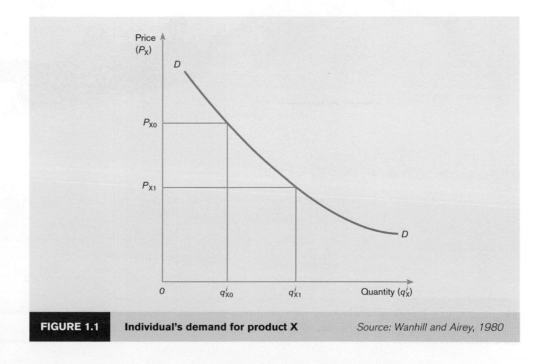

| FIGURE 1.1 | **Individual's demand for product X** | *Source: Wanhill and Airey, 1980* |

$$ei = \frac{\text{\% change in quantity}}{\text{\% change in price}}$$

It is conventional to consider *ei* in its absolute or positive value, thus we refer to an own price elasticity of demand as 1.0, 2.0, 3.0, etc., and not −1.0, −2.0 or −3.0. The critical value of *ei* is 1.0; for goods that have an own price elasticity greater than 1, demand is said to be elastic. Products exhibiting this property are goods that are normally viewed as luxury items – overseas holidays or dining out. When a good has an own price elasticity of demand of less than 1 it is classed as a necessity. For necessities, quantity adjustments respond sluggishly to price changes – food is classed as a necessity.

So far we have examined both individual consumer demand for a product and also single variables such as price. However, in truth the world is more complex than this and we need to extend the concept of demand schedules in two ways:

1 There are several factors other than price that affect a consumer's demand for a tourism product. These include prices of other goods, an individual's income and social tastes and habits. Economists find that it is not practical to consider variations in all the components at one time so they assume all components are constant except the one in question.

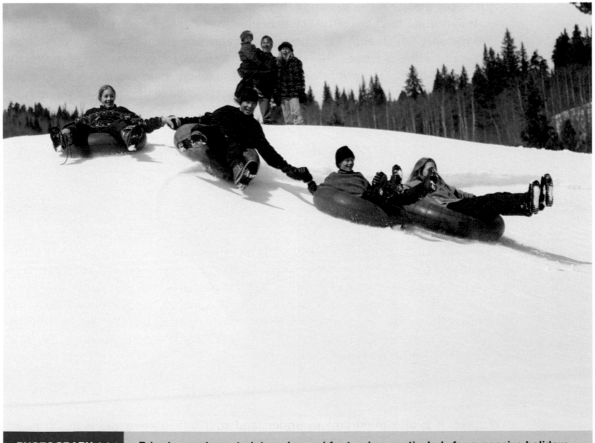

| PHOTOGRAPH 1.1 | Price is a real constraint on demand for tourism, particularly for expensive holidays such as winter sports |

| FIGURE 1.2 | Derivation of a market demand curve | Source: Wanhill and Airey, 1980 |

2 Tourism is not only concerned with individuals but also responses of the market to variations in the factors affecting demand. Since individual tourists make up the market, it is reasonable to suppose that market demand curves respond in a similar fashion to individual curves, hence a first approach is to sum the individual demand schedules to arrive at the market schedule. This is illustrated in Figure 1.2 which supposes that there are only two individuals in the market. The market demand schedule is derived from the horizontal summation of the two individual curves. We can see that the market curve has a distinct 'kink' where the two individual curves join: this arises because the market is assumed to consist of only two persons. As the number in the market increases so any kinks are ironed out and a more or less smooth curve results.

CONCLUSION

The generating region of Leiper's tourism system is influential in shaping the nature and scope of tourism flows around the world. As the tourism sector becomes more professional and knowledge-based, the techniques and approaches outlined in this chapter will be increasingly applied to the management of tourism demand. Approaches to the responsible consumption of demand, in other words, tourists exercising their 'right' to travel but doing so in a 'responsible' way, will become increasingly important if the integrity of destinations, environments and societies is to be preserved.

Definitions of tourism demand tend to be specific to particular viewpoints – for example, economists view demand in terms of schedules as described in this chapter. It is also important to understand that tourism demand is much more than just those who are travelling at any one point in time; indeed an understanding of the barriers preventing people from travelling is important. This is not just from the point of view of increasing society's access to travel, but also from a commercial point of view in increasing the viability of enterprises. Finally, this chapter has outlined some simple estimating techniques which allow you to calculate the potential of particular populations to travel.

Self-check questions

1 Make a list of the reasons why an individual may be in the 'no tourism demand' category.

2 Draft the elements of a 'responsible tourism behaviour code'.

3 List the reasons why an individual may fall into the 'potential tourism demand' category.

4 Identify 10 reasons why demand for international tourism has grown since 1945.

5 Review the concepts of demand substitution and demand redirection and provide two examples of each.

Essay questions

1 How might the market and individual demand curves for tourism differ from other commodities, such as, say, food?

2 Critique the concept of 'responsible tourism consumption'.

3 'The WTO's Global Code of Ethics for Tourism is impossible to police.' Discuss this statement.

4 Why is it difficult to come up with a universally agreed definition of tourism demand?

5 Identify and discuss the key barriers to tourism demand that an individual might experience.

Annotated further reading

Books

Jafari, J. (2001) *The Encyclopedia of Tourism*, Routledge, London.
A number of entries providing a definitive view of elements of tourism demand, the gravity model and other concepts written by the leading expert in each field.

Smith, S.L. (1996) *Tourism Analysis*, 2nd edn, Longman, Harlow.
A comprehensive handbook of analytical approaches, including demand estimation, various indices of demand and the models such as the gravity model.

Web sites

http://www.tourismconcern.org.uk

One of the first and most comprehensive pressure groups for the responsible consumption of tourism and a comprehensive resource.

http://www.world-tourism.org

The WTO's site is an excellent source for new initiatives in responsible tourism and the global code of ethics.

References cited

Mann, M. (1999) *The Good Alternative Travel Guide*, Earthscan, London.

Mathieson, A. and Wall, G. (1982) *Tourism: Economic Physical and Social Impacts*, Longman, London.

Tour Operators Initiative (2001) *Sustainable Tourism: The Tour Operators Initiative*, TOI, London.

Wanhill, S.R.C. and Airey, D.W. (1980) 'Demand for accommodation', pp. 23–44 in Kotas, R. (ed.), *Managerial Economics for Hotel Operation*, Surrey University Press, Guildford.

World Tourism Organization (1980) *The Manila Declaration on World Tourism*, WTO, Madrid.

World Tourism Organization (1994) *The Osaka Declaration*, WTO, Madrid.

MAJOR CASE STUDY 1.1
INDICATORS OF TOURISM DEMAND: TRAVEL PROPENSITY

In order to manage tourism demand we need to be able to measure and estimate the demand behaviour of different groups in society. One of the most useful indicators of effective demand in any particular population is travel propensity. This measure simply considers the penetration of tourism trips in a population. There are two forms of travel propensity:

1 **Net travel propensity** refers to the percentage of the population that takes at least one tourism trip in a given period of time. In other words it is a measure of the penetration of travel among 'individuals' in the population. The suppressed and no demand components will therefore ensure that net travel propensity never approaches 100% and a figure of 70% or 80% is likely to be the maximum for developed Western economies.

| PHOTOGRAPH 1.2 | **Propensities for travel in the developing world tend to be higher for those living in the cities than for rural areas** |

Source: Edward Webb/Rex Features

2 Gross travel propensity gives the total number of tourism trips taken as a percentage of the population. This is a measure of the penetration of 'trips', not individual 'travellers'. Clearly then, as second and third holidays increase in importance, so gross travel propensity becomes more relevant. Gross travel propensity can exceed 100% and often approaches 200% in some Western European countries where those participating in tourism may take more than one trip away from home per annum.

Simply dividing gross travel propensity by net will give the *travel frequency*, in other words, the average number of trips taken by those participating in tourism during the period in question. So, a worked example of travel propensity is as follows:

Out of a population of 10 million inhabitants:

3.0 million inhabitants take one trip of one night or more

i.e. $3 \times 1 = 3.0$ million trips

1.5 million inhabitants take two trips of one night or more

i.e. $1.5 \times 2 = 3.0$ million trips

0.4 million inhabitants take three trips of one night or more

i.e. $0.4 \times 3 = 1.2$ million trips

0.2 million inhabitants take four trips of one night or more

i.e. $0.2 \times 4 = 0.8$ million trips

In total 5.1 million inhabitants take at least one trip and there is a total of 8.0 million trips.

Therefore:

$$\text{Net travel propensity} = \frac{\text{Number of population taking at least one trip}}{\text{Total population}} \times 100 = \frac{5.1}{10} \times 100 = 51\%$$

$$\text{Gross travel propensity} = \frac{\text{Number of total trips}}{\text{Total population}} \times 100 = \frac{8}{10} \times 100 = 80\%$$

$$\text{Travel frequency} = \frac{\text{Gross travel propensity}}{\text{Net travel propensity}} = \frac{80\%}{51\%} = 1.57$$

A further refinement to these calculations can be made to allow us to assess the capability of a country to generate trips, an important activity when seeking new markets. This involves three stages:

- First, the number of trips originating in the country is divided by the total number of trips taken in the world. This gives an index of the ability of each country to generate travellers.

- Second, the population of the country is divided by the total population of the world, thus ranking each country by relative importance in relation to world population.

- Finally, by dividing the result of the first stage by the result of the second the 'country potential generation index' (CPGI) is produced.

$$CPGI = \frac{N_e/N_w}{P_e/P_w}$$

where N_e = number of trips generated by the country
N_w = number of trips generated in the world
P_e = population of the country
P_w = population of the world

An index of 1.0 indicates an average generation capability. Countries with an index greater than unity are generating more tourists than expected by their population. Countries with an index below 1.0 generate fewer trips than average.

An example will demonstrate the usefulness of this approach in understanding tourism demand, as follows.

Mexico is the world's fifth most populous country with 175 million inhabitants in 2001. In the same year Mexico generated 2.5 million outbound tourism trips, a very small number when compared to the potential of the population to travel.

In contrast, in the same year, the UK's population stood at 59 million and generated 58 million outbound trips. Why is there such a difference in outbound travel propensity between the two countries?

1 Economic factors – Mexico's economy collapsed in the late 1990s.

2 Social factors such as levels of education, living standards and population growth.

3 Locational factors – there are many destinations close to the UK and travelling within Europe is reasonably priced. In addition, the European tourism industry is mature and well developed, encouraging travel.

Source: Boniface and Cooper (1987), adapted from Burkart and Medlik (1975), pp. 53–60

REFERENCES

Boniface, B. and Cooper, C. (1987) *The Geography of Travel and Tourism*, Heinemann, London.

Burkart, J. and Medlik, S. (eds) (1975) *The Management of Tourism*, Heinemann, London.

DISCUSSION QUESTIONS

1 The notion of net travel propensity is important when estimating demand from populations with an above average travel frequency. Identify market segments in your country which might be expected to have a high travel frequency and explain why this is so.

2 Take a country of your choice and using Internet or other sources, calculate the 'country potential generation index' (CPGI). Compare your result with others in the class and explain the differences.

3 What factors in a country will lead to a high CPGI?

CHAPTER TWO
TOURISM CONSUMER BEHAVIOUR

INTRODUCTION

In the previous chapter we outlined basic definitions and concepts of demand and showed how the management of demand has changed since 1945. This probes more deeply into demand by providing an overview of the consumer decision-making process in tourism. There is no doubt that a grasp of consumer decision processes is essential if we are to understand and predict demand for tourism. Demand for tourism at the individual level can be treated as a consumption process that is influenced by a number of factors. These may be a combination of needs and desires, availability of time and money, or images, perceptions and attitude. In this chapter we review the major literature debates surrounding these concepts in order to explain how these factors influence individual behaviour in tourism.

Influences on consumer behaviour can be summarised as attitudes, perceptions, image, roles, motivations and determinants. A number of researchers have attempted to draw together these influences and to structure them in the form of models of consumer decision making. For tourism, these models have been adapted from more general approaches in the consumer marketing literature. As we will see this creates some issues in terms of the practical use of these models and their ability to capture the particular nature of the tourism purchasing decision.

LEARNING OUTCOMES

This chapter deals with the factors and influences which, when combined, will influence a consumer's demand for tourism. By reading this chapter you will:

- have a knowledge of the factors influencing the buyer decision process in tourism;

- in particular have an understanding of the theory of motivation;

- have an appreciation of the way that the roles and psychographics of tourists are linked to specific forms of tourism and tourist needs;

- have a knowledge of the key models that seek to explain the decision-making process for the purchase of tourism products; and

- be able to critique models of consumer decision making in tourism.

THE INDIVIDUAL DECISION-MAKING PROCESS

At the personal level it is clear that the factors influencing demand for tourism are closely linked to models of consumer behaviour. No two individuals are alike and differences in attitudes, perceptions, images and motivation have an important influence on travel decisions. It is important to note that:

- **attitudes** depend on an individual's perception of the world;

- **perceptions** are mental impressions of, say, a destination or travel company and are determined by many factors which include childhood, family, work experiences, education, books, television programmes and films and promotional images. Perception involves the encoding of information by individuals and influences attitudes and behaviour towards products but does not explain by itself, or when combined with attitudes, why people want to travel;

- **travel motivators** do explain why people want to travel and they are the inner urges that initiate travel demand; and

- **images** are sets of beliefs, ideas and impressions relating to products and destinations.

THE FUNDAMENTALS OF CONSUMER BEHAVIOUR AND TOURISM

It is important for tourism managers to research and understand the way in which tourism consumers make decisions and act in relation to the consumption of tourism products. While the term 'consumer' would seem to indicate a single concept of demand, the reality is that there is a whole diversity of consumer behaviour with decisions being made for a range of reasons. We need to study a tourist's consumer behaviour to be aware of:

- the needs, purchase motives and decision process associated with the consumption of tourism;

- the impact of the different effects of various promotional tactics;

- the possible perception of risk for tourism purchases, including the impact of terrorist incidents;

- the different market segments based upon purchase behaviour; and

- how managers can improve their chance of marketing success.

Many variables will influence the way consumption patterns differ. Patterns will change based upon the different products available and the way individuals have learnt to purchase tourism products. The variations are complex and therefore it is more practical to deal with general behavioural principles. These are often dealt with in a framework that includes the disciplines of psychology, sociology and economics.

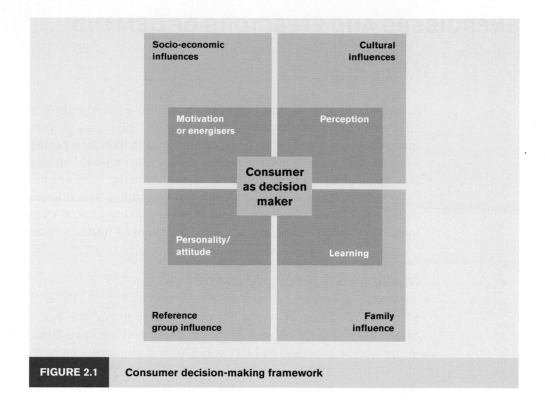

| FIGURE 2.1 | Consumer decision-making framework |

Figure 2.1 provides a simplification of some of the main influences affecting the consumer as decision maker. These are discussed within this chapter.

We can view the tourism consumer decision process as a system made up of four basic elements:

1 **Energisers of demand.** These are the forces of motivation that lead a tourist to decide to visit an attraction or go on a holiday.

2 **Effectors of demand.** The consumer will have developed ideas of a destination, product or organisation by a process of learning, attitudes and associations from promotional messages and information. This will affect the consumer's image and knowledge of a tourism product thus serving to heighten or dampen the various energisers that lead to consumer action.

3 **Roles and the decision-making process.** Here, the important role is that of the family member who is normally involved in the different stages of the purchase process and the final resolution of decisions about when, where and how the group will consume the tourism product.

4 **Determinants of demand.** In addition, the consumer decision-making process for tourism is underpinned by the determinants of demand. Even though motivation may exist, demand is filtered, constrained or channelled due to economic (e.g. discretionary income), sociological (reference groups, cultural values) or psychological factors (perception of risk, personality, attitudes). We look at determinants of demand in detail in Chapter 4.

ENERGISERS AND EFFECTORS OF DEMAND

Motivation

An understanding of motivation is the key to understanding tourist behaviour, answering the question of why people travel. The classic dictionary definition of motivation is derived from the word 'motivate' which is to cause a person to act in a certain way, or to stimulate interest. We can also refer to the word 'motive' which is concerned with initiating movement or inducing a person to act. As would be expected, many texts associated with tourism utilise the concept of motivation as a major influence upon consumer behaviour, taking general theories, such as that by Maslow, discussed below, and applying them to tourist's consumer behaviour.

Maslow's hierarchy model

Maslow's hierarchy of needs (Figure 2.2) is probably the best-known theory of motivation, perhaps because of its simplicity and intuitive attraction. The theory of motivation proposed by Maslow (1970) is in the form of a ranking, or hierarchy, of the arrangements of individual needs. The early humanistic values of Maslow seem to have led him to create a model where self-actualisation is valued as the level 'man' should aspire to. He argued that if none of the needs in the hierarchy was satisfied, then the lowest needs, the physiological ones, would dominate behaviour. If these were satisfied, however, they would no longer motivate and the individual would be motivated by the next level in the hierarchy.

Maslow identified two motivational types, which can be greatly simplified as:

- deficiency or tension-reducing motives;
- inductive or arousal-seeking motives.

Maslow maintained that his theory of motivation is holistic and dynamic and can be applied to both work and non-work spheres of life. He treats his levels of need as universal and innate, yet of such instinctual weakness that they can be modified, accelerated or inhibited by the environment. He also stated that while all the needs

Lower   1. Physiological – hunger, thirst, rest, activity

2. Safety – security, freedom from fear and anxiety

3. Belonging and love – affection, giving and receiving love

4. Esteem – self-esteem and esteem for others

Higher   5. Self-actualisation – personal self-fulfilment

FIGURE 2.2	Maslow's hierarchy of needs

are innate, only those behaviours that satisfy physiological needs are unlearned. Although a great deal of tourism demand theory has been built upon Maslow's approach there are a number of questions that Maslow does not answer:

- It is not clear from his work why he selected five basic needs.

- Why are the needs ranked as they are?

- How could he justify his model when he did not carry out clinical observation or experiment?

- Why did he never try to expand the original set of motives?

Tourism authors have borrowed extensively from Maslow, simply because he has provided a convenient set of containers that can be relatively easily labelled. The notion that a comprehensive coverage of human needs can be organised into an understandable hierarchical framework is of obvious benefit to tourism theorists.

Within Maslow's model, human activity is wired into predetermined, understandable and predictable aspects of action. This is very much in the behaviourist tradition of psychology as opposed to the cognitive approach, which stresses the concepts of irrationality and unpredictability of behaviour. However, Maslow's theory does allow for humans to transcend the mere embodiment of biological needs that sets them apart from other species.

To some extent the popularity of Maslow's theory can be understood in moral terms. It suggests that, given the right circumstances, people will grow out of their concern for the materialistic aspects of life and become more interested in 'higher' things.

The study of motivation in tourism

The study of motivation has been derived from a range of disciplinary areas which has led to a diversity of approach in tourism – an observation that holds true for many aspects of tourism studied in this book. This diversity is reflected in the approaches of various authors' discussions of how motivation influences tourists' consumer behaviour. The key approaches are outlined below.

DANN

Dann (1981) has pointed out that there are seven elements within the overall approach to motivation:

1 Travel is a response to what is lacking yet desired. This approach suggests that tourists are motivated by the desire to experience phenomena that are different from those available in their home environment.

2 Destination pull in response to motivational push. This distinguishes between the motivation of the individual tourist in terms of the level of desire (push) and the pull of the destination or attraction.

3 Motivation as fantasy. This is a subset of the first two factors and suggests that tourists travel in order to undertake behaviour that may not be culturally sanctioned in their home setting.

4 Motivation as classified purpose. A broad category which invokes the main purposes of a trip as a motivator for travel. Purposes may include visiting friends and relatives, enjoying leisure activities, or study.

5 Motivational typologies. This approach is internally divided into:
   (a) behavioural typologies such as the motivators 'sunlust' (search for a better set of amenities than are available at home) and 'wanderlust' (curiosity to experience the strange and unfamiliar) as proposed by Gray (1970); and
   (b) typologies that focus on dimensions of the tourist role.

6 Motivation and tourist experiences. This approach is characterised by the debate regarding the authenticity of tourist experiences and depends upon beliefs about types of tourist experience.

7 Motivation as auto-definition and meaning. This suggests that the way in which tourists define their situations will provide a greater understanding of tourist motivation than simply observing their behaviour.

Dann suggests that these seven identified approaches demonstrate a 'definitional fuzziness' which, if not clarified, may make it difficult to discover 'whether or not individual tourism researchers are studying the same phenomenon'.

MCINTOSH, GOELDNER AND RITCHIE

McIntosh, Goeldner and Ritchie (1995) utilise four categories of motivation:

1 **Physical motivators:** those related to refreshment of body and mind, health purposes, sport and pleasure. This group of motivators are seen to be linked to those activities which will reduce tension.

2 **Cultural motivators:** those identified by the desire to see and know more about other cultures, to find out about the natives of a country, their lifestyle, music, art, folklore, dance, etc.

3 **Interpersonal motivators:** this group includes a desire to meet new people, visit friends or relatives, and to seek new and different experiences. Travel is an escape from routine relationships with friends or neighbours or the home environment or it is used for spiritual reasons.

4 **Status and prestige motivators:** these include a desire for continuation of education (i.e. personal development, ego enhancement and sensual indulgence). Such motivators are seen to be concerned with the desire for recognition and attention from others, in order to boost the personal ego. This category also includes personal development in relation to the pursuit of hobbies and education.

PLOG

In 1974, Stanley Plog developed a theory which allowed the US population to be classified into a series of interrelated psychographic types. These types range from two extremes:

1 The 'psychocentric' type is derived from 'psyche' or 'self-centred' where an individual centres thoughts or concerns on the small problem areas of life. These

PHOTOGRAPH 2.1 **Motivations for tourism have changed over the years: in the new millennium motivations to see heritage sites and curiosity about the destinations have become dominant**

individuals tend to be conservative in their travel patterns, preferring 'safe' destinations and often taking many return trips. For this latter reason, market research in the tour-operating sector labels this group as 'repeaters'.

2 The 'allocentric' type derives from the root 'allo' meaning 'varied in form'. These individuals are adventurous and motivated to travel/discover new destinations. They rarely return to the same place twice, hence their market research label 'wanderers'.

The majority of the population fall in between these extremes in an area which Plog terms 'midcentric'. Plog also found that those who were at the lower end of income scales were more likely to be psychocentric types whereas at the upper income band there was more of a likelihood of being allocentric. In a later study it was observed that middle-income groups exhibited only a small positive correlation with psychographic types. This created problems because there were a number of psychographic types who could not, through income constraint, choose the type of holiday they preferred even if they were motivated towards it; after all, to be a wanderer around the globe can be expensive.

Plog's theory closely associates travel motivation to types of destination as shown in the first mini case in this chapter. Allocentrics, for example, will prefer destinations at the frontier of tourism, unspoilt and undiscovered by the travel trade. Psychocentrics on the other hand desire the comfort of a well-developed and 'safe' destination. While this is a useful way of thinking about tourists and destinations, it is more difficult to apply it. For example, tourists will travel with different motivations on different occasions. A second holiday or short-break weekend may be in a nearby psychocentric-type destination, whereas the main holiday may be in an allocentric-type destination. (See also Figure 7.1, p. 230.)

MINI CASE STUDY 2.1
Applying Plog's theory of travel motivation

Plog's psychocentric tourists are motivated by the safety and security of low-risk destinations where familiarity and continuity from visit to visit are clearly evident. Taking the example of the Alexander family from the United Kingdom, in the 1950s, they travelled each year from their home town in the north of England to the seaside resort of Blackpool. The constraints of factory holidays meant that they had to take the same two weeks holiday each year, staying in the same boarding house; indeed, they felt they were firm friends with the owners of the boarding house and were greeted warmly by name each summer. Of course, all their friends and workmates also had to take the same two weeks and, geographically, Blackpool was the easiest resort to reach by train from their hometown. Effectively, the town simply decamped to Blackpool for two weeks each year, creating the classic psychocentric profile of both traveller and destination – safe, familiar and with no surprises.

Mr and Mrs Alexander senior have not yet travelled overseas and in their retirement regularly return to Blackpool, but their son has long since tired of the psychocentric destinations of the English seaside. He has become the typical allocentric tourist, and is fortunate to have the income and lifestyle that allows him to adopt this role. Each year he visits a different international destination on the tourism frontier – Antarctica, Yemen, and the new destinations of the former Soviet Union. He is anxious to visit before they attract the mass market and, of course, he utilises the Internet for his bookings, travels light and is convinced that he is a 'traveller' not a 'tourist'.

DISCUSSION QUESTIONS

1 Draft a checklist of the characteristics of an allocentric-type tourist.

2 What might be the attributes of a psychocentric-type destination such as Blackpool?

3 Thinking about your last holiday, was it to a psychocentric or allocentric type of destination – and would holidaymakers visiting from different parts of the world to your own agree with you?

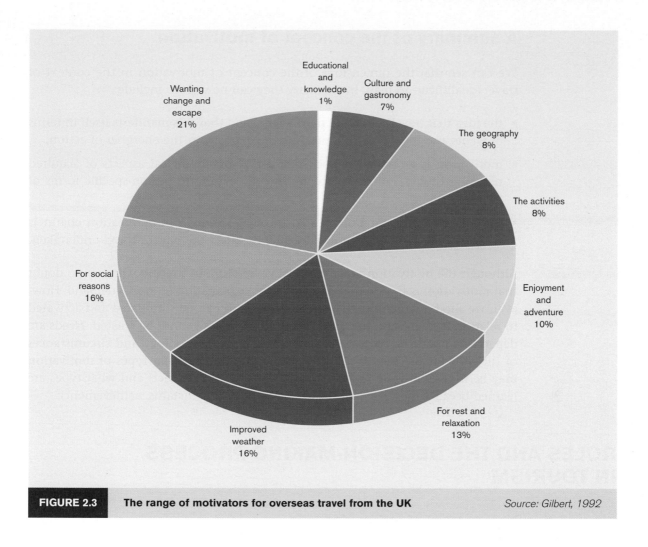

Educational and knowledge 1%
Culture and gastronomy 7%
Wanting change and escape 21%
The geography 8%
The activities 8%
For social reasons 16%
Enjoyment and adventure 10%
For rest and relaxation 13%
Improved weather 16%

FIGURE 2.3 **The range of motivators for overseas travel from the UK** *Source: Gilbert, 1992*

Smith (1990) tested Plog's model, utilising evidence from seven different countries. He concluded that his own results did not support Plog's original model of an association between personality types and destination preferences. Smith questioned the applicability of the model to countries other than the USA. In answer to Smith, Plog (1990) questioned the validity of Smith's methodology. Regardless of this defence, further controlled empirical studies will be required in order to ensure Plog's theory can be justified as a central pillar within tourism theory.

As we have shown, the concept of motivation as a major determinant of tourism behaviour is widely used by tourism authors. Yet most authors fail to provide a scientific basis for their motivation categories nor is any indication given of the proportion of tourists who would exhibit one type of motivation rather than another. An exception to this is shown in Figure 2.3. Here motivators were identified by research of a sample based upon a quota sample matched to the British Tourist Authority profile for overseas travel from the UK. The response involved individuals providing evidence of a cluster of motives, each of which is important as a determinant of demand.

A summary of the concept of motivation

We can see that the dimensions of the concept of motivation in the context of travel are difficult to map. In summary they can be seen to include:

- the idea that travel is initially need related and that this manifests itself in terms of wants and the strength of motivation or 'push', as the energiser of action;

- motivation is grounded in sociological and psychological aspects of acquired norms, attitudes, culture, perceptions, etc., leading to person-specific forms of motivation; and

- the image of a destination created through various communication channels will influence motivation and subsequently affect the type of travel undertaken.

Although the motivation literature is still immature in tourism, there is no doubt that motivation is an essential concept in the explanation of tourist demand. However, we should remember that while motivation can be stimulated and activated in relation to the 'want' to travel, 'needs' themselves cannot be created. Needs are dependent upon the human element through the psychology and circumstances of the individual. There is also the crucial question of what types of motivation may be innate in us all (curiosity, need for physical contact) and what types are learned because they are judged as valuable or positive (status, achievement).

ROLES AND THE DECISION-MAKING PROCESS IN TOURISM

Tourist typologies

Tourists can be characterised into different typologies or roles which exercise motivation as an energising force linked to personal needs. Utilising this approach, roles can be studied in relation to goal-orientated forms of behaviour or holiday choice activity. Therefore some understanding of tourist roles provides us with a deeper understanding of the choice process of different consumer segments.

The majority of authors who have identified tourist roles have concentrated on the assessment of the social and environmental impact of tourism or the nature of the tourist experience. Any definition or interpretation of tourist roles, such as those of motivation, varies according to the analytical framework used by the individual author. The initial ideas of role developed from the work of sociological theorists such as Goffman (1959). He suggested that individuals behave differently in different situations in order to sustain impressions associated with those situations. As actors have different front and backstage performances, participants in any activity vary their behaviour according to the nature and context of that activity. Consequently individual roles can be identified and managed according to social circumstances. Whereas tourists may vary considerably, we can discern a pattern of roles from the literature. Theoretical studies focusing on the sociological aspects of tourism role were developed in the 1970s through the work of Cohen (1972, 1974, 1984), MacCannell (1976) and Smith (1990).

The organised mass tourist
Low on adventurousness he/she is anxious to maintain his/her 'environmental bubble' on the trip. Typically purchasing a ready-made package tour off-the-shelf, he/she is guided through the destination having little contact with local culture or people.

The individual mass tourist
Similar to the above but more flexibility and scope for personal choice is built in. However, the tour is still organised by the tourism industry and the environmental bubble shields him/her from the real experience of the destination.

The explorer
The trip is organised independently and is looking to get off the beaten track. However, comfortable accommodation and reliable transport are sought and, while the environmental bubble is abandoned on occasion, it is there to step into if things get tough.

The drifter
All connections with the tourism industry are spurned and the trip attempts to get as far from home and familiarity as possible. With no fixed itinerary, the drifter lives with the local people, paying his/her way and immersing him/herself in their culture.

Familiarity

Institutionalised tourism
Dealt with routinely by the tourism industry – tour operators, travel agents, hoteliers and transport operators.

Non-institutionalised tourism
Individual travel, shunning contact with the tourism industry except where absolutely necessary.

Novelty

| FIGURE 2.4 | **Cohen's classification of tourists** | *Source: Boniface and Cooper, 1987, adapted from Cohen, 1972* |

61

The interaction of personality attributes such as attitude, perceptions and motivation allow different types of tourist role to be identified. One classification by Cohen is particularly useful and this is presented in Figure 2.4. He uses a classification based on the theory that tourism combines the curiosity to seek out new experiences with the need for the security of familiar reminders of home, reflecting Plog's ideas in Mini case study 2.1. Cohen proposes a continuum of possible combinations of novelty and familiarity and, by breaking up the continuum into typical combinations of these two ingredients, a fourfold classification of tourists is produced.

While destinations may be enjoyed as novel, most tourists prefer to explore them from a familiar base. The degree of familiarity of this base underlies Cohen's typology in which the author identifies four tourist roles: organised mass tourist, individual mass tourist, explorer and drifter (see Figure 2.4). Cohen described the first two roles as institutionalised and the latter types as non-institutionalised. Cohen was interested in classifying groups in order to understand not demand, but the effects or impact of institutionalised forms of tourism which he found to be authenticity issues, standardisation of destinations, festivals and the development of facilities. He also identified the impact of non-institutionalised forms of tourism upon the destination which he found acts as a 'spearhead for mass tourism' as well as having a 'demonstration effect' on the lower socio-economic groups of the host community.

Cohen's typology assists in formulating operational approaches to tourism research and forms a framework for management practice. Although it is not complete and cannot be applied to all tourists at all times, it does afford a way of organising and understanding tourist activity.

Role and family influence

As the fundamental social unit of group formation in society, the influence of a family on tourism demand is extremely important. A family often acts as the purchasing unit which may be supplying the needs of perhaps two or more generations. In addition, it socialises children to adopt particular forms of purchasing and acts as a wider reference group. Given the importance of family behaviour in the purchase of leisure products, we may want to question the preponderance of literature which treats consumer behaviour as an individual model of action. For example, the concept of motivation has been presented as essentially an individual one, yet the idea of 'shared motivators' takes into account that family and friends often influence holiday decisions.

Each member of a family fulfils a special role within the group. He or she may act as husband/father, wife/mother, son/brother and daughter/sister. Family decision making assigns roles to specific members of the family and decision making may be shared, or conducted by one person. One member of the family may be the facilitator, while information may be gathered by another. The family acts as a composite buying unit with the different role patterns leading to particular forms of tourism product purchasing.

The importance of image

An individual's awareness of the world is made up of experiences, learning, emotions and perceptions, or, more accurately, the cognitive evaluation of such experiences, learning, emotions and perceptions. Such awareness can be described as knowledge producing a specific image of the world. This image is critically important to an individual's preference, motivation and behaviour towards tourist products and destinations, as it will provide a 'pull' effect resulting in different demand schedules.

There are various kinds of definition adopted to describe the word 'image' in different fields. For example, the WTO defines image as follows:

- the artificial imitation of the apparent form of an object;

- form resemblance, identity (e.g. art and design); and

- ideas, conceptions held individually or collectively of the destination.

Following the work of Gunn (1972), the WTO suggests that the tourist image is only one aspect of a destination's general image, with the two being closely interrelated. Nobody is likely to visit a destination for tourism if for one reason or another he or she dislikes it. Conversely, a tourist discovery may lead to a knowledge of other aspects of an economic, political or cultural nature of that destination. The WTO further adds that the presentation of a **destination image** must allow for the fact that it is generally a matter not of creating an image from nothing but of transforming an existing image.

Tourist behaviour both of individuals and groups depends upon their image of immediate situations and the world. The notion of image is closely related to behaviour and attitudes. Attitudes and behaviour become established on the basis of a person's derived image and are not easily changed unless new information or experience is gained.

The holiday image

Mayo (1973) examined regional images and regional travel behaviour. Among other things he indicated that the image of a destination area is a critical factor when choosing a destination. Mayo further concluded that, whether or not an image is in fact a true representation of what any given region has to offer the tourist, what is important is the image that exists in the mind of the vacationer.

The tourist may possess a variety of images in connection with travel. These include the image he or she has formed of the destination, of the term 'holiday' itself, of the mode of transport he or she wishes to utilise, of the tour operator/ wholesaler or travel agency and of his or her own self-image. For example, it is probable that the term 'holiday' evokes different images for different people. However, it is likely that similar images of a particular holiday experience are held by people within the same segment of society and who have experienced a similar lifestyle or education.

Gunn (1972) identifies two levels of image. Viewed in terms of a country or destination, the 'organic' image is the sum of all information that has not been deliberately directed by advertising or promotion of a country or destination; this information comes from television coverage, radio reports, geography books, history books, what other people have said about the area, newspapers and magazines or the Internet. An imaginary picture is built up which is the result of all this information. The individual, following Gestalt psychology, attempts to make sense of it by forming a pattern or a picture of what he or she imagines the area to be like.

The second level of image is the 'induced' image. This is formed by deliberate portrayal and promotion by various organisations involved with tourism.

It is important to distinguish between these two levels since the induced image is controllable while it is more difficult to influence the organic image. Equally, the source of information is a significant influence upon a consumer's perception of its value. We can identify four stages in the development and establishment of a holiday image:

1 The first is a vague, fantasy type of image created from advertising, education and word of mouth and is formed before the subject has thought seriously about taking a holiday. This belief may be that people engage in taking holidays as a desirable activity.

2 The second stage is when a decision is made to take a holiday and then choices must be made regarding time, destination and type of holiday. This is when the holiday image is modified, clarified and extended. On completion of the holiday plans, the anticipatory image is crystallised.

3 The third stage is the holiday experience itself, which modifies, corrects or removes elements of the image that prove to be invalid and reinforces those that are found to be correct.

4 The fourth stage is the after-image, the recollection of the holiday which may induce feelings of nostalgia, regret or fantasy. This is the stage that will mould an individual's holiday concepts and attitudes and will promote a new sequence of holiday images influencing future holiday decisions.

MODELS OF CONSUMER BEHAVIOUR IN TOURISM

One approach to understanding tourism demand is to identify and evaluate the broader theories and models of consumer behaviour linked to purchasing behaviour. This is far from simplistic for we are faced with a proliferation of research within a subject area that has displayed significant growth and diversity. Perhaps the major utility of these models is to demonstrate the interrelationships of the key factors influencing consumer behaviour in tourism. We also have to understand the particular characteristics of a tourism purchasing decision as opposed to other products, and this includes the implications of tourism as a service activity. We can identify three phases that characterise the development of consumer behaviour theory:

1 **The early empiricist phase** covered the years between 1930 and the late 1940s and was dominated by empirical commercial research. This research was characterised by attempts in industry to identify the effects of distribution, advertising and promotion decisions. The basis for these models came mainly from economic theories relating to the company.

2 **The motivational research phase** in the 1950s was an age where stress was placed on Freudian and drive-related concepts. There was a greater emphasis placed upon in-depth interviews, focus groups, thematic apperception tests and other projective techniques. Activity was directed at uncovering 'real' motives for action which were perceived to lie in the deeper recesses of the consumer's mind. Much of the theory was based around the idea of there being instinctual needs which reside in the 'id' and are governed by the 'ego' which acts to balance unrestrained instincts and social constraints. The 'super ego' in turn was seen to embody values but to limit action on the basis of moral constraint. The major problem was the focus on unconscious needs which are by definition extremely difficult to prove empirically. Furthermore, they do not always translate into effective marketing strategies.

3 **The formative phase** of the 1960s can be seen as the formative years of consumer behaviour modelling. The first general consumer behaviour textbook became available in 1968 (Engel, Kollat and Blackwell) and other influential books such as Howard and Sheth (1969) followed soon after. The Howard–Sheth model of buyer behaviour is perhaps the most influential one, as it identifies the inputs to the consumer's decision-making process. During the formative phase, models of behaviour proved useful as a means of organising disparate knowledge of social action. The major theorists developed 'grand models' of consumer behaviour which have been subsequently utilised or transformed by authors interested in the tourism choice process.

These grand models can be found to share several commonalities:

- They all exhibit consumer behaviour as a decision process. This is integral to the model.

- They provide a comprehensive model focusing mainly on the behaviour of the individual consumer.

- They share the belief that behaviour is rational and hence can, in principle, be explained.

- They view buying behaviour as purposive, with the consumer as an active information seeker, both of information stored internally and of information available in the external environment. Thus, the search and evaluation of information is a key component of the decision process.

- They believe that consumers limit the amount of information taken in, and move over time from general notions to more specific criteria and preference for alternatives.

- All the 'grand models' include a notion of feedback, that is, outcomes from purchases will affect future purchases.

- The models envisage consumer behaviour as multistage triggered by the individual's expectation that a product will satisfy their needs.

THE BUYING DECISION PROCESS IN TOURISM

We subscribe to the approach of agreeing that consumer behaviour is purposeful and goal orientated. This places an emphasis on the free choice of an individual in the process of their consumption decisions:

Generally speaking, human beings are usually quite rational and make systematic use of the information available to them. We do not subscribe to the view that human social behaviour is controlled by unconscious motives or overpowering desires, rather people consider the implications of their actions before they decide to engage or not engage in a given behaviour. (Ajzen and Fishbein, 1975; 1980)

Figure 2.5 demonstrates that consumer behaviour is normally conceived as a process of stages. As part of this approach the decision to travel is the involvement of some or all of the following stages. The starting point is where a need is recognised and the individual is energised into becoming a potential customer. The stages can be thought of as:

- need arousal;

- recognition of the need – the prerequisite stage;

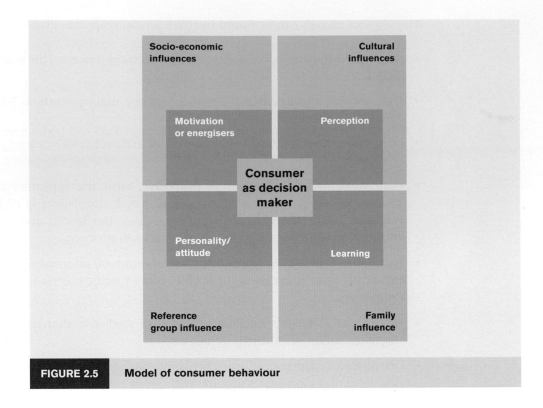

| **FIGURE 2.5** | **Model of consumer behaviour** |

- level of involvement – amount of time and effort invested in the decision process, e.g. degree of search for information;

- identification of alternatives – brands that initially come to mind when considering a purchase are referred to as the evoked set. However, friends, shop assistants, merchandise, leaflets, advertisements, etc. may provide a consideration step;

- evaluation of alternatives – comparisons are made of the salient attributes based upon criteria of the potential purchaser;

- decision choice made;

- purchase action; and

- post-purchase behaviour – the feelings an individual experiences after the purchase. Quite often with important purchases, such as travel, the purchaser will doubt the wisdom of their choice and have a need for reassurance to what is known as dissonance or disequilibrium. This psychological state is reduced by the means of guarantees or telephone help lines to deal with queries. It is also reduced by the welcome of someone on their return from their trip or experience.

Engel, Blackwell and Miniard (1986) classified models according to the degree of search or problem-solving behaviour by the consumer:

1 **Limited problem-solving models (LPS models)** are applicable to repeat or mundane purchases with a low level of consumer involvement. Apart from short trips near to home these are not applicable to tourism.

2 **Extended problem-solving models (EPS models)** apply to purchases associated with high levels of perceived risk and involvement, and where the information search and evaluation of alternatives plays an important part in the purchasing decision. Models of tourist behaviour fall into this category.

Given the high cost, risk factor and involvement of a tourism purchase, a number of models of consumer behaviour which seek to explain low involvement purchase behaviour are less relevant and therefore not considered here. The following models are all examples of EPS models.

Wahab, Crampon and Rothfield

One of the first attempts to provide some understanding of tourism purchase behaviour is to be found in the work of Wahab, Crampon and Rothfield (1976). These authors presented the consumer as purposeful and conceptualised his or her buying behaviour in terms of the uniqueness of the buying decision:

- no tangible return on investment;
- considerable expenditure in relation to earned income;
- purchase is not spontaneous or capricious; and
- expenditure involves saving and preplanning.

They presented a model of the decision-making process based upon the preceding 'grand models' of consumer behaviour and having the stages outlined in Figure 2.6.

Schmoll

Schmoll (1977) argued that creating a model of the travel decision process was not just a theoretical exercise, for its value could be found in its aid to travel decision making. His model was based on the Howard–Sheth (1969) and Nicosia (1966) models of consumer behaviour – see Figure 2.7.

Schmoll's model is built upon motivations, desires, needs and expectations as personal and social determinants of travel behaviour. These are influenced by travel stimuli, the traveller's confidence, destination image, previous experience and cost and time constraints. The model has four fields, each of which exerts

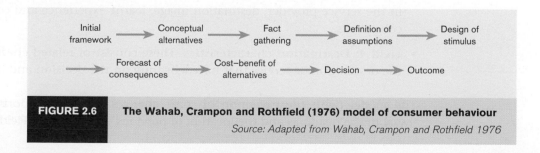

| FIGURE 2.6 | The Wahab, Crampon and Rothfield (1976) model of consumer behaviour |

Source: Adapted from Wahab, Crampon and Rothfield 1976

67

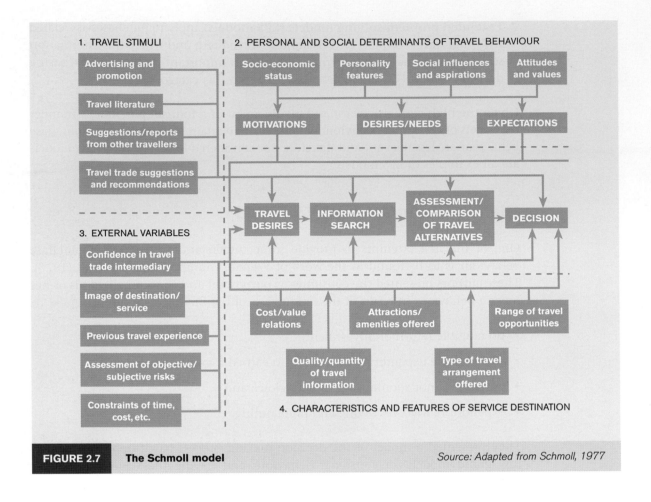

FIGURE 2.7   **The Schmoll model**   *Source: Adapted from Schmoll, 1977*

some influence over the final decision – according to Schmoll (1977): 'The eventual decision (choice of a destination, travel time, type of accommodation, type of travel arrangements, etc.), is in fact the result of a distinct process involving several successive stages or fields.'

- Field 1: Travel stimuli. This comprises external stimuli in the form of promotional communication, personal and trade recommendations.

- Field 2: Personal and social determinants. These determine customer goals in the form of travel needs and desires, expectations and the objective and subjective risks thought to be connected with travel.

- Field 3: External variables. These involve the prospective traveller's confidence in the service provider, destination image, learnt experience and cost and time constraints.

- Field 4: Destination characteristics. These consist of related characteristics of the destination or service that have a bearing on the decision and its outcome.

The model (with the exception of some changes which incorporate the word travel in the headings and the location of previous experience in Field 3) has been borrowed directly from the 'grand models' already discussed. In Schmoll's model there is no feedback loop and no input to attitude and values and therefore it is difficult for us to regard the model as dynamic. However, Schmoll does highlight many of the attributes of travel decision making which, while not unique in themselves, do influence tourism demand. We can include here decisions regarding choice of a mix of services which make up the product: high financial outlay, destination image, the level of risk and uncertainty, necessity to plan ahead and difficulty of acquiring completeness of information.

Schmoll, while highlighting some of the characteristics associated with the problem-solving activity of travel, simply reiterates the determinants of cognitive decision-making processes. Within Schmoll's work we are introduced again to the importance of image which plays a significant part in the demand process.

Mayo and Jarvis

Mayo and Jarvis (1981) have also borrowed from the grand theorist models. They have taken the basic Howard–Sheth three-level decision-making approach where problem solving is seen as extensive, limited or routinised.

Mayo and Jarvis follow the earlier theories by describing extensive decision making (destination purchase for them) as being characterised as having a perceived need for an information search phase and needing a longer decision-making period. The search for, and evaluation of, information is presented as a main component of the decision-making process whereby the consumer moves from general notions to more specific criteria and preferences for alternatives.

Mayo and Jarvis argue that travel is a special form of consumption behaviour involving an intangible, heterogeneous purchase of an experiential product, yet they then fail to develop an activity-based theory.

Mathieson and Wall

Mathieson and Wall (1982) offer a five-stage process of travel buying behaviour (see Figure 2.8). Their framework (as shown in Figure 2.9) is influenced by four inter-related factors:

- Tourist profile (age, education, income attitudes, previous experience and motivations).
- Travel awareness (image of a destination's facilities and services which are based upon the credibility of the source).
- Destination resources and characteristics (attractions and features of a destination).
- Trip features (distance, trip duration and perceived risk of the area visited).

In addition, Mathieson and Wall recognise that a holiday is a service product with the characteristics of intangibility, perishability and heterogeneity, which in one way or another affect the consumer's decision making. However, apart from pointing out that consumption and evaluation will occur simultaneously, the basis

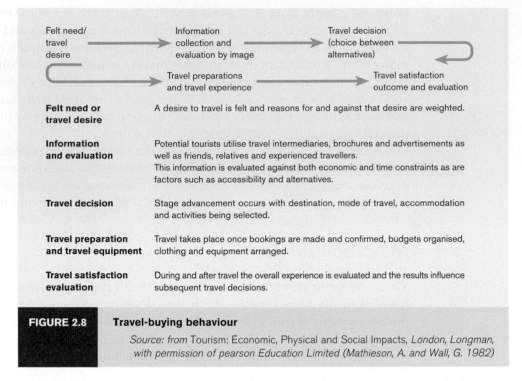

FIGURE 2.8   **Travel-buying behaviour**

Source: from Tourism: Economic, Physical and Social Impacts, *London, Longman, with permission of pearson Education Limited (Mathieson, A. and Wall, G. 1982)*

FIGURE 2.9   **The Mathieson and Wall model**

Source: from Tourism: Economic, Physical and Social Impacts, *London, Longman, with permission of Pearson Education Limited (Mathieson, A. and Wall, G. 1982)* of their model relies on the previously reviewed grand models. This is not to say that the model reflects the depth of insight of these models; on the contrary it only incorporates the idea of the consumer being purposive in actively seeking information and the importance of external factors. The model omits important aspects of perception, memory, personality and information processing, which is the basis of the traditional models. The model they provide focuses more on a product-based perspective rather than that of a consumer behaviourist.

Moscardo *et al.*

Moscardo *et al.* (1996) have provided a different approach to consumer behaviour by stressing the importance of activities as a critical link between travel and destination choice. They argue that motives provide travellers with expectations for activities, and destinations are seen as offering these activities. Figure 2.10 demonstrates this approach as an activities model of destination choice. In this model, Moscardo *et al.* have provided a useful practical outlet for the use of these models by marketers. They argue that activity-based traveller segments can be linked to destination activities through product development and communication strategies.

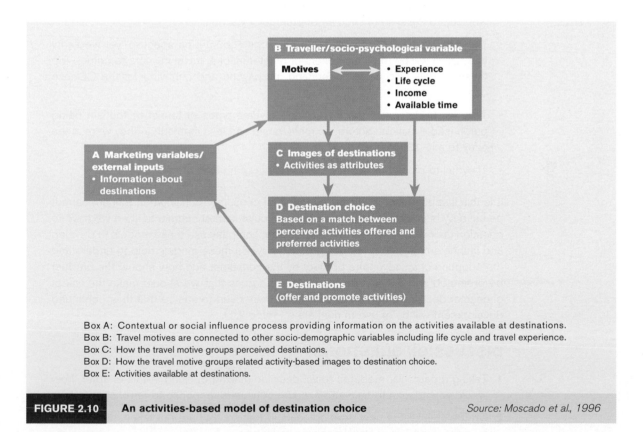

Box A: Contextual or social influence process providing information on the activities available at destinations.
Box B: Travel motives are connected to other socio-demographic variables including life cycle and travel experience.
Box C: How the travel motive groups perceived destinations.
Box D: How the travel motive groups related activity-based images to destination choice.
Box E: Activities available at destinations.

FIGURE 2.10   **An activities-based model of destination choice**   *Source: Moscado et al., 1996*

MINI CASE STUDY 2.2
Are models of consumer behaviour in tourism a waste of effort?

The tourism sector of a country can be crippled overnight by a terrorist incident, the outbreak of war, or a natural disaster. Yet if we cannot predict the response of the consumer to these types of incidents, should we be reassessing the role of consumer behaviour models? Of course, there is no doubt that models of consumer behaviour help us to understand the complexity of decisions taken to purchase travel and they assist in the understanding of how the various factors are related. However, models of consumer decision making in tourism have been criticised on a number of grounds (Swarbrooke and Horner, 1999):

- They are too theoretical and not grounded in any empirical testing – how, for example, would we test them against the observed change in behaviour in travel since the introduction of budget airlines across Europe?

- They are beginning to date and no new models have been developed since the mid-1990s, yet the travel sector has changed considerably – what, for example, is the impact of Internet bookings and information sources on such models?

- They do not help in the understanding of how the market would react to further 'shocks' to the system such as September 11, 2001.

- They view tourism from a Western developed-country perspective, yet we know that China will be the main generator of international travel in years to come – do these models help us to understand the psyche and behaviour of the Chinese consumer?

- They fail to recognise the increasingly diverse types of tourist or tourism being purchased – market sectors are more varied and less stable than they were in the early to mid-1990s.

- They fail to predict or identify the behaviour of tourists or markets.

It is this last point that is critical. If models of consumer behaviour in tourism cannot be used by marketers to fit products to particular market segments, then we have to question their use. How, for example, would a company use these models to develop and launch an adventure tourism product, how do these models help to understand the adoption of an adventure product by the consumer and how should the product be promoted and priced? Solomon (1996) argues that we should make the link of consumer decision models with marketing more overt to ensure that their continued development will be of use to marketers (Table 2.1).

DISCUSSION QUESTIONS

1 Taking a particular model of travel decision making outlined in this chapter, how would you adapt it to take into account consumer response to terrorist activity?

2 Draft a checklist of new developments in tourism that are not taken into account by current models of travel decision making.

3 Make a list of the classic features of a service product – do the current models of travel decision making adequately take these factors into account?

TABLE 2.1	Linking consumer decision models with marketing	
Issues at particular purchase stages	**Consumer considerations**	**Marketing considerations**
Pre-purchase stage	How does a consumer decide that he/she needs a travel product? What is the level of involvement/commitment on the part of the purchaser of a travel product? What are the best sources of information to learn more about alternative choices, and, given the intangible nature of the travel product, which sources have more authority and influence?	How are consumer attitudes toward travel products formed and/or changed? For example, why is the mass tourism experience, so popular in the 1970s, now less popular? What cues does the consumer use to infer which products are superior to others – a critical piece of information for promotion and positioning of travel products.
Purchase stage	Is acquiring a product a stressful or pleasant experience and does this influence the nature of intermediary used – or indeed whether an intermediary is bypassed? What does the destination and type of holiday arrangement purchased say about the consumer?	How do situational factors such as time pressure, family pressure or travel agent displays affect the consumer's purchase decision?
Post-purchase stage	Does the travel product provide pleasure or perform its intended function? How is the travel product consumed and are there environmental or social consequences to the travelling activity?	What determines whether a consumer will be satisfied with the travel experience or whether he/she will buy it again? Does this person tell others about his/her travel experiences and therefore affect their purchase decisions?

Source: Adapted from Swarbrooke and Horner, 1999; Solomon, 1996

CONCLUSION

Tourism marketing will become more effective if it develops a fuller understanding of what influences the tourist's consumer behaviour. This need has been highlighted since 2001 with the realisation that we could not predict travel demand response to 'shocks' to the system such as September 11 and the Bali bombings. To do this we require an appreciation of the way consumers behave and the way they recognise specific needs for travel, search for and evaluate information, make purchases and then evaluate what has been consumed as part of the tourism experience. This involves the need to understand some of the approaches to how motivation may function, the roles we adopt as tourists and how sociological changes will affect demand.

The understanding of the consumer is enhanced by the incorporation of these different variables into simplified models. Although these need improvement, they act as a guide to current thinking of how tourism demand may function. Nonetheless, these models of consumer behaviour in tourism remain at a relatively early stage of their development and significant levels of research are still required to clarify what are, effectively, subjective psychological influences upon buying processes in tourism. Indeed, they have been criticised on the grounds that they are too theoretical and offer little assistance to the tourism marketer. This said, they do perform a useful role in clarifying our thinking about the tourist decision-making process and in particular help us to understand the interrelationships of a range of complex variables.

Self-check questions

1 Draft a list of motivations for travel and, thinking of your last holiday, which one was dominant in your mind?

2 Consider tourist typologies that predominate at a tourist destination with which you are familiar.

3 Review the process you went through in the purchase decision process for the last holiday you took.

4 What factors differentiate a high-involvement purchase, such as tourism, from a low-involvement purchase, such as grocery shopping?

5 Consider a tourism product such as a tour operator's brochure – what cues are there to suggest the market targeted by the company?

Essay questions

1 Consider the factors that might motivate a tourist to travel to a range of different destinations.

2 Does the tourism industry takes full advantage of what is known about the buying decision process in tourism in respect of marketing?

3 How might the motivational 'push' of the tourist (e.g. sunlust versus wanderlust) affect the buying decision process for tourism? Identify the elements of the process which are likely to predominate for those motivated by sunlust and wanderlust.

4 'Designing consumer behaviour models for tourism is purely an academic exercise.' Discuss this statement.

5 Identify and discuss the relative importance of the major influences on a tourist's purchasing decision.

Annotated further reading

Books

Pearce, P. (1982) *The Social Psychology of Tourist Behaviour*, Pergamon, Oxford.
An excellent research-based text reviewing the major theories and applications of social psychology in tourism, including consumer behaviour.

Ross, G. (1998) *The Psychology of Tourism*, 2nd edn, Hospitality Press, Melbourne.
A text covering all the main elements of consumer behaviour and developing a model of tourist behaviour based upon social network theory.

Swarbrooke, J. and Horner, S. (1999) *Consumer Behaviour in Tourism*, Butterworth Heinemann, Oxford.
A thorough textbook reviewing all aspects of consumer behaviour and broader elements of tourism demand.

References cited

Ajzen, I. and Fishbein, M. (1975) *Attitude Intention and Behaviour: An Introduction to Theory and Research*, Addison Wesley, Reading, MA.

Ajzen, I. and Fishbein, M. (1980) *Understanding Attitudes and Predicting Social Behaviour*, Prentice Hall, Englewood Cliffs, NJ.

Boniface, B. and Cooper, C. (1987) *The Geography of Travel and Tourism*, Heinemann, London.

Cohen, E. (1972) 'Towards a sociology of international tourism', *Social Research* **39**(1), 164–82.

Cohen, E. (1974) 'Who is a tourist? A conceptual clarification', *Sociological Review* **22**(4), 527–55.

Cohen, E. (1984) 'The sociology of tourism, approaches, issues findings', *Annual Review of Sociology*, 1984, 373–92.

Dann, G.M.S. (1981) 'Tourist motivation: an appraisal', *Annals of Tourism Research* **8**(2), 187–219.

Engel, J.F., Blackwell, R.D. and Miniard, P. (1986) *Consumer Behaviour*, Dryden Press, New York.

Engel, J.F., Kollat, D.J. and Blackwell, R.P. (1968) *Consumer Behaviour*, Holt Reinehart and Wilson, New York.

75

Gilbert, D.C. (1992) *A Study of Factors of Consumer Behaviour Related to Overseas Holidays from the UK*, Unpublished PhD Thesis, University of Surrey, Guildford.

Goffman, E. (1959) *The Presentation of Self in Everyday Life*, Pelican, Middlesex.

Gray, H.P. (1970) *International Travel – International Trade*, Heath Lexington Books, Lexington.

Gunn, C. (1972) *Vacationscape – Designing Tourist Regions*, University of Texas Press, Austin, TX.

Howard, J.A. and Sheth, J.N. (1969) *The theory of Buyer Behaviour*, Wiley, New York.

MacCannell, D. (1976) *The Tourist: A New Theory of the Leisure Class*, Macmillan, London.

Maslow, A.H. (1970) *Motivation and Personality*, 2nd edn, Harper and Row, New York.

Mathieson, A. and Wall, G. (1982) *Tourism: Economic Physical and Social Impacts*, Longman, London.

Mayo, E. (1973) 'Regional images and regional travel consumer behaviour', pp. 211–18, in *TTRA Conference Proceedings*, Idaho.

Mayo, E. and Jarvis, L. (1981) *The Psychology of Leisure Travel*, CBI Publishing, Boston, MA.

McIntosh, R.W., Goeldner, C.R. and Ritchie, J.R.B. (1995) *Tourism Principles, Practices, Philosophies*, Wiley, New York.

Moscardo, G., Morrison, A.M., Pearce, P.L., Lang, C.T. and O'Leary, J. (1996) 'Understanding vacation destination choice through travel motivation and activities', *Journal of Vacation Marketing* **2**(2), 109–22.

Nicosia, F.M. (1966) *Consumer Decision Processes: Marketing and Advertising Implications*, Prentice Hall, Englewood Cliffs, NJ.

Plog, S.C. (1974) 'Why destination areas rise and fall in popularity', *Cornell Hotel and Restaurant Quarterly* **14**(4) (Feb.), 55–8.

Plog, S.C. (1990) 'A carpenter's tools: an answer to Stephen L.J. Smith's review of psychocentrism/allocentrism', *Journal of Travel Research* **28**(4), Spring, 43–5.

Schmoll, G.A. (1977) *Tourism Promotion*, Tourism International Press, London.

Smith, S.L.J. (1990) 'A test of Plog's allocentric/psychocentric model: evidence from seven nations', *Journal of Travel Research* **28**(4), Spring, 40–3.

Solomon M.R. (1996) *Consumer Behaviour*, 3rd edn, Prentice Hall, Englewood Cliffs.

Swarbrooke, J. and Horner, S. (1999) *Consumer Behaviour in Tourism*, Butterworth Heinemann, Oxford.

Wahab, S., Crampon, L.J. and Rothfield, L.M. (1976) *Tourism Marketing*, Tourism International Press, London.

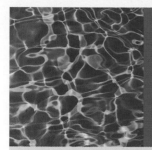

MAJOR CASE STUDY 2.1
THE IMPACT OF THE SEPTEMBER 11,
2001 TERRORIST ATTACKS ON THE USA
ON TOURISM CONSUMER BEHAVIOUR

INTRODUCTION

Bierman (2002) states that 'the marketability of individual destinations and global tourism is vulnerable to sudden changes in market perceptions' (p. 3). This implies that, as tourism is a discretionary activity, the majority of the market will change their behaviour in response to threats and danger. Here the relevance of consumer behaviour becomes clear and poses a new challenge for a new century – we must be able to understand how tourists' decision making changes in response to a threat such as terrorism. This is particularly the case given that an important part of a decision to travel and visit a destination is the perception of safety and security. If these perceptions are changed to being negative, then travel will not occur. One of the key issues here is that the words 'crisis', 'risk' and 'threat' did not enter the tourism sector's vocabulary until September 11, 2001 ('911'). As a consequence not only was the sector unprepared for the event, but information-gathering systems were not in place. In fact, one of the few benefits of the attacks has been the sector's new initiatives in gathering information on the impact of the attacks on travel patterns and intentions. This case study has relied heavily on the many sources of information about the changing consumer as a result of '911'.

Tourism has experienced crises in the past. Following both the Gulf War (1991) and the Kosovo crisis (1999) tourism growth was checked but recovered in the following year. Similar experiences followed other crises such as the attacks on tourists in Luxor (1997) and the Asian financial crisis of 1997/1998. Experience has shown that tourism is resilient and recovers from these incidents. However, immediately following '911' commentators said that 'this is different' and the tourism sector entered uncharted waters. Yet, in a sense history was proved correct, while global totals for tourism declined slightly in 2001 (by 0.5%) compared to 2000, the decrease was not as severe as had been initially feared. Admittedly, this is only the second time since 1945 that there has been a decline and the impact of '911' on key sectors such as the airlines has been devastating.

THE IMPACT OF '911' ON THE TOURISM SECTOR

Bierman (2002) has devised a rating scale for tourism crises ranging from DESTCON 5 where there is a minimal threat to the marketability of a destination; to DESTCON 1 where the marketability of not just one destination is threatened but it also has widespread or regional implications. '911' is rated as DESTCON 1.

The reasons for this are clear. Until 2001, the USA was the leading destination for international tourism. The short-term impact of '911' was a reduction of visitation to the USA and, in the long term, visitation is likely to remain depressed as draconian immigration measures are put in place at US borders. The impact of '911' on the USA is estimated to have cost 345,000 jobs in travel and tourism in the 12 months following '911', while in Washington DC, a city also attacked on September 11, in the immediate three months following the attacks,

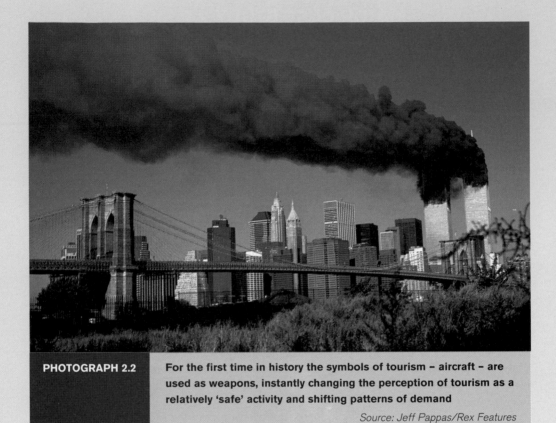

PHOTOGRAPH 2.2   **For the first time in history the symbols of tourism – aircraft – are used as weapons, instantly changing the perception of tourism as a relatively 'safe' activity and shifting patterns of demand**

Source: Jeff Pappas/Rex Features

hotel occupancy fell by 61%, hotel visitors fell by 400,000, job losses were 27,000 and the major tourist attractions in the city were closed for five months. These impacts were caused by consumers deciding not to travel, or restructuring their travel in response to fears of further incidents and perceived vulnerability of aircraft. It is therefore important that we understand how tourists' consumer behaviour has changed as a result of '911'.

CONSUMER TRENDS

Changing consumer behaviour as a result of '911' has impacted upon global patterns of tourism demand. The WTO (2002) has identified that a number of consumer trends were accelerated or initiated by '911' including:

- heightened cost consciousness – particularly as travel price comparisons are easier for consumers to make with the Internet;

- shorter booking times and a significant increase in last minute bookings following '911', a trend linked to price consciousness;

- growth in Internet and 'do-it-yourself' bookings, again closely linked to the first two trends above;

- shorter trips are taken;

- replacement of international trips by domestic trips;

- greater preference for holidays based on participatory motivations such as special interest, sports and environmental tourism; and

- greater preference for surface transport such as car and rail.

It was also evident that in the months immediately following '911' consumers were acutely aware of the increased 'physical' risk of travelling, fears enhanced by:

- increased airport security procedures;

- the introduction of armed sky marshals on aircraft;

- noticeably tightened immigration procedures; and

- saturation media coverage.

However, in the early months of 2002, the physical threat receded in consumer's minds and fears were more of 'economic' risk of redundancy and failing economies.

In respect of trying to influence consumer behaviour and encourage visitors to return to the USA, Bierman (2002) suggests that we should employ our understanding of consumer behaviour to segment markets at the time of crisis. His three segments are:

- **Stalwarts** – those with a strong affinity for the market. Domestic travellers would be an example here, as would the ethnic family market.

- **Waverers** – this group would normally visit the destination but do not have a strong family or emotional tie, hence they question their trip. However, they are also normally the first group to return once the crisis is over.

- **The disaffected** – the traditional holidaymaker who has no affinity to the destination and is immediately deterred from visiting by the crisis.

WINNERS AND LOSERS

In 2002, the WTO undertook an analysis of air bookings on the Amadeus system to 224 destinations (WTO, 2002). The booking periods chosen were August 2000 to February 2001 and August 2001 to February 2002, allowing the impact of '911' to be clearly discerned. The analysis shows that in total 18 million air bookings were lost as a result of '911', clearly demonstrating the devastating impact on the airline sector. It is also possible to identify in more detail the winners and losers from '911'.

The changed consumer trends identified above following '911' had a significant impact on redistributing global demand for tourism, with the major impact caused by a significant and immediate reduction of outbound travel from the Americas and Europe and a decline in inter-regional trips. Changing consumer behaviour in these key markets meant that certain destinations suffered due to '911' (WTO, 2002):

- countries perceived as being close to or connected to the 'war on terrorism';

- countries heavily dependent upon the USA market;

- countries dependent upon long-haul traffic.

On the other hand, those countries close to their major generating markets – such as Spain – were less affected, as were countries perceived as being safe havens – such as Australia – and other countries in Asia, also benefiting from growth in the China market which was unaffected by '911'. Also, where a country has a strong domestic market – such as Germany – this cushioned the impact of '911' on the tourism sector.

REFERENCES

Bierman, D. (2002) *Restoring Tourism Destinations in Crisis*, CABI, Wallingford.

World Tourism Organization (2002) *The Impact of September 11th Attacks on Tourism: The Light at the End of the Tunnel*, WTO, Madrid.

DISCUSSION QUESTIONS

1 Thinking of your own country, list the impacts of '911' on tourism behaviour.

2 Thinking of destinations around the world draft a list, supported with brief reasons, of those that you perceive as 'safe' and those that you perceive as 'unsafe'.

3 Make a list of crises that have impacted upon the tourism sector internationally since 1980 and, using WTO statistics, plot the growth rates of international tourism arrivals following the incidents.

CHAPTER THREE
MEASURING DEMAND
FOR TOURISM

INTRODUCTION

Following on from the last chapter that outlined consumer behaviour in tourism, we now turn to approaches to measuring patterns of consumer demand. In this chapter we describe and critically appraise the measurement of demand for both international and domestic tourism. We treat these separately for convenience, although it is recognised that international and domestic movements may be considered essentially the same activity. Certainly they have much in common. We consider why tourism demand is measured, what definitions are used and which statistics are normally compiled. We include a description of methods commonly used and an indication of their strengths and weaknesses.

Closely linked to the measurement of demand is the concept of collecting market intelligence and managing information. In tourism, this often means using secondary data (for example, data produced by national or regional government bodies), combined with primary data through market surveys. In the latter part of this chapter we provide a practical guide to market research for the tourism industry and, in particular, market surveys. The various stages of research are also explained, from the agreement of research purpose and objectives, through research design, data collection and analysis, to the reporting of the research. We also give emphasis to the importance of a manager making use of findings and feeding them into the decision-making process, as well as the emerging science of knowledge management and how it can be applied to tourism.

LEARNING OUTCOMES

In this chapter, we review the key issues associated with the measurement of tourism demand and the management of tourism information, to provide you with:

- an understanding of the reasons why we measure both international and domestic demand for tourism;

- a knowledge of the main methods used to measure tourism demand;

- a review of what is measured in respect of tourism activity;

- an appreciation of the difficulties of researching tourism markets and why tourism statistics must be interpreted with caution; and

- an awareness of the research process and how it might best be implemented in tourism.

DEMAND FOR INTERNATIONAL TOURISM

Why measure international tourism?

National governments are generally extremely keen to monitor and attach measures to the movement of people into and out of their countries. This is for a variety of reasons, many of which have nothing whatsoever to do with tourism, such as security, health and immigration control. The measurement of tourism movement, however, has increasingly been seen as important because of the effects of tourism activity on a country's balance of payments.

The balance of payments is a country's financial accounts. There are movements of monies into and out of these accounts. Any standard economics text will provide a detailed and proper explanation of the various components. An obvious way in which tourism has an impact on the balance of payments is through the spending of international tourists. We can identify two aspects here:

1 Residents of country X, who travel abroad, spend money abroad. This has a negative effect on the balance of payments of country X (and positive effects on the balance of payments of countries visited). With regard to the movement of money, this can be thought of as an import as far as X is concerned. It is referred to as an invisible import since there is no associated tangible good (such as a car or refrigerator).

2 Residents of a foreign country, who are incoming tourists to country X, spend money in X. This has a positive effect on the balance of payments of X (and corresponding negative effects on the balance of payments of the country of origin of the tourist). As far as X is concerned, the direction of the spending is such that it is considered to be an invisible export.

The two components described above combine to form what is known as the travel account for a country. A positive travel account means that spending by incoming tourists exceeds spending abroad by outgoing tourists, and the combined effect will be of benefit to the balance of payments. Many commentators argue that any comparison of the two types of spending is unfair, since they reflect different activities.

The above analysis does not take into account fares paid to international passenger transport carriers and the various secondary effects of tourist spending. Later in this book we consider the impacts of tourism in detail, including a comprehensive review of the economic impacts.

We can see, then, that governments are keen to measure the movement of international tourism, but particularly incoming tourism because of its economic benefits. There are, however, a number of other important reasons:

• Official records can be built up and trends in movements can be monitored over a period of time. This means, for example, that the effectiveness of the marketing arm of government can be monitored, or that any particular promotional campaign, which attempts to attract visitors from a particular country, can be assessed.

• In general, information about the origins of visitors, their trip and attitudes can be used for a variety of purposes in marketing or planning. This is true also for tourism organisations at regional and local levels, provided that data collected at international level can be disaggregated and still be reliable.

In addition, some commercial organisations, although a minority, can and do make use of international tourism statistics. An incoming tour operator or wholesaler, for example, needs to be aware of current trends in order that programmes can be adjusted accordingly. Similarly, international and national hotel chains monitor changes in demand as part of their intelligence activity.

Some definitions

In collecting any information on the movement of travellers, it is essential to decide who is to be included. Everyone would agree that a family on holiday should count in the figures, but what about a businessperson, or the crew of a passenger liner, or even a member of the armed forces on duty in a foreign land? See Figure 3.1 for the answers! We can identify a number of principles that should govern the formation of a terminology:

- Definitions should be unambiguous and easy to understand.
- Definitions should normally be consistent with established usage of the words concerned.
- Definitions should, as far as is reasonably possible, facilitate measurement.

There is a major difficulty concerning the word 'tourism' itself. The normal and everyday use of the word relates to pleasure travel, but it would certainly exclude business travel. This is unfortunately not in line with what has become accepted as standard in the tourism literature. It is standard practice to include, as tourists, not only people who travel for pleasure but also those who travel for the purposes of business, visiting friends and relatives, or even shopping. The reasons concern the use that is made of tourism statistics. After all, passenger transport carriers would wish for such a broad range of travellers to be included; a large number of hoteliers are interested in business travel because of the business it generates for them, and so on.

The definitions we give here are those that have become accepted. Figure 3.1 shows the breakdown of all travellers who cross international frontiers into those who are to be included in tourism statistics (to be called 'visitors') and those who are not. The decision as to whom to include is based on the purpose of visit. Visitors are divided according to whether or not there is an overnight stay in the country: if there is, then the visitor is deemed to be a tourist; otherwise he or she is a same-day visitor (previously called an excursionist). In summary, for the purposes of classifying international travellers:

- A visitor is a traveller who is included in tourism statistics, based on his or her purpose of visit, which includes holidays, visiting friends and relatives, and business. A fuller list is shown in Figure 3.1.
- A tourist is a visitor who spends at least one night in the country visited.
- A same-day visitor is a visitor who does not spend the night in a collective or private accommodation in the country visited. So, for example, those returning to ship or train to sleep are considered as same-day visitors.

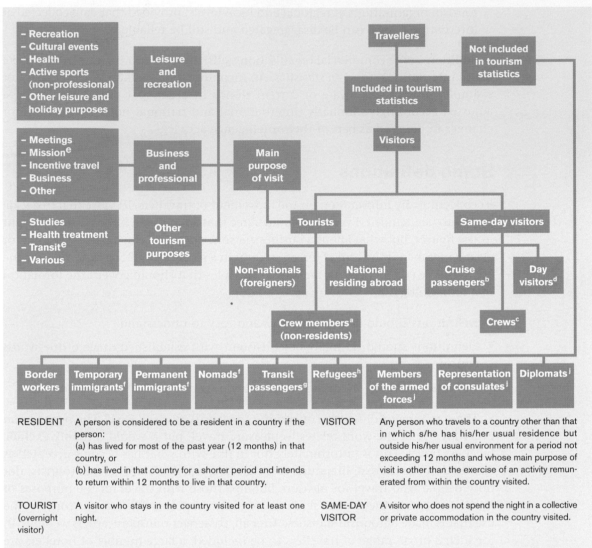

RESIDENT	A person is considered to be a resident in a country if the person: (a) has lived for most of the past year (12 months) in that country, or (b) has lived in that country for a shorter period and intends to return within 12 months to live in that country.	VISITOR	Any person who travels to a country other than that in which s/he has his/her usual residence but outside his/her usual environment for a period not exceeding 12 months and whose main purpose of visit is other than the exercise of an activity remunerated from within the country visited.
TOURIST (overnight visitor)	A visitor who stays in the country visited for at least one night.	SAME-DAY VISITOR	A visitor who does not spend the night in a collective or private accommodation in the country visited.

Notes:

[a] Foreign air or ship crews docked or in lay over and who use the accommodation establishments of the country visited.

[b] Persons who arrive in a country aboard cruise ships (as defined by the International Maritime Organization, 1965) and who spend the night aboard ship even when disembarking for one or more day visits.

[c] Crews who are not residents of the country visited and who stay in the country for the day.

[d] Visitors who arrive and leave the same day for leisure and recreation, business and professional or other tourism purposes including transit day visitors en route to or from their destination countries.

[e] Overnight visitors en route from their destination countries.

[f] As defined by the United Nations in the *Recommendations on Statistics of International Migration*, 1980.

[g] Who do not leave the transit area of the airport or the port, including transfer between airports or ports.

[h] As defined by the United Nations High Commissioner for Refugees, 1967.

[j] When they travel from their country of origin to the duty station and vice versa (including household servants and dependants and dependants accompanying or joining them).

FIGURE 3.1   **Classification of international visitors**   *Source: WTO, 2000*

What is measured?

The measurement of demand normally includes statistics of volume, value and profiles, as we describe in some detail below. In addition, during the collection of such data from visitors, questions are also often asked that relate to visitor opinions and attitudes.

VOLUME STATISTICS

The total number of international tourist arrivals to a country and the total number of international tourist departures from that country are key measures of demand. It can be seen that such measures are actually of trips. They are not counts of individuals since, for example, a businessman who makes 20 visits to a country will be counted 20 times. However, the numbers of trips and of individuals are related by the equation:

number of trips = number of individuals × average number of trips taken per individual

Estimates for any two of the variables in this equation will therefore provide an estimate for the third. The equation is general in the sense that it can be applied to any group of tourists. For example, the number of trips made in total by Japanese tourists to Ruritania in the year 2000 will be equal to the product of the number of individuals involved and the average number of trips they make to Ruritania.

A serious weakness in using international tourism arrivals, as far as most tourism suppliers are concerned, is that the length of stay is not taken into account. The length of stay is important for accommodation establishments, beach managers, retail outlets and so on, although not, of course, for passenger termini. A better measure of volume for many purposes is therefore total tourist nights. This also acts as a measure of likely impact on a tourist destination. It can be defined as follows:

total tourist nights = number of tourist trips × average length of stay (nights stayed)

VALUE (EXPENDITURE) STATISTICS

Total visitor expenditure is a simple measure of the economic value of foreign visitors to a country. It normally includes spending within a host country, and excludes fare payments made to international passenger carriers for travel into and out of that country. Similarly, the expenditure of outgoing tourists while abroad is a measure of the economic cost to a country due to its nationals travelling abroad. International tourism expenditure can typically be classified under the headings of accommodation, food and drink, entertainment, shopping and travel within the host country. For the purposes of comparison between countries, value statistics are often converted to US dollars.

VISITOR PROFILE STATISTICS

Profile statistics are made up of statistics relating to the visitor and those of the visit. Table 3.1 shows information typically collected.

TABLE 3.1	Visitor profile statistics	
The visitor	**The visit**
Age	Origin and destination
Sex	Mode of transport
Group type (e.g. alone, family)	Purpose of visit
Nationality or country of residence	Length of stay
Occupation	Accommodation used
Income	Activities engaged in
	Places visited
	Tour or independently organised

MEASUREMENT METHODS USED

Tourism statistics relating to international tourism are normally estimates rather than exact values. The reasons for this mainly centre on the fact that monitoring and measuring what are at times complex movements of people are not easy and are subject to error. We can most easily understand this when contemplating how to obtain detailed profile or expenditure information about tourists. Even the controls at international boundaries and currency controls do not normally work to provide accurate information.

Volume statistics are often obtained using counting procedures at entry and exit points to a country, or (for inbound tourism) sometimes through the use of registration forms at accommodation establishments. They can be supplemented by summaries of records kept by international passenger carriers, and by surveys of households, such as a national travel survey which will elicit information on foreign (outgoing) as well as domestic tourism. Research at tourist destinations also provides some information on the movement of international visitors to a country.

Procedures used at entry and exit points have normally been determined on the basis of administrative control and other reasons not specifically related to tourism. Tourism statistics are thus a by-product of the process rather than its main aim. Nevertheless, there are many countries that do make counts and collect information at frontiers for tourism-related purposes. Clearly, islands (such as Great Britain or those of the West Indies) have an advantage in this respect, since there are likely to be fewer entry/exit points anyway. A major problem with counting using accommodation establishments alone is that they give only partial coverage. No estimates would be possible for those staying with friends or relatives, for example.

Expenditure statistics are notoriously difficult to collect. We can derive them using foreign currency estimates from banks, or from suppliers of tourism services and facilities. These methods are cumbersome and normally not satisfactory. Increasingly, therefore, information is collected directly from the tourists themselves, through sample surveys of foreign tourists as they leave the country, and from nationals as they return from a foreign trip.

DEMAND FOR DOMESTIC TOURISM

Why measure domestic tourism?

Worldwide, relatively few people enjoy the opportunity to travel to and within countries other than their own. By far the most common form of travel is that by residents of a country within that country. International travel, although given high priority by segments of the populations of industrialised nations, is still very much a minority activity. As a very rough guide, we estimate that expenditure worldwide on domestic tourism may be worth up to ten times that on international tourism.

The WTO reported in 1984 that 'there are relatively few countries that collect domestic travel and tourism statistics', and the situation has not changed significantly since then. Much more information is available on international tourism. Why is this?

First of all, international travel involves, by definition, the crossing of a frontier. It is therefore easier to observe and monitor. Domestic tourism involves movement internally and is therefore more difficult to research. Countries that make use solely of registration forms at hotels miss out all aspects of domestic tourism that involve staying at supplementary accommodation establishments or with friends or relatives. A number of countries do not even try to measure domestic demand because it is considered unimportant owing to the nature of their own domestic tourism. For example, in many developing countries very little domestic movement involves staying in serviced accommodation, and so it does not compete with demand from international visitors. The benefits of collecting information always has to be set against its costs, particularly in a developing country where resources may be severely limited.

On the other hand, within the major international tourism-receiving countries of North America and Western Europe, domestic demand and international demand often compete with and complement each other. We can see this clearly in hotel lobbies, on beaches, in restaurants, at attractions and so on. So in countries such as the USA, Canada and the UK, the measurement of domestic tourism is important.

Use is made of domestic tourism statistics in a variety of ways:

- To measure the contribution of tourism to the overall economy. Although it is impossible to assess accurately, estimates can be produced that measure the effect of tourism on a country's gross domestic product.

- For promotion and marketing policies. Many countries promote themselves strongly as destinations to their own residents – in this sense, they compete with foreign destinations for their own tourists' spending.

- To assist area development policies. This can involve attempting to ensure a high quality of environment in the main tourism areas, as well as developing other areas to relieve congestion.

- To aid social policies. A statistical knowledge of holiday-taking habits by nationals is required, for example, for providing aid to the underprivileged, perhaps in the form of subsidies for socially orientated sites.

89

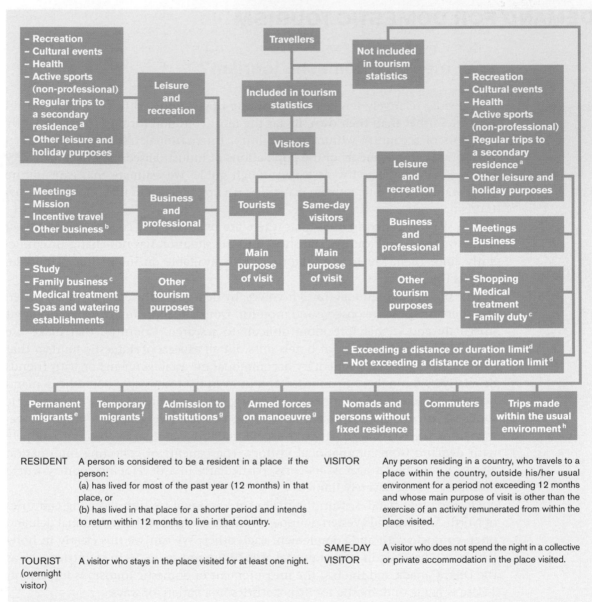

RESIDENT A person is considered to be a resident in a place if the person:
(a) has lived for most of the past year (12 months) in that place, or
(b) has lived in that place for a shorter period and intends to return within 12 months to live in that country.

VISITOR Any person residing in a country, who travels to a place within the country, outside his/her usual environment for a period not exceeding 12 months and whose main purpose of visit is other than the exercise of an activity remunerated from within the place visited.

TOURIST (overnight visitor) A visitor who stays in the place visited for at least one night.

SAME-DAY VISITOR A visitor who does not spend the night in a collective or private accommodation in the place visited.

Notes:

[a] Weekly trips to the place of second residence (whether owned, inhabited free of charge or rented) should be classified separately under leisure and recreation.

[b] Persons undertaking frequent trips within the country, e.g. crew members, drivers, tourist guides, salespeople, itinerant sellers, inspectors, artists, sportspeople.

[c] Attending funerals, visiting sick relatives, etc.

[d] Minimum distance and duration of minimum absence and duration of journey may be required for a person to qualify as a same-day visitor.

[e] For a period of more than 6 months, or the minimum time necessary to establish a new residence, including dependants.

[f] For a period of less than 12 months with the purpose of exercising an activity remunerated from within the place of destination, including dependants.

[g] Admission to a hospital, prison and other institutions.

[h] Trips of a routine character, part of a regular business schedule or frequent visits to a place for whatever reason.

FIGURE 3.2   **Classification of internal visitors**   *Source: WTO, 2000*

In addition to the above, local and regional tourism organisations and individual businesses make use of domestic tourism statistics as an aid to decision making.

Definitions of visitors vary country by country. When detailed accuracy is important it is advisable to check against the original source. Figure 3.2 gives definitions and classifications of internal (domestic) visitors as recommended by the WTO.

What is measured?

The measurement of domestic tourism demand covers similar areas to that of international demand: volume, value and visitor profile statistics. These can be presented for the country as a whole, but they are often more useful if they can be broken down to provide reliable information for specific destination areas. It is common for individual destinations to conduct their own research, and to complement their findings with the general data of a national study.

Measurement methods used

Statistics of domestic tourism are just like those of international tourism in that they are estimates, normally representing informed guesses and subject to different levels of error. Although some countries base them on returns from accommodation establishments, this does not provide proper coverage. It is increasingly common to collect information from the visitors themselves. This is normally done through sample surveys, and can take different forms, as follows.

HOUSEHOLD SURVEYS

Household surveys are based on a knowledge of the resident population, and provide a balanced view of domestic tourism for pleasure or business purposes. A structured sample of households is constructed and interviewers are employed to collect information using a questionnaire. Questions normally relate to past behaviour, covering trips already made, although studies of intentions are sometimes undertaken. Domestic tourism surveys, national travel surveys and holiday travel surveys (the latter excluding business travel) can all be based on household surveys, as shown in the first mini case study in this chapter. They also provide, as a matter of course, information on foreign travel by residents and also information on those who do not travel.

EN ROUTE SURVEYS

En route surveys are surveys of travellers during the course of their journey. Strategic points are selected to stop or approach people, who are then either interviewed or given a questionnaire or other documentation to complete in their own time for return by post. A major problem with this type of work is that the representativeness of the sample can be in doubt because of incomplete knowledge of traffic movement within a country.

MINI CASE STUDY 3.1
An example of household surveys: the United Kingdom
Tourism Survey

BACKGROUND

Prior to 1989 the four UK national tourist boards obtained estimates of domestic tourism volume and value from other surveys. The United Kingdom Tourism Survey (UKTS) came about, following reviews of statistical needs by and among the boards, as a result of a requirement for better data: better in the sense of being compatible over the UK as a whole, of covering aspects of tourism not covered by the earlier surveys, and of deriving from larger, and hence more statistically robust, samples (www.staruk.org.uk).

OBJECTIVES

The objective of UKTS is, first, to provide measurements of tourism by residents of the UK, in terms of both volume (trips taken, nights spent away from home) and value (expenditure on those trips and nights). Second, it is to collect details of the trips taken and of the people taking them. These objectives extend to:

- tourism by residents of any age;

- tourism for any purpose;

- tourism in the sense of trips away from home which last for one night or more up to a maximum of 60 nights; and

- tourism to any destination in any country of the world, using any accommodation type.

METHOD

The UKTS is a good example of how survey methodology changes to address both financial and technological change. The survey method for the ten years from 1989 to 1999 was a household interview. Each month, continuously, interviews were conducted face to face in the homes of a fresh representative sample of UK adults aged 15 or more. The sample used was a stratified random sample from the UK's electoral register, leading to named persons for interview. Up to four recalls were made at different times and on different days of the week: no substitutes were used in the sample. By this method, approximately 70,000 interviews were conducted each year in the course of fieldwork.

From the year 2000 onwards, the method changed to telephone interviewing and the sample was reduced to 50,000 adults. The sampling is achieved through random digital dialing with the interviewing spread evenly throughout the year. A particular change is that a longer time period is allowed to recall a respondent who is unavailable at the first time of calling. This is an important aspect when researching a market such as the UK where there is a large number of frequent travellers.

INFORMATION COLLECTED

The following information is collected by the UKTS:

- purpose of trip;
- number of nights away;
- accommodation used;
- transport used;
- activities undertaken;
- type of location;
- month trip started;
- booking method;
- demographics.

PUBLICATION OF FINDINGS

Findings are published annually.

Source: Adapted from The UK Tourist, *published jointly by the English Tourist Board, Northern Ireland Tourist Board, Scottish Tourist Board and Wales Tourist Board and* www.staruk.org.uk

DISCUSSION QUESTIONS

1 Tourism demand surveys are very expensive and compromises have to be made in their design to meet budgets. Do you think the public or the private sector should fund such surveys?

2 Draft a checklist of the differences between face-to-face and telephone interviewing.

3 Recalling past events is a critical element of this type of survey – can you remember your last three tourism trips in sufficient detail to answer the checklist of questions asked by the UKTS above?

DESTINATION SURVEYS

Surveys are often conducted at popular tourist destinations or in areas where there are high levels of tourist activity. They typically take the form of personal interviews by teams of interviewers. The information provided leads to estimates of the volume and value of tourism to the destination, of profiles of visitors and of their visits. Questions are also asked to elicit opinions about the destination and associated attitudes. It is difficult in this type of work to ensure that the sample of visitors is representative, though efforts are made to ensure a spread across appropriate days and weeks, and that interviews are conducted at a wide range of sites.

SURVEYS OF SUPPLIERS

Surveys of the suppliers of tourism services are sometimes undertaken in order to gain information on occupancy rates, visitor numbers, etc. Accommodation occupancy surveys are, in fact, common worldwide. In North America, airlines have been required through the Civil Aeronautics Board (in the USA) and the Canadian Transport Commission to produce origin and destination data.

USING TOURISM STATISTICS

Some words of caution

According to the WTO, international tourist arrivals in 2002 numbered 702.6 million, and receipts from world tourism amounted to US$474 billion. It is not so much the size of these figures that is so impressive, but the fact that anybody should know the value of tourism, the level of tourism demand or be able to work these figures out. In this chapter, we have detailed methods for measuring tourism demand and it is important to bear them in mind when interpreting the results.

Collecting tourism statistics is time consuming and complex. In some countries it is taken very seriously, to the extent that attempts are made to assess the size of potential errors. It is then possible not merely to provide a point estimate (that is, a single value) of, say, tourist numbers, but to give lower and upper bounds within which the true value is thought to lie. Some countries review their data collection procedures with a view to minimising errors subject to an acceptable cost. However, not all countries attach the same importance to tourism statistics in general, and to certain measures in particular. For example, the expenditure of incoming tourists normally has high priority attached to it, because of its positive contribution to the balance of payments. On the other hand, the number and spending of tourists who are visiting friends and relatives may be underestimated in countries in which measurement is through serviced accommodation establishments.

It is not surprising, then, that the interpretation of tourism data is fraught with danger. Key points to bear in mind are the following:

- Tourism statistics are normally estimates, often derived from sample surveys. As such, they are liable to various forms of error, many of which are impossible to quantify.

- For measurements which result from sample surveys, in general the smaller the sample size, the greater is the probable error.

- Even though the sample size for data relating to a region or country may give rise to acceptable levels of error, analysis of a subset of the data pertaining to a smaller area or region may not be feasible owing to the much reduced sample size.

- Sample size is not everything! The true random sampling of tourists who are, by their very nature, on the move is not normally possible. A sample has to be formally and carefully constructed.

- Where methodology in collecting data changes (even when it is for the better), it is dangerous to compare results.

- There are serious problems involved in attempting either to compare or to combine figures collected by different countries or organisations.

The final point arises because there is not only considerable variation in the methods employed by different countries, but also variation in the measures adopted. A notable example is that some countries count tourist arrivals (at least one night spent in the country visited), whereas others prefer to count visitor arrivals (this includes excursionists, i.e. those who do not stay overnight).

Interpreting tourism statistics

What then are we to make of the fact that we are told that international tourist arrivals in 2002 worldwide numbered 702.6 million? This total is certainly arrived at by grossing figures submitted to the WTO by governments or national bodies throughout the world. Each component value is subject to different levels of error, arising from different methodologies. It is clear, therefore, that the quoted figure is an estimate, and it is difficult to say how accurate it might be.

The points made above apply more generally than to total international tourist arrivals worldwide. They apply equally to many other situations in which data relating to tourists are collected: at resorts, attractions, passenger termini and so on. However, exact values are normally not what is important and, bearing in mind the shortcomings, we can see that tourism statistics often represent the best estimates available and also provide a guide as to true magnitudes. As a result, they have the following benefits:

- They often provide valuable trend data, where information is produced over a number of time periods.

- They contribute towards a database which may influence decision making, particularly in the areas of marketing, and planning and development.

- They enable the effects of decisions or changes to be monitored.

- They enable current data to be viewed in context.

- They provide a means of making forecasts.

RESEARCHING TOURISM MARKETS: THE VALUE OF RESEARCH

Many managers and organisations in the tourism industry attach great value to research and the knowledge that it delivers, using it to place themselves in a strong competitive position. Sound market intelligence is gained from a variety of formal and informal methods, and bridges the gap between the provider of the product or service and the consumer. Decisions such as those concerning product development and marketing activity can be based on research findings. Moreover, research can be used to highlight specific problems, and even to demonstrate to customers a caring attitude to customers.

We can see that marketing intelligence and marketing research in tourism can therefore:

- provide information for decision making;

- keep an organisation in touch with its market;

- identify new markets;

- monitor the performance of certain aspects of a business;

- draw attention to specific problems;

- monitor customer reaction to a service or facility;

- reduce waste; and

- demonstrate a caring attitude to the customer.

However, others view research with suspicion. It can be seen as an unnecessary cost, taking up valuable resources that could be used in a better way. There may just not be the time for it, given the high level of pressure under which many people work. Others may see research as an essentially academic activity with no real value for the business. In any case, some organisations are able to 'feed off' the research conducted and published by others with greater market share, or to make use of the findings and advice of national and regional tourist offices. These issues are further discussed in the major case study at the end of this chapter.

The potential benefits of research vary considerably by type of organisation and by size. Major airlines and international hotel chains, for example, collect and analyse data as an aid to making decisions. Individual hotels and attractions often conduct surveys of guests and visitors to gain profile information, opinions and satisfaction ratings. A small restaurant owner or retailer is unlikely to engage in formal research. All businesses monitor sales, however, and all good managers have an instinct for changes in the marketplace.

THE RESEARCH PROCESS

There is no standard way of approaching research. However, it is instructive to model the research process using the flow diagram shown in Figure 3.3, bearing in mind that stages shown often overlap in time rather than following the precise sequence implied. Some organisations generate research through a planning or marketing department that is able to identify research needs. The reporting of the outcomes can then be fed back into the department concerned for action, and an information base built up. Most organisations, however, generate *ad hoc* projects if and when the need arises.

Research can be undertaken 'in house' by an organisation using its own resources, or an external agency may be employed. In either case, the same principles apply and the process is essentially the same. There are numerous reputable

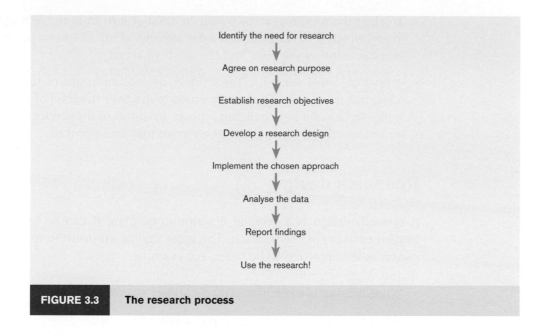

FIGURE 3.3 The research process

organisations – such as advertising agencies, market research agencies, consultants, academic institutions – that offer their services, and that either specialise in research or are experienced in research as part of their activity. A common practice when commissioning research is for the sponsor to issue a detailed brief. Following discussions, external agencies usually submit research proposals, often in competition, the successful one gaining a contract to undertake the research.

The principles we cover in the rest of this chapter are valid not only for research within the tourism industry, but also for students of tourism in a more academic setting. Research projects at all levels of study will benefit from the structure imposed by Figure 3.3.

Agreeing the purpose and setting objectives

Research based on a clear picture of its purpose is likely to lead to findings that will be of benefit. The overall purpose should be agreed by the major parties concerned. This is particularly important for the many public-sector projects in tourism that have to satisfy or are steered by representatives from a wide range of interested organisations.

The purpose is satisfied through the attainment of the research objectives set. The objectives should always be formally stated, and again agreed. This not only avoids later misunderstanding, but also gives a focus to the research. It is possible to match findings later with the objectives set in order to assess the success of the research. For example, the following research objectives are taken from a survey of educational visits to the National Maritime Museum:

- To elicit the profile of educational groups visiting the museum in terms of age, geographical location, sector of school and size of school group.

- To elicit the profile of visits by educational groups in terms of number of visits made, whether schools were on a day trip or staying in London, any publicity or event prompting the visit, and the mode of travel.

- A final objective related to the schools' use and opinions of the museum as an educational resource. The survey aimed to discover the level of use of the educational service and also to obtain schools' opinions of the service and the museum and to identify areas in which the service may be improved.

Research design

A research design is a detailed description or plan; it can be used to guide the implementation of the research. The most significant decision involved in design concerns the approach to be taken. For example:

- What reliance is to be placed on secondary sources?

- Should a sample survey or group discussions be used?

- Which survey technique should be used – personal interviews, telephone interviews or postal survey?

PRIMARY OR SECONDARY DATA?

Secondary data are those that have already been collected, possibly by some other individual or organisation and for some other purpose. In any country the most prolific source is government. Although its data are normally too general in nature to be of practical benefit, they often provide good background information. The same applies to data provided by other national and local bodies such as tourist offices. Before engaging in what may prove to be expensive primary data collection (that is, your own), it is worth a researcher identifying and assessing possible sources of information that could supplement primary data or even remove the need for it. There is no point in collecting information that already exists in an accessible form.

In particular, a tourism enterprise's own records are particularly valuable. Data can be taken from sales invoices, booking forms, general accounts, operating data, internal reports and so on. Many organisations have built up databases over a period of time, and these can form the basis of research data. Nevertheless, there are times when it is necessary to collect primary data, even though it is normal to supplement this with secondary data.

Methods of collecting primary data

In tourism, the most common method by far is the sample survey, either of visitors themselves or of businesses. The four main types of survey are personal interview, telephone interview, web-based survey and postal survey. The choice as to which to use depends on the nature of the research concerned, and takes account of the advantages and disadvantages of each method as demonstrated in the second mini case in this chapter.

Visitor surveys at attractions are often based on personal interviews using questionnaires at or near exit points. Telephone interviewing has become increasingly popular. It can be used in its own right or as part of an overall strategy. For example, an occupancy survey may involve contact by telephone, followed by a personal visit and the delivery of self-administered questionnaires. Postal questionnaires are often used when the manager does not have direct access to the user, or as a follow-up such as when a holiday is sold, using customer addresses. It is also possible to hand out questionnaires for self-completion: for example, on a return holiday flight or return coach journey. Web-based surveys using email or online survey forms associated with web sites, are growing in popularity and are particularly useful for more in-depth information, such as that required by the Delphi forecasting technique. There is also scope in tourism for the use of observation methods – in monitoring the popularity of displays or exhibits, or the movement of visitors at open-air sites.

It is possible to make use of modern computer technology in the collection of primary data. This can lead not only to improvements in accuracy, but also removes the need for data input at a later stage.

In a detailed study of attitudes or perceptions, it is probable that a qualitative approach will be taken in order to achieve greater insight and understanding. This might involve in-depth interviews or discussions with individuals, say with successful managers to analyse their decision-making processes. It can also involve the formation of discussion groups of between six and ten people, led by an experienced discussant. In this case the interaction between people can stimulate and encourage ideas, or draw out factors such as those that affect holiday choice.

PHOTOGRAPH 3.1 **Experience shows that in a tourism setting, survey respondents are more relaxed and willing to cooperate with surveys**
Source: Reed Kaestner/CORBIS

MINI CASE STUDY 3.2
Comparing data collection procedures

Major tourist attractions such as theme parks routinely research their markets to gain not only information on their market profile but also the opinions and satisfaction levels of their visitors. These attractions utilise different data collection procedures in their surveys but, of course, each procedure has its own strengths and weaknesses. Below we consider four of the most commonly used approaches for the collection of data at attractions.

PERSONAL INTERVIEW

Advantages:

- Initial interest can be aroused and visitors may then spend longer at the attraction.
- Complex questioning is possible on, say, visitors' likes and dislikes at the attraction.
- Visual aids and showcards can be used.
- Flexibility allows scheduling to be varied according to, say, the weather.
- Shows a caring attitude to the visitors at the attraction.
- Visitors are usually happy to cooperate.

Disadvantages:

- Time consuming for interviewer and visitor.
- Administratively difficult scheduling interviewers etc.
- It can be an expensive way to collect data as interviewers can be costly.

TELEPHONE INTERVIEW

Advantages:

- Close supervision and control is possible.
- Access is easy, call-backs are possible if the person who visited the attraction is not available.
- Response rates are usually good.
- Many interviews are possible in a given time period.

Disadvantages:

- Visual aids and complex tasks are not possible.
- Only verbal communication is possible.
- Interview is short (people hang up).
- For attraction surveys it relies on recall and the immediacy of the visit is lost.

POSTAL SURVEY

Advantages:

- Low cost.
- No intermediary, so answers are reliable and visitors would not answer in a certain way to 'please' the interviewer.
- Superior for sensitive questions (confidentiality must be stressed) on, say, satisfaction levels with the visit.

Disadvantages:

- Many variables are not controlled, since there is no interviewer.
- Mailing list is needed of visitors to the attraction.
- Response rates are low.
- Bias due to non-response.
- Detailed or long questionnaires reduce response.

INTERNET SURVEY

Advantages:

- Substantial cost savings over other survey methods.
- No cost to the respondent in replying.
- Response tends to be very quick.
- Instant feedback of undeliverable mail is useful in replacing respondents.
- Useful as a supplement to other survey methods – say, a follow-up on an interview at the attraction.
- Good for surveying specific populations such as teachers who have taken groups to the attraction.

Disadvantages:

- Sample bias due to the type of respondent – random sampling is virtually impossible.
- Evidence on response rates is contradictory.
- Needs high level of expertise to construct the survey.
- Ethical issues of sending unsolicited email.

Source: Adapted from Cooper and Latham, 1990; Tasci and Knutson, 2003

DISCUSSION QUESTIONS

1 For a survey of visitor satisfaction for a holiday island such as Majorca, draft a checklist of the main pros and cons for using each of the four methods outlined in the case study.

2 What are the main sources of tourism market information that lend themselves to collection by an Internet survey?

3 Of the methods in the case study, which is the most cost effective for a market survey of booking intentions?

Designing questionnaires

Questionnaires are by far the most common type of form used for primary data collection in tourism. They are difficult to construct, though much easier to criticise, and it is certainly sensible for a researcher to pass round his or her attempts to colleagues for suggested changes. Final versions are usually very different from early drafts. It is important to bear in mind the objectives of the research when constructing a questionnaire, as they give focus to it. The temptation to include questions not relevant to the study, but for interest's sake, should normally be resisted. Their inclusion can lead to a respondent tiring or losing interest, and put at risk answers to more important questions. The steps involved in the design of a questionnaire are as follows:

1 Plan what to measure, based on the objectives of the research.

2 Formulate the questions.

3 Decide on the layout and order of questions.

4 Pilot test the questionnaire.

5 Correct problems that arise and retest if necessary.

Here are some general guidelines for constructing or assessing the likely effectiveness of a questionnaire:

- Questions should follow a logical order; the questionnaire should flow.
- There should be a simple introduction and early questions should be straightforward.
- Language used should be appropriate to the respondent.
- Questions should be unambiguous.
- Avoid bias within a question, i.e. a question that suggests that a particular answer is acceptable.
- Do not tax the memory of the respondent.
- Instructions on the form (to interviewer or, in the case of self-completion, the respondent) should be highlighted.
- The questionnaire should be as short as possible.
- The form should be attractive, well laid out and easy to follow.

Sampling

Normally research in tourism seeks to gain information on a large number of people (or sometimes businesses). The term 'population', or 'universe', is used to describe all those under consideration. Examples of populations are all holiday-makers at a resort, all businesspeople using hotels in a city, all users of a leisure complex, or all visitors to an attraction.

For populations that are relatively small, say, the 17 coach operators who use a particular stop, it is possible to undertake a census. However, populations are usually large and it is not practical or cost effective to contact every single member. Instead, a sample survey is undertaken. The way in which a sample is constructed is a key element in the research process, since the sample must mirror the population from which it is taken. Then findings based on the sample will be valid for the population as a whole. The technicalities of sampling and the validity of making inferences about populations are complex, and are covered in texts on statistics and research methods.

There are a variety of sampling methods in use. The most common is what might be considered a 'loose' approach, where interviewers are given target numbers of interviews to achieve and are asked to contact a representative spread of people by age and sex. This almost certainly leads to a biased sample. At attractions and passenger termini, it is possible to take the selection of respondent away from the interviewer through the use of 'tighter' procedures such as systematic sampling (say, every twentieth person to pass an exit point).

It is difficult to construct with confidence a representative sample of visitors at a tourist destination such as a resort or within large recreation areas. This is because visitors are scattered over large areas and their movement is complex. It is normal to take account of the time of year (sample more heavily in the peak months) and to conduct interviews where tourists are likely to frequent (attractions, accommodation establishments, shopping centres, places of interest for destinations, popular sites for recreation areas).

Data analysis

Data from questionnaire returns or other data sheets can be input into computer files for analysis. The use of an appropriate software package speeds up the process and ensures accuracy within the analysis. The scope of analysis is also increased, because the relationships between variables can be examined in depth.

The first stage is often merely establishing counts or frequencies of response. These are often best expressed as percentages. Thus, 40% of visitors are in family groups, 80% arrive by car and so on. This is followed by the 'cross-tabulation' of variables, in which responses to one question are matched with responses to another. An example of output from this form of analysis is: 30% of holiday visitors to the hotel were dissatisfied with the leisure facilities, compared with only 5% of business visitors.

The use of counts and cross-tabulations is sufficient for the majority of studies. More detailed forms of analysis make use of higher-level statistics, and are common in project work undertaken by students registered for higher degrees.

Reporting research

An essential part of the research process is the final report. This is often accompanied by a formal presentation of findings. The level, method and timing of the reporting should be discussed and agreed at an early stage. Research results may well confirm what the manager already believed, and thus provide him or her with hard evidence to make his or her case to others. They can also lead to some surprises and to changes that were not anticipated. Effective reports should have a number of elements (Cooper and Latham, 1990), such as those listed under the following headings.

PRESENTATION

- Reports should be actionable.

- Findings and recommendations should be linked to objectives set.

- There should be a clear summary of findings and recommendations – it is normal for these to appear at the beginning.

- Language should be appropriate and clearly expressed. The main body of the report should be able to be understood by a non-technical manager. Appendices of technical detail should be included if relevant.

CONTENT

- Background information may be included.

- Research methodology should be included.

- Copies of forms (e.g. blank questionnaire) and letters used in the research should be included, normally as appendices.

- Details of analysis and tables should be clear and easy to understand.

- Diagrams may be used in addition to or instead of tables in order to enhance interpretation.

- Information should be full and complete.

- Appendices should be used for technical or other information that would otherwise detract from the reading of the report.

It is a waste of resources to commission research and then not consider the findings. Provided that the research purpose is clear from the beginning and that the objectives set were appropriate to it, the relevance to decision making should be clear. The research report then represents an objective view, relevant to the needs of the organisation.

CONCLUSION

The activity generated by tourism demand is prolific – in terms of both volume and revenue generated – and yet its measurement remains problematic at best and wholly inadequate at worst. Since many countries continue to derive their tourism statistics as a by-product of data gained for other, non-tourism-related, research, statistics for international and domestic tourism must be interpreted and utilised with caution and sensitivity.

Despite the difficulties, however, the measurement of incoming and outgoing tourism is crucial for economic and commercial reasons. In addition, the measurement of tourism activity, and an associated understanding of tourist motivations and profiles provides a wealth of information for the planning, management and marketing of tourism at the destination and an appreciation of consumer behaviour in tourism.

Self-check questions

1 Consider how you might approach the researching of tourism activity at a specific destination, reviewing the types of information you need to elicit from tourists and the methodology you might employ.

2 What might be some of the key problems in comparing tourism statistics from different areas and regions of the world?

3 Consider who should finance the collection of tourism information in your country.

4 Review the main stages of research and provide a tourism example of each.

5 Do you think there is a role for key international bodies such as the WTO to be more involved in the collection of tourism statistics? How might this involvement be manifested and where might the emphasis lie?

Essay questions

1 Why should tourism statistics be interpreted with caution?

2 Identify the major methods used to measure tourism demand and review the advantages and disadvantages of each.

3 Design a brief for a market survey for a tourist attraction to elicit both the current profile of visitors and their opinions of the attraction.

4 Why is domestic tourism demand difficult to measure?

5 What do you understand by the term knowledge management and how might it be used in tourism?

Annotated further reading

Books

Brent Ritchie, J.R. and Goeldner, C.R. (1994) *Travel Tourism and Hospitality Research. A Handbook for Managers and Researchers*, 2nd edn, John Wiley, Chichester.
A thorough handbook with authoritative entries on all of the main methods of collecting tourism information as well as guidance on research design, reporting and analysis.

Jennings, G. (2001) *Tourism Research*, John Wiley, Brisbane.
A comprehensive text covering all aspects of tourism research including research design, sampling, data collection, analysis and report writing.

World Tourism Organization (2000) *Data Collection and Analysis for Tourism Management, Marketing and Planning*, WTO, Madrid.
A comprehensive practical guide to collecting and analysing tourism information within a disciplined and coherent framework of statistics.

Web site

www.world-tourism.org
A comprehensive site with the definitive approaches to collecting tourism statistics, definitions and technical handbooks.

References cited

Cooper, C.P. and Latham, J. (1990) 'A layman's guide to market research for the tourist industry', *Insights*, English Tourist Board, London.

Tasci, A.D.A. and Knutson, B.J. (2003) 'Online research modes: waiting for leisure, tourism and hospitality researchers', *Journal of Hospitality and Leisure Marketing* **10**(3/4), 57–83.

WTO (1984) *Collection of Domestic Tourism Statistics*, WTO, Madrid.

WTO (2000) *Data Collection and Analysis for Tourism Management, Marketing and Planning*. WTO, Madrid.

MAJOR CASE STUDY 3.1
MANAGING TOURISM INFORMATION

There is no doubt that in today's 'knowledge economy', the role of information and knowledge is increasingly valued. Both nations and organisations are recognising that their competitiveness in the global marketplace depends upon their ability to capitalise on intellectual and knowledge-based assets, as opposed to the more traditional commodities. Tourism has been slow to adapt to this new way of thinking and reluctant to recognise knowledge as a key competitive tool for the private sector and a determinant of economic growth for governments. Yet, tourism, as one of the world's major economic sectors, will ultimately be required to adapt to these changes. One approach is to ensure the effective management of the massive volume of tourism information and statistics that is collected and which has been outlined in this chapter. The tool that is used for this management is known as 'knowledge management' (KM).

KNOWLEDGE MANAGEMENT

The concept of knowledge management (KM) arose in the 1980s and is defined as, 'the encouragement of people to share knowledge and ideas to create value-adding products and services' (Chase, 1997, p. 83). Essentially KM is a process by which research information and statistics are transformed into capabilities for an economic sector such as tourism by allowing organisations to use knowledge and skills to satisfy customers and exploit market opportunities. By adopting a KM approach organisations will increase their opportunity to become more profitable, efficient and competitive; operate more intelligently in the marketplace; and create learning, networked organisations.

In order to demonstrate how KM operates, Weggeman (1997) has designed a 'knowledge value chain' (Figure 3.4). The concept of the knowledge value chain clearly locates the key stages of knowledge management from knowledge generation to commercialisation and diffusion.

FIGURE 3.4   **The knowledge value chain**   *Source: Weggeman, 1997*

USING KM TO MANAGE TOURISM INFORMATION – FROM DATA TO KNOWLEDGE

This chapter has shown that measuring tourism activity is a major activity of governments generating a substantial amount of data. However, this case study suggests that the data generated could be more useful to the tourism sector if some general principles of knowledge management (KM) are followed. As tourism has become more professional, research has unquestionably grown, yet it has been largely market driven with tactical short-term objectives being the focus of attention. As a result tourism information has not been subject to a KM approach and some argue that the sector is not as competitive as it could be. This is not surprising considering that:

• Tourism has traditionally been service and product based and, with the exception of the distribution system and business administration, most tourism enterprises have been either unaware of, or slow to take up, the opportunities on offer from tourism research.

• The tourism sector is dominated by small-to-medium-sized enterprises, which are traditionally research averse.

• Tourism research has suffered from a lack of vision both by the bodies that provide money for research and surveys and the tourism industry itself – for which the research and surveys are often targeted.

• There is a perception that tourism is about play, recreation and having a good time.

• Tourism information has not been used effectively, and there is a reluctance to share information. As a consequence decisions are made without the benefit of the best information available.

There is no doubt that tourism data have proliferated in the last twenty years. This is due to a number of forces (Davidson and Voss, 2002):

• Globalisation has exposed tourism organisations to a wide array of organisations and competitors.

• The memory and processing power of information technology allied to the speed of communication of new media.

• The increased professionalism of the tourism sector means that information is sought.

• Changing organisational forms are creating freelance employees and knowledge workers.

But the availability of data is not enough as *data* are simply the raw numbers and facts of, say, the surveys outlined in this chapter. What is needed is for those data to be transformed initially into *information* by distilling facts and then creating *knowledge* that is the ideas, thoughts and beliefs which render the data useable by an organisation. As Davidson and Voss (2002) observe, knowledge has some interesting characteristics:

• It can be used without being consumed.

• One piece of knowledge can have many owners.

A great way to fly

SINGAPORE AIRLINES

A STAR ALLIANCE MEMBER ™

PHOTOGRAPH 3.2	**Large corporations are becoming true 'learning organisations' as they adopt the principles of knowledge management**
	Source: Keene

- One piece of knowledge can be in more than one place at any point in time.
- The cost of knowledge is heavily front loaded.
- Knowledge is unpredictable.

KM AND SINGAPORE AIRLINES

Singapore Airlines have adopted the principles of a KM framework in their business operations. Their KM approach has the following characteristics (Ahmed, Lim and Loh, 2002):

- Managing booking information – technology is an enabling tool for KM. Singapore Airlines have developed a sophisticated yield management and demand forecasting tool that allows them to sell seats on the same flight to different market segments, closely matching supply and demand.

- Sourcing information – KM identifies a range of sources of information for an organisation, including employees, customers and external sources (such as the competition):
  - The company sources ideas and information from its employees by newsletters, networking meetings and a 'staff ideas action scheme'.
  - Singapore Airlines has used market research to gauge customer attitudes to service levels. This information is then factored into the operation of the company. In addition, market research is carried out with 'knowledgeable customers' as well as the more traditional approaches of feedback forms and in-flight surveys.
  - Finally, Singapore Airlines regularly benchmarks against other service organisations – not just airlines – but also banks and other service delivery groups.

Singapore Airlines as a good example of how KM takes raw data and converts it to knowledge upon which the company can make both operational and management decisions.

REFERENCES

Ahmed, P.K., Lim, K.K. and Loh, A.Y.E. (2002) *Learning Through Knowledge Management*, Butterworth Heinemann, Oxford.

Chase, R.L. (1997) 'Knowledge management benchmarks', *Journal of Knowledge Management* 1(1), 83–92.

Davidson, C. and Voss, P. (2002) *Knowledge Management*, Tandem, Auckland.

Weggeman, M.C.D.P. (1997) *Kennismanagement. Inrichting en Besturing van Kennisintensieve Organisaties*, Scriptum, Schiedam.

DISCUSSION QUESTIONS

1 Review why it has taken tourism longer than other economic sectors to realise the value of a knowledge management approach.

2 From Singapore Airlines' point of view, what is the difference between data, information and knowledge?

3 Take a piece of research that you are familiar with in tourism; does it fit the knowledge value chain?

CHAPTER FOUR
TOURISM DEMAND DETERMINANTS AND FORECASTING

INTRODUCTION

This chapter focuses upon the key determinants of demand for tourism and goes on to show how an understanding of these underlying influences allows us to forecast tourism demand. It is difficult to generalise about the determinants of demand. There is, for example, a particular problem in terms of linking different levels of generalisation. At one level (in Chapter 2) we have already considered the individual's consumer behaviour with reference to tourism and analysed the various influences upon behaviour. In this chapter we consider specific determinants of demand at the individual level and go on to demonstrate how they can be aggregated to explain patterns and rhythms of tourism demand globally. In this way we can show that those countries with a high level of economic development and a stable, urbanised population are major generators of tourism demand.

An understanding of demand determinants is fundamental to forecasting future demand. For example, we can predict that effective demand for tourism will be highly concentrated among the affluent, industrialised nations. This information is important for managers and accurate forecasts in tourism are essential to inform decision making in both governments and the industry. The final section of the chapter examines the different approaches available to forecast tourism demand and the reasons why we should maintain forecasts, particularly the fact that tourism is a perishable industry and its assets such as beds or aircraft seats cannot be stored. There is no doubt that forecasts are necessary, despite the fact that some argue that as tourism is a volatile industry operating in a world of rapid and unexpected change, forecasts are increasingly irrelevant.

LEARNING OUTCOMES

The purpose of this chapter is to introduce and discuss determinants of demand and forecasting approaches. We then draw together the chapter by reviewing the major trends in the patterns of demand for tourism from historic and regional perspectives in the major case study. This chapter is designed to provide you with:

- familiarity with the determinants of demand which, at an individual level, are likely to affect propensity to travel;

- an understanding of social, technological, economic and political influences on tourism demand;

- an awareness of the reasons for forecasting demand for tourism;

- an understanding of the major approaches to forecasting demand for tourism; and

- an appreciation and explanation of the key historic and regional patterns of demand for tourism.

DETERMINANTS OF DEMAND FOR TOURISM

Determinants at the individual scale

Although an individual may be motivated to travel, the ability to do so will depend on a number of factors related to both the individual and the supply environment. These factors can be termed determinants of demand (**demand determinants**) and represent the 'parameters of possibility' for the individual – even within the developed world, many are unable to participate in tourism for some reason. For example, a certain level of discretionary income is required to allow participation in tourism, and this income, and indeed the type of participation, will be influenced by such factors as job type, life-cycle stage, mobility, level of educational attainment and personality.

Once a decision to travel has been taken, the ability to undertake the trip, and the nature of that trip will be determined by a wide range of interrelated factors. These can be broadly divided into two groups:

1 The first group of factors can be termed lifestyle, and includes income, employment, holiday entitlement, educational attainment and mobility.

2 The second group can be termed life cycle where the age and domestic circumstances of an individual affect both the amount and type of tourism demanded.

Naturally, these factors are interrelated and complementary. In a Western society, a high-status job is normally associated with an individual in middle age with a high-income, above average holiday entitlement, education and mobility.

Lifestyle determinants of demand for tourism

INCOME AND EMPLOYMENT

Income and employment are closely linked and exert important influences upon both the level and the nature of tourism demanded by an individual. Tourism is an expensive activity that demands a certain threshold of income before participation is possible. Gross income gives little indication of the money available to spend on tourism – rather, it is discretionary income that provides the best indicator; that is, the income left over when tax, housing and the basics of life have been accounted for. Clearly, two households with the same gross incomes may have very different discretionary incomes, although discretionary income is difficult to measure.

The relationship between income and tourism is a complex one. For example, certain tourism activities are highly sensitive to income – additional holidays and expensive pursuits such as skiing holidays are a particular case in point. The relationship is also characterised by the fact that, at the extremes of the income spectrum, tourism demand is strongly affected, whereas in the middle of the spectrum it is much more difficult to discern a clear relationship. For example, a very low discretionary income markedly depresses travel propensity. As discretionary income rises, the ability to partake of tourism is associated with the purchase of leisure-orientated goods, until, with a high discretionary income, travel may reach a peak and then level off as the demands of a high-status job, and possibly frequent business trips, reduce the ability and desire to travel for pleasure.

A fundamental distinction is between those in employment and those unemployed. The impact of unemployment on the volume of tourism demand is obvious, but the nature of demand is also changed by employment uncertainty. This encourages later booking of trips, more domestic holidays and shorter lengths of stay, and switches demand away from commercial accommodation to VFR, therefore leading to lower spending levels.

The nature of employment not only influences travel propensity by determining income and holiday entitlement, but it also has an effect upon the type of holiday demanded, as the mechanism of peer and reference group pressure is felt.

PAID HOLIDAY ENTITLEMENT

The increase in leisure time experienced by most individuals in the developed world since 1950 is well documented. However, the relationship between an individual's total time budget, leisure time and **paid holiday entitlement** is complex. A number of surveys suggest that, in a developed Western economy, individuals have anything from 35 to 50 hours free time a week at their disposal. This free time is greater for males, the young and single adults. Of this free time some two-thirds is spent around the home. However, to enable tourism, leisure time has to be blocked into two or more days to allow a stay away from home. While this obviously is the case with paid holiday entitlement, patterns of leisure time have changed over the past 20 years to allow three-day weekends, flexi time and longer periods of absence for those in employment.

A variety of holiday arrangements now exists worldwide, with most nations having a number of one-day national holidays, as well as annual paid holiday entitlement by law or collective agreements. Individual levels of paid holiday entitlement would seem to be an obvious determinant of travel propensity, but in fact the relationship is not straightforward and, rather like the income variable, it is clearer at the extremes. For example, low levels of entitlement do act as a real constraint upon the ability to travel, while a high entitlement encourages travel. This is in part due to the interrelationship between entitlement and factors such as job status, income and mobility. As levels of entitlement increase, the cost of tourism may mean that more of this entitlement will be spent at home.

Paid holiday entitlement tends to be more generous in developed economies and less so in the developing world. The pattern of entitlement is also responsible in part for the seasonality of tourism in some destinations simply because some of the entitlement has to be taken in the summer months. To an extent, this is historical and is rooted in the holiday patterns of manufacturing industries. It does, however, have an impact upon the nature of demand for tourism. In some countries, notably France, staggering of holiday entitlement has been attempted to alleviate seasonality.

EDUCATION AND MOBILITY

Level of educational attainment is an important determinant of travel propensity as education broadens horizons and stimulates the desire to travel. Also, the better educated the individual, the higher the awareness of travel opportunities, and susceptibility to information, media, advertising and sales promotion.

Personal mobility also has an important influence on travel propensity, especially with regard to domestic holidays. The car is the dominant recreational tool for both international and domestic tourism. It provides door-to-door freedom, can carry tourism equipment (such as tents or boats) and has all-round vision for viewing. Ownership of a car stimulates travel for pleasure in all but recessionary times.

RACE AND GENDER

Race and gender are two critical determinants of tourism demand, but the relationships are not clearly understood. Most surveys of participation in tourism suggest that it is whites and males who have the highest levels of effective demand for tourism. However, changes in society are acting to complicate this rather simplistic view. For example, in Japan, 'office ladies' are important consumers of travel.

Clearly for the purposes of analysing each variable, we have to separate them, but it must be remembered that they all are complementary and interrelated. Indeed this is such that some writers have attempted to analyse tourism or leisure lifestyles by performing multivariate analysis on the determinants of tourism demand and then trying to group individuals into particular categories. To date these analyses have met with limited success. Even where they have been commercially adopted as market segments it is difficult to correlate them with other variables such as media habits.

However, leisure or tourism lifestyles are considerations when viewing the important role of fashion and style in holiday choice. Tourism demand has always been susceptible to fashion and can be influenced perhaps more readily than demand for some other goods by marketing and promotional activity.

Life-cycle determinants of demand for tourism

The propensity to travel, and indeed the type of tourism experience demanded, is closely related to an individual's age. Although the conventional measurement is chronological age, 'domestic age' better discriminates between types of tourist demand and levels of travel propensity. Domestic age refers to the stage in the life cycle reached by an individual, and different stages are characterised by distinctive holiday demand and levels of travel propensity, as demonstrated in the first mini case for this chapter.

MINI CASE STUDY 4.1
Domestic age and tourism demand

Considering an individual's domestic age – or position on the 'domestic life cycle' (childhood, young adult, married, etc.) is an effective explanatory variable of travel behaviour. Here, we can see that there is a distinctive pattern of demand found at each stage in the life cycle. This is because at each stage in the life cycle individuals can be thought of as having:

- **preoccupations** – which are the mental absorptions arising from motivations;

- **interests** – which are feelings of what an individual would like to do, or represent the awareness of an idea or opportunity; and

- **activities** – which are the actions of an individual.

Each stage in the life cycle is characterised by particular combinations of these three factors. For example, in adolescence the preoccupation is with socialising and finding independence while in married adulthood the preoccupations are more with establishment and social institutions. As an individual progresses through life the combinations of the factors, and the nature of the factors themselves, change. At certain 'crisis' points the whole combination is 'unfrozen' and completely reformed. An example here would be having children. At this point in an individual's life, previous constraints and influences upon holiday taking are totally changed as holidays become more organisational and less geographical. The life-cycle framework can also be linked to lifestyle variables to provide a multidimensional analysis. In married middle age, for example, holiday entitlement, income and mobility are often at a maximum and this is reflected in the level of holiday taking (see Figure 4.1). Equally, companies such as Disney and McDonald's utilise the concept to win children as customers at an early age in order to retain them into later life. With the decline in birthrates in the developed world it is important to create hotel, activity and restaurant products that will socialise children to want to take certain types of activity holidays so as to encourage demand at a later stage in their life.

The domestic life cycle has a number of stages, as follows.

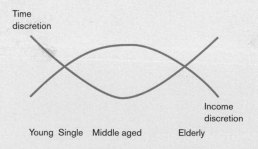

FIGURE 4.1	Traditional leisure paradox

CHILDHOOD

At this stage decisions are taken for the individual in terms of holiday taking although of course, children do have a significant influence upon their parents' decisions. By the age of 10 or 11 years some children take organised holidays with school or youth groups. These are usually domestic with self-catering arrangements.

ADOLESCENCE/YOUNG ADULT

At this stage, sometimes known as the bachelor stage, young single people, not living at home have a preoccupation for independence, socialising and a search for identity. Typically, holidays independent of parents begin at around 15 years, constrained by lack of finance but compensated by having few other commitments, no shortage of free time, and a curiosity for new places and experiences. This group has a high propensity to travel, mainly on budget holidays using surface transport and self-catering accommodation. Here the preoccupation is simply to 'get away' – the destination is unimportant.

MARRIAGE

Marriage represents the first 'crisis' in terms of unscrambling the preoccupations, interests and activities of an individual. Preoccupations turn to establishment and life-time investments. This life cycle stage can have a number of options. For example, newly married couples who are young and with no children may have few constraints on travel. Before the arrival of children young couples often have a high income and

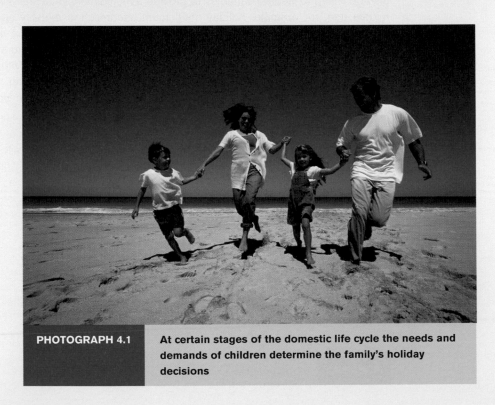

PHOTOGRAPH 4.1 **At certain stages of the domestic life cycle the needs and demands of children determine the family's holiday decisions**

few other ties, giving them a high travel propensity, frequently overseas. The arrival of children represents the second 'crisis' which coupled with the responsibility of a home may mean that constraints of time and finance depress travel propensity. Holiday preferences switch to domestic destinations, self-catering accommodation, and visiting friends and relatives. This is known as the full nest stage and constraints on travel will depend on the age of the children.

EMPTY NEST STAGE

As children grow up, reach the adolescence stage and begin to travel independently, constraints of time and finance are lifted from parents and their travel propensity increases. This is often a time for long-haul travel – the cruise market typically comprises this group.

OLD AGE

The emergence of early retirement at 50 or 55 years is creating an active and mobile group in the population of many countries who will demand both domestic and international travel. In later retirement, lack of finance, infirmity and often the loss of a partner act to offset the increase in free time experienced by this group. Holidays become more hotel based and travel propensity decreases.

The explanatory framework provided by the domestic life-cycle approach is a powerful one. It has implications for the supply of facilities, for the analysis of market needs of particular population groups (for example, the growing numbers of elderly people in some Western countries) and has clearly been used as a basis for market segmentation by tour operators and wholesalers. However, the life cycle as outlined in this chapter is only appropriate for developed Western economies and even here it is a generalisation as it does not consider, for example, one-parent families, divorcees or other ethnic groups living within Western economies.

Nonetheless, the concept of life cycle helps us to understand how situation-specific life-stage conditions exert a great influence on consumer behaviour. For example, the majority of recreational tourism in the USA is made up from the family market. The cycle is not just a progression by phase or age but represents likely fluctuations in disposable income and changes in social responsibilities. For example, the bachelor stage represents an individual living away from home with few responsibilities but with the need for affiliation with others and the likelihood of purchases of leisure and entertainment, personal care items and clothes.

DISCUSSION QUESTIONS

1 Draft a checklist of typical holidays at each of the main stages of the domestic life cycle.

2 How do tour operators use the domestic life cycle to segment their products?

3 Draft a checklist of the barriers to tourism that might be experienced at each stage of the domestic life cycle.

SUPPRESSED DEMAND FOR TOURISM

So far in this chapter the concern has been to identify factors that influence effective tourist demand. Yet tourism is still an unobtainable luxury for the majority of the world's population, not just in undeveloped and developing countries, but also for many in the developed world. There are a variety of reasons why people do not travel:

- Travel is expensive and demands a certain threshold of income before people can enter the market. It competes with other products for available funds.

- Lack of time is a problem for some individuals who cannot allocate sufficient blocks of time to stay away from home. This may be for business or family reasons.

- Physical limitations (such as ill health) are a significant reason for many people not travelling. In particular heart disease and mental/physical handicap act as a major constraint on travel.

- Family circumstances such as those who are single parents or have to care for elderly relatives may prevent travel.

- Government restrictions such as currency controls and visas may act as a real barrier to travel (both inbound and outbound) for some countries.

- Lack of interest/fear are real barriers for some individuals.

It is not uncommon for people to experience a combination of two or more of these barriers. For example, a one-parent family may find lack of income and time will combine with family circumstances to prevent tourism travel. Obviously it is just these groups who would most benefit from a holiday and tourism planners are increasingly concerned to identify these barriers and devise programmes to encourage non-participants to travel. Perhaps the best known example of this is the 'social tourism movement' which is concerned with facilitating the participation in travel by people with some form of handicap or disadvantage, and the measures used to encourage this participation.

MACRO DETERMINANTS OF TOURISM DEMAND

In the previous sections we identified a range of key determinants on tourism demand that operate at the individual level. In order to begin to understand patterns of tourism demand at a broader scale, it is necessary to find aggregate measures of these determinants. For example, taking the concept of travel propensity that we introduced in Chapter 1, we might expect travel propensity for a particular population to increase with such aggregate characteristics as:

- income;
- level of urbanisation;

- education levels; and

- mobility levels (such as car ownership).

However, it will decrease with characteristics such as:

- large household size; and

- increasing age.

At the aggregate level the relationship between travel propensity and the characteristics of a population is not straightforward. In particular, we must remember that the variables identified above are all related. A high travel propensity would be expected for a developed Western economy with a high degree of urbanisation, high incomes, small household sizes and high levels of mobility. Conversely, low travel propensities would be expected for rural societies with large family sizes and low incomes.

There are also a number of factors that will determine the propensity of a population to travel to particular destinations. We have already examined in detail the importance of destination 'image' in Chapter 2, and here the difficult issue of measuring promotional spend by a destination in creating the image needs to be considered. In addition, other relevant factors include economic distance, cultural distance and the relative cost of living at the destination. Economic distance, for example, relates to the time and cost of reaching a destination. Although the idea of 'friction of distance' can be used here, in practice distance alone is not the only consideration. For example, it is ironic that international destinations are often closer in economic distance terms than many domestic destinations. (It is easier, and often cheaper, for a traveller to reach the Spanish Costas from London, than it is to reach the Scottish island of Skye.) Cultural distance refers to the difference in culture between the origin area and the destination. For more adventurous travellers this acts to attract rather than to deter a visit. Costs at a destination are not an absolute quantity but have to be considered relative to the value of the traveller's own currency. This is graphically demonstrated by the ebb and flow of traffic across the Atlantic dependent upon whether the dollar or the euro is the stronger. Perception of price is also an important consideration – Switzerland is perceived by many as an expensive destination but in fact prices have fallen in recent years *vis-à-vis* many European currencies. However, measurement of such variables can be problematic. Clearly, there are many influences upon demand that can be labelled as determinants, as shown in Table 4.1.

TABLE 4.1	The major determinants of tourism demand	
Economic determinants	**Social-psychological determinants**	**Exogenous determinants (business environment)**
Disposable income	Demographic factors	Availability of supply resources
GNP per capita income	Motivations	Economic growth and stability
Private consumption	Travel preferences	Political and social environment
Cost of living (CPI)	Benefits sought	Recession
Tourism prices	Images of destinations	Technological advancements
Transportation costs	Perceptions of destinations	Accessibility
Cost of living in relation to destinations	Awareness of opportunities	Levels of development, infrastructure and superstructure
Exchange rate differentials	Cognitive distance	
Relative pricing among competing destinations	Attitudes about destinations	Natural disaster
	Amount of leisure time	Epidemics
Promotional expenditures	Amount of travel time	War, terrorism
Marketing effectiveness	Paid vacations	Social and cultural attractions
Physical distance	Past experience	Degree of urbanisation
	Life span	Special factors/Olympic games, mega events
	Physical capacity, health and wellness	
	Cultural similarities	Barriers and obstacles
	Affiliations	Restrictions, rules and laws

Source: Uysal, 1998

STEP ANALYSIS

When individual purchasing patterns and the influences upon them are aggregated to the national level it is possible to gain a clearer view as to the influences upon global patterns of demand for tourism. This is known as performing a **STEP analysis** – analysing the impact of:

S   **social factors;**
T   **technological factors;**
E   **economic factors; and**
P   **political factors.**

Social factors

Levels of population growth, its development, distribution and density affect travel propensity. In the second mini case for this chapter we outline the demographic

MINI CASE STUDY 4.2
The demographic transition and tourism

Population growth and development can be closely linked to the stages of economic growth of a society by considering the demographic transition where population growth and development are seen in terms of four connected phases.

THE HIGH STATIONARY PHASE

This corresponds to many undeveloped countries with high birth and death rates, keeping the population at a fluctuating, but low level. An example here would be Ethiopia where social and health conditions conspire to retain the country in this phase and render many forms of tourism impossible.

THE EARLY EXPANDING PHASE

Here high birth rates continue, but there is a fall in death rates due to improved health, sanitation and social stability. This leads to a population expansion characterised by young, large families. India is a good example of a country in this phase, it is unable to provide for its growing population and is gradually becoming poorer. Clearly, tourism is a luxury that cannot be afforded for many, although India has developed an inbound tourism industry to earn foreign exchange and there is a growing middle class that is travelling internationally.

THE LATE EXPANDING PHASE

Argentina demonstrates the classic features of this phase, having experienced a fall in the birth rate rooted in the growth of an industrial society and birth control technology. Most developing countries fit into the early expanding and late expanding phases with a transition to the late expanding phase paralleling the economic stage known as the 'drive to maturity' (Table 4.2, see page **125**).

THE LOW STATIONARY PHASE

This phase corresponds to the high mass consumption stage of economic development exemplified by the UK or Sweden (Table 4.2). Here, birth and death rates have stabilised at a low level, but for many European countries there are fluctuations as seen by the 'baby boom' of the late 1940s and early 1950s.

DISCUSSION QUESTIONS

1 For one country in each stage of the demographic transition, check the volume of international outbound tourism and explain the differences you see.

2 Draft a list of the key population characteristics of countries in the low stationary phase that influence tourism demand.

3 Taking the top twenty international tourism generating countries in the world, how many of them are in the low stationary phase?

transition as a powerful framework for understanding the influence of population factors.

Population density has a less important influence on travel propensity than has the distribution of population between urban and rural areas. Densely populated rural nations may have low travel propensities owing to the level of economic development and the simple fact that the population is mainly dependent upon subsistence agriculture and has neither the time nor the income to devote to tourism. In contrast, densely populated urban areas normally indicate a developed economy with consumer purchasing power, giving rise to high travel propensity and the urge to escape from the urban environment.

The distribution of population within a nation also affects patterns, rather than strict levels, of tourist demand. Where population is concentrated into one part of the country, tourism demand is distorted. This asymmetrical distribution of population is well illustrated by the USA where two-thirds of the population live in the eastern third of the country. The consequent east to west pattern of tourist flows (and permanent migrants) has placed pressure on the recreation and tourist resources of the Western states.

Social changes since the Second World War in the developed world have changed travel demand patterns. Most of these countries are experiencing a slowing of the birth rate, with some having projections of population decline. This, combined with extensions in life expectancy, has created an ageing population. In the past, the older generation in the 'third age' or 'grey panther' group is often made up of those who did not pay into pension schemes and consequently whose pension and benefits barely keep up with inflation. These groups and the unemployed are likely to adapt their lifestyle to basic activities and seek cheap travel activities. However, the post-war 'baby boomers' are now reaching retirement age and are demonstrating a significant demand for more 'upmarket' products.

Technological factors

There is no doubt that technology has been a major enabling factor in terms of converting suppressed demand into effective demand. This is particularly the case in terms of transport technology where the development of the jet engine in the late 1950s gave aircraft both speed and range and stimulated the variety of tourism products available in the international market to meet pent-up demand for international travel. Developments in aircraft technology have continued but so has the level of refinement and access to the motor car. Similarly, the development of information technology, and, in particular, the Internet, is a critical enabling factor in terms of tourism demand. Generally, technology acts to increase access to tourism by lowering the cost or by making the product more accessible. Examples here include developments in 'recreational technology' such as windsurfers, durable outdoor clothing, heli-skiing and heli-hiking, and off-road recreational vehicles.

Economic factors

A society's level of economic development is a major determinant of the magnitude of tourist demand because the economy influences so many critical, and interrelated, factors. One approach is to consider a simple division of world economies into the affluent 'north', where the countries are major generators and recipients of both international and domestic tourism, and the poorer 'south'. In the latter, some countries are becoming generators of international tourism but mostly tourism is domestic, often supplemented by an inbound international flow of tourists. In fact, the economic development of nations can be divided into a number of stages, as outlined in Table 4.2.

TABLE 4.2	Economic development and tourism	
Economic stage	**Some characteristics**	**Examples**
Traditional society Long-established land-owning aristocracy, traditional customs, majority employed in agriculture. Very low output per capita, impossible to improve without changing system. Poor health levels, high poverty levels.	**The undeveloped world** Economic and social conditions deny most forms of tourism except perhaps domestic VFR.	Parts of Africa, parts of Southern Asia.
Preconditions for take-off Innovation of ideas from outside the system. Leaders recognise the desirability of change. **Take-off** Leaders in favour of change gain power and alter production methods and economic structure. Manufacturing and services expand.	**The developing world** From the take-off stage, economic and social conditions allow increasing amounts of domestic tourism (mainly VFR). International tourism is also possible in the drive to maturity. Inbound tourism is often encouraged as a foreign exchange earner.	Parts of South and Central America;[a] parts of the Middle East,[a] Asia and Africa.
Drive to maturity[b] Industrialisation continues in all economic sectors with a switch from heavy manufacturing to sophisticated and diversified products.		Mexico; parts of South America.
High mass consumption Economy now at full potential, producing large numbers of consumer goods and services. New emphasis on satisfying cultural needs.	**The developed world** Major generators of international and domestic tourism.	North America; Western Europe; Japan; Australia; New Zealand.

[a] Countries that are members of the Organization of Petroleum Exporting Countries (OPEC) are a notable exception in these regions.
[b] Centrally planned economies merit a special classification, although most are at the drive to maturity stage.
Source: Boniface and Cooper 1987, adapted from Rostow, 1959

125

As a society moves towards the high mass consumption stage in Table 4.2, a number of important processes occur. The balance of employment changes from work in the primary sector (agriculture, fishing, forestry) to work in the secondary sector (manufacturing goods) and the tertiary sector (services such as tourism). As this process unfolds, an affluent society usually emerges and the percentage of the population who are economically active increases from less than a third in the developing world to half or more in the high mass consumption stage. With progression to the drive to maturity, discretionary incomes increase and create demand for consumer goods and leisure pursuits such as tourism.

Other developments are closely linked to the changing nature of employment. The population is healthier and has time for recreation and tourism (and has paid holiday entitlement). Improving educational standards and media channels boost awareness of tourism opportunities, and transportation and mobility rise in line with these changes. Institutions respond to this increased demand by developing a range of leisure products and services. These developments occur in conjunction with each other until, at the high mass consumption stage, all the economic indicators encourage high levels of travel propensity. Clearly, tourism is a result of industrialisation and, quite simply, the more highly developed an economy, the greater the levels of tourist demand.

As more countries reach the drive to maturity or high mass consumption stage, so the volume of trade and foreign investment increases and business travel develops. Business travel is sensitive to economic activity, and although it could be argued that increasingly sophisticated communication systems may render business travel unnecessary, there is no evidence of this to date. Indeed, the very development of global markets and the constant need for face-to-face contact should ensure a continuing demand for business travel.

Political factors

Politics affect travel propensities in a variety of ways. For example, the degree of government involvement in promoting and providing facilities for tourism depends upon the political complexion of the government. Governments that support the free market try to create an environment in which the tourism industries can flourish, rather than the administration being directly involved in tourism itself. Socialist administrations, on the other hand, encourage the involvement of the government in tourism and, through 'social tourism', often provide opportunities for the 'disadvantaged' to participate in tourism. Governments in times of economic problems may control levels of propensity for travel overseas by limiting the amount of foreign currency that can be taken out of a country or demanding a monetary bond to be left in the country while the resident is overseas. Government restrictions on travel also include visa and passport controls as well as taxes on travel. Generally, however, these controls are not totally effective and, of course, they can be evaded.

We can also identify inadvertent political influences – for example, a government with an economy suffering high inflation may find that inbound travel is discouraged. In a more general sense, unstable political regimes (where civil disorder or war is prevalent) may forbid non-essential travel, and inbound tourism will be adversely affected.

FORECASTING TOURISM DEMAND

In an industry as volatile as tourism and in times as uncertain as today, it is important for both governments and the tourism industry to have reliable and accurate forecasts to allow them to plan and make decisions for the future. The accuracy of a forecast is an essential consideration in any tourism management decision – too high a forecast and beds will lie empty, theme park rides will be unused and staff will be laid off; too low a forecast and opportunities will be missed, too few beds will be provided and theme parks will be congested. Essentially, these problems arise from the nature of tourism as a 'perishable' service industry – beds, rides and restaurants cannot be stored and this underlines the need for accurate forecasts of tourism demand.

Forecasting methods

There is a wide variety of methods available for forecasting tourism demand. Archer (1994) lists the factors that determine the choice of method to use:

- purpose of the forecast – this relates to the level of detail required and the scope of the forecast;
- the time period required;
- level of accuracy required;
- availability of information – there is no point in recommending a complex quantitative approach if the information is not available to support it; and
- the cost of the forecast and the available budget.

Managers can choose from two basic methods for forecasting tourism demand:

1 quantitative approaches; and

2 qualitative approaches.

However, in practice, the most successful forecasts are those that use a combination of these two methods, utilising the strengths of relative strengths of each.

QUANTITATIVE FORECASTING APPROACHES

There are numerous quantitative approaches to forecasting demand, ranging from the simplistic to the highly technical.

Causative models

At the complex end of the spectrum are causative models. These models attempt to predict changes in the variables that cause tourism demand and to analyse the relationship between those variables and the demand for tourism. The most well known of these approaches is econometric modelling, commonly using multiple regression. A mathematical relationship is sought that establishes demand as a function of influencing variables (such as the volume of populations, income of populations in the generating markets, price of the tourism product, promotional spending and time). The advantage of this approach is that it allows us to understand the underlying causes of tourism demand and to forecast how these will change in the future. It also allows us to ask 'what if' questions to see how demand will change under a certain set of circumstances.

However, for most managers who work within tourism such an approach is neither possible nor beneficial. It is far more important to be able to undertake relatively simple analyses in order to interpret demand data, and to highlight trends. These approaches are known as non-causal models and usually depend upon the extrapolation of past trends into the future.

Non-causative models

These models are often known as time series models. Essentially they rely on extrapolating future trends from the past and use techniques such as moving average, exponential smoothing and trend curve analysis. While these models can be criticised as inappropriate for a volatile industry such as tourism where past situations may not carry forward into the future, they do deliver surprisingly accurate forecasts. The worked example below shows how this approach can be used effectively by managers in tourism to provide estimates of future tourism demand.

Worked example

Table 4.3 shows the (artificial) quarterly demand for trips on the Smithson ferry over a five-year period. It is required to construct a model for this demand, and to produce forecasts for the following year. Even a cursory glance at the data shows us that demand is highly seasonal. Quarter 3 is the peak season of the year. By considering any of the four quarters over the five-year period, there is clear evidence of

TABLE 4.3	Demand (thousands of passengers)			
	Quarter			
Year	**Q1**	**Q2**	**Q3**	**Q4**
1	63	103	331	74
2	75	118	355	75
3	83	118	410	83
4	92	130	444	99
5	79	135	477	103

upward movement, so at this stage it is expected that the analysis will identify an increasing trend. It can be noted even at this stage that demand in year 5 quarter 1 is not in line with the previous values for the same quarter, and hence is unusual.

The aim is to construct a multiplicative model for the demand D; that is

$$D = T*S*R$$

where T is the trend value for that quarter, S is the seasonal index for that quarter, and R is the random or unpredictable element.

The first stage is to compute a four-quarter moving average. For each four consecutive values in the series, their average is calculated and is set against the middle of that time period. For example, take the four consecutive values starting with year 4 quarter 2; these values are 130, 444, 99, 79. Their average is 188 and this is set against the middle of the time period. Note that since the four values taken cover all quarters of the year, their average is 'de-seasonalised' (Table 4.3).

The four-quarter moving averages are now centred as shown in Table 4.4, so as to correspond with the given quarterly time periods. For example, the first two four-quarter moving averages 142.75 and 145.75 are averaged to give 144 (to the

TABLE 4.4	Demand (thousands of passengers)			
	Quarter			
Year	**Q1**	**Q2**	**Q3**	**Q4**
1 Original series	63	103	331	74
4-quarter m.a.		142.75	145.75	149.5
Centred m.a.			144	148
2 Original series	75	118	355	75
4-quarter m.a.	155.5	155.75	157.75	157.75
Centred m.a.	153	156	157	158
3 Original series	83	118	410	83
4-quarter m.a.	171.5	173.5	175.75	178.75
Centred m.a.	165	173	175	177
4 Original series	92	130	444	99
4-quarter m.a.	187.25	191.25	188	189.25
Centred m.a.	183	189	190	189
5 Original series	79	135	477	103
4-quarter m.a.	197.5	198.5		
Centred m.a.	194	198		

m.a. = moving average.

TABLE 4.5	Seasonal index of demand			
	Quarter			
Year	Q1	Q2	Q3	Q4
1			230	50
2	49	76	226	47
3	50	68	234	47
4	50	69	234	52
5	41	68		
Average (seasonal index)	48	70	231	49

nearest whole number). In this way each consecutive pair is converted to a centred moving average.

A table showing seasonal indexes can now be produced. The centred moving averages, having been constructed using all seasons of the year, are divided (one by one) by the demand figures of Table 4.3 to produce a seasonality factor for each period of time. The answers are normally multiplied by 100 to give a percentage. So, for example, using Tables 4.3 and 4.4, the seasonality factor for year 1 quarter 3 is equal to:

$$\frac{331}{144} \times 100 = 230\%$$

The average of the seasonal factors for each quarter is calculated and shown at the foot of Table 4.5. These four values are the seasonal indexes of demand.

Using standard simple regression analysis based on the centred moving averages of Table 4.4, trend values can be calculated for any time period. The regression line has the equation:

trend = 133.3 + 3.67*t

where $t = 1, 2, 3, \ldots$ is time starting with the value 1 at year 1 quarter 1, the value 2 at year 1 quarter 2, and so on. Incidentally, regression output gives a correlation coefficient of 0.99 indicating an excellent straight line fit to the centred moving averages. Substituting $t = 1, 2, \ldots, 20$ into the equation for the regression line, and taking trend values to the nearest whole number, leads to Table 4.6.

TABLE 4.6	Trend (thousands of passengers)			
	Quarter			
Year	**Q1**	**Q2**	**Q3**	**Q4**
1	137	140	144	148
2	152	155	159	163
3	166	170	174	177
4	181	185	188	192
5	196	199	203	207

Since the original demand data are to be modelled by the product $T*S*R$, dividing the values by the corresponding trend value and then by the appropriate seasonal index from the base of Table 4.5, produces for each period of time the random element R. For example, for year 1, quarter 1, it is calculated as:

$$\frac{63/48\%}{137} = 95.8$$

Table 4.7 represents a complete table of values of R, given to the nearest whole number. These values represent the extent to which demand is made up of the trend identified, combined with the seasonal index. Where the value of R is close to 100%, the random or unpredictable element is negligible in its effect. Only in the case of year 5 quarter 1 is there a sizeable effect on demand due to R. Demand in this quarter could not have been predicted (by this model) because of some random event (which would in practice probably be known).

In order to use the model of demand established to forecast future demand, it is simply a matter of forming for any particular future time period the product of the trend value for that period (found using the regression line equation), and the appropriate seasonal index from the base of Table 4.5. This method is only suitable for short-term forecasting.

Taking into account that passenger numbers throughout have been in thousands, the forecasts of demand for year 6 are as shown in Table 4.8.

Analysing patterns of demand over time

An analysis of tourism demand in the long term requires an examination of trends. A recommended first step in the search for a trend within demand data is to sketch a graph showing demand over time. It may be possible to describe the movement

TABLE 4.7	Residual index of demand (%)			
	Quarter			
Year	**Q1**	**Q2**	**Q3**	**Q4**
1	96	105	100	102
2	103	109	97	94
3	104	99	102	96
4	106	100	102	105
5	84	97	102	102

TABLE 4.8	Forecasts of demand for year 6
Quarter 1	101 000
Quarter 2	150 000
Quarter 3	504 000
Quarter 4	108 000

simply. The four diagrams in Figure 4.2 provide simple illustrations of patterns of demand over a period of time. The continuous lines drawn are suggested models which 'fit' the given demand values and which may then be used to describe the demand and, if required, to project future demand by extrapolation.

The process of formally fitting a line or curve to data to produce a model of demand is called trend curve analysis. In many cases, this can be done 'by eye', without employing statistical methods. Should the importance of the analysis require a more formal and rigorous approach, then standard regression analysis can be employed to find a curve of best fit. Software packages, such as spreadsheet or statistics, will perform what were once tiresome calculations and even inexpensive electronic calculators often have the facility to produce regression output. In this way, and using transformations of variables, a wide range of demand patterns can be analysed.

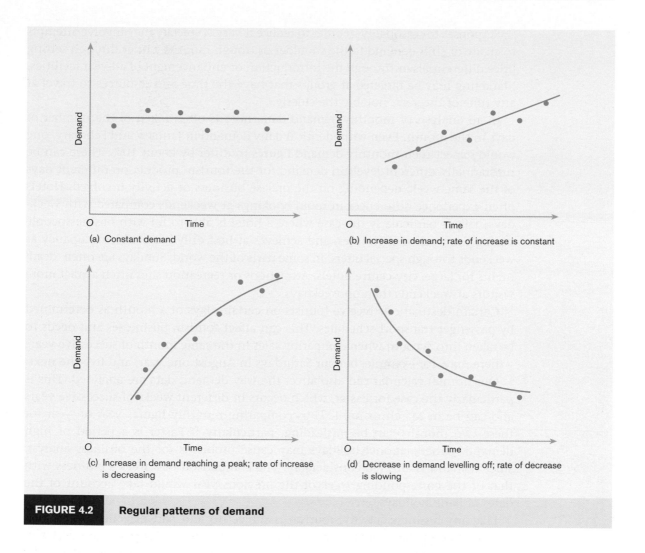

FIGURE 4.2   **Regular patterns of demand**

Seasonality

We know that within most patterns of demand in tourism, there are regular fluctuations due solely to the time of year. This phenomenon is called **seasonality**. It is often the result of changes in climate over the calendar year. Thus a destination that is essentially attractive because of its beaches and hot summers is likely to have a highly seasonal demand. The same applies to demand for holidays at a ski resort that has snow for only part of the year. There are, though, other influencing factors, such as the timing of school and work holidays, or regular special events held at a destination.

As tourism is a service industry, it is not possible to stockpile the product – a hotel room that is unsold on a particular night, an unsold seat on a flight or an unsold theatre ticket all have an economic value of zero. Seasonality of demand therefore causes major problems for the tourist industry. It can result in only seasonal employment for employees, and the under-use or even closing down of facilities at certain times of the year. It can also result in an over-stretching by some destinations and businesses at times of peak activity, to compensate for low demand off-season. This leads to over-crowding, over-bookings, high prices and ultimately to customer dissatisfaction and a worsening reputation.

Responses to seasonality in order to reduce it vary. Typically they involve attempts to create or shift demand to the shoulder or trough months, either through setting price differentials or through the introduction or enhancement of all-year facilities. Marketing may be targeted at groups that have the time and resources to travel at any time of the year, notably the elderly.

In an analysis of monthly demand data, note is often taken of the number of days in the month. Even with identical daily demand in January and February, one would expect their monthly demand figures to differ by about 10%. There can be substantially different levels in demand for the tourism product on different days of the same week, depending on the precise business or activity involved. Hotels often experience differences in room bookings at weekends compared with week-days. This is particularly the case where a hotel is able to fill with businesspeople during the week at high rates, and achieves at best only reasonable occupancy at weekends through special offers. In some parts of the world, Sundays are often 'dead' nights for large, city-centre hotels. Attractions or recreation sites often attract more visitors at weekends than on weekdays.

Certain destinations receive tourists on certain days of a month as determined by passenger transport schedules. This can affect tourism businesses and needs to be taken into account when comparing sales in the same month of successive years – there may, for example, be four Saturdays in August one year, and five the next.

Our normal calendar can also affect the way demand data are analysed. This is particularly the case for Easter, which occurs in different weeks of successive years and can be in March or April. Thus comparing monthly figures year on year for these two months can be misleading, particularly if Easter is a period of high demand. Other national holidays may cause problems for the business analyst, since demand is affected considerably. The comparison of a week's business with that of the corresponding week of the previous year would take account of the dates of bank holidays, etc.

Like any business activity, tourism is subject to and part of general economic cycles. Also regular events such as festivals, games or exhibitions cause cycles in tourism movement. As shown in the above section, tourism demand can be developed into formal and often complex models. However, it has to be recognised that even the most complete of analyses of a pattern of tourism demand provides a model that will vary from the true demand by some degree. All series contain elements of the irregular, random or unpredictable. These can take the form of sudden price changes, epidemics, floods, unseasonal weather or even wars.

QUALITATIVE FORECASTING APPROACHES

Qualitative approaches to forecasting demand are mainly used to product long-term trends, or to examine specific scenarios in the future such as environmental or technological influences, or the likely impact of a new product. While there are a number of techniques available, the most common ones are the Delphi technique and scenario writing.

The Delphi technique

The Delphi technique relies upon a panel of experts to deliver a consensus view of the future. The panel is selected according to their expertise and a questionnaire is

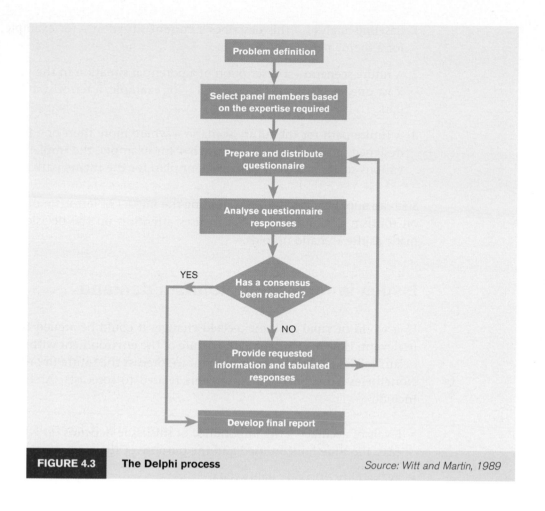

| FIGURE 4.3 | The Delphi process | Source: Witt and Martin, 1989 |

compiled relating to the particular future trend or forecast required. Once the panel members have completed the questionnaire, results are combined and circulated to the panel to give them chance to change their views, once they see the forecasts of other panel members. This process then goes through a number of iterations, often three or four, before a consensus forecast is reached (Figure 4.3).

There are significant advantages to this approach, as it does not rely on one individual view and can be tailored to particular needs. However, the Delphi technique can be expensive to implement and may be subject to the influence of a strong panel member; and its effectiveness depends on both the choice of questions and the selection of panel members.

Scenario writing

Scenario writing is not only a technique to forecast future tourism demand, but also an approach that clarifies the issues involved. It relies upon creating alternative hypothetical futures relating to particular 'states' or sets of circumstances that will impact upon demand in the future (Witt and Martin, 1989). It involves assessing the variables that we examined in the section on STEP analysis and then creating long-term scenarios of how they may change, based upon the current situation as a baseline. The steps in scenario writing are as follows:

1 Baseline analysis – this describes a current situation – for example, the market for a theme park.

2 A future scenario – a description of a potential situation in the future. Usually at least one such scenario is designed – for example, a terrorist attack on a theme park.

3 A future path for the future scenario – where more than one future scenario is designed, a path for each is written – for example, the implementation of the various stages of a crisis management plan for the theme park.

Such an approach is ideal for examining the impact of terrorism or natural disasters on tourism demand and also it focuses attention on the decisions that need to made as the scenario unfolds.

Issues in forecasting tourism demand

In a world of rapid and unexpected change, it could be argued that forecasts are irrelevant. However, the changing nature of the environment within which tourism occurs makes it all the more important to forecast the future in order to manage it. Nonetheless, there are some problems related to forecasts (Archer, 1994). These include:

- levels of accuracy – the importance of this issue depends on what is being forecast, the time horizon used and the purpose of the forecast;

- availability of good quality data;

- the influence of variables and events external to tourism – September 11, 2001 is a classic example here; and

- identification and quantification of the variables – it is often difficult to quantify variables we use in forecasting – for example, how do you accurately measure promotional spend?

CONCLUSION

This chapter has outlined a comprehensive range of determinants upon tourism demand at both the individual and aggregate level. Of course, it is important to recognise that, while we separate out these determinants for descriptive purposes, in fact they are all related – a person with a high income, access to cars, a good education and generous holiday entitlement is likely to travel more frequently than someone who has a low income, limited education and no access to a car. These determinants can be aggregated for different populations to allow us to predict and describe patterns of demand around the world. The case study at the end of this chapter shows that globally, demand remains – and is anticipated to remain – concentrated in the affluent, industrialised nations of the world where the determinants of demand at an individual level, such as income and paid holiday entitlement, predominate. This is what we would expect from the analysis of demand determinants. However, emergent nations in the East Asia and Pacific region, where economic power is becoming increasingly focused, are becoming major generators and receivers of tourism.

As a service industry, the assets of tourism are perishable as they cannot be stored. Add to this a volatile sector and a changing world and it is important that tourism managers have the techniques to forecast the future and thus control it. Here, both qualitative and quantitative approaches are critical in predicting flows and patterns of demand, in addition to numerical estimations of probable future tourism activity. Difficulties associated with forecasting and the models utilised are exacerbated by the fact that demand for tourism at the aggregated world level is characterised by uncertainty and a vulnerability to events that are uncontrollable. However, it is important for the tourism sector that we are able to forecast and manage the future and perhaps the best approach is to use a combination of both quantitative and qualitative approaches.

Self-check questions

1 Review the major determinants of demand at an individual level and assess their relative importance.

2 Draft a checklist of the reasons why access to a car is such an important determinant of tourism.

3 Review the key determinants of demand at an aggregate level and rank their importance for international tourism.

4 List three advantages of quantitative approaches to demand forecasting and three advantages of qualitative approaches.

5 Identify the top 10 international tourism-generating countries in the world and plot them on a world map – what does this tell you?

Essay questions

1 Taking a country or region of your choice, look at the patterns of demand for tourism and explain them in respect of social, technological, economic and political factors.

2 Identify the main determinants of demand for tourism and assess their relative importance.

3 Compare the advantages and disadvantages of each of the main approaches to forecasting tourism demand.

4 'In a world of unexpected and rapid change, forecasting tourism demand is a waste of time.' Discuss this statement.

5 Review the relevance of the life cycle and lifestyle demand determinants for the developing world.

Annotated further reading

Books

Brent Ritchie, J.R. and Goeldner, C.R. (1994) *Travel Tourism and Hospitality Research. A Handbook for Managers and Researchers*, 2nd edn, John Wiley, Chichester.
A thorough handbook with authoritative entries relating to tourism demand determinants and forecasting.

Witt, S.F. and Moutinho, L. (1989) *Tourism Marketing and Management Handbook*, 2nd edn, Prentice Hall, Hemel Hempstead.
An excellent handbook with key reviews of tourism demand determinants and approaches to forecasting.

Witt, S.F. and Witt, C.A. (1992) *Modelling and Forecasting Demand in Tourism*, Academic Press, New York.
A thorough and technical review of tourism demand forecasting.

World Tourism Organization (2001) *Tourism 2020 Vision – Global Forecasts and Profiles of Market Segments*, WTO, Madrid.
An excellent and comprehensive review of future patterns of tourism demand and the key changes in determinants across the world.

References cited

Archer, B.H. (1994) 'Demand forecasting and estimation', pp. 86–92 in Ritchie, J.R.B. and Goeldner, C.R. (eds), *Handbook of Travel, Tourism and Hospitality Research*, Wiley, New York.

Boniface, B. and Cooper, C. (1987) *The Geography of Travel and Tourism*, Heinemann, London.

Rostow, W.W. (1959) *The Stages of Economic Growth*, Cambridge University Press, Cambridge.

Uysal, M. (1998) 'The determinants of tourism demand: a theoretical perspective', pp. 79–98 in Ioannides, D. and Debbage, K. *The Economic Geography of the Tourist Industry*, Routledge, London.

Witt, S.F. and Martin, C.A. (1989) 'Demand forecasting in tourism and recreation', pp. 4–32 in Cooper, C.P. (ed.), *Progress in Tourism, Recreation and Hospitality Management*, Vol. 1, Belhaven, London.

MAJOR CASE STUDY 4.1
WORLD PATTERNS OF DEMAND FOR TOURISM

PATTERNS OF DEMAND: THE HISTORIC TREND

Since the Second World War, there has been rapid growth worldwide in international tourism (see Table 4.9). After the war increasing proportions of the populations of the industrialised nations were in possession of both the time (in the form of paid leave from employment) and the money (owing to increased disposable incomes) to engage in international travel. Supply to meet this increased demand for leisure tourism in particular was developed

TABLE 4.9	International tourism trends: arrivals and receipts worldwide, 1950–2002	
	Arrivals (thousands)	Receipts[a] (US$ million)
1950	25 282	2 100
1960	69 296	6 867
1970	159 690	17 900
1980	284 841	102 372
1990	455 900	264 100
2000	687 300	473 400
2001	684 100	459 500
2002	702 600	474 200

[a] Excludes international fare receipts.
Source: WTO, annual

mainly in the form of the standard, mass package tour. This was made possible by the arrival of the jet aircraft in 1958, and by cheap oil. Further, international travel was boosted by a substantial increase in business travel.

Over this period, international tourism has shown itself on a worldwide scale to be robust, showing resilience against such factors as terrorism and political unrest in many parts of the world, worldwide economic recession and fluctuating exchange rates. Even, the September 11 'shock' to the system had a lesser impact on this momentum than was at first feared, as discussed in Chapter 2. Generally, at times of economic growth, demand for travel has increased; on the other hand, during times of recession, demand has either remained constant or has soon recovered. This global experience of almost uninterrupted growth is not, though, equally shared by all destinations. For example, tourists tend to stay away from destinations that they rightly or wrongly perceive to be unsafe – this has clearly affected tourism to the Middle East and North Africa, and following September 11 other Muslim countries have also been affected. Other destinations might suffer because they are simply no longer fashionable.

The 1980s

As the market has matured, the average annual growth rate has tended to decrease. During the period up to 1980, international arrivals doubled every ten years or so. In contrast, the 1980s experienced a slowing of average annual growth rates to a little over 4%. Growth in the latter half of the decade was, in fact, more in line with that of the previous two decades and followed the slow growth of the early 1980s.

We can explain such unevenness of tourism demand by a number of major factors and events. The decade opened with economic recession which acted to dampen international travel, and volume did not really recover until 1984. The years 1984 and 1985 were record years with European destinations doing particularly well. However, the accident at the nuclear power plant in Chernobyl, in the then Soviet Union, combined with terrorist activity, the Libyan bombing incident and the weakening of the US dollar against other major currencies, all conspired to contribute to the depressing of demand for tourism. As a result, international travel was severely affected. The effect was not so much in terms of total numbers, which were up on the previous year anyway, but in terms of tourism flows and changes in types of trip taken. Many destinations suffered badly, whereas others gained. The second half of the decade saw a return to some sort of normality, both in terms of growth rates and in terms of types of trip taken.

The 1990s

The 1990s opened with the Gulf War and further economic recession, leading to great uncertainty for international tourism. In the short term, the build-up to the Gulf War, the war itself and the aftermath led initially to the virtual cessation of travel to the Gulf, the Eastern Mediterranean and North Africa. It not only depressed international tourism further afield, but also the economic recession experienced by the majority of industrialised countries was aggravated by it. The lessons of earlier years were that international tourism would recover and develop with new products, destinations and generating markets and indeed this has been the case, with tourism responding well to the growth in economic and social conditions and little or no slow down was seen in international tourism flows in the 1990s. In particular the decade was been characterised by the growth of overseas travel by residents of developing countries and the acceleration of multiple, but short-haul, trips from travellers in industrialised countries.

The new millennium

Tourism in the early years of the new millennium has been characterised by contrast. The millennium opened with optimism and the success of the Sydney Olympic Games, considerably boosting arrivals to Australia. However, the subsequent terrorism activities of September 11, 2001, the Bali bombings of 2002, war in Afghanistan and Iraq and the SARS outbreak in Asia severely affected the pattern of tourism demand. In addition, uncertainty, recessions in generating countries and tightened security at both borders and in the airline industry prompted consumers to holiday at home rather than internationally.

The terrorism incidents of 2001 saw international tourism arrivals decline by 0.5% over 2000. However, they recovered to grow by 2.7% in 2002, although as the industry struggled to attract the market, price competition depressed receipts from tourism in 2002.

PATTERNS OF DEMAND: THE REGIONAL DIMENSION

Table 4.10 shows the changes in the share of international tourism worldwide of the different regions over the 50-year period 1950 to 2000. Regional shares have to be viewed in the context of a greatly changing total, and so even a constant share represents substantial growth.

Europe and, to a lesser extent, the Americas have for some time dominated the international travel scene in terms of numbers of arrivals and receipts. More specifically, it is Western Europe and North America that have given rise to a high level of geographical concentration of movement.

In 2000, Europe accounted for well over half of all international tourist arrivals. We can identify a number of factors that explain the leading position held by Europe:

- Large segments of the population receive relatively high incomes, resulting in high levels of disposable income.

- Paid leave from work and a supportive social security system is normal in European countries.

- High proportions of the populations of, for example, Germany, France and the UK, attach very high priority to the annual foreign holiday and are reluctant to let it go even in times of recession.

- There is a wealth of both artificial and natural attractions.

- Demand for foreign travel is satisfied by a large tourist industry and the necessary infrastructure.

- Adoption of the euro in many countries has facilitated travel.

- International travel need not involve great distances, owing to the number of relatively small countries.

A number of these factors are equally applicable to North America. However, the sheer size of the USA and Canada means that the majority of their populations prefer to take domestic

TABLE 4.10	**Regional share of international tourism, 1950–2000**					
	1950 (%)	1960 (%)	1970 (%)	1980 (%)	1990 (%)	2000 (%)
(a) Share of arrivals						
Europe	66.5	72.5	70.5	68.4	63.5	57.8
Americas	29.6	24.1	23.0	18.9	18.8	18.4
East Asia/Pacific	0.8	1.0	3.0	7.0	11.4	15.7
Africa	2.1	1.1	1.5	2.5	3.4	3.9
Middle East	0.9	1.0	1.4	2.4	2.1	3.3
South Asia	0.2	0.3	0.6	0.8	0.7	0.9
(b) Share of receipts						
Europe	41.3	56.8	62.0	59.3	54.4	49.1
Americas	50.5	35.7	26.8	24.9	26.1	27.8
East Asia/Pacific	1.4	2.8	6.2	7.3	14.4	17.2
Africa	4.2	2.6	2.2	2.7	1.9	2.3
Middle East	2.3	1.5	2.3	4.3	2.5	2.5
South Asia	0.3	0.5	0.6	1.5	0.8	1.0

Columns do not necessarily add up to 100% because of rounding.
Source: Based on WTO data, annual

trips. Nevertheless, there are substantial numbers of North Americans who do engage in foreign travel each year, not merely within their own continent but also in long-haul trips. However, the impact of September 11 on both security measures at borders in the region, and also upon the psychology of the market, has seen the Americas share of the international market decline since 2001.

The shares of Europe and the Americas have fluctuated somewhat over the years, with some evidence of a decline in terms of both numbers of arrivals and tourism receipts. The clearest trend though has been the emergence of countries of the East Asia and Pacific (EAP) region as both receivers and generators of international tourism. The EAP share of arrivals worldwide was only 1% in 1960, but grew to 3% in 1970, 11% in 1990 and 16% in 2000. The increasing share is of an expanding market. This represents remarkable growth in a highly competitive environment.

We can see that the shares of international tourism of Africa, Middle East and South Asia have throughout the period 1950 to 2000 been small, though with a high level of fluctuation.

PHOTOGRAPH 4.2   **Asia is becoming a significant generator of international tourism**

Source: Jeremy Sutton Hibbert/Rex Features

As regions, they are not able to compete with Europe, the Americas and the EAP either in terms of generating or receiving large numbers of international tourists. The reasons for this are mainly economic. Destination countries within these regions can compete for specific markets from the major generating countries. Many, though, have been vulnerable to the effects of unrest and war, not necessarily in their own countries but near enough for them to be perceived as dangerous places to visit. In general, their incoming international tourism has suffered when business conditions have been depressed in the traditional tourism generating countries.

PATTERNS OF DEMAND: CHARACTERISTICS OF GENERATING MARKETS

It is essential for destinations to understand the origins of their tourists. Here, there are some generalisations that we can make as a specific country's market normally has the following features:

- It includes at least one of the four top generators of international tourism worldwide – Germany, the USA, Japan and the UK.

- It includes neighbouring states, since the distance and cost involved are relatively small.

- It includes countries further afield if, as is the case between the USA and Western Europe, air travel is available and at a cost within the reach of large segments of the population.

- It depends on the size of the population of generating states and their propensity to travel.

- It depends on ease of movement across borders.

- It depends on the real and perceived price of trips to the destination.

- It depends on the attractiveness of the destination.

- It depends on the social, cultural and historic links between countries.

- It depends on marketing activity and an appropriate supply in terms of sectors such as transport and accommodation.

WEB SITE

www.world-tourism.org

REFERENCE

World Tourism Organization (annual), *Tourism Highlights*, WTO, Madrid.

DISCUSSION QUESTIONS

1 Why is the East Asia and Pacific region set to become a major destination in the world?

2 Describe the impact of September 11, 2001 on international tourism demand patterns.

3 International tourism growth was phenomenal during the twentieth century. Identify some constraints to tourism in the twenty-first century that might slow this growth.

PART TWO
THE TOURISM DESTINATION

CHAPTER FIVE
THE ECONOMIC IMPACT OF TOURISM   150

CHAPTER SIX
THE ENVIRONMENTAL IMPACT OF TOURISM   194

CHAPTER SEVEN
THE SOCIO-CULTURAL IMPACT OF TOURISM   224

CHAPTER EIGHT
SUSTAINABLE TOURISM   258

CHAPTER NINE
TOURISM AND DEVELOPMENT PLANNING   296

INTRODUCTION

Part Two of this book examines the relationship between tourism and the destination. Because of the simultaneous nature of production and consumption within the tourism sector there are far more wide-reaching implications for this form of development than there are with many other development options. The chapters in this part take on an analytical flavour as they focus upon the multitude of models and approaches that have been used to investigate the various implications of tourism and its development. Each chapter examines the relevant models that have been used and compares and contrasts their efficacy.

The presence of tourists brings with it environmental and socio-cultural impacts as well as the economic impacts. Therefore the choice to pursue tourism as a development option needs to be made after considering all of the factors relating to its impacts and the resources upon which tourism will draw. Impact models if they are to be of use to tourism planners and policy makers must consider all of the effects of tourism (positive and negative) across all of the planes of influence (economic, environmental and socio-cultural) within a single analytical framework. An overarching aim of this part of the book is to put this fact into context and show how this can be achieved.

The main driving force that explains the relentless growth of the tourism industry over the past century is the economic benefits associated with it. Chapter Five examines both the economic significance of tourism to various destinations and how it can be measured and then goes on to look at the methodologies that have found favour in measuring its economic impact. To understand the economic significance of tourism it is necessary to look at the structure of the local economy and the level of dependence that exists upon the income, employment and foreign exchange earned from tourism. Where high levels of dependence are apparent there is concern that the destination becomes vulnerable because of tourism's sensitivity to factors outside of the control of the destination. This is particularly important as we start the twenty-first century in a world interrupted by terrorist activity. The ability to measure the economic significance of tourism using accounting practices such as tourism satellite accounts, provides governments with the facility to understand the importance of the sector but offers little opportunity for specific policy decisions. In order to understand the economic policy relevance of tourism to a destination it is necessary to turn attention to the economic impacts of tourism and their associated multiplier values.

The economic impact of tourism can be measured using a number of techniques of which *ad hoc* and input–output multiplier models have been the most important over the past 30 years or so. More recently there has been a growth in the adoption of computable general equilibrium models that provide the results that one normally expects from input–output models but with the added power of being able to simulate economic changes. Finally, this chapter looks at the often overlooked economic costs associated with tourism and its development and stresses the need for policy makers to focus on the 'net' economic benefits.

Chapter 6 examines the importance of the environment as a resource for tourism and the difficulties created by its use as a 'free' input to the tourism product. Attention is brought to the fact that tourism tends to suffer from a negative environmental image whereas in fact it has both negative and positive attributes. A range of environmental issues is discussed in order to demonstrate the scope of the topic and its importance. The importance of not being simply focused on the direct environmental effects is stressed together with ways of looking at the indirect and induced environmental consequences associated with production in general and tourism production in particular. Distinctions are drawn between environmental impact assessments (EIAs) and environmental auditing and the relative roles played by each.

The socio-cultural impacts of tourism are examined in Chapter Seven. This chapter begins with a review of the various approaches used to study tourism development and its implications for socio-cultural impacts. The major models that have been used to explain the development of tourism are combined to provide an overview that demonstrates the commonality of the models but highlights the inadequacy of the framework to produce solutions within a dynamic world. Fundamental issues regarding the cultural impact of tourism on host populations are put forward and questioned. Caution is expressed regarding the tendency to adopt biased views because of the focus of studies upon negative impacts. Positive contributions to socio-cultural aspects are discussed together with more specific negative issues such as crime, sex tourism and displacement. The chapter concludes by looking at some of the data sources available for the study of the socio-cultural impacts.

Much has been said in the literature over the past quarter of a century about the need to achieve sustainable tourism development. The definition and concepts are examined in Chapter Eight before an attempt to define sustainable tourism is made. The different types of sustainability are considered and the existence of any form of production that can be truly sustainable is questioned. Those factors working in favour of sustainable tourism and those working against are reviewed before attention is focused upon the two main ways forward in moving towards a more sustainable sector, limiting activity through thresholds and modifying the delivery and nature of the sector. The limits to development are discussed under the headings of carrying capacity and a great deal of discussion looks at the strengths and weaknesses of this approach. Concern is expressed about the use of the term sustainability as a marketing ploy rather than one with any real grounding and then some different types of tourism products are examined, including eco-tourism, drawing attention to their strengths and weaknesses.

There is a variety of models that have been put forward to explain general economic development and the role that can be played by tourism within such models is an important consideration. Chapter Nine starts by briefly looking at each of the main models and determining whether or not there is a role for tourism within general economic development. Once it is established that most of these models do provide a key role for tourism the chapter moves on to look at the characteristics of tourism that make it an attractive development option. Tourism planning takes place at different levels from international levels (such as the Caribbean or Europe) through to national and then to local planning levels. Each of these levels is discussed prior to looking at the key stages of the process of tourism development planning. The importance of each stage is considered followed by a brief look at the specialisms needed to construct tourism development plans. The chapter concludes by looking at what can go wrong and the reasons for plan failure.

CHAPTER FIVE
THE ECONOMIC IMPACT OF TOURISM

INTRODUCTION

This chapter examines the economic significance of tourism as well as the economic impacts associated with the industry. In the same way that the literature tends to exaggerate the negative impacts of tourism upon host societies and environments, so the positive impact of tourism upon economies is often over-stated. Therefore the positive and negative economic impacts of tourism will be discussed. An integral part of this chapter is a critical assessment of the methods of measuring economic impact drawing, particularly, on the application of multiplier analysis, **tourism satellite accounts** (TSAs) and computable generalised equilibrium models. All the multiplier models that are outlined in this chapter generate information that is valuable to policy makers and planners. It should also be noted that, within known limitations, **multiplier analyses** provide powerful and valuable tools for estimating and analysing the economic impact of tourism and comparing the performance of tourism with that of alternative industries.

LEARNING OUTCOMES

This chapter focuses on the economic impacts of tourism and is aimed to provide you with:

- an understanding of the economic contribution of tourism locally, nationally and internationally;

- an understanding of the methods used to estimate tourist expenditure and the way in which the significance of tourism can be measured;

- an appreciation of the positive and negative economic impacts of tourism activity; and

- a general knowledge of the approaches that may be used to measure the economic impacts of tourism and the strengths and weaknesses associated with each approach.

OVERVIEW

In spite of the many altruistic and well-meaning reasons sometimes put forward to support the case for tourism development, such as those originally proposed in the Manila Declaration (WTO, 1980a), it is the economic benefits that provide the main driving force for tourism development. Foreign exchange earnings, income and employment generation are the major motivations for including tourism as part of a development strategy. Tourist expenditure is as 'real' as any other form of consumption and international tourist expenditure can be seen as an **invisible export** from the host country, whereas domestic tourism can be seen as an 'export' from the hosting region to the other local regions. Domestic tourism can also in some instances, be seen as an import substitute for the national economy. Tourism activity can be seen as import substitution when tourists choose to take their vacation within the national economy rather than travel abroad.

International tourism activity is often easier to measure than domestic tourism activity because it involves custom/immigration procedures and currency exchange. Many countries collect information from visitor arrivals at the frontier providing a good source of data relating to the volume of arrivals, country of origin and purpose of visit. Currency exchange information is collected and monitored by central banks and this provides some useful information, but is by no means ideal, relating to tourist spending. Tourist expenditure can only be estimated with some degree of accuracy by undertaking specific visitor expenditure surveys, normally at exit points. Such surveys tend to be time consuming and costly. Some countries attempt to estimate the level and patterns of tourist spending from central bank statistics, while others try to economise by collecting tourist expenditure data at infrequent intervals (say, every five years). In order to use economic impact analyses for the purpose of tourism planning and development strategies it is important to have reliable flows of expenditure data. Therefore, visitor expenditure data should be collected by exit surveys each year, or at least every other year. This information can be collected along with demographic data and other variables that will help underscore other important surveys for, say the market research referred to in Chapter 17.

During the past few decades many economies have experienced growth in their service sectors, even when the more traditional agricultural and manufacturing sectors have been subject to **stagnation** or decline. The global importance of the service sectors can be identified by the introduction of the General Agreement of Trade in Services (GATS) following the Uruguay Round of negotiations. Tourism is the largest service-based industry and, as such, has been partly responsible for this service sector growth. In **developing countries**, the service sector is responsible for around 40% of **GDP** while in developed or industrialised economies it is responsible for more than 65% of GDP. In spite of its economic importance, the service sector has not been given adequate prominence in economic textbooks, which have tended to concentrate on the more traditional manufacturing industries. The dearth of material on service-based industries in the major textbooks can be, in part, explained (if not excused) by the lack of available and comparable statistics for service-based sectors. This shortfall in data is improving but, in general, it is tradition that has dictated the content of such books rather than pragmatism. The latter half of the 1980s saw a growing interest in the operation and performance of service industries. In 1986, it was observed that, because of the strength of **intersectoral linkages**, the

PHOTOGRAPH 5.1   **International tourism increases foreign exchange flows**   *Source: Travelex PLC*

service sector generally performs a more important function in the process of development than that suggested merely by looking at the service sector's contribution to a country's GDP. From the mid-1990s, the international world has been dominated by the service industries and they have also been responsible for the accelerated drive towards **globalisation**. International tourism activity enjoyed strong growth throughout the 1990s, often growing faster than other commercial services and at a rate that was almost twice as fast as international trade. Although the number of international tourist arrivals experienced a slight dip of just 0.5% in the period 2000 to 2001 (following the events of September 11, 2001) it recovered much of its growth impetus with the following year growing at 2.7% for 2001 to 2002. However, hidden within these overall growth figures is the fact that the number of international tourist arrivals to the Americas declined in 2001 (−6.1%) and 2002 (−4.4%). Each of the other regions showed a significant turnaround in 2002 and all recorded positive growth trends.

Recognition of the importance of the service sector to the world economy came in the form of the establishment of the General Agreement of Trade in Services (GATS). **GATS** grew out of the World Trade Organization's Uruguay Round of the General Agreement on Trade and Tariffs (GATT). The main declared purpose of GATS is the liberalisation of services. However, a brief examination of the slow-down in the growth of trade might suggest that GATS was introduced because the strong growth in service industries would accelerate the WTO's processes and influence.

Along with the movement towards the liberalisation of international trade has been the growth of *globalisation*. Globalisation refers to the result of a collection of forces that tend to change the way that the economic, political and cultural worlds operate. As the world becomes economically smaller, the concept of globalisation has taken on a more central position on the stage of global politics. From the earliest days when the world economy first started to transform from subsistence farming and fishing towards a market-based economy there has been a sustained growth in the geographical reach of businesses. However, this process of globalisation has been accelerating throughout the latter half of the last century. It has been referred to as a process in which the geographical distance between economic factors, producers and consumers becomes a factor of diminishing significance.

Tourism, as a major element of the service economy, has, for some time, been applauded for its sustained and rapid growth. However, not even its most ardent supporters would have forecast just how well it has been able to stand up to the pressures of global **economic recession**, even recessions that have severely damaged many of the world's major industries. The world has staggered from recession to recession over the past two decades and even the mighty giants of industry (such as IBM and Ford) have been forced to rationalise their activities. Although the purpose of this chapter is to examine the economic impact of tourism, it is useful to examine the economic significance of tourism to a number of countries, most notably the prime generators and/or recipients of international tourists. The economic significance of tourism is determined not only by the level of tourism activity that is taking place, but also by the type and nature of the economy being considered. For instance, the economic significance of tourism activity to a developing country may well be measured in terms of its ability to generate an inflow of foreign exchange or to provide a means for creating greater price flexibility in its export industries, whereas, for a developed or industrialised economy, the researcher may be looking at tourism's ability to assist **diversification** strategies and to combat regional imbalances.

The significance of tourism may be assessed in terms of the proportion of total global visitors attributable to individual countries, for here one can assess the relative importance of single countries in determining the volume of world travel. On the other hand, the significance of tourism may be examined with respect to the importance of tourist activity to the economy of each destination. This chapter examines both aspects in order to establish how some countries are extremely important as tourist generators and how other countries are highly dependent upon such tourism activity.

International tourism in selected countries

Recent events throughout the 1990s and early 2000s have had a profound effect on the pattern of international tourism. How long term these effects are will depend, to a large extent, on the future political and economic stability of the world. The financial crises that hit the **tiger economies** affected not only the flow of tourism activity but also the patterns. The events of September 11, 2001 and the subsequent conflicts in the Middle East have brought a significant change to the nature

TABLE 5.1	Principal tourist-generating countries, 1986–2002: expenditure (US$bn)			
Country	**1986**	**1990**	**1995**	**2002**
Germany	18.3	29.5	50.7	53.2
United States	26.0	37.4	45.9	58.0
Japan	7.2	24.9	37.0	26.7
United Kingdom	8.9	19.1	24.7	40.4
France	6.5	12.4	16.3	19.5
Top 5 countries	66.9	123.3	174.6	197.8
Rest of world	59.1	119.9	182.3	276.2
World total	125.0	243.2	356.9	474.0
Top 5 as % of world total	53.5	50.7	48.9	41.7

Source: Derived from WTO, 1988; 1992; 1997; 2003

of tourism flows. Therefore, although the global figures for international tourist arrivals and spending indicate a recovery path from the crisis period of 2001, the anatomy of that recovery portrays a different picture.

For instance, within Europe, international tourist arrivals to Spain increased by 4.6% in 2001 even though international tourist arrivals to Europe as a whole fell by 0.5%. Destinations such as the UK (–9.4%), France (–2.6%), Germany (–5.9%) and Italy (–3.9%) all recorded declines in the number of arrivals for that period. The following year (2001/2) showed a growth in international tourist arrivals to Europe as a whole of 2.3% with all countries except Switzerland, Poland and Portugal showing a positive growth over the previous year. As commonly occurs, tourist spending over these two years was more volatile than arrivals with Europe showing an overall decline of 1.7% in 2000/1 and a growth of 6.5% in 2001/2. The selection of countries for inclusion in tables of top generating and top recipient countries is at best difficult and at worst arbitrary. However, the countries selected in Tables 5.1 and 5.2 (China, France, Germany, Italy, Japan, Spain, the UK and the USA) have been included because they are among either the top five tourist-generating countries with respect to tourist expenditure and/or the top five countries with respect to tourism receipts.

TABLE 5.2	Principal destinations in terms of tourism receipts, 1986–2002: tourism receipts (US$bn)				
Country	**1986**	**1990**	**1995**	**1996**	**2002**
United States	20.4	43.0	61.1	64.3	66.6
Spain	12.1	18.6	25.3	28.4	33.6
Italy	9.9	20.0	27.5	27.4	26.9
France	9.7	20.2	27.5	28.2	32.3
China	1.5	2.2	8.7	10.2	20.4
Top 5 countries	60.3[1]	116.7[1]	160.5[1]	168.0[1]	179.8
Rest of world	77.3	144.4	232.6	254.7	294.5
World total	137.6	261.1	393.1	422.7	474.3
Top 5 as % of world total	43.8	44.7	40.8	39.7	37.9

[1] The top five countries prior to 2002 did not include China.
Source: Derived from WTO, 1988; 1992; 1997; 2003

Table 5.1 shows the principal tourist-generating countries, with respect to the level of their international tourist expenditure, over the time period from 1986 to 2002. It can be seen that, over the years covered by the table, the proportion of the world's total tourist expenditure attributable to the top five generating countries has fluctuated around the 50% level until the latter half of the 1990s, with a peak of just over 54% in 1988. However, this proportion has fallen to only 41.7% in 2002 and in spite of the events of September 11, the United States has overtaken Germany to regain its position as the prime generator of tourist expenditure. The UK has continued to grow strongly, quadrupling the amount of tourist spending generated over the 1986–2002 period. Conversely, Japan, with its economic crises has witnessed a 27% fall in the amount of tourist spending generated since 1995.

Table 5.2 shows the top five countries in terms of tourism receipts. The proportion of total global tourist receipts attributable to the top five countries has fluctuated around the lower half of the 40% range, with peaks of around 45% at the turn of the decade but falling to 40% by 1996. The USA has improved its position relative to the other top recipient countries, by increasing its receipts more than threefold over the ten-year period up to 1996. In 1986 the USA was responsible for 14.8% of the world total tourism receipts; in 1996 this figure had risen to 15.3%. China ranked as the 22nd destination by tourism receipts in 1986 and the rapid growth of tourism activity over the following 16 years has seen it rise to be fifth in the world ranking. It clearly has potential to move further up this list over the next few years.

A fact that becomes clear when examining the top tourist expenditure generating and receiving countries is the high degree of correlation between the listings. Tourism does not perform well as a global redistributor of income and wealth in the same way that it does for regional redistribution. This is particularly true if the relationship between developed and developing countries is considered. It is the developed and industrialised countries that tend to populate the lists in both the top generators of tourist expenditure and the top recipients.

The division between the performance of developed and developing countries is of additional significance when it is considered that, on average the industrialised countries are responsible for 70% of total world exports and yet receive over 70% of all tourism receipts, which contrasts with developing countries that are responsible for less than 30% of all world exports and received less than 30% of all tourist receipts.

Dependence upon tourism

Table 5.3 provides another way of examining the economic significance of tourism for countries by looking at dependence on tourism receipts (**economic dependence**) relative to total export earnings and gross national product (GNP) for 2001. It can be seen that among these developed economies, tourism receipts as a percentage of total export earnings ranges from the relatively unimportant 0.6% for Japan to the quite dependent 18.8% experienced by Spain. Confirming this dependency level the table also shows the percentage of **GNP** attributable to tourism receipts which shows that only 0.1% of Japan's GNP is attributable to tourist receipts but this figure rises to 5.6% for Spain. The final column in Table 5.3 shows the percentage and direction of change in the percentage of **GNI** attributable to tourism receipts when compared with the situation in 1995. Here we find that there is considerable volatility with Germany's dependence upon tourism receipts increasing as its GNI falters over the six-year period whereas the UK finds that its corresponding figure declines by 35% which reflects the effects of its declining tourism receipts in 2001 (as a result of the terrorist strikes in the USA) combined with a strong economy.

Two major problems that exist when making international comparisons of tourism expenditure and receipts are that the data are generally expressed in current prices and are standardised in US dollars. The problems created by this form of presentation is that (1) it does not take into account the effects of **inflation** and (2) movements in the value of the dollar exchange rate (which have been both frequent and dramatic over the past decade or so) will manifest as changes in the local value of tourist receipts and expenditure. The twenty-first century has started with very low levels of inflation but the US dollar has suffered as a result of its massive **trade deficit** and its involvement in the conflicts in Afghanistan and Iraq.

TABLE 5.3	Tourism receipts expressed as a percentage of total export earning and gross national income, 2001					
Country	Tourism receipts (US$m) (1)	Export earnings (US$bn) (2)	(1) as a % (2)	GNI[1] (US$bn) (3)	(1) as a % of (3)	% change over 1995
Spain	32 874	175	18.8	588	5.6	+16%
France	29 979	369	8.1	1 381	2.2	+16%
Italy	25 787	310	8.3	1 124	2.3	−8%
United Kingdom	16 263	385	4.2	1 477	1.1	−35%
United States	72 295	1 034	7.0	9 781	0.7	−22%
Germany	17 200	655	2.6	1 940	0.9	+29%
Japan	2 736	433	0.6	4 523	0.1	0%

[1] Gross national income (GNI) calculated using World Bank Atlas Method.
Source: Derived from Euromonitor, International Monetary Fund (IMF), International Financial Statistics

Table 5.4 takes the analysis one step further and examines the relationship between tourism receipts and expenditures in order to establish the net effect of travel on selected countries of the world. In 2002 the USA, France, Italy and China all had positive tourism balance sheets. That is, they earned more from international tourism receipts than their national residents spent as tourists outside of the country. However, Germany, the UK, Japan, the Netherlands, Hong Kong and the Russian Federation were all subject to a negative tourism balance sheet. That is, the normal residents of those countries spent more abroad on international tourism than the countries received from international tourism receipts.

There have been various attempts at finding consistent ways to measure the demand or the significance of tourism activity. The most universally accepted approach is through the construction of tourism satellite accounts.

Tourism satellite accounts

One approach to determining the economic significance of tourism to an economy is to construct tourism satellite accounts. This methodology has been approved and adopted by the United Nations and the World Tourism Organization in 2000.

TABLE 5.4	Tourism balance sheets for the top ten tourist spenders, 2002		
Country	International tourism receipts (US$bn)	International tourism expenditure (US$bn)	Balance (US$bn)
United States	66.5	58.0	8.5
Germany	19.2	53.2	−34.0
United Kingdom	17.8	40.4	−22.6
Japan	3.5	26.7	−23.2
France	32.3	19.5	12.8
Italy	26.9	16.9	10.0
China	20.4	15.4	5.0
Netherlands	7.7	12.9	−5.2
Hong Kong	10.1	12.4	−2.3
Russian Federation	4.2	12.0	−7.8

Note: A minus balance indicates where the country spends more than it receives through tourism activity.
Source: Derived from WTO, Tourism Highlights 2003

Tourism satellite accounts (TSAs) perform a different role from economic impact models that attempt to estimate the net economic benefits associated with tourism activity. To be of use TSAs must be built around an **input–output model** and they take a demand-orientated approach rather than the supply-orientated approach associated with input–output models. As the TSA name suggests they are a set of accounts that can be used to determine the size or significance of tourism within an economy, but not the impact of tourism. They are based on the national accounts data but this information is rearranged so that particular emphasis can be placed on tourism activities. Like input–output models, they also provide a means whereby tourism can be viewed in parallel with other industries and across international boundaries. The underpinning philosophy of TSA is to add credibility to tourism, which suffers because it does not fit into a single industry and its socio-economic impact is often difficult to measure.

MINI CASE STUDY 5.1
Tourism as a redistribution mechanism of wealth

Tourism has been lauded as an excellent vehicle for redistributing income from rich areas with abundant employment opportunities to poorer areas where employment opportunities are scarce. Consider domestic tourism in an economy such as France. The tendency is for people from the relatively affluent urbanised areas of, say, Paris to travel to less populated, poorer and more scenic rural areas. This results in a transfer of demand from the wealthier urban areas to the sparsely populated rural areas. Such transfers can stimulate investment and act as a catalyst for general economic development.

The same redistributive qualities of tourism have not been so apparent at the international level where the vast majority of tourism activity takes place between the wealthy industrialised economies. Tourism has done little to bridge the north–south divide. Indeed, it has been argued quite convincingly that tourism can exacerbate the income inequalities between rich countries such as the USA and less rich countries such as Kenya. The drive towards globalisation by some of the key elements of the tourism industry adds further substance to this belief.

The existence of economies of large-scale production, **comparative advantage** and the global nature of communications might suggest that any attempt to redress the imbalances will result in a misallocation of resources.

DISCUSSION QUESTIONS

1 Explain why tourism may act as an effective means of redistributing wealth at national level but often fails to do so at regional levels within an economy.

2 If the natural market forces are left to their own devices will tourism result in income redistribution that works in favour of the poorer segments of the population (nationally and internationally)?

3 What actions could be taken to encourage tourism to assist in redressing income inequalities without damaging the development of the industry?

In terms of the discussions in this chapter, the multiplier models are used to determine the economic impact of changes in tourist spending on the income, employment, government revenue and foreign exchange of any economy. They can also be used to identify **opportunity costs** by examining the effects of comparable changes in other industries. TSAs, on the other hand, offer a way of improving the estimation of the significance of tourism to an economy.

The concept of tourism satellite accounts is based on the need for a framework that will provide consistency over time and between countries and comparability between industries when calculating the significance of tourism to an economy. Providing the extensive data needs can be met with timely and accurate data the accounts should do much to promote the importance of tourism globally and within countries. There have been some serious concerns however, that some tourism satellite accounts have been constructed using data that are less than accurate. Such shortcuts will only serve to undermine the fundamental reason for implementing this accounting system.

THE GENERATION OF ECONOMIC IMPACTS BY TOURIST SPENDING

Tourists spend their money on a wide variety of goods and services provided by a wide range of businesses. For example, tourists purchase accommodation, food and beverage, transport, communications, entertainment services, goods from retail outlets and tour/travel services. This money may be seen as an injection of demand into the host economy, i.e. demand that is created by people from outside of the area of the local economy. In the case of international tourism, the tourist expenditure is a result of non-nationals spending within the national economy. In the case of domestic tourism the tourist expenditure is a result of spending by people that do not live within the local area in which the money is spent. However, the total value of international and domestic tourist expenditure represents only a partial and sometimes misleading picture of the economic impact. The full assessment of economic impact must take into account other aspects such as:

- **leakages** of expenditure out of the local economy;
- indirect and induced effects; and
- **displacement** and opportunity costs.

LEAKAGES OF EXPENDITURE OUT OF THE LOCAL ECONOMY

When tourists make expenditures within an economy the amount of money that stays within that economy depends upon the extent of leakages that occur. For instance, if a tourist purchases a carved wooden souvenir from a gift shop in Beijing, the extent of leakages will depend upon whether the carving was imported or made locally. If the carving was imported the tourist is really only buying the **value added** that was created within the local economy, i.e. the value of local transport, import, wholesale and retail margins, government taxes and duties, etc. The extent of leakages can result from demand-side factors such as the fact that different types of tourist and different types of tourist activity tend to be associated with differences in propensities to purchase imported goods. The leakages can also be associated with supply-side factors, particularly in developing economies where the local capacity to supply the needs of tourists may be small and there is consequently a high proportion of demand met through imported goods and services. Wherever money flows out of circulation, either by being spent on goods and services from outside or simply being withdrawn through savings, this constitutes a *leakage*.

161

THE MEASUREMENT OF ECONOMIC IMPACT

The measurement of the economic impact of tourism is far more involved than simply calculating the level of tourist expenditure. Indeed, estimates of the economic impact of tourism based on tourist expenditure or receipts can be not only inaccurate, but also very misleading. Before examining how the economic impact is measured, it is necessary to look at the different aspects of the economy that are affected by tourism expenditure.

To begin with, a difference can be drawn between the economic impact associated with tourist expenditure and that associated with the development of tourism. The former refers to the ongoing effects of, and changes in, tourist expenditure, whereas the latter is concerned with the one-off impact of the construction and finance of tourism-related facilities. The difference between these two aspects of impact is important because they require different methodological approaches. The calculation of the economic impact of tourist expenditure is achieved by using multiplier analysis and the estimation of the economic impact of tourism development projects is often achieved by resorting to **project appraisal** techniques such as **cost–benefit analysis**.

The measurement of the economic impact of tourist expenditure, if it is to be meaningful, must encompass the various effects of tourist spending as it impacts throughout the economy. That is, the direct, indirect and induced effects associated with tourist expenditure need to be calculated.

Direct, indirect and induced economic effects

Tourist expenditure has a 'cascading' effect throughout the host economy. It begins with tourists spending money in 'front-line' tourist establishments, such as hotels, restaurants and taxis, and then permeates throughout the rest of the economy. It can be examined by assessing the impact at three different levels – the direct, indirect and induced levels.

DIRECT EFFECTS

The direct level of impact is the value of tourist expenditure *less* the value of imports necessary to supply those 'front-line' goods and services. Thus, the direct impact is likely to be less than the value of tourist expenditure except in the rare case where a local economy can provide all of the tourist's wants from its own productive sectors.

INDIRECT EFFECTS

The establishments that directly receive the tourist expenditure also need to purchase goods and services from other sectors within the local economy, for example hotels will purchase the services of builders, accountants, banks, food and beverage suppliers, electricity and water, etc. Furthermore, the suppliers to these 'front-line' establishments will also need to purchase goods and services from other establishments within the local economy and so the process continues. The generation of economic activity brought about by these subsequent rounds of expenditure is known as the indirect effect. The indirect effect will not involve all of the monies spent by tourists during the direct effect since some of that money will leak out of circulation through imports, savings and taxation.

INDUCED EFFECTS

Finally, during the direct and indirect rounds of expenditure, income will accrue to local residents in the form of wages, salaries, distributed profit, rent and interest. This addition to local income will, in part, be re-spent in the local economy on goods and services and this will generate yet further rounds of economic activity.

It is only when all three levels of impact (direct *plus* indirect *plus* induced) are estimated that the full positive economic impact of tourism expenditure is fully assessed. However, there can be negative aspects to the economic impact of tourist expenditure.

Measuring the economic impact of tourist expenditure

At a national level, the WTO publishes annual tourist statistics for countries throughout the world. These statistics include figures relating to tourist expenditure, but it would not be correct to assume that these figures reflect the economic impact of tourist expenditure. These figures relate to how much tourists spend in a destination. They take no account of how much of that sum leaks straight out of the economy (paying for imported goods and services to satisfy tourist needs) or how much additional impact is experienced through the 'knock-on' effects of this tourist spending.

At a sub-national level the availability of tourist expenditure data is far more sparse. Some countries, such as the UK, undertake visitor expenditure surveys (for example, International Passenger Survey (IPS) and United Kingdom Tourist Survey (UKTS)) which allow expenditure estimates to be made at the regional level. However, it is often necessary to undertake specific tourist expenditure surveys to establish the tourist spend in particular areas.

In order to translate tourist expenditure data into economic impact information the appropriate multiplier values have to be calculated. The term multiplier is one of the most quoted economic concepts in the study of tourism. Multiplier values may be used for a variety of purposes and are often used as the basis for public sector decision making.

THE MULTIPLIER CONCEPT

The concept of the multiplier is based upon the recognition that sales for one firm require purchases from other firms within the local economy, i.e. the industrial sectors of an economy are interdependent. This means that firms purchase not only primary inputs such as labour and imports, but also intermediate goods and services produced by other establishments within the local economy. Therefore, a change in the level of final demand for one sector's output will affect not only the industry that produces that final good/service but also other sectors that supply goods/services to that sector and the sectors that act as suppliers to those sectors as well.

Because firms in the local economy are dependent upon other firms for their supplies, any change in tourist expenditure will bring about a change in the economy's level of production, household income, employment, government revenue and foreign exchange flows (where applicable). These changes may be greater than, equal to or less than the value of the change in tourist expenditure that brought them about. The term 'tourist multiplier' refers to the ratio of two changes – the change in one of the key economic variables such as output (income, employment or government revenue) to the change in tourist expenditure.

Therefore, there will be some value by which the initial change in tourist expenditure must be multiplied in order to estimate the total change in output – this is known as the *output multiplier*. In the same way, there will be a value that, when multiplied by the change in tourist expenditure, will estimate the total change in household income – this is known as the *income multiplier*. The reason why the initial change in tourist spending must be subject to a multiplier effect can be seen from Figure 5.1.

Figure 5.1 shows that the tourist expenditure goes, initially, to the front-line tourist establishments that provide the tourists with their goods and services. This money will be re-spent by the firms that receive it. A proportion of the money will leak directly out of the economy in the form of imports and savings (the tan boxes in the diagram). These imports may be in the form of food and beverage that the tourist consumes but are not provided locally, or in respect of services provided to the establishment by individuals or firms located outside the economy being analysed. Where the tourist consumes a product that has been imported into the local economy, they are only consuming the value added (**distributive trade**, importation, transport, local taxes, etc.) rather than the full cost of the product. The money paid to persons outside the economy cannot have any further role in generating economic activity within the local economy and, thus, the value of tourist expenditure that actually circulates in the local economy is immediately reduced. The remaining sum of money will be used to purchase locally produced goods and services, labour and entrepreneurial skills (wages, salaries and profits) and to meet government taxes, licences and fees. These effects are all known as the direct effects.

We can see from Figure 5.1 that money will flow from the tourism-related establishments to other local businesses. This money will also be re-spent, some of it leaking out as imports, some of it leaking out of circulation through savings and some going to the government. The remainder will be spent on labour and entrepreneurial skills and purchases from other businesses for goods and services. The businesses that receive money in payment for their goods/services will also make purchases locally, import goods and services and pay government taxes. These effects are known as the indirect effects.

During each round of expenditure, some proportion of money accrues to local residents in the form of income (wages, salaries and profits). Some of this money will be saved (by either households or businesses) and will cease to circulate in the

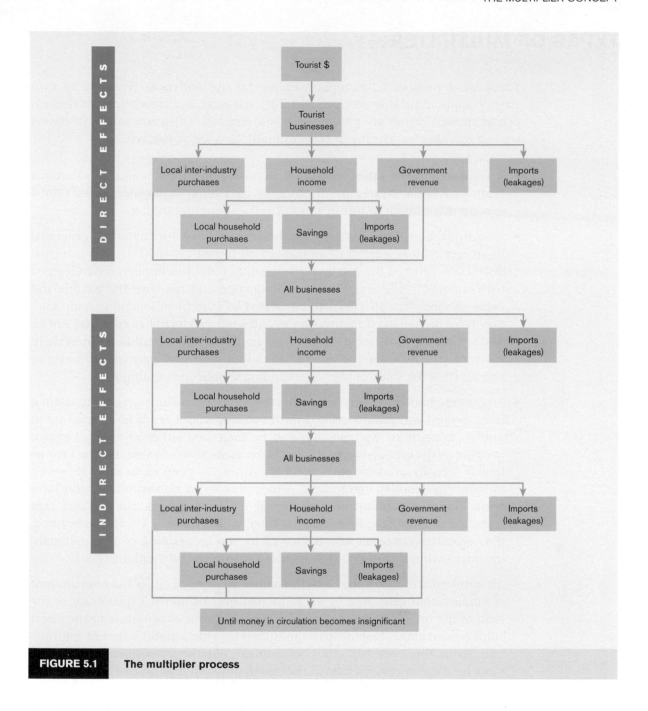

FIGURE 5.1 **The multiplier process**

economy, i.e. a leakage. The income that accrues to local households and is not saved will be re-spent. Some of it will leak out of the system as imports and some of it will go to the government as tax. The remainder will be re-spent as household consumption. This spending of income accrued as a result of the initial tourist expenditure will generate further rounds of economic activity – this effect is known as the induced effect.

The value of any tourism multiplier is meaningless unless it is qualified by both the methodology used to estimate it and the type of multiplier involved.

TYPES OF MULTIPLIER

There are a number of multipliers in regular use and each type has its own specific application. However, considerable confusion and misleading conclusions can be derived if they are misused or misinterpreted. This issue will be discussed later in this chapter. The major types of multipliers are as follows:

- A **transactions (or sales) multiplier** that measures the amount of additional business revenue created in an economy as a result of an increase in tourist expenditure. Similar to this in concept is the output multiplier.

- An **output multiplier** that measures the amount of additional output generated in an economy as a result of an increase in tourist expenditure. The principal distinction between the two multipliers is that output multipliers are concerned with changes in the actual levels of production and not with the volume and value of sales. Not all sales will be related to current production (some sales may have been made from inventories and some productive output may not be sold within the time frame of the model and, therefore, result in an increase in inventories). Therefore, the value of an output multiplier may well be larger or smaller than the value of the corresponding transactions multiplier.

- An **income multiplier** which measures the additional income (wages and salaries, rent, interest and profits) created in the economy as a result of an increase in tourist expenditure. Such income can be measured either as *national income* (*regional* in the case of domestic tourism) or as *disposable income*, i.e. the income that is actually available to households either to spend or to save. However, as mentioned earlier, the income, which accrues to non-nationals who have been 'imported' into the area, should be excluded because the incomes that they receive cannot be considered to be benefits to the area. On the other hand, the secondary economic effects created by the re-spending of non-nationals' incomes within the area *must* be included within the calculations.

- An **employment multiplier** which is a measurement of either the total amount of employment generated by an additional unit of tourist expenditure or the ratio of the total employment generated by this same expenditure to the direct employment alone. Employment multipliers provide a useful source of information about the secondary effects of tourism, but their measurement involves more heroic assumptions than in the case of other multipliers and care is needed in their interpretation.

- A **government revenue multiplier** that measures the impact on government revenue, from all sources, associated with an increase of tourist expenditure. This multiplier may be expressed in gross terms, that is the gross increase in government revenue as a result of an increase in tourist spending, or in net terms when the increase in government revenue is reduced by the increase in government expenditures associated with the increase in tourist activity.

Since the different types of multiplier are calculated using the same database they are closely interrelated. However, the concepts involved in each of the above multipliers are very different as are the magnitudes of each of the different multipliers calculated for the same economy. Some examples of these multiplier values are shown later in this chapter. Given the number of different multiplier concepts that are available it is not surprising to find that there has been some confusion over their interpretation. This confusion has been compounded by the fact that there are also a variety of methods that may be used to calculate each of the above multipliers.

METHODOLOGICAL APPROACHES

There are five major techniques that have been employed to measure the economic impact of tourism. Although they are often viewed as alternative approaches by many authors, with the exception of the base theory approach, each of the other methodologies plots out the natural evolution of a single concept as it struggles to overcome the inherent weaknesses and limitations. The five approaches are:

- base theory models;
- Keynesian multiplier models;
- *ad hoc* models;
- input–output analysis; and
- computable general equilibrium (CGE) models.

Base theory models

The basic assumption underlying base theory models is that there exists a stable relationship between each of the export sectors and the local sectors of an economy, so that changes in the level of tourist expenditure will create predictable and measurable changes the level of activity in local sectors. An example of this approach is given under the following sub-heading. Base theory multipliers are normally over-simplified formulations and are now rarely used.

MULTIPLIER ANALYSIS USING BASE THEORY

One early and interesting application of the technique by R.R. Nathan and Associates (1966) was used to calculate the short-run employment effects created by tourism expenditure in each of 375 counties and independent cities of Appalachia. The final model used took the form:

$$\frac{E}{E_{rx2}} = \frac{1}{1 - E_{rc}/E_r} \tag{5.1}$$

where E_r is total local employment, E_{rc} is local employment servicing local consumer demand and E_{rx2} is the direct change in employment created by a change in tourism expenditure.

Nathan Associates developed the multiplier model further, to measure long-term effects, by incorporating investment activity. This model took the form:

$$\frac{E_r}{E_{rx2}} = \frac{1 + i_2}{1 - E_{rc}/E_r} \tag{5.2}$$

where i_2 is a statistically estimated parameter (the value of which lies between 0 and 1) which relates the change in investment to the change in tourism activity.

This model is far too simplistic to be accurate in calculating tourism multiplier values.

Keynesian multiplier models

These multipliers are designed to measure the income created in an economy by an additional unit of tourist expenditure. The Keynesian multipliers were the first rigorous attempt at measuring the economic impact of an **exogenous change in demand**. The simplest formulation of the multiplier (k) is shown in equation (5.3):

$$k = \frac{1}{1 - c + m} \tag{5.3}$$

where 1 is the additional unit of tourism expenditure and leakages are the proportion of this expenditure which goes into savings ($1 - c$) and imports (m), i.e.:

$$k = \frac{1}{\text{leakages}}$$

To develop this model into a long-term formulation, which takes investment into account, is shown in equation (5.4):

$$k = \frac{1}{1 - c + m - i} \tag{5.4}$$

where i is the marginal propensity to invest.

Similarly the effects of the re-spending of money accruing to the public sector can be built into the model, and this is shown in equation (5.5):

$$k = \frac{1}{1 - c + m - i - g} \tag{5.5}$$

where g is the marginal propensity of the public sector to spend.

A typical Keynesian short-term multiplier model is shown in equation (5.6). The derivation of this model is given in Archer (1976):

$$k = \frac{1 - L}{1 - c(1 - t_i)(1 - t_d - b) + m} \tag{5.6}$$

where L = first round leakages out of the economy, t_i = the marginal rate of indirect taxation, t_d = the marginal rate of taxation and other deductions and b = the marginal rate of transfer payments.

The difference in the value of the multiplier created by applying exactly the same data to the short-term models shown in equations (5.3) and (5.6) highlight the dangers of relying on a model whose structure is too simplistic. For example, if we let L = 0.5, c = 0.9, m = 0.7, t_i = 0.16, t_d = 0.2 and b = 0.2 and calculate the income multipliers using first, the model shown in equation (5.1) and then again, using the more developed model shown in equation (5.6), the results are:

$$\frac{1}{1 - c + m} = \frac{1}{1 - 0.9 + 0.7} = 1.25$$

and

$$\frac{1 - L}{1 - c(1 - t_i)(1 - t_d - b) + m} = \frac{1 - 0.5}{1 - 0.9(1 - 0.16)(1 - 0.2 - 0.2) + 0.7} = 0.40$$

The two multiplier values derived from the same database are very different and would result in very different policy implications. However, even the more developed model shown in equation (5.6) is far too simplistic and is unable to measure variations in the form and magnitude of **sectoral linkages** and leakages out of the destination's economy during each round of transactions. Even the most complex and comprehensive Keynesian models developed for some studies are unable to provide the level of detail that is required for policy making and planning. One practical solution is to use *ad hoc* models.

Ad hoc models

The next step in the evolution of the multiplier approach was intended to overcome the 'broad brush' approach adopted by the Keynesian model wherein each sector was treated in an identical manner. The *ad hoc* models, although similar in principle to their Keynesian counterparts, are constructed specifically for each particular study. The simplest form of *ad hoc* model, using matrix algebra, is shown in equation (5.7):

$$A * \frac{1}{1 - BC} \tag{5.7}$$

where A = the proportion of additional tourist expenditure remaining in the economy after first round leakages, i.e. A equals the $(1 - L)$ expression in the Keynesian model, B = the propensity of local people to consume in the local economy and C = the proportion of expenditure by local people that accrues as income in the local economy.

The *ad hoc* model shown in equation (5.7) is too simplistic for serious application but more advanced models have been developed and used widely to calculate tourist multipliers to estimate the effect of tourist expenditure on income, public sector revenue, employment and imports. One such model, developed in the early 1970s (Archer and Owen, 1971) is:

$$\sum_{j=1}^{N}\sum_{i=1}^{n} Q_j K_{ij} V_i \frac{1}{1-c\sum_{i=1}^{n} X_i Z_i V_i} \tag{5.8}$$

where j = each category of tourist $j = 1$ to N, i = each type of business establishment $i = 1$ to n, Q_j = the proportion of total tourist expenditure spent by the jth type of tourist, K_{ij} = the proportion of expenditure by the ith type of tourist in the jth category of business, V_i = the direct and indirect income generated by unit of expenditure by the ith type of business, X_i = the pattern of consumption, i.e. the proportion of total consumer expenditure by the residents of the area in the ith type of business, Z_i = the proportion of X_i which takes place within the study area and c = the **marginal propensity to consume**.

The multiplicand equation (5.8) measures the direct and indirect effects of tourist expenditure while the multiplier measures the induced effects. In order to trace the flows of expenditure through successive rounds, separate equations are estimated for a range of V_i values. Examples of these are provided in the literature (see, for example, Archer and Owen, 1971).

Multiplier studies using *ad hoc* models are commonly used and examples can be found in the USA, the UK, South Pacific islands, Caribbean and elsewhere. More recent models have achieved even greater levels of **disaggregation**, even down to the levels of individual establishments.

Although models of this type can produce a large quantity of detailed and accurate information for policy-making and planning purposes, they are unable to provide the wealth of data yielded by the final methodological approach to be discussed, input–output analysis.

Input–output analysis

In order to overcome the subjectivity inherent in the *ad hoc* multiplier approach and to provide a more encompassing estimate of economic impact, the multiplier models commonly being used adopted the input–output framework. The input–output model approach presents a general equilibrium, rather than the partial equilibrium approach used in *ad hoc* models, to studying economic impacts. Input–output analysis begins with the construction of a table, similar to a table of national/regional accounts, which shows the economy of the destination in matrix form. Each sector of the economy is shown in each column as a purchaser of goods and services from other sectors in the economy, and in each row as a seller of output to each of the other sectors. The structure of an input–output table is shown in Figure 5.2. The table may be subdivided into three major quadrants. First, the inter-industry matrix (located in the top left-hand quadrant) details the sales and purchases that take place among the various sectors of the economy (for example, X_{11}, X_{12}, X_{13}, etc., are the sales of sector 1 to all other sectors within the economy, whereas X_{11}, X_{21}, X_{31}, X_{41}, etc., represent the purchases of sector 1 from all other sectors within the economy). Second, the bottom left-hand quadrant shows

SALES TO	INTERMEDIATE DEMAND Productive sectors						FINAL DEMAND Final demand sectors				TOTAL OUTPUT
PURCHASES FROM	Industry						H	I	G	E	
	1	2	3	4	...	m					
Industry 1	X_{11}	X_{12}	X_{13}	X_{14}	...	X_{1m}	C_1	I_1	G_1	E_1	X_1
Industry 2	X_{21}	X_{22}	X_{23}	X_{24}	...	X_{2m}	C_2	I_2	G_2	E_2	X_2
Industry 3	X_{31}	X_{32}	X_{33}	X_{34}	...	X_{3m}	C_3	I_3	G_3	E_3	X_3
Industry 4	X_{41}	X_{42}	X_{43}	X_{44}	...	X_{4m}	C_4	I_4	G_4	E_4	X_4
...	.	.	.	.	...	.	.	.	.	.	.
...					...						
Industry m	X_{m1}	X_{m2}	X_{m3}	X_{m4}	...	X_{mm}	C_m	I_m	G_m	E_m	X_m
Wages and salaries	W_1	W_2	W_3	W_4	...	W_m	W_C	W_I	W_G	W_E	W
Profits/ dividends	P_1	P_2	P_3	P_4	...	P_m	P_C	P_I	P_G	P_E	P
Taxes	T_1	T_2	T_3	T_4	...	T_m	T_C	T_I	T_G	T_E	T
Imports	M_1	M_2	M_3	M_4	...	M_m	M_C	M_I	M_G	M_E	M
Total inputs	X_1	X_2	X_3	X_4	...	X_m	C	I	G	E	X

(left side labels: Productive sectors; Primary inputs)

where:
X = Output
C = Consumption (households)
I = Investment (private)
G = Government expenditure

E = Exports
M = Imports
W = Wages and salaries
P = Profits and dividends
I = Taxes

Final demand sectors:
H = Household consumption sector
I = Investment expenditure sector
G = Government expenditure sector
E = Exports sectors

FIGURE 5.2 **Basic input–output transactions table**

each sector's purchases of primary inputs (such as payments to labour, W, profits, P, taxes, T and imported goods and services, M. Third, the right-hand quadrant shows the sales made by each sector to each source of final demand.

The simplest formulation is shown in equations (5.9) and (5.10) where, for ease of explanation, all forms of final demand are represented by a column vector ($\mathbf{Y}$).

$$\mathbf{X} = \mathbf{AX} + \mathbf{Y} \tag{5.9}$$

$$\mathbf{X} - \mathbf{AX} = \mathbf{Y}$$

$$(\mathbf{I} - \mathbf{A})\mathbf{X} = \mathbf{Y}$$

$$\mathbf{X} = (\mathbf{I} - \mathbf{A})^{-1}\mathbf{Y}$$

$$\Delta\mathbf{X} = (\mathbf{I} - \mathbf{A})^{-1}\Delta\mathbf{Y} \tag{5.10}$$

where $\mathbf{X}$ = a vector of the total sales of each sector of the economy, i.e. $[x_1 + x_2 + x_3 + x_4]$, $\mathbf{A}$ = a matrix of the inter-industry transactions within the economy, $\mathbf{Y}$ = a vector of final demand sales, $\mathbf{I}$ = an identity matrix (equivalent to 1 in simple algebra) and Δ = a change in a variable.

A change in the level of final demand (**Y**) will create an increase in the level of activity within the economy which manifests itself as changes in the output and sales of each sector. Further sub-models are required to calculate the effects on business revenue, public sector revenue, imports, employment and income. The model shown in equation (5.10) is still too simplistic for practical application and must be developed further.

For instance, in the simplified model discussed above, the imports of the economy are shown as a single row vector. However, the robust and flexible framework of input–output models allows the researcher to incorporate a matrix of import functions in order to draw distinctions between competitive and non-competitive imports. This is an extremely useful distinction because competitive imports are, by their very nature, far less predictable than non-competitive imports.

Incorporating an import function matrix which examines the trade-off between domestic production and competitive imports results in equation (5.10) being revised as follows:

$$\Delta X = (I - K^*A)^{-1} \, \Delta Y \tag{5.11}$$

where **K*** = a matrix where the diagonal values reflects the level of competitive imports associated with each sector which, when applied to the **A** matrix, reduces the domestic component of output by the required amount.

In this manner, changes in primary inputs (Δ**P**) created by a change in tourist expenditure (Δ**T**) will be given by:

$$\Delta P = B(I - K^*A)^{-1} \, \Delta T \tag{5.12}$$

where **B** = an $m \times n$ matrix of primary inputs.

Furthermore, the input–output model can be developed in order to provide information with respect to changes in employment levels brought about by changes in tourism expenditure. Let Δ**L** represent the change in employment and **E** be an $m \times n$ matrix of employment coefficients. The model will now take the form shown in equation (5.13):

$$\Delta L = E(I - K^*A)^{-1} \, \Delta T \tag{5.13}$$

Using this procedure, the labour usages of each productive sector can be incorporated on either a skill or educational requirement basis and this will allow the multiplier model to provide human resource planning information. Thus, multiplier models can provide information which will inform the future training needs for the destination.

In general, the input–output model can be as comprehensive as data, time and resources allow. Notwithstanding the fact that input–output analysis has been subject to criticism because of its general approach and the aggregation of firms into 'whole industries', the sectors of the model can be disaggregated to achieve the highest level of detail – even down to the level of individual establishments.

There are several weaknesses and limitations apparent with input–output models and most of them are the result of the restrictive assumptions upon which the model is based. For instance, the input–output model as discussed so far implicitly assumes that there are no such things as **supply constraints**. Supply constraints can inhibit the ability of an economy to supply the quantity and quality of goods and services needed to accommodate an increase in tourism expenditure. If capacity is inadequate to meet the additional demand and if insufficient factors of production, especially labour, are available, then additional tourism expenditure creates inflation and additional goods and services may have to be imported. Thus the size of the multiplier, if measured by an appropriate model, will fall. Within the input–output model framework the existence of supply constraints can be incorporated by building in a restrictions matrix that will channel unsupportable supply requirements into the import matrix. Such a work around has the disadvantage that it tends to act as a switch in the sense that it will either be 'on or off'. The reality of supply constraints is that there are likely to be some inflationary pressures that build as supply capacity is approached and such inflationary pressures may bring about other undesirable effects on the production function of many sectors within the economy. This is always a problem when the model that is being used is static rather than dynamic.

Most multiplier models are static in nature but can be made dynamic. Static models assume:

- that production and consumption functions are linear and that the intersectoral expenditure patterns are stable;

- that all sectors are able to meet any additional demands for their output; and

- that relative prices remain constant.

The first of these assumptions is that any additional tourism expenditure occurring will generate the same impact on the economy as an equivalent amount of previous tourism expenditure. Thus, any additional production in the economy is assumed to require the purchase of inputs in the same proportions and from the same sources as previously required. Similarly, any consequential increase in consumer demand is assumed to have exactly the same effect upon the economy as previous consumer expenditure. These anomalies arise because of the use of average rather than marginal production coefficients. The difference between the two often comes down to the existence or otherwise of economies of large-scale production and the stability of the production functions themselves.

With respect to the stability of the production functions, tourism, being a labour-intensive personal service, tends to be associated with fairly stable production functions. Thus, the use of average technical coefficients and the assumption of **linear homogeneity in production** tends not to be a serious drawback when using input–output analysis to study service-based economies. However, the problems of not being able to handle price changes are a major drawback of static systems.

Computable general equilibrium (CGE) models have been developed to overcome some of these limitations.

Computable general equilibrium (CGE) models

Computable general equilibrium models are constructed from a series of relationship equations that are compiled into social accounting matrices. Therefore, if constructed properly, CGE models allow for the effects of interaction between all elements of the economy unlike the input–output models that focus upon the supply side through output changes. For instance, CGEs can allow prices to vary and for resources in an economy to reallocated from one sector to others. This adds further to the flexibility afforded by input–output analyses. Furthermore, the CGE approach, because it is based upon a series of equations that explain the behaviour of individual sectors that are then simultaneously solved for the economy, means that changes from a wide range of sources (such as tax, price inflation, interest rate, exchange rate changes, etc.) can be analysed. In contrast the input–output approach is based on looking at the effect of an exogenous change in final demand on each of the different sectors of the economy. Although the addition of the dynamic aspects to the input–output framework are clearly welcome, there is much work to be done before such models can make significant improvements to the accuracy of impact estimates. Interregional input–output models have been constructed for many areas, such as that for the United Kingdom in the 1970s. These models incorporate trade flows (goods and services) between the regions and allow the researcher to estimate effects created in one region as a result of changes in another. However, to create realistic models the data requirements are enormous and at the end of the day there has to be some trade-off between accuracy and cost.

WEAKNESSES AND LIMITATIONS OF MULTIPLIER MODELS

Each of the multiplier model approaches outlined above contains several inherent problems that need to be overcome if they are to produce meaningful results. The majority of these problems stem from two distinct areas: the assumptions necessary to apply the models and the data needs.

Restrictive assumptions

Every economic model is founded upon a series of assumptions. The realism of those assumptions is clearly crucial to the model's performance – unrealistic assumptions will provide unrealistic results. During the early attempts at multiplier analysis the assumptions used were very restrictive. Sectors were all assumed to have the same propensities to import, employ labour, pay taxes and they were all assumed to be producing homogenous output. As the models have become more sophisticated, one by one these assumptions have been replaced with more realistic ones. The homogeneity of output can be overcome by the sectoral disaggregation, the differential needs for imports, tax liabilities and labour requirements can all be catered for within the post-Keynesian model structures. However, the greatest obstacles to improving the accuracy of estimates are found in the dynamics of the model. Most impact models are static in nature, providing a snapshot of an economy at one point in time. If the model is static it will not be able to reflect the effects of changes in relative prices, changes in production and consumption functions as a result of changes in relative prices and or supply constraints. To build these bridges and enhance the accuracy of the estimates, it is necessary to calculate price and income **elasticities of demand and supply**, relative returns on investment within dynamic capital markets and the effects of changes in interest and foreign exchange rates. In order to achieve this, it is necessary to know whether each sector is operating close to operational capacity because, as they move towards full capacity, pressure will be placed on the prices of some resources and this will affect other sectors as they compete for resources, and so on. This leads to the second category of problems, that is those associated with data deficiencies.

Recent attempts to build in such enhanced assumptions by using CGE models have not been too successful in overcoming these weaknesses and limitations. For instance, it is not uncommon for CGE models to assume that economies are always in full equilibrium at all times. This is clearly unrealistic for most economies. Many economies have some unemployment and are not populated by sectors that are all running at full capacity. Therefore models using such an assumption are likely to underestimate the true economic impact of an increase in tourism activities. Furthermore, CGE models tend to be based on assumptions that reflect developed market systems with relative prices constantly adjusting to reflect demand and supply circumstances. This is not always the case and can lead to inaccurate estimates. Finally, as pointed out by authors such as Miller (2002) and Cooper and Wilson (2002), most CGE models are heavily constrained by theory in the way that the dynamics are included and they typically do not perform well when subjected to statistical tests.

Data deficiencies

Secondary data (published and unpublished data) are rarely adequate to meet the requirements of the more demanding and advanced models. This means that researchers need to spend considerable time, effort and money collecting data for multiplier purposes.

Other data difficulties arise out of the nature of tourism itself as a multi-product industry directly affecting a large number of sectors in an economy. Tourist expenditure is spread across several sectors of an economy and accurate surveys of visitor expenditure are required in order to obtain an acceptable breakdown of this expenditure into its various components, e.g. accommodation, meals, beverage, transportation and shopping.

Furthermore, problems often arise when attempting to integrate this visitor expenditure into the categories disaggregated in the input–output table. Rarely are pre-existing input–output tables produced in a form sufficiently disaggregated to accept the detailed data derived from visitor expenditure surveys. In such cases, either the tourist expenditure data have to be compressed to fit the sectors already identified in the input–output table with a consequent loss in the accuracy of the results or else much time and effort has to be expended on disaggregating the existing input–output table.

If, however, an input–output (or alternative model) is constructed especially for the study, then the matrix can be arranged in a form which fits the tourist expenditure pattern and the data can be fed directly into the model. The development of the CGE models demonstrate the need to enhance the dynamic nature of the models but add considerable pressures to the data needs of the models. Rarely do we have sufficient information to calculate the effects of relative price changes on the allocation of resources within an economy. The movement of people from region to region as the relative prosperity of regions changes is, itself, a dynamic event and is determined by a host of economic, social and environmental factors. Foreign exchange rate data need to be considered on a global basis because international tourism is a global industry. Therefore, the data demands associated with making the models dynamic and sensitive to economic interactions between sectors and regions are formidable.

As economic impact models become more sophisticated and are able to reflect some of the dynamic processes it will be possible to estimate the 'net' economic benefits of tourism in a more meaningful way. As with any change in economic output, there is likely to be positive as well as negative economic impacts. To date the negative economic impacts have been sadly neglected by most model structures.

These negative economic impacts can manifest in a number of ways ranging from the misallocation of resources, an increase in the demand for public goods and infrastructure as a result of urbanisation, through to the displacement of existing business.

Negative economic impacts

The production of tourist goods and services requires the commitment of resources that could otherwise be used for alternative purposes. For instance, the development of a tourism resort in Spain may involve the migration of labour from rural to urban areas which brings with it economic implications for both the rural and urban areas – the former losing a productive unit of labour whereas the latter implying additional infrastructure pressure for health, education and other public services. If labour is not in abundance then meeting the tourists' demands may involve the transfer of labour from one industry (such as agriculture or fishing) to tourism industries, involving an opportunity cost that is often ignored in the estimation of tourism's economic impact. Furthermore, if there is a shortage of skilled labour then there may be a need to import labour from other countries such as Morocco and this will result in additional economic leakages as income earned from this imported labour may, in part, be repatriated (**repatriated income**).

Similarly, the use of capital resources (which are often scarce) in the development of tourism-related establishments precludes their use for other forms of economic development. To gain a true picture of the economic impact of tourism it is necessary to take into account the opportunity costs of using scarce resources for tourism development as opposed to alternative uses.

Where tourism development substitutes one form of expenditure and economic activity for another, this is known as the displacement effect. The displacement effect should be taken into account when the economic impact of tourism is being estimated. Displacement can take place when tourism development is undertaken at the expense of another industry and is generally referred to as the opportunity cost of the development. However, it is more commonly referred to when a new tourism project is seen to take away custom from an existing facility. For instance, if a destination such as St Lucia finds that its all-inclusive hotels are running at high occupancy levels and returning a reasonable yield on the investment, the construction of an additional all-inclusive hotel may simply reduce the occupancy levels of the existing establishments. This means that the destination may find that its overall tourism activity has not increased by as much as the new business from the development. This is displacement.

The size of multiplier values

The size of multiplier values will vary under different circumstances because it is dependent upon the patterns of tourist expenditure, the nature of an area's economy and the extent to which the various sectors of the economy are linked in their trading patterns.

A large number of tourism multiplier studies have been carried out since the 1960s. Table 5.5 shows the range of values of tourism output multipliers for a selection of industrialised countries, US states, cities and rural areas. The figures are only provided to give an indicative view of the relative size of output multipliers. Of course, the values will also depend upon the methodology used to calculate them and the following multiplier values were derived from the average of studies that used the unorthodox multiplier (output change as a result of a change in tourist expenditure) at the direct, indirect and induced level, using input–output analysis.

For policy-making and planning purposes, income multipliers are often seen to be the most useful because they provide information about national or local income rather than merely business output or turnover. Table 5.6 shows the range of income multiplier values for a variety of types of destinations. Care must be taken when comparing multiplier values between countries. First, the analyses may be undertaken over different time periods and, even though multiplier values tend not to be subject to drastic changes even over two decades, they do tend to increase as economies develop and improve their sectoral linkages. Second, and more importantly, using the different methodologies can make a significant difference to the values. For instance, input–output models, because they are based upon a general equilibrium approach, tend to yield significantly higher multiplier values than *ad hoc* models and, depending upon the level of comprehensiveness and

TABLE 5.5	The range value of tourism output multipliers for selected destinations
Country or region	**Tourism output multiplier**
Medium to large industrialised economies	2.00–3.40
Selection of US states	1.57–2.20
City/urban economies	1.24–1.51
Rural area economies	1.12–1.35

Source: Compiled by the authors from published articles and unpublished reports to governments

TABLE 5.6	The range of tourism income multipliers for selected types of destinations
Country or region	**Income multiplier**
National economies	1.23–1.98
Small island economies	0.39–1.59
US states and counties	0.44–1.30
UK regions and counties	0.29–0.47
UK cities and towns	0.19–0.40

Source: Compiled by the author from published articles and unpublished government reports

detail achieved in the *ad hoc* models, this difference may be as high as 30%. It has been suggested that input–output based multipliers often return higher multiplier values than their CGE counterparts (Dwyer *et al.*, 2003) because they may not pick up the negative effects created by relative price changes or demand displacement. However, there is a tendency for CGE models to underestimate the economic impact of tourism when they are based on assumptions of full capacity and market equilibrium.

It is also noticeable from Table 5.6 that the size of the income multiplier values tends to be correlated with the size of the economy. In general, the larger the economy, the higher will be the multiplier value, although there will obviously be some exceptions to this. The reason for this correlation is that larger economies tend to have a more developed economic structure which means that they have stronger intersectoral linkages and lower propensities to import in order to meet the demands of tourists, the tourist industry, non-tourist industries and the local population. The higher the propensity to import in order to meet local and tourist demand, the lower the income multiplier.

In addition to calculating the levels of output, income, employment and government revenue generated by additional units of tourist expenditure, multiplier analysis provides valuable information concerning its impact on a country's net foreign exchange flows. The impact model can be used to determine not only the direct import requirements necessary to meet the tourists' demands but also the indirect and induced imports required or generated as a result of the initial tourist expenditure. When all import requirements are summed and deducted from the international tourist expenditure the result will be the net foreign exchange flow. This can be further explored by examining the expenditure of local people when travelling abroad and a travel and tourism trade balance can be calculated.

The multipliers most vulnerable to criticism (and inaccuracies) are the employment multipliers. Therefore great care must be exercised in their interpretation. The data used for their measurement and the assumptions underlying the model constructions are more heroic for employment than for any other type of effect. The two major problems relate to the fact that:

- in the majority of studies employment is assumed to have a linear relationship with either income or output, whereas the available evidence suggests that this relationship is non-linear; and

- multiplier models assume that employment in each sector is working at full capacity, so that to meet any increase in demand will require additional employment. In practice, this is unlikely to be true and increases (or decreases) in the level of tourist expenditure will not generate a corresponding increase (or decrease) in the number of people employed.

In consequence, tourism employment multipliers should be interpreted as only an *indication* of the number of full-time equivalent (FTE) job opportunities supported by changes in tourist expenditure. Whether or not these job opportunities will materialise depends upon a number of factors, most notably the extent to which the existing labour force in each sector is fully utilised, and the degree to which labour is able to transfer between different occupations and between different sectors of the economy.

Table 5.7 shows the employment multipliers for several countries and regions. We can see that these employment multipliers are of a different magnitude from those relating to either output or income. This reflects the need for considerably larger amounts of tourist spending to generate one new full-time equivalent job opportunity.

Unlike the income and output multipliers, it is not possible to compare employment multipliers between different destinations when they are presented in this form. This is because the table figures show the number of full-time equivalent job opportunities created by 10,000 units of tourist expenditure where that unit is expressed in the local currency. Thus, differences in the unit value of local

TABLE 5.7	Tourism employment multipliers for selected destinations per 10,000 units of tourist expenditure (i.e. dollars, pounds or lira)
Country/city	**Employment multiplier**
Bermuda	0.44
Fiji	0.79
Jamaica	1.28
Malta	1.59
UK (Edinburgh)	0.37

TABLE 5.8	Standardised employment multipliers for selected destinations
Country	**Employment multiplier**
Jamaica	4.61
Mauritius	3.76
Bermuda	3.02
Gibraltar	2.62
Solomon Islands	2.58
Malta	1.99
Western Samoa	1.96
Republic of Palau	1.67

currencies will provide employment multipliers of different magnitudes. A more sensible way of making international comparisons of employment multipliers is to express them as a ratio of total employment generated to direct employment. Examples of this latter type of employment multiplier are shown in Table 5.8.

Table 5.8 shows that in Jamaica, for every new full-time employee directly employed as a result of an increase in tourist expenditure, a further 4.61 full-time equivalent job opportunities are created throughout the Jamaican economy. Again, we can see that the more developed the tourism economy, the larger the employment multiplier.

THE POLICY IMPLICATIONS OF MULTIPLIER ANALYSIS

Tourism multipliers measure the present economic performance of the tourism industry and the short-term economic effects of a change in the level or pattern of tourism expenditure. They are particularly suitable for studying the impact of tourist expenditure on business turnover, incomes, employment, public sector revenue and the **balance of payments**.

In the 1970s some economists argued strongly in favour of rejecting multiplier analysis as an appropriate technique for studying impact on the grounds that these models yield 'no useful guideline to policy-makers as regards the merits of tourism compared with alternatives' (Bryden, 1973, p. 217), yet a number of writers have shown that this is precisely the type of information which multiplier analysis can provide in a short-term context. For example, Diamond (1976) used an input–output model of the Turkish economy to measure sectoral output multipliers (for tourism and other sectors) in relation to four policy objectives that reflected Turkish planning priorities. His work demonstrated that multiplier analysis deals effectively with problems associated with short-term **resource allocation**.

MINI CASE STUDY 5.2
Tourism's contribution to global prosperity

INTRODUCTION

The growth of tourism activity throughout the last century has been phenomenal. As we start the twenty-first century tourism is universally acknowledged to be one of the world's largest industry. However, its significance for any given country can be measured using a variety of indicators such as:

- Tourism receipts as a percentage of gross national product.
- Tourism receipts as a percentage of export earnings.
- Tourism employment as a percentage of total employment.

In order to provide a framework for consistency the United Nations and the World Tourism Organization approved the recommendations and guidelines that set out the methodology known as 'tourism satellite accounts' in 2000.

TOURISM SATELLITE ACCOUNTS

This methodology provides an all-embracing approach to estimating and examining the size of the tourism industry. The aims of the tourism satellite accounts strategy were declared by the WTO to be:

- to increase and improve knowledge of tourism's relationship to overall economic activity in a given country;
- to provide an auxiliary instrument for designing more efficient policies in specific areas; and
- to create awareness among the various players not directly involved with tourism, of the quantitative importance of this industry (in monetary and physical terms) and by extension its role as an important economic factor in all the industries that produce the goods and services demanded by visitors.

Source: WTO, 2000b

The WTO went on to suggest that in order for tourism measurements to be credible they had to be based upon ongoing statistics and that they had to be comparable (in time and space) and consistent (i.e. conform to universally accepted accounting practices).

MEASURING TOURISM ACTIVITY

Given the wide range of tourism activity indicators that have evolved over the years, it would seem eminently sensible that a framework should be constructed that will achieve comparability over time and between countries. If such a structure can be built around the industries' manifold activities it would bring a greater sense of meaning to the statistics that are presented.

DISCUSSION QUESTIONS

1 Why do we need to measure tourism's economic activity?

2 If the individual components that make up the data required to create a set of tourism satellite accounts are examined it can be seen that, even with a standardised system in place (and adhered to) there are many problems in achieving consistency. What are these flaws and how can they be addressed?

3 The data that are used to construct the satellite accounts are, in practice, variable from destination to destination and sometimes foreign data and relationships are 'imported' to fill information gaps. Is this a valid way of filling information gaps and what are the dangers of adopting this approach?

However, resource allocation is not the primary use of multiplier analysis. The technique is most frequently used to examine short-term economic impacts where policy objectives other than the efficiency of resource allocation are considered important. A detailed input–output or CGE model, for example, can yield valuable information about the structure of an economy, the degree to which sectors within the economy are dependent upon each other, the existence of possible supply constraints and the relative capital and labour intensities of each sector.

Detailed multiplier models are suitable for:

- analysing the national or regional effects of public or private sector investment in tourism projects;

- simulating the economic impact, sector by sector, of any proposed tourism developments;

- examining the relative magnitudes of the impacts made by different types of tourism and by tourism compared with other sectors of the economy; and

- identifying the optimal tourism mix (those associated with relatively high net benefits)

For instance, a tourism input–output study of Jamaica examined the economic impact of tourism expenditure by purpose of visit, winter or summer visit, first and repeat visit in order to determine which tourists generated the highest level of income, employment and government revenue per unit of expenditure. This type of information can be used to target future marketing in order to maximise the desired benefits derived from tourism activity.

CONCLUSION

The economic impact of tourism on a host economy is generally positive but also carries with it some negative aspects. The literature is biased towards the positive aspects of economic impacts. It is important to establish how significant tourism spending is to an economy because this allows policy makers and planners to determine dependency and to develop strategies for the future. Of particular note is the fact that tourism spending tends to take place between the richer, industrialised countries rather than between industrialised and non-industrialised countries.

Tourism satellite accounts have been derived in order to present a clearer picture of the economic significance of tourism to a given destination. Built along similar lines to national accounts such tables provide insight into the contribution that tourism makes towards gross national product and the proportion of demand that is attributable to tourism activity. Such tables tend to be based around input–output models in order to provide an accurate picture. However, they are not impact models and further analyses are required in order to determine optimal policy decisions.

There have been a variety of attempts to develop models that will estimate the economic impact of tourism but only the *ad hoc*, input–output and CGE models are of sufficient accuracy and of policy use. The input–output and CGE methods provide the most comprehensive picture of tourism's economic impacts and also information that is useful to the tourism development planners. However, these models are also the most expensive type of impact model. The input–output methodology provides income, employment and government revenue multipliers as well as demonstrating the import requirements per unit of tourist spending. All of these different forms of economic impacts can be estimated at the direct, direct plus indirect and direct plus indirect plus induced levels of impact. This information has been successfully used to target market segments in order to enhance the economic benefits associated with tourist spending. Recent developments in the estimation of tourism impact analyses includes the combining of economic, environmental and social impact models with forecasting techniques in order to provide a comprehensive planning tool. There are weaknesses associated with economic impact models but most of these can be alleviated by the adoption of various procedures.

Self-check questions

1 Identify two policy areas that can be informed by knowing the (a) economic significance and (b) the economic impact of tourism?

2 Identify five different methods used to measure the economic impact of tourism.

3 Identify five different multipliers that can be derived from economic impact models.

4 What are the three different levels of economic impact in an economy?

5 What are the major areas of weaknesses in economic impact models?

Essay questions

1 Can tourism satellite accounts provide meaningful information for policy makers that cannot be provided by economic impact models?

2 Examine the relative advantages and disadvantages of each of the major types of tourism economic impact models.

3 What are the limitations and weaknesses of existing tourism economic impact models and how may some of them be overcome?

4 Given the reliability of tourism related statistics is it realistic to believe that the adoption of tourism satellite accounts will achieve the consistency and comparability that is the prime objective underlying their implementation?

5 What is the relationship between tourism satellite accounts and tourism economic impact models?

Annotated further reading

Books

Bull, A. (1998) *The Economics of Travel and Tourism*, Longman, Sydney.
An introductory text that covers many aspects relating to the economics of tourism.

Jafari, J. (2001) *The Encyclopedia of Tourism*, Routledge, London.
A comprehensive volume with definitive statements on every tourism term written by the leading expert in each field.

Sinclair, T. and Stabler, M. (1997) *The Economics of Tourism*, Routledge, London.
A text that covers a broad range of economic aspects relating to tourism.

Articles

Dwyer, L., Forsyth, P., Spurr, R. and VanHo, T. (2003) 'Tourism's contribution to a state economy: a multi-regional general equilibrium analysis', *Tourism Economics* 9(4), 431–48.
An examination of a recent multiplier application.

Frechtling, D. (1999) 'The tourism satellite account: foundations, progress and issues', *Tourism Management* 20(1), 163–70.
This article outlines the concepts and coverage of TSA and how it expands the scope of traditional tourism analysis. It outlines how the results may be employed in these analyses and explores the major issues of developing the TSA concepts and measurement techniques.

Jones, C., Munday, M. and Roberts, A. (2003) 'Regional tourism satellite accounts: a useful policy tool?', *Urban Studies* 40(13), 2777–94.
The authors examine some of the methodological difficulties in constructing a TSA at the regional level and the implications for deriving an effective tourism policy from such models.

1

Web sites

http://www.world-tourism.org

The World Tourism Organization provides an overview of the current state of international tourism through its tourism highlights as well as a catalogue of its publications and online data. In addition it provides viewpoints and summaries on a variety of tourism issues.

http://www.world-tourism.org/sustainable/concepts.htm
WTO Manila Declaration, 1980.

www.oecd.org

The OECD web site provides information relating to the economic indicators relating to OECD members it also provides information on a variety of economic policies.

References cited and bibliography

Archer, B.H. (1976) 'The anatomy of a multiplier', *Regional Studies* **10**, 71–7.

Archer, B.H. (1982) 'The value of multipliers and their policy implications', *Tourism Management* **3**(2), 236–41.

Archer, B.H. and Fletcher, J.E. (1990) *Multiplier Analysis*, Les Cahiers du Tourisme, Series C, No. 130, April.

Archer, B.H. and Owen, C. (1971) 'Towards a tourist regional multiplier', *Regional Studies* **5**, 289–94.

Bryden, J.M. (1973) *Tourism and Development: A Case Study in the Commonwealth Caribbean*, Cambridge University Press, Cambridge.

Cooper, A. and Wilson, A. (2002) 'Extending the relevance of TSA research for the UK: general equilibrium and spillover analysis', *Tourism Economics* **8**(1), 5–38.

Diamond, J. (1976) 'Tourism and development policy: a quantitative appraisal,' *Bulletin of Economic Research* **28**(1), 36–50.

Dwyer, L., Forsyth, P., Spurr, R. and VanHo, T. (2003) 'Tourism's contribution to a state economy: a multi-regional general equilibrium analysis', *Tourism Economics* **9**(4), 431–48.

Fletcher, J.E. (1989) 'Input–output analysis and tourism impact studies', *Annals of Tourism Research* **16**(4), 541–56.

Fletcher, J.E. and Archer, B.H. (1991) 'The development and application of multiplier analysis', pp. 28–47 in Cooper, C. (ed.), *Progress in Tourism, Recreation and Hospitality Management*, Vol. 3, Belhaven, London.

Fletcher, J.E. and Snee, H.R. (1985) 'The service industries and input–output analysis', *Service Industries Review* **2**(1), 51–79.

Leontief, W. (1966) *Input–Output Economics*, Oxford University Press, New York.

Milne, S.S. (1987) 'Differential multipliers', *Annals of Tourism Research* **14**(4), 499–515.

Miller, R. (2002) Preface to Cooper, A. and Wilson, A., *Tourism Economics* **8**(1), 5–38.

OECD (2001) *National Accounts*, OECD, Paris.

Sinclair, M.T. and Sutcliffe, C.M.S. (1982) 'Keynesian income multipliers with first and second round effects: an application to tourist expenditure', *Oxford Bulletin of Economics and Statistics* **44**(4), 321–38.

TCSP (1992) *The Economic Impact of International Tourism on the National Economy of Fiji*, a report published by the Tourism Council for the South Pacific, Suva, Fiji.

Wanhill, S.R.C. (1988) 'Tourism multipliers under capacity constraints', *Service Industries Journal* **8**(1), 136–42.

WTO (1980a) *Manila Declaration on World Tourism*, WTO, Madrid.

WTO (1980b) *Tourism and Employment: Enhancing the Status of Tourism Professions*, WTO, Madrid.

WTO (1988) *Yearbook of Tourism Statistics*, WTO, Madrid.

WTO (1992, 1997, 2002a) *Yearbook of Tourism Statistics*, WTO, Madrid.

WTO (2000b) *The Tourism Satellite Account (TSA): A Strategic Project for the World Tourism Organization*, Report by the Secretary General, Madrid, November 2000.

WTO (2003) *Yearbook of Tourism Statistics*, WTO, Madrid.

MAJOR CASE STUDY 5.1
TOURISM AND DAY VISITORS TO GIBRALTAR

Tourist and day visitor activity in Gibraltar includes staying visitors, cruise ship passengers and daytrippers across the land frontier. Gibraltar has become a shopping destination and the vast majority of visitors (arriving at the land frontier) do so to make purchases from retail outlets. In the year 2001 the total tourist expenditure was £145 million of which more than £85 million was on various forms of shopping.

The average party size of people visiting Gibraltar was just over 1.2 and the average length of stay was 1.3 days. This low average length of stay reflects the dominance of day visitors to the country overall. The day visitor content is also reflected in the fact that the two largest spending categories are shopping and duty free.

Staying visitors (the more traditional form of tourist activity) were responsible for just over £19 million expenditure. Day visitors from across the land frontier were responsible for more than £120 million and the remaining expenditure was split between cruise ship visitors (£4.219 million), yacht visitors (£353,000) and other visitors (£1.564 million). Other visitors were those that were entered as not known on the questionnaires.

Tourist expenditure by port of entry provides a similar picture with the tourist expenditure by each entry point being:

Air	£10.582 million
Sea	£7.113 million
Land	£127.616 million

Total tourist expenditure (£145 million) is associated with the following effects:

Direct income = £41.6 million
Direct plus indirect income = £68.5 million
Direct plus indirect plus induced = £91.5 million

Direct employment = 1,853 FTEs
Direct plus indirect employment = 2,760 FTEs
Direct plus indirect plus induced employment = 3,498 FTEs

(Note: The job and income effects are distributed across all of the sectors of the Gibraltar economy as the effects of tourist expenditure impact on virtually every area of productivity (directly and indirectly).)

Direct government revenue = £9.250 million
Direct plus indirect government revenue = £16.999 million
Direct plus indirect plus induced government revenue = £36.206 million

Direct import requirements = £54.346 million
Direct plus indirect import requirements = £76.077 million
Direct plus indirect plus induced import requirements = £97.046 million

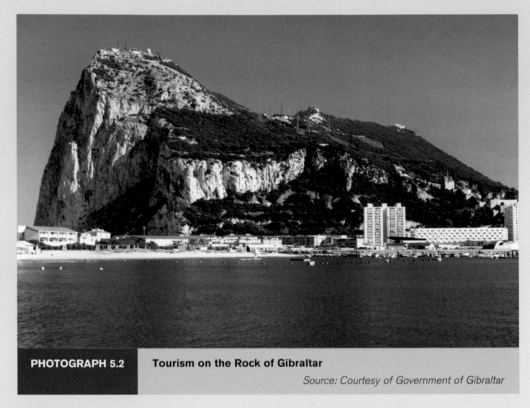

PHOTOGRAPH 5.2   **Tourism on the Rock of Gibraltar**

Source: Courtesy of Government of Gibraltar

The largest single component of tourist expenditure was attributable to those visitors arriving by land, where 7.1 million visitors spent £127.6 million. A major proportion of their total expenditure was on retail shopping. This is clearly a major export for Gibraltar and the direct level of income generated by day visitor spending amounts to £35.338 million, which increases to £58.587 million when the indirect effect is taken into consideration. The induced effect takes the total impact on income levels up to £78.178 million. This level of economic activity directly supports 1,515 FTE job opportunities and the economic activity stimulated by it supports a further 2,299 FTE job opportunities making 2,928 FTEs in total.

The government revenue derived from day visitor spending amounted to £8.239 million at the direct level, £15.035 million at the direct plus indirect level, and £31.417 million at the direct plus indirect plus induced level. The amount of imports required to meet the demands of this activity are £49.486 million directly, this goes up to £68.342 million when the indirect effect is included and up to £86.227 million when the induced effect is included.

THE VALUE OF TOURISM TO THE ECONOMY

Tourism has always been an important source of exports for Gibraltar. However, since the land frontier with Spain has been opened the economy's tourism industry has flourished. Visitors not only come to stay in Gibraltar but they also come as excursionists to explore the sights and heritage and also to shop.

Tourism in Gibraltar has changed beyond recognition compared with its performance in the 1970s and 1980s. The opening of the frontier with Spain has considerably altered both the volume and pattern of tourist spending.

The number of visitors to Gibraltar arriving by air in 1970 was 47,726 (21% of total arrivals). This figure was relatively stable through to the mid-1980s where after it grew rapidly to a peak of 162,438 in 1989 and then fell, just as rapidly down to a low of 66,219 in 1996 after which it has been growing steadily to the current level of visitors (92,535) in 2001 (just 1.27% of total arrivals). In contrast, the number of visitors arriving by sea was relatively stable through the period 1970 (92,943 – 78.7% of total arrivals) to the mid-1990s, but has shown a relatively steady increase from 1997 to the 2001 figure of 145,987 (2.0% of total arrivals). The major impact has been the change in the volume of visitors arriving by land. In 1970 this was zero as the frontier was closed between Gibraltar and Spain. In 1982 with limited access across the border the figure was 46,595 and this figure grew rapidly with the relaxation of border restrictions, to a stable base of 2,260,039 in 1985. Cross-frontier traffic has grown steadily since that time and the 2001 figure was 7,286,648 or 96.7% of total arrivals.

Clearly such a major change in shift away from the proportion of staying visitors arriving by air and sea in favour of day visitors crossing the frontier has changed the pattern of spend associated with visitors to Gibraltar. The volume and value of day visitors across the land frontier dominates the tourism statistics. This can be seen from the various tables shown below where items such as purchases of food and beverage, petrol, other shopping and duty free are significant elements of total expenditure. On the other hand, accommodation costs have become a minor part of the total tourist expenditure pattern.

The breakdown of tourist expenditure by type is shown in Table 5.9: it can be seen that shopping in total accounts for 79% of the total expenditure if the duty free and fuel sales are included under this heading and this further increases to more than 80.0% if the food and beverages bought in shops is included.

Table 5.9 shows how the £145 million total tourist expenditure in 2001 was distributed across the various categories. The importance of shopping and shopping-related activities is clear from this breakdown and once the different types of tourists are examined it can be seen that this influence is from the large number of land-based day visitors.

TABLE 5.9	Total tourist expenditure by category of spend, 2001
	% of total
Accommodation, food and beverage	10.7
Shopping	79.0
Transport etc.	4.8
Other	5.5
Total	**100.0**

189

TABLE 5.10	Staying visitors, 2001	% of total
Accommodation, food and beverage		50.8
Shopping		26.0
Transport etc.		5.6
Other		17.6
Total		**100.0**

STAYING VISITORS

Staying visitors in general spend around half of their total expenditure on accommodation and meals. Gibraltar is not an exception to this rule and some 50.8% of total spending was attributable to these two categories (see Table 5.10).

DAY VISITORS

The dominance of the day visitor to Gibraltar means that the total expenditure pattern of all tourists to Gibraltar reflects the day visitor pattern. It is a quite distinct pattern with shopping accounting for more than 87% of total spend. Given the volume of day trip visitors to Gibraltar this represents a significant amount of trade (see Table 5.11).

MULTIPLIER VALUES

The multiplier values associated with each form of economic activity within the Gibraltar economy are set out in Table 5.12. These are partial multiplier values in that they reflect the ability of each sector to generate output, income, and government revenue. These values should not be viewed judgementally. Variations between the direct, indirect and induced levels of income, government revenue or import impacts associated with one unit of output can be a result of many factors including the nature of the production function. For instance, the construction industry has a relatively high propensity to import because it imports the majority of its material inputs and these account for a large proportion of its total inputs. However, other sectors may import through wholesalers and this is reflected in the high import value of the wholesale sector. Labour-intensive sectors are likely to have higher than average income effects and those sectors that attract particular taxes and excise duties may be associated with high government revenue multipliers.

TABLE 5.11	Tourist expenditure, day visitors to Gibraltar, 2001
	% of total
Accommodation, food and beverage	4.5
Shopping	87.5
Transport etc.	4.4
Other	3.6
Total	**100.0**

Table 5.12 shows the direct plus indirect plus induced multiplier values, by sector within Gibraltar in 2000. As production functions and spending patterns tend to change slowly over time the values shown may be considered to be valid for up to a decade (assuming no drastic changes are made to the economic structure). The multiplier values associated with external trade may be considered to be complete multipliers and will differ to those shown in Table 5.12.

The income multiplier for tourism expenditure, at 0.6294 places Gibraltar in the lower half of the small island economies (0.39 to 1.59) range of income multipliers shown in Table 5.6. This is not surprising given the very small size of Gibraltar (see Table 5.13).

TABLE 5.12	Direct plus indirect plus induced multipler values (partial)			
Sector	Output	Income	Gov. rev.	Imports
Manufacturing	1.5259	0.8048	0.2343	0.6328
Electricity and water	2.1047	0.9495	0.3257	0.6478
Construction	1.5403	0.4925	0.2317	0.8375
Wholesale	1.4430	0.4976	0.2740	0.7186
Retail	1.6683	0.5639	0.2429	0.7019
Hotels	2.1224	0.9761	0.3167	0.4873
Restaurants	2.0259	1.0158	0.3057	0.4491
Transport	1.3677	0.5113	0.1446	0.6854
Communications	1.7403	0.8690	0.3711	0.5726
Financial services	1.3179	0.6697	0.1001	0.5001
R. est. and business services	1.7782	1.1678	0.3065	0.3551
Govt and welfare services	2.1806	1.2953	0.5606	0.4835
Other services	1.7425	0.9588	0.3090	0.5532

TABLE 5.13	Direct plus indirect plus induced multiplier values (complete)			
Sector	Output	Income	Gov. rev.	Imports
Tourism	1.7013	0.6294	0.2492	0.6678
Financial services	1.3179	0.6697	0.1001	0.5001
Other exports	1.4430	0.4976	0.2740	0.7186
Total	1.4657	0.5869	0.2105	0.6341

DISCUSSION QUESTIONS

1 What comparative analyses between the various sectors and types of final demand can you undertake given the above information?

2 Why do the complete multipliers differ from the partial multipliers?

3 What policy implications can be derived with respect to staying versus day visitors?

4 What limitations and words of caution should be applied to the results shown above?

5 What other information do you need to make the above more useful for the policy makers?

CHAPTER SIX
THE ENVIRONMENTAL IMPACT OF TOURISM

INTRODUCTION

Any form of industrial development will bring with it impacts upon the physical environment in which it takes place. In view of the fact that tourists must visit the place of production in order to consume the output, it is inevitable that tourism activity will be associated with environmental impacts. The identification of the need to follow an environmentally compatible pattern of tourism development is now well into its third decade but in spite of the fact that environmental issues are high profile, little has been achieved to ensure that future developments are environmentally sound.

LEARNING OUTCOMES

The objective of this chapter is to provide you with:

- an understanding of the physical impacts of tourism on the environment, both direct and indirect, positive and negative;

- a review of strategies and techniques that may be implemented to measure and quantify the impacts of tourism on the environment such as environmental impacts assessment;

- an appreciation of the difficulties of assessing environmental impacts; and

- real-life examples to encourage the application of theory to practice.

ENVIRONMENTAL IMPACT

At the end of the 1970s the **OECD** set out a framework for the study of environmental stress created by tourism activities. This framework highlighted four main categories of stressor activities including permanent environmental restructuring (major construction works such as highways, airports and resorts); waste product generation (biological and non-biological waste which can damage fish production, create health hazards and detract from the attractiveness of a destination); direct environmental stress caused by tourist activities (destruction of coral reefs, vegetation, dunes, etc. by the presence and activities of tourists); effects on the population dynamics (migration, increased urban densities accompanied by declining populations in other rural areas).

In 1992, the United Nations Conference on the Environment and Development, held in Rio de Janeiro, added further impetus to a debate that was growing stale and a new maxim emerged where 'Only whatever can be sustained by nature and society in the long term is permissible'. This new impetus was given the title **Agenda 21** to reflect the fact that it was a policy statement aimed at taking the world into the twenty-first century. What made Agenda 21 significant was the fact that it represented the first occasion when a comprehensive programme of environmental actions was agreed to be adopted by 182 governments. The Agenda was based around a framework of themes that were aimed at providing an overall strategy to transform global activity onto a more sustainable course. The matters addressed within Agenda 21 were not solely environmental because they included aspects such as human development and the redressing of the imbalance between rich and poor nations. However, many of the matters discussed and the strategies recommended were environmentally based.

Now in the twenty-first century and in spite of the programme's elegance and simplicity, the adoption of this maxim requires enforcement that is still far beyond the reach of most legislative frameworks and none of the recommendations made in Agenda 21 were legally binding to the 182 nations that approved its adoption. Furthermore, the implementation of this maxim requires that those charged with the construction of the necessary legislative framework be fully informed of the environmental repercussions of productive and consumptive activities. To date this is not the case. The literature on the environmental impacts of tourism is often biased, painting highly negative pictures of tourism with respect to its associated environmental impacts. In this chapter we examine the nature of environmental impacts, how they can be identified and measured and how this information can be integrated into the tourism planning process.

Tourism and the environment

The environment, whether it is natural or artificial, is the most fundamental ingredient of the tourism product. However, as soon as tourism activity takes place, the environment is inevitably changed or modified either to facilitate tourism or through the tourism production process. Environmental preservation and improvement programmes are now an integral part of many **development strategies** and such considerations are treated with much greater respect than they were during the first two-thirds of the last century. Relatively little research has been undertaken within a standardised framework to analyse tourism's impact on the environment. The **empirical studies** that have taken place have been very specific case studies – such as the impact of tourism on the wildlife of Africa, the pollution of water in the Mediterranean or studies of particular coastal areas and mountains. But the diverse areas studied, the varying methods used to undertake those studies and the wide range of tourism activities involved makes it difficult to bring these findings together in order to assemble a comprehensive standardised framework within which to work.

In order to study the physical impact of tourism it is necessary to establish:

- the physical impacts created by tourism activity as opposed to other activities;

- what conditions were like before tourism activity took place in order to derive a baseline from which comparisons can be made;

- an inventory of flora and fauna, together with some unambiguous index of tolerance levels to the types of impact created by different sorts of tourism activity; and

- the secondary levels of environmental impact that are associated with tourism activity.

The environmental impacts associated with tourism development, just like the economic impacts, can be considered in terms of their direct, indirect and induced effects. Again some of the impacts can be positive and some negative. It is not possible to develop tourism without incurring environmental impacts, but it is possible, with correct planning, to manage tourism development in order to minimise the negative impacts while encouraging the positive impacts.

Positive environmental impacts

On the positive side, the direct environmental impacts associated with tourism include:

- the preservation/restoration of ancient monuments, sites and historic buildings, such as the Great Wall of China (PRC), the Pyramids (Egypt), the Taj Mahal (India), Stonehenge and Warwick Castle (UK);

- the creation of national parks and wildlife parks, such as Yellowstone Park (USA), the Amboseli National Park and the Maasai Mara National Reserve (Kenya), Las Canadas (Tenerife), the Pittier National Park (Venezuela), Fjord Land National Park (New Zealand);

- protection of reefs and beaches, the Great Barrier Reef (Australia), Grand Anse (Grenada); and

- the maintenance of forests such as the New Forest (UK), Colo I Suva (Fiji).

Conservation and **preservation** may be rated highly from the point of view of researchers, or even the tourists. However, if such actions are not considered to be of importance from the hosts' point of view, it may be questionable as to whether they can be considered to be positive environmental impacts. When evaluating the net worth of preservation and conservation activities the opportunity costs associated with such activities must also be taken into account. African wildlife parks, such as Etosha National Park in Namibia, may result in the grazing lands of nomadic tribes being limited and hence constrain food production capability.

Negative environmental impacts

On the negative side, tourism may have direct environmental impacts on the quality of water, air and noise levels. Sewage disposal into water will add to pollution problems, as will the use of powered boats on inland waterways and sheltered seas. Increased usage of the internal combustion engine for tourist transport, oil burning to provide the power for hotel's air conditioning and refrigeration units all add to the diminution of air quality. Noise levels may be dramatically increased in urban areas through nightclubs and other forms of entertainment as well as by increased road, rail and air traffic.

Physical deterioration of both natural and built environments can have serious consequences:

- hunting and fishing have obvious impacts on the wildlife environment;

- sand dunes can be damaged and eroded by over-use;

- vegetation can be destroyed by walkers;

- camp fires may destroy forests;

- ancient monuments may be disfigured and damaged by graffiti, eroded or literally taken away by tourists (the Byzantine Fort in Paphos, Cyprus, for instance is a World Heritage Site subject to pilfering);

- the construction of a tourism superstructure utilises real estate and may detract from the aesthetics; and

- the improper disposal of litter can detract from the aesthetic quality of the environment and harm wildlife.

Examples of direct negative environmental impacts include:

- the erosion of paths to the Pyramids at Giza, Egypt by the camels used to transport tourists;

- the dynamiting of Balaclava Bay (Mauritius) to provide a beach for tourist use; and

- the littering of Base Camp on Mount Everest, Nepal by tourists and the erosion of the pathway to this site.

The building of high-rise hotels on beach frontages is an environmental impact of tourism that achieves headline status. This kind of obvious environmental rape is now less common than it was during the rapid growth periods of the 1960s and

1970s. In a number of countries, particularly island economies, the issue of land usage is often high on the agenda of planning meetings. Regulations have been introduced to restrict beachfront developments to a height no greater than that of the palm trees (as for example in Mauritius), or restrict development to a certain distance back from the beach (as in some parts of India).

Tourism activities can put scarce natural resources, such as water, under severe pressure. Tourists tend to be far more extravagant with their use of water than they are at home with estimates of up to 440 litres per person per day being made for areas around the Mediterranean. To put this into context, this is up to twice the normal usage of residents in urban areas of Spain or Italy. Some activities, swimming pools, golf courses require intensive use of these scarce resources and the latter can add further to the environmental impacts if fertilisers and weeding chemicals are used. Tourism Concern have estimated that the average golf course in tropical countries like Thailand requires 1500 kg of fertilisers, pesticides and other treatments per annum and use the same amount of water that would be consumed by approximately 60,000 village residents. Similar physical depletion can be witnessed in terms of deforestation as trees are cleared for land use and fuel.

Tourism is responsible for high levels of air and noise pollution through the transportation networks and leisure activities. Air transport is claimed to be a significant factor in global warming and tourism is responsible for the vast majority of international air transport. At the local level air transport near urban areas can cause severe pollution problems along with ground transport systems such as tour buses that use up resources in an attempt to maintain climate control for their passengers. Other forms of transport, such as jet skis, quad bikes and snowmobiles can create excessive noise pollution in coastal areas, national parks and areas of outstanding natural beauty. The noise from snowmobiles (particularly the older models) can be really intrusive when the area is a place of natural beauty. For instance, at the Yellowstone National Park the *Idaho News* reported that a survey showed that snowmobile noise could be heard for 70% of the time available at 11 out of 13 sampling sites. This noise and the pollution from snowmobiles adds further pressure on the wildlife and vegetation. Furthermore, the construction of additional roads and car parking facilities encroaches on wildlife habitats and the pollution from vehicles can be so severe that at times areas such as Yosemite Valley are enshrouded in smog and not visible from the air. The smog is harmful to all species of animal and vegetable (**UNEP**, 2004). The problems associated with littering (such as the high profile given to the littering by tourists at Base Camp on Mount Everest) present significant danger to wildlife as well as being unsightly and expensive to clear. Similarly, solid waste disposal, if not undertaken properly, can be a major despoiler of the environment in coastal areas, rivers, lakes and roadsides. Such pollution can also give rise to serious health risks to humans as well as wildlife. *Our Planet* magazine reported that the wider Caribbean region received 63,000 port calls from ships on an annual basis and that this activity alone resulted in 82,000 tons of rubbish. Given that cruise ships are responsible for 77% of the total waste generated this represents a major pollution problem for the islands where the cruise ship passengers create more than four times the daily rubbish than their local resident counterparts (*Our Planet* (UNEP) volume 10, no. 3).

It is also important to note that many environmental factors are interdependent – often in ways that are not yet fully understood. Damage to coral reefs by divers, cruise ship anchors, or through the construction of coastal developments will reduce the local diversity and population of fish and other creatures that may feed off the coral. This, in turn, may reduce the numbers of birds that feed on the fish and so on. In order to determine the full impact of environmental changes accurately, the **ecological system** and the way in which it responds to environmental stress must be understood.

The effect of any loss to **biological diversity** is an increased threat to the food chain, can imbalance species, soil formation and result in less ability to absorb greenhouse gases. A loss of biodiversity also hinders nature's ability to withstand the natural shocks caused by droughts, earthquakes, floods and hurricanes. Finally, it reduces the enjoyment that tourists experience when visiting areas by reducing the variety and wealth of flora and fauna available.

MINI CASE STUDY 6.1
Tourism and the environment: enemies or allies?

NAIROBI, 4 February 1999

Dr Richard Leakey, Director of the Kenya Wildlife Service, will today chair a round table to be attended by participants at the twentieth Governing Council session of the United Nations Environment Programme (UNEP) at its headquarters in Gigiri. The panellists will discuss the challenges of sustainable tourism and the approach needed to develop tourism while protecting and maintaining a healthy environment.

Richard Leakey will be joined by Jacqueline Aloisi de Larderel, the Director of UNEP's Division of Technology, Industry and Economics located in Paris.

'Putting tourism on a sustainable path is a major challenge, requiring partnership and cooperation within the tourism industry, and between the industry, governments and tourists themselves', said Klaus Toepfer, UNEP's Executive Director. 'To catalyse appropriate action UNEP, jointly with other international organisations, is promoting the definition and development of sustainable tourism through the publication of guidelines and handbooks, the exchange of successful experiences and the support of demonstration projects', he said.

The tourism industry commands an annual investment in capital projects of over $800 billion and ranks as a main sector of the world economy. It accounts for almost 11% of gross domestic product and is growing at an average rate of 4% yearly. With such a growth rate, increasing attention is being paid to the effect of tourism on the environment.

The effects of tourism on the environment are felt in several ways: resources are utilised to provide for the everyday comforts of visitors; utilisation of materials to produce souvenirs and destruction of the natural environment is caused by an influx of tourists. There is the pollution generated by tourists: discharge of untreated sewage into seas and rivers, carbon dioxide and nitrous oxide emissions from transport. There is also the impact of changes upon the social and cultural life of a country; the necessity to provide accommodation to support the tourism sector resulting in increased allocation of lands, sometimes in areas where the natural environment is irrevocably changed.

But there are numerous positive effects: countries receive the added revenue from the tourism industry; jobs are created; artisans find a booming market for their products and modern facilities and infrastructure are created which are beneficial to native populations.

In order for tourism to benefit important sectors of society and be sustainable, it must create a balance that takes account of the consumption patterns within the areas mentioned. Resource consumption and waste generation present a greater challenge to developing countries which do not have the technology to minimise their impact on societies. Threats generated by tourism are felt in both developed and developing countries. Resource consumption and waste generation are not easily handled by developing countries. Activities generate pollution: discharge of untreated sewage into seas and rivers, carbon dioxide and nitrous oxide emissions from transport and solid wastes all result in increased pressure on the environment of tourist sites.

It is important that all partners in the tourism sector adequately share the benefits that derive from tourism. A strong alliance should be forged for the tourism industry and the environment to enjoy a healthy coexistence in the future. In this regard, eco-tourism must not only be a conveniently used term it but must be meaningful. Eco-labelling is certainly not enough.

Source: News and Press Releases, United Nations Environment Programme GRID-Arendal, February 1999 (and see www.unep.org)

DISCUSSION QUESTIONS

The panel had to consider the following questions – give your viewpoint on each and justify your views.

1 How can societies ensure a more balanced distribution of the income generated from this booming industry?

2 Is eco-labelling the answer?

3 Should a percentage of profits from tourism businesses be earmarked for environmental conservation/development that will benefit the local population?

4 Are certification schemes needed to monitor eco-labelling?

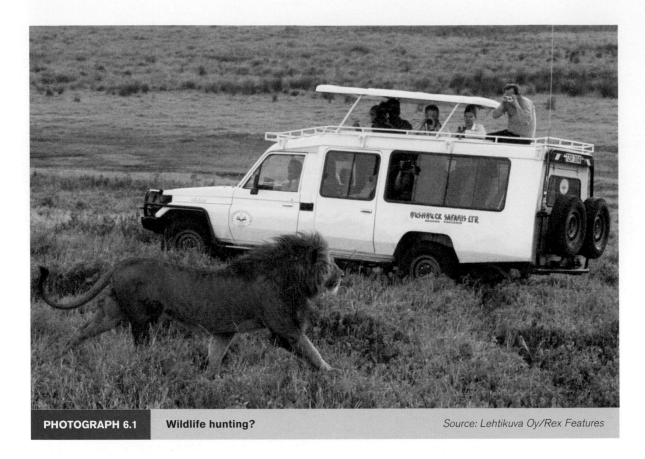

PHOTOGRAPH 6.1   **Wildlife hunting?**   *Source: Lehtikuva Oy/Rex Features*

ENVIRONMENTAL IMPACT ASSESSMENT

There are no generally accepted models for environmental impact assessment (EIA). In many environmentally sensitive tourism destinations the need for EIAs has become more frequent and expected when considering tourism development and its relationship with the environment. Many countries have now incorporated the need for EIAs within their planning legislation but even the absence of legislation to support environmental planning should not deter tourism planners from undertaking their own environmental impact assessment on proposed developments. Environmental protection is so much easier and less costly than environmental correction even when such remedial action is possible.

It is important to understand the motivation that underlies a particular environmental impact assessment before an appropriate methodology is selected. For instance, an EIA may be undertaken in order to determine a development's impact upon a specific ecology or even upon a single 'rare' species. This type of assessment may not require the evaluation of the environmental impacts in monetary terms. However, other EIAs may be instigated for the express purpose of determining the financial implications of environmental correction in order to reflect accurately the net economic returns of tourism activity or in an attempt to retrieve some of these costs from the industry. Furthermore, EIAs may be required in order to compare alternative developments in order to allocate resources in a manner that maximises the economic benefits of development while minimising the negative environmental impacts. In this case there is a need to take a general equilibrium approach which enables the researcher to compare and contrast development options not only between various tourism strategies but also between different industrial structures.

Finally, EIAs may be required simply to raise the profile of environmental issues. That is, future developments should not be evaluated solely in economic terms but in a more holistic manner that includes the effects upon the local environment. This approach allows the democratic processes of development choice to be fully informed. It also highlights the fact that environmental impacts and environmental audits should become a way of life for business organisations as well as governments and individuals.

Once the environmental consequences of our actions are recognised this information can be incorporated at every decision-making level to ensure the effective use of the planet's finite resources. Environmental awareness during the production and consumption processes may also bring long-term economic and social benefits. For instance, the effective use of scarce resources, particularly energy-related resources, can result in lower marginal costs of production. On the other hand, the careless or reckless use of resources during either the production or consumption processes can add to social resentment of tourism development. This may hinder future development and will certainly detract from the effective use of resources.

In spite of the fact that there is no single accepted framework for conducting EIAs, the true scope of environmental impacts should not be underestimated. Most forms of industrial development impact upon land use, energy consumption and other direct forms of physical impacts. However, to assess the overall environmental impact it is necessary to take into account the consequential impacts occasioned by the direct productive activity. In the same way that the economic impacts associated with tourism development can be direct and indirect, the same must be said for environmental impacts. If tourism activity requires the production of output from a diverse range of industries, including those that do not supply tourist goods and services directly, then the environmental impact associated with the output and production processes of these supporting industries should also be included in the overall evaluation. For example, if the level of tourism increases, and this causes hotels to increase their purchases from the building and construction industry, then the environmental damage created by that increased building and construction must also be included. This is also true with respect to the effects of the quarries that supply the builders and the transport system that facilitates it.

In some areas attempts have been made to construct tourism/environment balance sheets to assess the net effect of tourism development with respect to the environment. One such approach for Scotland concluded that tourism is an important sector of the Scottish economy and that, although there are widespread environmental impacts associated with tourism activity, they were only regarded as being serious in a few specific locations and that careful management could overcome these problems. In 1991 the UK Department of Employment set up a task force to examine the relationship between tourism and the environment in England and the report published under this same title supported the major views expressed by the Scottish Tourism Coordinating Group. However, this suggests that in places where the environmental impacts are serious over a wider range of areas then careful management may not be able to overcome these problems. In this latter case it may be questionable as to whether tourism development should be considered at all.

THE EIA PROCESS

It is important to identify environmental impacts associated with tourism development at an early stage because:

- it is easier to avoid environmental damage by either modifying or rejecting developments than it is to rectify environmental damage once a project has been implemented; and

- projects that rely heavily upon areas of outstanding beauty may become non-viable if such developments degrade the environment.

There is a variety of methods that may be used for EIA including checklists and network systems, but generally the EIA is a process that enables researchers to predict the environmental consequence associated with any proposed development project. To draw up a checklist of environmental impacts it is necessary to establish what potential impacts can occur as a result of tourism activity and Green's checklist is a fine example of the scope of what is involved.

GREEN'S CHECKLIST OF THE ENVIRONMENTAL IMPACTS CAUSED BY TOURISM

The natural environment

(a) Changes in floral and faunal species composition
- Disruption of breeding habits
- Killing of animals through hunting
- Killing of animals in order to supply goods for the souvenir trade
- Inward or outward migration of animals
- Destruction of vegetation through the gathering of wood or plants
- Change in extent and/or nature of vegetation cover through clearance or planting to accommodate tourism facilities
- Creation of a wildlife reserve/sanctuary

(b) Pollution
- Water pollution through discharges of sewage, spillage of oil/petrol
- Air pollution from vehicle emissions
- Noise pollution from tourist transportation and activities

(c) Erosion
- Compaction of soils causing increased surface run-off and erosion
- Change in risk of occurrence of land slips/slides
- Change in risk of avalanche occurrence
- Damage to geological features (e.g. tors, caves)
- Damage to river banks

(d) Natural resources

- Depletion of ground and surface water supplies

- Depletion of fossil fuels to generate energy for tourist activity

- Change in risk of occurrence of fire

(e) Visual impact

- Facilities (e.g. buildings, chairlifts, car parks)

- Litter

The built environment

(a) Urban environment

- Land taken out of primary production

- Change of hydrological patterns

(b) Visual impact

- Growth of the built-up area

- New architectural styles

- People and belongings

(c) Infrastructure

- Overload of infrastructure (roads, railways, car parking, electricity grid, communications systems, waste disposal, and water supply)

- Provision of new infrastructure

- Environmental management to adapt areas for tourist use (e.g. sea walls, land reclamation)

(d) Urban form

- Changes in residential, retail or industrial land uses (move from houses to hotels/boarding houses)

- Changes to the urban fabric (e.g. roads, pavements)

- Emergence of contrasts between urban areas developed for the tourist population and those for the host population

(e) Restoration

- Re-use of disused buildings

- Restoration and preservation of historic buildings and sites

- Restoration of derelict buildings as second homes

(f) Competition

- Possible decline of tourist attractions or regions because of the opening of other attractions or a change in tourist habits and preferences

Source: Green et al., 1990 (with permission from Elsevier Science)

In spite of the apparent comprehensiveness of this checklist it is evident that the listed aspects focus primarily on direct tourism activities and development. This is an inadequate approach because the indirect consequences must also be assessed. It is also important that environmental resources should be utilised efficiently. This means not only that they should be effectively used within the tourism industry but that this effectiveness should also be evaluated in relative terms in comparison with alternative economic development strategies. Only then can fully informed and sound rational planning decisions be made.

Once the potential impacts have been considered a checklist consisting of the fundamental elements at risk can be assembled. This checklist can then be used to form the basis of an evaluation matrix which will assess the impact of proposed developments on each of the fundamental elements according to whether the development will have no impact, minor impacts, moderate impacts or major impacts.

An EIA will examine:

- environmental auditing procedures;

- limitations to natural resources;

- environmental problems and conflicts that may affect project viability; and

- possible detrimental effects to people, flora and fauna, soil, water, air, peace and quiet, landscapes, cultural sites, etc. that are either within the proposed project area or will be affected by it.

Figure 6.1 sets out a typical process which an environmental impact assessment would adopt. A proposed development is put forward by a developer and this is initially assessed using the destination's environmental policy document as a performance indicator. Following this initial evaluation the proposal moves forward to site selection and undergoes a preliminary environmental impact assessment. This assessment can then be compared in more detail with the environmental performance indicators identified in the policy legislation/regulations in order to investigate potential conflicts.

Environmental indicators

There is a wide range of environmental indicators that can be used. However, few countries have instigated data collection procedures to monitor these environmental variables. The OECD (2004) provides an ongoing programme that highlights core environmental indicators. The development of harmonised environmental indicators with its member countries is pursued under the belief that there is no one universal set of environmental indicators but rather several sets intended to meet the needs of different purposes and audiences. More emphasis is now given to the conceptual framework of environmental indicators. The framework should include indicators that meet the criteria initially set out by the OECD in 1994 when it subdivided indicators into the following categories:

- climate change and ozone layer depletion;

- **eutrophication**;

- **acidification**;

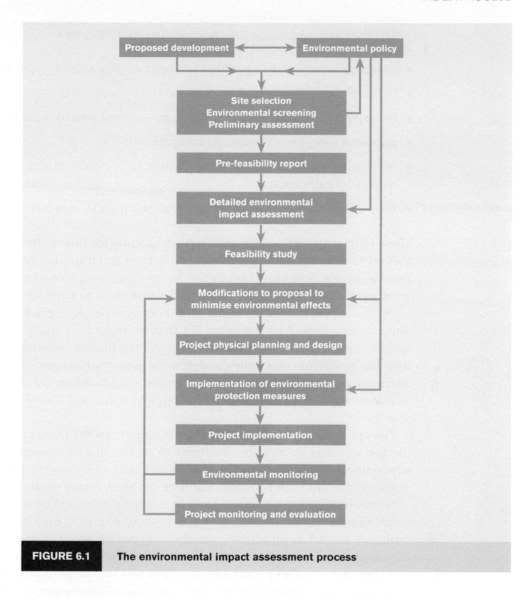

FIGURE 6.1   The environmental impact assessment process

- toxic contamination;

- urban environmental quality;

- biodiversity;

- cultural landscapes;

- waste;

- water resources;

- forest resources;

- fish resources;

- soil degradation;

- material resources; and

- socio-economic, sectoral and general indicators.

The criteria for indicator selection are that they should:

- provide a representative picture of conditions or society's response;
- be simple, easy to interpret and able to show trends over time;
- be responsive to changes in the environment and related human activities;
- provide a basis for international comparisons;
- be either national in scope or applicable to regional environmental issues of national significance; and
- have a threshold or reference value against which to compare it.

These criteria should be expanded further to allow for intersectoral comparisons if they are to facilitate future development planning and the optimum use of resources. Environmental indicators should not be confined to a role of simply measuring what we do, they should also provide information as to what we *should* do.

Once the preliminary assessment has been completed, a pre-feasibility study is undertaken followed by a detailed EIA that attempts to evaluate specific environmental costs and benefits. Again the results of the impact assessment are compared with the environmental policy and, if no serious conflicts arise, the proposal can move forward to a full feasibility study and modifications can be introduced to minimise any negative environmental impacts and bring the project in line with policy.

The physical planning and design of the project can then take place together with the introduction of measures designed to protect the environment in line with environmental policy. At this stage the project can be implemented and the project's development can then be monitored in terms of its future environmental impact.

However, if the EIA is undertaken in order to estimate the economic costs of correcting for the environmental impacts, or to compare the environmental performance of various industries, the above approach requires some modification. To examine impacts within a cohesive framework it is important that economic and environmental indicators are combined within a single model. This approach to EIA has been undertaken by researchers from Bournemouth University (UK) in studies for the government of Mauritius (1994) and the Wales Tourist Board (2002). The integration of economic, environmental and social impacts is essential if tourism strategies and choices are to be well informed and steps taken to prevent tourism development exceeding the carrying capacity of the destination. The Mauritius and Welsh models utilise the economic linkage information acquired during the input–output analysis (see Chapter 5) to provide the framework for estimating the indirect and induced environmental impacts associated with an industry's output level. The model relies only upon quantifiable environmental indicators in order to maintain objectivity. By constructing a set of environmental indicator coefficients that relate output by sector to environmental effects, planners are able to identify the environmental impact of any given change in the pattern or volume of production. The direct, indirect and induced environmental consequences of production in each industry can be assessed in exactly the same way that economic effects are measured. By utilising the economic linkage information to trace the consequential environmental effects of production, the model can provide a uniform framework for comparing not only the different types of tourism activity but also tourism with other forms of industrial activity. The confinement to measurable environmental indicators provides a platform for at least regional and national comparisons, and at best international comparisons. Because of the reliance on quantifiable variables the financial implications of production and consumption can also be estimated. Finally, because such models are constructed as interactive computer-based models, they are ideal for facilitating the **environmental auditing** process required of developments into the future.

ENVIRONMENTAL AUDITING

Unlike EIAs which focus on the effects of any given change in demand, environmental auditing represents a *modus operandi*, an ongoing process of monitoring and evaluation. The major differences between EIAs and environmental auditing are:

- environmental audits are generally voluntary in nature while EIAs tend to be written into the legislature and required as part of the planning approval process;

- environmental audits are part of an ongoing process – even a sense of attitude – rather than the one-off EIA studies; and

- environmental audits are concerned with performance and focus on how well a process is functioning. In this sense the environmental audit should become part of the organisational structure of private and public sector bodies alike.

However, one of these distinguishing features, the voluntary nature of environmental auditing, is also its Achilles' heel. Without the necessary legislation and regulation required to enforce the implementation and quality of environmental auditing, it is unlikely to be an effective environmental protector. Also, because tourism is a fragmented industry with no clear boundaries, the environmental auditing needs to be economy wide rather than solely aimed at tourism establishments. There is also an argument that common standards of environmental audits and performance indicators should be adopted on a universal basis because of the dangers of conflict if different industries pursue different environmental goals. All of these factors point to a single conclusion, namely, that environmental auditing is a macro rather than micro issue and that the distinction between EIAs and environmental auditing is becoming narrower. A more satisfactory solution is to adopt the general equilibrium EIA approach which encompasses all industrial output and consumption and facilitates the identification of consequential as well as direct impacts. In this way the EIA model can be a subset of the environmental audit process and be used to generate relative performance indicators that will act as benchmarks for each of the productive sectors within the economy. Legislation could then be drafted in such a way as to reward businesses that perform better than their industry average, thereby rewarding best practice.

Where environmental legislation and regulations are in force, then environmental auditing should be used to ensure that these legal and planning requirements are fulfilled. Where there are no legal or regulatory requirements, then environmental auditing should still be implemented in order to secure the long-term benefits associated with the effectiveness of appropriate development.

The environmental auditing process involves three distinct aspects:

1 An assessment of the system, how it functions and the implications of its operation.

2 A rigorous testing of the system to see how its performance compares with some optimal ideal or benchmark performance.

3 The certification of the results from the above comparisons.

Environmental auditing can take place at establishment and corporate levels for national and multinational businesses. However, with the recognition by many countries that the public sector has a vested interest in the development of tourism, environmental auditing should not only be incorporated into the legislature for private sector businesses, it should also be part of the operational remit of public sector divisions and departments. The adoption of environmental auditing can effect good use of resources as well as help create a good marketing image.

Finally, neither the public nor the private sector owns the environment. It is important that all of the stakeholders should be consulted when there are any proposals to implement development policies that will impinge or detract from the environmental store. These consultations can take many forms but should be undertaken well in advance of any implementation to allow proper time to consider and evaluate opposition and alternative strategies. The public announcement shown in Figure 6.2 demonstrates how such consultative procedures can be organised. In this example, the proposal for a second airport in Sydney, Australia, was under consideration and the public was being informed of the preparation of an EIA. It is commendable to note that the public were invited to attend preliminary information seminars prior to the release of the draft environmental impact assessment report. The airport development has not gone ahead but the consultation process did open up the forum for debate.

Having transgressed through the 'cautionary platform' of tourism research, the major thrust of experienced researchers is now one of acceptance. That is, there is an acceptance that destinations should not have the ideological stances of 'puritan' researchers imposed upon them. Indeed, destinations should have sovereignty over their own economic and environmental destiny providing that destiny does not impinge upon the destiny of others. Thus, if it is decided that tourism is an appropriate catalyst for economic development, it should not be suffocated under a barrage of concern for environmental conservation. Where tourism researchers can best help these destinations is to provide the framework for environmental auditing so that development may move forward in an optimal manner.

ENVIRONMENTAL ACTION PROGRAMMES

In addition to the development of viable and acceptable environmental impact assessment models, there have been a wide range of environmental initiatives undertaken in order to enhance the net effects of tourist activities and move towards some consideration of environmental sustainability. There are environmental protection agencies located at regional (for example, EU) and national levels

Second Sydney Airport proposal

The Commonwealth Government is assessing Badgerys Creek and the Holsworthy Military Area as potential sites for the Second Sydney Airport. An Environmental Impact Statement is being prepared to consider the impact of these proposals. Preliminary information is available on:

- **Flight Paths** information prepared by Airplan
- **Master Plans**
- **Road and Rail Access to the Sites**
- **Assessing the Impact of Noise**
- **Air Traffic Forecasts** information prepared by
  Commonwealth Department of Transport and Regional Development;

to assist you to understand these proposals. When the Draft EIS has been completed it will be released for public comment.

Come to a preliminary information session prior to the release of the Draft EIS

Helensburgh
Helensburgh Community Centre
Walker Street, Helensburgh
Tuesday 22 July, 6.00 pm – 9.30 pm

Penrith
Penrith Civic Centre
High Street, Penrith
Saturday 26 July, 10.00 am – 2.30 pm

Telephone Information Line: 1800 818 017

HOW TO FIND OUT MORE

- Fax the Community Access Centre on (02) 9600 9741
- Look up the internet at http://www.magnet.com.au/2sydair and e-mail us at 2sydair@magnet.com.au

FIGURE 6.2	**Public announcement for the new Sydney Airport**

Source: Advertisement from the Sun Herald, 6 July 1997, p. 9
© Commonwealth Department of Transport and Regional Development

211

throughout the world and further tiers of agencies at sub-national levels. Within Europe, the European Commission produces policy directives and guidelines in the form of **environmental action programmes** (EAPs) as well as commissioning wide-ranging research projects into the specifics of environmental issues. The latest EAP is the sixth such plan and will direct environmental policy throughout the first decade of this century. The European EAP targets four priority areas for urgent action with seven thematic strategies. These four areas include: climatic change; environment, health and quality of life; natural resources and issues relating to waste; nature and biodiversity. These are very broad areas and are impacted on by tourism in all of its forms. The European Environmental Bureau (EEB) sees the sixth plan as being particularly important in view of the fact that it will oversee the period of enlargement of the EU. These projects range from the sewage and waste disposal problems created by youth tourism in the eastern cantons of Belgium, through the more widely applicable case studies relating to coastal zone management, transport systems to the more specialised analysis of golf tourism and its ecological implications.

Within the USA the EPA provides national environmental policies while state EPAs provide local directives. The US EPA declared role is to protect human health and to safeguard the natural environment. The national agency works to develop regulations and enforce their implementation as well as commissioning research into environmental issues and providing support (policy and financial) to state EPAs.

In spite of the proliferation of environmental protection agencies since the 1980s there is still no consensus on the way that the environment should be protected from the activities of tourism. This in part may be the result of the fact that tourism's environmental impacts tend to be most obvious in specific areas rather than across nations. Unlike its position with respect to agriculture, energy and transport, the EU has so far failed to produce a comprehensive environmental policy with respect to tourism and much of the policy has been left to individual member countries.

Environmental impact assessments (EIAs) and environmental impacts statements (EISs) are studies that estimate the potential or expected environmental impacts of proposed actions or developments. In many countries EIAs or EISs are required (by legislation) for developments that exceed some minimum threshold level. For instance, in Mauritius an EIA is required on any tourism real estate development where there are more than nine tourism bungalows to be built. In Ghana EIAs are required if a planned hotel construction involves more than 40 rooms or if it is to be located within a national park, reserve, hilltop or island. However, the criteria for determining whether or not an EIA or EIS is required vary from always to only when there are significant environmental implications. The vagueness of the latter approach often renders environmental legislation impotent and even when there are detailed criteria there are quite often ways of circumventing the requirement, such as developing multiple adjacent sites where each site may be below the prescribed threshold and yet the development as a whole may vastly exceed that criteria.

To be effective environmental legislation must be enforceable, rigorous and be given as serious consideration as the financial aspects of the proposed development. The WTO produced a tourism and environmental publication in 1992 that illustrated 'an integrated approach to resort development' (Inskeep and Kallenberger, 1992) by referring to six case studies. These case studies covered a wide variety of resorts in Indonesia, the Republic of Korea, Mexico, Dominican Republic, Turkey and the Canary Islands of Spain.

In spite of the range of countries included in the case studies some general conclusions and recommendations could be noted. One major conclusion was that serious environmental problems can be prevented by the adoption of sound planning and development. The recommendations made by the authors encompassed not only the physical needs of integrated planning such as adequate infrastructure, the implementation of appropriate design standards and the need to integrate the resort planning exercise into the local or regional planning process, but also the organisational structures and training of human resources.

However, EIAs and EISs tend to apply to new developments. What can be done to mitigate the damage that is being done by the operation of existing sites? A survey undertaken by the United Nations Environment Programme (UNEP) revealed that more than 100 codes of conduct exist for national tourism organisations, the industry and tourists. For instance, environmental codes of conduct have been adopted by the Tourism Industry Association of Canada and the American

Society of Travel Agents as well as by national bodies and individual companies that are targeting the environmentally aware tourists and/or operating in particularly fragile areas. International organisations such as the World Tourism Organization and the World Travel and Tourism Council also promote environmental codes of conduct to the tourism industry.

While some countries have attempted to create an economic framework that will encourage best practice from an environmental point of view, and examples of these can be found in the national parklands of New Zealand, Africa and the Great Barrier Reef Marine Park of Australia, others have attempted to produce comprehensive environmental guidelines for developers. The WTO, UNEP and the EU have all published guidelines for the development of tourism in protected areas such as national parks.

Finally, some players within the private sector have been notable in their attempts to drive home greater environmental awareness and the pursuit of best practice. Large private sector businesses have adopted environmental management systems which contain four distinct elements:

1 An environmental review – base line impact studies that produce environmental inventories of the businesses activities and functions.

2 An environmental policy – a publicly stated set of identifiable and achievable objectives.

3 The design of an implementation and environmental system – setting out the mechanisms by which the objectives will be pursued.

4 An environmental audit – which can be used to measure the business's actual performance against its declared objectives.

Airlines such as KLM Royal Dutch Airlines and British Airways have been active in a number of ways. The former has been trying to increase the use of public transport by its employees and its customers and the latter has developed a series of environmental awareness events for managers, the creation of the Tourism for Tomorrow Awards programme and the adoption of energy-saving technology for its own activities. American Airlines developed a programme to standardise the approval procedures for chemical products in an attempt to reduce its purchases of environmentally harmful products, and ferry companies, such as P & O European Ferries, developed a cost-effective and environmentally friendly means of disposing of hazardous wastes.

Disney has been effective in forming a committee to evaluate the ways in which freshwater conservation measures can be combined with wastewater re-use and it has also provided its employees with the means to dispose of their personal hazardous wastes such as oils and other household chemicals safely. The European operations of CenterParcs are noted for their car-free resorts which provide a more healthy environment for guests and while the Maya Mountain Tours Company of Belize provides teaching facilities for students and researchers into environmental ethics, the Grecotel hotel chain ensures that all of its staff are trained in environmental issues. The Greek National Tourist Office uses policies of spatial zoning, visitor management plans, financial incentives and awareness campaigns in an attempt to drive home the need for better environmental management.

There are also dangers embodied in the growing awareness of environmental issues. With imperfect information the tourist can easily be misled into believing that specific tourist products are environmentally sound. This may encourage tourists to purchase tour operators' packages that are anything but environmentally friendly.

Finally, it is only the largest of private sector businesses that normally have the expertise and resources to implement their own environmental management systems. Given the fact that the tourism industry is dominated by **SMEs**, the full impact of environmental management systems will be relatively minor.

MINI CASE STUDY 6.2
Eco-tourism in Thailand: the thin end of the wedge?

ECO-TOURISM

Close-to-nature jungle safaris, scuba diving on pristine coral reefs, wilderness trekking to hilltribe villages . . . With no system of regulation in place, anyone can call themselves an 'eco-tourism' business and the money comes rolling in. But many tour operators have a strange idea of what being green means.

A boat run by a self-proclaimed 'eco-tourism' company is heading toward a pristine coral reef in the Andaman Sea. Once at the destination, the boat drops anchor in the open sea, instantly destroying myriad rich coral and the homes of many marine animals.

So much for Thai-style eco-tourism. To counter environmentally destructive mass tourism, the Tourism Authority of Thailand (TAT) launched the concept of eco-tourism here three years ago, but tour companies seem to have their own idea of what being green is.

Targeting the young and adventurous, companies advertise their jungle treks, diving trips and other 'close-to-nature' expeditions as eco-tourism. With no real concern for the environment, the surging popularity of nature tourism means an accelerated invasion of pristine areas and, as a result, more ecological degradation.

Ideally, eco-tourism is environmentally friendly and sustainable tourism which also benefits the local communities. But in fact, many eco-tourism ventures all over the country are destroying the very eco-systems they claim to protect. With poor planning and no benefits for the locals, eco-tourism often ends up providing little beside social tension and environmental degradation while leaving tourists feeling dissatisfied and cheated. Such problems have led to the fledgling eco-tourism industry coming under heavy fire as mere hype and sheer hypocrisy.

Pradech Phayakvichien, TAT's deputy governor of planning and development, said eco-tourism in Thailand needs time to mature.

'We're in the transition period. We need more networking and cooperation between concerned agencies such as government, non-government organisations, business operators, tourists and local communities in order to fulfil the objectives of eco-tourism,' he said.

One of the main factors in eco-tourism's failure, he said, is the lack of participation by local communities due to poor management skills and weak bargaining power against the tourism industry.

'They also lack information, expertise and money to manage the tourism business in their areas,' he said, adding that the government must intervene by giving financial assistance and expert advice to community eco-tourism operations.

At present, many communities are struggling with drastic social and environmental change resulting from the reckless behaviour of tourists and tour companies.

A case in point is the Umphang Wildlife Sanctuary where TAT launched its pilot eco-tourism project a few years ago despite the fact that the sanctuary, by law, does not allow human intrusion.

The project encouraged a large influx of trekkers and tourists far beyond the area's capacity. The sanctuary is now facing severe degradation. Like mass tourism, mass jungle trekking fattens the wallets of tour operators while hurting the eco-system and the hilltribe people's source of livelihood. The eco-tourism plague has spread far and wide to most other pristine areas in the country.

'No matter what you call it, mass or eco-tourism, it makes no difference to us local villagers because we never benefit from it anyway,' said Meeya Hawa, a villager in Jao Mai, a small Muslim fishing village in Trang province.

'Some of us may be hired as cheap labour in resorts or restaurants. But nothing more,' she said, adding that the environmental damage far outweighs the economic gains.

This quiet Muslim fishing village is located on beautiful Hat Yao beach and is a gateway to many virgin islands. Although the villagers see a large number of tourists passing through every year, they have no stake in tourism money.

'When the tourists come, they stay at comfortable resort hotels and ignore our small huts. They go to the islands by the resort's boat and eat at the resort's restaurant. And they throw garbage into the sea which we have worked so hard to preserve,' she said.

Only a handful of tourists stay in the villagers' homes, travel in their boats, or eat the indigenous food they cook.

What she wants, she said, is the kind of tourism which is run and managed by the community for the community.

215

Instead of letting individual villagers provide tourism services with the money going into personal pockets, Meeya said the environment will be more effectively protected if tourism is a community effort.

> **Many villagers are selfish and are doing their business without concern for the environment. Such tourism is short-lived and hurts the community as a whole.**
>
> **Meeya Hawa, *a Jao Mai villager and conservation activist***

'Community effort,' she said, 'will also give the villagers more bargaining power against tour companies.'

While TAT still has no concrete measures in place to support community-run eco-tourism, it acknowledges the role of non-governmental organisations (NGOs) in strengthening local community groups, a crucial condition for eco-tourism success.

For instance, the Thai Volunteers Service is working with the villagers at Jao Mai in Trang to develop community tourism which is environmentally friendly.

'They are on the right track although they lack marketing experience, which we have. If TAT and NGOs and the communities can work together, we can create tourism which benefits both the villagers and nature,' commented TAT's Pradech.

Kiriwong, a strong and tightly knit community at the foot of Khao Luang Mountain in Nakhon Si Thammarat, is a good example of community-based eco-tourism.

Apart from being the gateway to Khao Luang, the highest mountain in the south, the village's century-old forest orchards also attract a large number of visitors.

While rural Thailand lacks social security schemes, Kiriwong has a long history of community welfare funds and committed village groups. This community conscious-ness comes in handy when the village decides to regulate tourism activities in the wake of increasing numbers of tourists and environmental threats.

They set up Kiriwong Eco-tourism Club under its Tambon Administrative Council to draw up rules and regulations for tourists to prevent environmental degradation.

Nipat Boonpet, the club secretary, said Kiriwong has limited the number of mountain trekkers to only thirty a month. Each trekker pays about 3,000 baht for a four-day trek which covers food, accommodation, luggage carriers, sightseeing, contact fees, and a donation to the community.

'The Khao Luang mountain is like the roof of our houses. We have to safeguard it, otherwise it might collapse which would mean big trouble for us,' he said.

All profits go back to Kiriwong's community welfare funds.

Kiriwong's income from its eco-tourism business is secondary since the community lives primarily on their forest orchards.

'We keep our tourism business small because we want to avoid the mistakes of other tourist spots,' said Nipat. 'We're often tempted though, because tourism is easy money. But we have to constantly ask ourselves if we want to lose our roots or have our families break down by opening up our community too much and too soon.'

Not all tourists are happy with Kiriwong's arrangement though. The fee, they say, is too high, thus making nature trips to Khao Luang unaffordable to students with no income.

The mountain, they add, belongs to everyone and the Kiriwong villagers have no right to claim ownership and to charge people.

Flooded by complaints, Kanittha Ponoum, director of TAT's Nakhon Si Thammarat office, said Kiriwong 'misinterprets its role' and should lower the fee and give preferential treatment to students as a compromise.

Although Kiriwong is considering a new fee structure, it insists that charges are essential to limit the number of tourists to a level within nature's carrying capacity.

'Tourists only think of costs in terms of what they pay for food, travelling and accommodation. Nature for them is free. It is not,' said Nipat of Kiriwong.

According to Pradech, tourists also must change their behaviour for eco-tourism to succeed. Although TAT is stepping up its domestic eco-tourism campaign, Pradech said Thai tourists in general lack environmental concern for the places they visit.

The number of tourists has increased every year. This means more pressure on nature and local communities.

Short of a real revolution in environmental awareness among tour operators and tourists alike, eco-tourism will remain just another hyped-up marketing strategy while short-sighted tourist businesses continue to erode the natural environment on which they depend.

Source: Article taken from the Bangkok Post, Saturday 10 May 1997

DISCUSSION QUESTIONS

1 By developing eco-tourism is there a danger that we encourage tourism to develop in areas that are too sensitive to sustain tourism activity?

2 Once tourism development has started is it only a matter of time before the level of activity increases beyond its environmental capacity?

3 What policies and systems could be used to try and control the nature and type of tourism development in such cases?

CONCLUSION

Environmental impacts are not unique to tourism and tourism receives a disproportional share of criticism for its negative environmental impacts. Environmental impacts manifest themselves at the direct, indirect and induced levels and all three levels of impact should be taken into account during the process of assessment. The methods of assessment available to researchers have been developed in a piecemeal fashion, limiting their usefulness for generalisations. However, the adoption of a matrix approach, utilising input–output modelling structures, provides the most promising outlook for a universally acceptable framework for the study of such impacts. International agencies, through statements such as Agenda 21, have declared their intentions to develop an environment-friendly approach to policy making. Similarly, national governments are responding to the pressures from these international bodies as well as from their own populations, to move towards a more environmentally friendly development path. Finally, the private sector (at least as represented by the larger businesses) is responding to pressures by implementing environmental management systems.

There is an overwhelming need to bring some credibility to the study of environmental impacts and this can be achieved by focusing upon the objective environmental indicators, such as those listed by the OECD, rather than subjective data sets that may only have local relevance.

Self-check questions

1 With respect to the environmental impacts associated with tourism activity, list three positive and negative impact examples at the (a) direct (b) indirect, and (c) induced levels of impact.

2 What made Agenda 21 so unique?

3 Explain briefly the difference between environmental impact assessments (EIAs) and environmental audits.

4 What are the major difficulties associated with trying to identify the environmental impacts caused by tourism activity?

5 How would you define eco-tourism?

Essay questions

1 'The environment is often an un-priced element of the tourism product which distorts the workings of the market system. This prevents the market from achieving an optimal level of tourism activity.' Discuss.

2 Environmental resolutions have been made on the international stage for more than 20 years. Why have they had so little impact on the environmental performance of the tourism industry?

3 'When assessing the environmental impact of any sector of production all environmental consequences of that production should be examined not simply the direct effects.' Discuss.

4 What general conclusions can be drawn from the analysis of tourism's environmental impacts?

5 What are the processes involved in implementing an environmental management system and what are the weaknesses involved from such an implementation?

Annotated further reading

Books

Gunn, C. A. and Var, T. (2002) *Tourism Planning*, 4th edn, Routledge, London and New York.
Provides a comprehensive overview of tourism development.

Hall, M. C. and Page, S. J. (2002) *The Geography of Tourism and Recreation: Environment, Place and Space*, 2nd edn, Routledge, London and New York.
This book provides a broad overview of tourism development in terms of demand, supply and impacts.

Middleton, V.T.C. with Hawkins, R. (1998) *Sustainable Tourism, A Marketing Perspective*, Butterworth Heinemann, Oxford.
A book rich with case studies that examines the feasibility of sustainable tourism and the role of marketing in driving the industry in that direction.

Articles

Buckley, R. (2003) 'Ecological indicators of tourist impacts in parks', *Journal of Ecotourism* **2**(1), 54–66.
The author discusses the importance of indicators which are discriminating, quantifiable, actionable, sensitive, ecologically significant, integrated, and feasible in practice. Emphasis is given to the need for indicators that reflect the priority conservation values of the protected areas concerned, and the types of use, and not merely for management processes.

Garcia, C. and Servera, J. (2003) 'Impacts of tourism development on water demand and beach degradation on the island of Mallorca (Spain)', *Geografiska Annaler Series A. Physical Geography* **85**(3–4), 287–300.
Paper includes a focus on over-reliance of tourism and includes economic impacts and benefits. Also states poor planning development has led to strain on resources and resulted in the dwelling capacity being exceeded. Mallorca demonstrates an unsustainable situation.

219

Gossling, S. (2002) 'Global environmental consequences of tourism', *Global Environmental Change* **12**(4), 283–302.

In 2000, almost 700 million international tourist arrivals were counted worldwide. Even though a global activity of this scale can be assumed to have a substantial impact on the environment, its consequences have never been assessed and quantified. In this contribution, five major aspects of the leisure-related alteration of the environment are investigated: (1) the change of land cover and land use, (2) the use of energy and its associated impacts, (3) the exchange of biota over geographical barriers and the extinction of wild species, (4) the exchange and dispersion of diseases, and (5) a psychological consequence of travel, the changes in the perception and the understanding of the environment initiated by travel.

Web sites

http://www.earthsummit2002.org/es/2002/bergen/energy_summary.htm
The Earth Summit web site sketches out the major issues discussed at the Earth Summits including the latest discussions relating to environmental sustainability.

http://www.environment.gov.au/
The Australian Environmental portal provides information relating to the Australian environment.

http://www.epa.gov/
This is the USA's Environmental Protection Agency web site and includes material on US policies on environmental issues relating to tourism.

http://www.greentourism.org.uk/
The tourism and environment web site demonstrates how Scotland is working towards creating a framework for environmentally sustainable tourism.

http://themes.eea.eu.int/Sectors_and_activities/tourism
The European Environmental Agency acts as a portal for information relating to environmental aspects in Europe including tourism.

http://www.uneptie.org/pc/tourism/sust-tourism/env-3main.htm
The United Nations Environmental Programme covers a wide range of environmental topics including this section which looks at sustainable tourism.

References cited and bibliography

Burnett, G.W. and Conover, R. (1989) 'The efficacy of Africa's national parks: an evaluation of Julius Nyere's Arusha Manifesto of 1961', *Society and Natural Resources* **2**, 251–60.

Cohen, E. (1978) 'The impact of tourism on the physical environment', *Annals of Tourism Research* **5**(2), 215–37.

de Kadt, E. (1979) (ed.) *Tourism: Passport to Development?*, Oxford University Press, New York.

Getz, D. (1986) 'Models in tourism planning', *Tourism Management* **7**(1), 21–32.

Green, D.H., Hunter, C.J. and Moore, B. (1990) 'Applications of the Delphi technique in tourism' *Annals of Tourism Research*, **17**, 270–9.

Inskeep, E. (1991) *Tourism Planning: An Integrated and Sustainable Development Approach*, Van Nostrand Reinhold, New York.

Inskeep, E. and Kallenberger, M. (1992) *An Integrated Approach to Resort Development: Six Case Studies*, WTO, Madrid.

Lorch, J. and Bausch, T. (1995) 'Sustainable tourism in Europe' in *Tourism and the Environment in Europe*, EU, Brussels.

Mathieson, A. and Wall, G. (1982) *Tourism: Economic, Physical and Social Impacts*, Longman, Harlow.

OECD (1994) *Environmental Indicators*, OECD core set and Paris.

OECD (2004) http://www.oecd.org/searchResult/0,2665,en_2649_34283_1_1_1_1_1,00.html

UNEP (2004) http://www.uneptie.org/pc/tourism/sust-tourism/env-3main.htm

Welford, R. and Gouldson, A. (1993) *Environmental Management and Business Strategy*, Pitman, London.

MAJOR CASE STUDY 6.1
TOURISM DEVELOPMENT IN FRAGILE
ENVIRONMENTS: THE ARCTIC

Tourism development has spread across the globe and now even encroaches on the Arctic. Over the past two decades the level of tourism has grown steadily and there are now almost one million visitors travelling to this fragile area each year. The experience of two world wars raised awareness of the Arctic region to the troops involved in the conflicts in that area. This, together with the technological developments of television and more recently the Internet, has led to the increasing demand from tourism. The Arctic provides breathtaking views and images on our screens and this whets the appetites of tourists. The proximity of some of the highly fragile areas to populated areas such as Scandinavia and Svalbrad means that large numbers of people need only travel short distances to access the area. Physical disturbance and noise affects all countries within the Arctic region and garbage is rapidly becoming a major aspect of the areas environmental degradation. It is argued that tourism development in the Arctic has both positive and negative benefits. The positive benefits manifest through the preservation of endangered species such as whales and seals living in their natural habitats. Tourism in the Arctic can raise people's awareness of the plight of these endangered creatures and the fragility of the natural environment. This may put pressure on those that hunt whales and seals to cease this activity before the species are extinct.

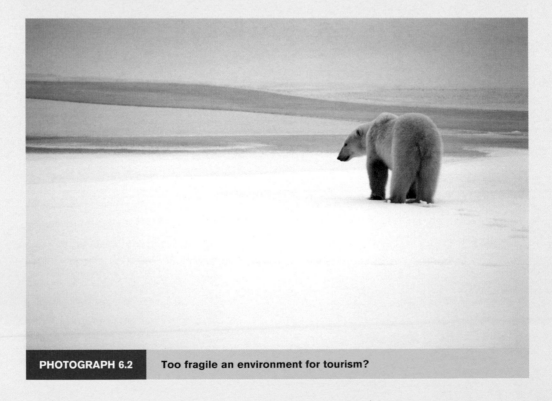

PHOTOGRAPH 6.2   **Too fragile an environment for tourism?**

The negative impacts of close to one million visitors per annum include the pollution created by cruise ships, aircraft that fly people further into the area, increasing road networks, human waste and increased human contact with the endangered species of flora and fauna.

A project known as 'Environment and Tourism in the Arctic' was implemented in 2000 to develop a definition of sustainable tourism for this fragile area. The definition used is that: 'Tourism has to be based locally, and shall give a reasonable economic benefit to the local society. Tourism may not have negative influences upon, or conflict with, business or culture in the local society, but has to contribute to the positive development of local society. Tourism nay not damage nature and environment. In principal, it should be sustainable for ever.' Furthermore, the WWF has set out ten principles to guide the development of tourism in the Arctic which include:

1 Making tourism development compatible with the environmental aims of the area.

2 Supporting the preservation of the wilderness and biodiversity.

3 Adopting sustainable uses of resources.

4 Minimising consumption, waste and pollution.

5 Respecting the local culture.

6 Protecting and respecting historic sites.

7 Ensuring local communities benefit from tourism development.

8 Using properly trained staff.

9 Make learning a part of the tourist experience.

10 Adopting safety rules and guidelines.

Source: http://www.ngo.grida.no/wwfap/core/about/tourism_guidelines/ten_principles_english.html

The local populations in the Arctic region have a significant say in the whether and how tourism development will take place. The key guiding principle that seems to be taking hold is that tourism development should take place for the local population and not for international tourists. Given the strong link that the local population place between the land and survival it is hoped that this will develop a clear understanding of the regions fragility to any visitors.

DISCUSSION QUESTIONS

1 What are the merits and de-merits of developing tourism in areas such as the Arctic?

2 If tourism is to be permitted in areas that are environmentally fragile what measures should be taken to control the development of such tourism and how can such measures be enforced?

3 When the fragile resources are unique, who are the stakeholders?

CHAPTER SEVEN
THE SOCIO-CULTURAL IMPACT OF TOURISM

Tourism is a product that is based upon simultaneous production and consumption. For tourism output to have occurred the tourists must visit a destination and consume the product of the sector *in situ*. There is a wide range of **service industries** in the world, but there is often no need for the consumer to visit the place of production in order to consume the product. However, tourism is a personal service and, as such, can only be consumed by the tourist visiting the destination. The implications of this for the destination's population is that not only will it be subject to the changes created by the stimulation and change in direction of the local economy, it will also come into contact with an alien population during the production process. Changes in economic growth and development will always be associated with changes in the socio-cultural characteristics of an area. As the population becomes wealthier and healthier, their wants and needs change and this influences their spending choice and lifestyles. However, because tourism brings visitors into contact with the local population it adds further dimensions to the socio-cultural change.

The contact between visitors and local residents can be beneficial or detrimental to the host population depending upon the difference in cultures and the nature of the contact. Much of the literature on social impacts is biased in that it focuses attention upon the detrimental impact of tourism on the host population. Similarly, little attention has been paid to the fact that there can also be socio-cultural impacts on the tourist population, which can again be either positive or negative. In reality socio-cultural impacts tend to contain a mixture of both positive and negative strands and these impacts affect both hosts and guests.

LEARNING OUTCOMES

The learning outcomes of this chapter may be defined as:

- identifying those aspects of socio-cultural behaviour that are most susceptible to tourism activity and most likely to be influenced and changed as a result of it;

- understanding the various approaches to studying the socio-cultural aspects of tourism and the relationship between them;

- providing a framework for the study of the relationship between tourism development and socio-cultural impacts; and

- encouraging the reader to understand key concepts.

THE NATURE OF SOCIO-CULTURAL IMPACTS OF TOURISM

The aim of this chapter is to outline the nature of socio-cultural impacts, to examine those contacts that are positive and those that may be deemed to be negative. In order to do this it is important to include an examination of the process of tourism development because the speed and nature of development can be a major influence on the magnitude and direction of socio-cultural changes. The chapter will also investigate the causal factors for socio-cultural impacts, suggest possible methods for measurement and outline some policy implications.

The socio-cultural impact of tourism is manifested through an enormous range of aspects from the arts and crafts through to the fundamental behaviour of individuals and collective groups. The impacts can be positive, such as the case where tourism preserves or even resurrects the craft skills of the population or the enhancement of cultural exchange between two distinct populations. The impacts can also be negative, such as the **commercialisation and bastardisation** of arts, crafts and ceremonies/rituals of the host population. The impacts can also detract from cultural exchange by presenting a limited and distorted view of one of the populations.

A factor often overlooked by researchers is the socio-cultural impact of tourism on the visitor population. For instance, the growth of UK tourists visiting Spain throughout the 1960s and 1970s resulted in culinary and beverage changes in the UK (paella and Rioja wine being two Spanish products that benefited from this exchange). Visitors to Australia would often find it hard to resist adopting the beach-based lifestyle and the barbecue when they return home. There is evidence of socio-cultural impacts, ranging from the clothes we wear, the food we eat and our general lifestyles and attitudes, which can all be influenced by places we visit.

There is a tradition of viewing the socio-cultural impacts as a combined effect because of the difficulty in distinguishing between sociological and cultural impacts. This distinction is also somewhat artificial given the fact that sociological and cultural effects overlap to a large extent. There is also a tradition of examining the socio-cultural impacts of tourism purely in terms of the contact that takes place between the host and visiting populations: this is a very limited approach. The true socio-cultural impact of tourism is far reaching and encompasses direct and indirect effects in a manner similar to the economic impacts. Again, some of these consequential impacts may be beneficial while others may be seen as detrimental. These matters will be explored in greater detail below.

APPROACHES TO THE STUDY OF SOCIO-CULTURAL IMPACTS OF TOURISM

There are a variety of ways in which we can examine the relationships between tourism development and socio-cultural and socio-economic changes. Authors such as Cohen (1984) looked at the study of socio-cultural impacts from four different but overlapping viewpoints:

1 Tourism impact studies.

2 Host guest interaction.

3 Tourist systems.

4 Tourists and their behaviour.

The studies that have taken place have ranged from those that have attempted to provide formal models to explain tourism development and the host guest interaction (such as that by Butler (1980), Doxey (1975) and Smith (1989)). Although none of these models has met with a great deal of success, they have created frameworks within which researchers can examine appropriate issues. Many of the other studies relating to the socio-cultural impact of tourism have been specific case study approaches which have lacked the universal rigour that allows the development of an over-arching theoretical understanding.

The development of the tourist product is inextricably linked to the contribution that tourism development can make to general economic development. In fact, the relationship between tourism development and general economic development can be studied under the heading of dependency or core–periphery theory, which relates to the enrichment of metropolitan areas at the expense of under-developed **peripheral areas**. Studies of dependency theory often cite examples of the Caribbean and the South Pacific to highlight not only the economic and political dependence resulting from tourism activity, but also the socio-cultural dependence. However, the issues are more far reaching than the effects upon small island developing states (SIDS) and we find that all countries that are in the tourism business experience socio-cultural changes as a result of tourism activity. In some countries, such as Spain, the dynamics of socio-cultural change have been found to be surprisingly rapid as the effects of tourism development in Costa Brava demonstrated in the late 1960s and early 1970s.

The development of the tourism product will, to some extent, be determined by the type of tourism activity that takes place. This, in turn, will be partly determined by the nature of the destination and the socio-economic characteristics of the tourists. Similarly, the magnitude and direction of the economic and sociological impact of tourism on the host population will be partly determined by the type of tourism product.

The impact brought about by the interaction of hosts and tourists is a well-documented phenomenon, and the findings of researchers, such as Smith (1989) in her book on the **anthropology of tourism** have rapidly gained acceptance in the academic world. The categorisation of tourists into '**typologies**' is now accepted as an orthodox tool in the study of socio-cultural impacts. Authors such as Doxey (1975) have explored the changing relationship between guests and hosts through his construction of his Index where that relationship travels from a state of euphoria, through apathy to annoyance and ends up with a state of open antagonism as the visitor presence becomes more and more pronounced. Plog (1977) and Butler (1980) both used the dynamics of change as part of their explanatory models, but here they were looking at the changing fortunes of the destination as the visitors revised their perceptions.

The typology of tourists

Typology is a method of sociological investigation that seeks, in this instance, to classify tourists according to a particular phenomenon, usually motivations or behaviour. A simple example of a typology which has implications for the development of the tourism product is shown in Table 7.1:

- Package tourists – usually demand Western amenities, are associated with rapid growth rates and often lead to the restructuring of the local economy.

- Independent tourists – usually fit in better with the local environment and social structure, are associated with relatively slow growth rates and often lead to local ownership.

A more detailed typology, such as the one devised by Valene Smith, relates the type of tourist to volume and adaptation levels.

Before examining the different approaches that can be used to study the socio-cultural impacts of tourism it is important to consider some fundamental matters relating to these impacts that are often ignored by researchers. In spite of the fact that some researchers regard socio-cultural change as one of the evils of tourism development, any form of economic development will, by definition, carry with it implications for the social structure and cultural aspects of the host population.

TABLE 7.1	Typology of tourism: frequency of types of tourist and their adaptations to local norms	
Types of tourist	**Number of tourists**	**Adaptation to local norms**
Explorer	Very limited	Accepts fully
Élite	Rarely seen	Adapts fully
Off-beat	Uncommon but seen	Adapts well
Unusual	Occasional	Adapts somewhat
Incipient mass	Steady flow	Seeks Western amenities
Mass	Continuous flow	Expects Western amenities
Charter	Massive arrivals	Demands Western amenities

Source: Smith, 1989. Reprinted by permission of the University of Pennsylvania Press

This is true for both international and domestic tourism development. To condemn tourism development because it will inevitably bring with it socio-economic change is tantamount to consigning a destination to a cultural museum. This choice can only come from the host population and not from external researchers who become too embroiled in the sociological resources that are used in the tourist transactions. Furthermore, to criticise researchers for forecasting future growth levels of tourism and manpower requirements on the grounds that such forecasts ignore the fact that these employees are members of families is to deny the whole essence of sound tourism planning. Successful tourism development can only be achieved by undertaking rigorous quantitative and qualitative research.

The speed and concentration of tourism development are also important influences on the magnitude and direction of social impacts and must be taken into account when attempting to attribute the cause of socio-cultural impacts. The nature of the tourism development process and its impact on the host population can be categorised into a variety of subsets and the analyses of each of these subsets can shed additional light on the type and source of impacts attributable to tourism development.

With respect to the speed of development a broad analytical approach would suggest that if tourism develops rapidly, the accompanying change to the economy would create a new power structure. In contrast, slow tourism development tends to be associated with small, locally owned developments with less change to the power structure.

THE TOURISM DEVELOPMENT PROCESS

Studies that look at the socio-cultural impact of tourism on specific types of destinations according to their resource base are quite common (see for example, Gill and Williams (1994), Price (1992), Stokowski (1996)). Although tourism development can take place in a wide variety of forms, a typical development scenario considers the tourism product as it grows from infancy to maturity and looks something like this:

- A few tourists 'discover' an area or destination.

- In response to this discovery, local entrepreneurs provide new or special facilities to accommodate the growing number of visitors and service their needs. More importantly, they provide the means to attract more visitors in the future.

- The public sector provides new or improved infrastructure to cater for the inflow of visitors.

- Finally, **institutionalised or mass tourism** is developed, which is commonly resort based and sold as a package. It is based upon large-volume production techniques in order to exploit economies of large-scale production in marketing, accommodation and transport, such as high payload factors for aircraft.

Many regional and national tourism development plans have attempted to shortcut the above tourism evolution cycle by aiming for the final stage of mass tourism straight away, but few destinations can make this leap without first securing outside capital and expertise and incurring severe social stress.

Unfortunately, there is no single coherent body of knowledge or theory which comprehensively explains tourism development. Evidence, such as it is, is rather piecemeal and comes from a number of disparate case studies. Furthermore, the situation is compounded by the fact that different disciplines approach the subject matter in different ways, and although many aspects of the studies may overlap, it is difficult to tie the different conclusions together into a single body of thought.

The different approaches may be categorised under the following headings:

- psychological;
- sociological;
- socio-economic.

THE PSYCHOLOGICAL BASIS OF TOURISM DEVELOPMENT

In Chapter 2 we introduced Stanley Plog's (1977) approach to a typology of tourists and in this chapter we have reiterated how useful such typologies can be in the study of socio-cultural impacts. Plog devised his classification in terms of **psychographic analysis**, and in this way attempted to explain why resort destinations appear to follow a pattern that causes them to rise through a period of development and then fall into a period of decline. He saw a continuum of market segments with two diametrically opposed groups occupying either pole (see Figure 7.1). In 2004, Stanley Plog revisited his earlier work and modified the categories of tourists,

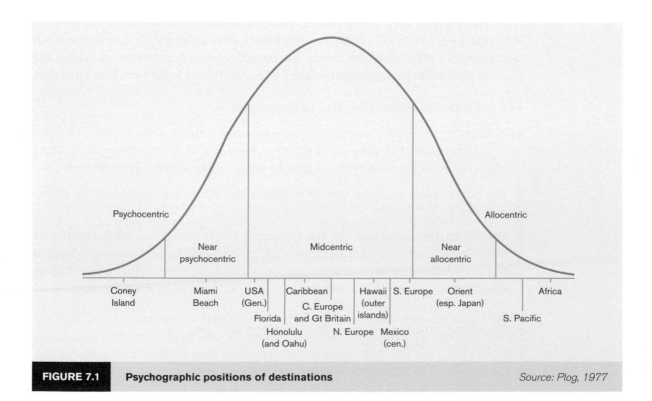

| FIGURE 7.1 | **Psychographic positions of destinations** | *Source: Plog, 1977* |

replacing the allocentrics with venturers and the psychocentrics with dependables (Plog, 2004). Plog also updated his chart in 2003.

Plog's theory suggests that the tourist segments can be divided into different psychographic traits, i.e. allocentrics, near allocentrics, midcentrics, near psychocentrics and psychocentrics. The polar extremes of these groups can be described as exhibiting the following characteristics:

- **Allocentrics** seek cultural and environmental differences from their norm, belong to the higher income groups, are adventurous and require very little in the way of tourism plant.

- **Psychocentrics** seek familiar surroundings, belong to the lower income groups, are unadventurous and demand a high level of tourism plant.

According to Plog's framework, a resort may typically begin by attracting a small number of allocentrics (trendsetters), similar to Smith's explorers, but will soon develop in order to attract larger numbers of visitors. Using Plog's terminology this development will move the resort into and through the near allocentrics and then into the midcentrics. During this process the allocentrics will be alienated and they will move on to look for new destinations to 'discover'.

Resorts that have a strong competitive advantage, in terms of climate, location or top-quality tourism plant, such as DisneyLand in Florida, USA, may continue to thrive in the midcentric market. However, many resorts will tend to lose favour (perhaps because they are considered by tourists to be too commercialised) and continue their drift towards the psychocentric markets by offering lower tariffs, more comprehensive packaging and more scheduling of activities – the complete 'no-surprise vacation'.

Contrary to original thoughts concerning Plog's theory, this process of rise and decline is not immutable. Such a process may have seemed inevitable for many resorts in the past but, once decision makers realise that limited tourism development can be an attractive means of growth, they may develop tourism plant that is compatible with the environment and the indigenous characteristics of a region, and target them at the 'desired' market segments. Alternatively, recognition of the importance of quality tourism plant can allow destinations to maintain a midcentric position in the market continuum.

THE SOCIOLOGICAL BASIS OF TOURISM DEVELOPMENT

The sociological basis of tourism development can be subdivided into (a) the social phenomenon of tourism and (b) the socio-economic basis underlying tourism development.

Several factors of the modern world can be identified as the seeds from which international tourism has grown into an inescapable social phenomenon:

- Population growth.

- Increasing urbanisation and the overwhelming pressures of urban life which create the desire to escape.

- Growth in communications and information technology, creating awareness and stimulating interest.

- Changes in mobility and accessibility, brought about largely by the growth of air transport and private motor car ownership.

- Increased leisure time and longer periods of vacation, together with rising real incomes in the wake of sustained economic growth.

- Increases in world trade for business tourism.

When examining the factors that are associated with tourism development it is interesting to note that they can also be categorised according to whether they are *push* factors or *pull* factors. By this we mean that some factors generate a desire to escape (*push*) such as urbanisation, overcrowding, pollution or even tedium, whereas other factors such as specific events (Olympics) or climate and natural phenomena generate a magnetism that attracts tourists (*pull*). There are a number of factors that will influence the attitude of people towards tourism at both domestic and international levels. These include the following:

- **Age.** The age of the tourist will, within certain boundaries, influence the type of tourism activity pursued. For instance, there is likely to be less demand from the elderly for trekking and mountaineering vacations than from other age groups. Similarly, the greatest demand for tourist destinations with a hectic nightlife is likely to be from the 18–35-year-old age group. Of course there are always exceptions to these rules.

- **Education.** There is a tendency to associate the more adventurous and independent vacations with the more educated portion of the population. These would include Plog's allocentrics as well as Smith's explorers and élite travellers.

- **Income levels.** Income levels have an obvious influence on the decision of people to travel, the location to which they travel, the nature of the activities undertaken while away and the mode(s) of transport utilised.

- **Socio-economic background.** The previous experiences of people will play an important role in determining the type of holiday they will consume in future time periods. For instance, children from the higher **socio-economic groups**, who are accustomed to frequent trips abroad, are likely to continue this pattern throughout adulthood.

In addition to the socio-economic characteristics of the tourists, the tourism development process, together with its implications for socio-cultural impacts, should be examined. This approach encompasses all three approaches discussed so far – the psychological basis for tourism development, the sociological basis and the socio-economic basis for tourism development. In general there is a *direct* socio-cultural impact which occurs as a result of the contact between the host population and the visitors. De Kadt (1979) suggests that there are three broad categories of such contact:

1 When the tourists buy goods and services from the hosts.

2 When the hosts and tourists share a facility such as the beach, a train or bus, a restaurant or bar, etc.

3 When tourists and hosts come together for the prime purpose of cultural exchange.

232

The first two of these types of contact are associated with the majority of the negative aspects of social contact, whereas the third type of contact is generally considered to be positive in nature. To draw comparisons between this work of de Kadt and the typology-based research of Smith, it is evident that the explorer/ adventurer tourist is most likely to take part in the latter, positive type of interaction – providing a favourable association between this type of tourist and their socio-cultural impacts. However, the mass and charter tourist is more likely to be pre-dominantly concerned with the first two types of contact, thereby making their presence generally unfavourable from a socio-cultural impact point of view. A crude conclusion can be drawn from this somewhat simplistic approach – the negative types of interaction are by far the most common and the positive types of contact are relatively rare.

The '**demonstration effect**' is also an aspect of the *direct* socio-cultural impact of tourism. Tourists influence the behaviour of the host population by their example. This is an area where tourism development is at a distinct disadvantage when compared with the use of alternative industries as a means to economic development. Tourism is a product that requires simultaneous production and consumption. Although international tourism may be seen as an export industry, in the same way as, say, oil or automobiles, it has the disadvantage that the consumer must visit the place of production (the factory) in order to consume it. This means that tourism will bring with it the physical presence of tourists and this will stimulate changes in the behaviour and dress style of the host population.

It is not even necessary for tourists to come into direct contact with members of the host population for the demonstration effect to take place. Those members of the host population who are influenced by the behaviour of the tourists are likely to influence other members of their community by their changed attitudes and behaviour. This can be classified as an *indirect* socio-cultural impact. More-over, if tourism development is successful, new employment opportunities created by the increased activity will be the harbinger of social change in the same way that any form of economic development will change the consumption habits, the location and the behaviour of the local population. These changes will be stimu-lated further by the introduction of new or enhanced forms of communications, transport and infrastructure primarily provided for tourism development. These latter factors may also be considered to be *indirect* socio-cultural impacts but this time they are associated with many types of economic development, not just tourism. However, the diversity of productive sectors associated directly and indir-ectly with the tourism industry is such that these types of socio-cultural impacts will probably be more widely spread as a result of tourism development than any other industry.

As an economy grows and develops there will probably be an increase in income levels and the proportion of the population involved in the monetised sector. This will alter the consumption patterns of the local population. Such changes, if they include consumer durables such as television, videos and radio, will expose the local population to a greater range of wants and, in so doing, speed up the process of social change. These effects, because they are a result of increased income levels and consumer spending, may be seen as being *induced* socio-cultural impacts. This latter type of socio-cultural impact will also be evident irrespective of the type of economic catalyst that generated the development and is not uniquely attributable to tourism development.

233

The magnitude of the direct socio-cultural impact associated with tourism development will also be determined by the extent of the difference in socio-cultural characteristics between hosts and guests. Inskeep (1991) suggests that these differences include:

- basic value and logic system;

- religious beliefs;

- traditions;

- customs;

- lifestyles;

- behavioural patterns;

- dress codes;

- sense of time budgeting; and

- attitudes towards strangers.

To add further complexity to our understanding of the problems, the speed of development and change will have an important role in determining the magnitude of the socio-cultural changes because time allows for the process of adaptation. Compounding the issue further is the fact that the tourists' cultures when abroad (it is probable that the tourists will represent several different cultures) are different from the tourists' cultures at home. In other words, tourists often take on different attitudes and adopt different codes of behaviour when they are on vacation and away from their normal environment.

As discussed earlier, the socio-cultural impacts associated with tourism can be either positive or negative. One of the positive impacts highlighted by de Kadt was the exchange of cultural information, ideas and beliefs. But tourism can also be used to help stimulate interest in, and conserve aspects of, the host's cultural heritage such as in Petra, Jordan, York in the UK and Machu Picchu (the lost city of the Incas) in Peru. This is a significant positive socio-cultural impact and extends over ancient monuments, historic sites, arts, crafts and cultural ceremonies and rituals. If tourists appreciate the cultural heritage of a destination, that appreciation can stimulate the hosts' pride in their heritage and foster local crafts, traditions and customs.

The negative socio-cultural impacts are sometimes the result of *direct* contact and the demonstration effect and these can distort the traditional crafts and customs into shorter, commercialised events that offer the host community little in the way of rich cultural experience. Negative socio-cultural impacts can also be generated if the tourism development is not managed properly and the full economic potential of that development is not realised. For instance, foreign employment in tourism-related jobs and foreign investment in tourism projects both add to the local resentment of tourism development. The exclusion of hosts from certain tourist facilities (such as private beaches, casinos and transport services such as the Sky Train in Bangkok where locals have been excluded by high prices and limited flexibility off the tourism route) will further increase the pressure of resentment and may create conflict between the host population and the tourists.

As with any form of economic development, the new income-earning opportunities created by tourism development are unlikely to be evenly distributed across the destination. This may give rise to some members of the host community feeling resentful and antagonistic towards tourism development. Tourism destinations such as Jamaica in the Caribbean have experienced social problems because tourism development was confined to the north and western coast, although more recently attempts have been made to redress this imbalance. In tourism's favour, it is generally developed in areas where there is little in the way of competing industries (particularly manufacturing); therefore it helps provide employment opportunities in areas where they may be most needed. The creation of job opportunities with higher wage rates than those paid by the more traditional industries of fishing and agriculture can create social pressures between hosts who occupy these posts and their families and peers who do not.

A major problem can also occur because of a real (and sometimes only apparent) difference in wealth between the tourists and their hosts. It is true that there are occasions when the tourists are generally much wealthier than the hosts with whom they come into contact. However, this difference may be exacerbated by the fact that tourists exhibit spending patterns and behaviour that is very different from their norm, simply because they are on vacation. The normal spending habits of tourists is not information readily available to the average host. Furthermore, the difference in wealth between tourist and host may not be as severe a problem as initially perceived given the fact that the vast majority of international tourism takes place between industrialised countries and not between industrialised and developing countries.

When attempting to measure the level of irritation generated by tourist–host contact, Doxey (1975) drew up the following Index:

1 **The level of euphoria** – the initial thrill and enthusiasm that comes along with tourism development results in the fact that the tourist is made welcome.

2 **The level of apathy** – once tourism development is underway and the consequential expansion has taken place, the tourist is taken for granted and is now only seen as a source of profit taking. What contact is made between host and guest is done so on a commercial and formal footing.

3 **The level of irritation** – as the industry approaches saturation point, the hosts can no longer cope with the number of tourists without the provision of additional facilities.

4 **The level of antagonism** – the tourist is now seen as the harbinger of all ills, hosts are openly antagonistic towards tourists and tourists are regarded as being there to be exploited.

5 **The final level** – during the above process of 'development' the host population has forgotten that all they once regarded as being special was exactly the same thing that attracted the tourist, but in the rush to develop tourism circumstances have changed. The social impact has been comprehensive and complete and the tourists will move to different destinations.

Although we have discussed a wide range of approaches to the study of the socio-cultural impact of tourism, there are some very strong common strands. If

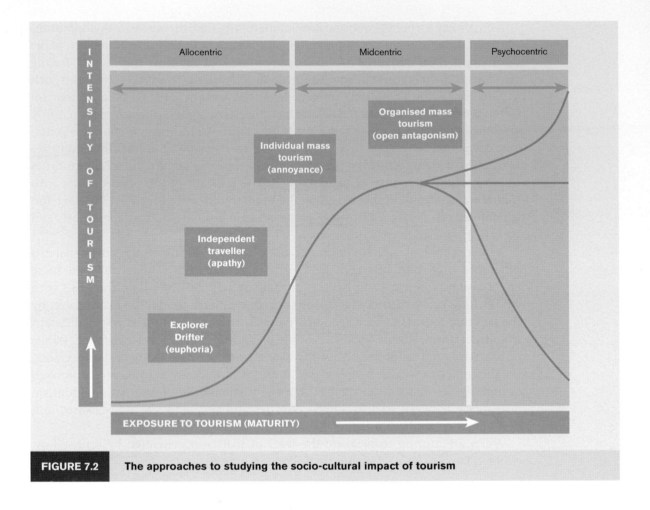

FIGURE 7.2   **The approaches to studying the socio-cultural impact of tourism**

the typology used by Valene Smith is linked to the host guest interaction suggested by Doxey, within the framework proposed by Butler and Plog then the commonality can be seen. Figure 7.2 shows each of these theories combined within a two-dimensional frame.

Although Figure 7.2 presents the various approaches within a single framework, the framework is a static one. This means that it is still hampered by the fact that the dynamics of the process are not reflected and thus its practical applicability is severely limited.

SOME GENERAL NEGATIVE SOCIO-CULTURAL IMPACTS OF TOURISM

There is a wide variety of ways that the development and operation of tourism can create social tensions and impact on the integrity of the local culture. The most obvious and direct effect is the bringing together of two different cultures and this is an issue that threads its way throughout this chapter. However, the socio-cultural impact of tourism may arise from some general but less obvious factors.

Economic factors

The majority of tourism activity takes place between the industrialised economies of the world. However, where tourism takes place between the industrialised and the less developed destinations or regions, there can be an enormous imbalance of economic power between the tourists and the hosts. Where tourists are much wealthier than the people with whom they come into contact there is likely to be some attempt at emulation as well as some resentment. This may be reflected in behaviour, dress and spending patterns. Furthermore, where tourism results in the migration of labour from rural to urban areas and attracts workers from the traditional sectors, there could be a growing inequality in the wealth of the local residents as some of them enjoy the higher wages of the tourism sector. This can also lead to social tensions. But it should be borne in mind that the latter channel of economic inequality will be present with any form of economic development.

The tax burden on the local residents may be increased in order to meet the growing demands for better infrastructure (roads, water supply, sewage treatment, etc.). Where tourism drives improved infrastructure without the costs being reflected in the tourism product, there will be growing social tension as residents may struggle to meet the higher tax demands.

Labour factors

The economic factors demonstrated how tourism can attract workers from other industries. The level of antagonism with respect to tourism can be exacerbated where the employment opportunities for workers within the tourism industry are limited to lower level, front-line workers. In such cases the senior and middle management positions are filled by experienced staff from outside the country (often from the country that has provided either the investment or the tourists). Even where a significant proportion of the managerial staff are locals, their contact with other non-local staff and the tourists may cause a change in their consumption habits so that they have a high propensity to consume imported goods.

Although tourism may be an industry that is associated with higher wages and salaries than the more traditional industries such as farming and fishing, there are many cases where the working conditions are found to be less than desirable. Child labour, casual contracts, part-time jobs with no training are all too common. The International Labour Organization (ILO) estimate that some 10–15% of all employees in the tourism industry are below the age of 18 years. Children under the age of 12 years are frequently employed in developed and developing countries to work in tourism-related businesses. This again, is not unique to tourism as child labour has always been apparent in the primary sectors (such as agriculture) and manufacturing sectors (such as textiles).

Behavioural and demonstration factors

If the tourists are not aware of, or care for, the local customs they may behave in a way that creates severe social friction between tourists and residents and, ultimately between the residents themselves. The planet is rich in customs and

237

MINI CASE STUDY 7.1
Income inequality in Taman Negara National Park, Malaysia

In Western Malaysia, the Taman Negara National Park is a privately owned park and resort which can house 260 visitors at a time. The park employs 270 people and 60% of the staff in the administrative headquarters are locals. In 1999 these local staff earned about US$120 a month; for comparison, Malaysians living off the land at that time were earning on average about US$40 a month.

Despite the positive effects of increased park employment, the difference in income between the two local groups has led to social tension and driven up boat fares and the cost of everyday goods. Little of the tourism money generated by the park stays in Malaysia, and park employees spend almost 90% of their income outside the region or on imported goods. Thus local inhabitants, whose culture has been marketed to attract tourists, benefit only to a very limited extent. Indeed, many have taken to illegal hunting and fishing in the park, contrary to its protective regulations.

Source: ILO report on human resources development, employment and globalisation in the hotel, catering and tourism sector, 2001 from http://www.ilo.org/public/english/dialogue/sector/techmeet/tmhct01/tmhctr2.htm; *report for discussion at the Tripartite Meeting on Human Resources Development, Employment and Globalization in the Hotel, Catering and Tourism Sector, Geneva, 2–6 April 2001, International Labour Office, Geneva*

DISCUSSION QUESTIONS

1 'The income and employment inequalities experienced by any country or region as their economy develops may lead to social tensions and a change in the lifestyles and behaviour of the population. This is not a condition unique to tourism development and should be accepted rather seen as a criticism of the tourism industry.' Discuss.

2 Would it be better from a socio-cultural point of view, to isolate tourists from the local population by putting them into private resorts or to integrate them by developing tourism into existing sites?

3 What policies could be implemented to mitigate some of the tension that has been experienced at Taman Negara National Park?

every custom gives the tourist an opportunity to adapt to the local norms or to insult their hosts, often without ever knowing that they have done so. Slurping of soup may be seen as being the result of poor table manners in the UK but is an expression of appreciation in China; putting your chopsticks vertically into the bowl of rice in Japan is a symbol of death and is usually only seen in funeral ceremonies; showing the soles of your shoes is considered offensive in a number of countries including Thailand and Iran; inappropriate dress in Muslim countries can cause offense, so too can inappropriate consumption (such as alcohol) or nude sunbathing in countries that may be conservative in this respect.

SOME SPECIFIC NEGATIVE SOCIO-CULTURAL IMPACTS OF TOURISM

There are many destinations in the Middle East, the Far East, the Caribbean and the South Pacific that would find the lack of adherence to local social behaviour codes difficult to tolerate. Those that are exposed to such inappropriate behaviour or dress codes may find that, over time, they come to accept them and even emulate such behaviour, causing tension between the residents.

Resource use factors

Tourism is about real estate development and thus will place high demands on land use. These demands will compete with alternative local use and may result in land price inflation. Where land price inflation occurs it can create social tension as local residents are competed out of their properties.

Environmental and cultural damage resulting from tourism can lead to social tension. This is a common problem in areas where there are heritage sites and examples can be found in places like Paphos where there was open pilfering by the tourists and residents from the site of the Byzantium Fort. It is not only the man-made heritage that is being stolen, precious and irreplaceable fossils in areas such as the Petrified Forest of Arizona are also subject to looting by smugglers and tourists. Similarly, where the social tensions increase there can be vandalism and wilful damage to heritage sites.

Competition between locals and tourist businesses for local resources is commonplace, such as the use of a beach or mountain area. The economics of the situation gives the tourist businesses the upper hand in such competitions and the locals often find that their use of the facilities are removed or downgraded.

SOME SPECIFIC NEGATIVE SOCIO-CULTURAL IMPACTS OF TOURISM

Sex

The fact that tourists will travel abroad to enjoy uninhibited casual sexual encounters is not a new phenomenon. Sexual exploitation has grown as rapidly as tourism in many destinations. The early European tourists were to some extent motivated by the liberal attitude towards sex in some of the Third World countries they visited. More recently a major tourism market has grown up around **sex tourism** and destinations such as Thailand, The Gambia and some of the Central European countries have actively marketed the sexual content of their products. The proliferation of **AIDS** has done much to dampen the rapid growth of this element of the tourism industry but it is still a significant part of the market. It is questionable whether tourism created the social disruption associated with the sex trade or whether the sex trade has stimulated the tourism market. But, as with all forms of prostitution, it is impossible to be conclusive as to the rights and wrongs of either party. Certainly the growth of paedophile activity is one element of the tourist industry that is outlawed in many of the tourist-generating countries and can only be pursued under the guise of international tourism. The United Nations defines

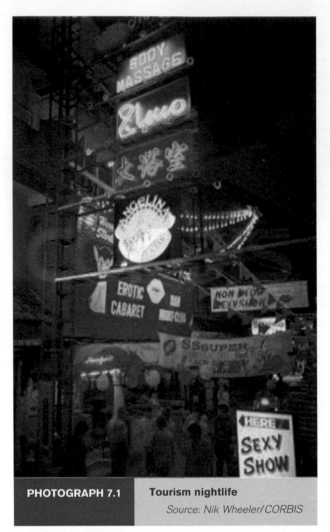

PHOTOGRAPH 7.1	Tourism nightlife
	Source: Nik Wheeler/CORBIS

sex tourism relating to children to be 'tourism organised with the primary purpose of facilitating the effecting of a commercial sexual relationship with a child'. The growth of such activities is often supported by a network of facilitators ranging from pimps and brothels through to the seemingly more respectable taxi drivers and hotel workers. The Internet has only added to the problem by creating an international communication network that can market these services on an international scale. So prolific is this problem that agencies such as ECPAT have been set up to campaign against child prostitution. The acronym stands for 'End Child Prostitution, Child Pornography and Trafficking of Children for Sexual Purposes'.

The future development of tourism using specific sexual activities as its main catalyst may be in doubt in the current world of AIDS and other sexually transmitted diseases. However, many tourists from industrialised countries may expect to relax their sexual morals during a vacation and this can lead to a thin line being drawn between destinations that are primarily trading on sex and those that offer an environment wherein tourists can relax their sexual morals.

MINI CASE STUDY 7.2
The trouble with TOURISM WITHOUT AIDS by Paschal Eze

Not a few members of the global travel trade had berated my TOURISM WITHOUT AIDS campaign as unnecessary. 'This is a blackmail,' one had posited. And as far as he was concerned, a campaign for equitable tourism in Africa was more pressing. Another email writer shared the same sentiment, opining, 'Young man, there are more pressing issues in the global travel and tourism industry than HIV/AIDS.' To yet another member of the trade, I deserved the question, 'Are you saying tourism is synonymous with AIDS?' His understanding was that the campaign would only succeed in discouraging some people from tourism activities. But the truth is that as long as the earth remains, people will continue to travel for 'pleasure . . . holiday, business, family affairs, mission, meeting and family purposes'. And as they do so, they will continue to be exposed to high-risk social behaviours like casual sex, drunkenness and intravenous drug use which engender the spread of HIV/AIDS.

Many people on holiday tend to behave as though they have just been liberated from long-drawn bondage. They indulge in habits that are not the least healthy, with

HIV/AIDS as a very possible offshoot. I agree that the travel industry in Africa is fraught with leakages which need to be squarely addressed. But I also know that HIV/AIDS is the most potent threat to this industry to which many African countries look up for the much needed foreign exchange. It takes no strain to find out that most of the countries said to have the highest prevalence of HIV/AIDS in Africa are notable tourist destinations. The eco-tourist haven of Botswana that had been touted by the West as having the fastest growing economy is today under the suffocating grip of the HIV/AIDS pandemic.

Kenya, another African country seen as a more popular destination than Botswana, has not been spared the claws of HIV/AIDS as people die in their hundreds daily. Able-bodied men and women, I mean. Hotels and tourism establishments are recording very high turnover of staff and contending with the very low productivity of members of their staff who are living with HIV/AIDS. Some of them, especially members of the entertainment/animation teams as well as those in room service, contracted the virus through unprotected sex with infected tourists and spread it to members of their families.

Are some African destinations not being promoted as havens for sex tourists? Are poverty and ignorance not turning some African youths into sex slaves, prostitutes and gigolos? How many paedophiles of European and American extraction pollute countries in South East Asia in the name of tourism?

Sensitive questions, aren't they? Yet, campaigning against these ills is anathema to many destinations, the fear being that people will be discouraged from visiting them. If Senegal is today a reference point in HIV/AIDS control, it is partly because of the regulation of the activities of commercial sex workers who are registered and regularly counselled and screened. Good thing its neighbouring country, The Gambia, established a task force in 2000 to rid its Tourism Development Area of gigolos and prostitutes, among others.

Are there destinations in Africa that preach safe sex among tourism workers, tourists and members of host communities? Perhaps, none! If only there can be a change of attitude on the part of tourism authorities, tour operators, ground handlers, hoteliers and hotel workers and the rest of the travel and tourism industry, the heavy toll HIV/AIDS is taking on the industry would be minimised.

The truth should be told about the relationship between TOURISM AND AIDS even if it hurts. It is not enough to tell us about the multi-billion dollars worth of transactions in the global travel and tourism industry yearly or about the top ten destinations and source markets.

People need to know the human cost involved.

Source: http://www.unique.gm/menaa/gamtourism.htm

DISCUSSION QUESTIONS

1 Is the choice of destinations one of having tourism, with the risk of increasing health risks that have devastating consequences, such as AIDS, or not having tourism at all?

2 Commercial sexual exploitation has developed in parallel with the growth in tourism. Is the commercial sex industry simply a matter of local control and regulation or is it an issue that should have international intervention?

3 Discuss the socio-cultural and ethical issues of the tourist sex industry and any actions that may be undertaken to control it.

241

Crime

The link between tourism and crime is hard to establish. Many writers, such as Mathieson and Wall (1982), have suggested the link but find it hard to establish whether crime increases simply because of the increased population density (urbanisation) or whether it is more specifically associated with tourism. Clearly the presence of large numbers of tourists carrying relatively large sums of money and valuables with them provides a source for illegal activities including drugs trafficking, robbery and violence. Brazil, Florida, and Jamaica are just three of the many destinations that have been the subject of international press coverage because of acts of violent crimes against tourists. Tourists are sometimes obvious victims of crime where they are clearly identifiable by language or colour and can be expected to be carrying significant sums of money with them.

Tourism is often the catalyst for the growth of gaming activities and a number of destinations have used casino developments as a means to attracting tourist spending. Unless properly monitored and controlled, such developments can induce social behaviour that is detrimental to social cohesion.

Where hotels attempt to protect their guests by the use of armed agents this can often inflame the social tension between tourists and local residents.

Health

The problem of AIDS has already been mentioned. However, there are other less newsworthy diseases that can be transmitted when people from different communities interact, such as the recording of more than 8,500 cases of malaria in the UK largely through tourists and **VFR** traffic. Although often not fatal, these illnesses can cause social and economic stress to the host population who may have less immunity to the diseases than the tourist population. Where tourism growth is rapid and unplanned there can be infrastructure failures that lead to health hazards.

Other aspects

Following the lead of Cohen (1988) it is possible to categorise the key themes that characterise the interface between culture and tourism. There are a variety of ways that such categories can be constructed but the following issues reflect the major concerns that are currently being debated:

- **Commodification** – where the demands of tourism lead to the mutation and sometimes destruction of the meaning of cultural performances and events. Tourists are likely to have different time frames and expectations to local residents and this may result in religious rituals and traditional ethnic customs and rites being changed to suit the needs and wishes of tourists. This process is sometimes referred to as reconstructed ethnicity.

- **Staged authenticity** – where 'pseudo-events' are presented to satisfy tourists' needs for new (simulated) experiences such as the Fijian firewalkers (see below).

- **Standardisation** – where the tourists' search for the familiar leads to a loss of cultural diversity.

- **Alien cultural experiences of tourists** – which examines the apparent inability to enjoy meaningful cultural experiences without travelling to different environments.

COMMODIFICATION

Commodification is a long-standing criticism relating to tourism's effect on culture and art. Crafts, ceremonies and rituals are often driven into an exploitation stance, abbreviated, made more colourful, more dramatic and spectacular in order to capture the attention and imagination of an audience that often does not possess the underlying knowledge/experience that would make the unadapted version appealing. Countless examples can and have been cited, from the sale of concrete paving slabs with carvings of Bob Marley on them in Jamaica, the *Bula Fiji* carved wooden knives and clubs, to the Polynesian dances of Western Samoa and the limbo dancers of the Caribbean. Where culture becomes a commodity for financial transactions it is difficult to be objective. Although it is true that the demands of people from alien cultures who are operating on a very tight and sometimes fixed time budget are very different to the local demands, it is sometimes this foreign demand that enriches and/or preserves decaying and dying skills and performances.

STAGED AUTHENTICITY

With growing public awareness regarding cultural and ethnic differences there has been increasing demand for tourism products that offer cultural authenticity. That is, environments where the tourists can 'get behind the scenes' to meet and observe the real people. Although, in the Plog sense, this may be considered a great leap forward in perception and understanding by volume tourists and a movement back from the psychocentric scale of the tourist market, it can also be regarded as being a signal for impending cultural devastation for some destinations. This represents the social impact dilemma of post-1980 tourism development.

In order to differentiate their product from other tourism products on the market destinations have highlighted environmental, climatic and cultural differences. In this last instance, they are using their cultural heritage as a promotional device to attract increasing numbers of tourists. Although this may be considered to be a positive step in achieving greater awareness concerning cultural differences and, perhaps, a greater empathy between tourist and host, it also exposes a deeper layer of the sociological structure and thereby risks further 'contamination'.

However, there are ways of differentiating the tourism product, providing tourists with sufficient cultural exposure to satisfy their demands while preserving the true cultural identity of the host population. One such way is the use of staged authenticity whereby the host population provides a more realistic performance of cultural heritage than existed before, but still ensures that the tourists do not manage to penetrate behind the stage curtains. Figure 7.3 demonstrates the concept and dangers of staged authenticity.

| FIGURE 7.3 | Levels of cultural penetration |

In Figure 7.3 the arena is divided into three distinct areas:

A – the previous level of tourist penetration into the host culture;

B – the new level of cultural penetration that is considered to be authentic by the tourist but is, in fact, staged authenticity; and

C – the true cultural heritage of the host society that maintains its integrity by keeping tourists on the other side of the firewall curtain.

Although effective in the short term, this approach to cultural impact containment can lead to increasing levels of penetration when the firewall curtains are continually retreating in order to provide greater tourist experiences and diversity within a competitive market. Even if the social firewall does not retreat there is a danger that some of the tourists will manage to penetrate beyond the curtain. Eventually there will be nowhere for the host population to maintain the integrity of their culture. There is an additional danger in the form of a *gradual* cultural impact. The very act of staging the authenticity of the culture can blur the true boundaries of the local heritage and, in so doing, distort the cultural heritage that is being maintained behind the firewall curtain.

It has also been argued that the so-called authenticity of culture is a fleeting moment in the development calendar. Culture is a dynamic living concept and changes continually in order to capture and embrace the needs of society in the present time period. From this point of view culture continually runs through a process of being invented and re-invented and that, in this sense, all of culture can be defined as staged authenticity.

An example of the dynamics of cultural performances can be seen in the Fijian firewalkers. Like the limbo dancers of the Caribbean, the firewalkers of Fiji are, today, almost exclusively found in cultural centres or hotels. In fact, they can be found wherever tourists are willing to exchange money for the privilege of watching these ancient customs that are packaged and transformed into dinner-side entertainment.

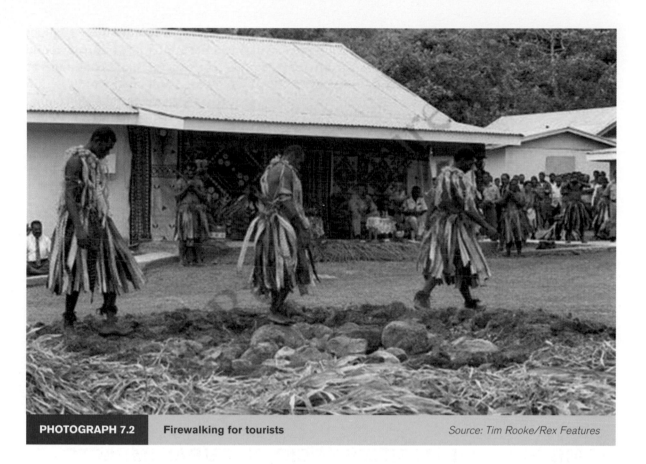

| PHOTOGRAPH 7.2 | Firewalking for tourists | Source: Tim Rooke/Rex Features |

The Fijians who perform the ritual known as *Vilavilairevo* (which translates literally into 'jumping into the oven') accept that the walking across the heated stones of a *lovo* (earth oven) is now a commercial event. It is rarely performed as a sign of respect for powerful and important visitors and never as a commemorative ritual to celebrate (and test the legend of) *Tui Qualita*. Nor does it any longer signify the conquering of the *lovo* in which a defeated warrior may be buried and baked. The tourists who visit Fiji often have no prior information about the origin of this particular form of firewalking but it does little to detract from the spectacular and impressive displays. The fact that the tourists, in spite of any narrative that may accompany the firewalking events, are unaware of the true meaning and significance of the ritual does not mean that tourism's mutation of the custom has created a gulf between host and visitor. That gulf existed prior to the performance and may well be one of the reasons why the tourist chose that destination. The commercialisation of the event in itself is also not wholly bad in that it generates much-needed currency for communities and, given its redundancy as part of modern-day Fijian culture preserves a custom and instils pride in the history and culture of the Fiji people.

STANDARDISATION

Tourists, although they may search for unfamiliar environments and cultures, often search for familiar facilities. Examples such as McDonald's demonstrate this effect quite clearly. This introduces a number of factors into the development scenario. First, there is the development of superstructure that might be quite different to that normally found in the local environment. Second, the operation of those facilities may introduce work practices and systems that are different to those normally found in the local economy, particularly their employment structures and conditions as well as their purchasing strategies. Finally, by building familiar structures within unfamiliar environments there is a loss of diversity that is as real to the socio-cultural environment as the loss of a species may be to biodiversity. This issue becomes more problematic as you move into the high volume tourist markets where destinations must not appear too strange if they wish to capture large segments of the market.

ALIEN CULTURAL EXPERIENCES OF TOURISTS

This issue revolves around the apparent inability of tourists to take part in or enjoy meaningful cultural experiences within their home environment. As with many of the aspects that underlie the motivation of tourists, it is not so much the inability of tourists to enjoy meaningful cultural experiences within their home environment, indeed many do so without even recognising the fact, it is more the reflection that tourists search for different – *or alien* – experiences. The desire to experience different climatic experiences (sun, rain or snow) and different environmental experiences (deserts, rainforests, cities or rolling green fields) are willingly accepted. Therefore, it is not an absurd proposition to suggest that tourists may actively seek out cultural experiences that are deliberately different from their norm – indeed such motivation is becoming an increasingly important aspect of twenty-first-century tourism.

SOME GENERAL POSITIVE SOCIO-CULTURAL IMPACTS ASSOCIATED WITH TOURISM

Tourism fosters local pride

Tourism can inspire pride in a destination's heritage. Often we forget the value of the things that surround us and only when seen through the eyes of tourists do we revalue our culture. Ceremonies and rituals that have become jaded over time and can lose their appeal to local residents. Tourism can put new life into such ceremonies and make them come alive once more. The same is true regarding old skills and crafts that, without tourism may have ceased to exist in a modern world where they lose relevance. Of course, it can be argued that if these skills or crafts were past their sell by date and would have ceased to exist then they should be allowed to have a peaceful natural death and not be preserved as something that is 'quaint' for the sake of tourism.

Tourism for socio-cultural awareness and peace

Tourism takes people to new places and broadens their understanding and knowledge of other cultures and environments. This is an educational process and is an important part of the industry. If channelled properly this education can lead to a greater awareness, sympathy and admiration for other societies. This cultural exchange that takes place between tourists and local residents can help foster peace between communities. So strong is the belief in the relationship between tourism and peace that in 1986 the International Institute for Peace through Tourism (IIPT) was set up. The IIPT has organised several conferences since its inception and in November 2000 made the Amman Declaration that set out the fundamental objectives of the IIPT and those that were aligned to the movement. This was ratified by more than 450 delegates from 60 countries and included the chief executive officers of 22 major international tourism corporations. The Amman Declaration was a far-reaching document that attempts to incorporate socio-cultural, environmental and economic objectives under a single banner.

Tourism provides shared infrastructure

When tourism is developed in a destination the local infrastructure is often enhanced to meet the needs of this development. The local community can find that the quality of their life is significantly enhanced through being able to enjoy this improved infrastructure. This can be as simple as the increased health afforded by improved water supply and sewage treatment to the more complex issues surrounding the provision of an airport and access to regular international flights. New sporting venues, entertainment facilities, restaurants and a better range of food and beverage available for consumption are just some of the many positive side-effects that tourism can create for the local population.

Tourism can provide direct socio-cultural support

The tourism industry can provide much-needed funds to help restore heritage sites or conserve natural and cultural sites. Examples of such good practice can be found on the Tour Operators Initiative web site http://www.toinitiative.org/good_practices/case_studies.htm. They include examples such as the Travel Walji's case where the company is not only providing direct financial support to conservation in the Karakorum region of South Asia but is also providing indirect support to the area through its tourism development aid.

Tourism can yield enormous socio-cultural benefits as well as devastating costs. The net effect depends upon the responsibility exercised by the various stakeholders of the industry including the public and private sectors as well as the tourists and residents. To be able to evaluate the net socio-cultural benefits of tourism it is necessary to be able to measure the benefits and costs in an objective and acceptable framework.

METHODS OF MEASURING THE SOCIO-CULTURAL IMPACT OF TOURISM

Data collection

The socio-cultural factors influenced by tourist activities are, in general, the most difficult ones to measure and quantify. Whereas the economic and many of the environmental indicators do lend themselves to objective measurement, the

247

socio-cultural impacts are often highly qualitative and subjective in nature. The nature of socio-cultural impacts can range from those impacts that are obvious and measurable, such as the outbreak of particular types of disease and/or infection, to those that are hard to identify and measure such as changes in customs and codes of conduct. On the other hand, there are those impacts that may be identifiable, such as increased crime rates, drug abuse and prostitution, but are difficult to attribute to tourism rather than to other factors of influence (such as media intrusion).

There is a wide range of data sources that may be utilised in order to examine the social impact of tourism. It is important to recognise that some of these data may not be exclusively related to tourism activity. Where causes of variable changes are multivariate then deeper analysis must be undertaken in order to filter out other influences. Complete filtering is unlikely to be possible.

Data collection sources can be categorised into primary and secondary. Primary data can be collected by undertaking household and visitor surveys. This method of data collection is time consuming and costly. It is also sometimes difficult to maintain the appropriate level of objectivity and the resident awareness questionnaires require very careful construction if they are to provide data that are both unbiased and in a form that is user-friendly. Other forms of primary data collection include the interviewing of **focus groups**, **key informants**, **Delphi analyses** and participant observation. Table 7.2 distinguishes between interview/questionnaire/Delphi approaches and those that use observation techniques.

There are a variety of secondary sources for gathering information with respect to socio-cultural impacts. These include criminal activity statistics, notification of infectious diseases statistics, employment and unemployment data, newspaper reports/articles and other media coverage. Some of these data are quantitative in nature whereas others are quite subjective and care must be taken in the interpretation. Table 7.2 distinguishes between those data that are collected, assimilated and tabulated for other purposes, and information (largely qualitative) that can be gleaned from scanning past and present newspaper cuttings, television and radio news and documentary programmes and other media forms of covering current affairs.

The two fundamental means of assessing socio-cultural impacts in a destination are by surveying both tourists and local residents. There are several factors that should be taken into account when undertaking a local resident survey.

First, it is important, as with all sampling procedures, to obtain a representative sample of the population. This may seem obvious, but several social impact studies have relied entirely upon random sampling of the immediate population (those directly in the vicinity of the tourist facilities). In order to gauge the true impact and its level of penetration it is important that the survey population is seen as being wider than this. Second, it is important to establish whether or not the respondent correctly identifies who is a tourist. The misperception as to what constitutes a tourist can render local resident surveys misleading. Third, in areas subject to seasonality, it is also important to undertake the survey at different times of the year. Quite often a good indicator of the magnitude of the social impact of tourism is how quickly the levels of awareness, resentment and other characteristics decline once the peak season recedes. Where there is a significant level of decline shortly after the peak season one can assume that the impacts, although severe during the peak period, are not too deeply embedded in the local population. Where remedial action is required in visitor management flows or **infrastructural**

	Primary data		Secondary data	
Indicators (changes in)	Survey	Observe	Data	Media
Crime rates/levels	X		X	X
Prostitution		X	X	X
Drug abuse	X		X	X
Promiscuity	X	X	X	X
Gambling	X		X	X
Family relationships	X		X	X
Social values	X	X	X	X
Creative expressions	X	X		X
Traditional ceremonies	X	X		X
Safety levels	X		X	
Health	X		X	
Community organisations	X		X	X
Infrastructure	X	X	X	X
Collective lifestyles	X	X		X
Economic independence	X		X	X
Population dispersion	X		X	
Cultural commercialisation	X	X	X	X
Host/tourist hostility	X		X	X
Demonstration effects	X	X		
Economic and social dualism	X		X	X
Psychological stress	X		X	X
Living standards	X		X	X

TABLE 7.2   Data from different sources

investment, there is every chance that these actions will be successful. If the levels of resentment continue to run high during the off-peak periods then there is a distinct possibility that any remedial action will need to be fundamental even to the point of reducing the peak levels of tourism flows.

In order to complement the work that has already been undertaken in the field of economic and environmental impacts and to provide a common framework for the analysis of socio-cultural impacts, researchers at Bournemouth University have attempted to embed the process of socio-cultural impacts within the economic and environmental model structure. The inclusion of socio-cultural impacts within such a model allows for the direct, indirect and induced impacts to be considered as well as providing a vehicle for the study of social and cultural changes as a result of other (non-tourism-related) factors.

At this point in time the number of socio-cultural variables that can be included at such a detailed and quantifiable level are limited but include indicators such as:

- the ratio of tourists to host population;

- the number of contacts between hosts and guests for transactions;

- the number of contacts between hosts and guests while sharing facilities;

- the number of contacts between hosts and guests for socio-cultural purposes;

- differences between host and guest age distributions;

- percentage of local population coming into contact with tourists;

- percentage of population working in tourism-related industries weighted by indirect and induced employment;

- tourist/host clustering; and

- the nature of tourism.

The above data should be collected and analysed at relatively frequent intervals. Some of these data are readily available in most countries and systems can be put into place to show those ratios on a weekly or monthly basis. Others are more difficult to acquire and may only be available at discrete time intervals.

CONCLUSION

This chapter has examined the nature and determinants of the socio-cultural impacts associated with tourism development. In so doing, the nature of the tourism development process has been explored and the influence of socio-economic factors in driving the development of tourism. The typological studies undertaken by researchers such as Smith and Plog have provided a framework which facilitates the further development of socio-cultural impact methodologies and that framework can be used to show the commonalities of the models suggested by Butler and Doxey. But, it was noted, this framework is static and is severely limited by the nature of the variables used. The development of tourism can have specific implications for incidents of crime and health, as well as influencing the individual and collective lifestyles of the local population. It was also noted that there are positive aspects to tourism's socio-cultural impacts and that these should not be neglected when evaluating the performance of tourism in a given destination. It is also important to recognise the fact that tourists can also transmit socio-cultural impacts back to the populations of the originating countries.

The problems associated with measuring either the desirability of preserving the cultural heritage of a destination or determining how this is influenced by the presence of tourists make it a difficult area of research. The staged authenticity approach to tourism development can provide a firewall in order to maintain the integrity of the local cultural heritage. However, staged authenticity can also act as a catalyst for further cultural penetration and act as the 'thin end of the wedge' for further intrusion.

There are data available that can be used to analyse the magnitude and direction of socio-cultural impacts and these were examined in order to suggest a framework for an integrated tourism impact model.

Self-check questions

1 What are the major approaches to studying the socio-cultural impacts of tourism?

2 What models have been put forward to explain the development of tourism and its impact on the local population?

3 Identify three direct positive socio-cultural impacts of tourism and three indirect positive socio-cultural impacts of tourism.

4 Identify three direct negative socio-cultural impacts of tourism and three indirect negative socio-cultural impacts of tourism.

5 What are the major difficulties involved in measuring the socio-cultural impacts of tourism and what sources of data are available?

Essay questions

1 'It is not the *absolute* characteristics of the tourists that determine the degree of socio-cultural impact on a destination, it is the *relative* difference between the profiles of the tourists and those of the local population that is important.' Discuss.

2 Examine the commonalities and differences between the tourism typology studies, the life-cycle theories and the work of Doxey as a means to studying the determination of socio-cultural impacts.

3 'The lack of a base line from which to measure tourism's socio-cultural impacts and the inability to isolate changes from other sources such as television and films makes it impossible to determine the impacts of tourism.' Discuss.

4 Are the socio-cultural impacts associated with tourism development necessarily negative?

5 What key variables can be used to measure the magnitude, scope and direction of socio-cultural impacts? Outline the weaknesses and strengths of these variables.

Annotated further reading

Books

Duval, D.T. (2004) *Tourism in the Caribbean: Trends, Development, Prospects*, Routledge, London.
A book that examines a wide range of tourism issues in the Caribbean, including the cultural implications and tourism impacts at historic sites.

Gartner, W.C. and Lime, D.W. (2000) (eds) *Trends in Outdoor Recreation, Leisure and Tourism*, CABI, Wallingford, Oxford.
A comprehensive collection of papers examining the implications of tourism for development, the economy, society and on the environment.

Krippendorf, J. (1987) *The Holiday Makers – Understanding the Impact of Leisure and Travel*, Heinemann, London.
The author places his arguments in favour of responsible tourism in the context of Maslow's pyramid of needs and looks at the demands and effects of the tourists once they have satisfied their basic demands.

Mathieson, A. and Wall, G. (1982) *Tourism: Economic, Physical and Social Impacts*, Longman, Harlow.
Although somewhat dated it still provides a very readable journey into the impacts of tourism upon society and culture.

Smith, V.L. and Eadington, W.R. (eds) (1995) *Tourism Alternatives: Potential Problems in the Development of Tourism*, University of Pennsylvania Press, Philadelphia, PA.
A reflection on the socio-cultural impacts of alternative forms of tourism development.

Articles

Berno, T. (1999) 'When a guest is a guest: Cook Islanders view tourism', *Annals of Tourism Research* **26**(3), 656–675.
This article reports the findings of cross-cultural psychological research undertaken in the Cook Islands. It is argued that differences in the ways that hosts and guests conceptualise tourism in the Cook Islands are related to the socio-cultural and psychological impacts of the industry.

Brunt, P. and Courtney, P. (1999) 'Host perceptions of socio-cultural impacts', *Annals of Tourism Research* **26**(3), 493–515.
This paper investigates community perceptions of the socio-cultural impacts of tourism and examines the extent to which they coincide with their classifications made by academic writers.

Graburn N.H.H. and Barthel-Bouchier, D. (2001) 'Relocating the Tourist', *International Sociology* **16**(2), 147–158.
This article traces the arrival and the subsequent debates about the place of the tourist in sociology. The sociology of tourists focused first on their economic and then their physical and socio-cultural impacts, in the stereotypical case of mass

tourists of the metropolis visiting historical and peripheral locations. More recently, Graburn and Smith differentiated tourists by class, gender and lifestyle, and then by national origin.

Web site

http://www.theepicentre.com/Destinations/customs.html
The Epicentre web site provides a rich tapestry of different customs and culinary traditions adopted by a wide range of countries.

References cited and bibliography

Butler, R.W. (1980) 'The concept of a tourist area cycle of evolution: implications for management of resources', *Canadian Geographer* **24**(1), 5–12.

Cohen, E. (1984) 'The sociology of tourism: approaches, issues and findings, *Annual Review of Sociology* **10**, 373–92.

Cohen, E. (1988) 'Authenticity and commoditization in tourism', *Annals of Tourism Research* **15**, 371–86.

de Kadt, E. (ed.) (1979) *Tourism: Passport to Development?*, Oxford University Press, New York.

Doxey, G.V. (1975) 'When enough's enough: the natives are restless in Old Niagara', *Heritage Canada* **2**(2), 26–7.

Gill, A. and Williams, P. (1994) 'Managing growth in mountain tourism communities', *Tourism Management* **15**(3), 212–20.

Inskeep, E. (1991) *Tourism Planning: An Integrated and Sustainable Development Approach*, Van Nostrand Reinhold, New York.

Jafari, J. (1987) 'Tourism models: the sociocultural aspects', *Tourism Management* **8**(2), 151–9.

Mathieson, A. and Wall, G. (1982) *Tourism: Economic, Physical and Social Impacts*, Longman, Harlow.

Murphy, P.E. (1985) *Tourism: A Community Approach*, Methuen, New York.

Plog, S.C. (1977) 'Why destination areas rise and fall in popularity', Kelly, E.M. (ed.), in *Domestic and International Tourism*, Institute of Certified Travel Agents, Wellesley, MA.

Plog, S.C. (2004) *Leisure Travel: A Marketing Handbook*, Pearson Prentice Hall, Upper Saddle River, New Jersey, p. 59.

Price, M.F. (1992) 'Patterns of the development of tourism in mountain environments', *Geojournal* **27**(1), 87–96.

Smith, V.L. (1989) *Hosts and Guests: The Anthropology of Tourism*, 2nd edn, University of Pennsylvania Press, Philadelphia, PA.

Stokowski, P.A. (1996) *Riches and Regrets: Betting on Gambling in Two Colorado Mountain Towns*, University Press of Colorado, Niwot, Colorado.

Stokowski, P.A. (2000) 'Assessing social impacts of resource-based recreation and tourism', pp. 265–74 in Gartner, W.C. and Lime, D.W. (eds), *Trends in Outdoor Recreation, Leisure and Tourism*, CABI, Wallingford, Oxford.

Stymeist, D.H. (1996) 'Transformation of Vilavilairevo in tourism', *Annals of Tourism Research* **23**(1).

MAJOR CASE STUDY 7.1
UDAIPUR AS A LEARNING CITY
Background for study on tourism in Udaipur,
winter 2001

Tourism has been highly touted as a route to the development of a city or environment. It professes to bring much-needed revenue and employment to the inhabitants of the place, while simultaneously claiming to preserve its cultural, historical, or natural 'attractions'. These arguments are currently being used by the Rajasthan government in its mission to expand tourism in the state (an estimated expenditure of nearly Rs 1,200 crore (27.7 million US$)). Because Udaipur and its surrounding villages are targets within this development plan, it is relevant and pressing to consider the influence these new policies/plans will have on the people of Udaipur, their economy, environment, culture and social relationships.

The following background paper seeks to bring out critical points from the *Rajiv Gandhi Tourism Development Mission for Rajasthan* (the most current proposal on tourism development in Rajasthan), as well as to highlight pertinent information about tourism. This article can be used as a starting point from which to generate critical and creative ideas for the further exploration of tourism.

THE PLANS OF THE RAJASTHAN GOVERNMENT

Annexure B in the *Tourism Development Mission* lists eight areas for which the growth of tourism in Rajasthan is important:

1 Employment generation

2 Poverty alleviation

3 Empowerment of women

4 Survival of rural artists

5 Upliftment of rural artists

6 Improvement in urban and rural infrastructure

7 Better image, quality of life and attitude of people

8 Revival of traditions and heritage conservation and management

These points form the comprehensive plan to uplift and empower the people of Rajasthan through an economy based in tourism – the largest growing industry in the world. This plan seeks to include urban and rural areas, as well as women, in increasing incomes, improving infrastructure, and encouraging full-spectrum participation.

From this list, we can roughly draw four categories by which to understand tourism:

1 tourism as an economic industry;

2 the environmental implications of tourism;

3 the effects of tourism on social relationships; and

4 the impact of tourism on culture, arts and language.

These categories are not mutually exclusive; they overlap and interact in a variety of ways. However, for the purpose of this case study the focus will be on the fourth aspect the impact of tourism on culture, arts and language.

The impact of tourism on culture, arts, and language

'[W]hen we travel, we buy a product, a product that includes people. Travel offers an exciting chance (for those who can afford it) to buy or become, if only for a little while, a part of another culture.'

Deborah McLaren

Tourism in Udaipur, as in the whole of Rajasthan, largely highlights its traditional crafts and cultural and historical monuments. By creating more access to rural areas and artisans, the government sees two levels of benefits. One, tourists have increased interest in rural regions; and two, rural economies are uplifted as artisans and other members of the community have the ability to capitalise on their traditional skills (with possibilities even for world travel, the *Tourism Development Mission* suggests). Further, by making historical and cultural sites attractive for corporate investment, more funds can enter the state. For example, the *Tourism Development Mission* suggests an 'Adopt-a-Monument Scheme' for corporate and institutional donors. It also seeks to lease out premier heritage sites to internationally acclaimed hotel chains. By functioning on a competitive bid system, the government hopes to bring in a hefty sum of money, while simultaneously attracting big names to develop the heritage and culture of Rajasthan.

There are several questions to be asked here. First, can rural life serve as a tourist attraction? By turning traditional ways of living and the production of crafts into tourism products, people compromise their cultures and common functions of their lives. The 'products' that sell best become the focus of work and life. This not only distorts traditional meanings and uses, but it also contributes to the disappearance of those crafts that do not sell. In addition to crafts, there is concern that innovations and knowledges are being pirated and patented as 'intellectual property'. Tourists enter forests, farmlands and sacred places and walk away with local plant or wildlife, healing treatments, grains, spices, etc. This 'bio-piracy' results not only in economic loss, but also in the loss of living systems.

In considering the cultural and historical impacts of tourism in Udaipur, the major touristed sites in the *Tourism Development Mission* include Jag Niwas, City Palace and Saheliyon-ki-Bari. If these sites are turned solely into sources for corporate income generation (they are not far from there), how will they lose meaning for the community? A cultural or historical site represents different qualities and values to a community – whether through use, religious significance, location, etc. When the 'ownership' of such a site shifts to a single party for economic benefit, the community associations to that site – largely cultural – also change. This may be reflected in a loss of perceived responsibility to a site, loss of traditional access and use, and resentment when cultural or historical significance is perverted.

Author's note: Udaipur, known as the City of Dawn, or the Jewel of Mewar, is set at the edge of seven lakes. It is a place of beauty and has significant heritage resources including gardens, museums, palaces and temples.

Source: http://www.swaraj.org/shikshantar/ulc_tourism.htm

DISCUSSION QUESTIONS

1 Can rural life be sustainable if it is used as a tourism product?

2 If income generation becomes dependent upon the 'sale' of culture and heritage, how is this likely to distort the future development of those resources?

3 If crafts and skills only survive because of their value to tourism should we be concerned if some crafts and skills disappear?

CHAPTER EIGHT
SUSTAINABLE TOURISM

INTRODUCTION

This chapter investigates the concept, definition and practical applications of sustainable tourism. Sustainability has become a fashionable term with respect to tourism development and operation. However, there is a significant amount of confusion relating to the meaning of sustainability and whether or not such a thing is achievable with respect to the tourism sector. The chapter looks at the historical background of sustainability and how it applies to tourism activity. Following a debate about the origin of the term and its definition in general, the implications of the concept for tourism are considered. The threshold levels of destinations are examined under the heading of carrying capacity, a fundamental aspect of sustainability. Carrying capacity is associated with economic, environmental and social impacts as well as the ability of the tourism product to withstand degradation as flows increase. Finally, no discussion on sustainability would be complete without looking at the alternative tourism products that have been put forward in the name of sustainability.

LEARNING OUTCOMES

This chapter focuses on the sustainability issues relating to the development and operation of tourism activities and is intended to provide you with:

- an understanding of the concept of sustainability and an appreciation of the difficulties associated with trying to derive a universally acceptable definition;

- an appreciation of how the sustainability issue pervades all aspects of the tourism process and applies to all of the **stakeholders** involved in the tourism process;

- a recognition of the different ways that tourism can pursue sustainability objectives and the limitations likely to be experienced;

- an understanding of the concept of carrying capacity and the difficulties involved in applying that concept in the real world; and

- an insight into alternative forms of tourism, including eco-tourism products and how they attempt to improve the sustainability of tourism and what there limitations may be.

HISTORICAL BACKGROUND

Sustainability is now one of the most common concepts used in tourism development discussions. At the same time it is also one of the least understood concepts and both academics and practitioners are still a very long way from reaching a consensus regarding its definition. The analytical framework of sustainability is broad, encompassing economics, environmental and socio-cultural issues while using ethics and the platforms of intra- and inter-generational equity as the instruments of the debate. Type **'sustainable development'** into an Internet search engine and you will find 4.5 million listings with more than 1.5 million relevant references. Sustainable tourism produces 1.5 million listings with more than 250,000 relevant references. There are literally hundreds of definitions of sustainability. The movement towards today's environmental sustainability platform can be traced back to the late nineteenth century when the first formal signs of concern about the planet upon which we live manifested themselves in the formation of protection societies and national parks (Yellowstone National Park, USA, 1872; Royal Society for the Protection of Birds, UK, 1889, National Trust, UK, 1894). National Parks were formed in many Commonwealth countries (Australia, Canada and New Zealand) towards the later stages of the nineteenth century and within the UK at the start of the twentieth century. Economics has never been far away from the issues of sustainability because of its focus upon the optimum use of scarce resources and sustainability issues have been explored for the best part of a century. The 1960s was a catalytic decade that saw the first major movements towards mass concern for the planet, perhaps in response to the post-war period of rapid economic development and special changes together with the realisation of the planet's fragility fuelled by the first images of Earth from space. The early 1970s witnessed the first United Nations (UNEP) Conference on the Human Environment (Stockholm, 1972) which produced an action plan for the environment based on:

1 the global environmental assessment programme (Earthwatch);

2 environmental management activities; and

3 international measures to support the national and international actions of assessment and management.

The Stockholm Conference resulted in the commissioning of the World Conservation Strategy (WCS) (1980) which can be seen as the implementation arm of the human environmental action plan in that its focus was on explaining how development and conservation could work together. The next landmark in the pathway to sustainability was the Bruntland Report (1987) which stated that one of its primary goals was to:

help define shared perceptions of long-term environmental issues and the appropriate efforts needed to deal successfully with the problems of protecting and enhancing the environment, a long-term agenda for action during the coming decades, and aspirational goals of the world community. (Bruntland, 1987: ix)

The Bruntland Report has been criticised on the grounds that many of its predictions and concerns did not materialise but it provided an invaluable platform for the debate on the north–south poverty divide as well as underscoring the global concerns that had been the outcome of the Stockholm Conference. Within five years of the Bruntland Report the Earth Summit was held in Rio Janeiro (1992) putting down a landmark for sustainability in the form of broad action strategy that is known as Agenda 21. The good intentions that came out of the 1992 Summit still apply today what has been lacking has been any significant action to implement the resolutions that came out of the Summit. This was the main focus of the Johannesburg Summit of 2002. The next decade or so will be the test to see if there is a genuine will among governments to implement the global strategies and actions that were set out more than a decade ago.

Any form of production and consumption will have sustainability implications and therefore the debate of sustainable development should rightly encompass all forms of activity. Tourism in particular comes under the sustainability spotlight because (a) production and consumption tends to take place in areas where the natural or man-made resources are fragile (for example, areas of natural beauty, coastal areas, heritage buildings, etc.) and (b) the environment and culture are often used as a major component of the product without being subject to the price mechanisms that apply to many natural resources.

DEFINITIONS OF SUSTAINABILITY

The Bruntland Report (1987) defined sustainability to be 'meeting the needs of the present generation without compromising the ability of future generations to meet their own needs' and it went on to identify some basic principles of sustainability. These identified needs were to:

- take an holistic approach to planning and strategy;

- protect the environment (biodiversity) and man-made heritage;

- preserve the essential ecological processes;

- facilitate and engage public participation;

- ensure that productivity can be sustained into the long-term future; and

- provide for a better level of fairness and opportunity between different countries.

The last identified need in the above list could be in direct conflict with the overall definition of sustainability that the Bruntland Report used. This is the debate between intra-generational equity and inter-generational equity. If the latter objective is pursued without concern for the former than there is an implicit assumption that the distribution of wealth and opportunity in the present day is somehow optimal and this is not a point that many would be able to defend.

Murcott (1996) lists 57 definitions of sustainability that range from the early definitions proposed by Coomer (1979) that suggested that a sustainable society is not a no-growth society but one that lives within the self-perpetuating limits of its own environment, through the WCS (1980) definition that focused its attention on maintaining the essential ecological processes, to the more recent suggestion by Choucri (1997) who argues that it is the process of managing social demands without eroding life support properties or mechanisms of social cohesion or resilience.

The vagueness of the definitions and, according to Butcher (1997), the hypocrisy that often accompanies the international organisations that have flaunted sustainable development on the global stage have tended to undermine the principles of sustainable development and have done little to enhance the implementation of sustainable practices around the world. To be effective any objective must possess certain characteristics. They should be clear, unambiguous, non-conflicting, measurable and achievable. The reality of sustainable development as it has been defined to date is that it fails on nearly all of these counts. On that basis alone sustainable development cannot be considered to be achievable.

The term 'sustainable development' could be replaced by terms such as 'wise use' or 'sound planning' as they have in the past, but even here it is too vague and still begs any mechanism by which it could be measured or achieved. Economists could argue that all resources should be properly costed and included within the market process so that rational decisions can be made on the basis of complete information. But the issue is much wider than the economics of the environment, the planet's heritage and culture is also part of the system and these too should be included within the decision-making processes.

The responsibility of pursuing sustainability is also a matter of some importance because it is not simply the responsibility of the international organisations or the governments that support them. Industry has a key role to play in recognising the importance of social responsibility and long-term objectives. Consumers are also an important stakeholder in the quest for sustainability yet both industry and consumers are driven by short-term needs and objectives that work counter to the long-term goals of sound planning and sustainability.

The proponents of sustainability can be subdivided into two schools of thought, those that may be classified as strong or full sustainable supporters and those that may be deemed to be weak or partial sustainable supporters. In order to examine the two schools it is necessary to define the different types of resource that are subject to depletion or degradation. Simplistically we can categorise them into four types of capital stock:

1 Human – the population, welfare, health, workforce, educational and skill base.

2 Physical – productive capital such as machinery equipment, buildings.

3 Environmental – man-made and natural resources, biodiversity.

4 Socio-cultural – well-being, social cohesion, empowerment, equity, cultural heritage.

These four categories of capital stock are shown in Figure 8.1. In reality there are significant overlaps between these categories. However, they do serve to explain the differences between the two schools of thought and the concept of sustainability.

At any point in time there is a given stock of each form of capital. These capital stocks can be used for production that will be either consumed or invested

FIGURE 8.1   Sustainability and capital stocks

back into the capital stock. The strong sustainability proponents would argue that sustainability meant that the level of each of these individual capital stocks must be maintained for future generations. The weak sustainability proponents would argue that the total capital stock (i.e. the sum of all four categories) must be maintained but that it is possible to deplete one stock in order to increase another. Clearly some of the capital stocks are responsive to investment. Education and health services are two ways of improving the quality of the population and workforce and this stock can be increased over time by such investment. In the long term there are likely to be diminishing returns to such investments. The physical capital stock is that capital used for productive purposes and this can and is being invested in all the time both for replacement purposes and for new investment to increase productive capacity. Some aspects of the environmental capital can respond to investment, the creation of national parks, cleaning up rivers, preventing air and noise pollution being examples on the natural environment side and with respect to the built environment, the construction of new homes, shopping malls, hotels, etc. However, there is clearly a trade-off between these two elements of the environmental stock. Bridging the environmental capital stock with the socio-cultural stock there is also scope for investment in temples and monuments. Finally, with respect to the socio-cultural capital stock it is possible to invest in customs and traditions by training and raising the profiles of them within the local population and to visitors to ensure their continuity.

If the strong sustainability approach is adopted there is a serious question mark over any form of production because, although it is possible to invest in some of the capital stocks and to restore their levels, it is not possible to increase the level of others without adopting a no-growth stance. For instance, new physical capital cannot be created without depleting some of the environmental capital stocks. Wherever land or raw materials are used then this represents a depletion of that capital stock and unless alternative land or raw materials can be recovered from elsewhere such a process will have a finite future and cannot be sustained.

DEFINITIONS OF SUSTAINABLE TOURISM

With respect to tourism the definition of sustainability has not achieved any better success. Using the Bruntland definition as its starting point the World Tourism Organization defines sustainable tourism to be:

Sustainable tourism development meets the needs of present tourists and host regions while protecting and enhancing opportunity for the future. It is envisaged as leading to management of all resources in such a way that economic, social, and aesthetic needs can be fulfilled while maintaining cultural integrity, essential ecological processes, and biological diversity, and life support systems. (World Tourism Organization)

There have been many variations of this definition used by regions and countries around the world. For instance, the Organization of East Caribbean States (OECS) provides the following definition:

The optimal use of natural and cultural resources for national development on an equitable and self-sustaining basis to provide a unique visitor experience and an improved quality of life through partnership among government, the private sector and communities.

Whichever definition of the hundreds that have been published seems most relevant, the key factors that come out of the debate on definitions of sustainability are that sustainability requires appropriate consideration of the long-term economic, environmental, socio-cultural and political well-being of all stakeholders. That to achieve such long-term goals requires the engagement of all of the stakeholders involved in the production and consumption process.

SUSTAINABILITY OF TOURISM

Tourism is not an industry that sits easily within the concept of sustainability. International tourism, for instance, involves major transport components, cultural mixes and fierce resource competition. Examining each aspect of sustainability with respect to tourism activity and development paints a depressing picture.

Economic aspects working against sustainable tourism

To work within the parameters of 'wise use' or 'sustainability' it is important that the net long-term economic benefits are optimal. The economic impact of tourism, discussed in Chapter 6, means that tourism competes with other industries for the use of factors of production, as such it can stimulate price inflation by driving up the cost of land and labour. It attracts workers from rural areas who may have been employed in the traditional industries causing the output levels in those industries to fall. Scarce investment funds may be attracted to the tourism industry on the promise of rapid returns and foreign exchange inflows. This can distort the allocation of resources in the longer term and lead to structural unemployment. Where tourism development takes place in industrialised urban areas the above may not present severe obstacles but to less developed countries or sparsely populated regions the effects associated with the development of tourism can be economically traumatic.

Environmental aspects working against sustainable tourism

Airlines are responsible for a major aspect of air pollution and the vast majority of air transport is for tourism purposes. Tourism is about real estate development and so it competes for land use and depletes the natural environmental stock as it does so. Tourism activities can be severely disruptive to biodiversity from the extreme activities of hunting and fishing to the less obvious disruptions through wildlife observing and hill walking. The spectacular is often headline material such as the effects of boats, anchors and pollution on the coral reefs in the Caribbean. The unusual also captures headlines such as visitors to the Antarctic, the degradation of the environment at Everest Base Camp, the erosion of ancient monuments. The increased presence of tourists in the tombs of the Valley of the Kings, Egypt can raise the humidity levels by several percentage points and this increases the erosion from pollutants. The less spectacular is no less devastating such as the increased use of fossil fuels for energy consumption and water desalination, the construction of roads, airports and sea ports to cater for the travel of tourists. The introduction of large numbers of visitors to environmentally fragile areas will always be accompanied by tension between the natural environment and tourism.

Socio-cultural aspects working against sustainable tourism

Tourists, whether they come from the explorers that Valene Smith suggests adapt to local norms or the mass tourists who do not adapt at all will always have socio-cultural impacts on the local community. They may be through natural curiosity where the empathetic visitor is intrigued by local customs and traditions so they go to observe and that observation can set in motion a commercialisation process that will sooner or later change the events. Or it could be the psychocentric visitor who wishes no surprises, does not wish to get involved but, through the demonstration effect of their behaviour, dress and customs alter the corresponding behaviour, dress and customs of the local residents. Because tourism requires the tourists to visit the destination these negative impacts are bound to be a threat.

Irrespective of the difficulties encountered when trying to define sustainable tourism in a useable and acceptable manner there are approaches that can be

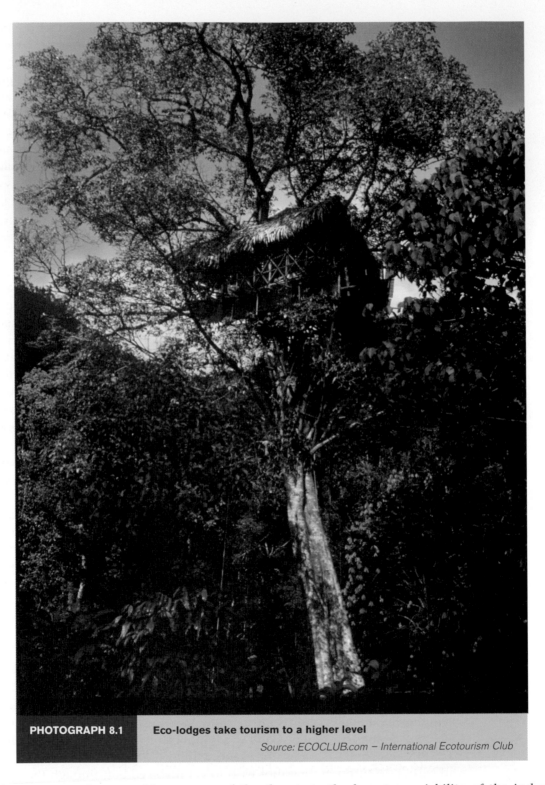

PHOTOGRAPH 8.1	Eco-lodges take tourism to a higher level

Source: ECOCLUB.com − International Ecotourism Club

taken to mitigate some of the threats to the long-term viability of the industry. One approach is to set limits on the future growth of tourism in each destination. This would not necessarily improve the net benefits derived from tourism for any destination and in those destinations where tourism was already creating problems it would not secure its long-term viability. Another approach is to change the behaviour of the stakeholders in the tourism industry to make the products currently provided more sustainable. This could involve better socio-cultural and environmental management within businesses together with better awareness and behaviour from tourists towards the destination's environment and culture. It would also probably require some changes to the economic structure and power balance between the businesses involved in the supply chain of tourism products so that local factors were fully and equitably included within the market processes. The third approach is to replace the current (unsustainable) tourism products with new products that are sustainable.

To be successful it is likely that a combination of all three approaches will be necessary. That is, there will need to be a change in the behaviour of stakeholders with businesses, tourists and local residents behaving more responsibly, with limits or thresholds being placed on developments and activities (carrying capacity) and with new products being introduced that have greater empathy with the local environment and culture. The following discussion examines the issues surrounding the identification of carrying capacity for a destination.

Thresholds and carrying capacity

The fact that tourism activity impacts on the social, cultural, environmental and economic aspects of a destination brings with it certain implications for sustainability. Even with a more aware tourism industry or more environmentally friendly types of tourism activity there will be thresholds beyond which the negative impacts easily outweigh the economic advantages. It would be unrealistic to assume that these impacts could be eliminated altogether and therefore, the volume of tourists and the type of activity they pursue will have a direct implication for sustainability. If it is assumed that there are both positive and negative impacts associated with tourism and that the net effects are likely to diminish as the volume of tourism increases there will be certain thresholds beyond which additional tourists will create unacceptable net impacts (economically, environmentally or socially). Exceeding these thresholds is likely to affect every facet of tourism development. For instance, exceeding:

- physical thresholds will limit the volume of tourist flows and expose tourists to safety hazards;

- environmental thresholds will also limit the tourist flows by creating secondary problems, such as health hazards, or detract from the attractiveness of a destination;

- social and cultural thresholds will generate resentment and antagonism towards tourists from the host population;

- tourist flow thresholds will affect the satisfaction levels of tourists and cause them to search elsewhere for a better product; and

- economic thresholds will result in misallocation of resources and factors of production.

The main difficulty with which we are faced is finding the level of the thresholds beyond which tourism should not venture. As with the definitions of sustainability, defining these thresholds and the carrying capacity implied by them is a difficult task. Scientists from a wide range of specialist fields have attempted, with varying degrees of success, to provide a working definition of carrying capacity. For instance, ecologists might define carrying capacity as 'the population of an identified species which can be supported throughout the foreseeable future, within a defined habitat, without causing permanent damage to the ecosystem upon which it is ultimately dependent'. If this type of definition is transferred to the human species some modifications must be made unless the 'defined habitat' is taken to be the planet as a whole. That is, the territorial boundaries are not unique or limiting in terms of the ability of the species' population to survive. What happens within one territorial boundary may well influence the long-term viability of the species in others.

With respect to tourism, one approach is to adopt Hardin's (1991) formulation of human impact and simply transfer it to tourism such as that set out below:

tourism's impact = tourist population × tourist impact, per capita

However, this is not sufficient and such a definition fails to reflect the variety of influences relating to the nature of the tourist activity, the vulnerability of the destination, technological change and so on.

Carrying capacity has been defined as 'the maximum number of people who can use a site without an unacceptable alteration in the physical environment and without an unacceptable decline in the quality of experience gained by visitors' (Mathieson and Wall, 1982). Note that the use of words like 'acceptable' means that there will be alterations and decline and this means that sustainability in its purest sense will not be achieved. Note also that the term 'tourist presence' is used as opposed to the more simple notion of tourist numbers. This is because it is necessary, when attempting to identify the levels of carrying capacity, to weight the absolute numbers of tourist arrivals to take account of a number of factors as follows:

- the average length of stay;

- the characteristics of the tourists and hosts;

- the geographical concentration of tourists;

- the degree of seasonality;

- the types of tourism activity;

- the accessibility of specific sites;

- the level of infrastructure use and its spare capacity;

- the extent of spare capacity among the various productive sectors of the economy.

Another aspect rarely touched upon in the literature is the fact that different tourists interact with each other in different ways. For example, destinations in the Caribbean, such as St Lucia, draw their tourists from a variety of countries, but the majority of tourists come from the US market and a significant number come from European countries. The problem here is the fact that the Caribbean is a relatively inexpensive destination for the American market, which is close by, whereas it is a relatively expensive destination for the European market, because of the high cost of transport involved in the package. This means that European tourists are more likely to be of a higher socio-economic grouping than their American counterparts. This problematic mix can shorten the **tourist satisfaction** ratings quite significantly, suggesting that, from the tourists' point of view, carrying capacity may be as much influenced by the mix of tourists as by the volume of tourists.

When attempting to determine or identify carrying capacity, it is essential that tourism presence is measured in some unambiguous manner. One possibility is to discuss carrying capacity in terms of *tourism units* where a tourism unit is a standardised concept based upon tourist numbers weighted by some composite factor derived from the above influencing elements. In this way each destination is likely to have different carrying-capacity levels. However, the derivation of some standardised unit is difficult. For example, there are problems to be encountered if the number of day visitors is to be incorporated into the overall tourist numbers. This is because day visitors tend to be associated with different levels of impact per hour per tourist from those of their staying counterparts. The shorter the stay of tourists the more pressing will be the sense of time budgeting and the higher will be the level of expenditure per unit of time.

Composite indicators can be constructed to provide some insight into the threshold levels of tourism activity. For instance, McElroy (2004) discusses the strengths and limitation of a Tourism Penetration Index (TPI) for selected Caribbean islands where the index is based on per capita visitor spend, average daily density of visitors (in aggregate) and hotel rooms per square kilometer. The use of such indices is highly questionable given that they do not take into account temporal variations (seasonality), the spatial spread and size of the island (which influences the density indicator) and the retention of revenue from tourism. Many other factors could also be included such as the geographical spread of economic activity, the nature of visitor host interactions, etc. but these data are expensive and time consuming.

An issue already raised above is that the carrying capacity definitions tend to include the term 'acceptable'. However, the question that needs to be asked is to whom should a change be acceptable or unacceptable? If, as in the case of social impacts, the host population is the body that should consider the acceptability of developments, how is this reflected in policies? In a perfectly democratic political system then we could argue that the residents would be able to register their views on proposed developments. However, such perfect democracy may be hard to find? Furthermore, much tourism development is driven by the private sector who may take a much narrower perspective of the issues surrounding development.

The issue becomes even more complex with respect to any environmental carrying capacity. Who should consider and vote on the acceptability or otherwise of a project that brings environmental impacts? The environment itself may signify changes and species of flora and fauna may suffer from development but they do not have a vote. How will environmental acceptability be considered and voiced within the planning framework?

The above issues relate to all aspects of carrying capacity, perhaps with the exception of the acceptability of developments to tourists. Visitor satisfaction surveys are frequently undertaken by many destinations to monitor acceptability. Furthermore, if the carrying capacity in this respect is exceeded, tourists will vote with their feet and go elsewhere.

In spite of the problems involved in converting this theoretical definition of carrying capacity into an operational tool, it does fit in well with modern development strategies that increasingly incorporate attempts to impose some constraint on the ultimate level of development to prevent damaging impacts on the environment and society or to avoid the risk of over-dependence.

The dynamics of carrying capacity

The literature on carrying capacity, rather like the literature on tourism development planning, gives the impression that it is in some way static or absolute. The very word capacity makes one think of a specific level like filling the seats on a boat or an aircraft, but nothing could be further from the truth. Carrying capacity is an extremely fluid and dynamic concept. As with many human traits, exposure to stimuli brings with it acceptability. Socio-cultural tolerance levels change over time with gradual exposure to tourists. If, for example, a small island destination goes from 100 to 1,000,000 tourists in the space of a year it is likely that the socio-cultural, economic and environmental impacts will be devastating. Take the same destination and increase the volume of tourists by the same amount over a 50-year period and the discernible impact is likely to be far less. People become accustomed to change – it does not make the change any less but it does make it more acceptable. Economies too are better at adjusting to structural change that takes place over a long time period, rather than dealing with rapid changes. Sufficient time will allow for the necessary linkages and support services to be brought into place and, in consequence, allow the destination to optimise its benefits from tourism. Even the environment, or at least the local population's concern for it, may be better able to cope if change comes slowly and proper visitor management systems can be implemented to mitigate negative impacts.

In effect the carrying capacity of today will not be the carrying capacity of tomorrow. In the 1950s few of the top tourist destinations in the world could have imagined the volume of tourists that they are playing host to today. This dynamic characteristic of carrying capacity, together with the difficulty in finding a universally acceptable definition has resulted in some bodies, such as the United States National Park Service, choosing to adopt an alternative terminology, that of '**limits of acceptable change**' (LAC), as their planning indicator.

Therefore, carrying capacity is a dynamic concept in the sense that the threshold levels that determine carrying capacity are likely to grow over time, providing that the development of tourism is sound. Unplanned rapid development could easily result in low tolerance levels and carrying capacities of much lower values.

Other factors influencing carrying capacity

In addition to the characteristics of the tourists and their hosts, there are a number of other factors that will influence the carrying capacity of a destination. It has already been noted that the speed of change is an important factor. The difference between the tourists and hosts is also an important consideration. It is not the absolute characteristics of either population group that is important, but the relative difference. This is one reason why domestic tourism is often, but not always, more acceptable than international tourism in terms of the socio-cultural impacts.

If the demographic profiles of tourists are similar to those of the host population, particularly in relation to age distribution, socio-economic grouping and religion, then the socio-cultural impact of increasing tourist numbers is likely to be relatively low. On the other hand, major differences in any of these factors can result in significant socio-cultural impacts even though the number of tourists in both scenarios is the same.

The fact that there are four broad groups of capacity indicators, economic, environmental, socio-cultural and tourist satisfaction levels gives rise to some difficulty in establishing exactly what the carrying capacity of a specific destination may be. It is likely that, for any given destination, the carrying capacity will be reached in just one of these areas before it is reached in the rest. Thus, a destination may find that tourism activity brings pressure to, say, the local ecosystem before it creates any significant threats to the social structure, the culture or the economy. This means that, regardless of the threshold limits in these latter areas, the carrying capacity for this destination is dictated by the vulnerability of the ecosystem. In order to move away from the qualitative to the quantitative approach for determining carrying capacity it is necessary to delineate the different areas of study (outlined overleaf) and examine the processes by which carrying capacity is determined and how it may change over time.

The process of determining carrying capacity

Figure 8.2 outlines the process by which carrying capacity is influenced and can be measured. The diagram shows the broad groups of factors that determine carrying capacity along with the different stages that can influence the magnitude and direction of the impacts and hence the carrying capacity. The different areas of the flow diagram are set out under the following subheadings.

LOCAL FACTORS

There are many local factors that will influence the magnitude and direction of impacts but what is important, besides the nature of the local factors, is the relative difference between the local factors and the tourist counterparts and the speed of change. Looking at individual factors we can see how complex the issues are.

Social structure

The social structure of the destination is vital in determining the scale and nature of any impacts. For example, taking two extreme views, the social structures of London, New York and Sydney are more able to absorb and tolerate the presence of tourists than cities such as Apia in Western Samoa or Port Louis in Mauritius. The former can tolerate the presence of tourists without incurring any significant changes to their social structures because those changes have already occurred. They are larger in population and cosmopolitan in structure, making them more adaptable to change. The latter have relatively small populations, the extended family system is still largely intact (particularly in Apia) and they are not as cosmopolitan in structure. Therefore, some societies can accept large-volume tourism with little obvious effect while others cannot. In general, the smaller the local population, the more dramatic will be the social impact of tourism, particularly if that tourism is based upon large-volume tourist flows.

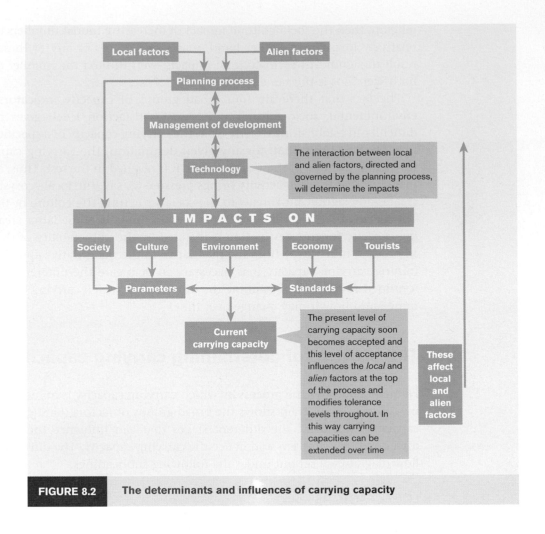

FIGURE 8.2   **The determinants and influences of carrying capacity**

Cultural heritage

The cultural heritage of a destination is very important when attempting to determine the impact and carrying capacity. The more unusual the cultural background, the more attractive a destination may become to potential tourists. Ironically, the more unusual the cultural background, the more likely it is to be adversely affected by the presence of tourists. The end result is either the destruction of the cultural heritage or, more probably, the distortion of the local culture through staged authenticity, over-commercialisation of cultural features and traditions, such as dances and costumes, religious ceremonies, arts and crafts. The destination can soon become in danger of becoming a caricature of itself.

Environment

The environment *will* be changed by the presence of tourists no matter how sympathetic they may be or how careful the tourism activity is planned. The environment can be either artificial or natural. In general the former is more resilient to tourism impacts than the latter. Environmental change is inevitable and will be more obvious and pronounced in those areas that are sparsely populated and not subject to frequent high-volume tourist visits. The more fragile and unique an environment, the more vulnerable it is to change from the presence of humans. It is important to remember that the environment is also changed by many factors, not just tourism, and it is often difficult to isolate those effects created by tourists from those created by other factors.

Economic structure

The economic structure will determine the benefits and costs associated with tourism activity. In general, the more developed and industrialised the economy, the more robust and adaptable it will be. As economies grow and diversify, so too do the skills of the workforce. This, together with a more refined capital system, allows such economies to respond and adapt to the changes brought by tourism. These countries will be able to secure the greatest benefits from tourism activity while incurring the minimum costs. In contrast, economies that are not sophisticated may find that rapid developments in tourism can distort the allocation of resources quite drastically and set up importation habits that may be difficult to break in the future.

Tourism development, particularly rapid development, tends to be resort based and this may bring with it the economic problems associated with:

- migration from rural to urban areas; and

- the transfer of labour from traditional industries to tourism and its related industries.

Economies have to be mature to be able to adjust to these pressures.

Political structure

The political structure can affect the impacts of tourism and its carrying capacity in a number of ways. To begin with, political instability will deter tourists and therefore hinder tourism development. Some groups of tourists are more sensitive to political instability than others but few tourists are unaffected by the prospect of political instability. The political structure may also have direct influences upon tourism development if, in reflecting the ideals and beliefs of the population, it is decided that tourism development should be constrained or even discouraged. Some countries limit tourism development by restricting the number of visas issued within any given year (Bhutan, for example), whereas others may increase the costs of obtaining visas or make the acquisition of visas difficult, thereby restricting them to only the most determined. The political openness may well reflect the willingness of society to welcome tourism development and this may either raise or lower the carrying capacity thresholds.

Resources

The availability of local resources (labour, capital, land, etc.) is likely to have a major influence on the acceptability and desirability of tourism development, and even on the form that development takes. Where resources are scarce, competition for them will be high and the opportunity cost of using these resources for tourism will also be high. The local infrastructure is also part of the resource base.

273

If tourism development means that the local infrastructure will be over-utilised then this will create a capacity constraint (at least in the short term) that may well become operative before any of the other carrying capacity constraints are approached. If the infrastructure is over-utilised because of tourism development then this may well breed resentment and hostility among the local population and then the social impact of tourism will create a carrying capacity constraint.

On a more positive note, tourism development may well result in an improved infrastructure, which will also be available to hosts as well as tourists and this may increase the carrying capacity level by enhancing the lives of the local community.

ALIEN FACTORS

Tourist characteristics

Clearly, the characteristics of the tourists who visit any given destination are an important factor in determining the social and cultural impact of tourism on the host community. For instance, tourists who belong to the mass or charter groups are more likely to have a greater social and cultural impact than those who belong to the explorer, adventurer and ethnic tourist categories. The former tends to demand Western amenities and bring their culture with them without adapting to the local norms and customs. The latter tend to be far more sympathetic towards local customs and traditions and actively seek them out as part of their vacation experience. This, however, is not always the case. The important factor is the relative difference between tourists and hosts. The greater the difference between the host's and the tourist's social and cultural backgrounds, the greater the impact and consequent change. Tourist characteristics also include visitor expenditure patterns, mode of transport, structure and size of party, age, educational background, income and purpose of visit. All of these factors will influence the nature and magnitude of the impacts on the host community.

Carrying capacity is centred around tolerance levels:

- how tolerant the ecological system is to tourist intrusion and activity, as well as those activities created as a result of tourism activity;

- how tolerant the socio-cultural structure is to the introduction of foreign cultures, ideal and beliefs; and

- how much tolerance there is within the economic structure.

However, carrying capacity is also about the tolerance levels of the tourists. A destination that is considered to be over-crowded by the tourists has exceeded its carrying capacity and, in consequence, will find its tourist arrivals diminishing or the composition of tourists changing. The composition of tourists may change as the destination lower prices in an attempt to shore up falling numbers. The tolerance level of tourists introduces a further complication into the issue of determining carrying capacity. Different categories of tourists will display different levels of tolerance with respect to deviations from their expected experience.

Figure 8.3 demonstrates how tolerance levels associated with different types of tourist and within different types of resort may change. The figure represents

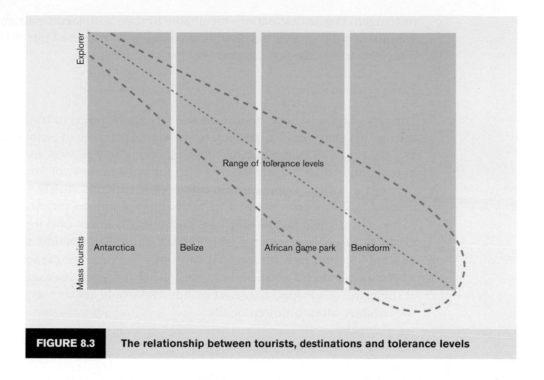

FIGURE 8.3   **The relationship between tourists, destinations and tolerance levels**

two planes. The horizontal plane depicts the nature and characteristics of the destination with a range moving from the fragile and vulnerable, such as Antarctica, through the vulnerable but less fragile areas, such as the Galapagos Islands, to the more organised and controlled but nevertheless vulnerable game parks, such as those found in Kenya, right through to the full-blown totally dedicated destinations such as Hawaii and Benidorm in Spain.

The vertical plane represents the type of tourist and ranges from the explorer to the mass tourist as you move down the plane. The diagonal line running from the top left-hand corner through to the bottom right-hand corner demonstrates the 'fit' between tourist and destination. Thus, starting in the top right-hand corner we find that the explorer will seek out the fragile but exclusive destinations such as Antarctica. At the bottom left-hand corner, reading across the horizontal plane and down the vertical plane we find that the mass tourist will seek out the no-surprise destinations such as Benidorm. The range along the line, between these two polar extremes also shows the 'fit' between the characteristics of the tourist and the destination. The dotted lines that run alongside the central diagonal line represent the tolerance levels. By this we mean that each type of tourist will be associated with an average given level of tolerance with respect to how close a destination may match her or his expectations. Thus, the explorer may generally be regarded as being fairly intolerant of significant deviations from her or his expectations. If the destination does not live up to expectations he or she will quickly seek alternative destinations. At the other extreme, the mass tourist is generally more tolerant of deviations from the expected. Thus, the corridor of tolerance increases in size as we move away from the top left-hand corner. The tolerance levels of destinations can also be seen in this diagram in the sense that the central diagonal line still shows the 'fit' between tourist and destination, but the corridor of tolerance may also relate to the destination's tolerance to changes in tourism. Fragile destinations are unable to cope with significant changes in the volume of tourism whereas the more commercial purpose-built destinations are more able to absorb such deviations.

Types of tourist activity

The types of tourist activity pursued will be closely linked to the characteristics of the tourists who take part in them. However, the presence of certain activities, such as gambling, can bring specific social problems and stresses that are far greater in magnitude than those associated with the same number of tourists undertaking different activities. Gambling can bring with it increased risks to the host community (and to other tourists) in terms of exposure to prostitution, drugs and crime. All of these factors will help create much lower carrying capacities than might normally be associated with tourism. It need not be just the emotive cases of gambling and prostitution that can limit the carrying capacity. Destinations with very fragile ecosystems or with, say, rare bird species, may suffer more severely at the hands of the special interest groups who would actively seek out and disturb the habitats, albeit unintentionally.

Planning management and technology

Planning is concerned with the organisation of factors in order to manipulate future events. The management of tourism is the process by which plans are put into practice. Changes in technology will have direct and indirect effects on the difficulties associated with the planning and management tasks. Given the interaction between local and alien factors within the host environment, the planning and management process should aim to secure the maximum positive benefits (as dictated by the planning objectives) while incurring the minimum costs. Figure 8.2 shows that the planning, management and technology factors act as a funnel between the 'raw' interaction of the local and alien factors and the impact that this interaction has on the destination. The more successful the planning and management, the lower will be the levels of negative impacts and the greater will be the carrying capacity. The dynamic nature of this process is such that suitable developments combined with appropriate visitor flow management will 'naturally' select the required tourist market segments, while allowing the local factors the amount of time and space needed to adapt to the alien factors. The end result is a destination that can enjoy both growth and sustainability (growth + sustainability = development).

IMPACTS

The local and alien factors, manipulated by planning and the management of tourism development, will result in impacts on the social structure, culture, environment and economy, and upon other tourists. Impacts are the yardsticks of carrying capacity, but they are derived variables. The task to the planner and tourism management specialists is to ensure that the appropriate impacts occur.

Parameters

The impacts that occur reflect the nature and magnitude of change brought about by the interaction between tourists and hosts, given the management and planning

MINI CASE STUDY 8.1
Sustainable development networks (SDNs) for Grenada

BACKGROUND

The report of the Rio Conference, Agenda 21, identified a number of important aspects of information technology and electronic networks for sustainable development. These included:

- The wide range of users and providers of information.

- The need to develop the capacity to provide and use information.

- The need for appropriate information.

- The widening gap between the information rich and poor.

- The potential of electronic networks.

The sustainable development network programme initiated by the UNDP in 1989 has established some twenty SDNs that are viewed by many governments as an indispensable tool for implementing national Agenda 21s.

In a review of Chapter 40 of Agenda 21, Roberto Bissio (Director of the Third World Institute [IteM]) wrote:

> **The large proportion of the analysis and recommendations devoted to electronic networking clearly demonstrates an unprecedented understanding by the Earth Summit that we are not dealing here with just another technology (no other heads of State conference ever praised the virtues of fax, phone or telegraph) but with a substantial reformulation in the way people deal with each other on a global scale. The Earth Summit itself was an impressive demonstration of the potential of electronically assisted networking.**

The importance of information for small island developing states (SIDS) is unquestionable. Information represents market power and can lead to economic success. Yet many small island states are not able to enjoy levels of information similar to their large national competitors. This suggests a role for collaboration in the process and dissemination of information.

The information required for decision making in the context of sustainable development poses far greater challenges including the following:

- The collection of different types of data to determine the status and trends of the planet's ecosystem. (e.g. biodiversity, global warming).

- The setting and acceptance of global standards relating to the categories and the quality of the data collected.

- The identification and adoption of acceptable indicators of sustainable development.

- The integration of information from many different disciplines.

- The need to disseminate information among departments and organisations.

277

THE CHALLENGES FACING GRENADA

In 2002 the United Nations called for a thorough review of the Barbados Program of Action that was adopted in 1994. As of January 2004 there are 41 nations that are recognised as SIDS by the UN. The limited resources and the many other associated problems such as transport difficulties and the isolation of small island developing states, typified by islands such as Grenada, in the Caribbean, makes these challenges even greater. It is essential to provide assistance with the establishment of access to the global electronic networks and, without in any way limiting that access, provide guides to the information that is particularly relevant to the needs of small island developing states. SIDSNET is not a duplication of other networks; it is a guide to the world of networks for people and information relevant to the sustainable development of small island developing states. Decision and policy makers in the governments of small island developing states clearly need access to the most up-to-date information about the latest technological innovations and policies which are best able to deal with threats to the fragile ecosystems for which they are responsible.

Source: Adapted from http://www.upei.ca/~meincke/barbpap.htm

DISCUSSION QUESTIONS

1 Consider the above with respect to tourism development and identify the type of data that could be shared between governments that would benefit tourism planning.

2 Identify the ways in which technology could assist governments in creating such a network.

3 Where data are available across national boundaries who should be responsible for collecting and maintaining such data banks?

that has been implemented. The parameters can be identified as the changes that take place to the local and alien factors as a result of different levels and types of interaction. They are *factual* in the sense that they are devoid of value judgements and simply relate tourist host interaction and tourist presence to changes in the social, cultural, environmental and economic factors.

Standards

The standards may be seen as acceptable limits applied to the parameters. They refer to the value judgements imposed by the host and tourist populations with respect to how much a variable may change without incurring irreversible or undesirable damage to the nature of tourism and the environment in which it takes place.

Carrying-capacity determination

Carrying capacity is the dependent variable. It is not possible to over-emphasise the word variable because it is not a fixed value based on tourist presence. The dynamic nature of carrying capacity is based upon the changing tolerance levels of each of the determining factors as a result of both exposure and management.

The feedback over time, between carrying capacity and the local and alien factors, will be responsible for increasing/decreasing the magnitude of acceptable tourist presence. The carrying capacity will also feed back into the planning and management stages in order to inform and enhance the processes of visitor and destination management.

If the carrying capacity is exceeded, with respect to any of the impact areas, the tourism development process will be hindered and the development may be considered unsustainable. The damage created by exceeding the carrying capacity may be related to any of the impact areas or in terms of tourist satisfaction, but the end result will be the same. Either the destination will experience diminishing numbers as its tourism industry declines – tourists pursuing alternative destinations – or the mix of tourist arrivals may change, making it increasingly difficult for the destination to achieve its declared planning objectives.

The vulnerability of different destinations to tourist presence will be a major factor in setting the acceptable standards to be maintained during the management process. To illustrate this point the plight of World Heritage Sites can be examined. The very nature of World Heritage Sites means that they are not only finite but also irreplaceable and the successful management of such sites is vital. The World Heritage Convention requires that the international community cooperates to ensure that measures taken to protect and conserve these sites are effective. The management of these sites is almost always translated into access control. The management of Keoladeo National Park in India relies upon the access provided by the restricted number of trained guides or by bicycles and specified trails set out for the tourists. In other areas more arbitrary, but still restrictive, limits are set such as the 11,800 visitors per annum allowed to view the resident gorilla families. Alternative strategies can also be used, such as the spacing of tourist visits, or restrictions based on a specific aspect of a destination in order to manage its overall tourism development.

Measurement criteria

Carrying capacity is subject to multiple determination and as such, each of the separate components must be investigated. Tables 8.1 and 8.2 are provided to give some guidance to the variables that may be measured, the thresholds that may be encountered and the effects of over-exploitation.

Clearly, understanding the implications for each of the indicators is an important aspect of being able to determine the thresholds of successful tourism development. As mentioned earlier in this chapter, setting limits on tourism activity is only one aspect of striving towards successful tourism development. Destinations can also work towards changing the behaviour of the stakeholders involved in the tourism process either by creating an appropriate economic framework or by investing in awareness campaigns. They can also encourage the development of more sustainable forms of tourism activity. Given that both of these strategies work towards meeting tourism demand in a way that minimises the net negative impacts they can be considered within the same framework.

280

TABLE 8.1	Variables and thresholds	
Impact on	**Variable**	**Threshold(s)**
Economy		
Dependency	Contribution to GNP	Diversity/imports
Finance	Level of investment	Availability of funds
Labour	Employment	Shortages/training
Price inflation	Consumer price index	Social costs/distribution
Wealth	Income growth/distribution	Wage inflation/imports
Environment		
Changes	Species/populations	Extinction/balance of population
Hazards	Fires, erosion, pollution	Costs/risks
Viability of wildlife	Urbanisation	Land usage/species count
Physical resources		
Access	Cost/time/volume	Congestion/hazards
Accommodation	Number/size/quality	Occupancy
Attractions	Number/size/type	Access/available land
Land	Proportion of land usage	Land price inflation
Transportation	Cost/capacity	Congestion/hazards
Infrastructure	Investment/quality	Capacity/health risks
Political framework		
Strategies	Goals range/scope	Conflicts, goals missed
Resources	Expenditure/revenue	Budgetary deficits
Cooperation	Partnerships	Lack of participation/funds
Society-culture		
Population	Migration	Distribution/infrastructure
Living standards	Real income/wealth	Inflation
Values	Crime/drugs/health	Social disruption/costs
Traditions	Participation/quality	Occurrence/characteristics

TABLE 8.2	Scale of development and its effect on impacts and carrying capacity	
Effect on	**Small scale dispersed**	**Large scale concentrated**
Accommodation		
Range of products	Highly limited	Diverse
Range of prices	Low/medium	Low/medium/expensive
Seasonality	Peaked	Wider but more problematic
Size of business	SME	SME to international
Ownership	Local	Non-local
Characteristics of facilities		
Range	Highly limited	Diverse
Finance	Local	Mixed local/foreign
Usage	Peaked	High volume
Need for support	Low	High
Labour market		
Demand/supply	Learning by doing	Demand for high skills
	Local labour	Mixed local/migrant labour
	Constrained by local supply	Increased migration
Transport		
Infrastructure	Limited	High but congestion during peaks
Supplier	Private sector	Greater public supply
Stimulating supply	Low-level effect	High-level effect

Sustainable tourism products

Terms such as 'eco-tourism' and 'alternative tourism' have taken a prominent position in tourism literature (academic and marketing) since they were introduced in the mid-1980s. Eco-tourism has been misused as a term both intentionally, as a marketing ploy, and unintentionally due to a lack of understanding and in common with the term sustainability, there has been considerable debate about an acceptable definition. Wight (2001) points out that the World Tourism Organization estimated that some 10%–15% of global tourism could be classified as eco-tourism in 1997. However, within that same year the WTO revised this estimate to 20%. It is hard to find any credibility in these proportions given the dominance of mass tourism in total global tourism activities. Eco-tourism is unequivocally linked to natural tourism attractions rather than their man-made counterparts and environmental sustainability is often found to be a core component of such a product's definition. However, it is also accepted that many definitions of eco-tourism include some reference to indigenous cultural sustainability. According to Weaver (2004) a further factor that is associated with definitions of ecotourism relate to their educational or learning opportunity components. Once all of these aspects are incorporated into a single tourism product it can be seen that eco-tourism will not appeal to the masses at present. The masses seeking sand, sea, sun vacations within a wide variety of areas that may or may not also be areas of outstanding natural beauty. Eco-tourism demands a high level of interpretation whereas the mass tourism product does not. This is not to say that mass tourism products would not benefit from greater interpretation.

Both eco-tourism and alternative tourism imply small-scale, indigenous low-key activities. Where the former holds the preservation of the natural environment at its core, the latter may not necessarily do so. Indeed the latter may simply be at the beginning of the tourism development process for a destination soon to be enveloped in a more commercial package as the product develops. Eco-tourism suggests that it has in place constraints that will prevent or inhibit uncontrolled development. However, both forms of tourism activity can provide a temporary runway for the take-off of the destination as it moves towards mass tourism. There is no product currently on the market that could come close to being classified as mass sustainable tourism. The presence of large numbers of tourists in high densities with the necessary infrastructure for transportation and public health and safety defies the laws of sustainability.

The 1980s also saw the emergence of the 'Three Rs' being applied to sustainability in the corporate world. The fact that the corporate world was even thinking about sustainability was a huge leap forward, although the cynics would argue that they were paying lip service to a concept that would pay dividends in terms of increased sales. Tour operators such as Thomsons did not find sustainable touism products to be the 'hot' products that this line of thinking promised. The three Rs were:

- Reduce

- Reuse

- Recycle

The very fact that these words were being used in corporate circles represents a major shift in attitudes towards the environment and social responsibility. Middleton (1998) expanded this list to 10 Rs which included:

- Recognise

- Refuse

- Replace

- Reduce

- Reuse

- Recycle

- Re-engineer

- Retrain

- Reward

- Re-educate

Although some of the additional Rs may be considered to be contrived and there is considerable overlap between several of them, the list does serve to show just how far away the three Rs were from presenting a significant step towards sustainability. Furthermore, a major **R** in the form of 'Responsibility' was not included in the Middleton list. Middleton's marketing approach provides some good examples of the issues relating to sustainable tourism.

MINI CASE STUDY 8.2
Sustainability and accreditation schemes in Costa Rica

Sustainable tourism development meets the needs of present tourists and host regions while protecting and enhancing tourism for the future. It is envisioned as leading to management of all resources in such a way that economic, social and aesthetic needs can be fulfilled while maintaining cultural integrity, essential ecological processes, biological diversity and life support systems. (WTO, 2001)

Eugenio Yunis (Head of Sustainable Development of Tourism, WTO) highlighted WTO's support of the Sustainable Tourism Stewardship Council (STSC) in its attempt to create a global accreditation scheme. He stated that the WTO has been studying sustainability in tourism for nearly one decade. They continue to be concerned with how to demonstrate a company's commitment to sustainability to the various parties of the tourism supply chain. The proliferation of certification schemes has created confusion among consumers and suppliers as to which standards ensure that practices on the ground are sustainable. WTO supports the need to increase the number of companies seeking certification, promote certification in the marketplace, and raise standards used by certifiers. Consumers, tour operators and others in the tourism trade need to know the validity of the certificates on a global level.

WORLD TOURISM ORGANIZATION, 2002

There are a large number of existing accreditation schemes, such as ISO 9001, Total Quality Management (TQM), Swiss Tourism Quality Label (Q), ISO 14001, SA 8000, Green Globe, Costa Rica Tourism Label and Australian National Ecotourism Accreditation Programme (NEAP). Some of the schemes are limited by the fact they refer to processes and systems such as ISO 14001 (ISO is an international certification process to show that companies have met the standards for the integration of environmental and safety systems and procedures), whereas others refer to products and or services and require certain social-ecological standards such as the Costa Rica Tourism Label. All of the schemes are limited in some way either by region, types of business or the scope of coverage (environmental, socio-cultural and economic sustainability). For instance the Costa Rica Tourism Label has developed a certification-for-sustainable-tourism scheme that assesses how businesses interact with:

1 physical and biological factors;

2 infrastructure and services;

3 external factors;

4 socio-economic aspects of Costa Rica (the interaction of tourism businesses with the local community).

To measure and fix these different levels, the Certification for Sustainable Tourism (CST) programme provides a system of 'sustainability levels', attaching a scale ranging from 0 to 5, in which each number indicates the relative position of the firm in terms of its sustainability. This scheme provides a way to classify the tourist firms in terms of 'levels' in a system very similar to the commercial categorisation of hotels by means of the stars system.

DISCUSSION QUESTIONS

1 Critically appraise the WTO statement on sustainability and, by so doing, demonstrate its limitations as a vision of sustainable tourism development.

2 If an accreditation scheme such as Green Globe is operated for profit what are the possible implications for achieving sustainability?

3 Consider what indicators you would use to measure the sustainability performance of a hotel in Costa Rica and would the indicators differ from those used if the hotel had been located in New York, USA? If so in what ways?

SUSTAINABILITY AS A STRATEGY

In spite of the difficulties involved in trying to find an acceptable definition for sustainability that will have practical value and the enormous problems in trying to measure crucial factors such as a destination's carrying capacity, there is a way forward. Sustainability more than anything else involves a process of recognition and responsibility. Recognition that the resources which are used to produce the tourism products are expendable and vulnerable. Responsibility for the wise use of these resources rests across all stakeholders from the governments and planners, through the industry that delivers the product to the tourists and their hosts who temporarily co-exist within the destination. A sustainable strategy must engage all of the stakeholders in the planning of tourism. The involvement of local resident participation is as difficult to achieve in practice as trying to get the industry to behave in a more environmentally and socially sympathetic manner.

From an environmental point of view there have been numerous attempts at trying to 'green' the industry. These attempts have been in the form of awareness campaigns through to certification schemes but none of them has been successful to date. The major problem has been the failure of the companies and organisations that have touted their certification programmes to demonstrate to the industry that certification truly saves them money or generates additional demand. Tourists are still largely driven by the pleasure factors of the product rather than their social and environmental conscience. Therefore consumers must share their responsibility because without a demonstrable demand for certified green products the certification process will not be embraced by the industry without some form of supporting legislation. The certification companies have by and large failed to put credible programmes into the marketplace because the enforcement that must accompany certification is expensive and time consuming making it an unwelcome burden on the industry. The only effective way of providing such certification schemes would be through a non-profit public sector body in the same way that health and safety standards are enforced.

The only practical way forward from a planning point of view is to develop integrated impact-modelling tools. One such tool is described in Mini case study 8.3 and demonstrates the use of fully integrated impact software. This model was developed by staff at the International Centre for Tourism and Hospitality, Bournemouth University, and provides a valuable planning tool that demonstrates the interrelatedness between each of the different types of impact, analyses them with a unified framework and allows these impacts to be examined from either forecasted future impacts or from those drawn as hypothetical case studies.

Economic sustainability for tourism requires holistic planning across all industrial sectors. It must also reach beyond the destination to make sure that intermediaries such as tour operators are not able to circumvent or put undue pressure on the planning processes. The formation of partnership chains throughout the industry would be one way to achieve this but is unlikely to ever happen given the competitiveness of the tourism industry and the predominance of SMEs. The quality of the tourism product demands staff training that is universally acceptable and the economic environment must make environmentally and socio-culturally sound behaviour the best economic choice.

Environmental sustainability in tourism requires greater awareness and knowledge about the impacts and ways of translating those impacts into the economic marketplace. The responsibility of tourists and businesses must be made clear and there needs to be a legislative system that penalises failure to abide by those systems. The indirect and induced environmental consequences of activities must be included in the calculation of their market prices but it must also be recognised that environmental and social systems change over time as a natural consequence of development and such changes need to be accommodated.

MINI CASE STUDY 8.3
User-friendly interactive planning software – a schematic
presentation of a tourism planning tool kit

The model encourages data collection with respect to planning variables. Once the empirical data are inputted they are subjected to the input–output methodology to obtain the economic and environmental direct, indirect and induced effects. The socio-cultural impacts are evaluated using ratios, for example host-to-guest ratios, penetration levels, etc. The results obtained from the model are generated in terms of multiplier values and absolute economic impact values (i.e. income, employment and import implications of a given level of tourist spending). The forecasts of arrivals are produced using an auto-regressive linear function. This type of model can be used to estimate the future likely impacts based upon current trends, or to test hypothetical changes to existing patterns of spending or arrivals.

CONCLUSION

Sustainability is a difficult concept. It is complex and hard to define and, if taken literally, the pot of gold at the end of the sustainability rainbow may be considered to be unattainable. However, this should not detract from the ambition of trying to achieve sound tourism planning and for the stakeholders in tourism to find ways of making the most efficient use of the resources and ensuring that tourism has a long-term future. To do this there will come a time (already reached in many destinations) where there is need to limit development to some pre-determined threshold. This brings into play the notion of carrying capacity. Carrying capacity can only be examined in a case-by-case situation because it is sensitive to location, the type of tourist activity, the difference in cultures between tourists and guests, the speed of tourism growth and the temporal dimension of development. Time is a great healer and it allows destinations to adapt and adjust to the presence of tourists and their associated impacts. Thus, carrying capacity is a dynamic rather than static concept.

Carrying capacity thresholds may manifest themselves in economic, environmental, socio-cultural and political structures. The determination of carrying capacity at any one point in time will be the type of impact with the greatest change relative to its impact threshold. Once the carrying capacity threshold has been reached in one of these variables it will limit or change the tourism development process if that process is not to suffer long-term damage. The major influences on the level of carrying capacity are the differences between the nature of the tourists and their activities and those of the local population, weighted by the speed of change.

In addition to limiting the nature and volume of tourism activity there is a need to modify the behaviour of the stakeholders in tourism. The behaviour of the industry and tourists should reflect the needs of the local destination. Eco-tourism and alternative tourism products have been around since the 1980s but many of them owed their title to a marketing approach rather than any real attributes of the product. The eco-tourism product is essentially natural resource based and is dependent upon low-volume tourist activity. This is useful for the sustainability of tourism in a specific area but offers little scope for the sustainability of global tourism which is largely made up of the mass sand, sea and sun tourism products. It is important to examine the relationship between the impacts of tourism and the scale and dispersion of tourism activity. In general, small-scale dispersed tourism activity is likely to have a lower impact level than large-scale concentrated tourism development. However, small-scale dispersed tourism activity is unlikely to be able to cater for the major tourist market segments. The only hope of making this latter type of activity 'green' is through the recognition and adoption of appropriate corporate responsibility by the private sector combined with a fully engaged public participation in the planning of tourism.

Self-check questions

1 Define sustainability.

2 What are the major obstacles to achieving sustainable development?

3 What methods can be used to make tourism more sustainable than it is at present?

4 What is meant by the term 'carrying capacity'?

5 How sustainable are sustainable tourism products?

Essay questions

1 Critically appraise the attempts that have been made to find a universally acceptable definition of sustainability. What are the major stumbling blocks and how might they be resolved?

2 What do you understand by the term 'carrying capacity' and what are the problems encountered when trying to define it?

3 'Carrying capacity is a dynamic concept.' Discuss.

4 'The carrying capacity of any given destination is influenced more by the speed of tourism development and the *relative* differences between tourists and hosts than it is by their *absolute* characteristics.' Discuss.

5 In what ways should the behaviour of the stakeholders in tourism be modified to move the industry towards a more sustainable future?

Annotated further reading

Books

Gartner, W. and Lime, D. (eds) (2000) *Trends in Outdoor Recreation, Leisure and Tourism*, CABI Publishing, London.
A collection of edited papers that deal with a wide range of planning and policy issues related to tourism. The book provides in-depth analyses for the more advanced student.

Gunn, C.A. and Var, T. (2002) *Tourism Planning*, 4th edn, Routledge, London and New York.
Provides a comprehensive overview of tourism development.

Inskeep, E. and Kallenberger, M. (1992) *An Integrated Approach to Resort Development: Six Case Studies*, WTO, Madrid.
A collection of case studies that explores the issues relating to planning in the real world. The cases would have provided greater insight if they had been more varied but nevertheless the book provides good insight into many of the issues involved in tourism planning.

Middleton, V.T.C. with Hawkins, R. (1998) *Sustainable Tourism, A Marketing Perspective*, Butterworth Heinemann, Oxford.
A book rich with case studies that examines the feasibility of sustainable tourism and the role of marketing in driving the industry in that direction.

Shaw, G. and Williams, A. (2002) *Critical Issues in Tourism: A Geographical Perspective*, Routledge, London.

Articles

Luiz, A. (2003) 'Sustainable tourism development: a critique', *Journal of Sustainable Tourism* **11**(6), 459–475.
The author provides a brief critique of some of the many weaknesses in the sustainable tourism literature. It explores six issues that are often overlooked but which must be addressed in research: the role of tourism demand, the nature of tourism resources, the imperative of intra-generational equity, the role of tourism

in promoting socio-cultural progress, the measurement of sustainability, and forms of sustainable development. Finally, it is argued that in order to transform research on sustainable tourism to a more scientific level, a systems perspective and an interdisciplinary approach are essential.

Stem, C.J., Lassoie, J.P., Lee, D.R. and Deshler, D.J. (2003) 'How "eco" is ecotourism? A comparative case study of ecotourism in Costa Rica', *Journal of Sustainable Tourism* **11**(4), 322–347.
The authors question the contribution of eco-tourism to conservation and community development, citing negative impacts, such as solid waste generation, habitat destruction, and socio-cultural ills.

van Fossen, A. and Lafferty, G. (2001) 'Contrasting models of land use regulation: community, government and tourism development', *Community Development Journal* **36**(3), 198–211.
In this paper the authors assesses the capacity of local communities and sub-national governments to influence patterns of tourism development, within the context of a globalising economy. Through a comparison of the contrasting examples of Hawaii and Queensland, the paper indicates the consequences of different approaches to land-use regulation. It points to the importance of planning and policy processes that integrate community interests, in order to achieve long-term, sustainable tourism development.

Web sites

http://www.gdrc.org/uem/eco-tour/eco-tour.html
A useful site listing codes of practice, definitions, tools and strategies for sustainability and links to the accreditation companies and organisations.

http://www.waksberg.com/research.htm
René Waksberg's site is an invaluable research tool for all those interested in tourism in general and contains a large section of links relevant to sustainable development.

www.unesco.org/whc/nwhc/pages/sites/s_f9.htm
This UNESCO site contains a list of cultural and heritage sites, it discusses the management of protected areas and sustainable tourism in general.

References cited and bibliography

Bruntland Report (1987) World Commission on Environment and Development (1987) *Our Common Future*, OUP.

Butcher, J. (1997) 'Sustainable development or development', in Stabler, M.J. (ed.) *Tourism Sustainability – Principles to Practice*, CAB International, pp. 27–38.

Butler, R.W. (1997) 'The concept of carrying capacity for tourism destinations', pp. 11–22 in Cooper, C.P. and Wanhill, S.R.C. (eds), *Tourism Development: Environmental and Community Issues*, Wiley, Chichester.

Choucri, N. (1997) 'Global system for sustainable development research TDP-MIT', Unpublished notes, MIT, Cambridge, MA, January.

Coomer, J. (1979) 'The nature of the quest for a sustainable society', in Coomer, J. (ed.) *Quest for a Sustainable Society*, Pergamon Press, Oxford.

Duval, D. (ed.) (2004) *Tourism in the Caribbean: Trends, Development, Prospects* in the series edited by M. Hall, Contemporary Geographies of Leisure, Tourism and Mobility, Routledge, London.

Gartner, W. and Lime, D. (eds) (2000) *Trends in Outdoor Recreation, Leisure and Tourism*, CABI, New York.

Hardin, G. (1991) 'The tragedy of the unmanaged commons: population and the disguises of providence', in Andelson, R.V. (ed.) *Commons without Tragedy*, Savage, MD.

Johnson, P. and Thomas, B. (1994) 'The notion of capacity in tourism: a review of the issues', pp. 297–308 in Cooper, C.P. and Lockwood, A. (eds), *Progress in Tourism, Recreation and Hospitality Management*, Wiley, Chichester.

Mathieson, A. and Wall, G. (1982) *Tourism: Economic, Physical and Social Impacts*, Longman, Harlow.

McElroy, J. (2004) 'Global perspectives of Caribbean Tourism', pp. 39–56 in Duval, D.T. (ed.) *Tourism in the Caribbean*, Routledge, London.

Middleton, Victor T.C. with Hawkins, Rebecca (1998) *Sustainable Tourism: A Marketing Perspective*, Butterworth Heinemann, Oxford.

Murcott, S. (1996) http://www.sustainableliving.org/seminar96/murcott.htm

Weaver, D.B. (2004) 'Manifestations of ecotourism', pp. 172–86 in Duval, D.T. (ed.) *Tourism in the Caribbean*, Routledge, London.

Wight, P. (2001) 'Ecotourists: not a homogenous market segment' in Weaver, D. (ed.) *The Encyclopaedia of Ecotourism*, CABI, Wallingford, UK.

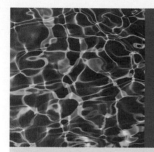

MAJOR CASE STUDY 8.1
ENCOURAGING SUSTAINABLE TOURISM: CHANTING THE ECO-TOURISM MANTRA IN INDIA

If there is an ideal eco-tourism destination in India, it is Sikkim. This Eastern Himalayan state of India with its pristine mountains, crystal-clear lakes and rich cultural and natural diversity is fast gaining popularity. Attracting some 200,000 tourists a year, of which 12,000 are foreigners, it has witnessed a 15% growth in the past three years. Rustam Vania reports on the country's potential for eco-tourism development.

Recognising the opportunities this sector offers to Sikkim, the Chief Minister Pawan Chamling says, 'The enormous biodiversity of Sikkim is for the people. Sikkim cannot afford to have large polluting industries. Along with education, computers and agro-based industries, eco-tourism is a way towards sustainable development for us.' The state has had a record of taking tough decisions to protect the environment.

Tree felling has been severely restricted, grazing has been banned in the reserved forests and attempts are being made to make Sikkim a plastic-free state. Eco-tourism is seen as the developmental option for the future. Inaugurating the South Asian meeting on eco-tourism in the state capital Gangtok in January (2002), Union tourism minister Jagmohan grandly announced, 'We want to make Sikkim a model of eco-tourism for India and the world.'

The state government now has a tourism plan, which includes orchid tourism – over 454 species of orchids are found in the region, – and butterfly parks – 50% of the butterflies of the Indian subcontinent are found in Sikkim. 'We should target this high-value market. Last year, ten groups came from rhododendron societies across the world, spending over Rs 80 lakh,' says K.C. Pradhan, retired chief secretary of Sikkim and a keen promoter of rhododendron tourism.

Pema Gyaltsen, from Yuksom in Western Sikkim understands the gap between rhetoric and reality. 'We don't want the government to dole out tin sheets to spruce up our houses for tourists . . . We want to know about guest management skills, a greater share in tourism benefits,' he demands.

Worried that with the rush to the pristine corner of the Eastern Himalaya will come garbage, deforestation and immigration – and no economic benefit to the local people – Gyaltsen and a group of young people have formed the Kanchenjunga Conservation Committee (KCC) to start a conservation education programme for tourists and porters.

OLD WINE IN A NEW BOTTLE?

The Indian government has also discovered the eco-tourism *mantra*. The National Tourism Policy, 2002, is keen to promote of nature and cultural destinations. It plans to market just about everything – from coastal resorts, cruise destinations, to traditional cuisines, to 'village tourism', to adventure tours in the Himalaya, to wildlife. It chants the right words about sustainability and community involvement, saying that eco-tourism 'should be made a grassroots, community-based movement through awareness, education and training of local community as guides and interpreters'.

But plans are easy to make, difficult to undertake. India's track record in tourism, leaving aside nature tourism, is abysmal. According to government documents, a majority of tourists visiting India rate facilities – from roads to accommodation – as average or poor. No wonder, the country gets less than 0.38% of the share of tourists of the world – fewer visitors than tiny Singapore. In nature tourism too – the 'tiger tourist' kind – policy is equally disjointed. The National Action Plan 2002, prepared by the Ministry of Environment and Forests, plans to 'use increased tourism revenue entirely to augment available resources for conservation'.

Yet, on the ground, the handling of the increasing number of tourists in national parks tells an entirely different story. Park management is ill prepared to deal with tourists and without this, tourism is creating new problems – increasing pressures on the carrying capacity of these protected areas on one hand, and sharpening tensions between the park and the local community, which is not benefiting from the visitor's economy, on the other.

TIGER TOURISTS

Take Ranthambore – a prized tiger reserve in the Aravalli Hills. Tourism has boomed here. Big hotel chains, from the Tata-owned Taj hotels to the luxurious Oberois have set up shop here. Many say, this is former US president Bill Clinton's legacy. His visit to Ranthambore has made it a popular destination, attracting – according to some estimates – over 60,000 tourists last year. Tourists pay phenomenal rates – from Rs 10,000 to Rs 30,000 a night – in some of these hotels, which promise a ride into the park for a near certain view of the tiger.

PHOTOGRAPH 8.2   Indian tigers attract the tourists

So what does the tiger reserve itself gain from this increased tourist traffic? The economics are simple. Indian visitors pay Rs 25 per visit and foreigners Rs 200 as park fees. In addition, Rs 200 for a video camera and Rs 125 for a jeep come to the park. The rest – from hotel rooms, to guides, to jeeps and canters (a small bus) – stays with the industry. G.V. Reddy the park director concurs, 'We only earn from the park entrance fee. I feel a 10% fee should be paid per tourist by hotels to the park.' In the absence of a policy, tourism is adding to the pressures working against conservation. Reddy says they have no legal control over where hotels are erected. Hotels are mushrooming in the buffer zone around the park.

The only control Reddy and his colleagues have is to restrict entry. They have done this by limiting the number of jeeps into the park. The park management signs a contract with the operators, binding them to the rules. But as may be imagined, this has led to a virtual goldmine for the jeep operators and their jeeps are booked months in advance. The money for hiring jeeps and guides is not shared with the tiger they market.

Contrast this with the National Wildlife Action Plan 2002–2016, which says that all tourism receipts and the penalties collected in a protected area should go to a local trust fund headed by the park manager. It should be used in the proportion of 70% for community benefit works and 30% for park management and development activity, not covered by the protected area's budget.

And what of the local people? The wildlife action plan says, 'preference in regular or occasional employment has to be given to local people'. Yet, opportunities for employment generated by tourism in Ranthambore, as in most parks, are unevenly shared. Ran Singh, a guide in the park, grumbles, 'Hotels employ trained staff from outside and the forest department rarely hires locals for development work or as forest guards within the park. On the other hand local villagers often lose crops to animals from the park.'

Now, with the entry of the big 'outside' hotels, local jeep operators, who ferry tourists within the park, are an unhappy lot too. These hotels are buying their own fleets of jeeps so that they can milk the benefits directly.

To conserve the park, local people are faced with severe restrictions on grazing and fuelwood collection, but no benefits. It is not surprising that villagers living near the park feel it is for foreigners only. Their alienation and desperation makes for annual 'battles' between desperate graziers with slingshots and helmet-wearing park officials.

More hopefully, managers of the Periyar National Park in the Western Ghats of Southern India are creating tourism products that they hope will not only benefit the local communities but also help the short-staffed and poorly funded forest department to achieve their conservation goals. With funding from the Global Environment Facility's (GEF), park authorities working on an eco-development project have created committees to work with villagers on creating alternative livelihood options and enhanced agricultural productivity.

Members of one such eco-development committee have set up the Periyar Tiger Trail project, which includes 23 former poachers, who previously made a living by trading forest goods illegally. This eco-tourism project is a joint collaboration between the Kerala Forest Department and the ex-vanaya-bark collectors' eco-development committee.

The ex-cinnamon bark poachers turned tourist guides' intimate knowledge about plants and animals and their survival instincts make them ideal guides for eco-tourism activities. Besides taking small groups of tourists on foot into the forest, they also assist forest guards in patrolling. The intelligence network of the park authorities has improved tremendously. Poachers have been caught redhanded. A fast regeneration of cinnamon trees is seen in Periyar forests and an unprecedented 89 cases of sandalwood poaching were reported since the scheme was launched.

The idea of eco-tourism is still at a nascent stage in India and the country is beginning to see the first steps towards guidelines and policies.

This is a shortened version of an article, originally titled, *Eco-tourism: Scrambling for Paradise*, which first appeared in *Down to Earth* (31 July 2002), published by the Centre for Science and Environment in Delhi, India. (The photograph did not appear in the article.) © People & the Planet 2000–2004 (excluding photograph)

Source: http://www.peopleandplanet.net/doc.php?id=1759 (*posted 30 September 2002*)

DISCUSSION QUESTIONS

1 With such nature-based tourism products as these in India how should the authorities attempt to balance the economic, environmental and socio-cultural costs and benefits of tourism? In particular, who should pay for paradise and who should benefit?

2 Comment on the control strategies referred to above such as that of product diversity (such as the orchid tourism) to that of controlling tourist entry and consider what other types of strategies might be implemented to work towards sustainability.

3 Is there scope for accreditation schemes in such an environment; if so what sort of scheme would you recommend and why?

CHAPTER NINE
TOURISM AND DEVELOPMENT PLANNING

INTRODUCTION

Any form of economic development requires careful planning if it is to be successful in achieving the implicit or explicit objectives that underlie the development. In this chapter we show that tourism development, because it is a multisector activity and because it brings with it the environmental, social and economic impacts discussed in Chapters 6–8, requires considerable planning if it is to be successful and sustainable. The role of tourism within the major general economic development theories is examined. We also show that the development of tourism will not be optimal if it is not undertaken as a partnership that engages all of the stakeholders rather than being left entirely in the hands of private sector. The private sector tends to be associated with a myopic view that is focused upon short-term profits whereas the public sector is often associated with a conservative approach towards development. We therefore identify in this chapter that tourism development planning requires careful cooperation and coordination of both the public and private sectors together with the engagement of the local community. This chapter also demonstrates that the emphasis of tourism development planning has moved away from the rigid 'grand design' **master plan** in favour of more flexible and reactive development plans. This change in approach is, in no small way, due to the recognition that development is not a finite concept. Development is infinite and takes place in an ever-changing environment. Therefore development plans should attempt to facilitate the desired objectives while taking into account the changing factors that influence not only the objectives but also the means of achieving them.

LEARNING OUTCOMES

The objectives of this chapter are to ensure that you:

- understand how tourism fits into the general theories of economic development;

- understand the importance of integrated tourism planning and development, development planning layers and the role of the community in this respect;

- are able to identify characteristics of the tourism product that have implications for tourism planning and development; and

- can outline the major steps involved in the tourism planning and development process.

TOURISM AND ECONOMIC DEVELOPMENT THEORIES

There have been a number of theories put forward to explain the process of economic development (see Nafziger, 1997). A few of the more influential economic development theories in their time include:

- The English classical theory of economic stagnation.
- Marx's historical approach.
- Rostow's identification of stages of economic growth.
- Vicious circles of demand/supply and investment.
- Balanced and unbalanced growth theories.
- Theories of dependence.

It is possible to examine the main threads of these theories in order to identify whether or not there is a role for tourism within the more general theories of economic development. Although it should be noted that since the 1970s there has been a tendency to move away from the grand theoretical notions of economic development and instead use a more specific, case by case, approach. Nevertheless, it can be helpful to look at the characteristics of tourism development within a framework of general economic development.

English classical theory of economic stagnation

This theory grew out of the classical writings of early economists Malthus, Mill and Ricardo. To understand the concept of the theory it needs to be noted that such writers were very much influenced by Newtonian's physics with its belief that life was never random and was ordered by some 'grand design'. Of the various assumptions employed by the classical economists, the operation of this theory can best be seen by focusing upon just two of them: that in the event of no technological progress, output was constrained by the scarcity of land, and the law of diminishing returns.

In Figure 9.1 it can be seen that additional units of labour with a fixed amount of land increase output per unit of labour significantly when the labour is increased from 1 to 3. However when a fourth unit of labour is added the increase in output, although positive, is not as great as the previous increase. The increase in output achieved when the fifth and sixth units of labour become progressively less. If more than six units of labour are added the output starts to decline as diseconomies of large scale are experienced.

The theory also suggests that the long-term wage rate, the natural wage rate, was at the subsistence level. Therefore, in spite of short-term deviations from the natural wage rate, it would always tend to return to the natural level.

Under this theory, if food production increases, wages rise and the extra food available means that the population becomes healthier and grows. As the population increases there are more mouths to feed and more units of labour with the fixed supply of land. As the labour force is increased the average wage rate falls and

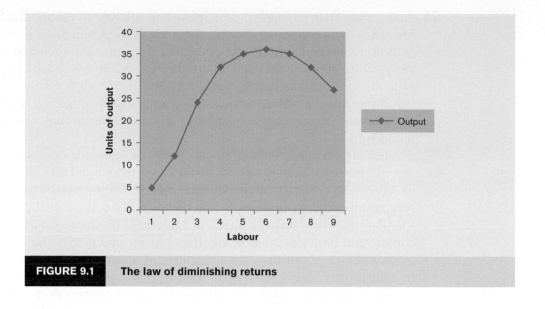

FIGURE 9.1 The law of diminishing returns

continues to do so until the subsistence wage rate is reached. If the wage rate falls below subsistence level then the population declines and the scarcity of labour forces the average wage rate back up to its natural level. Given the lack of any technological progress, the only way to mitigate against the diminishing returns is to increase the capital accumulation per worker. But even here, the classical economists had tied themselves into an economic straightjacket. The need to acquire profits and interest payments in return for increased capital stocks requires the existence of increased availability of surplus value (output less the cost of labour) but the diminishing returns assumption means that the surplus diminishes and hence the return on capital. With dimishing returns on capital there is reduced incentive to increase the capital per worker and the route to economic stagnation and decline is set. There are good grounds for viewing the English classical theory to be a theory of doom and gloom.

The flaws in the theory are many and include the neglect of technological progress that can multiply the output per worker manifold. Also, the assumption that population growth was uniquely determined by prosperity is also found to be wanting particularly in industrialised countries where voluntary birth control has stabilised population levels. The ownership of capital and land is not necessarily the prerogative of the private capital owners. State ownership of capital and land may result in a different set of objectives that may allow continued growth.

Marx's historical approach to development

Marx's historical materialism approach to development is framed within a dynamic world rather than based on the static scenario used by the classical economists. Within this dynamic view of development, changing technology, enhanced organisation of production and the development of human skills all work together to provide lubricant for the engine of change. The world, as seen by Marx and Engels, moved naturally from **feudalism** to **capitalism**, to **socialism** and then to **communism**. The economic consequences of the rise to capitalism include demand expanding more slowly than productive capacity and an increase in monopolistic power that forces out small businesses creating a segment of the population of workers who are without property. The dynamics of this result in what Marx referred to as a reserve army of unemployed that acts as a buffer to absorb the shocks as the economy expands and contracts during business cycles. The result is a series of crises where the ownership of productive capacity is repeatedly challenged by the educated proletariat until communism is established and socialism through the state, becomes redundant.

There are a number of flaws in Marx's view of economic development, including the observed facts that revolution when the proletariat did take the state happened in Russia rather than the West at a time when Russia was one of the least developed capitalistic countries in Europe. The theory relies upon their being a conflict of the objectives held by capitalists and those held by the proletariat. If there is no conflict and both sides realise that they can prosper if they both decide to share a fast growing output then the dynamism of Marx's theory takes a serious blow. In spite of this, Marx's theory still finds a great deal of support from those either discontent with the distribution of wealth in their country or those worried about the threats of the recent trends towards globalisation and the dominance of multinational corporations.

Rostow's theory of growth and development

The processes of change identified within Marx's dynamic world were not evenly distributed. If an historical view is taken, the existence of the pre-capitalist societies was spread over long periods of time with little evidence of significant changes to economic life. It was the recognition that there were five distinct stages through which economies pass as they develop that led to Rostow identifying the stages in his influential work (Rostow, 1990). The five stages were:

1 The (pre-industrial) traditional society.

2 The pre-conditions for economic take-off.

3 Economic take-off.

4 Self-sustained drive towards maturity.

5 The age of mass consumption.

Rostow's work was more a collection of identified sequential trends rather than a theory. The tenet of Rostow's paper is that there is a natural inertia that needs to be overcome before self-sustained development takes place. This inertia is overcome by a build up of transport investment; enhanced organisation and production in agriculture; increased imports – particularly capital. These three factors Rostow refers to as the pre-conditions for take-off. The pre-conditions were deemed to have been met when countries experience a rapid increase in net investment, have a major leading economic sector with strong linkages to other sectors and have in place the necessary infrastructure to support the development of modern industries.

Once the pre-conditions for take-off have been met and take-off started the economy is deemed to be on a route of self-sustained consistent growth. This stage is associated with migration from rural to urban areas, a developed labour force and a state system that provide stability. This process of self-sustained growth will continue until it matures into a stage of mass consumption where the ownership of durable goods such as automobiles, white goods and other equipment are considered to be the norm.

Rostow's view of economic development was more influential within government circles where it presumably struck some familiar chords in US government offices, than it did within academic circles. Rostow's academic peers received his theory with mixed views and it was severely criticised by some as being too vague, overly-simple and impossible to test. His theory was also criticised on the basis that it lumped together a wide range of countries under the category of traditional economies irrespective of their resources, history or structure. The theory relating to the role played by net investment in breaking down the natural inertia of economies is not supported by empirical evidence and there is no demonstrable reason as to why the components of each stage should not occur at any time in the development process rather than only in the stage to which Rostow refers. A fundamental criticism of Rostow's theory is that it implicitly assumes that development today will mirror the development process that was experienced by today's developed countries. This ignores the effects of international linkages and trade as well as assuming that today's developing countries all have the same objectives for development that were pursued by the industrialised countries of today.

Vicious circles of demand/supply and investment

This theoretical approach suggests that countries are poor because they always have been. The poverty leading to poverty premise can be examined from either the demand side or the supply side in order to arrive at the same conclusion. From the demand side it is suggested that if a country is poor then the levels of income will be low. This means that the level of demand for goods and services will also be low and therefore there is no incentive for entrepreneurs to invest in additional productive capacity. This means that the amount of capital per worker remains low, productivity remains low, and this sustains the link between low income and low demand. From a supply side there is a suggestion that low income levels present few opportunities for saving and this means that there is little in the way of capital availability to invest in productive capacity. With low investment there is low capital per worker and this maintains the low productivity which leads to low income and savings.

These mechanisms are appealing from the point of view of simplicity but it is their simplicity that gives most cause for concern. The link between income levels and savings at national level is not as obvious as this theory suggests. Corporate saving is an important element of total savings and in many cases the marginal propensity to consume may not be significantly higher than in industrialised countries where there are constant forces trying to induce consumers to spend more. The simplicity of the theories also suggests a level of volatility that is not apparent in national economies. For instance, a small injection of additional demand would lead to the opportunity to invest in additional capital per worker, leading to additional productivity, higher income levels and higher demand. This would expand the economy out of its poverty trap.

Balanced and unbalanced growth approaches

These theories are variants of a theme and relate to whether development occurs across all sectors or whether there is development in a few leading sectors that will act as a catalyst for development across the economy as a whole. The balanced growth theory suggests that it not possible to overcome the natural inertia in a stagnant economy by only investing and developing a few export sectors. There is indivisibility in infrastructure that requires a broader development platform if it is to be successful and investment decisions often have linkages with other invest- ment decisions without which they would not be viable. As an alternative there is the suggestion that unbalanced growth, where investment occurs in just a few leading sectors is far more achievable with resources of developing countries and that these leading sectors will drag the other sectors up in their wake.

Dependency theory of development

The dependency theory of economic development suggests that the ability of an economy to achieve autonomous development is determined by its dependency upon other capitalist countries. The greater the dependency upon other capitalist economies the lower the ability to achieve economic development. Proponents of this theory cite the colonial periods as evidence of foreign powers exploiting less developed countries in order to grow richer as a result of their relationship – even to the point of de-industrialising them. There are many instances where colonialism can be seen to have such a negative impact on a colony's economic development, although it is often difficult to determine how much development would have taken place without colonialism. Furthermore, there are many countries that were never colonised and that have remained under-developed, such as Afghanistan and Ethiopia. Nevertheless, there are few people who would argue that colonialism and dependency did not lead to the suffocating of indigenous development forces through:

- migration of workers from rural to colonial organised urban areas;
- 'cropping' the best workforce members to work in colonial offices;
- foreign trade on unfair terms; and
- opening of local markets to foreign companies.

The development theories and tourism's role

Within the English classical theory of development there is no clear role for any industry beyond the limits imposed by the scarcity of land. Tourism development is a form of real estate development and as such it will add to the pressures on the use of land without providing a way of breaking down the constraining factors associated with diminishing returns.

As a vehicle or catalyst of change, there is a clear role for tourism within Marx's theory of development. Tourism can speed up the process of change because it has product characteristics (see below) that enable it to develop quickly and help the transfer process perhaps from capitalism through to socialism and eventual communism. However, there are elements of the industry that thrive on exploiting economies of large scale production (natural monopolies such as airlines) that would resist the movement from capitalism to more egalitarian-based systems. But, overall, tourism can be seen as an excellent driving force for economic, social and political change.

If the role of tourism is examined with respect to Rostow's stages of economic development there is clearly a strong role that can be played by tourism. The development of the transport and infrastructure, together with the import of capital that is seen as a pre-condition for take-off is a fundamental part of most tourism development. Thus tourism can be used as a catalyst to overcome the inertia of developing countries. The organisation of agricultural production is also often associated with the injection of the additional demand presented by tourism development.

Tourism could play a significant role within the vicious circle theory of development simply by either injecting additional demand into an economy or by providing a stimulus to investment. The introduction of tourism under this theory of development would result in an expanding economy when viewed from either a demand or a supply side.

In either the balanced or unbalanced growth theory approaches there is a clear role for tourism within the theories, either as part of the overall broad balanced approach to development or as one of the leading sectors in an unbalanced approach. Why tourism would be chosen as a lead sector within the unbalanced approach to development can be found in the extent of linkages that tourism has with other industries within an economy. Often they are far more widely spread and of deeper significance than those traditionally found with primary goods markets such as agriculture or fishing.

It is not difficult to relate modern-day tourism traits to the dependency theory of development. There are often fears about dependency both on tourism as an industry and as a dependency upon foreign suppliers (particularly tour operators and transport companies) as they are the lifeline of tourism development. As such the dependency theory is more an explanation of under-development rather than one that tries to explain development. There is a role for tourism but it can be either a stimulant or an inhibitor of development depending upon ownership of the tourism establishment.

In summary, of the major theories that have attempted to enhance our understanding of the economic development of countries, there is a major role that can be played by tourism except in the case of the English classical theory where there is little scope for any industrial sector other than the latitude offered by the availability of land and its relationship with population (see Table 9.1). Tourism leads the global economy as an engine of development as we enter the twenty-first century. Its growth performance has been nothing short of astonishing over the last half of the twentieth century. The result of this is that tourism is a development option that most governments fondly embrace.

When the discussion turns to 'sustainable' development the key economic development theories discussed above are all found to be lacking as they do not encompass the environmental and socio-cultural aspects that must be considered if sustainability is to be explored. Nor does the market system fully reflect the true cost of resources upon which so much of tourism depends. This is a topic that is explored in Chapter 11.

TABLE 9.1	The role for tourism in major development theories
Theories	**A role for tourism**
English classical theory	×
Marx's theory	✓
Rostow's theory of growth	✓
Vicious circle theory	✓
Balanced/unbalanced	✓
Dependency theory	✓

INTEGRATED PLANNING AND DEVELOPMENT

There are a variety of approaches that may be adopted when planning for the development of any industry or any economy. One can take a proactive stance and develop strategies to secure the desired development path. This approach requires deep and thorough understanding of not only the local economy and its structure, limitations and strengths, but also the probable effects of external factors, how they may impinge on the local development process and what form these external effects are likely to take. Alternatively, one can adopt the reactive stance of chaos theory. This approach is based upon the premise that there are too many variables, internally and externally, to be able to plan. These variables cannot be controlled nor can they be predicted with sufficient levels of accuracy. Therefore, it is better to develop reactive schemes in order to be in good order to meet the unexpected rather than to attempt a proactive but indeterminable development path. This latter approach has been likened to training policy makers on flight simulators so that their reactions develop in positive and enlightened ways. However, both proactive and reactive approaches can use such an analogy. Pilots are trained to fly to pre-determined paths and schedules while, at the same time, they are trained to be able to react sensibly to unexpected events. The same may be said about tourism development planning. To rely purely on reactive policy solutions is to forsake the prospect of optimising tourism development.

A second issue that has given rise to much academic debate during the 1990s is the notion of sustainable development (see Chapter 8). Although much that has been said about sustainable development is sound from an academic viewpoint, it is neither innovative nor radical. The notion that we must look forward to future generations when we are planning to consume finite resources is commendable and such notions should also be transferred to all other production and consumption activities, not just tourism. Furthermore, the term 'sustainable development' is a misnomer and has led to much confusion. Development has sometimes been confused with the concept of growth and it is *this* misunderstanding that has caused the increased volume of literature to be published proclaiming the call for sustainable development. In reality, development has to be sustainable to be classified as development at all, otherwise it is short-term growth. Most textbooks that attempt a definition of development include some statement about self-sustained growth. However, the allocation of finite resources to productive activities is not sustainable unless technological inventions and innovations can find alternative resources in the future. There is a danger in inhibiting specific forms of tourism activities in order to reduce the immediate impacts of tourism in the short term because such remedial actions may unleash far more devastating and less sustainable impacts in the future. Clearly, there is no simple answer to the sustainability debate. Only to state that development planning has *always* been concerned with sustainability issues and it is only 'bad' planning that has given so much impetus to these recent debates.

Tourism and development

If tourism is to be incorporated into a country's development plan it must be organised and developed according to a strategy constructed on sound foundations. These foundations should take account of the coordination of the tourism-related

MINI CASE STUDY 9.1
Can we turn back the clocks in Benidorm?

Tourism development planning articles and books often discuss the issues as if they were starting from a no-tourism situation. The reality is that most tourism activity takes place in well-developed economies with significant investments in infrastructure and tourism plant. Resort areas such as Benidorm, Spain, have been subject to major tourism investment, the environment has changed beyond recognition and the local culture has changed from one based upon a traditional fishing village to one based on a high-density international visitor culture. Many of the local residents have been displaced by the development of tourism facilities, the increased cost of land and housing and the 'invasion' of alien cultures. It is not possible for the environment to revert back to its original state nor would it be economically viable to attempt such a reversal of development. Too much investment has taken place and too many jobs are at stake.

The future of these resorts is partly determined by the local authorities and the respective national governments, the tour operators, the tourism businesses and the other local stakeholders. Future development can take place, either in the form of

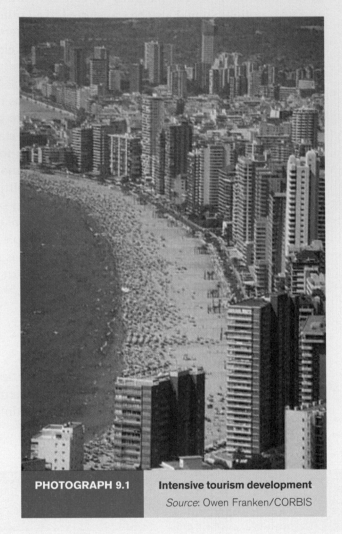

PHOTOGRAPH 9.1	**Intensive tourism development**
	Source: Owen Franken/CORBIS

new investment in facilities and infrastructure or in terms of maintenance investment to keep tourism plant up to date. The tourism strategies for resorts such as these will be significantly different to those constructed to support tourism development in virgin areas.

DISCUSSION QUESTIONS

1 What are the planning implications for tourism strategies in Benidorm?

2 Given that it is not possible to turn back the clock on areas where environmental and socio-cultural impacts of tourism have been so devastating, what development options are left to the policy makers? Comment on a possible way forward that includes the economic viability of the area.

3 One way to preserve the environmental and socio-cultural integrity of areas of Spain that have not yet been touched by tourism is to ensure that future developments take place in areas such as Benidorm and that tourism development in the unspoiled areas is avoided or kept to the low-volume, low-impact variety. Discuss.

sectors, and the supply and demand for the tourism product. The process of development planning involves a wide cross-section of participants who may bring with them goals that are conflicting. Furthermore, different stakeholders may well bring with them incompatible perceptions about the industry and the development process itself. Before looking at the process of tourism development planning it is worth considering some of the advantages and disadvantages associated with selecting tourism as a catalyst for general development.

TOURISM PRODUCT CHARACTERISTICS

The tourism product is unique in terms of the range and diversity of activities encompassed. Few products can compete with the wide variety of activities included under the heading of tourism. Tourists can add to this uniqueness by bringing their own extra dimension to the product. Furthermore, the tourism product must be consumed within the geographical boundaries of the destination in which it is offered. The producers of the tourism product, however, are not always confined to the local economy and in this growing age of globalisation tourism may include transport businesses, accommodation owners, tour operators, travel agents and information providers that are based outside of the destination. As with any personal service, production and consumption occur simultaneously and, in the case of tourism, such production affects most other sectors (directly and indirectly) of the economy. As seen elsewhere in this book, this **simultaneity of production** and consumption also creates specific social (and to some extent, environmental) impacts not normally associated with the production of other goods and services.

TOURISM AS A MEANS OF WEALTH REDISTRIBUTION

Tourism is widely recognised to be one of the fastest earners of foreign exchange and one of the most effective income redistribution factors in many countries. Although able to provide strong redistribution effects within an economy when residents of urban areas spend some of their income in the less populated poorer regions of their country, it has been disappointing as a vehicle to redress the global economic imbalance between north and south. Nevertheless, it has provided a valuable source of foreign exchange to the smaller developing countries that find it difficult to compete in the tangible goods markets.

Domestic tourism is a very effective means of redistributing income between different areas within a national economy. This is because tourism tends to take place in the more sparsely populated scenic areas where there is little in the way of manufacturing industry. Therefore tourism provides the opportunity to create employment and income in areas with limited alternative sources. Thus, English residents head for Cornwall, the Peak District, Scotland and Wales for the domestic trips, the French leave Paris *en masse* in August and generally head south. The mass exodus of people out of the cities throughout Europe, the Americas and Australia during the main vacation periods is evidence of this domestic redistribution at work.

The literature on international tourism as a means of income redistribution is somewhat deceptive. Many of the articles written about tourism development tend to focus upon economically, environmentally and/or socially vulnerable destinations. This is because they provide a more visible stage on which to examine each of the consequences of tourism development. However, in reality, the vast bulk of international tourist movement takes place between industrialised countries. To support this viewpoint it can be noted that in 2002 more than 88% of total international tourist arrivals in Europe came from other European countries and that globally more than 80% of international tourist arrivals tend to be residents within the region where they arrive. In terms of the north–south debate, tourists escape the industrialised countries to visit other industrialised countries and the south enjoys little in the way of a significant share of the wealth created by tourism. This is a fact that should be borne in mind when examining the global consequences of tourism development.

TOURISM AS A LABOUR-INTENSIVE INDUSTRY

Tourism, in common with most personal service industries, is labour intensive. For developing countries with surplus labour and for industrialised countries with high levels of unemployment, tourism provides an effective means of generating employment opportunities. In general, at a time when the labour:capital ratio is moving strongly against labour in most production industries, the importance of the labour-absorbing qualities of tourism cannot be overlooked. However, in many countries there are labour shortages and it is not uncommon to find these countries importing labour to work in their tourism industries. Under such circumstances one might question whether these countries have a comparative advantage in tourism and whether or not their factors of production would be better employed in alternative industries.

Even in those situations where there is an abundance of labour it may be the case that there are other factors of production that provide arguments in favour of development routes other than through tourism. Where there are clear indications that the local destination would benefit from the employment created by tourism, this view should be tempered by the characteristics of the labour force generally associated with tourism-related establishments. The employment profile of large hotels, for example, tends to yield a relatively flat occupational pyramid such as that shown in Figure 9.2. This means that middle and senior management posts are relatively scarce compared with the high number of low-skill employees. Such an occupational pyramid results in a lack of career development and, consequently, a lack of staff motivation. A point also worthy of consideration is the predominance of females and young people employed in tourism-related establishments.

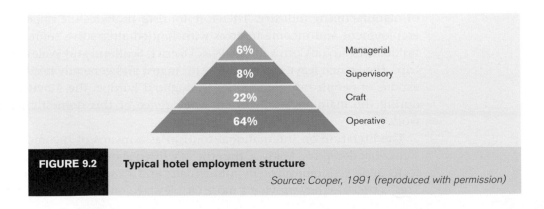

6%	Managerial
8%	Supervisory
22%	Craft
64%	Operative

FIGURE 9.2 **Typical hotel employment structure**

Source: Cooper, 1991 (reproduced with permission)

Attempts have been made to increase the height of the occupational pyramid by, for example, the introduction of departments and layers of middle management posts in luxury hotels. This, it was hoped, would provide a much-needed impetus to career prospects and motivation. However, recent experience suggests that there has been a reversal of this trend with 'de-layering' and the career development prospects in large hotels is not significantly different from that exhibited three decades ago. Thus, although tourism may provide a quick and ready means of increasing the number of employed people in the local economy, its contribution to long-term development may be questionable. To expand this argument further it is necessary to consider the secondary employment effects associated with tourism development and here one can find a much broader range of skill requirements and career development paths. Therefore, although the direct employment effects of tourism may be subject to some limiting characteristics, the indirect effects do not suffer in the same way.

TOURISM AND ON-THE-JOB TRAINING

The development of travel and hospitality skills in the local labour market is unlikely to make large demands on educational resources. The educational qualifications of those employed in the accommodation sector are heavily weighted in favour of those with only a rudimentary education. This is undesirable both from the point of view of the future of the industry and in terms of the overall development of the destination. There is often an urgent need for training and education at all levels in both the private and public sectors. However, industry often chooses to ignore this need and to enjoy the benefits of a cheap and plentiful labour market, and the public sector is often more concerned with the short-term goal of achieving employment opportunities rather than the development of a well-educated and qualified labour force. There is an unquestionable need for education and training in the tourism and hospitality industries and the reliance upon untrained labour with on-the-job training is responsible for many poor-quality tourism products. These destinations fail to compete with high-quality tourism destinations that, in consequence, are able to charge higher prices and enjoy more buoyant demand for their products.

The poor quality and inadequate education and training related to the tourism and hospitality industries is an aspect that has been known for almost two decades, as Table 9.2 demonstrates. From a short-term growth point of view rather than as a development option, this educational profile has both positive and negative implications. On the positive side it means that the labour force for tourism growth can be mobilised relatively quickly. The training can be undertaken on the job, which means that units of labour can be brought in quickly from either the unemployed or, as is often the case in developing countries, from agriculture and fishing industries. On the negative side, the lack of educational qualifications found in tourism-related businesses means that the growth of tourism does not necessarily result in a more educated labour force – one of the factors perceived to be an important ingredient in the economic development process.

THE STRUCTURE OF THE TOURISM INDUSTRY

One of the more notable features of the tourism industry is the proportion of the total businesses that are classified as small and medium-sized enterprises (SMEs).

TABLE 9.2	Level of training in tourism	
Level	**Supplementary activities (%)**	**Activities (%)**
University	1	3
Other higher education	4	5
Secondary		
Higher	30	45
Lower	34	40
No qualifications	31	7

Source: WTO, 1980

The nature of tourism as a personal service industry tends to make it attractive to individual and family entrepreneurs. The proliferation of small businesses brings with it both advantages and disadvantages. In the first instance it facilitates quick start-ups and flexible supply sources that can respond rapidly to fluctuations in demand. It is also an industry that, from the outside, does not appear technically daunting and thus encourages budding entrepreneurs to enter the industry. There are few **barriers to entry** in the sense that businesses can be started with small amounts of investment and there is room for **product differentiation** to provide some monopolistic power to the smallest businesses. However, these advantages can also be the source of the industry's worst problems in terms of:

- inadequate staff training (unstructured informal training);

- too high a debt/equity ratio leading to business failure (borrowing on the good will of the business); and

- inefficiency problems because of a failure to capitalise on economies of large-scale production.

Although the vast majority of business establishments in tourism may be considered to be SMEs, a significant proportion of the total output of the industry is attributable to the larger national and multinational corporations. Nevertheless, there is certainly scope for a wide range of business structures within tourism from bed and breakfast units through to international hotel chains, from independent sightseeing flight operators to national airline giants. Each type of business has its own operating characteristics with a tendency for the smaller firms to be more labour intensive and dependent upon local suppliers; to the larger companies that make extensive use of capital and bulk purchase from a global warehouse.

PROTECTIONISM

The simultaneity of production and consumption of tourism means that the tourist must travel to the destination to enjoy the product. This makes tourism unique as an export industry. The consumers of international tourism (the importing country) often fail to recognise their tourist spending overseas as an import and hence do not see it as a serious threat to the level of employment in their own countries. Thus, tourism tends to escape the danger of being singled out for **protectionism** or trade retaliation, except as part of a general macroeconomic policy which restricts foreign exchange allowances to correct balance of payment problems. Having said that, it is often the existence of foreign exchange restrictions in many of the developing regions of the world that explains the relatively slow rates of growth in interregional tourism (as, for example, in South East Asia). Similarly, when countries are faced with currency crises (such as the UK in the 1960s and 1970s and currency crises in Malaysia in the 1990s) the government of the day imposes restrictions on the amount of currency that outbound tourists can convert.

MULTITUDE OF INDUSTRIES

Tourism is a composite industry product. That is, it is composed of the output of the travel, accommodation and food and beverage, retail, entertainment sectors plus many others. This means that its economic and development impacts are felt quite widely from the initial impact onwards. It also tends to suggest that tourism has strong linkages with many other sectors of the economy and it is the strength of these linkages that determine the value of the output, income and employment multipliers associated with tourist expenditure.

The variety of industries included under the umbrella of tourism means that there are a variety of employment opportunities generated by tourism activity. This may stimulate the labour market and the delivery of vocational training.

PRICE FLEXIBILITY

Many developing countries are dependent upon the world market prices for primary agriculture produce for their foreign exchange receipts. That is, the prices of, say, cocoa, sugar, rice, etc., are determined in world commodity markets where individual countries have very little say in determining the final price of the goods. Tourism, on the other hand, provides a source of foreign exchange that is subject to some degree of control by the host country. Product differentiation, either through natural endowments or man-made resources, can provide some price-setting power. The greater product differentiation that is either innate or can be engineered, the greater the **monopolistic power** and hence the greater freedom a destination has in setting its own price. Product differentiation can be based on natural factors ranging from broad aspects such as climate (Florida, Bermuda and Iceland as examples) to specific natural attractions (such as Victoria Falls, Great Barrier Reef and Grand Canyon). Differentiation can also be achieved through socio-cultural aspects, heritage (such as the Pyramids of Egypt, the Great Wall of China and Stonehenge in the UK) and even in terms of the quality of the tourism product itself. Basically, it does not matter what aspect is used to differentiate the product providing there is sufficient demand for it. However, tourism is also highly **price competitive**.

PRICE COMPETITIVE

The bulk of the tourism market, which is resort tourism, is extremely price sensitive and, consequently, internationally competitive. The effects of currency fluctuations on the number of international arrivals and the volume of tourist expenditure adequately demonstrate this fact. Although most mass tourism destinations claim a high degree of product differentiation, a brief examination of the major tour operators' brochures selling sun, sand and sea products will show that the major battleground is fought not on hotels, the quality of beaches or the sea, but the price of the package. Price competition is a fundamental feature of the budget tourism market for both destinations and operators.

SEASONALITY

A striking feature of tourism in many countries is the way in which the level of activity fluctuates throughout the year. This is not a characteristic unique to tourism – agriculture is also an industry used to seasonal fluctuations in activity – but the majority of industries are not subject to the degree of seasonality experienced by tourism establishments. Seasonality in tourism can be caused by either supply factors, such as those mentioned above, or demand factors such as the availability of tourists to travel at different times of the year. For instance, international holiday packages aimed at attracting family groups from Europe or the USA would need to bear in mind that the availability of most families will be determined by the school holidays. The effect of this can be seen by searching for flight costs during school term periods and those during school holidays periods. The latter tend to be associated with a premium price tag. Therefore the forces of seasonality attack the consumption of the product from both sides of the market, demand and supply.

Irrespective of the cause of the seasonality in the tourism industry, it tends to be reflected in:

- employment (casual/seasonal staff);

- investment (low annual returns on capital);

- pricing policies (discounted off-season prices).

From an economics point of view, any business subject to seasonal fluctuations in demand for its output is faced with a dilemma. If it purchases sufficient resources to meet the peak load demand, then it will have to carry spare productive capacity for the remainder of the year. If it gauges its resources according to the average level of demand it will spend part of the year carrying spare capacity and be unable to meet the peak-load demand level. Alternatively, it can take on variable resources (staff) to meet the peak-load demand and then shed these variable factors of resources during the off-season. Although attractive from the point of view of the profit and loss account, this widely practised solution does nothing to improve employer/employee relations. Also, there is an inherent waste in taking on staff each year on a temporary basis, investing in human resources (by training) and then losing that investment at the end of the main season.

In order to offset some of the costs associated with seasonality many hotels and operators offer holidays for off-season periods with heavily discounted prices. By offering lower prices it is possible to induce visitors to a destination at a time when they would otherwise not visit. However, there are limits to such discounting. First, the revenue that establishments receive during the off-season must *at least* cover the variable costs of production. If this is the case then, by opening in the off-season, they will be able to maintain their staff and, perhaps make some contribution to their **fixed costs**. Second, the discounting of off-season packages should not be so great as to damage the desirability of the main season product.

There are also destinations that do not suffer much from seasonal variations and this provides them with a competitive advantage by allowing them to operate at a higher throughput of tourist activity across the year without suffering from as much socio-cultural and environmental impacts as their seasonal competitors.

HIGH OPERATING LEVERAGE/FIXED COSTS

Many of the tourism-related industries are subject to high levels of fixed costs. That is, there is a large capital element that must be committed before any output is produced. In industries subject to this type of cost structure (e.g. airlines and hotels) the volume of sales becomes the all-important factor. This aspect is shown in Figure 9.3, where the vertical axis measures revenue and costs, and the horizontal axis depicts the quantity of output produced during the time period under consideration. The break-even output for the non-tourism industry is represented by Q1 whereas Q2 shows the break-even output for the tourism industry. The cost curve C_1 relates to the cost function of a non-tourism industry and C_2 relates to the cost function of a typical tourism-related industry. We can see that both industries are subject to the same variable-cost structures (that is why the two cost functions run parallel to each other) but the tourism-related industry is subject to a higher fixed-cost element. The end result is that the break-even point for the tourism-related industry (BEP_2) is much higher than that for the non-tourism industry, thus the volume of output becomes all important for high fixed-cost industries. The break-even point refers to that level of revenue and output that will just cover the costs involved in producing the output.

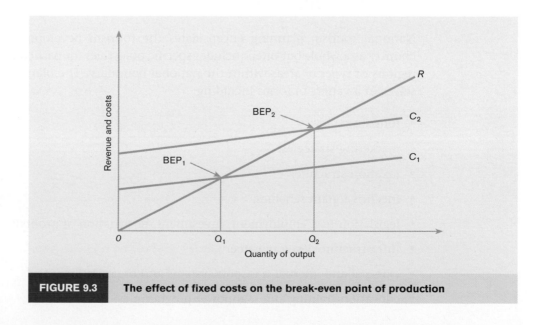

| FIGURE 9.3 | The effect of fixed costs on the break-even point of production |

The pre-occupation with volume displayed by industries that have high operating leverages can also influence the mindset of the national tourist organisations. Many tourist destinations base their tourism development plans on volume figures. Countries the world over tend to celebrate the fact that visitor numbers exceed some *magical* annual threshold and many countries still express the targets/objectives of their development plans in terms of bed spaces and tourist nights. However, the presence of tourists in itself is not the main objective of any of these destinations. The primary aims are economic and the indicators of performance and targets should be expressed in economic rather than volume figures and/or constrained by environmental or social indicator values.

Clearly, there is overwhelming evidence to support the view that there are a number of factors related to the tourism industry which make it an attractive development option. But some of these factors may make it less attractive if they are not controlled or alleviated by proper planning.

DEVELOPMENT PLANNING LAYERS

Tourism development planning can take place at international, national and sub-national levels.

International tourism planning

At the international level organisations such as the WTO, EU, OECD, Caribbean Tourism Organisation (CTO) and the Tourism Council for the South Pacific (TCSP) all undertake, albeit limited, forms of tourism planning. This level of planning is often weak in structure, detail and enforcement. It is generally provided in a guideline form in order to assist the member states.

National tourism planning

National tourism planning encapsulates the tourism development plans for a country as a whole but often includes specific objectives for particular sub-national regions or types of areas within the national boundary. The plans manifest themselves in a variety of forms including:

- tourism policy;
- marketing strategies;
- taxation structure;
- incentive/grant schemes;
- legislation (e.g. employment, investment, repatriation of profits);
- infrastructure developments;
- external and internal transport systems and organisations; and
- education/training and manpower programmes.

Regional/local tourism planning

Regional and local tourism planning deals with specific issues that affect a sub-national area. It tends to be much more detailed and specific than its national counterpart and can vary quite significantly from area to area. For instance, there may be areas where tourism development is to be encouraged and others where specific types of tourism facilities, such as a casino, are actively discouraged. Such plans may relate to a state within a country, to a county, a city or even a local resort area.

However, there are constraints on how different regional plans can be from other regional plans or from the national plan. Certainly they should not detract from the overall aims and objectives of the national plan or those of another region. Ideally, the sub-national plans should work in harmony with the national plan as far as local conditions will allow.

Plans at all levels should include consideration of how information is transferred to the consumer – the tourist. It should also be borne in mind that what you *do not* tell the tourist is often as vital as what you *do* tell them. This is particularly true from the point of view of visitor management when attempts are made to direct the tourists towards some specific regions but away from others. Such information can be disseminated through a variety of media including the Internet which is becoming increasingly important as a tool for tourism development and marketing. However, traditionally the following media have been used:

- visitor orientation centres;

- tourist information centres;

- advertising brochures, maps, magazine articles and broadcasting;

- self-guided tours and trails;

- official guides;

- posters and displays.

The above can all be seen as a means to visitor awareness and can be used to support more formal programmes run by tourism officials.

THE TOURISM DEVELOPMENT PLANNING PROCESS

The concept of planning is concerned with organising some future events in order to achieve pre-specified objectives. Integrated planning and development is a form of comprehensive planning: comprehensive because it integrates all forms of planning – economic, physical, social and cultural. Planning should not be seen as a static concept, rather it attempts to deploy the best strategy in a world of changing internal and external influences. Although planning as a dynamic concept can take a variety of forms, there is a consistent structure that can be applied to the process of planning. That structure is set out in Figure 9.4.

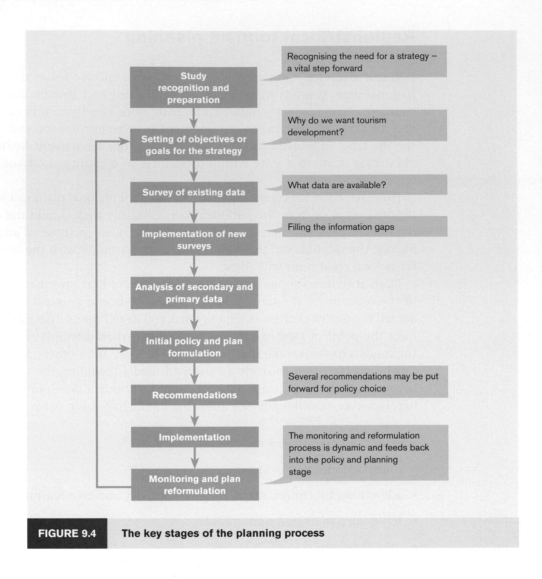

FIGURE 9.4   The key stages of the planning process

Study recognition and preparation

The study recognition and preparation are really concerned with the recognition by the planning authorities (normally the government), the private industry and the local community that tourism is a desirable development option, together with some awareness of the constraints within which it must develop. The fact that it is recognised that a strategy is required is an important indication that the government and people are aware of the complexity of the tourism industry and its need for coordination.

Setting of objectives or goals for the strategy

In order to design a development plan successfully it is necessary to have a clear understanding of the objectives that are to be achieved by the development of tourism. A common mistake in tourism development planning is to lose sight of the reasons why tourism has been selected as a development option. If it is the case that tourism is seen as the most appropriate vehicle for generating foreign exchange and employment opportunities, these goals should be embedded in the development plan from the start. This helps to avoid the problems encountered when the objectives are set down in terms of visitor numbers or annual guest nights.

Some major objectives, commonly found in tourism development plans, are set out below:

- To develop a tourism sector that, in all respects and at all levels, is of high quality, though not necessarily of high cost.

- To encourage the use of tourism for both cultural and economic exchange.

- To distribute the economic benefits of tourism, both direct and indirect, as widely and to as many of the host community as feasible.

- To preserve cultural and natural resources as part of tourism development and facilitate this through architectural and landscape design which reflect local traditions.

- To appeal to a broad cross-section of international (and domestic) tourists through policies and programmes of site and facility development.

- To maximise foreign exchange earnings to ensure a sound balance of payments.

- Attract high-spending 'up-market' tourists.

- Increase employment opportunities.

- Aid peripheral regions by raising incomes and employment, thus slowing down or halting emigration.

It is important that the objectives set out in the development plan are *clear*, *unambiguous*, *non-conflicting* and *achievable*. We can see from the above list of objectives that these examples are not specific in nature, thus it would be difficult to assess whether or not the objective had indeed been achieved. Also, some of the objectives may be conflicting, particularly those relating to the type of tourist to be attracted and their desired impact. Where the objectives are vague and/or conflicting, the tourism development plan is doomed to failure from the start.

Survey of existing data

Before setting out on the data collection stage it is vital to undertake an existing data search. Although this may sound obvious, there are many instances where data that are crucial to tourism development planning are collected and held by government agencies not expressly concerned with the planning process. Thus, when researchers go out into the field to collect **primary data** they are told that businesses have already supplied this information. The authors have come across incidences where no fewer than five hotel surveys were being conducted concurrently. This is not only wasteful in terms of time and resources, it also depletes the goodwill of the business community.

Implementation of new surveys

Once the existing data are known and the scope of the planning objectives have been set, the information gap can be filled by undertaking primary data collection. The data requirements for development planning are quite comprehensive and include:

- tourist characteristics/travel patterns;
- tourist attractions;
- accommodation facilities;
- other tourist facilities;
- land availability and use;
- economic structure – all sectors;
- education and training needs and provisions;
- environmental indicators;
- socio-cultural characteristics;
- investment and available capital – all sectors;
- public and private sector organisations; and
- relevant legislation and regulation.

All of the above factors are considered with respect to both their existing states and their projected states within the development plan's time scale.

The survey of existing data and primary data collection should generate an awareness of the importance of good-quality data for planning, management and monitoring purposes. The authorities should implement a long-term strategy of data enhancement by setting up a management information system that is flexible enough to accommodate the collection of new data when they become available and to encompass issues not necessarily identified within the current strategy.

Analyses

Once the objectives have been formulated, the analytical framework chosen will determine the precise sets of data to be collected. Once collected, the data are analysed by considering a wide range of issues. The major issues to be considered generally fall into four subject areas:

1 **Asset evaluation.** This area of analysis examines the existing and potential stock of assets, the ways in which they can be developed and the probable constraints on that development. The asset evaluation should also include an appraisal of the infrastructure in order to determine whether or not further investment is required. The asset evaluation should begin with a broad approach looking at assets across a wide range of sectors and their alternative uses. The evaluation could then be focused to concentrate on the tourism-related assets and how they should be best employed within that framework.

2 **Market analysis.** The market analysis is clearly a crucial component of a sound development plan. The market analysis undertaken during tourism development planning is sometimes too narrow in scope to be of optimum use. Initial issues that need to be addressed concern global, regional and country market trends by type of tourism activity. Another fundamental question is 'Why do tourists come to this destination?' Too many development plans of the past have relied upon the assumption of constant market share and this is not a valid assumption. To appraise the development plans, attempts must be made to determine whether or not the proposed developments are appropriate, the markets that are likely to be attracted by these developments and the price level or **tariff structure** that should be adopted. The market analysis must also incorporate a study of developments in competitive markets and/or in competitive modes of transport. Generally these issues will be tackled within a competitive and comparative advantage study that incorporates a SWOT analysis.

3 **Development planning.** A major issue to be studied under this heading is the time phasing of the development plan in order to ensure successful implementation. The possible sources of funding of the development are examined and the appropriate level of foreign funding (if any) is calculated. The analysis section encompasses all issues, such as the number of foreign employees, the marketing strategy to be adopted, investment incentives, organisational structures and training programmes.

4 **Impact analyses.** The impact analyses should be all embracing, covering issues such as the probable effects that the development will have on the host community and the environment, the economic implications in terms of key indicators (employment, income, government revenue and foreign exchange flows) and the probable economic rates of return. Analyses should also examine the risks involved and the sensitivity of the results to changing assumptions. The integration of economic, environmental and socio-cultural impact analyses is a vital advancement to tourism planning tools which took place in the closing years of the twentieth century. The incorporation of a forecasting model, so that future economic, environmental and social impacts can be assessed, is equally crucial. Tourism researchers are constantly striving to develop enhanced planning tools for use in tourism development and models, such as those developed within the International Centre for Tourism and Hospitality Research, Bournemouth University, will play a major part in providing the framework for future tourism planning exercises.

The analyses set out above are of both a quantitative and qualitative nature and most of these issues must be faced before a move can be made towards formulating policy recommendations.

Policy and plan formulation

The results from the analyses of the survey data are unlikely to yield a unique solution and, instead, will tend to suggest a number of possibilities for development strategies. The process from here is one of formulating draft plans on the basis of each policy option derived from the analyses. The alternative plans are then evaluated in terms of their potential economic, physical and socio-cultural costs and benefits, together with any possible problem areas that may result from the implementation of each plan. The plans that achieve the most objectives while not exposing the destination to potentially serious problems are then selected and drawn up in full. Finally, a 'preferred' plan is drafted for policy consideration.

Recommendations

The preferred plan that has been selected on the basis of the analyses, having now been completed in detail, is submitted to the authorities by the planning team. This submission is sent to the authorities, together with recommendations concerning the optimum methods of developing tourism in the destination and, in so doing, achieving the plan's objectives. It is more than likely that the planning team will present the authorities with a selection of recommendations that all fulfil the requirements of the preferred plan. It is at this stage that feedback between the authorities and the development plan team is essential in order to focus attention on issues where attention is needed and to play down areas where it is not. During the process of these discussions the final development plan is formulated. Therefore, the recommendations stage should really be regarded as a period of dialogue between the planning team and the policy makers.

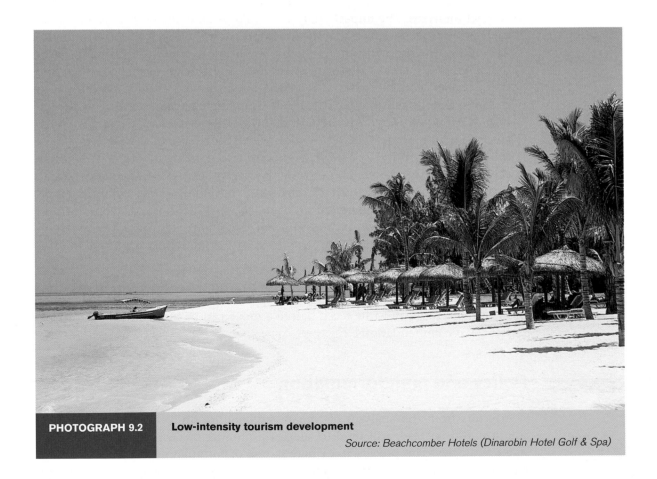

PHOTOGRAPH 9.2   **Low-intensity tourism development**

Source: Beachcomber Hotels (Dinarobin Hotel Golf & Spa)

Implementation of the plan

The methods of implementing the development plan will have been considered throughout most stages of its construction. Thus, during the secondary data survey stage attention will have been paid to many aspects that relate to implementation – such as the existing legislative and regulatory frameworks. By the time that the implementation stage is reached, all of the necessary legislation and regulation controls will have been brought into effect. Furthermore, the methods used to facilitate public debate and discussions relating to the development will have been devised and enquiry and appeal mechanisms will be in place. During the implementation stage particular attention will need to be paid to the phasing of the plan and the critical path analyses will have highlighted areas that may be the cause of concern.

Monitoring and reformulation

Once the development plan has been implemented it must be closely monitored in order to detect any deviations that may occur from the projected path of development. Any such deviations, and there will probably be some, must be analysed in order to assess how they will affect the development plan and its objectives. Once this secondary analysis has been completed, the research team can report back to the authorities with recommendations as to how the plan and its policy recommendations should be modified in order to stay on target. External and internal factors may influence the performance of the strategy and it is important that the monitoring systems enable the research team to be fully informed about all relevant changes. Furthermore, even with the best-laid plans, unexpected events do occur and it is here that the reactive policy skills of the research team and policy makers come into play. For instance, there could be outbreaks of disease that are of international headline importance (the outbreak of the plague in India), the foot-and-mouth crisis in the UK, terrorist activities (Bali, Cairo, London, Madrid and New York) or a destination may be deemed to be unsafe by governments (such as – at various times – Cyprus, Indonesia, Saudi Arabia and Sri Lanka) that cause the international flows of tourists to deviate from their expected path. Even positive developments in competing countries, such as the liberalisation of South Africa, can have unforeseen effects on other destinations. It is important that the research team is aware of how sensitive the strategy is to each of the conceivable variables and how best to react to such events. Even then the tourism plan is likely to face inconceivable events where the research team and policy makers will have to rely upon intuition.

MINI CASE STUDY 9.2
How do you plan for the unexpected? Turkey 1999

In August 1999 an earthquake struck Turkey causing severe damage in its highly populated north-western region that is responsible for almost one-third of the country's total economic output. Many companies were badly affected by the earthquake with factories demolished and severe disruption to the infrastructure. Even those companies that did not suffer directly from the effects of the earthquake closed down production so that employees could help friends and relatives that were affected by the disaster.

TOURISM AFFECTED

Tourism is an important export industry for Turkey and was already under pressure from the threat of terrorism by Kurdish rebels. The news and images of the effects of the earthquake combined with the existing threats of terrorism by Kurdish rebels will have a significant impact on the 10 million visitors that normally visit the region.

The cost of repairing the earthquake damage is likely to be high and some reports have estimated it to be in the region of $30–40 bn. This will severely limit the funds available to boost the faltering tourism industry. These unexpected events came at a time when the Turkish economy was already under attack on a number of fronts including a government deficit of $20 bn and an inflation rate of 50%.

DISCUSSION QUESTIONS

1 Although it is impossible to forecast every disaster that may beset a destination, what steps can Turkey take to mitigate the impact of such disasters on the tourism industry?

2 What are the priorities of a government in relation to the tourism industry when faced with unexpected disasters such as the Turkey earthquake?

3 Are there any pre-disaster steps that governments such as Turkey can take to deal with events if and when they do occur?

The development plan team

The development plan team will need considerable expertise and experience in the formulation of such plans. In general, the team will consist of four groups of specialists, falling into the broad categories of technical services, marketing specialists, planners and economists. In more detail, the likely spread of specialist skills will include:

- market analysts;
- physical planners;
- economists;

- environmental scientists;
- infrastructure engineers;
- transport engineers;
- social scientists;
- draughtsmen and designers; and
- legal experts.

The plan will be constructed over a period of time and this time can be broken down into five distinct phases.

1 **Identification and inventory of the existing situation.** This phase includes:

    (a) characteristics and structure of current consumer demand;
    (b) study of consumer choice;
    (c) current land use, land tenure and land-use control;
    (d) existing natural and artificial attractions;
    (e) ecosystem factors – particularly those considered to be vulnerable;
    (f) economic structures and the capacity thresholds of industries;
    (g) labour force skill mix and educational base, together with availability;
    (h) accommodation facilities;
    (i) tourist services facilities;
    (j) infrastructure facilities and their capacities;
    (k) transport facilities and their capacities;
    (l) graphic presentation of physical inventory.

The above data will be used to establish the adequacy of existing structures and facilities, the classification and cost organisation of existing facilities (together with an index of standards currently achieved), and the economic impact of present tourism activity. This then leads on to the second phase.

2 **Forecasts for the future.** This phase will include forecasts of future demand and probable tourist movements and needs. This will be complemented by an analysis of the implications of these forecasts for future production levels of each relevant service and good, together with the infrastructural requirements. Anticipated standards of service will be examined and the economic forecasts of local repercussions will be estimated.

3 **Plan formulation.** The formulation of the plan will include proposed programmes of market organisation and promotion, comprehensive land-use and control planning, detailed infrastructural plans and the economic, environmental and social evaluations associated with the proposed development plan. Again it is likely to include a graphic presentation of land use and infrastructure, together with a mapping of social impacts and the constraints imposed by the environmental considerations.

4 **Specific project development.** This phase will include an analysis of specific policies and projects for marketing, and tourism management. The physical planners and architects will draw up selections of alternative layouts relating to specific projects and alternative solutions to infrastructural development problems will be developed. Costs of the alternative projects and infrastructural schemes

will be assessed, along with the economic analysis of the various possible investment projects. Once the specific projects have been selected from the various
alternatives these will, again, be subject to graphic presentations. The local environmental issues will be assessed and methods of alleviating problems will be set
out. Examples of environmental planning actions could be broadly based, such
as the treatment of raw sewage and the maintenance of water quality, or highly
specific, such as the planned periodic movements of footpaths to prevent serious
erosion. Matters relating to visitor orientation programmes, visitor management
and interpretation will all be considered and set out within this phase.

5 **Implementation.** The implementation programme will be set into motion with
   construction and supervision, technical and managerial assistance in tourism
   development projects, and financial analysis, and the recommended infrastructure
   investment programme will commence. The implementation stage will include
   the setting up of the continuing monitoring and re-evaluation activities to ensure
   that the strategy is performing optimally and so that adjustments can be made
   swiftly if the circumstances (internally or externally) change.

TOURISM DEVELOPMENT PLANNING: WHEN IT GOES WRONG

Even the best-laid plans can be knocked off course or fail because of unexpected
events. Disaster management is an important element of modern-day planning and
tourism is subject to a wide range of disasters including earthquakes, hurricanes,
outbreaks of infectious diseases and acts of terrorism. A large number of tourism
development plans are, to varying degrees, unsuccessful. Given the fact that such
plans operate in an environment that is constantly changing because of forces
acting outside the control of the authorities, often outside the geographical area
of the destination, perhaps this is not surprising. For instance, the terrorist attacks
on the USA on September 11, 2001 have changed tourism flows in ways that
have severely damaged the tourism development plans of many Caribbean states.
However, many plans fail as a result of inadequacies in the development plans
themselves. Discussions about this latter type of failure can be broken down into
two categories: failure at the design stage and failure at the implementation stage.

Design stage plan failure

Many of the tourism development plans that fail do so because, at the design
stage, they follow no more than the basic formulation of tourism development.
Consider the basic tourism development plan in Figure 9.5. A plan of this structure
will provide a general framework for state and municipal/local investments and
will help to guide and evaluate the proposals of private developers. However, this
type of plan structure lacks the analytical detail and scope necessary for a successful tourism development plan. Quite often this absence of analytical components
is a reflection of the planning bodies who carry out the construction of the plan,
bodies lacking in planning expertise and experience.

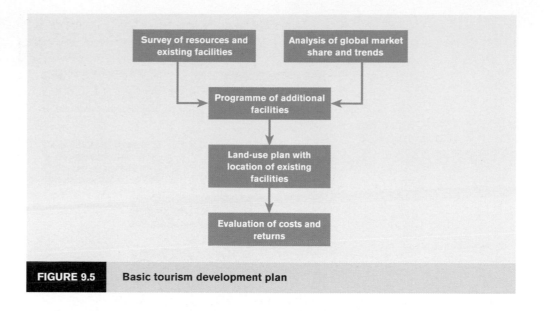

FIGURE 9.5 Basic tourism development plan

More importantly, the plan does not give a clear statement with respect to its objectives – objectives must be achievable, unambiguous and non-conflicting. The plan also fails to take into account the wider issues relating to environmental and social impacts because it is driven uniquely by its financial returns. One of the dangers of drawing up development plans in order to seek external funding is that the myopic view of financial profit and loss accounts may cause the planners to overlook some of the fundamental issues involved. This may well result in a plan that will fail financially as well as structurally.

The development plan takes no consideration of the impact of tourism on the host community, the environment and the economy. The projects are only evaluated on a financial basis (profit and loss accounts) and take no account of social costs and benefits.

Too much emphasis is placed upon physical development, i.e. supply-led tourism development without proper consideration of returns to capital investments and effects on the market. The plan structure fails to make adequate market assessment. The global approach of examining tourist flows from the tourist-generating countries and projecting forward to future time periods under the assumption that all destinations will receive their fair share, fails to address the fundamental issue of *why people want to come to this particular destination*. Unless this issue is addressed future projections can be wildly off target.

Taking the above points into account, the basic development plan structure can be modified as in Figure 9.6.

Implementation stage plan failure

Problems encountered at the implementation stage are largely, but not exclusively, concerned with miscalculations regarding the use of land and the control of land usage. Tourism is, after all, an activity largely involved in real estate development. The type of land difficulties encountered during the implementation stage include the following:

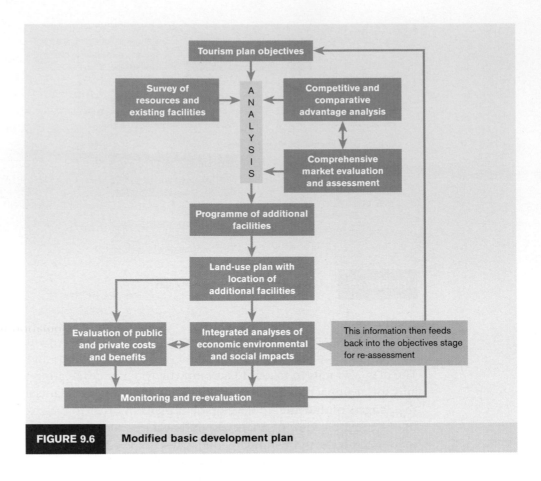

FIGURE 9.6 Modified basic development plan

- Those that actually undertake the development are sometimes more concerned with real estate speculation rather than the operation of tourist facilities. Thus, the motivation for development (particularly when incentives are on offer) may be more to do with capital gain than the tourism product. Such speculative development can lead to poorly designed facilities which are inefficient to operate, or facilities situated in poor locations.

- Development often takes place on the basis of a high debt/equity ratio using land values as security for the loans. This may lead to financial failure when property sales and operating profits do not materialise.

- The planning authorities often underestimate the difficulties that can be encountered when attempting to control the use of land. The only certain way of controlling land usage is by ownership.

- Failure to introduce the required planning legislation quickly enough to implement the development plan, or the lack of ability to enforce such legislation.

- If the specific sites earmarked for development are 'leaked' prior to the implementation of the development plan, land speculation and price inflation is likely to follow. This will alter the economic evaluations and may turn a viable project into a certain failure.

Other problems that may be encountered include the following:

- Failure to coordinate intermediaries in the travel trade, private sector development and public sector provision. Tour operators are an extremely influential component of the tourism process. If left to market forces then oligopolist behaviour can put severe pressure on the economic profitability and local benefits derived from tourism will suffer. Lack of coordination between public and private sectors can result in supply bottlenecks, affecting most aspects of the tourism product; damage the economic benefits associated with the tourism activity; adversely affect visitor satisfaction; and consequently cause the plan to miss its targets.

- Poor communications and infrastructure.

- Inadequate procedures to deal with public opposition and representations concerning the proposed development. A lack of such a mechanism can slow the development process down considerably and result in plan failure.

One of the most common scenarios from unsound tourism planning policies is over-exploitation – when the carrying capacity thresholds of a destination are exceeded such as in Aya Napa in Cyprus where the local population was displaced by tourism development or Benidorm in Spain during the rapid growth stages that created pressures on infrastructure, water supply, health and safety. Such excesses tend to lead to a decline in the quality of the tourism product and, ultimately, to a decline in the 'quality' of tourists, i.e. tourists associated with greater undesirable impacts and lower spend. Under such circumstances the destination may find some or all of the following indicators:

- ecological imbalance through over-use of resources;

- outbreaks of diseases through infrastructural failure;

- congestion, queues and economic inefficiencies;

- deterioration of natural and artificial environment through over-use;

- resentment towards tourists;

- increases in criminal activities; and

- destruction of host community's values.

Although some of the above problems can be alleviated, such as improving the infrastructure to reduce the health risks of water and sewage treatment failure, some of them cannot. The effects of over-exploitation can be minimised, however, by diverting pressures. For instance, ecological imbalances can be tackled by:

- appropriate visitor flow management;

- fencing-off areas subject to over-use;

- providing alternative routes and facilities for tourists to relieve others;

- dispersing tourists over wider or to different areas;

- zoning tourism-related activities;

- educating tourists and hosts to limit socio-cultural damage; and

- encouraging more positive local involvement in tourism activities.

One of the most well-tried techniques is that of access control – the volume or flow of tourists can be controlled economically through prices, or physically, through closures, limiting parking facilities, transport or issuing quotas.

There are, of course, dangers associated with these remedial actions. For instance, dispersing tourists to other areas or to a wider area can sow the seeds for greater long-term problems if the source of the over-exploitation is not harnessed. Dispersing tourists temporally by extending the tourist season can reduce the time that some destinations need to recover from the industry's activities. Re-directing tourism flows may alleviate damaged areas in the short term, but only to replace them with newly damaged areas in the longer term. Such dispersion can also conflict with the prime objectives of the tourism plan. Zoning brings with it many limitations and problems, particularly in border areas. Therefore, when the remedial actions are implemented they should be seen as short-term alleviation methods until the true source of the problems can be tackled.

Finally, the issue of quality should be embedded in all aspects of tourism development planning. The issue of quality is vital for successful tourism development and should manifest itself in the structure and nature of the plans, the educational institutions that train the management and labour force and the monitoring and evaluation of the tourism development process. There are destinations, such as Mauritius and some Indonesian resorts, that owe their competitive advantage to the 'quality' of their tourism product and use 'quality' as a means of product differentiation. Quality should not be confused with high price or up-market tourism. It is just as important to strive for quality in a bed and breakfast or one-star hotel as it is in a five-star hotel or resort. However, when quality is the only factor leading to a competitive edge, then the development of the destination is vulnerable because quality is replicable by other destinations. This means that quality should be considered as a vital part of any tourism development strategy if the strategy is to achieve long-term success.

CONCLUSION

Tourism, as an industry, fits well into the various economic development theories that have been put forward over the past couple of centuries. The only theory that does not provide a positive role for tourism in achieving general economic development is the English classical theory which provides little hope for any industry. The remaining theories all suggest that tourism would be a useful component of general economic development.

The successful development of tourism requires the construction of a development plan or strategy that is flexible and thorough. Flexibility is required in order to adjust and reformulate in response to internal and external changes. Thoroughness is required because of the complexity of the tourism industry and the economic, environmental and social consequences of its development. The issue of 'sustainability' is no more than sound planning because development requires that the path chosen is one that is in some way sustainable. Although the process of tourism development planning will be specific from destination to destination there are processes that need to be followed at national and sub-national levels and these processes provide the framework for tourism development planning.

Tourism development plan failure, when it occurs, is likely to be attributable to failures at either the design stage (inadequate planning structure) or the implementation stage. Both forms of failure are common but in many instances there are remedial actions that may be taken to alleviate some of the problems encountered by failure. Finally, it is important that authorities have contingency plans in place to deal with unexpected events that may knock the tourism strategy off course.

Self-check questions

1 Which theories of economic development provide the best basis for tourism as a catalyst for economic development?

2 What are the major steps, and their sequence, that need to be undertaken as part of the planning process?

3 What reasons can be cited to explain tourism development plan failure at the design stage?

4 Why do tourism master plans/strategies fail at the implementation stage?

5 List the characteristics of the tourism product that influence its attractiveness as a development option. In so doing identify whether the characteristic provides a positive or negative influence when considering tourism as a development option.

Essay questions

1 What indicators can be used to measure economic development and what are their weaknesses or limitations?

2 Tourism development is a complex issue that requires a complex solution. What factors make tourism planning complex and how can they be catered for within the planning process?

3 'It is better to plan tourism development and fail than it is to allow tourism to develop in an unplanned manner.' Discuss this statement incorporating the various forms of plan failure that can occur.

4 What characteristics make tourism an attractive industry for economic development?

5 What are the characteristics of the tourism product that make planning such an important aspect of successful development?

Annotated further reading

Books

Gartner, W. and Lime, D. (eds) (2000) *Trends in Outdoor Recreation, Leisure and Tourism*, CABI Publishing, London.

A collection of edited papers that deal with a wide range of planning and policy issues related to tourism. The book provides in-depth analyses for the more advanced student.

Gunn, C.A. and Var, T. (2002) *Tourism Planning*, 4th edn, Routledge, London and New York.
Provides a comprehensive overview of tourism development.

Inskeep, E. and Kallenberger, M. (1992) *An Integrated Approach to Resort Development: Six Case Studies*, WTO, Madrid.
A collection of case studies that explores the issues relating to planning in the real world. The cases would have provided greater insight if they had been more varied but nevertheless the book provides good insight into many of the issues involved in tourism planning.

Nafziger, E.W. (1997) *The Economics of Developing Countries*, 3rd edn, Prentice Hall, Upper Saddle River, USA.
An excellent book on theories of economic development and the issues relating to the development process.

Swarbrooke, J. (1999) *Sustainable Tourism Management*, CABI Publishing, London.
This book examines the definition of sustainable tourism and looks at tourism management in practice from around the world.

Articles

Ceron, J-P. and Dubois, G. (2003) 'Tourism and sustainable development indicators: the gap between theoretical demands and practical achievements', *Current Issues in Tourism* 6(1), 54–75.
This paper outlines the historical context in which indicators appeared, and links this to the need for improving information systems.

Ghina, F. (2003) 'Sustainable development in small island developing states' *Environment, Development and Sustainability* 5(1–2), 139–65.
This paper explores the status of sustainable development in small island developing states (SIDS). It is the position of this paper that issues related to environmental vulnerability are of the greatest concern. A healthy environment is the basis of all life-support systems, including that of human well-being and socio-economic development.

Lino Grima, Ä.P., Horton, S. and Kant, S. (2003) 'Introduction: natural capital, poverty and development', *Environment, Development and Sustainability* 5(3–4), 297–314.
Can development occur without running down natural resources in an unsustainable way? The concept of natural capital offers a way for those with divergent views (ecologists and economists for example) to discuss this difficult question. Four aspects are examined:

1 The role of institutions in facilitating sustainable development.

2 Examples from (eco)tourism illustrate the potential – and limits – of applicability of the concept.

3 Measurement issues for natural capital are then considered.

4 The concept is applied to agricultural strategy in fragile lands, where the trade-off between the environment and development is likely to be most severe.

Some implications for future research and policy are developed.

Poirier, R.A. (1995) 'Tourism and development in Tunisia', *Annals of Tourism Research* **22**(1), 157–71.
Economic liberalisation policies, externally imposed structural requirements, and Tunisia's comparative advantage have led the government to pursue tourism on a large scale. The growth of this sector has been phenomenal as evidenced by large-scale hotel resort enclaves for Europeans and supportive infrastructural commitments by government and the private sector.

References cited and bibliography

Ashworth, G. and Dietvorst, A. (1995) *Tourism and Spatial Transformations: Implications for Policy and Planning*, CAB, Oxford.
Bodlender, J. and Gerty, M. (1992) *Guidelines on Tourism Investment*, WTO, Madrid.
Chopra, S. (1991) *Tourism and Development in India*, Ashish Publishers, New York.
Cooper, C. (1991) *Progress in Tourism, Recreation and Hospitality Management*, John Wiley & Sons, Chichester.
de Kadt, E. (1979) *Tourism, Passport to Development*, Oxford University Press, Oxford.
Edgell, D. (1990) *International Tourism Policy*, Van Nostrand Reinhold, New York.
Hall, C.M. and Jenkins, J.M. (1994) *Tourism and Public Policy*, Routledge, London.
Inskeep, E. (1993) *National and Regional Planning, Methodologies and Case Studies*, WTO/Routledge, Madrid/London.
Inskeep, E. and Kallenberger, M. (1992) *An Integrated Approach to Resort Development*, WTO, Madrid.
Jansen-Verbeke, M. (1998) *Leisure, Recreation and Tourism in Inner Cities*, Routledge, London.
Johnson, P. and Thomas, B. (eds) (1992) *Perspectives on Tourism Policy*, Mansell, London.
Kinniard, V.H. and Hall, D.R. (eds) (1994) *Tourism Development: The Gender Dimension*, Belhaven, London.
Lawson, F. (1995) *Hotels and Resorts: Planning, Design and Refurbishment*, Butterworth Heinemann, Oxford.
Murphy, P. (1997) *Quality Management in Urban Tourism*, Wiley, New York.
Nafziger, E.W. (1997) *The Economics of Developing Countries*, 3rd edn, Prentice Hall, Upper Saddle River, USA.
Rostow, W.W. (1990) *Stages of Economic Growth: A Non-Communist Manifesto*, 3rd edn, Cambridge University Press, Cambridge.
WTO (1980) *Tourism and Employment: Enhancing the Status of Tourism Professions*, WTO, Madrid.

MAJOR CASE STUDY 9.1
A THREE-YEAR TOURISM STRATEGY FOR NEW ZEALAND, 2003–2006

Tourism New Zealand has won acclaim for its '100% Pure New Zealand' campaign which was launched before the millennium. To build from that success it has launched a strategy for the next three years that will attempt to identify and attract the 'target market' for New Zealand. The strategy is built around a market that Tourism New Zealand has categorised as 'Interactive Travellers®', defined as regular international travellers who consume a wide range of tourism products and services. They are travellers who seek out new experiences that involve engagement and interaction, and they demonstrate respect for natural, social and cultural environments. A summary of the strategy is shown below.

The Strategic Plan presents Tourism New Zealand's plans for the three-year period, 2003 to 2006. Tourism New Zealand is explicitly emphasising important tourism outcomes, with the activities undertaken by Tourism New Zealand being considered as important in helping to stimulate sustained economic growth in New Zealand. This plan is presented at a time when international visitor arrivals have reached two million and expenditure is estimated to be NZ$6.1 bn in foreign exchange during the year ended December, 2002. This makes tourism one of New Zealand's top foreign exchange earners.

STRATEGIC PERSPECTIVE

Strategic goals:

- Increase the number of international holiday tourists to New Zealand by 1.32 million by 2006.

- Increase the percentage of Interactive Travellers® of the 2.55 million forecast arrivals in 2006.

- Increase the number of Interactive Travellers® considering New Zealand as a tourist destination.

- Improve our capacity to monitor the quality of the visitor experience and disseminate this information to stakeholders.

ORGANISATIONAL SUCCESS INDICATORS

As an organisation, Tourism New Zealand will know that its strategy (as articulated in the framework) is working when the following occur.

Reputation

Government, industry and other key stakeholders confirm in a variety of ways their regard for and confidence in Tourism New Zealand's performance, advice and contribution to the interests and priorities of industry and government.

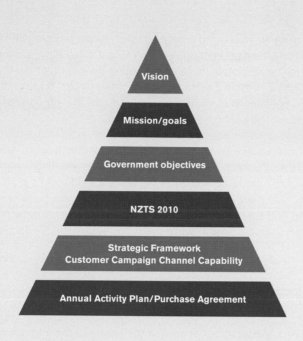

Excellence

Tourism New Zealand reliably delivers quality outputs, provides quality stakeholder experiences, meets external requirements, shares appropriate information and knowledge freely, smoothly manages risks, commits resources prudently, sustainably and with its priorities in mind and provides workplaces that enable staff to do their best work.

PERFORMANCE MONITORING

Tourism New Zealand will monitor its performance against this Strategic Plan by way of reporting required for the Purchase Agreement and Annual Report, and will communicate progress against the Strategic Plan annually to all of our key stakeholders.

The context of the strategy

The growth of tourism has been considered within the context of current government policy and direction, the New Zealand Tourism Strategy (NZTS) 2010, feedback from industry stakeholders and the New Zealand Tourism Board. Tourism New Zealand's activity over the next three years falls into the three broad areas of:

- Campaign
- Channel
- Capability

Key to this is identifying New Zealand's target market, those people whose motivations best match the New Zealand tourism offering, working to establish New Zealand as the ultimate holiday destination for these people while also meeting the needs of the tourism industry and other key stakeholders. The New Zealand Tourism Strategy 2010 tasks the tourism industry with addressing the implications of tourism growth and how this growth can best be managed at a sustainable level for the country.

Tourism New Zealand know through research that the indigenous culture of a country is a strong motivator and source of holiday satisfaction for the type of global travellers they want to attract to New Zealand. Tourism New Zealand is working to infuse Maori culture through all aspects of the global campaign as we see Maori tourism's profile grow. By attracting visitors who will take care of the environment while they are here, who will travel to the regions, spend more and go home 100% satisfied, Tourism New Zealand hopes to increase foreign exchange earnings per visitor, while managing a sustainable tourism industry for the future.

Development objectives

1 CHANNEL
Focus the distribution channel to better service the needs of the interactive traveller.

APPROACH

- To develop the capability of the travel distribution industry to market New Zealand tourism product internationally.

- To increase the value of New Zealand's Internet presence to visitors, the tourism sector and the media/travel media.

- To foster the alignment of air capacity and anticipated market demand.

OUTPUT

- Trade training and facilitation.

- Internet – online marketing.

- Market support – offshore.

2 CAPABILITY

Manage systems to influence the quality of the visitor experience for the Interactive Traveller®.

APPROACH

- To deliver a quality system for the tourism industry ensuring that visitor experience delivery mirrors international marketing promise.

- To foster development and packaging of high-quality, high-yield products for all seasons.

- To ensure regional New Zealand has high awareness of the implications of targeting the Interactive Traveller®.

OUTPUT

- Product development and marketing.
- NZ – market support.

The external environment

Tourism New Zealand's ability to operate effectively in offshore markets is subject to a number of external pressures:

- Significant world events (such as war and terrorism).
- Slowing economic performance in some economies.
- The value of the $NZD and exchange rate fluctuations offshore.

Tourism New Zealand is cognisant of the impact that significant world events (such as war, threats of terrorism and economic recessions) have on the tourism industry and has therefore put in place several strategies to ensure that the key stakeholders are adequately prepared and able to respond should such events occur. These strategies were developed in early 2003 after discussion with the industry and include:

- Re-establishing our global tourism trend monitoring activity.
- Holding firm to the 100% Pure New Zealand campaign investments.
- Monitoring the impacts on air capacity to/from New Zealand and work to protect this wherever possible.
- Where appropriate, move marketing emphasis and PR focus on key markets which demonstrate an early propensity to recover, i.e. Australia, Japan and the UK.
- Encouraging our tourism industry to have confidence about recovery prospects (based on past events) and not be pressured into reducing margins.

New Zealand's requirements

New Zealand's requirements in the medium to long term are best summarised within the NZTS 2010 as:

- Securing and conserving a long-term future.
- Marketing and managing a world-class visitor experience.
- Working smarter.
- Being financially and economically prosperous.

The inferences for the target market

New Zealand's target market is one that:

- Desires authentic engagement and active participation.
- Is environmentally aware.

- Seeks discovery and/or new experiences.
- Has high levels of sociability.
- Has high(er) discretionary income.

The 'Interactive Traveller®'

Based on the work and research undertaken to date, this visitor, with motivations aligned to the products that New Zealand has to offer has been defined as the 'Interactive Traveller®'. The Interactive Traveller® has a global mindset – is aware that he/she is part of a much larger world, so therefore keeps him/herself informed of what is happening in it. More specifically, the Interactive Traveller® is someone who:

- Consumes a wide range of tourism products and services.
- Seeks out new experiences that involve engagement and interaction with natural, social and cultural environments.
- Having sought these new experiences, is then keen to share experiences with others.
- Respects the environment, cultural and societal values of others.
- Is considered a leader by his/her peers.
- Uses technology to enhance his/her life.
- Values authentic products/experiences as opposed to having a 'trend' consciousness.

Source: Tourism New Zealand 3-Year Strategic Plan 2003–2006

DISCUSSION QUESTIONS

1 The identification of 'ideal visitors' to New Zealand is an important element of the strategy but the delivery of a product that satisfies the needs of these 'ideal visitors' represents a different challenge. How would you work towards creating the 'ideal product' for these visitors?

2 In order to optimise the economic benefits of visitors to New Zealand it is important to ensure that tourists are given spending opportunities. With the emphasis that this strategy has on the natural environment, what strategies would you include to ensure that the tourists spend their money in a way that benefits the New Zealand population?

3 What are the major strengths, weaknesses, opportunities and threats to this strategy? How would you monitor and fine-tune the strategy's performance?

PART THREE
THE TOURISM SECTOR

CHAPTER TEN
ATTRACTIONS   344

CHAPTER ELEVEN
ACCOMMODATION   384

CHAPTER TWELVE
INTERMEDIARIES   420

CHAPTER THIRTEEN
TRANSPORTATION   460

CHAPTER FOURTEEN
PUBLIC SECTOR AND POLICY   502

INTRODUCTION

In Part Three, we turn our attention to the tourism sector and public sector organisations that influence and support tourism demand and supply. We have adopted an analytical and evaluative approach to this section, identifying the main subsectors that, when combined, constitute the tourism sector. We have focused generally on providing insights into the operating characteristics, trends and issues that dominate tourism and, specifically, upon attractions, accommodation, intermediaries, transportation, and public sector organisations. Although these do not represent an exhaustive range of enterprises, they do illustrate the dominant characteristics of the tourism sector and demonstrate key operational practices.

Leiper defined the tourism 'industry' as 'the range of businesses and organisations involved in delivering the tourism product' and, in the light of his model of the tourism system (as discussed in detail in 'An Introduction to Tourism'), these businesses and organisations represent a key element. However, despite the unique nature of tourism and the differing attributes of the individual sectors, there are common characteristics, trends and issues that are evident across the board:

- The low level of **concentration** in a sector where small businesses dominate despite the fact that a relatively few, large corporations have market prominence.

- The high ratio of **fixed costs** to **variable costs** which has considerable implications for financial stability and which dominates tactical and strategic operation.

- The high levels of customer contact, demanding staff to be highly trained in both operational aspects and customer care.

- The low levels of technological adoption across much of the sector.

- The general lack of marketing and human resource management expertise remains a constraint in all sectors of tourism, albeit to varying degrees.

- The importance of location *vis-à-vis* access to markets.

- The **perishable** nature of the product for all tourism sectors demands continued investment in reservation and yield management systems.

- The prevalence of seasonal and irrational demand patterns, involving enterprises in the use of promotional and pricing strategies.

- The inconsistent adoption of the principles of sustainability, environmental auditing and EIA techniques.

- The increasing degree of **vertical**, **horizontal**, and **diagonal integration** throughout the sector.

- The increasing adoption of **collaboration** within and across the various sectors of the tourism sector.

- The traditional outlook of service industries and, arguably, the so-called 'under-management' of the tourism sector which means that the sector as a whole is vulnerable to ideas and takeovers from other industrial sectors.

- Conversely, the increasing professionalism of the sector.

These are issues and difficulties that dominate tourism as a whole, irrespective of subsector. Nevertheless, it is also possible to isolate the key sectors and attribute more detailed and precise characteristics to each; thus, we have divided this section into five chapters. This said, it is important that the reader understand the complex linkages and interrelationships that exist between the various individual tourism sectors and the mutual dependency of one sector on the next. It is the objective of this section, therefore, to highlight these complex relationships and to explore the implications of these on tourism as a whole.

In Chapter Ten, the focus of attention is on the attractions segment of the tourism sector, incorporating natural and artificial attractions. Attractions are integral to the tourism product, often providing the primary motivation for tourist visits, yet they continue to receive a patchy and undisciplined coverage in the literature. We use this chapter to explore many of the issues associated with the development and management of attractions as well as consider some of the possible visitor management techniques that may be implemented to address the adverse social, cultural and environmental impacts of tourism at both natural and artificial sites.

Chapter Eleven is concerned with accommodation, perhaps the most visible and ubiquitous of all sectors of tourism. The scope and size of the sector is explored and the relationship between this subsector and the complete tourism product is discussed. We also evaluate many of the key issues that are currently influencing the accommodation sector such as hotel consortia, yield management, the potential of information technology, the new-found emphasis on environmental issues and the role and importance of quality and branding.

Chapter Twelve introduces and reviews the role of intermediaries in the packaging and distribution of the tourism product. The distribution of the tourism product is unusual insofar as it is achieved, almost exclusively, by intermediaries, rendering the distribution channel extremely competitive and susceptible to fierce power struggles and damaging price wars. The structure of the distribution channel and the respective roles of intermediaries make the distribution of the tourism product very risky, particularly in light of the precarious economics of tour operation/wholesaling and the intense financial pressures that dominate their operation. The chapter also explores online developments and the increasing consolidation and concentration of tourism intermediaries.

Chapter Thirteen concentrates on transportation for tourism and offers a thorough review of the issues which dominate this sector. Particular emphasis is placed on the changing competitive framework with a focus on the development of low-cost airlines and the continued expansion and popularity of cruising.

Finally, in Chapter Fourteen, we concentrate on those public sector organisations that are crucial to tourism and discuss the role of governmental intervention in tourism. We consider the importance of public sector involvement in tourism and review its current, and changing, role: increasingly, the public sector is withdrawing from tourism and private sector organisations are being encouraged to step in. However, it is argued here that, while tourism must involve participation and funding by the private sector, there are many clear and powerful reasons why the public sector must remain involved:

- Many core tourist attractions – such as landscapes, culture and built heritage and architecture – are public goods and, to this end, public sector involvement is at worst desirable and at best, crucial.

- Many activities such as planning, research, resource allocation, management and regulation can be undertaken most effectively – and most impartially – by the public sector.

- The lack of expertise in the tourism sector in certain key areas (such as marketing), and the domination of small businesses with inadequate funds to promote themselves sufficiently, provides a compelling argument for continued involvement of the public sector.

We also use this chapter to demonstrate the global and local policy frameworks for tourism and to provide an overview of the likely administrative structure of a national tourist office (NTO). In addition, the impact of the public sector in respect of its demand and revenue management roles (marketing, promotion and information provision) and its supply and cost management roles (planning controls, building regulations, land-use decisions, market regulation, market research, and planning and investment incentives) are also considered in detail.

It is clear that, while the individual sectors of tourism are interlinked and, to some extent, are mutually dependent upon each other, there is a potential for conflict within and between sectors. This may be attributed to the fact that each sector is working to its own agenda with a view to its own profit maximisation. One of the primary objectives of the public sector, therefore, is to temper over-ambitious individual providers and sectors and to provide a strategic approach to product development, distribution and marketing for the overall benefit of the destination. However, it may be argued that the intermediaries are perhaps the most powerful determinants of the ultimate success or failure of a destination in terms of revenue, market share and visitor numbers, since it is in the hands of the intermediaries that influence is exerted most directly on tourism demand.

In the next five chapters, we explore many of the key issues in respect of the above and provide the reader with a greater understanding and appreciation of the tourism sector, its core business and its operating practices.

INTRODUCTION

For many tourist destinations around the world, it is their attractions that often serve as the catalyst for tourist visits. Attractions are numerous, diverse, fragmented geographically and often have limited resources at their disposal for purposes of management. In order to shed some light on the management complexity and diversity of development of attractions this chapter is broken down into four main sections. The first section introduces the nature and purpose of attractions, their characteristics, and issues pertinent to both natural and man-made attractions. The second section builds on this foundation by exploring a range of issues relating to their development. The third section concentrates on the management of attractions with issues of ownership, the problems of cost structure, pricing and revenue generation, the employment and training of staff, and attempts to counter seasonality featuring strongly. The final section outlines the variety of visitor management techniques in existence and attempts made by operators of attractions to manage visitor impacts in a more sustainable manner. This leads on to the issue of sustainable tourism development in which the object is to manage tourism growth in a manner that ensures that tourists do not destroy by pressure of numbers the very attractions they come to see. In this discussion, the choice – or balance – between regulation and market solutions is discussed with a closing discussion on the impact on attraction authenticity of 'modern' attraction management.

LEARNING OUTCOMES

Attractions are an integral part of the tourism product and, in this chapter, we focus on providing you with:

- a review of the nature, purpose, and classification of attractions;

- a discussion of the roles and responsibilities of the public and private sectors in respect of the development and management of tourist attractions;

- a consideration of all issues associated with the management of attractions;

- an analysis of environmental issues in respect of attractions; and

- an evaluation of strategies that have been developed with a view to alleviating environmental and visitor impacts of tourism at attractions.

THE NATURE AND PURPOSE OF ATTRACTIONS

Attractions provide the single most important reason for leisure tourism to a destination. Many of the components of the tourist trip – for example, transport and accommodation – are demands derived from the consumer's desire to enjoy what a destination has to offer in terms of 'things to see and do'. Thus a tourist attraction is a focus for recreational and, in part, educational activity undertaken by both day and stay visitors that is frequently shared with the domestic resident population. Attractions also serve a variety of different purposes, some unrelated to tourism. For example, attractions often have an explicit educational purpose, are often central to the protection, or in fact creation, of cultural identities, and can contribute to the conservation and protection of many historic sites. This variety of 'sense of purpose' is important in that it helps explain why attractions are often so difficult to manage. Attractions often have to accommodate the numerous wishes of their stakeholders, the various expectations of different visitor groups (often from different countries), meet the needs of owners, and serve on occasion as **attraction 'icons'** for national governments in international marketing strategies. Examples of this are the use of images of the Coliseum when marketing Rome, the use of Table Mountain when marketing South Africa, or those of the London Eye, sponsored by British Airways, when promoting London and the UK overseas.

PHOTOGRAPH 10.1 **British Airways London Eye, one of London's more recent 'iconic' attractions which features in much of the UK's international marketing and publicity material**

Source: Newscast

In addition to the above, there are many examples where attractions have played a catalytic role in the regeneration of an area or destination. The success of the Guggenheim in Bilbao, Spain and the National Museum of New Zealand and its contribution to the development of Wellington as a destination are two examples of 'best practice'. Such **'flagship'** attractions can be used to pull in visitors, meet needs of local residents, and develop stronger tourism activities within the destination. While a destination rarely survives long term on the basis of one attraction, it can be the key pump-primer in more sustainable development of a destination.

With such diversity present within the attractions' sector, the uniform definition and categorisation of attractions has proved elusive, as has the ability of many attractions to share 'best practice' both from attractions of a similar kind and from attractions elsewhere around the globe. It is also worth noting that it is a common feature of tourist attractions that they are shared with the host community. This in turn may give rise to conflict in popular destinations, where tourism is perceived to cause problems of crowding, traffic congestion, environmental damage and litter. There can thus be little doubt that the management of tourist attractions is in no way a straightforward exercise.

CHARACTERISTICS OF ATTRACTIONS

There are many different types of attraction, and a number of attempts have been made to classify them. Classification is possible along a number of different dimensions:

- ownership;
- capacity;
- **market or catchment area**;
- permanency;
- type.

Early attempts at classification were according to type, distinguishing between natural resources and artificial 'man-made' features or products. Man-made features were as follows:

- Cultural – religion, modern culture, museums, art galleries, architecture, archaeological sites.
- Traditions – folklore, animated culture, festivals.
- Events – sports activities and cultural events.

Natural resources included national parks, wildlife, viewpoints and outstanding natural phenomena such as Uluru (Ayers Rock) in Australia or the Niagara Falls in Ontario, Canada. An alternative and more complex approach is that designed by Clawson and Knetsch (1966) and shown in Figure 10.1. In one diagram, Clawson and Knetsch linked the classification of attractions in a spatial sense, according to their proximity to markets, to their level of uniqueness and to their intensity of use. Clawson's approach is flexible and best utilised as a way of thinking about attractions. For example, a major historic building is clearly a resource-based attraction, but it may extend its market by adding a user-orientated element, such as a small theme park or garden development, as has occurred with many of the stately homes and palaces in Britain and continental Europe. Parks Canada has adopted a variant of Clawson's ideas to provide functional zones related to use in their parks (Mini case study 10.1).

MINI CASE STUDY 10.1
Functional zoning applied by Parks Canada

Parks Canada has developed a classification of its park resources based heavily upon Clawson's ideas. In effect, the zones range from Zone I, a pure resource-based zone, through to Zone V, a pure user-based zone. Between the two extremes, a continuum of zones is maintained through appropriate planning and management strategies:

- **Zone I**   Special preservation areas: small and specific areas designated for a particular reason, such as the presence of endangered species. Entry is strictly controlled and access is by permit.

- **Zone II**   Wilderness: areas with specific natural history and/or environmental value. Activities include dispersed hiking and some camping.

- **Zone III**   Natural environments: access is compatible with the environment and this is the first zone where motorised access is allowed. However, this access is to the edge of the zone; entry beyond this is via strategically located trails.

- **Zone IV**   Recreation areas: includes campsites, boating, skiing and motorised access. Interpretative services are designed to explain and protect the environment.

- **Zone V**   Park services: includes centralised visitor support services, park administration offices, etc., which are all located and designed to blend in with the surroundings. In some parks this zone is located outside the park boundary.

DISCUSSION QUESTIONS

1 For a destination/country of your choice, allocate its range of attractions according to the ideas advocated by Clawson. What is the overall balance of attractions in your chosen destination/country and what challenges does this 'balance' contribute to the overall management of the attractions' product?

2 What particular management issues may be unique to wilderness-based attractions?

3 Propose your own form of classification of attractions and suggest how this may or may not benefit the future management of attractions.

Source: Adapted from Murphy, 1985

User orientated	Intermediate	Resource based
Based on whatever resources are available. Often artificial developments (city parks, pools, zoos, etc.). Highly intensive developments close to users in large population centres. Focus of user pressure. Activities include golf, tennis, picnicking, walking, riding, etc. Often highly seasonal activities, closing in off-peak.	Best resources available within accessible distance to users. Access very important. More natural resources than user-orientated facilities, but experience a high degree of pressure and wear. Activities include camping, hiking, picnicking, swimming, hunting and fishing.	Outstanding resources. Primary focus is resource quality with low-intensity development and artificial facilities at a minimum. Often distant from users, the resource determines the activity (sightseeing, scientific and historic interest, hiking, mountain climbing, fishing and hunting).

Activity paramount ← → Resource paramount
Artificiality ← → Naturalness
← Intensity of development →
Distance from user →

FIGURE 10.1	**Clawson's classification of recreation resources**

Source: Adapted from Clawson and Knetsch, 1966; Boniface and Cooper, 1987

PHOTOGRAPH 10.2	**The Grand Canyon, one of the world's 'iconic' natural attractions**

Source: Grand Canyon National Park

FIGURE 10.2 **Classification of attractions** *Source: Leask, 2003*

In this chapter, for purposes of analytical convenience, we have adopted the more recent classification shown in Figure 10.2. Although not exhaustive, Figure 10.2 identifies the principal features of classification used in various settings and demonstrates the diversity of the attraction product around the world. At the core of the recent classification rests the core product offered by the attraction, which represents the resource/attributes that attract visitors in the first place. Also within the core are those aspects of the attraction, which contribute to its presentation, such as interpretation, and generation of additional income and revenue streams – a facet of most attractions irrespective of their natural or man-made origins. Going further, it will be appreciated that the initial classification may be subdivided again into attractions that are site specific because of the physical location of facilities and therefore act as a destination, and attractions that are intangible and ephemeral because they are events. For events, it is what is happening at the time that is important, rather than the location. Thus some of the most spectacular events in the form of parades or carnivals take place in large cities, for example, the Pamplona Bull Run in Spain or the Calgary Stampede in Alberta, because cities provide access to a large market and have the economic base to support them. Such **'hallmark' events** are becoming increasingly popular as a means of developing tourism. The growth in cultural tourism, for example, is forcing many destinations to try and turn important events in the local calendar into hallmark events.

Site and event attractions can be complementary activities. Staging a festival of the countryside can enhance the appeal of a country park, and similarly for the performance of a Shakespeare tragedy in the courtyard of an historic castle. Events are frequently used to raise the image of a destination, a factor that lies behind the very competitive bidding for **mega-events** such as the Olympics. They are also used to give animation to object-orientated attractions, such as museums, to encourage new and repeat visitors, particularly in the off-season.

The extent to which attractions are in fact 'natural' or 'man-made' represents the next stage of classification. Natural attractions include country parks in Britain, lakes in Canada, mountains in Switzerland and the coast in Spain, for example. Man-made attractions, however, are more commonly the results of the history and culture of a country which leaves a legacy of historic monuments and buildings, but also includes specially created entertainment complexes such as theme parks, of which the most well known are the Walt Disney parks, originating in California, but now reproduced in Florida, Tokyo and near Paris, with one further park due to open soon in Hong Kong. One could, in fact, go one stage further and subdivide the man-made category into those attractions that were created specifically for tourism, such as Disney's theme parks, and those that were created originally for purposes other than tourism. Historic houses, castles and monuments would all come under this category of man-made attraction. It is these types of attractions in particular that often have the greatest challenges in maintaining their **authenticity**, the addition of cafés, restaurants and gift shops for purposes of income generation often diluting the 'purity' of the attraction product.

The varying approaches to the management of natural and man-made attractions and the different pressures they have to face help explain their inclusion here. For example, while the Grand Canyon may have management objectives that focus on conservation issues and the management of visitors, theme parks have at their core objectives of entertainment and income generation. The division between natural resources and artificial attractions, however, is not always clear cut. Many natural attractions require considerable inputs of infrastructure and management in order to use them for tourism purposes. This is the case of water parks, ski resorts, safari parks, aquaria and many attractions based on nature. This infrastructure may also be put in place to protect the resource from environmental damage. In many countries, it is no longer possible to have open public access to many forests. Specific sites are designated for cars, caravans and camping, and there are colour-coded trails for walkers.

Man-made attractions that are the legacy of history and culture also share with natural resources the fact that they cannot be reproduced without considerable expense and alterations to their authenticity, unlike attractions designed principally for entertainment. They therefore deserve greater protection and management input to guard against excessive use. Such attractions are commonly in the control of the state. A good example is Stonehenge in the UK, which exhibits all the features of being resource based and non-reproducible, so that for some time too many visitors have threatened it. Measures to resolve this have included the construction of a new visitor centre some distance from the monument and putting a cordon around the stones to prevent them being further defaced by touching and, in some instances, chipping of the stones by capricious visitors. From this it follows that when looking at the development of attractions, we can place them on a scale that has at one end those that have been built or designed for visitor purposes such as theme parks, which are in the minority, and at the other, cultural resources and facilities that were neither for visitors nor can be adapted for them. The bulk of attractions would then be spread out between these two poles.

The next basis upon which classification can be attributed is the pricing policy adopted for access to attractions, that is whether or not access is either free or where an admission charge is required. Many countries around the world offer free access to their national museums, galleries and monuments – such attractions considered by governments to be the national heritage of the population at large (tax concessions are often also connected to such a strategy). This is not always the case, however, with the demise of the public purse sometimes serving as the catalyst for the levy of admission charges at previously 'free' attractions. Understandably, the contrasting objectives between the public and private commercial sector operators of attractions, affects the operational and management approaches adopted. More recent studies, however, suggest that the increasingly competitive markets that attractions now find themselves in are leading to greater commonality of management practice, because once paying visitors are introduced to attractions in the public and voluntary sectors, then pressure builds up for the visitor experience, in support of admissions, to become the marketed output, as in the commercial sector. This is something that is often resisted by the curatorial staff of these attractions, who are rightly concerned about the authenticity of the visitor experience. For example, in the 1980s, the Victoria and Albert Museum was heavily criticised for using the marketing strap-line 'Ace caff with quite a nice museum attached!' to stimulate a re-appraisal of the museum by the public; a marketing strategy that would be considered quite acceptable today.

The market in which the attraction draws its visitors represents the final classification in Figure 10.2. For example, while Universal Studios' theme parks may have an international audience, The Eden Project in England a national audience, and the wineries of Western Australia a regional audience, the majority of attractions have a much smaller local audience. Clearly the nature of the market and the volume of visitors may well determine the nature and management of the product offering, particularly with regard to pricing, visitor spend and interpretation.

NATURAL ATTRACTIONS

In the instance of natural features it is often the quality of the resource that provides the attraction, whereby location becomes secondary. Their appeal is both national and international. Thus tourists come from all over the globe to enjoy the Himalayas in Nepal, the Blue Ridge Mountains of Virginia, or the Ring of Kerry in Southern Ireland. Traditionally, water-based resources, either coastlines or lakes, have always been the most important tourism resource and still are, but with more frequent holiday taking, the countryside and panoramic scenery have witnessed increasing usage. However, natural amenities are not only confined to the landscape but also include, for example, climate (which accounts for the dominant tourist flows being north–south to sun resorts), vegetation, forests and wildlife.

The most common aspect of natural resources is that they are generally fixed in supply and are able to provide only a limited amount of services in any given time period. But in many cases, the services provided by this fixed stock of natural amenities can be put to several different uses. Thus if it is proposed to increase the land available for tourism and recreation purposes, it may often be at the expense of other land users, say, industry. There is therefore a trade-off that must take place

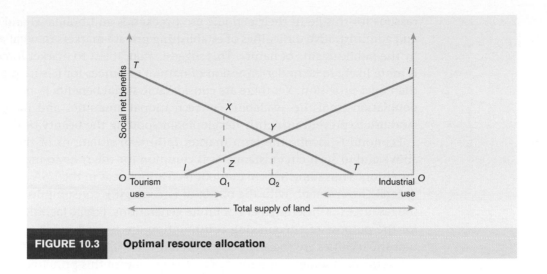

FIGURE 10.3 **Optimal resource allocation**

to ensure that the resource is used to the best advantage of society. This is demonstrated in Figure 10.3: the vertical axis represents the **social net benefits** (social benefits less social costs) of using a given area of land for tourism or industrial purposes. The schedule TT illustrates how these net benefits decline as more land is made available for tourism and similarly for the schedule II which applies to industrial use. At Q_1 the social net benefit from the last portion of land devoted to industry is measured by the distance ZQ_1, while that for tourism use is given by XQ_1. Clearly, the net benefits obtainable from tourism use are much greater than those that can be gained from industrial use and so it will pay society to switch land from industrial designation to tourist use. The optimal point will be at Q_2 where the net social benefits from each use are equalised. By undertaking such a move, society increases social net benefits by the amount XYZ, for the total gain from tourism use is XQ_1Q_2Y but this must be offset by a loss to industry of ZQ_1Q_2Y.

The essence of land-use planning and the legislation that enforces it is to determine some optimal allocation in the manner shown by Figure 10.3. In this way land is zoned for a variety of uses, from tourism and recreation through to urban development, and when disputes occur as to use it is customary to hold some form of public inquiry in which the benefits and costs of alternative choices are evaluated to reach an appropriate decision. Most governments maintain strict planning controls on alternative uses of land, whether it is publicly or privately owned. Thus social considerations via the political process are the main driving force behind land allocation. In the case of privately owned land, social choice may be enforced through compulsory purchase by the state. In some cases the stark choice presented in Figure 10.3 is nullified in practice because multiple land use is possible. National parks in Britain, such as the Lake District, for example, include residential, farming, forestry, recreational activities and small-scale production within their boundaries.

Market failure and public provision

One of the problems concerning the provision of outdoor areas for leisure purposes on a large scale is that they are rarely commercially viable in terms of the investment costs and operating expenditure necessary to establish and maintain them. The reasons for this lie in their periodic use (weekends and holidays) and the political and administrative difficulties of establishing private markets in what are perceived by the public as gifts of nature. This suggests that, if left to market forces, the result is more likely to be under-provision of natural resources for leisure purposes rather than over-provision. Yet there are considerable social benefits to be enjoyed by the population from the availability of recreational amenities and in the control of land use to prevent unsightly development spoiling the beauty of the landscape.

Economists ascribe the term **market failure** to situations of the kind outlined above and in such circumstances it is common for the state to make the necessary provision. Thus some 85% of outdoor recreation areas in the USA are owned by the Federal Government, with the object of encouraging consumption and protecting the resource for the enjoyment of future generations. Public facilities made available for the purpose of encouraging consumption are termed merit goods, to indicate that the facilities are socially needed even if the willingness to pay for them in the marketplace is somewhat limited. The recognition of this principle in the USA goes back to 1872 with the enactment of the Yellowstone National Park. In Britain, planning and development for tourism purposes is largely a post-1945 phenomenon, commencing with the National Parks and Access to the Countryside Act in 1949, though it was not until the 1960s that positive action in the field of tourism and recreation provision really got going. The worldwide growth of tourism has prompted many other countries to enact similar legislation to manage natural resources in a way that will sustain their use for consumption, while at the same time providing protection against over-use.

There is another aspect of state provision: the so-called **public or collective good**. The principal feature of such goods or services is that it is not realistically possible to exclude individuals from consumption once they have been made available. Private markets for these goods would quickly disintegrate because the optimal strategy for the individual consumer is to wait until someone else pays for the good and then to reap the benefits for nothing. Thus if the good or service is to be provided at all, it may be consumed by everyone without exception and normally without charge at the point of use. The natural environment is a typical example of a public good and the growing pressure of tourist development has created concern for the environment in a number of countries. The point of issue is that public goods form no part of the private costs facing the tourism developer and are therefore open to abuse through over-use. In response the state, in addition to enforcing collective provision out of taxation, regulates individual behaviour through legislation to preserve environmental amenity. For example, in Bermuda tourists are not allowed to hire cars, but only mopeds, while on the Greek island of Rhodes, vehicles are banned from the touristically attractive town of Lindos. Mauritius has a planning law that restricts buildings to a height no greater than the palm trees. In practice, this means hotels of only two storeys and thus permits adequate screening on the seaward side. Where legislation is considered impractical, or overly restrictive, then the approach is to try to change behaviour through educational awareness campaigns. The purpose of such codes is to disseminate information and persuade tourists that on their own volition they should avoid damage to the environment and adverse socio-cultural impacts. These codes apply not only to visitors; there are also industry codes to educate staff and the business community in the recycling of materials and respect for the environment, as well as codes for the host community to help in understanding tourism and the benefits it brings, so as to encourage better relationships between hosts and guests.

Managing the attraction resource

Given a fixed amount of natural resources for leisure purposes, it is only possible to alter the supply by adopting different use patterns. Critical to this is the generally accepted premise that tourists should not destroy through excessive use the natural features that they came to enjoy. This view is encapsulated in the concept of sustainable tourism development, which argues that economic growth is only acceptable if it can maintain, at a minimum, the stock of tourist assets intact from one generation to another. Emphasis tends to be placed on the natural environment because it cannot be directly substituted for artificial facilities, and the danger of irreversible damage appears more likely. This danger is also present with man-made attractions such as historic artefacts, but here the concept is more subjective in that it has to do with authenticity; namely, at what point does repair and replacement of stone, say, on an historic monument owing to erosion and visitor damage, mean that it is no longer authentic? This is further complicated by the fact that perception seems to vary according to the nature of the historic artefact under consideration – whether it is glassware, tapestry, a sculpture or features of a building.

It has already been noted that the application of capital, labour and management to the natural environment is often necessary to render them suitable for tourist use, as in the case of a beach resource. This permits more intensive use of the beach provided that the necessary safeguards are put in place to prevent over-exploitation of the free availability of the resource in its role as a public good. One way of achieving this is to restrict accommodation provision to match the desired density of the population on the beach. A high-quality resort would aim at allocating 20 square metres per person, compared with 10 square metres per person for a budget resort. In other situations, the degree of inaccessibility may be used to control visitor numbers. This is illustrated in Figure 10.4, which demonstrates the inverse relationship between visitor numbers and difficulties of access and is also indicated in Clawson's classification (Figure 10.1). The latter may be due to time, distance or restrictions imposed by the managing authority. For example,

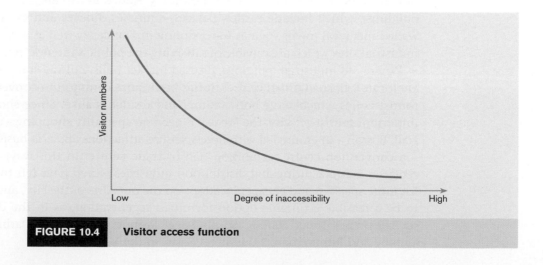

FIGURE 10.4   **Visitor access function**

with natural attractions that draw visitors both at the national and international level, it is common for the authorities to implement 'park and ride' schemes so as to control the flow of cars in the area. Another popular strategy is the use of 'honey pots', whereby a variety of attractions, shops, restaurants and accommodation are clustered around one or two viewpoints to create a complex capable of absorbing a high population density.

The honey pot concept augments natural attractions with artificial, user-orientated attractions capable of drawing visitors away from the rest of the natural resource area. It is well known, for example, that the demand for domestic tourism and recreation facilities arises, in the main, from urban areas but that pressures on attractions and rural areas generally decrease with distance from city centres. Hence greater opportunities for protection and management of natural sanctuaries for wildlife and vegetation can be found by locating them in areas remote from urban environments. As the city centre is approached so there is a need to provide purpose-built facilities to cope with day excursions and weekend trips. Depending on the climate and country these will include seaside or lakeside resorts, mountain resorts, health centres, spas, and themed and nature parks. Within the city boundary there will be a requirement for town parks, and sport and leisure complexes. Thus as the volume of leisure demand increases so the need to augment natural attractions with artificial facilities arises. In this respect, cities such as Amsterdam, St Petersburg and Istanbul have always been great magnets for tourists because of their historical and cultural resources. For these same reasons, cities everywhere are becoming tourist destinations in their own right rather than just places where people live and work. Today's better-educated traveller is looking for experiences that combine educational interest and entertainment, with the result that cultural tourism is expanding worldwide and, with it, the growth in urban tourism.

MAN-MADE ATTRACTIONS

Many man-made attractions are products of history and culture. The range of museums and art galleries in the world's top tourist destinations is usually extensive and many are subject specific, for example, the Rijksmuseum in Amsterdam, or Chicago's Museum of Science and Industry. Added to this are numerous historic buildings, which include castles, palaces, churches, houses and even completely walled medieval towns such as Carcassonne in France, as well as a variety of early industrial sites which are capable of satisfying the public's interest in bygone times.

Where old industrial buildings, disused market halls, railway stations and docks are located close to urban centres, it has been quite common to convert them into tourist zones which serve both visitors and residents alike. Since shopping is an important tourist activity, the focus has been on speciality shopping – as in Faneuil Hall, Boston – intermingled with hotels, leisure attractions and also business facilities – a convention centre, exhibition hall or trade centre. In this way, tourism has replaced manufacturing and distribution industries which have left the inner core for more spacious and cheaper locations on the outskirts of the city, and has proved to be a feasible economic option for urban regeneration, as in the development of Baltimore's Inner Harbor, South Street Seaport, New York, Darling Harbour, Sydney and Birmingham's Gas Street Basin in the UK.

Over and above the attractions left by historical legacy, there are numerous engineered attractions whose principal role is one of entertainment. Such attractions are user orientated and are capable of handling thousands of visitors per day: they include theme and leisure parks, sporting venues, theatres and all-weather holiday centres. Theme parks will also include an educational function, for example, Futurescope in France, as well as providing exciting 'white knuckle' rides in the form of roller coasters, runaway trains, log flames and oscillating 'pirate' ships.

One of the most famous theme parks (in the true sense), Colonial Williamsburg in Virginia, USA, is a living museum. It was originated by establishing an old city within a new one and the staff creating a time capsule of the colonial period of America through role play and using the technology of the day. Its success has drawn in a range of partners to propagate the cultural richness of the state of Virginia. A similar re-creation has taken place at Beamish in the north of England. The museum has been positioned at a time just before the First World War and staff demonstrate the technology and converse with visitors in the way of life of that period. As far as possible the houses, shops, transport system, goods and artefacts are genuine articles of the time that have been brought to the site from all parts of the UK. In this manner, Beamish and Colonial Williamsburg have crossed the boundary between a theme park and a museum. In so doing they have captured the public's imagination by allowing participation. The public is now attuned to experiencing the sights and sounds of the era being witnessed, which gives opportunities for using technology creatively to enhance the visitor experience. We know that ultimately it is the visitor experience that is the marketed output of tourist attractions. The acceptance of the content and style of this experience is determined by fashion, which has its own dynamic that is born out of the spirit of enquiry and competition within society to alter its patterns of consumption and value systems.

To this extent, animals in captivity in the form of zoos or safari parks are no longer acceptable to many people and there is a marked decline of interest in static attractions and object-orientated museums, unless they are national collections or they are best presented in this way, as for example jewellery. The quest for improving the attraction experience forces theme and leisure park operators to install more complicated rides and challenging entertainment as the public seeks to increase the skill content of their consumption. Similarly historic properties, museums and gardens change their displays and feature special exhibitions/events to maintain interest. Some attractions are fortunate enough to be able to tie themselves to regular events aimed at an enthusiast market, for example automobile rallies, for which demand is more or less continuous.

DEVELOPING ATTRACTIONS

Already it is clear that the range of attractions is extensive and that there are numerous variations in respect of the product concept or creativity of the design and its appeal. This we will term the '**imagescape**' to match the use of the word 'imagineers' by the Disney Corporation when describing its designers. The concept is based on the fact that all attractions, in some part, measure their performance by the number of visitors, the quality of the experience they give them, and the

| **FIGURE 10.5** | **The attraction product** | *Source: Wanhill, 2003* |

memories that they take home to ensure repeat visits or the spread of 'word-of-mouth' recommendation. To enhance the experience, the modern approach is to place tangible objects, say, a thrill ride or a collection of museum artefacts (despite their intrinsic value), within the context of a specific theme or image in a particular setting or environment; hence the word 'imagescape'.

This approach is consistent with the post-industrial societal views espoused by Pine and Gilmore (1999) in their seminal publication, *The Experience Economy*, where it is argued that the production system should be re-engineered to add value through marketing experiences. This implies producing services with attached goods, rather than the traditional mass production process in which commodities are uniformly produced and sold on price. In this way, customers are able to receive a package that relates to their needs. Following this viewpoint, Figure 10.5 offers an abstract perspective of an attraction product where the core element is represented by the 'imagescape' – the idea of which is to communicate the fundamental nature of the visitor experience to the potential target markets.

Clearly a variety of 'imagescapes' are possible. Examples may include 'art and media', 'childhood', 'fame and notoriety', the 'human body', 'myths and fantasy', the 'natural world' and 'war and conflict' to name but a few. Adopting the concept of the 'imagescape', a range of projects planned for the future include the Wetlands Park in Hong Kong, a 10,000 square metre educational 'conservation' attraction, a 'Pop Century Resort' to be developed by Disney in Florida which offers a 2,880-room 'time-capsule' resort to celebrate 50 years of pop culture, and Europe's largest indoor adventure park in Bremen, Germany, with a space centre theme. Further developments include the ambitious 'Habitat for Humanity' in Georgia, a global village and discovery centre which aims to show visitors life and customs in some of the world's poorest countries, and 'Mystery Park' in Switzerland which represents a 700,000 square metre all-weather attraction which focuses on the world's great mysteries and the unexplained.

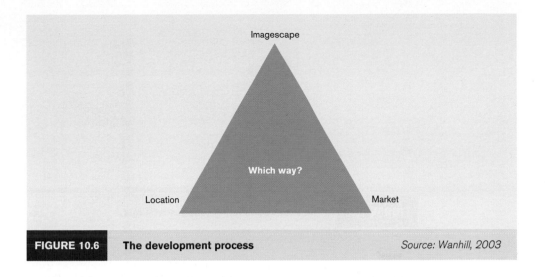

FIGURE 10.6   **The development process**   *Source: Wanhill, 2003*

The attraction development process

When contemplating attraction development the ideal process from a demand standpoint is one of Market → Imagescape → Location. In reality, however, this demand-led sequential process is seldom implemented, it only applying to '**foot-loose' attractions** that have flexibility across all three aspects in order to generate economic success. Given that most attraction developments are constrained more often than not by their location, type and ownership, a more common process – especially in the instance of regeneration – is one of location → imagescape → market (see Figure 10.6). Most important, however, is not perhaps the sequential order of development but the fact that location, imagescape and market are inextricably bound up with one another. If site selection becomes at most a second choice, this throws greater weight on to the market–imagescape mix in order to achieve visitor numbers commensurate with notions of the economic viability of the attraction. How in reality these three factors are balanced clearly depends upon the overriding objectives of the attraction and the status of its owners.

The market–imagescape mix

What is clear from the above is that both market and imagescape are inextricably linked to each other *vis-à-vis* the development of attractions, as evidenced in Figure 10.7. That type of attraction which carries the least commercial risk is that identified in Q1, that of '**me too' attraction development**. The fact that parallel attractions already exist in the marketplace ensures that the creators of the attraction are able to benefit from previous market performance and the passage of trends over a specified time period. One of the dangers of 'me too' developments is that assumptions are often made, incorrectly, that if a concept works in one location then it will automatically work elsewhere. It is also a problem in some countries with the over-development of heritage attractions – often perceived as a 'quick-win' for politicians, but frequently short of visitors after the initial spurt of interest. Before giving the 'green light' to such attractions it is advisable to

Image	Current	New
Market		
Current	Q I 'Me too' attraction	Q II 'Grand inspiration' attraction
New	Q III 'New version' attraction	Q IV 'Wonder' attraction

FIGURE 10.7   **The attraction market–imagescape mix**   *Source: Wanhill, 2003*

evaluate the likely displacement of visitors from other attractions and so anticipate the genuine additionality, if any, to the destination in question.

Success in delivering '**grand inspiration' attractions** in QII, is clearly dependent on the imagescape meeting the needs and expectations of the market. Pre-market evaluation of the concept is difficult in that the market is frequently unaware of what the concept will look like. More common is a reversal of the sequence of project evaluation in that the volume of visitors required to make the attraction both feasible and viable at a price the market is prepared to pay is first estimated. Even if this is successful, however, there still remain the problems of raising finance and finding a suitable location. The fact that most available land is owned by the public sector is a hindrance in that very few local or regional authorities have the vision to foresee the positive impact of such attractions.

'**New version' attractions** in QIII represent the preservation of existing image-scapes in content and format, albeit in new locations and accessible to new markets. The expansion of the Disney concept to Japan, Paris and now Hong Kong represents a good example of this type of development. Despite some initial problems with its theme park near to Paris, Disney has continued to build its theme park business by adopting 'new version' strategies. For established attractions, meeting the needs of new and future markets may require a much greater leap forward in terms of imagescape development for the new version to be successful, something that was achieved successfully by the opening of the Guggenheim in Bilbao.

Those attractions that carry with them the highest level of risk are labelled '**wonder' attractions** as identified in QIV. This type of attraction represents projects on a grand scale that deliver significant economic impacts on their location. Because the development of such attractions contains considerable risk and uncertainty, it is fair to say that very few examples of attraction development would sit in this category: Disney's EPCOT (opened in 1982) and Sydney's Opera House (opened in 1973) are two examples of success, though only after a financial struggle, particularly the Opera House, which came in ten years late and fourteen times over budget. London's Millennium Dome is an example of how a development can go off course! This can be attributed to political interference and a lack of clarity in the marketplace of what it was supposed to be. It was designed as a celebration for the Year 2000, but was judged by the press as a commercial attraction, so that the out-turn of 6.5 million visitors for the year as against a forecast of 12 million was declared a financial 'disaster' in the media and the political arena, and an embarrassment to the government. With the clear majority of all attraction developments achieving annual attendance levels of 200,000 and below it is no surprise that investments of the above scale are few and far between. The risks are high and the funding required is such that they tend to proceed with the support of governments and large leisure corporations working in partnership. That said, if the balance is right the potential benefits to accrue from success are considerable. With regard to the innovation process with 'wonder' attractions, the departure from existing imagescapes is common in that the new attraction often sets the standard for others to follow and an inspiration for subsequent development.

In trying to develop a successful attraction, the discussion above leads to the conclusion that the creativity of the imagescape needs to connect to the needs and expectations of the market. In the majority of cases, attractions as a product group tend to defy business logic in that they are frequently supply led with many being developed for purposes other than tourism and in other economic sectors. Although this is maybe obvious with regard to many public attractions such as museums, monuments and historic houses, it is also true for many 'themed' attractions such as Disney, in that the Disney characters were established 'icons' long before the development of the theme parks in California and Florida. This, and to

MINI CASE STUDY 10.2
Snoasis

Plans to develop the world's biggest indoor ski slope in the Suffolk countryside, a few miles outside of Ipswich, represent a perfect example of the development of a 'new version' attraction in the UK. With a number of large indoor ski centres already operational across mainland Europe and the UK, Snoasis plans to take the concept further by combining the major attraction of the world's biggest indoor ski slope (with a near 100-metre vertical drop and a width of 75 metres), with the planned development of a four-star 350-room hotel and 350 self-catering lodges and accommodation for students, catering facilities and a wide variety of other attractions including 14 different winter sports disciplines. With the intention to accommodate 'Olympic standard' training facilities 'quality' underpins the entire proposal which will offer a year-round winter sports centre with broad appeal to a variety of markets. Market analysis conducted to date suggests that the attraction is likely to have sufficient wide-reaching appeal to attract a very large and regular visitor base. Not only is it expected to appeal to the domestic family audience, it is expected also to tap into the winter sports market, domestic day visitors and the overseas family market. The planned product mix for Snoasis includes:

- an external ice hockey rink and speed skating rink;
- full-length dry-run bobsleigh track;
- ice climbing walls and cross-country ski run;
- an 18-hole golf course;

- water sports facilities;

- horse riding;

- multipurpose indoor sports centres;

- a health and fitness centre;

- a 7,000-seat multipurpose arena with ice rink and practice rink;

- outdoor sports pitches and 8-screen multiplex cinema;

- state-of-the-art 24-lane ten-pin bowling centre;

- 12 restaurants, 6 bars and cafés and 24-hour store;

- national winter sports academy;

- a 100,000-square foot casino and nightclub and mixed-use development, compromising office, residential and commercial space.

It is believed that the above mix will create a sufficient volume of activity that it will eventually be considered as a destination in its own right: the attraction dovetailing neatly with the current trends for activity and adventure-based tourism, health tourism and the burgeoning popularity for extreme sports. This said, planning consent is still required from the local authority: the sheer scale of the attraction creating a significant planning dilemma for Mid-Suffolk District Council. Although the attraction is planned on the redundant Blue Circle Industries cement works at Great Blakenham, local authority support is essential to drive the project forward. With the anticipated attraction of 2.5 million visitors annually and the creation of around 3,000 jobs (direct and indirect) once construction is complete, the proposed attraction clearly offers many benefits. As a 'brownfield' development, Snoasis meets many of the sustainable principles of development, as is it likely to serve as a major driver for economic development in the vicinity. It is also hoped that Snoasis will deliver an 'iconic' project-style landmark for the area and represent the catalytic focus for the wider East Anglian economy similar to the Baltic Exchange in the north-east of England, the Eden Project in the south-west of England, and the Guggenheim in Bilbao, Spain.

DISCUSSION QUESTIONS

1 What visitor trends may support the development of a Snoasis-type attraction in a region/country of your choice?

2 How would you categorise Snoasis according to Wanhill's ideas on the 'market–imagescape' mix and why?

3 What are likely to be the principal challenges facing the management of Snoasis and where are its most significant competitive threats likely to come from?

Source: Adapted from Spanner, 2003; Locum Destination Consulting, 2003; www.mid-suffolk-dc.gov.uk/environment/planning/snoasis/plans; www.mid-suffolk-dc.gov.uk/environment/planning/snoasis

a large extent the future of attraction development appears to lie with the development of new products that customers recognise by 'association': the development of corporate brand attractions being a perfect example of this, such as the Guinness Storehouse in Dublin, Ireland and Niketown in the USA. Investments of this kind may be regarded as **brand extensions** or **brand stretching**.

MANAGING ATTRACTIONS

The sheer diversity, geographic fragmentation, varying pattern of ownership and funding, scale and market–imagescape mix are such that the management of visitor attractions can be a very complex and demanding proposition. This applies especially with regard to attempts made to date in developing a cohesive national strategy for visitor attractions, which in turn, creates a sound strategic platform for the management of individual attractions. Work by Middleton (2003) outlines those conditions upon which a national strategy for visitor attractions would be beneficial. Such conditions include:

- the situation where destabilising effects of a sudden massive injection of un-anticipated capital into an already saturated market;

- where large, newly opened projects are putting established attractions at a significant disadvantage;

- instances of major expenditure on other major urban regeneration projects;

- situations where there is a steady decline of local authority annual revenue funding for traditional attractions such as museums and galleries;

- where the industry structure is one in which the great majority of attractions are small businesses, with only a very small percentage of larger attractions capable managerially and financially of marketing themselves professionally and organising their own data collection; and

- where there is a lack of management information and where the attractions sector is populated by more non-commercial 'public' institutions than by commercial 'private' businesses.

If the majority of the above conditions are in place, Middleton identifies seven key components that ought to be considered for action recommendations in any national strategy for visitor attractions. The seven factors are:

- the collection and dissemination of effective research on a comparable basis and which covers both demand and supply-side perspectives;

- application of expertise to the analysis and communication of trends and their implications in terms that the majority of smaller attractions will be able to understand and respond;

- advice, and perhaps support, on assessing quality of visits and providing customer assurance via benchmarking initiatives;

363

- collection and dissemination of good practice examples in visitor attraction management and operations;

- coordination and possibly funding for/provision of training and management development;

- influence over funding bodies concerning the criteria they apply to bids from new and existing attractions including advice to government on the way in which taxes in the sector are imposed and collected; and

- influence and advice to public-sector bodies, especially local authorities, that they may consider in relation to their own decisions on planning and funding activities for attractions in their areas.

Moving away from the notion of a national strategy, however, a number of issues are fundamental to the day-to-day management of visitor attractions.

Economic aspects

As with natural resources, a great many man-made tourist attractions, because of their historical legacy, are not commercially owned. They are owned by central government, in the case of national collections, quasi-public bodies which are at an 'arm's length' from the government, local government and voluntary bodies in the form of charitable trusts. Ownership status is in fact one of the key determinants of attraction management. Leask (2003, p. 11) for example, concludes that ownership proved to be a 'key independent variable with regard to determining the entire approach to attraction management'. This was particularly to be the case for 'managing revenue and overall yield, visitor management strategies and the management of environmental impacts at attractions'.

Issues of ownership

PUBLIC OWNERSHIP

Publicly owned attractions may receive all or a substantial part of their funds from general taxation either directly or via grant-in-aid for quasi-public bodies. They are thus provided in the manner of a **merit good** and in so doing impose a degree of coercion on everyone, as individuals are not free to adjust the amounts that are made available. This is shown by Figure 10.8: the schedule SS is the quantity of, say, museum services supplied to each person as a result of public provision. The distance $0t$ represents the amount of income foregone per person in terms of tax and A the demand curve of individual A and similarly for B. At a tax cost $0t$, A demands only Q_A museum services while B demands Q_B. Clearly, the supply of services exceeds A's demand by XY, but falls below B's demand by YZ. It follows therefore that public provision is likely to generate political debate and lobbying as individuals try to alter the amounts produced to suit their own requirements. In market-orientated economies the trend has been towards charging for national museums in order to cut public expenditure, though there is still resistance among certain sections of the community, including museum managers, who feel that museums

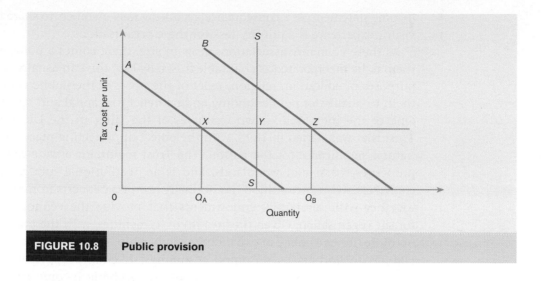

FIGURE 10.8   **Public provision**

have a public obligation requirement. As a consequence, only voluntary admission donations have been introduced in some instances, with a recommended minimum contribution, while other museums have simply refused to charge for admission in exchange for tax breaks, but the trend is one of introducing user charges.

It is evident from the above discussion that the classification of goods and services into public and private provision is by no means clear cut. It is up to society to decide upon the dividing line through the political process. Nevertheless, governments do have to make everyday decisions on which projects to promote. This is particularly true of tourist attractions, because they are frequently sponsored by local authorities and voluntary organisations who look to central government for grant assistance. To aid decision making, economists have devised the analytical framework of cost–benefit analysis, which takes a wider and longer look at project decisions. The diversity of tourism expenditure is such that the most feasible method of assessing government support is to look at the impact that spending by visitors to the attraction has a local income and employment via the multiplier process. Implicit in this process is the requirement that the normal financial checks will be undertaken to ascertain whether the project is able to sustain itself operationally: if not, then it will need permanent subsidy if it is to proceed.

VOLUNTARY ORGANISATIONS

Many museums and events have arisen out of the collections or interests of a group of enthusiasts who come together to provide for themselves and others collective goods and services which are unlikely to have any widespread commercial appeal (market failure) and are equally unlikely to be of sufficient importance to attract central provision by the state. These organisations are in effect clubs and normally have non-profit aims. But in contrast to the public sector, they are not able to raise funds from taxation and so in the long run must cover their costs out of income. Yet, unlike the private commercial sector, many find their income source is not made up principally of admission charges and visitor spending inside the attraction, and those that do will have a different pricing policy than commercial operators. Membership fees, gifts and bequests often take on a far greater significance in the income statement. As a consequence, recruiting new members to share the collective visitor experience is a priority task for these organisations.

As these voluntary associations grow in size, there comes a point where it pays them to be incorporated as charitable trusts. By law, this can usually only be for the purposes of education, religion, relief of the poor, or the public good, and allows them to qualify for public funding and tax relief for capital and revenue expenses. One of the most well-known examples of the latter in the UK is the National Trust that was started in 1895, with the object of protecting places of historic and natural significance for the nation. The Trust maintains a wide range of historic properties, parks and woodlands, and is an institutional model that has been copied elsewhere. Acquisition has normally been via bequests from previous owners together with substantial endowments that provide the economic foundations for the organisation. Given the breadth of its facilities, with the potential of taking on more, it has a policy of expanding membership, since its objective, as any other club, is to encourage consumption amongst like-minded persons. However, it is also careful to hedge the demand risk by receiving income from a variety of sources, namely, admission charges from non-members, shops and catering, grants and donations, sponsorship, events and services rendered, for example, lecture programmes. On the cost side, like other voluntary societies, the Trust benefits from some labour inputs and materials being provided free of charge. An events example is the Sealed Knot society, which undertakes re-enactment battles of the English Civil War (1642–51). Similarly, there are several military history associations in the USA that undertake re-enactments of events that took place in the American Civil War (1861–65).

COMMERCIAL SECTOR

For the commercial attractions the rules of market economics apply. They are required to make profits so as to contribute a return on the capital invested. In theory this return, at a minimum, should be equal to the current cost of raising money for investment purposes, and for new or 'venture' projects considerably more. In situations where attractions are owned by multiproduct firms or conglomerates, the ability of the facility to contribute to the cash flow of the overall business is often given a higher priority than return on capital. Production industries frequently have long lead times between incurring costs and receiving revenues. In these circumstances, the ownership of subsidiaries capable of generating ready cash inflows into the organisation on a daily and weekly basis can contribute greatly to total financial stability.

The principal economic concern of most commercial attractions are the same ones that face many other tourist enterprises, namely their cost structure and the seasonal nature of demand. Furthermore, for user-orientated attractions, fashions and tastes also play a considerable part. As noted earlier, theme park owners have to add new rides and replace old ones long before they are physically worn out simply to maintain attendances. Historic properties and museums can fall back on the intrinsic value of their buildings and collections, but even here presentation and interpretation have become more important. The Major case study at the end of this chapter provides a very pertinent example of commercial 'theme park' attraction development and identifies many of the contemporary issues and future challenges faced by commercial attraction operators.

Costs

Typically, the cost structure of tourist attractions is made up of a high level of fixed, and therefore unavoidable, costs in relation to the operational or variable costs of running the enterprise. The main component of the fixed costs is the capital investment required to establish the attraction in the first place and capital additions from new development. The economic consequence of having a high level of fixed costs is to raise the break-even point in terms of sales or visitor numbers as shown in Figure 10.9. The revenue line from sales to visitors over a given time period is represented by R. The lines C_1 and C_2 are total cost schedules according to different visitor numbers: the slope of these cost schedules is determined by the variable costs incurred per visitor (marginal costs) and where they cut the revenue and costs axis determines the level of fixed costs. It may easily be seen that with overall fixed costs of F_1 the break-even point (BEP_1), which is at the intersection of R and C_1, is achieved at V_1 level of visitors. If fixed costs are set at F_2, then the number of visitors needed to break-even rises substantially to V_2, which increases the amount of risk in the successful running of the operation. This also has an impact on location, because for user-orientated attractions population catchment areas in terms of ease of access to the site are of prime importance. The greater the visitor numbers required in order for an attraction project to break-even, the fewer are the number of acceptable locations. It follows from this that government initiatives to stimulate the development of tourist attractions largely hinge, for their success, on the amount of assistance that can be given to help with the capital costs of starting up the project. This assistance may be in the form of cash grants, subsidised ('soft') loans, shared ownership, the provision of benefits-in-kind such as land, infrastructure and access routes or a combination of any of these. For example, the site for Disneyland Paris was obtained at 1971 agricultural prices, in spite of the fact that it had already been zoned for urban development. As a rule, cash grants are perceived by the commercial sector as the most effective form of financial help.

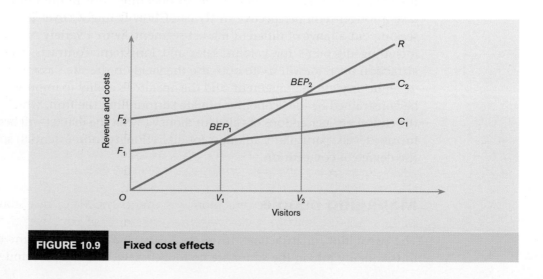

| FIGURE 10.9 | Fixed cost effects |

FIGURE 10.10 **Market orientation**

Pricing policy

The effects of having high fixed costs also spill over into pricing policy. The difference between the price charged for admission to an attraction and the variable
or marginal cost of providing the visitor experience for the customer is the contribution margin per customer towards paying the fixed costs and meeting targets
on profitability. As shown in Figure 10.10, where the contribution margin desired
is low because fixed costs are low, the marginal cost of supplying an additional unit
is relatively high and so provides a good guide to setting the price level. This is
known as cost-orientated pricing. On the other hand, where there are high fixed
costs, the admission charge has to be set considerably above the **marginal cost** of
provision, in order to ensure a high contribution margin to meet the financial costs
of servicing the investment that has been sunk into the attraction. In this instance,
the marginal cost of provision is no longer a good guide to pricing and the enterprise
is forced to take a market-orientated stance in its pricing policy. The difference
between the admissions price and marginal cost is the range of price discretion that
the organisation has, for it must cover its operating costs in the short run, but may
take a longer-term perspective in terms of how it might cover its fixed costs. By
seeking out a range of different market segments with a variety of different prices,
including discounts for volume sales and long-term contracts, the commercial
attraction operator will try to optimise the yield on the site's assets. This is termed
'revenue or **yield management**' and the operator's ability to improve the yield will
be constrained be the economic climate surrounding the firm, which will include
the customers' perceptions of value for money ('what the market will bear'), personal
income levels, particularly amounts for discretionary (non-essential) spending, and
the degree of competition.

Managing people

The perception of attractions in recent years *vis-à-vis* employment has changed
in that many jobs in the sector are no longer viewed as low paid and seasonal but

represent opportunities that offer real benefits and long-term development. This is reflected in a gradual improvement in good management, recruitment, training, appraisal procedures and the development of career structures. Many of these points were noted by Swarbrooke back in 1995 when identifying those issues deemed important for the future success of managing visitor attractions. It was noted also that attractions would have to contend with flatter organisational structures and the empowerment of staff, an increased emphasis on quality and a growth in performance-related pay for valued employees.

Despite recognition of much of the above by many attractions there still remains across the leisure sector in the UK a considerable skills gap. This was noted by Keep and Mayhew (1999) whereby, in particular, information technology and customer care skills were deemed to be lacking, with little evidence of training for volunteers. These points were also noted by Watson and McCracken (2002; 2003) in their study of attractions in Scotland. A number of key environmental factors were highlighted as significant drivers for future change, notably developments in technology, legislative changes (including requirements on health, safety, and employment issues), and external socio-economic trends. Irrespective on one's particular viewpoint, it is clear that attractions need to continue to acquire more professional approaches to the recruitment, development, and overall management of people, if the sector as a whole is going to sustain growth and popularity in the years to come, and at best catch up with their more 'professional' sector neighbours (such as transportation, intermediaries and the hospitality sector) in managing their workforce.

Managing seasonality

Seasonality becomes an issue in tourist attractions because the product, the visitor experience, cannot be stored. This being the case, it is peak demand that determines capacity and user-orientated attractions are frequently designed to a standard based on a fixed number of days per annum when capacity is likely to be reached or exceeded. This implies that at most times of the year the attraction has too much capacity. The level of investment is therefore more than what would be required if the product was storable. In turn, seasonality can affect pricing policy as presented in Figure 10.11. SS is the supply schedule representing the incremental cost of expanding visitor numbers. D_2D_2 is the demand for the visitor experience in the main season, while D_1D_1 is the off-season demand. Market clearing requires a policy of seasonal price differentiation, charging P_2 in the main season and P_1 in the off-season. However, in practice many attraction managers are opposed to seasonal pricing, because, they argue, it simply reacts on customers' perceived value for money. Visitors feel that they are being overcharged because they are unable to come in the off-season. To counter this perception problem, attraction operators tend to narrow seasonal price ranges and offer additional product benefits, in the form of free entrance to different parts of the site, to those visitors coming when the attraction is not busy.

Another method of smoothing the difference in prices is to charge a two-part tariff. Instead of the major contribution to fixed costs being borne by main season visitors, the admission price is made up of a fixed charge to meet the requirement to cover fixed costs in the long term and a variable charge depending on the level of usage. While most attractions pay attention to segmented pricing techniques for

FIGURE 10.11   **Seasonal demand**

groups, senior citizens, children and schools, the dictates of yield management do require operators to address the seasonal and spatial limitations of demand in their pricing policy.

Managing visitors

Price has often been used as a method of regulating demand and enforcing exclusivity as in luxury resorts such as Malibu and the Maldives, or in luxury hotels, for example the Mandarin and Shangri La hotels in Asia. To be able to use price to limit the number of visitors requires that consumption should be excludable – only those who pay can benefit from the visitor experience. But this is frequently deemed undesirable in the case of natural resources or the historical and cultural artefacts of a country, either because they are public goods, so that it is not practical to exclude consumption, or because they are merit goods whereby it is to the benefit of society that consumption should be encouraged. Even commercial attractions would have difficulty in using price as the sole regulator of visitor numbers. In any one year such attractions have a variety of peaks and troughs, which would therefore entail a whole range of different prices. In Western economies, the public does not respond well to wildly fluctuating prices and so all attractions resort to some non-price methods to manage visitor flows.

A number of possible actions exist to manage visitors at busy times and thereby avoid congestion and improve the visitor experience. These start with marketing and information provision and go through to techniques that can influence the visitor's behaviour on the site. Some attractions have adopted deliberate demarketing at peak times, but where they are nationally or internationally known this is only of limited effectiveness. First-time visitors to capital cities nearly always want to see the principal landmarks: Prague Castle in the Czech Republic, the Grand Palace in Bangkok, and the Empire State Building in New York City. The first step at any site is to deal with car and bus traffic, if only to prevent congestion building up and blocking main roads. Once on site, visitors can be channelled using internal transport systems, for example land trains, where distances involve a considerable amount of walking. For theme parks, queue management is often necessary for popular attractions and rides, so that excessive waiting does not detract from the visitor's enjoyment. This may be achieved by ensuring that the queue line passes through a stimulating environment, with the ability to view the attraction as the latter is approached, by providing entertainers and by using markers to indicate the length of time people will have to wait at different stages of the queue.

Environmental impacts

The concern for the tourism environment, be it natural or artificial, is linked with the notion of sustainable development. Rarely in history has any society willingly absorbed the imposition of a variety of outside cultures upon it, yet, in the interests of generating local economic activity and employment, this is precisely what host communities are expected to do with regard to the development of tourism. The situation is depicted in Figure 10.12. Suppose the local economy is positioned at *A* and the desire is to increase employment. The adverse consequence is where such a policy can only be accomplished by a move from *A* to *B*, which trades off employment against environmental quality. The concept of sustainable tourism development argues that economic growth and environmental quality are not mutually exclusive events. By changes in technology to improve the use of resources, controlling waste and managing visitor flows to prevent damage to non-renewable tourism resources, it is possible to reach a position such as *C* in Figure 10.12.

Going 'green' can build a platform for long-term growth by offering a better tourist product, saving resources and raise the public's perception of the tourism industry. Sustainable development thus offers a way to escape the 'limits to growth' syndrome illustrated by a move from *A* to *B*. But care of the environment is more than just preservation or protection: some of the key principles that should govern environmental policy for the implementation of any tourism development plan are:

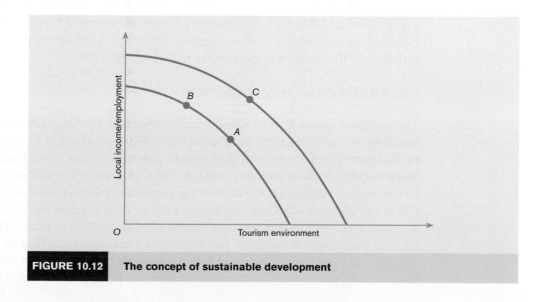

FIGURE 10.12 The concept of sustainable development

TABLE 10.1	Tourism in relation to the environment	
Tourism to environment		**Environment to tourism**
Opportunities		**Opportunities**
Commercial returns for preservation of built environment and natural heritage.		Fine scenery and heritage as visitor attractions.
New use for redundant buildings and land.		Eco-tourism based on environmental appreciation.
Increased awareness and support for conservation.		
Threats		**Threats**
Intrusive development.		Off-putting, drab environments.
Congestion.		Pollution hazards on beaches, in water, and in rural and urban areas.
Disturbance and physical damage.		Intrusive developments by other industries.
Pollution and resource consumption.		

- recognition of a two-way relationship between tourism and the environment, yielding possibilities of conservation through tourism;
- visitor management to reduce pressure;
- environmental improvement for the benefit of residents and visitors;
- sensitive development that respects and, if possible, enhances the environment;
- responsible operation through ecologically sound practice in tourism businesses and the means of travel.

The significant feature that is not always given the coverage it deserves in the media is the existence of a two-way relationship between tourism and the environment, as illustrated in Table 10.1. The tendency in the discussion of the impacts of tourism has been to give weight to the negative aspects of tourism on the environment rather than the positive opportunities that are available.

REGULATION OR MARKET SOLUTIONS?

The question posed is how should the mechanism for sustainable development work? In market-orientated economies the policy preference is for solutions based on the principle that the **'polluter' should pay**, thus prices should reflect not only the economic costs of provision but also the social costs. The different approaches to the impact of visitors on the tourism environment are shown in Figure 10.13. DD is the demand schedule and at low rates of tourist consumption, say, V_1, the social cost per unit (SC) is equal to the economic cost (EC) of usage. Thus up to V_1 current consumption does not interfere with future consumption or damage the resource. If only current demand is considered then the resource would be used to a level V_2 with visitor expenditure settling at point B. This results in resource

FIGURE 10.13   **Control versus market solutions**

depletion to the extent that *SC* is as high as point *A*. The market solution is to drive consumption back to V_3 by imposing a tourist tax *CE* on usage to compensate for the renewal cost of the resource.

The difficulty with market solutions is that, as discussed elsewhere, many natural attractions have public good properties whereby consumption is non-excludable and there is an element of public resistance to charging for a nation's heritage which is presumed to belong to all, although some museums and galleries do discriminate between domestic and foreign visitors, through having, say, a local residents' 'privilege' card. In such situations there is little choice other than to control visitor flows by influencing behaviour and/or to follow a programme of continual repair and maintenance. The significant aspect of many environmental matters is that the sheer number of agents involved in tourism, both public and private, with very different objectives and performance measures, make it virtually impossible to achieve concerted action other than through a regulating agency that has the force of law, which leaves little scope for market economics. The British experience, for example, has been that rarely have visitors or tourist businesses been charged directly for the social and environmental costs generated by their actions. The money is paid indirectly through general taxation and most of the burden of coping with congestion, litter and visitor management falls on the public sector, particularly local authorities. To this extent the government tries to take account of the influx of visitors in its support grant for local provision of public services. This is not to say that the 'polluter pays' principle through the application of 'green' taxes may not be appropriate in certain circumstances. Thus the Australian authorities raise a specific charge on visitors to the Great Barrier Reef, a popular destination that is under considerable environmental pressure.

The pure conservation solution requires that demand is driven back to V_1 by simply limiting the number of visitors, so that no social costs are incurred whatsoever and any social benefits that may be gained by expanding demand to V_3 are ignored. Such a position contrasts strongly with the ideas expressed in Table 10.1. A more extreme situation, one in which society becomes over-zealous in its actions, is depicted by V_4 in Figure 10.13. *CAC* represents the combined average cost curve of the tourism plant in the community. If demand is forced back to V_4 it may be seen that this plant is no longer viable, for the average cost of supply (point F) is greater than the average visitor spend (point G), and so in order to survive in the longer term the tourism enterprises have to be subsidised by an amount $EFGH$. One of the paradoxes of tourism is that those who do not see that their income is directly dependent on the tourism industry are frequently opposed to it, yet closing down the tourism plant reverses the multiplier process. Quite soon local businesses and employment are affected, and the economic rationale for the community may be impaired, which can affect the very jobs of those who are opposed to tourism development.

Regulation and market solutions to manage the tourism environment are not necessarily mutually exclusive. A compromise is to assign quotas at the conservation level V_1 to tourist enterprises, but at the same time allowing market forces to work by levying a graduated environmental charge on those businesses exceeding their quotas. The object here is to position society as near as possible to point C in Figure 10.13. To ensure that allocations are adjusted in an optimal manner, businesses are allowed to buy and sell quotas so as to reach a level appropriate to their own organisation.

Clearly, the model depicted in Figure 10.13 is not static. In times of growth this is of benefit, for it is politically less painful to refuse planning permission for new projects than it is to regulate existing operators. Over time it is expected that new technologies for maintenance and repair, and improved visitor management techniques will enable the SC schedule to be shifted to the right. This should allow a greater number of visitors to be handled at a lower cost to the environment, which is the essence of the sustainable tourism development argument depicted in Figure 10.12.

Attraction authenticity

It is the concern of social researchers that tourists should be given a genuine appreciation of the destination they are visiting. In too many cases, it is argued, tourists are given the impression that the destination is some idyllic fantasy world, and that they are fooled into this by attractions, particularly events, that are staged and may have little relevance to the culture of the country. Thus the tourists do not see the real landscape and way of life of the host community. This implies a loss of authenticity in the visitor experience. Of course, some tourists do not want an authentic experience: the purpose of going to leisure or theme parks to participate on the rides is for entertainment and excitement.

The ideal situation is considered to be where both the host community and the visitor see the experience as authentic. However, given mass tourism flows, it is virtually impossible to meet the curiosity of visitors without staging events and certain aspects of historic attractions. Many historic properties in Britain stage period tableaux to give visitors an impression of what living was like at those times. The visitor knows that they are staged, yet at the same time every effort is made to give the most authentic representation possible, even including the reproduction of smells, as in the Jorvik Centre in York, which places visitors in a 'time car' to travel around the re-creation of a Viking village. Authenticity becomes questionable when the destination tries to conceal the staging of an event by giving visitors the impression that what they are seeing is real, when in fact it may be an artificially created event or belong to a time gone by and have no place in the current life of the community. Historic and cultural staging presents the visitor with the salient features of a community's heritage and reduces the need for encroaching on the private space of the host population. It may also generate pride and interest among the local community who have previously taken these aspects for granted.

CONCLUSION

Attractions are an integral – and important – component of the tourism product. As we note in early chapters, certain attractions are so alluring in their own right that they provide the sole motivation for a visit. However, for most attractions to survive and flourish, other elements of the tourism product must also be on offer at a destination, at a complementary level, quality and price, to support the attraction and to provide the tourist with the necessary supporting infrastructure and superstructure.

As an area of investigation and study, tourist attractions are becoming increasingly important. Their contribution to the overall tourism product has been recognised and, as new technology-based innovations have been applied in this domain, the profile of many tourist attractions has risen dramatically.

Attractions remain the focal point for new visitor management and control techniques which aim to alleviate the pressure of large numbers of tourists and to ensure natural resources are protected and sustained.

While there remains a debate about the effectiveness of these strategies, there exists also discord as to who should be responsible for investing in the development and maintenance of resources which are enjoyed by many groups, including the local community. The role of the public sector versus the private sector in attraction investment and management has become an important issue as both strive to balance the oft-conflicting needs of user groups and to enhance the quality of the attraction experience for all.

Self-check questions

1 With reference to the contents of this chapter, what would you see as the main customer segments that are attracted to national parks?

2 In classifying attractions, how would you compare theme parks to, say, museums?

3 What are the main factors affecting the establishment of a new large-scale theme park attraction?

4 LEGOLANDs are a reflection of the Lego toy. What other themed attractions are reflections of industrially produced products? Consider the advantages and disadvantages of this type of development.

5 How do you see attractions developing in the future?

Essay questions

1 Critically evaluate existing methods of classifying attractions and examine the value of developing a single national strategy for attractions in a country of your choice.

2 Review the roles and responsibilities of public and private sector bodies in the provision and maintenance of tourist attractions in a country, area or region with which you are familiar.

3 Evaluate the implications on other aspects of the tourism system (such as tourism demand) as a result of the mix of attractions present at a given destination.

4 Assess the effectiveness of visitor management techniques employed at a tourist attraction known to you.

5 What role can 'hallmark projects' such as Disneyland Paris play in the development of tourism?

Annotated further reading

Books and articles

Fyall, A., Garrod, B. and Leask, A. (2003) *Managing Visitor Attractions: New Directions*. Butterworth Heinemann, Oxford.
This book provides a valuable contribution to the literature by providing a selection of contemporary themes, written by experienced academics and practitioners in the field. The book explores the nature and purpose of attractions, aspects relating to the development, management and marketing of attractions, and future trends and market developments.

Stevens, T. (2000) 'The future of visitor attractions', *Travel and Tourism Analyst* **1**, 61–85.
This report introduces a series of valuable insights into the future direction, development and management of visitor attractions. It has a truly international focus and identifies the significant shift in visitor trends expected over the coming years.

Swarbrooke, J. (2000) *The Development and Management of Visitor Attractions*, 2nd edn, Butterworth Heinemann, Oxford.
The second edition of this landmark textbook provides a highly suitable foundation for the study of visitor attractions. It is comprehensive in coverage and provides the reader with a considerable supply of examples from around the world.

Web sites

http://www.iaapa.org
A very comprehensive site provided by the International Association of Amusement Parks and Attractions (IAAPA). Membership of this site provides extensive coverage of a wealth of market information, current developments and trends, as well as a wide range of very useful links to other related web sites.

http://www.thrillnetwork.com

This site provides extensive news, facts and figures, and park trends and developments in the domain of theme parks. Although with a strong US orientation, coverage is comprehensive and insightful and useful from both a leisure and research perspective.

References cited

Boniface, B. and Cooper, C. (1987) *The Geography of Travel and Tourism*, Heinemann, London.

Clawson, M. and Knetsch, J. (1966) *The Economics of Outdoor Recreation*, Johns Hopkins University Press, Baltimore, MD.

http://www.locum-destination.com (accessed 21 January 2004).

http://mid-suffolk-dc.gov.uk/environment/planning/snoasis/plans (accessed 21 January 2004).

http://mid-suffolk-dc.gov.uk/environment/planning/snoasis (accessed 21 January 2004).

Keep, E. and Mayhew, K. (1999) *The Leisure Sector*, Skills Task Force Research Paper No. 6, DFEE Publications, London.

Leask, A. (2003) 'The nature and purpose of visitor attractions', pp. 5–15 in Fyall, A., Garrod, B. and Leask, A. (eds), *Managing Visitor Attractions: New Directions*, Butterworth Heinemann, Oxford.

Locum Destination Consulting (2003) *Snoasis: Market Analysis Summary*, Locum Destination Consulting, Haywards Heath.

Middleton, V.T.C. (2003) 'A national strategy for visitor attractions', pp. 270–83 in Fyall, A., Garrod, B. and Leask, A. (eds), *Managing Visitor Attractions: New Directions*, Butterworth Heinemann, Oxford.

Murphy, P.E. (1985) *Tourism: A Community Approach*, Methuen, London.

Pine II, B. and Gilmore, J. (1999) *The Experience Economy*, Harvard Business School Press, Cambridge, MA.

Spanner, G. (2003) 'Snoasis: I wish it could be Christmas eeeverydaaayy . . .', *Locum Destination Review*, Winter, 50–2, Locum Destination Consulting, Haywards Heath.

Swarbrooke, J. (1995) *The Development and Management of Visitor Attractions*, Butterworth Heinemann, Oxford.

Wanhill, S. (2003) 'Interpreting the development of the visitor attraction product', pp. 16–35 in Fyall, A., Garrod, B. and Leask, A. (eds), *Managing Visitor Attractions: New Directions*, Butterworth Heinemann, Oxford.

Watson, S. and McCracken, M. (2002) 'No attraction in strategic thinking: perceptions on current and future skills need for visitor attraction managers', *International Journal of Tourism Research* **4**(5), 367–78.

Watson, S. and McCracken, M. (2003) 'Visitor attractions and human resource management', pp. 171–84 in Fyall, A., Garrod, B. and Leask, A. (eds), *Managing Visitor Attractions: New Directions*, Butterworth Heinemann, Oxford.

MAJOR CASE STUDY 10.1
LEGOLAND

LEGO THEME PARKS

Background

The LEGOLAND parks come under the Global Family Attractions division of the LEGO Company and, as they are branded parks, their history and development has been, and still is, very much bound up with the core business of the company, which is toy manufacturing. Since the early 1960s, the company has become truly international: it has 57 subsidiaries spread around 30 countries, with worldwide sales of its product in over 130 nations. It is wholly owned by a Danish family, the Kirk Christiansens, which is somewhat unusual for a company of its size, with some 8,000 employees and a turnover over US$ 1 billion, prior to the virtual standstill of the toy market in 2003. The basis of the company's growth has been the eight-stud plastic brick that offers creative play to children in the form of a new toy every day. This may be appreciated when it is realised that the mathematics of combinations dictates that six bricks can be combined in 102,981,500 ways.

PHOTOGRAPH 10.3 **The entrance to the LEGOLAND Windsor theme park, a truly global tourism brand** *Source: LEGOLAND Windsor, The LEGO Company*

History

Understanding some of the history of the company is significant for comprehending the development of the LEGOLAND parks as they are a cross between the usual themed ride park and the 'brand'. The story begins with Ole Kirk Christiansen establishing his joinery and carpentry business in Billund, Jutland, in 1916. But, like most of Denmark, Billund was an agricultural area that suffered greatly during the interwar depression and in order to find alternative employment, since construction work had come to a halt, Ole started manufacturing wooden products in 1932, both household goods and toys, seeing particularly good prospects for the latter, since children will always need playthings. In 1934 he called both his toys and his company LEGO, which is an abbreviation for the Danish words *leg godt*, meaning 'play well'. He also inscribed his aim on a wooden sign in his workshop that read 'Only the best is good enough', which has remained the motto of the company to this day.

The next major step took place in 1949 when, based on the ideas of an English inventor, Hillary Page, the company produced interlocking plastic bricks, but at that time sold only in Denmark. In 1954 Ole's son, Godtfred, realised that the bricks could be worked into countless combinations and developed the 'LEGO System of Play', which was introduced into the Danish market in 1955, using a town plan as the basis for building houses, shops and other buildings with small plastic bricks. But the breakthrough came in 1958, when the company patented a way to improve the clutching strength of the bricks (and therefore structural stability) by placing inner tubes inside the hollow underneath part. In 1960 the wooden toy workshop burnt down and the company decided to concentrate on a single product idea: the LEGO building bricks. This 'one-brand company' phase was to last until 1979, when Kjeld Kirk Christiansen (Godtfred's son) took over as managing director and developed the product along the following lines: Duplo for the 1–3 year olds; LEGO System for the 3–9 year olds; LEGO Technic for the 9–16 year olds; and LEGO Dacta for use in schools.

The parks

As shown in Table 10.2, there are currently four parks, one of which is still establishing itself. The accepted thesis in the 'post-Fordist' society is that to retain market position, suppliers should no longer sell goods with attached services but rather services with attached goods to create experiences so that each customer receives a bespoke package. It might be thought that the first park, opened at Billund in 1968 and generating around 625,000 admissions in that year, is an early development of this concept, but the reality was somewhat more indirect and personal, as it was born out of Godtfred's frustrations with disruptions caused by visitors to the factory and the desire to halt this and find an alternative solutions to cater for the needs of visitors.

Its development came about from three sources of inspiration:

- Godtfred had seen a miniature park in Holland, which gave the idea for the 1-to-20 scale Miniland to be found in every park today;

- Godtfred was impressed with the Louisiana movement in modern art and hired its chief of exhibitions, Arnold Boutrup, to mastermind the development of the park;

- the creative ability of his cousin, Dagny Holm, in using the brick to make outstanding models.

Nevertheless, it has turned out that the Billund park, unlike its replicas Windsor and Carlsbad in California, which principally serve the domestic resident populations, has become a flagship

379

TABLE 10.2	LEGO global family attractions				
LEGOLAND	**Opening year**	**Area (hectares)**	**Visitors 2000 (millions)**	**Visitors 2002 (millions)**	**Design standard (millions)**
Billund, Denmark	1968	10	1.56	1.59	Site restricted
Windsor, UK	1996	60	1.49	1.45	1.40
Carlsbad, CA, USA	1999	52	1.40	1.31	1.80
Günzburg, Germany	2002	140	–	1.32	1.50

international tourist attraction that reaches sacrosanct status amongst LEGO enthusiasts, since it is regarded as the natural home of LEGO. Replication has only served to elevate the standing of Billund, which is now suffering from too many visitors on peak days, but this is difficult to control through 'de-marketing' methods because they are tourists, many being international, who are hard to reach through normal communications channels such as local radio announcements telling listeners that the park is likely to be full early on today.

The gap in park development is also explained upon personal lines, arising from the involvement of the company in a consortium to create the Hansa-Park in Germany during the late 1960s. This was not a success and LEGO withdrew from the venture, leaving Godtfred determined neither to cooperate with anyone in the park business nor to undertake any park expansion outside Billund. At the beginning of the 1990s, under Kjeld's stewardship, the latter policy was changed and park development was seen as a way of growing the market for the core business. The planning for the Windsor project was started in 1990 and since opening it has been an undoubted accomplishment. The parks are planned along the following guidelines:

- The overall strategy is that their design and existence is to support the toy sales, thus, for example, Castle Land/Hill is themed on the LEGO Castle Play System and the Dragon Ride contained within it tends to be the most popular activity. It is probably the most important themed area when it comes to linking the brand, the product and the company.

- Prospective locations are in regions where sales are substantial and there is strong brand awareness.

- They are family parks for children aged between 2 and 13 years and the investment requires a resident catchment area of around 20 million, with about 50% or more being target families.

- They should be located in an established tourist area yielding a steady flow of visitors.

- They should be within attractive rural surroundings with planning permission for leisure development.

- The minimum site requirement is 40 hectares.

- Support services in terms of suppliers and general tourist infrastructure should be locally available.

Designing theme parks revolves around market penetration rates in terms of the defined catchment area, and therefore the number of rides and attractions that would warrant the estimated penetration rates at the proposed admission charges. This requires considerable financial investment and in current terms the LEGOLAND parks cost about US$ 160–180 million each to build: to date, the company has financed these internally. The latter gives advantages in decision speed and ensuring minimal information leakages to competitors. For this money, taking LEGOLAND Deutschland as an example, there are around 40 rides and attractions covering 12 hectares of land, with a further 20 hectares allocated for parking and the remainder of the site will be used for administration, park expansion, woodlands and other 'green' areas. LEGOLAND Deutschland has a full-year staff of about 120 and a seasonal workforce of around 600 employees. Sponsorship of attractions is accepted but there is no franchising. The company mimics Disney in quality and this it sees as being achievable only through complete control so that every day can be seen as 'fresh as springtime' by the visitors.

Given that LEGO toys have a worldwide distribution, the aim is to develop each park optimally, but in a way that specifically supports the brand. A significant aspect of the development of the park at Carlsbad was to increase the US exposure of the toy and so boost market penetration. It follows therefore that the parks have a high degree of commonality in their imagescapes, save where local cultural adjustments are clearly necessary. Thus Legorado in Billund, which has a Wild West imagescape, is not suitable in California in the light of current American cultural attitudes towards this period of their history. As a counterpoint to the company's strategy, it should be noted that a new line of toys can fail or have a short lifetime, while investment in new rides in the parks is expensive as they have to be written off over four to six years. The risk is therefore that the parks end up with rides that have no reference to the LEGO product portfolio. The hybrid nature of the parks also has consequences for performance measurement: for example, it is customary to measure capacity in theme parks by ride throughput, but the LEGO parks have a great deal of 'soft' capacity in the form of workshops where model makers are on display and give advice to visitors. Similarly, Miniland is a passive visual activity that can absorb a variable number of visitors. Calculating the return on capital employed is also problematic as the role of the parks in uplifting toy sales creates a longer pay-back time.

Future strategy

Towards the end of the 1990s the company set itself the mission statement of being the strongest global brand amongst families with children by 2005. But although acclaimed as the toy of the last century and widely admired by developmental psychologists for the scope it offers for children's inventiveness and experimentation, and by parents for creativity and the quiet absorption that results, the brick has been a casualty of the advance of high-tech gadgetry (with instant action and gratification) for older age groups of children against the simpler toys (and in this case a 'make and create' toy) of yesteryear. This has seen sales growth fall back, forcing the company to trim its costs and embark on new developments. The company fought back with the introduction of robotics (LEGO Mindstorms), Bionicle (LEGO Technic) and licensing agreements with the Walt Disney Corporation, Lucas Licensing Ltd (Star Wars) and Warner Bros (Harry Potter) to obtain characters. It will be readily appreciated that, from the perspective of the parks, the LEGO Company has no iconic children's characters as can be found in the theme parks of Disney or Universal Studios. However, these new products are fashion items, matching the achievement of the films as with the Harry Potter figures, and in 2003 the company saw a significant fall in its global sales with no new films coming on stream. Plans have been mooted for further parks in Japan and the USA (Florida being an obvious choice), but these are very much dependent on the fortunes of the company in the turbulent global market for toys, which has recently demonstrated a renewed interest in construction products, and the performance of the most recent parks.

Source: Adapted from Wanhill, 2003

REFERENCE

Wanhill, S. (2003) 'Economic aspects of developing theme parks', pp. 39–57 in Fyall, A., Garrod, B. and Leask, A. (eds), *Managing Visitor Attractions: A New Direction*, Butterworth Heinemann, Oxford.

DISCUSSION QUESTIONS

1 Under what circumstances are LEGO likely to develop a fifth park in either the USA or Japan?

2 What alternative development or 'diversification' strategies are open to LEGO in the next five to ten years?

3 To what extent does the 'hybrid' nature of the theme parks limit international expansion?

CHAPTER ELEVEN
ACCOMMODATION

INTRODUCTION

Accommodation or lodging is, by a long way, the largest and most ubiquitous subsector within the tourism economy. With few exceptions, tourists require a location where they can rest and revive during their travels through, or stay within, a tourism destination. There is great diversity in the size, type, and organisation of this accommodation, while as a sector, it is extremely heterogeneous.

In this chapter, we are primarily concerned with those establishments and organisations that provide places of rest and revival on a commercial and organised basis. We therefore give rather less consideration to lodging in the **visiting friends and relatives (VFR)** sector. This chapter, therefore, is mainly concerned with fully or partially serviced accommodation, self-catering accommodation, accommodation support facilities, and accommodation within mobile transportation such as cruise ships, ferries, trains and airliners. These accommodation types vary in their importance and contribution to both domestic and international tourism. There are also close links between accommodation providers and other sectors within tourism where the cross-sectoral characteristics of tourism organisations are increasing with integration in the tourism industry. For example, hotels are major providers of leisure, sporting and entertainment facilities as well as business and conference services. Likewise, accommodation's relationship with transportation is one of long standing but it is one that is increasing in its sophistication and complexity, as transport providers recognise that accommodation can be an attraction to guests in its own right and not just a necessary service to be provided en route.

LEARNING OUTCOMES

During this chapter, we will focus on the accommodation sector and some of the issues that currently influence it. The learning outcomes for this chapter, therefore, may be defined as:

- identifying and assessing the scope of the hospitality industry;

- understanding the structure of the accommodation sector, the role of brands and the different ownership models that predominate;

- assimilating the sector's historical development and the effect of this on today's operation; and

- discussing some of the key issues that dominate the sector today and that will influence its future development.

ACCOMMODATION AND THE TOURISM PRODUCT

In the context of the tourism sector in general, accommodation rarely has a place or rationale in its own right. It is rare for a tourist to select to stay in a hotel or other form of accommodation for its own sake. Rather, the choice is made because the accommodation provides a support service for the wider motivation which has brought the visitor to the destination, whether for business or leisure purposes. It is arguable that some resort hotels may fall outside this generalisation in that guests may choose to stay at Gleneagles in Scotland because of the accommodation experience that such hotels provide but, generally, this motivation will be coupled with the desire to avail of a wider tourism product within the resort or locality.

Accommodation is a necessary component in the development of tourism within any destination that seeks to serve visitors other than daytrippers. The quality and range of accommodation available will both reflect and influence the range of visitors to a location. As such, achieving the appropriate balance of accommodation to meet the destination's strategic tourism development objectives can be a challenge. It is arguable, for example, that the inability of traditional destinations such as the Isle of Man in the UK to create new market opportunities in the wake of the decline of its traditional visitor base (family holidays) was directly linked to its old and inflexible accommodation stock. We can identify situations where accommodation is seen as part of the overall tourism infrastructure without which tourists will not visit the location. It therefore also assists in attracting wider investment in the tourism product at the locality. For example, the province of Newfoundland, in Canada, built four hotels in strategic locations as part of its tourism development strategy in the early 1980s. Accommodation can also feature as an element in wider economic development strategies. Similarly, the town of Akueryi, in Iceland, built and operates a hotel at a deficit because it is seen as an essential support facility for wider economic development, particularly in the fisheries sector. Accommodation, therefore, has an integral but varied role as part of the wider tourism product.

Accommodation also plays an important role in the overall economic contribution which tourism makes at a local and national level. It is difficult to generalise about the proportion of total tourist expenditure that is allocated to accommodation because this varies greatly according to the market, accommodation type and nature of product purchased. As a very general rule, perhaps 33% of total trip expenditure is allocated to this sector. This figure decreases in the case of fully inclusive packages to, say, the Mediterranean resorts where intermediaries negotiate low-cost bulk purchases of apartment or hotel rooms. By contrast, the proportion may be considerably higher in the case of domestic tourism where transportation costs are, generally, lower than is the case with international travel. Accommodation may be sold as a '**loss leader**' to promote expenditure on other components of the tourism product. Off-season 'offers' are frequently promoted whereby hotel rooms are provided 'free' on condition that guests purchase a specified minimum in terms of food and beverage. This strategy recognises important dimensions of the accommodation sector:

- demand is highly volatile and fluctuates on a seasonal and weekly basis; and
- accommodation can act as the catalyst for a range of additional sales opportunities within complex tourism and hospitality businesses – traditionally, casino

hotels have discounted accommodation in anticipation of generating considerable profits from customers at the gaming table while golfing hotels may seek to generate profits from green fees rather than room revenues.

Indeed, accommodation pricing in general is a complex and, sometimes, controversial area. Rack room rates (those formally published as the price of the room) are rarely achieved and extensive discounting for group bookings, advance reservations and corporate contracts are widespread. Fixed pricing is only successful and commonplace within the budget hotel sector. Yield, measured against potential, rarely runs at much more than 60% in the mid- to upper-market levels of the hotel industry and yield management systems are in place, within most large companies, in order to maximise achieved rates while optimising occupancy potential. Managing contracts in order to maximise yield is also an important strategy for accommodation units with the objective of replacing low-yield groups or aircrew business with higher-yield business or fully inclusive tour (FIT) guests.

DEFINING THE ACCOMMODATION SECTOR

Hotels

Hotels are undoubtedly the most significant and visible subsector within accommodation or lodging. Although a highly varied collection of properties in most countries, hotels are the tourism subsector that provides the greatest total employment in global terms and probably accounts for the highest level of receipts. The traditional view of a hotel was an establishment providing accommodation as well as food and beverage services to short-stay guests on a paying basis. This view has influenced most attempts to define hotels. But, as we shall see later in this chapter, this is a somewhat inadequate description in view of the growth of ancillary activities commonly associated with the hotel sector (leisure, business, etc.) and the withdrawal of many hotel companies from the operation of food and beverage services entirely.

In most countries of the world, hotel businesses are dominated by small, family-owned operations, which have developed hand-in-hand with the tourism sector often earlier in the twentieth century and, in particular, since 1945. Thus, the typical hotel business is represented by 30-bedroom seafront establishments in resorts, country house hotels or the wide range of city properties. This small business sector has, in many parts of the world, declined in importance in recent years, faced with the challenge of branded multiple operators offering a range of products from budget to luxury. The cost of re-investment in order to meet changing consumer demand combined with the marketing and operational challenges posed by technology have forced many hotels of this kind out of business. Those that do survive successfully in the contemporary tourism industry do so because they have recognised the importance of niche marketing by tailoring their products and services to meet the specific niche requirements of identified market groups. An important survival strategy for small, independent hotels is membership of a marketing consortium representing similar operations at a national or international level. Best Western and Golden Tulip are two of the best known international **consortia** while Scotland's Best represents a similar approach but within a niche geographical market.

The group or chain component of the hotel subsector accounts for between 5% and 10% of the property stock in most European countries but this figure is much higher in South East Asia and in North America. In terms of the bedroom inventory of most countries, the percentage penetration of groups/chains is rather greater:

- up to 30% of the total in the UK; and

- over 50% in the USA.

This reflects the fact that hotels that are part of multiples tend to be considerably larger (and generally more recently built) than independents. The almost universal trend in the hotel subsector is for multiples to gain market share from independent operators within expanding markets.

Ownership and management of hotels reflect the growing complexity of business formats within the private sector generally. There are three major operating models with various combinations:

1 Hotel companies may *own and operate* the hotels which operate under their name or they may have a part equity stake in the property.

2 Alternatively, the hotel may be operated and owned by a *franchise partner* – this is a rapidly growing business format, especially within the budget market. Franchises may be operated at an individual property level or as part of a master franchise arrangement whereby a company owns or operates a large number of properties, typically at a national or regional level, under the umbrella of an established brand or brands. Hospitality Franchise Systems (HFS) is an American company that operates master franchises on behalf of a number of established brands but manages these franchises, in large part, through individual local franchisees and owners. HFS is, thus, frequently referred to as the world's largest hotel company although its actual ownership is minimal.

3 Finally, the hotel company may *manage the property on behalf of an owner* – this is a common format at the top end of the international market, to be found in the portfolios of major companies such as Hilton, Hyatt, Inter-Continental and Marriott.

A major influence on the publicly quoted hotel sector in recent years has been that of increasingly focused performance demands placed upon operators by stock market investors. In the past, especially in Europe, average return on investment within the hotel sector was considerably below that achieved in other industrial and service sectors. This reflects, in part, the small business structure of hotel companies as well as perceptions of an operating culture which set hotels apart from other businesses – one where the focus was on hospitality rather than profitability. The view was that the two were, in some way, incompatible. This perception lost its primacy in North America some time before influencing the European industry. The success of many Asian companies in combining the two objectives of profitable service and excellence has led to change in Europe as well. Companies such as

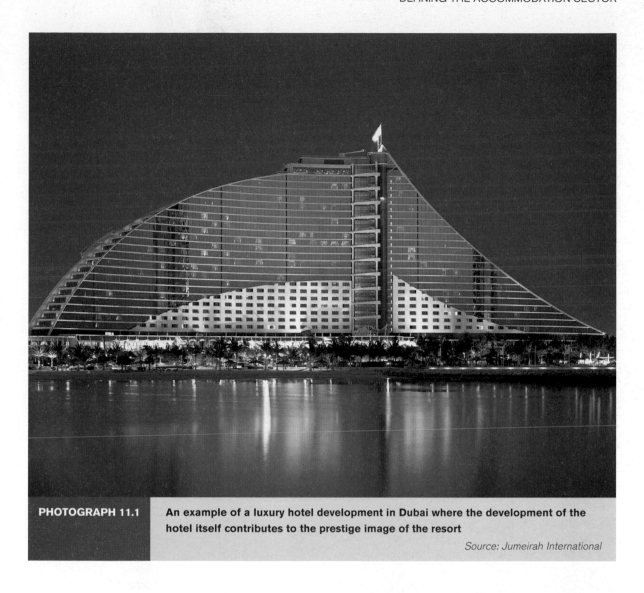

PHOTOGRAPH 11.1	An example of a luxury hotel development in Dubai where the development of the hotel itself contributes to the prestige image of the resort

Source: Jumeirah International

Accor, Granada and Whitbread, each owners and operators of a portfolio of different hotel brands, now operate to profit criteria designed to satisfy 'City' interests as their first priority. In this context, Le Meridien's Welcome Charter (Mini case study 11.1) demonstrates that hospitality and profitability *can* be entirely compatible with objectives within the accommodation sector.

Guesthouses, bed and breakfasts, farmhouse accommodation, inns

This subsector brings together a number of different types of operation with the common characteristics of offering accommodation plus some food and beverage (often just breakfast) in a small, family-style environment. Such properties may provide many similar facilities to smaller hotels although the category also includes simple and limited operations where guests may share facilities and, indeed, meals with their hosts.

MINI CASE STUDY 11.1
Le Meridien

This case study contains an extract from Le Meridien/Forte Grand's *Welcome Charter Manual* which contains guidelines for all departments within the company's hotels. The Charter is the outcome of a guest survey conducted within 20 hotels and 5000 members of the chain's 'Carte Noire' loyalty programme. In this case, we include the section entitled 'Welcome basics' which is applied to all departments of the hotel.

WELCOME BASICS

Mission statement

To be the Number One for quality and consistency in the international up-market hotel business.

Brand positioning

An international brand of hotels of four-star level and above, which serves business and leisure guests, and is European in character, French in origin and integrated with local culture.

We will deliver superior profitability by recognising that our guests are the most important people in our business and our employees are our most important resource. Suppliers will be treated as partners.

Respect for oneself and for guests

PERFORMANCE CRITERIA

APPEARANCE

- Uniforms must be impeccable and complete at all times (including polished shoes).

- Badges must be worn at all times.

- A neat appearance is essential:
  - neat, conventional hairstyle
  - tasteful, subtle makeup
  - discreet jewelry.

- Immaculate hygiene at all times.

LANGUAGE

- A warm, but never familiar approach.

- Direct, but not arrogant or vulgar.

- Distinct, precise diction.

- Controlled physical gestures.

- Greet the guest in the local language if appropriate but converse with them in the language that suits them best.

POSTURE

- Maintain dignified poise in every situation.

Caring for guests

PERFORMANCE CRITERIA

THE SMILE

- The most universal of all languages.

- Understood by everyone and the starting point for all welcome actions.

CONSIDERATION

- Know how to recognise and anticipate the expectations of our guests.

- All times, show courtesy and willingness to please.

LISTEN

- Know how to listen to a guest in order to assimilate both requests and complaints accurately.

- Never argue with a guest.

BE AVAILABLE

- Know how to stop doing something in order immediately to satisfy a request from a guest.

- Do not let guests repeat the same request to several departments. Do it for them.

Professionalism

PERFORMANCE CRITERIA

RESPONSIBILITY

- Always keep a cool head – whatever the circumstances.

- Know how to reassure guests.

- Remain vigilant to constantly ensure guest safety.

EFFICIENCY

- Respond quickly and ensure that guest requests are always followed through.

OFFER A CHOICE

- Always find and propose alternatives to guests to avoid ever being unable to satisfy them.

RELIABILITY

- Always honour a promise made to a guest.

PROVIDE INFORMATION

- Keep informed in order to be able to keep guests informed.
- Always inform guests if unforeseen circumstances arise which may cause problems.

NURTURE A TEAM SPIRIT

- Make a positive contribution to the hotel's overall friendly atmosphere.
- Always support each other since guests notice this.

Source: With thanks to Le Meridien

DISCUSSION QUESTIONS

1 How might Le Meridien assist employees to achieve the requirements detailed in the case study?

2 How might Le Meridien measure the effectiveness of the charter?

3 What other suggestions can you make that would further enhance working relationships between staff members?

Internationally there are significant contrasts in the operation of this subsector:

- In the UK, bed and breakfast and guesthouses enterprises are not significantly different, although the former require fewer controls or licences in order to operate. Indeed, it is a subsector where many operators take guests on a seasonal or sporadic basis and, as a result, can offer a flexible accommodation resource to a city or locality, available for use as and when required but without large fixed costs, particularly in terms of labour.

- Bed and breakfast enterprises in the USA, however, tend to be rather more sophisticated in their approach and comprehensive in their services. In European terms, they resemble inns or small hotels and are frequently members of national or regional marketing consortia.

- In Canada, inns are similar and can be grouped together on a themed or regional basis for marketing purposes. The Heritage Inns of Atlantic Canada is one example and membership depends upon a number of criteria, of which one is age – all properties must have been built before 1930. Some Canadian inns offer very sophisticated facilities. One example is the Spruce Pine Acres Country Inn in

Port au Port, Newfoundland, which is a modern, purpose-built facility with just six bedrooms but its services also include a licensed dining room, a well-equipped meeting room and a business centre with Internet access.

Farmhouse accommodation is a central component in the growing international agri-tourism movement. Not only has this become a major feature of tourism development in a number of countries such as Ireland and New Zealand, but it is also a component in the development plans of countries in Eastern Europe and Asia.

Accommodation is, generally, similar to that afforded by bed and breakfast operations but the context is different. Provision is usually within a working farm environment and guests may be able to participate in various aspects of the agricultural working routine as part of their stay. Marketing of farmhouse accommodation includes consortia operating at a national and/or international level.

Small, independent operators across this subsector face significant challenges from the growing budget hotel sector, especially in Europe. In physical product terms, there may be considerable similarities between the two in terms of their bedrooms – indeed, budget properties may well exceed the competition in this respect. For example, the growth of the budget sector has forced the generally unregulated family-style sector in the UK to upgrade facilities or to cease operating. As a result, many such operations now provide en-suite bathrooms, multichannel television and tea and coffee-making facilities.

Self-catering accommodation – apartments, cottages, gites, etc.

Self-catering accommodation is an important and varied component of the lodging sector within tourism. Essentially, what such properties have in common is a combination of accommodation with additional recreational areas and the facility to prepare food on a personal basis. Apartments form a major element within the accommodation available in many Mediterranean resorts but the sector also includes:

- individual cottages and gites – frequently adapted from normal residential use; and

- purpose-built cottage colonies developed and marketed as a distinct brand – for example, Rent an Irish Cottage, established in 1968 by Shannon Development (a public sector body) but subsequently sold off to private interests in the early 1990s.

Self-catering holiday accommodation may be rented as part of a vacation package, through an agency or independently direct from the owner. Alternatively, holiday accommodation ownership is a major component in the tourism industries of some countries and specific destinations. This is so much so in some places that in the off-season, communities can be just a fraction of those at peak periods. In some countries, ownership of a country or beach cottage is commonplace and not confined to the wealthy – this is certainly true of Norway and its seaside or mountain *hutte*. Where holiday homes are not purpose built but purchased within the normal housing market, they can create considerable distortion to the local property market and resentment within local communities which may see prices rise and young people unable to buy into the local housing market.

It is quite common for local residents' homes to form the accommodation for self-catering vacations. This may be through a number of mechanisms:

- House-swap schemes by which a family from, say, Sweden, exchanges homes for a month with counterparts (often in the same professional or work area) from Canada; the exchange may include use of vehicles and responsibility for pets as well as accommodation.
- Major events can also prompt local residents to vacate their homes in favour of visitors on a pay basis – something that happens throughout the world when major sporting events take place in particular.

Campus accommodation

Campus accommodation includes facilities that are used both within and outside the tourism sector. For much of the time, most campus accommodation is used on a semi-permanent basis by students, as many readers of this book will know. However, increasingly, universities and colleges seek to utilise a resource that is under-used during major periods of the year when students are on vacation. Accommodation is, therefore, widely used not only for conference and meetings purposes, but also as a leisure location, especially by campuses close to scenic or vacation areas. In addition, some campuses include permanent hotel-style facilities, designed for short-term visitors such as those attending executive development modules in business schools. Generally, the trend is towards up-grading of facilities in campus accommodation so that its use for non-student lets is competitive with other accommodation providers.

Time-share

Time-share is a form of period-constrained (i.e. one or two weeks a year) self-catering, holiday home ownership which provides additional benefits to owners in the form of possible access to other similar properties in resorts throughout the world. Many time-share properties also provide a range of additional services and facilities, including food service and sports/recreation so that they have much in common with resort hotels. Pressure selling of time-share has gained the sector a bad reputation in some countries.

Youth accommodation

Youth travel is an important, growing and little researched sector of the tourism market. The extent of such travel and the specific facilities designed to meet its needs vary greatly between countries. Young people tend to utilise accommodation at the low cost end of the market – bed and breakfasts, youth hostels such as those run by the Youth Hostel Association (YHA), Young Men's Christian Association (YMCA) and Young Women's Christian Association (YWCA) and their local equivalents as well as campsites.

Specialist accommodation providers to the youth market, such as youth hostels in many countries, YMCA/YWCAs and **backpacker hostels** in Australia, have moved from offering simple, frequently dormitory-style accommodation, to providing greater comfort, a more sophisticated product and more comprehensive services. In some cases, there is little to distinguish these providers from equivalently priced hotel products – the YMCA in Hong Kong is a good example. These trends reflect changing youth market demand, expectations and travel experience together with the increasing affluence of young people in many countries.

Camping and caravan sites

An important component in the domestic and international tourism of many countries is that where visitors bring their own accommodation to the destination in the form of tents, caravans or trailers. The accommodation levels provided on these sites has improved greatly from the camping experience of earlier generations but is still restricted in terms of space and privacy. An important provider, within tourism, is the subsector offering sites for campers or caravaners. Such sites may be basic fields with few if any utilities provided or sophisticated resort locations including a range of comfort services as well as leisure, food service and retail options.

Some sites offer permanently sited tents or caravans and tourists travel to the locations for a one- or two-week stay. Companies, such as Eurocamp, package these site holidays in Mediterranean locations for north European clients on very much the same basis as hotel or apartment-based fully inclusive packages. Permanent caravan sites include vehicles for short-term let, as well as those owned by visitors who may use the accommodation on a regular basis throughout the season.

Medical facility accommodation

This area is not normally seen as part of the tourism industry although facilities in hospitals, especially private institutions, are close to the best available within tourism accommodation. However, some specialist medical facilities also offer quality accommodation to relatives and friends. This may be true of premium children's hospitals, for example.

Nursing homes and other long-stay facilities for the elderly, likewise, are not normally associated with tourism. However, this market has attracted increasing attention from hotel companies such as Accor and Marriott who have developed a long-stay product for the seniors market which is a hybrid of a luxury hotel and a nursing home, offering medical as well as leisure facilities within the one establishment.

In Eastern Europe, countries such as Romania have spa tourism where resorts offer integrated medical treatment and hotel accommodation at all levels from the very basic to the very luxurious.

Cruise liners and ferries

Long-distance passenger liners were, of course, the main form of transport for those wishing to travel transatlantic, or otherwise intercontinental, in the era that preceded the development of wide-bodied jets. Such liners provided functional accommodation to all but first-class passengers, designed as a necessary facility and ancillary to the prime purpose of transport. Likewise, ferries provided functional but limited accommodation services.

The growth of cruising from European and North American ports in the 1960s grew as an alternative use for the now-redundant liners and little attempt was made to alter the form of accommodation or the attendant facilities provided. Accommodation management also retained a marine and functional ethos. The building of dedicated cruise ships has changed the focus of on-board services from one where the main purpose was on transport to an environment where the cruise itself became equally important to the destinations visited. The popularity of the 'cruise to nowhere' concept in South East Asia testifies to this. Modern cruise ships have more in common with all-inclusive resorts than with traditional marine transport. From an accommodation perspective, they are designed to offer comfort, facilities and service comparable to that of equivalent resort hotels. Indeed, the terminology used and the culture is that of hotel services.

Ferries, too, have changed in a similar way, particularly those offering longer services between, for example, the UK and Scandinavia or Spain.

Trains and aircraft

Although luxuriously appointed accommodation as part of train travel has a long history, the more common model was that akin to seaborne comfort. The natural constraints of space, which railways impose on sleeping accommodation, are difficult to overcome and, as a result, most overnight sleeper facilities remain basic and functional. However, there has been a revival of luxury, on-train accommodation, spearheaded by companies such as Orient Express in Europe and between Singapore and Bangkok, as well as by a number of operators in India, Australia and South Africa. These trains, either modernised versions of old rolling stock or purpose built, provide hotel comforts to the maximum permitted by space constraints.

Aircraft are faced with similar space constraints in providing sleeping accommodation for regular fare-paying passengers. A number of first-class products make claims to provide bed-like comfort for long-haul travellers. However, by comparison with their hotel equivalents, even the best of these products is akin to dormitory-style accommodation with a lack of real space or individual privacy.

Visiting friends and relatives (VFR)

While outside the commercial accommodation sector, VFR tourists generally, but not exclusively, utilise facilities within the homes of their family or friends. As a result, their economic contribution to a community or region may be limited but, nonetheless, VFR constitutes a major element within the tourism industries of many countries, especially domestic tourism. In many developed countries, as family ties continue to weaken, it is likely that the VFR option may be used by fewer and fewer people. Where the return home is to a society that is markedly different from that where the tourists originate (for example, Afro- or Irish-American visitors to their roots), it is quite likely that commercial accommodation providers will be used for VFR visits although payment may well be by the host family rather than the visitors.

THE DISTINCTIVE NATURE OF ACCOMMODATION

In addition to the heterogeneous nature of the accommodation industry discussed above, the hospitality and accommodation sector is distinct from other industries in three areas.

The first of these areas is the concept that hospitality and accommodation comprise both tangible and intangible factors. The tangible aspects of hospitality and accommodation would include the physical surroundings, the equipment needed to provide hospitality and accommodation, the decor, the location and perhaps the food and beverage that were consumed by the guest. The management of the tangible aspects of hospitality and accommodation are complex and guests will make judgments concerning the appearance and surroundings of a commercial accommodation provider in comparison to their expectations. Similarly, while the provision of food and beverage at its most basic level merely satisfies basic human needs, the dining experience often forms an integral aspect of the overall accommodation experience and the provision of food and beverage is considered important as it will influence accommodation guests' lasting memories. In addition, the management of food and beverage is further complicated by the guest's not unreasonable expectation to be provided with food and beverage that has been appropriately and hygienically produced and served.

In comparison, the intangible aspects of hospitality and accommodation are potentially much more complicated than the tangible aspects and would include the atmosphere present in an establishment and, importantly, the service that the consumers of the hospitality and accommodation product experience.

Most hospitality and accommodation products are a combination of both tangible objects and intangible performances or experiences. For example, a guest's experience in a hotel restaurant will involve the combined effect of numerous intangible activities – including the acquisition of supplies, the preparation of the meal, and the serving of the meal. The tangible components behind all this – the building, the interior decor, the kitchen equipment, the table, the chairs, the cutlery and of course the food items are obviously necessary for the service. However, it is argued that the intangible service activities make up the key product offering.

It might be argued that the hospitality or accommodation element comprises a combination of both tangible and intangible factors. The tangible/intangible emphasis will depend on both the accommodation provider and the activity. For example, in a commercial hotel there will be greater emphasis on intangible aspects concerning the concierge activity, while, in contrast, the tangible aspects of accommodation provision will outweigh the intangibles.

The second area concerns the inseparability of the production and consumption of goods and services in the hospitality and accommodation sector. Essentially this means that the guest has to be present during the production and consumption of the accommodation provision – the guest has to be present during the overnight stay. This is in contrast to the provision of a physical good, such as a washing machine that may be manufactured in Germany but consumed in the Czech Republic.

The concept of inseparability in the provision of goods and services in the hospitality and accommodation sector further means that the goods and services consumed by the guest or customer have no lasting value. While it is recognised that the guest will benefit from staying in a hotel overnight, apart from the memory of the stay, the guest will experience no lasting physical benefit from the experience. Similarly, eating a meal in a hospitality provider will satisfy the customer's hunger; however, that customer will start to feel hungry again in four or five hours. Compare this to the purchase of a washing machine which will continue performing the task for which it was bought for a number of years.

The third area that distinguishes accommodation from other industries is the fact that it is immediately perishable. Essentially this means that accommodation cannot be stored and if it is not sold for any given night, the opportunity for the sale is lost forever. Even if all subsequent nights are full due to a sudden surge in demand, lost revenue from the previous empty night can never be recovered.

Unlike most goods, accommodation is highly perishable and cannot be stored for future sale. Demand, therefore plays an especially significant role in the production and delivery of accommodation. In certain accommodation situations where demand is steady, for example, in the prison service, the concept of perishability does not pose a significant problem. However, the majority of accommodation providers experience severe fluctuations in demand resulting in a significant problem for accommodation managers.

THE MANAGEMENT OF COMMERCIAL ACCOMMODATION

While it is recognised that the management of commercial accommodation provision is a complicated business and it is out with the scope of this chapter to discuss all aspects of this activity, this section aims to highlight two fairly unique aspects of the management of commercial accommodation.

First, the concept of overbooking is a relatively common activity within commercial accommodation. Overbooking is the act of selling more rooms than are actually available in an attempt to ensure that the accommodation element of the business is full. This activity has increased in popularity due to the number of reservation cancellations and no shows that are experienced in commercial accommodation provision. For example, according to the reservation system, a hotel might be fully booked. However, guests' plans may change resulting in their cancelling their reservation, or not informing the hotel and just not turning up. Depending on the time of year, the level of cancellations and no shows might be as high as 15% and in order to combat this, hotels will regularly overbook by a similar amount.

Overbooking is, however, a sensitive activity and should a guest with a reservation turn up then technically, the hotel has breached the contact with that guest. Due to potential legal liability and the substantial damage to the hotel's reputation and goodwill, some hotels have completely eliminated the practice of intentional overbooking. Others continue to take that risk in an effort to ensure that their hotel is completely full.

Second, and in an effort to manage the reservation system more closely and as a means of ensuring the maximum number of rooms are full at any given time, accommodation providers have increasingly been adopting concepts such as yield management. Donaghy, McMahon and McDowell (1995) consider that yield management is a **revenue maximisation** technique with aims to increase the net yield (or revenue) through the predicted allocation of available accommodation capacity to pre-determined market segments at optimum price. First developed in the airline industry (which also suffers from acute perishability) yield management has been adopted by many commercial accommodation providers. Essentially, yield management means that the accommodation provider sells accommodation to the right people at the right price and at the right time. Practically speaking, the accommodation provider might examine historical reservation charts in an effort to identify periods of low demand. Thereafter these rooms which have proved difficult to sell in the past will be subject to marketing, advertising and discounting as a means of stimulating demand. The accommodation provider will adopt a flexible pricing policy based on the number of rooms available and the demand for those rooms. Indeed, the cost of accommodation might increase the closer to the date the reservation is made. Thus it is usual for guests to be paying a variety of rates for staying in the same type of room, in the same hotel, on the same night. This activity will also assist accommodation providers in identifying periods of high demand and ensuring that rooms are not sold at a discounted rate, thus maximising yield.

SECTORAL OVERLAP

The accommodation sector may or may not exist in organisational isolation from other sectors of the tourism economy. In other words, there are operations that provide accommodation facilities and nothing else to their customers – some budget hotel products, self-catering cottages and campsites are examples of businesses where there may be minimal horizontal integration with other activities in tourism. By contrast, there are operations where accommodation is just one of a range of integrated tourism services provided by the one organisation. All-inclusive resorts and cruise ships, offering a wide range of entertainment, leisure, retail and food service facilities in addition to accommodation, provide good examples. The problem, from a definitional point of view, is that terms in the accommodation area are used very loosely so that the word 'hotel' may be employed to describe a small, family-owned bed and breakfast establishment, a budget hotel, a luxury country house property or an integrated resort such as Gleneagles in Scotland. As a result, official definitions are rarely of much value and are mainly used in order to regulate or grade the sector.

An important trend, in the hotel sector, is the disaggregation of accommodation from other aspects of hotel services, particularly in the moderate and economy sectors of the marketplace. The customer may not always be aware of this disaggregation because it frequently represents a business rather than a service arrangement. Hallam and Baum (1996) discuss the growing trend towards out-sourcing food and beverage services within hotels, to either individual operators or to branded chain restaurants, allowing some hotel companies to concentrate on high-yield, low-cost accommodation provision while ensuring that their customers have access to appropriate food service opportunities. Other concepts such as Embassy All-Suites, in the USA, and Travelodge in the budget sector in the UK, have been designed as almost exclusively accommodation providers, encouraging guests to make use of external food service, leisure and entertainment facilities. This disaggregation process appears to represent a growing trend in the tourism industry at one end of the market. At the other end, increasingly sophisticated integrated all-inclusive resort provision points in the opposite direction.

399

SECTOR ORIGINS AND INFLUENCE OF THE UNITED STATES

Accommodation has been a travel requirement since the first trading, missionary and pilgrimage routes were established in Asia and Europe in pre-Christian times. The basis of such accommodation was, generally, non-paying with travellers provided with a roof and sustenance as part of religious obligation or in the hope that similar hospitality might be offered to the host in the future. Possibly the first reference to commercial accommodation provision in Europe comes from thirteenth-century Florence but an identifiable commercial accommodation sector cannot really be identified until the late eighteenth century when coaching inns in Britain developed in response to organised stagecoach travel and the first large hotels were opened in France and the USA. The dawn of the railway era stimulated hotel development in many countries of Europe and elsewhere and the railway companies were among the main promoters of hotel building, proximate or integral to main termini in cities such as New York, London or Edinburgh. In many respects, these were the first hotel multiples or chains with which we are familiar today.

The latter half of the nineteenth century also saw increased travel stimulate the development of some of the great luxury hotels of the major capital cities of the world, many of which continue to set standards of luxury for the industry today. Hotels such as the Waldorf Astoria in New York, the Savoy, Dorchester and Claridges in London and the Ritz in Paris all date from this era. Raffles in Singapore and the Taj Mahal in Mumbai, while somewhat different in the motivation for their establishment, also date from the same period and represent a tradition of European-style accommodation or hotel keeping which provided the dominant model until superseded by the American approach in the late 1940s and early 1950s. At the other end of the luxury scale, the growth of popular and accessible tourism options in most industrialised countries stimulated the development of low-cost seaside accommodation in resorts such as Deauville, Douglas, Blackpool and Atlantic City.

The post-1945 period saw the development of the American model of accommodation management and operations. Dominated, in its early days, by concepts of standardisation, risk avoidance and the application of Fordian principles of mass production, the American model is one that has spawned most of the major hotel corporations which increasingly dominate the international accommodation sector: Hilton, Hyatt, Holiday Inn, Sheraton, Inter-Continental all have their origins in this concept of the hotel, although not all the companies in question are American owned today.

The American influence on the contemporary accommodation or lodging sector has been profound and it is arguable that this source continues to dominate new ideas, products and systems. The European concept of professional hospitality has been very important, especially in translating service from the *mine host* environment of the small hospitality business into larger organisations in all parts of the world. Similarly, the more recent influence of Asian service cannot be underestimated. The American contribution has been to apply successive industrial models to the accommodation sector and thus create the foundations of an industrial sector from what was a loose amalgam of small business enterprises. While the American influence has been most noticeable within the hotel sector, the impact has been felt in other subsectors such as bed and breakfast and cruise liners. The American influence has been wide ranging and we will only address a selection of examples here.

- The mass mobility of millions of Americans, previewed in the 1930s and a true reality in the post-1945 era created roadside demand for value and informal accommodation which led to the motel concept, the forerunner of today's chain budget or economy lodge. With minimum service, these largely family-run operations were opened along all main highways in the country and established a new form of accessible and low-cost accommodation available to a segment of the population which, previously, had been unable to afford conventional hotels. The heyday of the motel was the 1940s and 1950s before they were over-taken by the chain or franchise alternatives of the major lodging companies. However, the old style, independent motel is still to be found in more remote parts of the USA – a journey along Highway 1 through Maine and to the Canadian border is one past a large number of such businesses to which few changes or compromises to modernity have been made since their opening some 50 years ago.

- The creation of the standardised chain offering common services, prices and reducing the risk in accommodation choice for the frequent traveller is commonly attributed to Kemmons Wilson and the foundation of the Holiday Inn chain. Nickson (1997, p. 126) expands on this story:

Kemmons Wilson developed the idea for Holiday Inns (the first one opened in 1952) after the experience of what he called 'the most miserable vacation of my life' (Lee, 1985 [cited in Nickson, 1997]). This was the result of the unpredictable quality and prices of motels which Wilson had experienced. As a result of this, Holiday Inn was based and developed on the notion of concept standardization, to ensure operational control and guest consistency.

- Wilson also introduced franchising into the accommodation sector on a large scale for the first time, thus facilitating rapid growth for his concept and, at the same time, applying strict operating standards and consistency to a previously unregulated area of the tourism industry.

- Holiday Inn was one example of the growth of hotel chains or groups, some standardised and some not, which became an important feature of the American lodging industry – household names such as Hilton, Hyatt, Inter-Continental, Marriott and Sheraton all have their origins from this period when multiple hotel operations were unusual elsewhere in the world and, where they existed, rarely operated under the banner of a common brand name.

- The strength of the emerging American hotel chains, coupled with US-led commercial and travel growth, created the first major wave of internationalisation in the accommodation sector. Nickson (1997) talks about this:

...internationalisation process which drew heavily on the certainties offered to the American hotel chains in their home country. Thus as these firms begin to serve markets outside of their home country, they did so in a resolutely *American way.*

It is arguable that the major impact of this early internationalisation in the hotel sector was to create models and set standards which newer, non-American entrants into this market have adopted and enhanced, without ever losing the key flavour of their origins. Nickson argues that recent dilution of American ownership in the international hotel sector represents a shift of influence to Asia and Europe in terms of the sector's culture. Given the strength of early American influence on what we know today as the international hotel, this argument is, at least, open to debate.

- Finally, in this context, the American lodging model has given respectability to minimalism in terms of service and services within the accommodation sector. American lodging, from motels onwards, have increasingly accepted the business benefits of the separation of food service from accommodation in operational and ownership terms (Hallam and Baum, 1996) or, indeed, its total elimination which is commonplace in the modern budget or economy property.

The accommodation sector, today, is moving from traditions that were predominantly national to a more international stage, although the truly global accommodation brand, in the sense of Coca-Cola or Kellogg's, remains some way off. Companies are, increasingly, looking to investment that is international in focus so as to create brand awareness on a larger scale, to the benefit of domestic businesses and those in the countries of investment. American companies are developing elsewhere because of perceived saturation in the marketplace at home where reinvestment in tired mid-market, franchised properties is of greater need than the creation of additional capacity. European and Asian companies see the opportunity to bring the distinctive flavour of their brands (for example, Novotel and Mandarin Oriental) to new markets. Competition in the accommodation sector, therefore, increasingly exists at an international level but is complemented by strengthening and up-grading of many independent or small chain operators at a local level.

QUALITY ISSUES AND GRADING IN THE ACCOMMODATION SECTOR

In common with all areas of tourism, the accommodation sector in any one location is a product of local and global forces representing historical, political, economic, socio-cultural and technological factors. The interplay of these environmental determinants is the main cause of the sector's heterogeneity.

Comparison, therefore, becomes difficult between subsectors within accommodation and between operations in different countries and regions of the world. There are few meaningful frameworks or criteria that can compare the physical product attributes and ambience of, for example, Ashford Castle in the west of Ireland with its focus on the traditional in the style of the landed aristocracy and the ultra-modernity of the Ritz Carlton, Millenia, Singapore, situated in the heart of that urbanised city state. Both offer excellence within their own location and context but their physical product is completely different. Where comparison may be ventured is in terms of service quality but this dimension presents numerous problems of, in particular, subjective assessment.

Quality comparisons are attempted through various accommodation grading and classification schemes. These, generally, operate on a national or regional basis within countries and may be run by either public (e.g. tourist board) or private sector (e.g. the Automobile Association (AA) or the American Automobile Association (AAA)) organisations. Attempts to introduce transnational systems within, for example, the EU, have failed largely because of diversity within the industry of each country.

Accommodation classification or grading may be applied to all subsectors but is predominantly used with respect to hotels, guest houses, farmhouse accommodation, bed and breakfast establishments and campsites. There is a difference in focus and purpose between classification and grading:

- **Classification** may be defined as 'the assignment of hotels to a categorical rating according to type of property, facilities, and amenities offered' (Gee, 1994). This is the traditional focus of most schemes.

- **Grading** in contrast emphasises quality dimensions. In practice, most national or commercially operated schemes concentrate on classification with quality perceived to be an *add-on* which does not impact upon the star rating of an establishment.

The purposes of accommodation classification are varied. They include:

- *standardisation* – to establish a system of uniform service and product quality that helps to create an orderly travel market distribution system for buyers and sellers;

- *marketing* – to advise travellers on the range and types of accommodation available within a destination as a means of promoting the destination and encouraging healthy competition in the marketplace;

- *consumer protection* – to ensure that accommodation meets minimum standards of accommodation, facilities, and service within classification and grade definitions;

- *revenue generation* – to provide revenue from licensing, the sale of guidebooks and so forth;

- *control* – to provide a system for controlling general industry quality; and

- *investment incentive* – to give operators incentive to upgrade their facilities and services in order to meet grading/classification criteria.

Accommodation classification, however, is not without problems. One of these relates to the subjectivity of judgement involved in assessing many key aspects of both the tangible and intangible elements of the accommodation experience such as personal service or the quality of products. As a consequence, many classification schemes concentrate, primarily, on the physical and quantifiable attributes of operations determining level of grade on the basis of features such as:

- room size;

- room facilities, especially whether en-suite or not; and

- availability of services – laundry, room service, 24-hour reception.

However, this is commonly done without any attempt to assess the quality of such provision or the consistency of its delivery. Other problems with classification schemes include:

- political pressures to offer classification and grading towards the top end of the spectrum to most hotels, thus creating a top-heavy structure;

- the cost of administering and operating a comprehensive classification assessment scheme, especially where subjective, intangible dimensions are to be included;

- industry objections to state-imposed, compulsory schemes; and

- the tendency of classification schemes to encourage standardisation rather than individual excellence within hotels.

Mini case study 11.2 is an extract from the research study undertaken prior to implementing changes to the Scottish Tourist Board's (STB) scheme. Within this scheme, star grading (one to four stars) is based exclusively upon assessment of quality and will provide the headline information for consumer choice and information. Information on facilities will be provided in directories and similar publications. Thus, a small establishment, excelling in its service but limited in the range of facilities available for guests, could be graded as five star while a large, international property with a full range of product attributes (leisure, business) could be graded as three star on the basis of the quality of its service and products.

MINI CASE STUDY 11.2
Scotland's Commended Hotels

Scotland's Commended Hotels (SCH) is best described as an association of individually owned and managed country and town house hotels, ranging within the four- to five-star quality range. The hotels pride themselves on the individuality of their products and services, with a particular emphasis on quality ambience and personal attention to guest needs. The consortium came into being in 1990 when the British Tourist Authority discontinued its development promotion of distinctive regional and product collections.

SCH is a cooperative, organised on a membership basis with a democratic, participative structure, operating to an elected board of directors. The focus of the organisation is on achieving consensus in its strategies and operations and thus ensuring that its members have shared market positions and stated values. The main purpose of SCH is to market the products and services of its membership within the domestic and international marketplace; to promote cooperation and guest referral; and to obtain purchasing advantage, on behalf of members, through volume arrangements.

SCH has 66 full members, who represent 1,159 bedrooms, an average property size of 17.5 bedrooms. Membership criteria include the requirement that hotels:

- are independently owned and managed;

- have high standards of food and beverage;

- are graded as a minimum of Four-Crown Highly Commended within the STB's grading scheme;

- have a maximum of 40 bedrooms;

- are individual and original in character; and

- that members are actively committed to SCH and participate in the activities of the consortium, particularly through brochure display and referral.

The strengths of SCH can be summarised as follows:

- association of top, independently owned hotels all having the same stated values;

- in comparison to the identified competitor organisations, it is a low-cost consortium to join;

- variety of hotel types, which are individual, personally managed and not standardised;

- comprehensive geographic spread, good range of prices, with quality products at each price level;

- strong market proposition of collectively good products;

- members directly involved in selling the products;

- STB support of the only cohesive consortium that represents the Scottish hotel product.

With thanks to Dr Alison Morrison, The Scottish Hotel School

DISCUSSION QUESTIONS

1 From an organisational perspective, what effects, both positive and negative, can you identify that would occur as a consequence of an independently owned hotel becoming part of Scotland's Commended Hotels?

2 How would you exploit the characteristics of member hotels when marketing the SCH product?

3 What benefits and opportunities might be provided to staff who are employed in one of SCH's hotels?

Quality and quality assessment are rooted in the culture and context of the country in which they are located. As a result, a five-star or deluxe hotel in South East Asia will be significantly different from a property which purports equivalence in Turkey or in Brazil. At best (and even this is debatable), classification can provide a guide to national standards. Even this is not always the case. In Spain, for example, the level of tax which a hotel pays is related to its grade, with five-star properties paying more than twice the amount of four-star hotels. As a consequence, there are few five-star hotels in Spain and a clustering of four-star properties covering a wide range of standards. Hotels such as Sofitel, Inter-Continental and Crowne Plaza are classified as four star when, elsewhere in Europe, these hotel brands would attract higher levels. Indeed, neighbouring Sofitel and Novotel properties in Madrid are both classified as four star, making a mockery of parent company Accor's branding intentions where they are clearly differentiated.

Probably the major difficulty faced by hotel classification schemes in Europe and North America is how to include the growing number of budget or economy hotels within schemes without creating unworkable ambiguities. The modern budget or economy hotel room contains a comprehensive range of simple but comfortable furnishings and facilities in a spacious, clean and modern environment. The comfort to be found in such rooms is primarily related to the physical product and is, generally, offered with minimum levels of service. One effect of the growth within this sector has been to create very real problems for hotel classification systems which find it difficult to accommodate physical comfort with the absence of services available to the guest. There is also perhaps an issue with the increasing supply of **boutique**

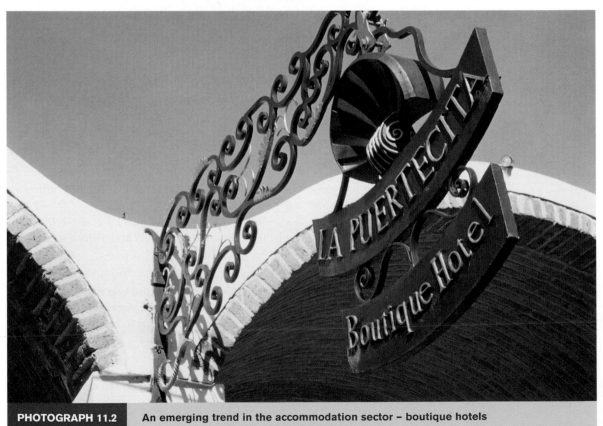

PHOTOGRAPH 11.2   **An emerging trend in the accommodation sector – boutique hotels**

Source: Dave G. Houser/CORBIS

hotels across Europe in that due to the 'unique' nature of their proposition they do not lead themselves easily toward 'standardised' classification systems.

The AA in the UK have created a special category to cater for budget accommodation, called 'lodges', as did the STB as early as 1993. The STB (1996) states:

The introduction of this category [lodges] acknowledges the popularity and growing provision of purpose built bedroom accommodation designed primarily to provide convenient overnight accommodation for short stay visitors. Many establishments of this nature do not provide meals or offer lounge facilities and are unlikely to meet the requirements of a normal Crown classification. These establishments will usually have 100% of bedrooms en suite and have restaurant or dining facilities nearby.

Budget hotels, in Europe, are a response to changing customer needs and expectations and their importance can be dated from the mid-1980s. Prior to their development, the consumer in search of low-cost accommodation would have patronised one of the large number of small, independent hotels, guesthouses or bed and breakfast establishments, generally at the unclassified, one- or two-star level, to be found in all Western European countries. Products and services were very varied – just the problem faced by Kemmons Wilson in the USA some 30 years previously. The option of quality, low-cost and modern accommodation in the form of budget hotels, branded under names such as Formule 1, Travelodge, Travel Inn and Campanile, has moved a significant volume of demand away from traditional operators and resulted in both widespread upgrading of facilities and business failure in this sector.

As a consequence, the overall quality of bedroom accommodation in the lower-priced segments of the Western European lodging industry has improved significantly over the past two decades. The quality gap between this sector of the market, measured in physical product terms, and that provided by mid- to upper-sector hotels (three to five stars) has decreased greatly as a result and, with the growing impact of low-cost technology, this is a gap that is likely to narrow further. It is a reasonable expectation that, just as en-suite facilities, hot beverage equipment, international direct dialling (IDD) telephones and satellite television services are virtually the norm throughout much of the accommodation range, additional benefits (fax, Internet) will become available to properties at all levels and simultaneously.

The challenge for higher-priced and graded accommodation providers, therefore, is to ensure clear market differentiation between their offering and that of the budget sector. However, as up to 50% of the custom of budget hotels in the UK is from the business market, this suggests that, at present, they are not particularly successful in doing so. The key differentiation that they are able to offer, given that physical attributes no longer provide such clear water, is that of service in its widest sense. There is considerable evidence that there is an accommodation market that is able and willing to pay considerably more for the benefits that attentive, individualised and problem-solving service provides. Balmer and Baum (1993) provide a theoretical explanation for this, based on the work of Herzberg.

Accommodation organisations place increasing emphasis on their ability to respond positively to the service demands of their customers and companies such

407

as Ritz Carlton and Marriott have established international reputations for their focus on service. (Mini case study 11.1 was taken from Le Meridien's Welcome Charter, designed to provide new staff with an induction into the group's service quality standards.)

THE ACCOMMODATION SECTOR AND ENVIRONMENTAL ISSUES

The accommodation sector is not one that we generally think of as evoking images of pollution and environmental degradation. However, the structure of the sector, with operational units widely dispersed in some of the most fragile natural environments as well as within ancient and historic cities, means that its environmental impact can be very significant at both macro and micro levels. Indeed, visitors' fascination with the most fragile natural, historic and cultural environments may create demand for accommodation in locations that, otherwise, would be totally off the beaten track.

The accommodation sector's impact, in environmental terms, is varied and complex. The key areas are included under the following subheadings.

Water use

Tourists are high consumers of water and many major tourist destinations are located in areas of potential or actual water shortage. Much of the water that visitors use during their time is within accommodation units – for baths, showers, in the swimming pool, laundry, maintaining green and attractive garden areas and sports facilities such as golf courses. Generally, tourists are less likely to visit destinations or stay in accommodation where there are restrictions on the use of water or where its quality is substandard. However, the long-term impact of unregulated water use by tourists can be very significant. In parts of southern Spain for example, the permanent lowering of the water table affects other economic activities, notably agriculture. Likewise, rice farmers in Phuket, Thailand, have had restrictions placed on their cropping seasons in order to preserve water for tourists. Sectors of the accommodation industry have responded to the pressures of a finite water supply and also the increasing tendency to charge businesses for consumption by activating varied water conservation measures. Towel re-use opportunities are in place in many hotels, whereby guests are asked to indicate which of their towels require laundering and which can be re-used. Some hotels, such as the Holiday Inn in Phuket, has its own water treatment plant which permits sufficient treatment of waste water to allow for its use in the hotel's gardens and leisure facilities.

Energy use

Reducing energy use, whether for heating in a winter climate or air-conditioning in hot climates, has clear environmental as well as financial savings to the business concerned. The Hong Kong Guide identifies practical routes to energy conservation within all departments of hotels. Computer technology permits the more effective control of energy, whether heat, air-conditioning or light and it is possible, for example, to close down rooms, corridors or whole blocks automatically if vacated by guests.

Recycling

Re-use of paper products from reception and administrative areas, replacement of individual shampoo sachets in bathrooms with dispensers and the avoidance of disposable tableware are examples of how the accommodation sector can recycle items normally bound for disposal.

Waste disposal

Accommodation operations, especially large hotels, create large amounts of liquid and solid waste which requires sensitive disposal. In some situations, especially small island locations such as the Maldives, disposal is a major problem and solid waste may need to be shipped off-island for disposal. In some countries, hotels quite freely dispose of liquid waste directly into the sea or rivers. This can be seriously damaging to health and the environment.

Fragile nature

Hotels and other accommodation units, located within fragile natural environments (such as safari lodges) pose major threats to the fauna and flora of such locations. Such environments need to be managed with appropriate sensitivity so that guests are not disappointed in their experience but, at the same time, their presence does not destroy the very resource they have come to experience.

The critical concern here is one of the education of both employees within accommodation units and of their guests in the importance of environmental sensitivity and responsibility. The accommodation sector's role, in environmental and conservation terms, is not entirely negative. The contribution to the conservation and, indeed, enhancement of historic houses and castles in many parts of the world, adapted for hotel use, cannot be ignored for these are properties which may otherwise not have found another suitable use without conversion to accommodation facilities.

INFORMATION TECHNOLOGY AND THE ACCOMMODATION SECTOR

In common with all other areas of services and, indeed, most areas of tourism, the accommodation sector is increasingly influenced by developments in the information and communications technology field. In many respects, technology has permitted the creation of highly labour efficient and quality product budget or economy units by centralising all non-customer contact functions (reservations, marketing, finance) and allowing the property to concentrate on the delivery of a limited but consistent product. Technology impacts both at the unit level, within accommodation, and in terms of macro marketing and financial aspects:

- **Unit level.** Technology is the key to the efficient management of resources at unit level – energy, stock, human and financial. The training implications, for effective use of technology in the small accommodation business, is an issue that is not widely recognised.

- **Macro level.** The significant development at this level is the increasing dominance of global distribution system (GDS) as the lead method of securing market share and marketing advantage for major accommodation brands. At the same time, cost of participation within GDS means that small companies and independent operators may be excluded from this technology-driven avenue of reaching key customers unless they are able to establish sufficient market presence through participation in an established consortium such as Best Western.

HUMAN RESOURCES AND THE ACCOMMODATION SECTOR

Service-intensive businesses within accommodation are also labour intensive and are always likely to remain so. This is despite considerable improvements in:

- productivity through use of technology;
- training;
- systems efficiency; and
- management effectiveness.

There are few significant labour-saving initiatives that can drastically reduce the level of employment in, say, housekeeping. By contrast, the budget or economy sector is able to provide a quality product without significant service levels through minimising the level of staffing employed.

In spite of significant changes to the use and productivity of labour within the sector, accommodation remains an area that provides employment opportunity for a wide range of skills and aptitudes, reflecting not only the diversity of businesses that operate under the accommodation umbrella but also the variety of tasks that working in the sector demands. In many communities, accommodation businesses contribute socially by providing employment opportunities for people who would find it difficult to work in other sectors of the economy. Accommodation also provides relatively easy access to employment for new immigrants (legal and illegal) as well as those entering the labour market for the first time (school leavers, students). These positive dimensions must be counterbalanced by recognition of perceived and actual problems with respect to work conditions, pay and general industry image issues, especially in developed countries.

CONCLUSION

In this chapter, we have addressed the largest and, arguably, the most important subsector within tourism at a domestic and international level. The purpose of the chapter has been to demonstrate the position of accommodation within the wider tourism sector and to show how its diversity meets the requirements of virtually all tourism market groups. The origins of the accommodation sector are considered and the dominant influence of the US model of commercial hospitality discussed. Issues such as standardisation, the management of standards and the accommodation sector's environmental responsibilities are addressed.

Accommodation is a rapidly changing sector within tourism and, as a consequence, it is an area where many businesses are casualties in the face of competition from new products and service/product standards. It is unlikely that the pace of change will slow in the foreseeable future.

Self-check questions

1 What are the particular aspects regarding the management of budget accommodation? Illustrate your answer using various sector examples.

2 Given its diversity, how can the accommodation sector provide meaningful comparisons of quality?

3 Review and discuss the key issues facing the accommodation sector and their likely impact in the future.

4 What are the benefits, to the small independent hotel, of participating in a marketing consortium?

5 What are the unique characteristics of accommodation? Can you think of any other special features that characterise the accommodation industry that are not found in other service businesses?

Essay questions

1 Critically examine the impacts on the wider accommodation sector of the trend toward greater consolidation and concentration among international hotel groups.

2 Recent years have seen a significant growth in the demand for and supply of budget-style accommodation. To what extent has this trend impacted on the future strategic direction of other 'non-budget' hotels and hotel groups?

3 Evaluate the application of yield management techniques across the full range of accommodation types. What are the benefits and drawbacks of its application in each?

4 Examine the extent to which online developments and Internet bookings may have changed customers' buying behaviour toward their choice of hotel.

5 What factors have underpinned the development of resort-based hotels and to what extent are future tourism trends compatible with such developments?

Annotated further reading

Books

Kandampully, J. (2002) *Services Management: The New Paradigm in Hospitality*, Pearson Education Australia, New South Wales.
This book adopts a services management approach to the study of hospitality and provides a critical overview of four key aspects for readers. The first part of the book introduces and examines the service paradigm while the second part explores the domain of services quality. Part Three then introduces the area of marketing of services before concluding in the fourth part with an examination of services growth and the pursuit of excellence. A very interesting book which provides some valuable insights for readers.

Olsen, M., West, J. and Tse, E. (1998) *Strategic Management in the Hospitality Industry*, John Wiley & Sons, New York.
This book explores the dynamics of strategy in the context of hospitality. It introduces the various stages of the strategic management process and offers a number of very useful examples which blend the theoretical and practical aspects of strategy. The book closes with valuable coverage of managing service quality and the relationship between leadership and strategy.

Rutherford, D.G. (2002) *Hotel Management and Operations*, John Wiley & Sons, New York.
A very useful book which examines the various management and operational aspects of the hotel sector.

Yu, L. (1999) *The International Hospitality Business: Management and Operations*, Haworth Hospitality Press, New York.
This book provides a comprehensive overview of the international hospitality industry and is primarily designed to cover the complex and difficult issues faced by hospitality managers when they are assigned to work overseas. The book introduces the international business context, the geography of hospitality developments, and provides a very useful overview of the differences in cultural, political and economic systems throughout the world. The book also provides valuable accounts of organisational structures and development strategies as does it offer comprehensive coverage of the various hospitality management functions. The book concludes with a look to the future and those issues impacting on the industry in the years to come.

Web sites

http://www.ehotelier.com
A very comprehensive 'news and features'-related web site of the international hotel sector. The site provides a 'one-stop shop' for the hospitality researcher.

http://www.shangri-la.com
The corporate web site of the Shangri-La corporation. In addition to the consumer aspects of the web site, there exists a good supply of material for those wishing to keep abreast of developments within the corporation.

http://www.wiredhotelier.com
Another very comprehensive 'news and features'-related web site with considerable coverage of the international hotel sector. It provides a valuable resource base for practitioners, academics, researchers and students with a wealth of useful information online.

References cited

Balmer, S. and Baum, T. (1993) 'Applying Herzberg's hygiene factors to the changing accommodation environment: the application of motivational theory to the field of guest satisfaction', *International Journal of Contemporary Hospitality Management* **5**(2), 32–5.

Donaghy, D., McMahon, U. and McDowell, D. (1995) 'Yield management: an overview', *International Journal of Hospitality Management* **14**(2), 139–50.

Gee, C. (1994) *International Hotels: Development and Management*, Educational Institute of the American Hotel and Motel Association, East Lansing.

Hallam, G. and Baum, T. (1996) 'Contracting out food and beverage operations in hotels: a comparative study of practice in North America and the United Kingdom', *International Journal of Hospitality Management* **15**(1), 41–50.

Nickson, D. (1997) 'Continuity or change in the international hotel industry', pp. 213–28 in Foley, M., Lennon, J. and Maxwell, G. (eds), *Hospitality, Tourism and Leisure Management: Issues in Strategy and Culture*, Cassell, London.

STB (1996) *Quality Assurance*, Scottish Tourist Board, Inverness.

MAJOR CASE STUDY 11.1
SHANGRI-LA HOTELS

INTRODUCTION

The story of Shangri-La Hotels and Resorts was created in 1971 when a deluxe hotel was founded in the city of Singapore. Today, Hong Kong-based Shangri-La Hotels and Resorts is the largest Asian-based deluxe hotel group in the region. In addition, it is regarded as one of the world's finest hotel management companies, receiving international awards and recognition from prestigious publications and industry partners. The chain comprises 44 deluxe hotels and resorts in key cities of Asia and the Middle East and most sought-after leisure destinations. Six of these are Traders Hotels, the sister brand that was established in 1989 to deliver high-value, mid-range, quality accommodation to the business traveller.

The name Shangri-La was inspired by James Hilton's legendary novel, *Lost Horizon*:

> ...he felt an extraordinary sense of physical and mental settlement.
> It was perfectly true; he just rather liked being at Shangri-La.

A tranquil haven in the mountains of Tibet, Shangri-La casts a spell on all who reside there. Today, Shangri-La stands as a synonym for paradise. And even though mythical in origin, the name perfectly encapsulates the genuine serenity and service for which Shangri-La Hotels and Resorts have come to be recognised.

Currently, there are two main brands within the Shangri-La group. These are:

The 38 hotels and resorts bearing the Shangri-La logo represent the majority of establishments within the chain. Located in city and resort destinations, without exception, these hotels operate at the top end of the market and provide five-star luxury. With the majority of hotels situated in the Asia/Pacific region, the company currently operates:

1 2 hotels in Australia

2 13 hotels in China

3 2 hotels in Hong Kong SAR

4 2 hotels in Fiji

5 2 hotels in Indonesia

6 7 hotels in Malaysia

7 1 hotel in Myanmar

8 4 hotels in the Philippines

9 2 hotels in Singapore

10 1 hotel in Taiwan

11 1 hotel in Bangkok

12 1 hotel in Dubai

An additional two properties are scheduled to open by the end of 2004.

The modern and sophisticated Shangri-La 'S' logo not only resembles uniquely Asian architectural forms, but also reminds the beholder of majestic mountains reflected in the waters of a tranquil lake.

The second main brand within the group is:

Hotels operating under the Traders Hotels brand offer mid-level service and facilities with the Shangri-La service guarantee. Currently there are six Traders Hotels operating in China (2), Myanmar, the Philippines, Singapore and Dubai with a further operation being developed in China and scheduled to open at the end of 2004.

Utilising a chop – the traditional seal of quality used by Chinese traders for 5,000 years – the Traders logo reflects the brand's philosophy of offering the business traveller first-rate quality with the greatest value for money.

Group aim and objectives

The overall aim of the Shangri-La group is to delight customers by providing quality and value through distinctive service and innovative products. In order to achieve this, the company has identified eight guiding principles. These are:

1 ensuring leadership drives for results and with the aim of working together as one team;

2 to make customer loyalty a key driver of the business through consistency in delivery of service, delighting customers in every customer contact and ensuring that executives have a customer contact role;

3 the encouragement of empowerment and therefore demanding decision making at customer contact point;

4 the commitment to the financial success of individual operating units and the company as a whole in both the short and long term;

5 the creation of an environment where associates may achieve their personal and career goals;

6 the demonstration of honesty, care and integrity in all relationships.

7 ensuring that procedures are customer and employee friendly and are suitably enabled by technology; and

8 the guarantee that the organisation will be environmentally conscientious and provide safety and security for customers and associates.

SHANGRI-LA CARE

Shangri-La are committed to highly personalised guest service and therefore recruits for attitude and trains for skills. The acclaimed training programme, Shangri-La Care, is divided into three modules and in line with the group's strategic plan to be an industry leader, ensures that all members of staff undergo the modules within six months of joining the group.

Shangri-La Care is a living culture within the group, strongly supported by the top management and continuously cascaded through the organisation. All hotels are required to allocate a specific budget for training and development, and the general manager is personally responsible for ensuring that all the allocated funds are appropriately spent.

Module one – Shangri-La hospitality from caring people

Launched in 1996, this module addresses how to make guests feel special and important by focusing on the five core values of Shangri-La Hospitality: Respect, Humility, Courtesy, Helpfulness and Sincerity. It also emphasises the value of 'Pride Without Arrogance' as the service hallmark.

Module two – delighting customers

Launched in 1998, this module focuses on the importance of guest loyalty and how it can only be achieved by delighting guests on a continuous basis. It emphasises that employees must be guest obsessed and willing to 'go the extra mile', be flexible and never say no and have the ability to anticipate guests needs and respond appropriately and quickly.

Module three – recover to gain loyalty

Launched in 2003, this module highlights the importance of recovery when a mistake is made. Emphasis is placed on the concept that when recovery is done well, it is often an opportunity to gain further guest commitment and loyalty. However, recognition is placed on the fact that if there is no or poor recovery, the lifetime value of the guest is lost in addition to at least 25 others who may hear of the incident through word of mouth. Therefore, this module teaches the five steps to recovery – Listen, Apologise, Fix the problem, Delight – the Extra Mile – and Follow-up.

AWARDS

Regarded as one of the world's finest hotel companies, Shangri-La is consistently recognised as an industry leader in readers' polls of prestigious publications worldwide. For example, in

2003 and 2004 the company received nine awards, including Preferred Hotel Chain (*TIME*, Asia), Best Asia Pacific Hotel Group (*Travel Weekly*, UK), Best Business Hotel Brand in Asia-Pacific (*Business Traveller*, Asia-Pacific), Best Hotel Chain in Asia (*The Asset*), Best Overseas Hotel Group (*The Guardian* and *The Observer*, UK) and Best Hotel Chain for Business and Vacation in Asia (*Asiamoney*).

In addition, individual hotels consistently receive awards from international publications. For example, in 2003, the Shangri-La Hotel, Sydney received the awards of 'One of the World's Top Hundred Best Hotels' (*Conde Nast Traveller*, UK) and 'One of the Best Foreign Hotels' (*Daily Telegraph*, UK).

PRESERVING NATURE

As a result of Shangri-La's commitment to environmental awareness, 20 hotels have received ISO 14001 certification, the international environmental management system standard.

This certification is only awarded to organisations which are able to show ISO 14001 compliance throughout all operations. These environmentally friendly and cost-efficient practices include installing energy-saving light bulbs, biodegradable cleaning materials, water restrictors, and sewage treatment facilities to prevent water pollution.

All properties follow an environmental management system (EMS) manual which helps to identify and address the immediate and long-term impact of the hotel's operations on its local environment. And every six months, the Lloyd's Register of Quality Assurance sends a representative to inspect the hotels to ensure not only that the system is being maintained but that continual environmental improvement is achieved by setting new environmental objectives and targets.

Amongst efforts to continually improve its contribution to local environments, the organisation has recently transferred from coal to diesel at Shangri-La Golden Flower, Xian; changed to low sulfur diesel at the Island Shangri-La, Hong Kong; and are changing from coal to gas at its Beijing properties.

Shangri-La Hotels and Resorts is a founding member of the Asia Pacific Hotels Environmental Initiative. In accordance with the group's environmental policy, all Shangri-La and Traders hotels have 'Green Programs' to identify ways to reduce wastage, eradicate practices that damage the environment and generally promote environmental awareness.

SHANGRI-LA PEOPLE

The Shangri-La Group endeavours to attract and retain talented people. The reasoning behind this is a belief that motivated staff who share the organisation's goals are key to maintaining and improving upon the standards of excellence by which the company has come to be known. There is a recognition that a commitment to a complete career path and the provision of a working environment where all people are valued and involved is essential to be able to become a preferred employer.

Therefore the company believes that the ideal Shangri-La employee is created by a combination of nature and nurture, thus great emphasis is placed on hiring people with the right attitude and potential. Thereafter the organisation strives to equip its people with the necessary skills through appropriate training and development. Consequently, each year a minimum 2% of payroll expenses is invested in the training and development of employees.

TRAVEL PARTNERS

Shangri-La have negotiated reciprocal arrangements with a variety of airline partners. Currently, customers of 33 airlines can earn airline points by staying with Shangri-La.

Source: www.shangri-la.com, 5 October 2004

DISCUSSION QUESTIONS

1 Why do you think that Shangri-La Hotels and Resorts have created the Traders Hotel brand?

2 What are the key aspects of Shangri-La Hotels and Resorts that differentiate this company from other major hotel organisations?

3 Shangri-La Hotels and Resorts appear to adopt a relatively unique approach to the management of their human resources. How do you consider that this approach assists in achieving their overall aim?

CHAPTER TWELVE
INTERMEDIARIES

INTRODUCTION

In this chapter we show that the principal role of intermediaries is to bring buyers and sellers together. For travel and tourism, intermediation comes about through tour operators or wholesalers assembling the components of the tourist trip into a package and retailing the latter through travel agents, who deal directly with the public. However, as this chapter shows, this is not the only way by which the tourist product reaches the customer and we discuss several other distribution channels. The structure of intermediation is complicated by the fact that some retail agents and some of the principal suppliers, such as airlines, also act as tour wholesalers. Much of this trend has been driven by 'online' developments and the rapid adoption of electronic technologies in facilitating the supply of and demand for tourism products. Online travel trends will be explored in this chapter with their impact on the traditional industry examined.

In this context, the chapter outlines the roles played by the retail travel agent and the tour operator consecutively. We point out the differences between the North American and European travel trade systems, although our main emphasis is on the commonality of the underlying principles governing their activity. The conceptual aspects of tour operation are relatively straightforward but the implementation requires considerable organisation and planning, particularly in view of the time lags involved. We therefore discuss the main stages of tour operation in some detail. Finally, the factors making for market dominance are analysed.

LEARNING OUTCOMES

The focus of the chapter is the packaging and distribution of the tourism product. By the end of this chapter, therefore, you will:

- be familiar with the nature and structures of intermediation and the arguments for and against dis-intermediation of distribution channels in tourism;

- be aware of 'online' developments and the increasing consolidation and concentration of tourism intermediaries;

- be familiar with the operating characteristics, roles and functions of retail travel agents and tour operators;

- have an understanding of the process of distribution; and

- be aware of the financial constraints on the operation of intermediaries and the difficulties these inflict.

THE NATURE OF INTERMEDIATION

In all industries the task of **intermediaries** is to transform goods and services from a form that consumers do not want into a product that they do want. For everyday household requirements, this is performed mainly through holding bulk supplies and breaking these down into amounts required by individuals, as well as bringing the goods to the marketplace. In tourism the situation is somewhat different, for it is quite possible to buy the components of the tourism trip (accommodation, transport, excursions and entertainment) directly from producers. This dispenses with the need for a middleman. Traditionally, this has not happened to any great degree because the linkages (termed distribution channels) between the suppliers of tourism products and their potential customers are imperfect.

Given the above situation, we can see that it is possible for intermediaries to improve distribution channels and so make markets by bringing buyers and sellers together. It is argued that distribution channels often influence both consumer behaviour, and determine the ability of the industry to respond to consumers' requests efficiently. Distribution channels quite clearly help determine the competitiveness of suppliers and destinations. The bulk of this work falls upon the tour operator or wholesaler who packages the main components of the tourist trip into a single product and sells this at one price through retail travel agents or, particularly in North America, airline sales offices. By and large, the role of the retail travel agent has been to provide an outlet for the actual sales of tours, tickets and travel services, such as insurance or foreign exchange, to the public.

Benefits

By making markets, travel intermediaries bestow benefits on producers, consumers and the destination. These benefits include the following:

Producers:

- Are able to sell in bulk and so transfer risk to the tour operator, though wholesalers do attempt to cover themselves by including release clauses in agreements. These may vary from four or more weeks to seven days.

- Can reduce promotion costs by focusing on the travel trade, rather than consumer promotion, which is much more expensive.

Consumers:

- Can avoid search and transaction costs in both time and money by being able to purchase an inclusive tour.

- Gain from the specialist knowledge of the tour operator and the fact that the uncertainties of travel are minimised. For example, cruising and coach tours are attractive to senior citizens because the holiday starts the moment they board the ship or coach.

- Often gain most from lower prices, notably in the case of resorts dealing with large numbers of visitors as in the Mediterranean, Mexico and Hawaii. In such destinations wholesalers are able through their buying power to negotiate discounts of up to 60% off the normal tariff.

Destinations:

- Especially in developing countries where budgets are limited, may benefit considerably from the international marketing network of tour operators. However, it is naive to expect, as some countries do, that this should be a responsibility of these companies.

Clearly some disadvantages do exist. For the producer, use of intermediaries will reduce – or result in the loss of – margins, and their degree of marketing control and influence over the process of distribution. It is also likely that ultimate customer service will be beyond their control with most attention being directed at the channel intermediaries rather than the end consumer. For the consumer, further concentration and consolidation of tourism intermediaries may actually reduce choice and increase prices while for destinations, if they become overly dependent on intermediaries for bookings, they are very much susceptible to the 'whims' and 'vagaries' of the marketplace.

Structure

A schematic diagram of the structure of distribution channels is shown in Figure 12.1. Independent travellers put their own itinerary together. This they can do by purchasing the key components of accommodation and transport directly from suppliers, from their own outlets, or via the retail travel agent. It is common in domestic tourism for consumers to purchase their trip requirements directly because they usually have good product knowledge and ready access to a telephone to make reservations. However, in order to boost the market for the domestic product in Britain, the national and regional tourist boards have produced commissionable brochures which they distribute in a number of ways: directly through

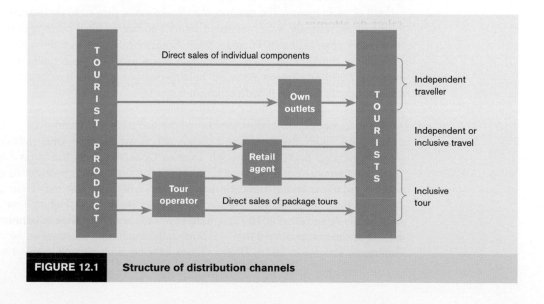

FIGURE 12.1   **Structure of distribution channels**

the mail in response to inquiries or from a mailing list (termed direct response marketing), through TICs, or by persuading the travel trade to give the tourist boards' brochures rack space in their shops. These brochures simply give the public a portfolio of products to choose from, which avoids the tourist boards being classified as 'organisers' according to the EU Package Travel Directive.

It is not uncommon for airlines, bus and shipping companies to have their own outlets in large cities from which the public may purchase travel products directly. Airlines are particularly keen to secure their presence in the market by locating offices on flagship sites in capital cities. These serve both the trade and the public, and are especially important in cities such as Bangkok, Berlin, New York or Hong Kong where not only are there large numbers of business travellers, but also many overseas holidaymakers travelling independently. International hotel chains also use individual establishments (such as retail shops) for selling rooms in other properties belonging to the group. This has become increasingly easier with the continual development of more sophisticated reservation systems.

The founding companies of today's travel trade, Thomas Cook (see Mini case study 12.1) and American Express, are both travel agents and wholesalers, and so history is on the side of the retail agent that buys directly from producers. Through agency agreements (which, in the United States, are requirements set by what have been historically termed conferences representing the domestic and international airlines, shipping companies and railways), retailers sell the individual components of the trip, such as transport tickets, accommodation, and excursions, but they

MINI CASE STUDY 12.1
Thomas Cook AG

With its origins going back as far as the mid-1800s, Thomas Cook has grown from a one-man excursion 'organiser' to a major multinational organisation employing over 28,000 people across five continents. Thomas Cook's first European tour took place during the summer of 1855 whereupon two significant innovations arose. The first, the hotel coupon, enabled travellers to pay for hotel accommodation and meals instead of using money. The second, the circular note, proved to be the forerunner for the travellers' cheque, which enabled tourists to obtain local currency in exchange for a paper note issued by Thomas Cook. Such innovation has been a feature of the evolution of the Thomas Cook empire ever since with today's organisation employing over 2,000 employees alone as 'holiday designers', their role being to develop travel products for its multitude of target markets.

After a turbulent period of development in the early 1900s, Thomas Cook benefited considerably from the post-war holiday boom, which saw one million Britons travelling abroad by 1950. Although Thomas Cook remained the largest and most successful company in the industry, the 1960s brought with it ever-increasing competition from numerous new players who sought to under-cut Thomas Cook. Acquired by a consortium of the former Midland Bank, Trust House Forte and the Automobile Association in 1972, a number of radical changes were implemented to withstand the competitive threat – including its again highly innovative Money Back Guarantee scheme in 1974. Thomas Cook later became a wholly owned subsidiary of the Midland Bank Group and began to concentrate on long-haul, rather than short-haul package tours market.

After celebrating 150 years of operation in 1991, Thomas Cook was acquired from the Midland Bank by Westdeutsche Landesbank (WestLB), Germany's third largest bank, and LTU Group, Germany's leading charter airline, in 1992. Eventually, Thomas Cook became a wholly owned subsidiary of WestLB before entering a period of rapid growth which saw the acquisition of Sunworld, Time Off and Flying Colours in quick succession. This period of growth for Thomas Cook then culminated in merger with Carlson Leisure Group's UK travel interests and the subsequent formation of JMC in 1999.

The new millennium saw the acquisition of Thomas Cook by C&N Touristik AG, an acquisition which was eventually approved by the European Community in March 2001. Recognising the heritage and respect for the global travel brand that is Thomas Cook, C&N Touristik AG re-named themselves as Thomas Cook AG and are now able to benefit fully from being one of the most recognised and most respected brands in the world.

Today, Thomas Cook AG offers what it refers to as 'The Whole World of Travel' for it has interests across the entire travel 'value-added chain' including airlines, hotels, tour operators, travel and incoming agencies. The Group encompasses 33 tour operators, approximately 3,600 travel agencies, a portfolio of 76,000 controlled hotel beds, a fleet of 84 aircraft and as stated at the beginning of the case, a work-force which numbers around 28,000. With representation in the sales markets of Germany, the UK, Ireland, France, Belgium, Luxembourg, the Netherlands, Austria, Hungary, Poland, Slovakia, Slovenia, Egypt, India and Canada global sales were in the region of €8 billion in the financial year 2001/2002 with the company serving in excess of 13 million customers. Significantly, almost 80% of the turnover was generated in its key origin markets of Germany and the UK, with the remaining 20% attributed to its other markets.

For the future, the group is to adopt a new brand strategy in that Thomas Cook will be rolled out as a brand across all markets and all levels of the 'travel-value-added' chain. It is hoped that this act will reinforce the fact that with 160 years of history behind it, Thomas Cook remains the longest-serving and internationally best-known name in travel.

DISCUSSION QUESTIONS

1 Compare and contrast the development of Thomas Cook AG with a tour operator of your choice. To what extent can other operators compete with over 160 years of travel industry experience?

2 What markets are likely to be of interest to Thomas Cook in the future that today remain untapped?

3 How may advances in technology and developments in 'online' booking impact on the future success of Thomas Cook AG?

Source: www.thomascook.info

426

PHOTOGRAPH 12.1 Thomas Cook, holidaymaking in the 1950s. Although a major player in the business of travel intermediation, Thomas Cook has over 160 years of travel industry experience

Source: Advertising Archive

may also put together their own brand of tours, overbrand another tour operator's brochure or have a specialist wholesaler put together a brochure for them. Own branding is a practice that is much more common in North America than in Europe, as is the use of travel counsellors to assemble specially tailored packages for clients.

As a rule, travel agents make the bulk of their money from selling **inclusive tours** and airline tickets. In Europe most inclusive tours are associated with foreign travel, whereas in North America domestic trips are the dominant source of inclusive tour sales. The importance of business travel has led to the growth of agencies, usually belonging to a chain, dealing solely with this aspect of tourism, to the extent of providing 'implants' in major corporations solely for the purpose of covering their travel needs.

The most common way of distributing foreign holiday travel in Europe is through inclusive tours packaged by tour operators and sold by travel agents. Some holiday packages are marketed directly to the public by wholesalers and at one stage it was thought that the electronic revolution through the establishment of global airline GDSs, such as Sabre, Worldspan, Galileo or Amadeus, with their attendant alliances with hotel companies, transport operators and activity providers, would lead more and more tours to be sold in this way, especially when there could be cost savings of 10% or more.

However, this method of selling has been slow to capture the public's attention and the percentage share of the market held by **direct-sell** holidays is still behind that of products purchased by more traditional means. It has also been put forward that the increasing sophistication of the travelling public, combined with the ease of making reservations, would lead to the demise of the package holiday and dis-intermediation of the tourism distribution system. For example, Buhalis (2003, p. 271) suggests that 'as the Internet on the one hand allows principals and destinations to promote their products online and on the other enables consumers to develop and purchase their own itineraries online and unaided, the future of travel agencies looks questionable'. Principals in this instance may be a tour operator or wholesaler, a hotel or a transport company. Buhalis goes on to state that the 'high dependence of travel agencies on information and communication in order to perform their role, in combination with the reluctance to take advantage of the emerging technology, places traditional agencies in an extremely vulnerable position'. Table 12.1 identifies some of the developments and trends in the marketplace affecting travel agencies while Tables 12.2 and 12.3 outline some of the arguments both for and against **dis-intermediation** of travel agencies and tour operators.

While it is true that more people are travelling independently, evidence to date suggests that traditional purchasing patterns are holding firm in many markets (especially 'grey' markets and those on a low budget), for it still remains the case that operators can negotiate cheaper arrangements through their bulk purchasing power, and they are also able to respond to the public's demands by building in more options to their package offers.

Integration, consolidation and concentration

The term **integration** is an economic concept to describe formal linking arrangements between one organisation and another. **Vertical integration** is where the linking occurs along the production process, for example, when an airline establishes

TABLE 12.1	Some developments and trends in the marketplace affecting travel agencies

- Tourism principals and suppliers are eager to control costs of distribution, improve their communication function and bypass the use of agencies by developing Internet-based interfaces with consumers.

- Commission capping or termination by a number of international airlines.

- Development of 'no-frills' airlines that perform most of their reservations online.

- Increased computer literacy and confidence among consumers.

- Emergence and rapid development of electronic intermediaries.

- Expansion of customer relationship management systems and their gradual integration with loyalty schemes.

- eTicketing eventually will enable the entire process of making reservations and purchasing tourism processes paperless.

- Traditional intermediaries (such as Thomas Cook) re-engineering their processes in order to update their offering, improve customer satisfaction and remain competitive.

- Tourism destinations develop regional systems to enhance their representation, boost their image and attract direct bookings.

Source: Based on Buhalis, 2003

its own tour operating company, as in the case of British Airways or Lufthansa. The latter are examples of vertical integration forwards into the marketplace, of which the most common in terms of intermediaries is where a tour wholesaler acquires through merger or purchase a retail travel chain. In Britain, the largest tour operator, Thomson Holidays, is part of the Preussag AG group of companies. Thomson not only has a chain of retail outlets, Lunn Poly, but also has its own airline, Britannia Airways. Of the other major operators in Britain, MyTravel has its own airline, also called MyTravel, and retail chains, Going Places, Travelworld and MyTravel, while First Choice owns Air 2000 (see Table 12.4).

Tour operators owning airlines provide an example of vertical integration backwards and this is also common among scheduled airlines who form alliances with (and even own) multinational hotel chains and surface transport companies to secure trading advantages over their rivals. One of the widest range of integrated activities may be found in the French conglomerate Groupe Accor. Originally known for its hotel operations, Groupe Accor's interests now include all aspects of tourism, as can be seen in Figure 12.2.

Looking at developments over time, it appears that the degree of vertical integration varies with the **product life cycle**. We illustrate this in Figure 12.3 at the early stage of development, as in the case of Thomas Cook, there is a high degree of vertical integration as there are few suppliers. But as demand expands so specialists develop to increase the efficiency of the distribution channel. Operators are bound together by their mutual interest in helping the market to grow. As the market matures, competitive pressures for market share force companies to seek the benefits of forming vertical links. These include:

TABLE 12.2	Arguments for and against the dis-intermediation of travel agencies
Arguments for the dis-intermediation of travel agencies	**Arguments against the dis-intermediation of travel agencies**
• Travel agencies currently add little value to the tourism product, as they primarily act as booking offices. • Travel agencies merely manage information and undertake reservations. • Travel agencies are biased, in favour of principals who offer override commissions and inhouse partners. • Experienced travellers are much more knowledgeable than travel agencies. • Visiting travel agencies is inconvenient and time consuming. • Commissions to travel agencies are often inadequately trained and inexperienced. • Gradual increase in independent holidays and a decrease in package holidays. • Technology enables consumers to undertake most functions at home. • Electronic travel intermediaries offer great flexibility and choice. • Re-engineering of the tourism industry (e.g. electronic ticketing, 'no-frills' airlines, airline commission capping, loyalty schemes) facilitates dis-intermediation.	• Travel agencies are professional travel advisers and offer valuable services and advice. • Travel agencies use expertise to save consumers' time. • Technology is difficult to use and expensive to acquire for individuals. • Much of the market is computer illiterate. • Electronic intermediaries primarily serve the business market and are more expensive. • Travel agencies can achieve better prices through the right channels and deals and by buying in bulk or through consolidators. • Travel agencies offer a human touch and a human interface with the industry. • Travel agencies reduce the insecurity of travel, as they are responsible for all arrangements. • Internet transactions are not secured or reliable yet and consumers are not willing to provide credit card details.

Source: Based on Buhalis, 2003

- economies of scale through the linking of complementary activities, investing in new technologies and improved management expertise in, say, foreign exchange transactions, forecasting and marketing;
- cutting out the middleman by being able to control costs and quality standards under the umbrella of one organisation;
- securing supplies and increasing buying power; and
- protecting market position by guaranteeing retail outlets on prime high street sites.

It is important to note that vertical integration forwards does not necessarily have to come about through ownership. Control may be exercised by franchising. This is a licensing agreement whereby the parent company grants another, usually smaller,

429

TABLE 12.3	Arguments for and against the dis-intermediation of tour operators
Arguments for the dis-intermediation of tour operators	**Arguments against the dis-intermediation of tour operators**
• Tour operators add little value to the tourism product, as they act primarily as aggregators. • Tour operators manage information and package products in a unified and mass approach. • Ultimately principals have the responsibility for serving tourism products. • Tour operators often offer biased advice and direct consumers to principals who offer override commissions and higher profit margins or to inhouse companies. • Experienced travellers are much more knowledgeable than many tour operators and now have the ability to research and develop individualised packages for their needs. • Tourism packages are often not inexpensive, as tour operators need to add administration and marketing costs. • Often the terms and conditions of packages are unfavourable for consumers and principals. • There is an increase for demand of independent holidays, especially by young, experienced and educated travellers. • The re-engineering of the tourism industry and particularly the development of 'no-frills' airlines facilitates disintermediation.	• Tour operators offer professional travel services and develop tourism packages by aggregating packages from disparate services, offered by individual principals. • Many holidays allow a degree of flexibility and are sometimes themed. • Tour operators develop packages based on extensive research and experience. • Tour operators manage to reduce the total price of the packages by operating charter airlines and by negotiating prices with principals. • The Internet is still inadequate and unreliable, especially for destination-naive or inexperienced travellers. • A large part of the market is computer illiterate. • Tour operators reduce the insecurity of travel, as they are responsible for all arrangements and can compensate consumers should products fail to reach specifications.

Source: Based on Buhalis, 2003

firm the right to sell its products and use its brand name, but in return the firm should not sell the products of its competitors. In Germany, the package holiday business was developed by the major retail groups, such as Karstadt, Neckermann and Quelle in the 1960s. They already had the advantage of retail shops and mail order systems to distribute their products. Owing to stricter cartel laws, further expansion through vertical integration was difficult, so they developed market power through mutual shareholding agreements and a system of tied agency licensing, which gave them exclusive outlets for their products and protected their profit margins.

Another organisational aspect of the travel trade sector that should be considered is **horizontal integration**. This occurs when two tour operators or two travel agents amalgamate, either through merger or takeover. This strategy was very prevalent amongst retail travel chains in Britain during the 1980s and became known as

TABLE 12.4	Integration in UK tour operations			
	MyTravel	**Thomson**	**Thomas Cook**	**First Choice**
Status	UK plc	Subsidiary (Preussag)	Subsidiary (C&N)	UK plc
Largest tour brands	Airtours Direct Holidays Panorama Cresta Bridge	Thomson Skytours Portland Crystal Magic	JMC Style Neilson Club 18–30	First Choice Unijet Meon Hayes & Jarvis
Travel agents	Going Places Travelworld MyTravel	Lunn Poly	Thomas Cook	Travel Choice
Airline	MyTravel	Britannia	JMC Thomas Cook* BAH*	Air 2000

* Under joint venture with British Airways.
Source: Adapted from Horner and Swarbrooke, 2004

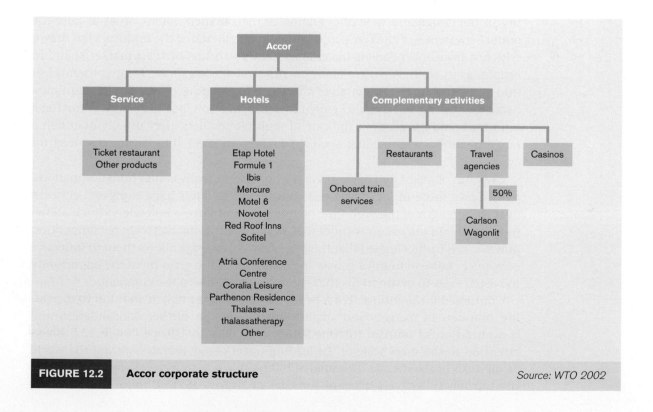

| FIGURE 12.2 | **Accor corporate structure** | *Source: WTO 2002* |

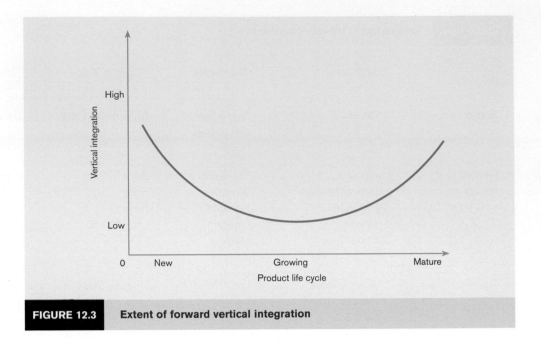

| **FIGURE 12.3** | **Extent of forward vertical integration** |

the 'march of the multiples'. The reasons for this are similar to those for vertical integration but also include the spatial dimension of extending the geographical spread of outlets to ensure representation in all regions. Thomas Cook and Lunn Poly in Britain, and American Express and Ask Mr. Foster in the USA, are examples of major chains that have increased their geographical representation.

For the retailers, horizontal integration strengthens their buying power with regard to wholesalers. They support this by developing their own corporate identity in the design and style of operation of their branch outlets, so as to raise the public's awareness of the company. Naturally, the march of the multiples has drawn criticism from independent travel agents owing to loss of their market share. In Britain, as in North America, many small travel agencies have formed themselves into consortia to give themselves the same negotiating power as the multiples. Large tour operators have also grown by amalgamation, but instead of enforcing a uniform brand image, as in the case of multiple retailers, they usually maintain a range of products, including acquired brands, to meet the consumer's need for choice.

Criticism of major tour operators and wholesalers usually comes from destinations, particularly those in less-developed countries. The latter have expressed concern over the strength of the economic buying power of large wholesalers which allows them to obtain prices below those that would occur in markets where competition prevails. It is further argued that their specialist knowledge allows them to influence consumer choice in tourism-generating countries and so gives them the opportunity to switch sales to destinations that are more profitable to the company.

Continued integration activity, be it vertical or horizontal, in addition to increasing numbers of mergers and acquisitions has led to further consolidation and concentration of tourism intermediaries, especially in Europe. Table 12.5 draws attention to the sheer scale of the leading travel conglomerates around the world at the turn of the decade. Dominated by the primary tourist-generating countries the top ten collectively account for sales of nearly US$150 billion. The leading

TABLE 12.5	Major global travel conglomerates				
	Company	Headquarters	Sales (US$ billions)	% – travel	Sales – travel (US$ billions)
1	Carlson Companies*	USA	31.4	–	–
2	American Express	USA	22.1	79	17.4
3	Japan Travel Bureau*	Japan	14	100	14
4	Preussag	Germany	19.2	48	9.3
5	Airtours**	UK	6.5	100	6.5
6	Accor	France	6.6	94	6.2
7	C&N Touristik***	Germany	4.2	100	4.2
8	Rewe (Touristik)	Germany	35.5	10	3.7
9	First Choice	UK	2.7	100	2.7
10	Groupe Kuoni	Switzerland	2.5	100	2.5

* 1999 sales.
** Now MyTravel.
*** Now Thomas Cook AG.
Source: Adapted from WTO, 2002

European tour operator is Preussag of Germany. A recent entrant into the tourism industry, Preussag divested itself of its shipbuilding and mining activities and invested heavily in travel and tourism. After acquiring TUI of Germany in 1997, Thomas Cook and Carlson UK were purchased in 1998 with Thomson Travel of the UK added to the portfolio in 2000. Preussag also own a significant stake in Nouvelles Frontières of France with further acquisitions planned. To satisfy the demands of the European Union, however, Thomas Cook was sold to C&N Touristik AG, now Thomas Cook AG, in December 2000. This trend of consolidation and concentration shows no signs of abating with most key players seeking greater economies of scale, market coverage and visibility, market presence, and in turn, greater control and influence in the marketplace. Multidistribution strategies, multichannel advertising and communication, and an ability to manage yield through sophisticated pan-company systems give the major players significant economic advantage in the marketplace. For example, in Germany, nearly 80% of trade is in the hands of just five tourism wholesalers while in the UK, a similar percentage of the market is controlled by only four companies.

The major beneficiaries of consolidation are clearly consumers and shareholders with consumers in a number of markets benefiting from highly competitive price wars, and shareholders in terms of their rising stock values. A note of caution is necessary here, however, as the cost of consolidation for some companies has been excessive and threatens to damage their very existence in the future. This is made clear in the case of MyTravel in the UK where the rush for growth has delivered severe financial problems and a question mark over the companies future independence (see the Major case study 12.1 at the end of this chapter).

For the independent sector, of which there still remain many, the future demands greater differentiation, and an ability to deal with barriers that increase with consolidation, most notably in the form of price wars. Whether it is increased levels of service provision or a focus on niche destinations or travel products, independents are likely to experience more, rather than less competition from an ever-more consolidated sector in the future.

Online travel

The significant development and growth of **online travel**, predominantly on the back of the development of information technologies and telecommunications plus phenomenal growth of the Internet and electronic commerce, has been one of the great success stories for tourism generally, and tourism intermediaries in particular. The volume of online tourism-related transactions is anticipated to reach over one-third of all e-transactions in the near future with considerable implications for intermediaries and their competitors across the wider tourism industry – and none more so than for the four major global distribution systems which still dominate the distribution of travel products, notably Sabre and Worldspan, which dominate in the USA, and Galileo and Amadeus, which are market leaders in Europe. Back in 1996, Sabre was the first GDS to venture online with its launch of Travelocity.com, a virtual agency. At the same time, Expedia.com was launched by USA Networks (see Mini case study 12.2). This was then followed by Amadeus.net in 1997 by Amadeus Global Travel Distribution and the purchase of TRIP.com by Galileo International in 2000. After just three years in operation, Travelocity.com and Expedia.com were among the ten largest US distributors of travel products in terms of revenue. In Europe, Lastminute.com was launched in 1998 and eBookers.com in 1999 demonstrating that new methods of online communication were able to cross entry barriers to a market previously outside the scope of new players.

One of the biggest contributors to the growth in the purchase of e-tickets has been the rise and rise of discount 'no-frills' airlines, especially across the USA and Europe. The principal catalysts for change were Southwest Airlines in the United States and easyJet and Ryanair in the UK and Ireland respectively. Whereas Southwest Airlines dominates the US online market with sales in excess of US$1.5 billion (over a quarter of its overall sales), online sales for easyJet are in excess of 90% of its business. For airlines generally, although they are subject to the same rules as travel agencies, they often are able to offer special rates and exclusive deals and so motivate consumers to purchase tickets directly rather than via a travel agent. This incredible growth has been in a remarkably short time period and reflects most dramatically how certain parts of the wider tourism industry have capitalised on changing trends in technology and their greater acceptance by the consumer. In response to the fierce competition from the 'no-frills' carriers and the growth of virtual intermediaries, many international airlines are coming together in order to compete head-on with the new players. For example, in December 2001, the virtual intermediary Opodo was launched by nine European airlines with an initial focus on the German, French, Italian and British markets. Collectively, Air France, British Airways, Lufthansa, Alitalia, Iberia, KLM, Aer Lingus, Finnair and Austrian Airlines have used Amadeus technology to develop a serious competitor to existing players. One cautionary note is the move by some airlines to withdraw commissions to online agencies. Although this may represent a temporary initiative it does introduce an element of uncertainty for the future relationship between producers and intermediaries in their search for finding the most effective and cost-efficient means of reaching the final consumer.

The fact that there remains in some parts of the market much caution with regard to the use of virtual intermediaries explains in part the development of **'click-and-mortar' agencies** whereby a combination of online and offline services – often in the form of a network of traditional travel agencies and/or call centres – are a

MINI CASE STUDY 12.2
Expedia

Launched in 1996 by Microsoft, Expedia.com was the first e-intermediary to enter the online travel market by a non-travel organisation. With a very broad product offering which encompassed all aspects of the tourism product, Expedia grew very quickly, entering the UK market in 1998 and being voted Europe's primary travel site in August 1999. Expedia grew exponentially to the extent that Expedia Inc., the parent group, was floated on the Nasdaq stock exchange at the end of 1999. A year later, the UK site – Expedia.co.uk – launched web-enabled phone (WAP) and personal digital assistant (PDA)-compatible platforms whereby travellers could access essential travel information enroute. At the same time, Expedia held 25% of the major online market for travel products in the USA with reservation income reaching a staggering US$1.8 billion. Expedia was second only to Travelocity in the USA, the e-intermediary developed by the Sabre Holdings Corporation which recorded a market share of 35% in 2000.

The success of Expedia continued apace in that significant revenue gains in 2001 led to the acquisition of a controlling interest in Expedia Inc. by USA Networks. USA Networks owns five TV networks and plans to take advantage of this technology by launching a new travel channel in the United States. Eventually, Expedia's new owners hope to develop a totally interactive TV-based product which combines traditional TV viewing with shopping. In the near future, Expedia has three key strategic targets, notably:

1 to increase reach and distribution through awareness raising advertising and developing links with partners;

2 to increase conversion rates – whereby browsers are turned into buyers – and develop improved, deeper and more rewarding relationships with customers;

3 to increase cross-selling through the introduction of a range of ancillary products.

DISCUSSION QUESTIONS

1 Identify some of those factors which may still inhibit some individuals from making reservations 'online'.

2 What travel products are most conducive to being purchased 'online'?

3 How may small, independent travel agents and tour operators compete with the proliferation of 'online' specialists such as Expedia?

Source: Horner and Swarbrooke, 2004

PHOTOGRAPH 12.2   **One of the new e-intermediaries in the global marketplace, Expedia has tapped into the power of the Internet and offered customers considerable choice online**

Source: Expedia.co.uk

strategic response to the concerns of many. In addition, many traditional players are now developing the reverse in that they are developing a web presence to complement their traditional business.

In addition to the above, and consistent with traditional intermediaries and the wider tourism industry, consolidation is occurring also in the virtual marketplace. In the USA alone in 2001, the top five industry leaders controlled nearly 60% of the online travel market. Clearly, the speed with which online travel has developed is remarkable. The speed with which consolidation has begun to impact the structure of the industry is even more remarkable, however, in that in the space of seven to eight years a number of the new players are now re-writing the rules of competition for the established conglomerates.

THE ROLE OF THE RETAIL AGENT

As has begun to become apparent from the above discussion, the primary task of travel agents is to supply the public with travel services. This they do on behalf of their suppliers or 'principals', the latter being a trade term. An agent may also offer travel-related services such as insurance or foreign exchange. For providing these services, the agent is rewarded by commission from the principals. Traditionally, commission amounts to 10% of the selling price, but this is normally 1% or 2% less for airline tickets, hotel bookings and rail travel. Insurance will usually generate commission of around 30% and car hire can, on occasions, make considerably more than the basic 10%. Sales of travellers' cheques and currency will yield no more than about 2%. However, by dealing with preferred suppliers and achieving specified sales targets, agents can achieve '**overrides**' which are extra commission amounting to about 2.5% of sales. As discovered in the previous section, however, commissions are not always forthcoming in the new arena of **e-intermediaries**. Commission rates in the future, both for traditional and virtual players are likely to be the subject of much negotiation and debate.

How a retail travel agency should set about discharging its primary function is a matter for discussion. Where an agent has no wholesaling function and therefore does not share in the risk of tour production by holding stock, it is suggested that the agent's main concern should be the choice of location to ensure ready availability of the principals' products in the market place. The agent has access to a principal's stock through the reservation system and here efficiency is important. The customer expects instant confirmation and staff at the agency do not want to waste time with repeated telephone calls. Instant availability on a computer screen permits the staff to share the booking process with the customer to reinforce the buying decision. This approach to the role of the retailer likens the agent to a 'filling station' for travel: creating demand is the responsibility of the principals. If demand is given, then controlling costs is the best way for the agent to maintain profitability.

An alternative view argues that the acquisition of product knowledge and the assumption of the risks involved in assessing the extent and nature of demand is the job of the agent. The agent should thus take on the role of a travel counsellor to give the public impartial advice and seek to generate business in the local market area. Many countries have national associations for travel agents that also act as

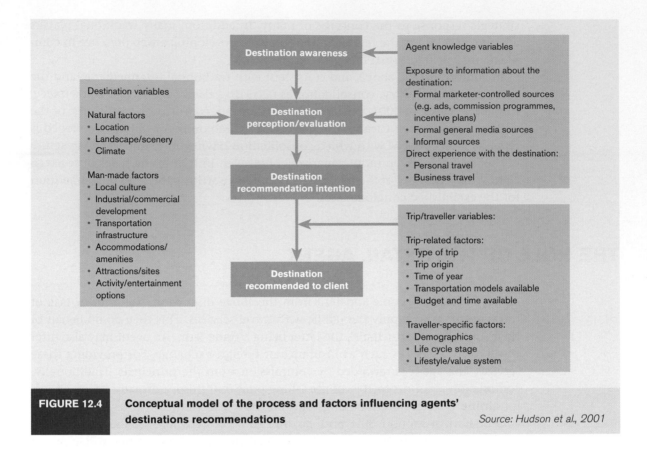

Destination awareness

Agent knowledge variables

Exposure to information about the destination:
- Formal marketer-controlled sources (e.g. ads, commission programmes, incentive plans)
- Formal general media sources
- Informal sources

Direct experience with the destination:
- Personal travel
- Business travel

Destination variables

Natural factors
- Location
- Landscape/scenery
- Climate

Man-made factors
- Local culture
- Industrial/commercial development
- Transportation infrastructure
- Accommodations/ amenities
- Attractions/sites
- Activity/entertainment options

Destination perception/evaluation

Destination recommendation intention

Trip/traveller variables:

Trip-related factors:
- Type of trip
- Trip origin
- Time of year
- Transportation models available
- Budget and time available

Traveller-specific factors:
- Demographics
- Life cycle stage
- Lifestyle/value system

Destination recommended to client

FIGURE 12.4 **Conceptual model of the process and factors influencing agents' destinations recommendations**

Source: Hudson et al., 2001

regulating bodies: the Association of British Travel Agents (ABTA) in Britain and the American Society of Travel Agents (ASTA) in the USA. The code of conduct of ABTA requires agents to take an active promotional role.

It has already been noted that the counselling role has been far more prevalent in North America than in Europe. It appears that in Europe the tour operator's brochure, together with advertising and promotion, and more recently use of the web, has held greater sway in destination choice. Thus, although there are many local exceptions, travel agents in Europe have tended to conform to the filling station model. The concept of impartial advice is also questionable in that while agents want to meet their client's needs, they are also mindful of the different rates of commission on offer and any bonuses, particularly in instances where they are owned by their principals. Figure 12.4 represents a conceptual model of the process and factors influencing agents' destination recommendations and highlights the potential for 'switch selling' to take place. 'Switch' or 'directional' selling can be described as a 'sale or attempted sale by a vertically integrated travel agent of the foreign package holidays of its linked tour operator, in preference to the holidays of other operators' (MMC, 1998, p. 4).

However, one of the features of the expansion of corporate chains has been not only their purchase of prime retail sites, but also their efforts to improve staff competencies and the provision of specialists, as well as providing better career prospects in a sector which is well known for relatively low pay.

Retail agency economics

Traditionally the retail travel trade has been characterised by ease of entry. This is because the retailer carries no stock and so capitalisation is relatively low. All that is required is a suitable shop front and the acquisition of agency agreements from tour operators to sell their products. It is then up to the marketing skill of the agent to establish the business within the locality. If the agent wishes to offer air transport services worldwide, which is essential for dealing with business travel, then it is necessary that the agent holds a licence from IATA. This requires a thorough investigation of the agency by IATA, particularly the qualifications and experience of the staff.

In the USA virtually all retailers are members of both IATA and the Airlines Reporting Corporation (ARC) which allows them to sell both international and domestic air tickets. This is because the major part of an agent's income in the USA is obtained from the sales of airline tickets. An ARC appointment is essential for retail agents in the USA and normally enables an agent to obtain other licences without difficulty. In Britain the extra cost of obtaining IATA membership tends to deter smaller agencies and leads them to specialise in selling inclusive package holidays which avoids the need for an IATA license.

A representative breakdown of the operating accounts of a medium to large travel agent is shown in Table 12.6. The example is drawn on European experience and is standardised to one million currency units of turnover. Table 12.6 gives an indication of the items that enter the **operating account** and shows that inclusive tours and air tickets are by far the most important sales items. The item for other transport tickets includes sales arising from acting as an agent for rail, shipping and coach companies. Miscellaneous includes independent bookings of hotels, theatres, etc., foreign exchange transactions and the sale of travel goods such as luggage, sports items, first aid kits and travel clothes.

The most important item of income to the agent is commission and since there exists considerable pressure on commissions in some markets, it will be appreciated that the ability of the agent to generate turnover is crucial, particularly for the independent retailer. The latter has been doubly squeezed: first, by fierce competition from the multiples and virtual intermediaries, second, from the fact that the relative cost of holidays has fallen in real terms while overheads have been generally increasing. Other income in the revenue statement includes interest earned on clients' deposit money. For accounting purposes this is a profit item which is only indirectly sales related. It could be excluded here and added into the net income statement afterwards.

The largest item of cost is remuneration to staff (including payments to directors or owners). The difficulty that independent agents have experienced in trying to expand turnover has tended to make them cost orientated in the operation of their businesses. Controlling costs, especially for the smaller agent, has been the short-term recipe for survival and this in turn has served to keep staff salaries low, which creates difficulties in both attracting experienced staff and retaining existing staff. The problem is often compounded by cutting advertising, training and investment in new technology. Administration costs include printing, stationery, insurance, bonding levy, legal and professional fees, bank charges, accounting and record keeping, and any travel that may be incurred. Accommodation expenses refer to charges arising from occupation of the premises.

439

TABLE 12.6	Travel agency operating accounts
Item	**Currency units**
Sales	
Inclusive tours	530 000
Air tickets	330 000
Other transport tickets	49 000
Insurance	10 000
Car hire	3 000
Miscellaneous	78 000
Total	1 000 000
Revenue	
Commission	96 000
Other income	5 000
Total	101 000
Costs	
Payroll expenses	46 500
Communications	12 000
Advertising	3 000
Energy	1 500
Administration	6 500
Repairs and maintenance	500
Accommodation expenses	12 500
Depreciation	2 500
Total	85 000
Net income	16 000

Source: Trade information

Although the independent retailer can compete with the multiple and virtual intermediary on the basis of the level of personal service, the argument for raising commission rates is a strong one. Ideally, the retailer is looking to wholesalers to provide a wide range of products that are regularly being upgraded, and that are capable of generating volume sales at high margins. The difficulty is that in a competitive environment higher commission rates may simply be countered by the multiples and virtual intermediaries offering larger discounts.

THE ROLE OF THE TOUR OPERATOR/WHOLESALER

Since the dominant international leisure tourism flows are north–south to sun resorts, it is not surprising that much of the work of tour operators and wholesalers is bound up in providing single destination inclusive or package holidays. Multi-centred holidays are more common on long-haul travel where the period of stay may extend to three weeks, and there is still a buoyant market for coach tours which were the main form of package holiday before the arrival of low-priced air travel in the 1950s. The first business to introduce the modern form of package holiday was the British company Horizon (later acquired by Thomson), when, in 1957, in order to circumvent exchange controls by paying the whole price in the country of origin, it marketed combined transport and accommodation arrangements to Corsica.

At its most fundamental, tour operating is a process of combining aircraft seats and beds in hotels (or other forms of accommodation), in a manner that will make the purchase price attractive to potential holidaymakers. As we noted earlier, tour wholesalers achieve this through bulk buying which generates economies of scale that can be passed on to the customer. Despite the increasing popularity in the use of operators' web sites, the most essential link in this process remains the tour operator's brochure which communicates the holiday product to the customer. The brochure must include within it:

- illustrations which provide a visual description of the destination and the holiday;

- copy, which is a written description of the holiday to help the customer match the type of product to his or her lifestyle; and

- price and departure panels which give the specifications of the holiday for different times of the season, duration of stay and the variety of departure points.

Large tour operators and wholesalers normally sell a wide portfolio of tours and therefore have a range of brochures. For instance, there will be separate brochures for summer sun and winter sun holidays, ski holidays, long-haul travel and short breaks. Popular destinations may have tour operators' brochures dealing solely with holidays to that country or region, for example, Greece, Florida or Turkey. Research has shown that the place to visit is often the first holiday decision made by some travellers. The brochure is designed to encourage customers to buy and is often the only information they might have concerning the resort until they arrive there. However, it cannot be a comprehensive travel guide. The number of pages is limited by considerations of cost and size, and operators try to put as much detail about accommodation and resorts as they can in the space available, but in so doing, they must also conform to the legal requirements of the consumer protection legislation that exists in the country where the brochure is marketed. Clearly, the contents of the brochure must be consistent with the brand image each operator is trying to convey, as they will each be competing for the customer's attention on travel agents' brochure racks.

Principal stages of tour operating/wholesaling

Although the conceptual principles of tour operating are easy to follow – linking transport and accommodation to produce a package that can be offered in a brochure – the practicalities of the tour-operating cycle require careful planning, preparation and coordination. For example, media advertising in support of the brochure must be booked well in advance, particularly if numerous channels are to be used. The process of brochure production is initiated early on in the cycle to ensure that printing deadlines are met. There are myriad tasks to be performed, not only by separate divisions within the tour company, but also by outside contractors. The task of coordinating all these activities usually falls upon the marketing department.

Because of the complexity of organising package trips, there are tour operators and wholesalers who do not put together their own programme. They simply contract the work out to a wholesaler and pass on the bookings as they come in. An example of this are organisations known as *affinity groups*. They range from travel clubs whose members may have ethnic ties with particular countries, to professional associations who may arrange to have their meetings in different parts of the world.

Figure 12.5 presents a stylised layout of an operating cycle for a large-scale summer programme selling one million or more holidays. From initial research to the commencement of sales, the period spans some 14 months and, to first departures, 21 months. For winter programmes and short breaks, which are normally smaller in volume, the corresponding preparation periods are somewhat less. The example shown should not be taken as definitive since, by nature of the very many activities that are being performed and the differing objectives of tour companies, there will always be variances on timings; for example, spreading the season into April or curtailing it at the end of September or in mid-October.

RESEARCH

Key outcomes of research are the forecasts of overall market size and the changing patterns of holiday taking. These will assist in the selection of destinations, which in turn will be constrained by conditions of access, the extent of the tourist infrastructure and the political climate of the host country. In terms of destination choice, a specialist tour operator is able to respond far more quickly to changing market conditions than the volume or mass tour operator. The latter usually has long-term commitments to existing destinations which may include capital tied up in resorts. From destination choice, the research process will enable the operator to derive a market strategy, whereby one of four main options is possible. The first, market penetration suggests that the destination continues to appeal to existing markets with the same product but through more manipulation of the elements of the marketing mix. The second, product development suggests that the destination develops a new product to appeal to its existing market while thirdly, market development suggests that the existing destination product is targeted to new segments

ACTIVITY	Year 1					Year 2												Year 3									
	Aug	S	O	N	D	Jan	F	M	A	M	J	J	A	S	O	N	D	Jan	F	M	A	M	J	J	A	S	O
Research																											
• Review market performance	X																										
• Forecast market trends		X																									
• Select and compare new and existing destinations			X	X																							
• Determine market strategy				X	X																						
Capacity planning																											
• Tour specifications						X	X																				
• Negotiate with and contract suppliers						X	X	X																			
Financial evaluation																											
• Determine exchange rates							X																				
• Estimate future selling prices								X																			
• Finalise tour prices								X	X																		
Marketing																											
• Brochure planning and production							X	X	X	X																	
• Brochure distribution and launch									X	X																	
• Media advertising and sales promotion										X	X	X	X	X	X												
• Market stimulation											X	X	X														
Administration																											
• Recruit reservation staff									X																		
• Establish reservation system								X	X																		
• Receive reservations by telephone and viewdata							X	X	X	X	X	X	X	X	X	X	X		X	X	X	X	X	X	X	X	X
• Tour accounting and documentation							X	X	X	X	X				X	X	X		X	X	X	X	X	X	X	X	X
• Recruit resort staff								X	X	X										X							
Tour management																											
• Customer care at resort											X	X	X	X	X						X	X	X	X	X	X	X
• Customer correspondence											X	X	X	X	X							X	X	X	X	X	X
• Payment of suppliers										X	X	X	X	X							X	X	X	X	X	X	X

FIGURE 12.5 **Tour-operating cycle of an abroad summer programme**

within the wider market. Fourthly, destinations could diversify in that they develop totally new products for new markets – a strategy that brings with it slightly higher risk than the preceding three strategy options (see Ansoff 1988).

CAPACITY PLANNING

The market forecasts can be used to plan total capacity, which, together with the market strategy, will set tour specifications by type, destination and volume. Once the tour programme has been planned, negotiations for beds and aircraft or coach seats may take place. Bed contracts may take two forms: an allocation or a guarantee. An allocation operates on a sale or return basis with an appropriate release date. This type of contract is usually negotiated with medium-grade hotels and above, where opportunities for re-sale are generally easier. The risk is thus transferred from the tour operator/wholesaler to the hotelier. In turn the hotelier covers this risk by making contracts with several operators and quoting variable rates. With a guarantee, the wholesaler agrees to pay for the beds whether they are sold or not. Such a commitment naturally brings with it a cheaper rate than an allotment and is commonly applied to self-catering properties for the purpose of obtaining exclusive contracts.

Aircraft seats may be contracted in a variety of ways. The largest tour operators and wholesalers are likely to have their own airline and some airlines, particularly in the USA, also have tour wholesaling divisions or companies. In other circumstances, the tour operator may contract an aircraft for the whole season (a 'time charter'), for specified flights (a 'whole plane charter'), or purchase a block of seats on a scheduled service or a chartered airline (a 'part charter'). The use of scheduled services tends to be for specialist tours (which are often escorted) or tailor-made packages for customers. As scheduled flights are likely to work on a break-even 'load factor' of 60% or less, airlines are prepared to give good discounts for inclusive tour excursion fares.

Where an operator has contracted for a time charter, it is important to maximise the utilisation of the aircraft. The underlying principle is that charters should be operated back-to-back, namely that the plane should fly out with a new tour group and return with the previous group. Empty flights (known as 'empty legs') will arise at the beginning and end of the season, and these must be allowed for in the costing of seats. In summer the aircraft is likely to be used for three return trips or 'rotations' per day (two in winter) following the flight patterns shown in Figure 12.6. Aircraft may be used to rotate from one point of departure to a range of destinations or from a variety of departure points to one destination, or a combination of the two.

However, in the interests of protecting scheduled airlines from unfair competition through charters taking their normal traffic at peak times, aviation authorities have usually imposed operating restrictions on charter airlines. These may include the following:

- The trip must be an inclusive tour which implies the provision of accommodation as well as an airline seat.

- Airport terminals used by passengers must be the same on both the outward and return journeys.

FIGURE 12.6 **Time charter aircraft flight patterns:**
(a) 'w' pattern;
(b) radial pattern

- The air ticket must be for a round trip and is neither transferable nor part-usable in the sense that the holder may not use the return portion without having first travelled on the outbound flight.

Within the EU, competition policy dictates that such restrictions are no longer valid, for they are not appropriate to a policy of transport liberalisation or deregulation.

FINANCIAL EVALUATION

We can see from Figure 12.5 that tour operators and wholesalers have to finalise prices some eight months or more before the first tour departs. Apart from the usual hazards of forecasting so far in advance, there are several inherent risks that must be accounted for. These are:

- contracts with local suppliers are commonly made in the currency of the destination country;
- the currency for payment of airlines is usually US dollars;
- airlines maintain the right to raise prices in response to increases in aviation fuel costs; and
- alterations in dues, taxes or fees levied by governments.

Tour operators and wholesalers cover these risks (termed '**hedging**') by trying to build in anticipated changes in exchange rates for the purposes of determining tour prices and then buying forward the foreign exchange required at an agreed rate in order to meet contractual obligations, and by bringing in surcharges at the point of final billing of customers. Because the latter have proved unpopular, operators have tried to avoid their negative impact by offering no-surcharge guarantees, limiting the amount of surcharge liability, or offering cancellation options. In this context, it is worth noting that surcharges are often regulated by consumer protection legislation, as in the **EU Package Travel Directive**, which requires that latest date for price revisions (about a month before departure) must be included in the contract and that any significant alterations to the contract give the customer the right of cancellation without incurring penalties.

MARKETING

Brochure production starts several months prior to the publication date with initial agreements about printing arrangements. It is usual for the layout of the brochure to be undertaken by a specialist design studio following the guidelines laid down by the tour operator's own staff. A variety of styles may be considered before the final choice is made. Particular attention is paid to the front cover to make sure that it conveys the right message to the target market segment and to ensure that it is likely to stand out on the travel agent's brochure racks. The draft final document is scrutinised for errors and corrected, with the pricing panels being left to the last possible moment before full production, to allow for any unforeseen economic changes.

It is important for the brochure to be launched well before the summer season starts because there is a section of the market that likes to book early in order to guarantee the destination and to take advantage of any promotional prices. The pattern of brochure distribution depends on the nature of the tours being offered and a trade-off between the costs of sending to all agents in order to maximise brochure exposure and limiting the number of outlets in the knowledge that the majority of the business will come from a minority of agents. Specialist wholesalers offering high-priced trips will restrict the number of retailers and in so doing convey the message of product exclusiveness to the customer. In any event, they are unlikely to be in a position to support a large network of travel agents. For cost-effective reasons even mass tour operators limit the number of agents they appoint and, as indicated previously, very large wholesalers often have their own retail travel chain to distribute their products.

Monitoring the progress of advertising and sales campaigns is achieved through booking patterns. Typically operators are looking for capacity utilisation factors of 85–90% in order to break-even. Past experience enables wholesalers to establish reference booking patterns so as to compare actual with predicted bookings. Tour operators/wholesalers reserve the right to cancel or 'consolidate' holidays, for example, merging flights or combining itineraries and switching accommodation, if the demand take-up is insufficient. This makes it relatively easy for operators to test new products in their brochures. However, on the supply side, merging charter flights is not normally feasible for a summer programme after January because of the cost of airline cancellation charges. Large operators benefit here by having their own airline.

On the demand side, consolidation is a common source of annoyance to customers and leaves the travel agent with unenviable task of advising his or her clients of the changes. Tour operators defend this practice on the grounds that if they where unable to use cancellation or consolidation to reduce over-capacity, then the average price of a holiday would rise. Underestimating demand is less of a difficulty because there is usually some flexibility in the system for procuring extra flights and accommodation. On the other hand, tour operators protect themselves against cancellation by their clients. Refunds are normally arranged on a sliding scale, so that the cancellation of a holiday six or seven weeks before departure may only result in a lost deposit, but after that the amount of the purchase price returned falls relatively sharply to zero for a cancellation only a day or so before departure.

Owing to the negative effects of consolidation on customers and the wider impacts this may have on public relations, tour operators and wholesalers prefer to use market stimulation techniques to boost sluggish booking patterns. Such tactical marketing (as opposed to strategic) methods will depend upon the time available and may vary from increasing advertising expenditure through special discounts for booking by a certain time, to substantial price cuts some six to four weeks before departure. Critical to obtaining last-minute sales is a network of retailers linked by viewdata into the operator's own computer reservation system so that price promotions may be quickly communicated to the travelling public. Consumers, in turn, have recognised the bargains on offer and these have, over the years, encouraged later booking.

ADMINISTRATION

Owing to the seasonal nature of tour operation, the extra staff required to run the reservation system and represent the operator/wholesaler overseas are recruited and trained when needed, with only a core being employed all year. Frequently the same staff come and work for the same operator every year, which reduces the need for training.

The reservation system holds the tour operator's stock of holidays and careful attention is paid to matching the information held by the system to that contained in the brochure. Normally, travel agents make direct bookings through computer terminals in their own offices, but many agents still have to make telephone bookings, either because they are dealing with small operators who do not have electronic systems in place or there is a need for clarification of the product on offer.

TOUR MANAGEMENT

Specialist tour operators are most likely to offer escorted tours whereby a tour manager accompanies holidaymakers throughout the whole of their journey in order to oversee arrangements. For the volume package tour market, the function of the operator's resort representative is to host the tour. This involves meeting the tourists when they arrive and ensuring that the transfer procedures to the places of accommodation go smoothly. The representative will be expected to spend some time at the resort before the start of the season checking facilities, noting any variations from the brochure and, with the authority of the company, requesting discrepancies to be put right. During the holiday, the representative is required to be available to guests at the various hotels to give advice and deal with the many problems that may arise, as well as supervising (and sometimes organising) social activities and excursions.

After the holiday the operator/wholesaler will receive customer correspondence that will include compliments, suggestions and complaints. Most correspondence can be dealt with by a standard letter and justified complaints may receive a small refund. For serious complaints, national travel associations may offer arbitration services which can reconcile disputes before steps are taken to instigate legal proceedings.

Tour operator economics

We have already considered many of the economic aspects of tour operation in our discussion of the benefits of intermediation and the way in which a tour programme is put together. Essentially the mass tour operator or wholesaler relies on the economies of scale generated by bulk purchase and this in turn allows individual packages to be competitively priced to the consumer on the basis of a high take-up rate of offers made.

Once the tour operator/wholesaler is committed to a programme, the financial risks are substantial, irrespective of tactical risk avoidance strategies such as late release clauses, surcharges and consolidation. This is because most of the costs of running the programme, if it is to run at all, are unavoidable and therefore fixed. The marginal or variable costs of selling an extra holiday are very small, which accounts for the large discounts on offer for 'late-availability' trips that give the customer only a short period of notice (sometimes just a few days) before departure.

LEVERAGE

The financial structure of tour operation is illustrated in Figure 12.7. R is the revenue line which increases with the level of capacity utilisation and C_1 the total cost line attributable to running the tour programme. It may be seen that C_1 cuts the revenue and costs axis some way above the point of origin. The latter is caused by the high level of fixed costs in relation to the variable costs of tour operation. The financial term for this is a 'high operating leverage'. By way of contrast, C_2 is

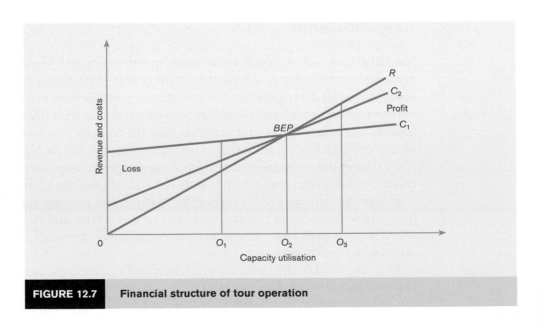

FIGURE 12.7 Financial structure of tour operation

a total cost line which has a low operating leverage: fixed costs are relatively small when compared to the steeply rising variable costs.

Consider a tour operator who is planning a break-even capacity utilisation level of O_2, but demand is such that O_3 holidays are sold. Clearly, O_3 is well above the break-even point (BEP) and so the operator makes substantial profits as shown by the difference between R and C_1. A firm that has a low operating leverage would not do so well, as can be seen from the difference between R and C_2. Conversely, if the tour operator did not manage to achieve targeted break-even sales and the realised utilisation was some way below the required level, say, O_1, the losses can be severe and may result in the collapse of the operator. We show in Figure 12.7 that a firm with a low operating leverage would not be so badly affected.

There is thus considerable financial risk associated with tour operation and this acts as a deterrent to entry. Specialist operators cover this risk by dealing with niche markets, and using scheduled airline services and high-grade hotels for which reservations may be readily cancelled if the minimum number of confirmed bookings for the tour are not met. The major tour operators address this financial risk by securing their market position through vertically integrating their operation both forwards and backwards. The **tied agency** scheme in Germany was particularly effective in allowing the large tour operators to profit from their market position. It is in the middle ground, among wholesalers who have neither their own chartered aircraft (and so must purchase a part charter) nor their own retail network, where the financial risk tends to be at its highest. These are the tour operators that are most likely to go out of business when demand falters. To safeguard the public from lost holidays or from being stranded abroad when a tour operator collapses, most governments have legislation dealing with bonding arrangements, though the fund is not always sufficient to meet the losses or extra expenses incurred.

SALES MIX

During the 1950s holiday tourism was largely centred around the traditional summer break at a coastal resort, but rising affluence, longer holiday periods and an increasing desire to travel have led to an expansion in the degree of market segmentation. Tour operators and wholesalers have responded to changing consumer preferences by diversifying their portfolio of products. This in turn has helped to spread risk and generate all-year business. Thus most major tour operators have winter and summer programmes.

Table 12.7 presents the sales mix that would be appropriate for a large European operator offering summer sun holidays to Mediterranean resorts. Most holiday movements in Europe are still towards beach destinations in summertime, though winter holidays have increased their market share in response to more frequent holiday taking. Minimum rated packages are effectively the transport cost only, with nominal accommodation provision so as to comply with the legal definitions of an inclusive tour.

PRICING

The price of an inclusive holiday in a wholesaler's brochure will be bounded above by what the market will bear and below by the cost of providing the holiday. Thus

TABLE 12.7	Sales structure of a large tour operator
Sales	**Percentages**
Summer inclusive tours	60
Winter inclusive tours	25
Minimum-rated packages	10
Excursions and insurance	4
Interest on deposits	1
Total	100

Source: Trade information

customers expect exclusive holidays to be relatively expensive and so price is used as an indicator of quality, which in turn gives the tour operator the opportunity of securing higher margins. The volume market for inclusive tours is sold competitively on price. Hence operators will consider a range offers, taking account of a number of factors, namely:

- seasonal effects – the range of variation between low- and peak-season prices is usually around 20 to 30%;

- exchange rate movements;

- competitors' prices and the degree of product differentiation;

- promotional pricing to encourage early booking and late-availability discounts;

- market segmentation pricing, with special offers for senior citizens, young people and families with children below a certain age; and

- discounts for affinity group travel.

The price structure for a typical mass market inclusive tour undertaken within Europe is shown in Table 12.8. Competition keeps profit margins low, and so the emphasis is on volume sales and cost control to sustain net income. In these circumstances, the importance of hedging on foreign exchange is readily appreciated, because uncovered fluctuations in exchange rates may easily erode slender profit margins. This does not entirely remove the risk, for the tour operator/wholesaler still has to predict the amount of business going to each destination.

TABLE 12.8	Price structure of a 14-night inclusive tour
Item	**Percentages**
Price	100
Direct costs	
Accommodation	40
Air seat (including taxes)	36
Transfers, excursions, etc.	2
Agent's commission	10
Total	88
Gross margin	12
Indirect costs	
Payroll expenses	4
Marketing	3
Office expenses	2
Total	9
Net income	
Trading profit	3
Interest on deposits	1
Total	4

Source: Trade information

AIR SEATS

For wholesalers who operate their own airlines or secure whole plane or time charters, an important element in determining the tour price is the costing of an air seat. This is calculated from the following formula:

$$s = \frac{dR}{(d-1)LN} + t$$

where s = unit seat cost per round trip, d = number of aircraft departures, R = aircraft cost per rotation, L = load factor, N = number of seats per flight and t = airport tax.

As an example, consider an aircraft of 250 seats contracted on a time charter for 30 departures. The rotation cost is calculated at 50,000 currency units, the load factor at 90% and airport tax is ascertained to be 5 currency units. By substitution into the above formula, the unit seat cost per return flight is:

$$s = \frac{30 \times 50,000}{29 \times 0.9 \times 250} + 5$$

$$= 235$$

Note that the number of departures in the denominator of the equation is reduced by 1 to allow for empty legs.

STRATEGIC POSITIONING

History has shown that while there are no major constraints on entry into travel wholesaling, the mass holiday market in any country tends to be dominated by only a handful of companies. The tour operator/wholesaler has no monopoly over airline seats or hotel beds and product standards are easy to emulate. This being the case, the lessons of success indicate strategic market positions secured by a combination of the following factors:

- economies of scale through bulk purchase and volume distribution;
- low-cost distribution network together with national coverage;
- developing new products and markets, and adopting new technologies;
- competitive pricing;
- multibranding to attract different market segments; and
- product differentiation to avoid competing on price alone.

As with major retail stores and supermarket chains, volume throughput and national presence are critical to the success of a mass tour operator. This being the case, in a European context, it is unlikely that any wholesaler can compete effectively, particularly on price, in the mass market segment with sales of under a million holidays. When account is taken of the organisation structure needed and bonding requirements of around 10% of turnover if belonging to a recognised trade association with its own reserve fund, but as much as 25% otherwise (EU Package Travel Directive), it will be appreciated that the costs of entry into the volume market do act as a considerable deterrent. However, once the volume market has been penetrated, the substantial fixed costs involved are easily transferable to rival operations.

The factors giving rise to a winning strategy are also the cause of a high degree of sales concentration in the tour operation industry, leaving small operators to create their own distinctive market share through specialised holidays. The economics of the industry are such that this situation is one that can only continue, for the large operators are prepared to defend their market position by diversifying their products, even into specialist areas, by multibranding to reach economic sales levels in particular markets quickly, by undertaking price wars and generally enforcing the success criteria outlined above.

CONCLUSION

We have used this chapter to review the way in which the individual elements of the tourism product may be packaged together for convenience and then distributed to the market efficiently. There are important variations in the way in which this procedure is executed in different regions of the world but, as a result of the predominant north–south flow in tourism, it is the northern countries of the world that have developed the most sophisticated network of distribution to satisfy the volume of market demand.

However, it is important to remember that the distribution of the tourism product is the aspect of the tourism system that has the most potential for change over the next few years as new technology permeates the marketplace and direct access to the tourism product becomes even more prevalent.

Self-check questions

1 Review and discuss the roles of travel agencies and tour operators.

2 Identify the benefits and drawbacks of further consolidation and concentration in the distribution channel in tourism.

3 Compare and contrast differences in the distribution of the tourism product between the USA and Europe.

4 Identify potential threats to the continued dominance of travel agencies and tour operators and assess the likely impact of technological progress in respect of distribution.

5 What are the implications of 'switch selling' for both the tourism intermediary and the consumer?

Essay questions

1 Critically discuss the arguments for and against dis-intermediation of the distribution channel in tourism.

2 To what extent is bonding still important in the travel industry?

3 'It is an impossible task for trade associations to represent fairly the rights of consumers when their obligations are to their members.' Discuss.

4 Critically explore the benefits and drawbacks of the adoption of a multichannel strategy for a tour operator of your choice.

5 Critically discuss the future strategic options for independent intermediaries in light of the trend toward further consolidation and concentration in the tourism industry.

Annotated further reading

Books

Buhalis, D. (2003) *eTourism: Information Technology for Strategic Tourism Management*, Pearson Education, Harlow.

This book provides an extensive overview of the digitisation of all processes and value chains in the tourism and hospitality industries. It explores in depth the impacts of information communication technology (ICT) across all tourism sectors as well as providing a useful debate as to how the application of ICT is fundamental to the future competitiveness of the tourism industry.

Buhalis, D. and Laws, E. (2001) *Tourism Distribution Channels: Practices, Issues and Transformations*, Continuum, London.

This is a very useful text which explores the nature, dynamics, interactions, and complexities of tourism distribution channels. It is extensive in its academic coverage and comprehensive with regard to its international mix of case examples.

WTO (2002) *Tourism in the Age of Alliances, Mergers and Acquisitions*, World Tourism Organization, Madrid.

A very credible account of the increasing concentration and consolidation of the global tourism industry. Detailed analysis of each sector of tourism is provided with critical discussion relating to current and future issues for each sector, including tourism intermediaries, to encourage future debate.

Web sites

www.abta.com

This very useful web site provided by the Association of British Travel Agents offers a wealth of information for the UK travel trade and consumer. With 85% of the UK's package holidays sold through ABTA members the site is comprehensive in its coverage of all aspects of travel and tourism. ABTA's Code of Conduct is a strong feature of the site as is its coverage of issues relating to arbitration, disability and financial protection.

www.travelmole.com

Travelmole provides an excellent resource base for students, academics and practitioners in travel and tourism. It contains extensive news reports on all sectors of tourism and is comprehensive and contemporary in its coverage.

www.tui.com

This corporate web site provides some valuable insights into the TUI AG organisation, its products, markets, and range of business units, and serves as an excellent resource base.

References cited

Ansoff, M.I. (1988) *The New Corporate Strategy*, Penguin, London.

Buhalis, D. (2003) *eTourism: Information Technology for Strategic Tourism Management*, Pearson Education, Harlow.

Horner, S. and Swarbrooke, J. (2004) *International Cases in Tourism Management*, Elsevier Butterworth Heinemann, Oxford.

Hudson, S., Snaith, T., Miller, G. and Hudson, P. (2001) 'Travel retailing: "switch selling" in the UK', pp. 172–84 in Buhalis, D. and Laws, E. (eds), *Tourism Distribution Channels: Practices, Issues and Transformations*, Continuum, London.

MMC (1998) *Foreign Package Holidays*, HMSO, London.

WTO (2002) *Tourism in the Age of Alliances, Mergers and Acquisitions*, World Tourism Organization, Madrid.

MAJOR CASE STUDY 12.1
MYTRAVEL GROUP PLC

MyTravel Group plc is a significant player in the market for all-inclusive holidays and other leisure travel services across the UK, Ireland, northern Europe, and North America. With its head office in Manchester in the UK, the MyTravel Group is supported with regional bases in Denmark, and Florida in the United States. At the end of 2003, the group had over 10.5 million customers, 22,000 employees, over 100 principal brands and 900 retail travel agents. The company is thus considerable in size, scope and market reach with it including also the possession of 56 aircraft, 120 resort properties (including joint ventures and associates) and 4 cruise ships.

MyTravel Group plc began life in 1972 as Airtours when its founder, David Crossland, acquired two travel agency outlets in Lancashire in the UK. Through further acquisitions and the organisation of package holidays Airtours expanded very quickly to the extent that by 1986 it was handling in the region of 290,000 customers per annum. In the same year, Airtours sold its travel agency business which, by then, comprised 21 outlets. The money generated was used to fund further expansion of the tour operating business – via strategies of horizontal and vertical integration – to the extent that it was eventually floated on the London Stock Exchange in 1987 with a market capitalisation of £28 million. Since flotation, a number of significant developments have taken place. For example between 1987 and 1995, Airtours developed Eurosites, a camping operator with sites across Europe, began short (mostly one-day trips) to major European cities, and acquired Pickfords Travel Service Limited, in addition to acquiring Hogg Robinson Leisure Travel Limited, the Aspro Travel Group, and the Tradewinds brand. Once the acquisitions were completed, Airtours launched their 'Going Places' brand which sought to bring together their retail shops under one umbrella. There then followed the introduction of a ski-based programme, followed by the acquisition of the Scandinavian Leisure Group (SLG), and their first entry into the fly/cruise market with the acquisition of the MS *Seawing* and MS *Carousel* cruising ships. After acquisition of further travel agents Airtours diversified by acquiring Late Escapes, a telephone sales business – a move that was in response to the emerging change in travel booking patterns taking place in the market. Toward the end of this period, Airtours also acquired Sunquest Vacations – one of Canada's largest tour operating businesses.

The next seven years saw yet more growth and expansion in a number of sectors. Hence, between 1996 and 2003 a strategy of acquisition continued with established names such as Sun International SA of Belgium, Cresta Holidays Limited and Bridge Travel Services Limited, both weekend break specialists, Direct Holidays Limited (as its name suggests a tour operating business specialising in the direct sell market), the Panorama Holiday Group (a specialist in Tunisia), and Travelworld, a travel agency business with outlets based in the north of England. The years 1999 and 2000 saw yet more acquisitions with a variety of European-based tour operating businesses coming into the Airtours family. Expansion further afield saw the acquisition of DriveAway Holidays Pty Limited – an Australian car-renting and leasing company – and Kemwel, a similar operation in the United States. In May 2000, an ambitious e-commerce strategy was developed, named MyTravel, including the launch of www.mytravelco.com. The wider e-commerce strategy offered a more holistic approach in that appropriate content and product features were integrated with distribution and customer relationship management. The strategy was multichannel in that customers could purchase products and services from a multitude of technology platforms with a high degree of personalisation. For example, in addition to a wide range of holidays, flight-only offers, tailor-made itineraries, charter flight tickets, cruises and numerous holiday extras, Airtours gave customers the facility to create their own personal portfolio of dream destinations. It also includes LateEscapes – a holiday auction site – virtual tours, independent hotel reviews, a magazine and world weather reports.

Perhaps the most significant change for the future was that which occurred in 2002 – the rebranding of the company name Airtours plc to MyTravel plc. This move incorporated the development of a multichannel distribution capability with MyTravel.com in the UK, Scandinavia and America. Thus, the new e-commerce strategy served as the driver for the new group company name – MyTravel Group plc – the e-developments driving organisational change. This period also saw the launch of MyTravel Lite – the group's low-fare airline and the first UK budget airline used by a UK tour operator – and the rebranding of the Airtours international and premier fleets to MyTravel Airways. Flying from Birmingham, Manchester and London Gatwick in the UK, MyTravel Lite destinations across Europe include Paris, Alicante, Amsterdam, Barcelona, Malaga, Murcia, Palma, Faro, Pisa and Tenerife.

Quite clearly expansion over the past two decades has been considerable to the extent that MyTravel is estimated to control in the region of 17% of the package holiday market in the UK alone. Through its constant acquisition of related businesses and ambitious plans for development MyTravel is a considerable player in the marketplace – its wide portfolio of brands bringing it tremendous power in the marketplace, particularly in Europe.

However, more recent developments have served as a cause for some concern in that a number of overly optimistic forecasts led to a financial crisis to the extent that in 2003, the company reported a loss of £358.3 million after making a loss of £20.4 million in 2002. As a consequence of the loss in 2002, a wave of bad publicity emanated from the press and in turn, many people withheld bookings for fear that the company would suffer financial collapse, thus making the summer 2003 period particularly challenging. In order to rectify the situation as much as possible a number of measures were implemented. First, the chair of the board of directors – David Crossland – retired, and a number of other directors left their posts. Second, the company decided to re-focus on its core business and divested a number of its related businesses. Third, a considerable cost-cutting strategy was implemented – which included redundancies – and a reduction in capacity in the tour operation business took place in light of very difficult trading conditions and the considerable pressure to offer heavy discounts on a vast array of products.

For the future, as the results for 2003 show, the outlook for MyTravel is perhaps a little uncertain as the share price remains low, the environment for travel and tourism is beset with uncertainty, and re-establishing confidence with customers, the industry and investors alike has perhaps proved more challenging than was originally thought. The fact that the 2003 loss excludes £26.9 million for goodwill amortisation and an exceptional operating item of £373.9 million has not helped matters. This said, a number of measures are continuing apace. These include further revisions of previous accounting estimates and an improvement in management information and control systems. Due to the severity of the losses a number of business units are continuing to be sold with disposals in the United States already bringing in around $250 million in much-needed cash to the company. One problem remains, however, lower bookings and significant pressure on margins for the bookings being made. A reduction in the size of aircraft fleet is being planned as is a reduction in the number of cruise ships belonging to the group and the portfolio of guaranteed beds – all in an attempt to reduce risk levels.

In many ways, MyTravel Group plc is experiencing a 'reality check' after the heady growth days of the 1990s and the combined impact of severe external events such as SARS and 9/11 and a loss of internal management control, whereby the very existence of the company was clearly threatened. One thing is guaranteed for the future of MyTravel – change will continue to occur and the outcome of such changes is more likely to remain uncertain in the short to mid-term. That said, the dramatic climb and 'wobble' of the company in recent years serves as an excellent example of the dynamics and complexities of travel and tourism intermediation in an environment which is far from stable.

Source: Horner and Swarbrooke, 2004; www.mytravelgroup.com *(accessed 12 February 2004); MyTravel Group PLC Annual Report & Accounts 2003*

REFERENCE

Horner, S. and Swarbrooke, J. (2004) *International Cases in Tourism Management*, Elsevier Butterworth Heinemann, Oxford.

DISCUSSION QUESTIONS

1 To what extent is the pattern of growth of MyTravel Group PLC typical of other large travel companies throughout the world?

2 What are the benefits and drawbacks of adopting multichannel distribution strategies for tourism companies such as MyTravel?

3 How compatible is the launch of its very own 'no frills' airline 'MyTravel Lite' with its other airline and tour operations business?

CHAPTER THIRTEEN
TRANSPORTATION

INTRODUCTION

Tourism is about being elsewhere and, in consequence, the main function of transport in the tourism system is one of transit, carrying tourists between generating regions and the tourist destination regions. This relationship has traditionally been regarded as 'chicken and egg'. Adequate transportation infrastructure and access to generating markets is one of the most important prerequisites for the development of any destination. In most cases mass tourism has been developed in areas where extensive transportation networks were in place and the potential for further development was available. The fact that in most destinations worldwide, the traveller can find adequate hospitality and leisure facilities close to transportation terminals demonstrates this point.

On the other hand, tourism demand has stimulated the rapid development of transportation. As millions of tourists expect to be transported safely, quickly and comfortably to their destinations at a reasonable cost, the transportation industry has had to adjust in order to accommodate this increased, and also more sophisticated, demand. In response, technology has allowed new vehicles with improved speeds and operating efficiencies to develop.

In this chapter we provide a framework for the analysis of passenger transportation operations for tourism. We explore the modes and elements of transportation, examine issues such as regulation of transport and its environmental impacts, and perform a competitive analysis for the major modes of transportation. Finally, the chapter illustrates the major future political, environmental and economic trends that are expected to influence tourist transportation.

LEARNING OUTCOMES

The primary objective of this chapter is to demonstrate the importance of transportation to the overall tourism product and to illustrate their interdependence. Transport is responsible not only for physically moving demand for tourism to supply regions, but also for transporting tourists once they arrive at the destination. With this in mind, on completion of this chapter, you will have:

- an understanding of the major modes of transportation for tourism and the competitive advantages and disadvantages of each;

- an appreciation of the influence of political developments on transportation for tourism;

- a knowledge of the purpose and impact of regulation in transportation;

- an awareness of issues and future trends that will have an impact upon transportation for tourism; and

- an understanding of transport as a tourist attraction.

TRANSPORT AS A COMPONENT OF THE TOURIST PRODUCT

Transportation is an essential element of the tourist product in three ways:

- the means to reach the destination;

- a necessary means of movement at the destination; and

- in a minority of instances it is the actual tourism attraction or activity.

Transport as transit

By far the most important contribution of transport is as a means of transit, which accounts for 90% of tourist use of transport. It is a derived demand, which is not undertaken for its own sake but merely as a means of getting from the tourism-generating region to the tourism destination. This can produce significant operational difficulties because the transport operator has little control over the demand for such services. The busiest tourism routes are those linking originating regions, which display high levels of income and leisure time with popular tourist destinations. For example, there remain large traffic flows between affluent countries of northern Europe and countries with Mediterranean resorts in southern Europe. The future prospects for such routes are more a function of the relative affluence of the former and the relative attractiveness of the latter than they are of any actions taken by the transport operator. Furthermore, tourism is a fragile industry and traffic flows can undergo significant change instantaneously as a result of a natural catastrophe, conflict or instance of political instability such as displayed by the fall in transatlantic air travel in the immediate aftermath of events post-September 11, 2001 (**9/11**).

Not only is the size of demand outside the control of the transport operator, so to are the patterns of demand. The derived nature of transport demand means that factors such as climate, restrictions to vacation entitlement from work, religious festivals and the dates of school holidays all influence when the demand for tourism transport occurs creating peaks and troughs. For cold-climate regions such as northern Europe there are clear periods of peak-seasonal demand from June to mid-August, but within this pattern there are more subtle peaks, particularly day-of-the-week peaks. In many destinations such as the UK, Denmark or the ski resorts of the Alpine region of North Tyrol and Salzburg there is a preference to travel on Saturdays for main holidays, heavily influenced by accommodation providers, many of which only accept Saturday-to-Saturday bookings. The growth of short-weekend break holidays has contributed to Friday travelling peaks on some modes of transport.

The potential operational problems of these peak periods of demand are created because like many service industries, transport production cannot be stored, it is consumed at the point of production. Therefore to meet demand at peak periods the transport operator has to provide extra capacity which may then be under utilised during the **off-peak** periods. If one is not careful serving peak demand can become unprofitable. Transport operators must take care to ensure the revenue earned (which could be over a relatively short peak period) exceeds the full costs of providing the capacity, including all fixed costs, which are incurred over the whole year. The most commonly cited examples of **peak** capacity are related to fleet size. Coach companies, rail operators and airlines all have potential for the fleet size to be determined by the peak season with some vehicles not really required to meet off peak demand. However, the operational problems extend to other elements of the transport system such as the terminal. For example, Palma Airport (Majorca), has three passenger terminals, but only fully utilises all three during the peak summer season (and indeed only on certain peak days of the week during this season); one of the terminals is mothballed for the off-peak winter season.

Transport operators have powers to generate or increase levels of demand or even influence patterns of demand, although only marginally. Their most powerful tool is price. For instance, very low prices can be used to generate or stimulate extra demand during the off-peak period. Nevertheless, very low fares to Majorca in January may well increase demand for air services during that off-peak month, but it will not generate passenger numbers to match those of the peak period and with the low fares, overall yields will, of course, be low. Operators can also charge higher fares for peak days of demand to reduce fluctuations. UK rail operators have higher leisure fares for travel on Fridays and many charter airlines in Europe have traditionally charged higher fares for Saturday travel.

Despite being a derived demand, transport for transit can be viewed as part of the leisure experience with the journey being important for some categories of visitor. The view from the coach or the excitement of flying are examples of potential enjoyment. However, for the business traveller, transport may be seen as a necessary evil and is associated with a frictional element. The degree to which travel is part of the leisure experience has been analysed as some form of continuum. It is dependent upon:

- the mode of transport (some modes are intrinsically more enjoyable than others);
- the personality of the tourist;
- the frequency with which the tourist uses that mode;
- the group with whom one travels (supervising young children will, for instance, add stress to the journey).

However, increases in traffic flows have resulted in increased congestion contributing to unscheduled and unacceptable levels of delay which it is argued has reduced the pleasure of travelling for a range of modes from driving (still often portrayed as a pleasure activity by motoring manufacturers in their advertising campaigns) to air travel, and while still very rare, instances of air rage and road rage are increasing.

Transport at the destination

Once at the destination, visitors make use of taxis, rental cars, scheduled bus and coach services, and rail and, dependent on the destination, even ferries. For longer excursions where the country is seen as the destination area scheduled domestic air

463

may be used and rail may increase in significance. Travel in the destination area accounts for around 10% of tourist use of transport. This, of course, involves tourists sharing scheduled local transport services, which were not specifically designed for their use, with the local population. Sometimes this provides an ideal fit with the two markets complementing each other. This is true of tourism to major cities such as Amsterdam, Helsinki, Boston, and Brisbane where tourism demand for bus and metro services tends to commence after 9.30–10.00 a.m. when the peak period of local use for commuting to work is over. Therefore tourists provide an opportunity for the transport operator to earn additional revenue at a time when there is spare capacity. Special product developments such as off-peak travelcards allow unlimited travel but only after the morning peak. This can help the operator control and manage this division, although some conflicts between local and tourist use during the early evening peak may be unavoidable. In other locations there can be conflicts between tourist and local requirements. The vintage bus fleet in Malta is more suited to tourists than the local population whereas ticketing policy does not reflect the needs of tourist users well. Visitor expenditure figures illustrate the importance of transport as an element of the product. Transport at the destination can represent as much as 15% of international visitor expenditure within a large country such as Indonesia.

Some transport operators in destination areas tailor products specifically for tourism such as the half-day and whole-day coach excursion to attractions in the surrounding region. Sightseeing tours on the top of a double-deck bus with the roof removed are familiar sights in many destination areas, particularly cities. Having first begun in capital cities such as London, the concept has over recent years expanded and in 2001 Guide Friday, the largest operator of such tours, were operating in 30 UK destinations and 7 European destinations (Robbins, 2003). A more recent development pioneered in the US are 'Duck Tours' which undertake a sightseeing tour using a Second World War amphibious landing craft, with a short water-based section included on the tour route. These tours do give the tourist mobility around the destination area and on the bus tours tickets are valid all day so one can hop on and off. However, for many the vehicle itself becomes the attraction and perhaps they rightly fall under the next section.

Transport as the tourist attraction

Increasingly, there are instances of transport, both within and between countries, becoming an attractive tourist product in its own right. The largest mass market is the cruise industry (see the Major case study at the end of this chapter). Other examples include:

- railway products – the Palace on Wheels (India), the Blue Train (South Africa), the Orient Express and the Eastern & Oriental Express;
- sea products – day trips by ferry in the Baltic Sea and across the English Channel;
- canal cruises in a narrow boat.

MODE OF TRANSPORT

The most obvious way of analysing transport is by mode. There are four major modes of travelling:

- road;
- water;
- rail;
- air.

The choice of mode of transport by the visitor is related to purpose of travel. Table 13.1 provides an indicative structure for modal choice. Furthermore, the visitor's choice of mode of transport is affected by:

- distance and time factors;
- status and comfort;
- safety and utility;
- comparative price of services offered;
- geographical position and isolation;
- range of services offered; and
- level of competition between services.

The relative importance of these major influences upon modal choice will vary from one visitor type to another although visitor types are no longer as homogeneous as previously assumed; some inclusive tour passengers will elect to travel business class by scheduled air rather than by charter and a significant percentage of passengers using low cost airlines are business passengers. Mini case studies 13.1 and 13.2 analyse modal choice decisions.

Increasingly transport operators are attempting to identify segments of demand for which specific categories of service will appeal. In Europe coaches now offer degrees of comfort and service unheard of in the 1970s, while ferry companies have become expert in organising a range of centred or varied itineraries for motorists holidaying overseas with their own car.

TABLE 13.1   Mode of transport and visitor type with examples of product types

Visitor type	Road		Air		Sea/water		Railways
	Car	Coach	Scheduled	Charter	Ferry	Cruise	
Holiday – inclusive tour	Car hire Fly drive	Coach tour	Packages – long haul – city break	Medium/short-haul packages	Ferry package	World cruise	Orient Express
– independent	Touring private car	Scheduled coach	Self-packaging – Internet – low-cost carrier	Seat only to – villa – time-share	Private car		7- or 14-day ticket
Business and conference	Company car	Executive coach	Fully flexible fare		High-speed catamaran		TGV or Bullet Train
VFR	Private car	Scheduled service	Cheapest fare		Private car		Excursion fare
Other special and common interest, e.g. religion	Car hire Private car	Coach charter	Cheap or flexible fare	Group travel			Group fare
Same-day visitors (excursion)	Private car	Scheduled excursion fare	Scheduled excursion fare	Special flights	Coach/car excursion	Local day cruise	Day excursion fare

MINI CASE STUDY 13.1
Differences in travel time and modes of travel – Thailand

BANGKOK TO SELECTED LOCATIONS IN THAILAND

Bangkok to	Distance one way (kms)	Airfare scheduled carrier US$	Airfare low-cost or budget carrier US$	Rail fare US$	Coach fare US$
Chiang Mai	569	50–63	20–41	32	16
Khon Kaen	369	35–44	18–33	25	10
Phuket	693	58–72	23–44	N/A	19
Hat Yai	773	65–81	26–44	36	21

TIME TO TRAVEL ONE WAY ACCORDING TO MODE

	Air	Rail	Coach
Bangkok–Chiang Mai	70 mins	12 hrs	10 hrs
Bangkok–Khon Kaen	55 mins	7 hrs	6 hrs 30 mins
Bangkok–Phuket	70 mins	–	13 hrs
Bangkok–Hat Yai	90 mins	14 hrs	14 hrs

Notes:
1 Air fares based on one-way economy service; conditions may vary according to fare paid but taxes included.
2 Coach fare normally offers a reclining seat on a luxury bus.
3 Train is air-conditioned with a berth on an overnight service.
Sources: Carriers' published materials

The above tabulation shows the time to travel to selected destinations in Thailand by the different modes of travel available. Domestic travel within countries is characterised by significant differences between modes. These differences can be of the order of a ratio of 10 to 1 when comparing air with rail/and or road although such comparisons do not take account of travel time from the city centre to the airport whereas road and rail termini are usually located in city centres. A one-hour journey by air may involve up to two additional hours given check-in, travel to/from the airport, and baggage reclaim time. Travel by air from the capital city in a country to various regional centres is often undertaken by the national or state carrier and governments often see it as a necessary service for regional development.

Rail and road services which compete with air will vary from country to country but will depend on the infrastructure of track and highway provided by public authorities. Normally the competitor rail and road services will be cheaper than air but will be slower over large distances especially for locations in excess of 1,000 km from the point of origin. The emergence of low-cost air carriers in countries such as Thailand may change these traditional distance, time and cost relationships.

Prior to the year 2000 there was little competition between domestic air carriers in Thailand with the state carrier Thai Airways predominant and expensive. Bangkok Airways was the main alternative air operator especially to holiday islands like Koh Samui. It has developed a reputation as a 'boutique carrier' offering service in excess of its rivals but also charging premium fares on the routes that it monopolised.

Changes occurred in the early part of this decade partly as a result of deregulation of certain industries in Thailand in response to World Trade Organization pressures, and partly from pressures from other international agencies involved in the restructuring of the Thai economy post the Asian financial collapse of the late 1990s. The restructuring and consideration of privatisation of the state carrier Thai Airways was also taking place. There were pressures to open up certain destinations outside of Bangkok such as Chiang Mai and to make it a regional hub for business and tourism for the Mekong group of countries. Low-cost air operations that developed in Australia and Malaysia were examples that could easily be followed in Thailand (see Mini case study 13.2).

Apart from the Thai government's encouragement for new carriers to develop in the regions and between these and surrounding countries, there has been the development of Orient Thai Airlines known as 'One Two Go' who as an alternative domestic carrier have tried to introduce innovative marketing tools, such as:

- a smart card topped up with cash but increased in value for frequent users/flyers;

- turn up and fly; and

- booking using smart technology at shopping centres as well as on the Internet;

Low-cost flights are seen no different than turning up for a coach trip. For example, Air Asia which developed in Malaysia, has a Thai subsidiary and the innovative pricing of tickets makes alternatives of travel by train or coach seem unattractive in terms of the time and convenience. The alternatives before this new era of domestic competition were not attractive. Apart from the Eastern and Oriental Express, the luxury train form Singapore to Thailand running through Malaysia, the alternatives by normal train are not attractive either domestically or on an international basis. Bangkok–Chiang Mai by train can take 12 to 14 hours but by air just over an hour.

Express buses and minibuses have been in use in Thailand for some time and a high proportion of domestic travellers will take this mode of transport especially at times of national holidays and festivals because it is traditional and it is the cheapest mode.

DISCUSSION QUESTIONS

1 What are the main factors affecting modal choice for tourism journeys?

2 What barriers exist to the development of mass travel by air within a country or region?

3 How might railway and coach companies respond to increased competition from low-cost domestic air operators?

COMPONENTS OF THE TRANSPORT SYSTEM

We can identify four basic elements in any transport system, namely:

- the way;
- the terminal;
- the vehicle; and
- the motive power.

These elements vary for each transportation mode but performance is dependent on the interaction of these four elements. Speed, capacity, safety, security and even perceived quality of service for each mode is dictated by the weakest element in the system.

The way

The way is the medium of travel over which the vehicle operates. It may be purely artificial such as roads and railways; or natural, such as air or water. Railways and inland waterways restrict vehicles to movement, very specific patterns, or pathways while road offers a much greater degree of vehicle flexibility over the route network. At first sight, air and sea would appear to allow unlimited flexibility but international regulations and conventions dictate otherwise. Significant areas of airspace over a country are reserved solely for military use and the civil airspace is delineated into air corridors and controlled by **air traffic control (ATC)** systems utilising sophisticated computer systems and comprehensive radar coverage. Likewise, although less rigorous, there are designated shipping lanes. In considering transport modes, the availability of the way is very important and requires considerable investment. A shortage in capacity leads to inefficient services, congestion and unscheduled delays. Currently in the UK congestion on the rail network has led the **Strategic Rail Authority (SRA)** to reduce the number of services on some routes in an attempt to improve reliability. In contrast, mainland Europe, where land is at less of a premium, has expanded rail capacity with the addition of new high-speed lines. Capacity overload on the ATC system can result in planes having to circle busy airports for significant amounts of time awaiting a landing slot. Traffic congestion on roads is a phenomenon familiar to many in developed and developing countries.

The terminal

Public transport terminals give the passenger access to the vehicle, or act as an interchange between different modes of transport. Not all modes need to have sophisticated terminals, buses and coaches for instance can and do operate from roadside locations although town and city centre terminals are often more substantive. Perhaps the most complex terminal is an airport and the dramatic growth in air transport worldwide has witnessed the development of many new airports in recent years (Hong Kong, Kuala Lumpur and Athens).

In fact, most terminals are becoming integrated transportation points as they can act as interchanges where travellers can transfer between vehicles or modes. Switzerland has examples of integrated rail and air transport with rail termini at the airports of Zurich and Geneva further linked to main rail routes and then the post-bus to the final destination. Airports can be used as transfer points between aircraft, often organised into the well-structured patterns of arrival and departures required for hub airports in the hub and spoke route networks initially developed

PHOTOGRAPH 13.1 Heathrow Airport, Terminal 5 is a £4 billion investment set to open in spring 2008. As well as the core terminal building there will be two further satellites, extensions to the Heathrow Express and Piccadilly Line, a multistorey car park and a hotel. Terminal 5 will cater for 30 million passengers annually and is set to house the entirety of British Airways' operation at Heathrow   *Source: BAA, Artist's Impression*

in the deregulated US domestic market, but also must interface with other modes of travelling, such as the car, coach or train.

The design of terminals and the amenities they offer depend heavily upon the type of journey and mode of transportation involved, as does the length of time spent at the terminal. Air will generally require the longest visit with arrival at the airport required one to two hours (or even longer where security measures dictate) prior to scheduled departure. Travellers will also tend to allow excess time for infrequently undertaken long-distance rail journeys whereas arrival will be just in time for shorter frequent and familiar rail journeys such as commuting. The basic requirement is for toilet facilities and light refreshment although the long time the passenger is held as a captive customer creates retail opportunities which airport terminals seek to exploit fully with up to 60% of airport revenue from retail activity. This share appears to be falling in European airports following the abolition of duty-free sales for passengers travelling within the EU in June 1999 (Graham, 2003). Main line city centre terminals for intercity rail traffic have also sought to exploit retail opportunities (Liverpool Street and Victoria Stations in London).

For private transport such as the car there is still a requirement for the user to access the vehicle and for the vehicle to access the way although there is no designated terminal where this must happen. The relative importance of the terminal is often and easily overlooked. The comfort and convenience of the journey can be influenced as much by the experience at the terminal as by the experience on the vehicle. Airlines seek to gain a competitive advantage for high-yield first- and business class passengers with the use of **VIP** lounges. Airports also demonstrate the importance of the terminal in the capacity of the overall transport network. All terminals need sufficient capacity for both vehicular movements and also for passenger movement. In the case of the airport these activities are separated. The vehicle movements are airside, predominantly measured as **air traffic movements** (ATMs) and catered for by runways (together with the capacity of ATC). The use and availability of taxiways, the number of parking stands for planes and the number of exit points on the runway for smaller planes that do not need the full length of the runway, all dictate the number of ATMs an airport can handle each hour. Shortage of capacity to meet forecast demand at London airports in 2015 (DETR, 1997) led to the proposals set out in the aviation paper of December 2003 to develop a second runway at London Stansted followed by a possible third runway at London Heathrow (DFT, 2003a).

Passenger capacity is a function of the terminal facilities to handle the passengers carried by the ATMs. Essential facilities include check-in, baggage handling and baggage reclaim, passport, immigration and customs controls as well as the shopping and refreshment facilities. Since 1985 virtually all increases in airport capacity in London have been achieved by the development of more terminals. However, squeezing more capacity into airports brings its own problems. Maximum runway throughput can only be achieved with queuing aircraft (on the ground for take-off and in stacks for landing) which itself affects reliability (Graham, 2003). Airlines publish longer scheduled flight times to allow for the delays in an attempt to retain punctually and yet despite this over 25% of flights from many European airports such as Madrid, Rome, Paris (Charles de Gaulle – CGG – and Orly) as well as London are over 15 minutes late. The position in the USA is equally difficult with congestion well documented. Additional runway capacity will be a major requirement in many destinations if growth rates are to be maintained.

The vehicle

The carrying unit is the actual transportation medium: the vehicle that facilitates the movement. The nature of vehicles has been influenced by numerous factors, which include travel demand, and technological developments, as well as the other elements of the mode, particularly motive power. In the past few decades developments have occurred in the carrying units which have enabled greater speed which usually, but not always, resulted in greater efficiency and sometimes improved consumer comfort. Executive style coaches with on-board services, airline-style reclining seats on trains and railway-viewing cars and flat seats in airline business class are all examples of improved comfort.

The motive power

Finally, and perhaps the most important, motive power is the key element in transportation development. Natural power of horse-drawn carriages and sailing vessels provided the initial energy for transportation. The exploration of steam power provided the opportunity for the radical introduction of steam ships and railways which were such a driving force behind the creation of mass tourism in Europe while the internal combustion engine stimulated the development of road and air transportation. Finally, jet propulsion enabled air transportation to be competitively priced and gave aircraft both speed, range and increased vehicle size. The combination of speed (which allowed the vehicle to make more return trips each 24 hours) and increased vehicle size dramatically reduced operating costs per seat km (Doganis, 2002) enabling these savings to be passed on to the consumer in the form of lower fares. Not all technological advances led to increased efficiency. Concorde, which was withdrawn from passenger service in 2003, had relatively poor productivity despite its very high speed, largely as a result of the low vehicle capacity (approximately 100 seats) and was only viable operating predominantly a business service with a premium fare. Likewise, the hovercraft offered high-speed sea crossings but a combination of high fuel consumption and poor reliability in rough weather prevented its development into the mass mode that was predicted in the 1960s.

Speed of travel has largely stabilised in the last decade with no major technological advances. Naturally the speed for any mode is governed by the interaction of the various components. Cars can move faster than 70 mph (100 km per hour) but limitations of the way mean that maximum speed limits are required for the safety of other road users (both car drivers and, where there is no segregation, pedestrians, cyclists and so forth). The rail industry even more clearly demonstrates the limitations the way imposes on vehicle speeds. Most of the alignment of the national rail networks date back to the nineteenth century when they were constructed. Whilst new high-speed rail vehicles have developed, this technology, pioneered by the **Train de Grande Vitesse** (TGV) network in France, cannot be adopted onto existing track due to track alignment and particularly the angle of bends. The solution of matching the vehicle speed to the way is to build a new high-speed rail link as adopted with the development of the TGV in France, and copied in much of Europe including very recently the UK with the opening of the first phase of the High-Speed Channel Tunnel rail link in 2003. Attempts to run faster trains over existing track is a much more technologically difficult project, although the development of tilting trains, first attempted by the ill-fated **advanced passenger train** (APT) project in the UK in the early 1980s, is now coming to fruition with Virgin Trains. Amtrak's attempts to introduce high-speed trains in the US market, where rail has a significantly lower share than Europe, has run into technical difficulties although the journey time from New York to Boston has been reduced from five hours to four.

Vehicle size has also stabilised in the last decade for most modes, although the economies of scale achieved by bigger cruise vessels has seen the introduction of increasingly large vessels (see Major case study). There have been no major advances on plane size, the latest Boeing 747–400 series has a longer range but carries a similar number of passengers as previous models, although development of a larger long-haul jet is now underway. In fact, there is a fundamental difference of opinion between the two main manufacturers. While Boeing have dropped their project for a larger plane on the grounds that the trend in large deregulated markets such as the US domestic market is for airlines to offer more frequent services with smaller planes, the European Airbus consortium have developed the super-jumbo A380 with a planned capacity of 555 passengers in tri-class seating (more if limited to one-class economy-type seating), for introduction in 2005 with an 800-seater plane on the drawing board. They see the new plane as valuable to airlines flying on heavily trafficked routes and that continued capacity problems at many airports make it attractive to many airlines. Over the last 20 years the emphasis has been on developing larger medium-sized jets such as the Boeing 767, the 777 and the various airbuses. Boeing have settled for their 7E7 named the Dreamliner to come into service in the year 2008 – it will have no more than 250 seats but will be 20% more fuel efficient than current competitor models. The major developments in motive power and vehicle technology are illustrated in Table 13.2.

The recent history of transport for tourism is characterised by changes in technology but the emphasis is moving to more environmental considerations. Engine technology has resulted in more fuel-efficient engines helping to reduce emissions including greenhouse gasses (CO^2). Car engine efficiency has improved by 1.5% per annum (Royal Commission on Environmental Pollution, 1994) and the rate of technical progress is accelerating (RAC Foundation, 2002). The last two decades have seen quieter engines, particularly in the case of aircraft, where new EU regulations regarding noise emissions are being phased in.

The development of fuel-efficient technology has been encouraged by the rising cost of fuel caused by a number of major incidents:

1 In 1973–74 the Arab–Israeli War.

2 In 1978–79 the Iranian crisis.

3 In 1991 the Gulf War.

4 War in Afghanistan in 2001.

5 War in Iraq in 2003.

Air charter operators and low-cost carriers now need to use new fleet rather than, as in the early 1970s, second-hand older equipment. Indeed, airline operations illustrate the changing cost structure over time and this can be seen by considering fuel as a percentage of operating costs; in 1973 for international scheduled

473

474

TABLE 13.2   **The historical development of tourism: recent changes in transport**

	1930s	1940s–1950s	1960s–1970s	1980s–1990s	2000 on
Air	Civil aviation established. Travel is expensive and limited.	Propeller technology. Travel still limited. Basic terminals. 400–480 km/h.	Jet aircraft. Boeing 707. Cheap fuel. 800–950 km/h. Charters take off.	Wide-bodied jet 747. Extended range. Fuel efficient. No increases in speed except Concorde.	Concorde withdrawn. Megacarriers emerge of 500–800 seats. More fuel-efficient carriers – Boeing Dreamliner.
Sea	Ocean liners and cruises. Short sea ferry speed less than 40 km/h.	Little competition from air. No increase in speed.	Air overtakes sea on N. Atlantic. Hovercraft and faster craft being developed.	Fly-cruise established. Larger and more comfortable ferries. Fast catamarans developed.	Even larger cruise ships such as *Queen Mary II.*
Road	Cars 55 km/h. Coaches develop.	Cars 100 km/h.	Cars used for domestic tourism. Speed 115 km/h.	Speed limits in USA. Rise in car ownership rates. Urban congestion. Green fuel. Improved coaches.	LPG-powered and hybrid vehicles.
Rail	Steam era. Speed exceed cars.	Railways at peak.	Electrification. Cuts in rail systems: some resorts isolated.	High-speed networks develop in Europe. Business products offered – memorabilia and steam.	Even faster trains to 300 kph.

services, fuel accounted for 12% of total costs but rose beyond 25% by 1980. With the introduction of fuel-efficient aircraft during the ensuing decade, this item of variable cost was reduced; in 1989 fuel accounted for 14% of all costs and currently ranges between 10% and 20% of total costs.

A COMPETITIVE ANALYSIS

Modern passenger transportation is a very complex and competitive industry. This competition is expressed between the various modes and vehicles of transportation, between different companies and even between countries.

In this section we provide a competitive analysis of transportation modes, based on consumer behaviour variables. These variables have been identified as:

- safety;
- price/cost;
- time/speed;
- distance;
- convenience;
- departure and arrival times;
- reliability;
- availability;

- flexibility;
- service quality;
- comfort/luxury;
- incentives;
- ground services;
- terminal facilities and locations;
- status and prestige;
- enjoyment of trip.

Road transport

The car dominates road transport, which is almost the perfect tool for tourist use offering the following attractions:

- the control of the route and the stops en route;
- the control of departure times;
- door-to-door flexibility;
- the ability to carry baggage and equipment easily;
- the ability to use the vehicle for accommodation in the case of recreational vehicles and caravans;
- privacy;
- the freedom to use the automobile once the destination is reached; and
- the low perceived cost.

Some nations tend to utilise a car much more than others for recreation and tourism. This is, in part, dependent on levels of economic development which itself influences levels of car ownership among the population but also is dependent upon geography (average distances travelled for tourist trips), climate and the cost, quality and availability of alternatives. Nevertheless, the car share is very high in developed countries. Trips by car account for approximately 90% of the pleasure/personal and business trips taken by Canadian and US residents, for almost 60% of the total holiday trips in Europe and over 70% of all UK domestic holiday trips.

Growth rates of traffic over the last 50 years have been phenomenal. For instance, in the UK the modal share of the car for all journey purposes has grown from 35% of all passenger kilometres in 1955 to 85% by 2002 (DFT, 2003b). However, over the same period both disposable time and disposable income have increased resulting in far more travel overall so the increase in vehicle kilometres is eight-and-a-half-fold. Likewise traffic volume in the USA increased by 76% between 1980–2000. The leisure and tourism share of all this traffic is not insubstantial. Around 13% of all passenger kilometres are accounted for by holiday trips but daytrip excursions and appropriate VFR traffic would increase the 'tourism' share to nearly 30% of all kilometres.

These dramatic growth rates of car use are now considered unsustainable by governments in many developed countries as car users are imposing huge costs on others which they do not directly pay for (termed '**externalities**'). The contribution of cars to greenhouse gas emissions is high at around 20% (RAC Foundation, 2002) and growing despite improving engine efficiency. They also affect local air quality and produce VOCs which are linked to asthma and other respiratory complaints, generate huge costs to society in terms of congestion, road accidents and the sheer visual intrusion of large numbers of vehicles can reduce the attractiveness of tourist destinations, most particularly popular rural locations such as national parks.

Traffic growth rates in developing countries may be even higher if high rates of economic growth are coupled with significant population growth. Ironically higher levels of car ownership can be seen as proof of economic success by governments and yet the externalities of car use are equally as problematic.

The UK government has set out a number of policies at least to reduce the rate of traffic growth if not to see absolute traffic levels fall (DETR, 1998) but recent developments have seen the concept of road pricing, charging the motorist directly for using the most congested parts of the road network at the most congested times, gain ground. The introduction of congestion charging for a central core area of London between 7.00–18.30 on weekdays in February 2003 has attracted international attention. While it is not the first road-pricing scheme, schemes such as road pricing in Singapore pre-date it, it is the first on this scale. Early results have exceeded expectations with traffic falls of 18% and congestion reduced by 30% over the first year of operation. Stockholm plans to trial a similar scheme from 2005.

Other forms of road pricing are aimed at long-distance travel in the form of motorway/autobahn/interstate highway tolls. They have a relatively long history in Europe and the USA and were introduced in the UK for the first time in 2003 (M6 Toll) and again increases in the level of charges can be used as a tool to manage traffic growth. Both forms of road pricing have the advantage of narrowing the price advantage of the car over other forms of public transport by placing a greater element of car-use costs at the point of use. Currently the point-of-use cost of a car is very low (petrol costs plus, perhaps, a little extra for vehicle maintenance) and the price advantage is enhanced for family groups of three–five people. However, if the cost of car travel rises too steeply, there are fears that tourism growth rates may slow or even move into decline.

The coach

In many developed countries the scheduled bus and coach networks have seen significant decline of passenger numbers. However, the coach still plays a role in the tourism market divided into three sectors. First, scheduled long-distance coaches are used as an alternative usually to rail or car to travel to the destination although long-distance coach services in the USA (for instance, Greyhound & Trailways) are in direct competition with air. This mode is particularly useful for short and medium-distance journeys. It has traditionally attracted the elderly and inexpensive markets and the stereotype is of the lower occupational or social groups and the over-50s market. Beyond a certain threshold distance, lack of comfort and the relatively slower speed compared with other modes has to be traded-off against cheaper and more attractive pricing structures. The coach network is more dense than the rail network offering more destinations and can be quicker than rail in areas where there has been investment in new roads versus an aging rail system (northern Portugal). For some destinations it may be the only public transport alternative.

The second sector is the coach tour. Again the market traditionally attracts an over-50s' market, but often from higher socio-economic groups and attracting passengers from car-owning households. The break from driving, the scenic views from the coach and the social interaction with the other coach passengers are all attractions for this type of holiday.

The third sector is the hired coach. This has traditionally been employed at the destination by groups for transfers to and from the terminal most notably airports on inclusive tour holidays. In addition, sightseeing trips and tours are normally conducted by coaches or minibuses. Safaris in particular use the adapted microbus for sightseeing and game watching, for instance in Kenya.

The importance of the coach market can be overlooked. It is estimated coaches carried 860 million US passengers in 2000 with the vast majority (90%) carried on privately hired vehicles.

Railway transport

Overall the rail share of travel for holiday purposes is traditionally not high. However, the rail shares for certain corridors (especially high-speed lines) are higher as is the share for city centre to city centre traffic and for business and conference traffic. Railway terminals are often located in city centre locations compared to airports which are often located 20 or 30 kilometres away from the centre which increases their attraction for this market. For rail the main competition between modes is often based upon the time and distance comparison, city centre to city centre, compared with air. Beyond a certain distance, some visitors see rail as being too cumbersome and tiring and it is then that notions of adventure and sightseeing take over as the attractions of the rail mode (Figure 13.1). However, the traditional model demonstrated in Figure 13.1 is beginning to break down with rail services losing out to low-cost air carriers on many routes at distances significantly below 500 kms. One factor contributing to this is price. Rail has very high fixed costs (track, signalling, engineering costs) which either result in high fares (UK) or very high levels of subsidy (France, Germany) or a combination of both.

Trains are a relatively 'green' form of travel both in terms of fuel efficiency and also in terms of emissions, although the performance of ageing diesel trains has

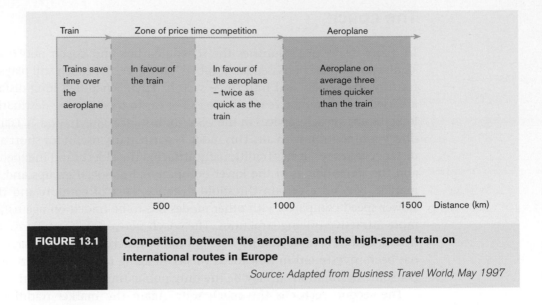

| FIGURE 13.1 | **Competition between the aeroplane and the high-speed train on international routes in Europe** |

Source: Adapted from Business Travel World, May 1997

recently been criticised. Electric trains are much more fuel efficient than cars per passenger km travelled. Rail also has a hugely better safety record than car travel.

The **EC** has been pressing for increased competition on rail networks throughout Europe (European Commission Directive 91/440/EEC) but the impact of rail privatisation in the UK has not been entirely beneficial to this mode of transport and is now unlikely to be copied by other countries. (For further studies on UK rail privatisation see Kain, 1998 and Welsby and Nichols, 1999.)

Although train operators try to emphasise the rest and relaxation of travel by train, rarely do they offer high-quality services throughout the network of a country so journeys involving a change from main high-speed lines to branch lines are more variable. The luxury and comfort attributes are therefore limited to journeys between 200 to 500 kilometres between major cities where airlines are currently making inroads.

The most important reasons from travelling by train are:

- safety;
- the ability to look out of the train and see en route;
- the ability to move around the coach;
- arriving at the destination rested and relaxed;
- personal comfort;
- centrally located termini;
- environmentally friendly form of transport; and
- decongested routes.

The traditional market for the train has been regarded as the independent holiday visitor, particularly the VFR category; they may also attract a significant 'fear of flying' market. Although in the USA trains are considered a second-rate means of passenger transportation, in Western Europe trains hold a valuable market share of passenger traffic, primarily because of policies of protectionism and subsidy by the respective governments. However, the introduction of high-speed and intercity services, such as the TGV in France, has improved the level of service and comfort offered. The opening of the Channel Tunnel in 1993 has created rail demand from London to Paris and Brussels. In addition, there is a tendency to change the image and function of trains towards an environmentally friendly, traditional, stylish, relaxed, reliable and consumer-orientated form of transport.

Sea transport

In broad terms, we can divide water-borne transport into short sea ferry transport and ocean-going cruises. Other categories exist such as inland waterway craft and small pleasure craft, but assume less significance as a means of transport as they are more destination products in their own right. Cruising should also be thought of as a holiday product as much as a mode of transport. Ferry services, which include or exclude vehicles, can provide lifeline services to islands as well as a focus for visitors who normally are packaged holidaymakers, independent or same-day visitors. Catamaran tend to be faster than conventional forms of ship technology but, in general (unless for short sea commuting such as between Hong Kong and Macau), business visitors tend to choose other modes of transport. Owing to the vagaries of the sea, visitors either like, accept or dislike this means of transport. Geographical factors tend to determine the provision of ferry transport leaving some destinations heavily dependent upon such links. Examples include:

- Aegean island hopping or travel to and from the Greek mainland; or

- channel crossings such as the English Channel, Irish Sea, the Cook Strait between the North and South Islands of New Zealand, and the Baltic Sea.

As far as the transportation of vehicles and merchandise is required on short sea crossings, ferries offer inexpensive, reliable and safe services. Ferry transportation is the only possibility in the case of remote and small islands which have no airport. This situation can be found in Greece, where there are only 15 airports to serve 95 inhabited islands. In this case, large ferries provide coastal shipping services linking the mainland ports and islands as well as the islands with each other. Furthermore, smaller regional ferries undertake transportation between the islands, especially during the summer peak period.

However, in many cases, air can be a viable alternative to sea transportation between larger islands and the mainland. The main advantage of ferry operators when compared with air transportation is price, combined with the fact that passengers can carry their own vehicles and use them at the destination. The popularity of motoring holidays and self-drive packages as well as the introduction of roll-on–roll-off facilities which enable the ports to handle a much greater volume of vehicles demonstrate the increase of passenger demand for ferry services.

In Europe, the gradual liberalisation of air transportation, the decrease of air fares, the construction of the Channel Tunnel and the development of alternative modes of travel have forced the ferry companies to improve the luxury of their vessels considerably, to increase the cruising speed, to increase their size and to install leisure facilities. Routes with longer crossings can enhance the leisure facilities – casinos, cabaret bars, cabins – to offer a consumer-orientated service.

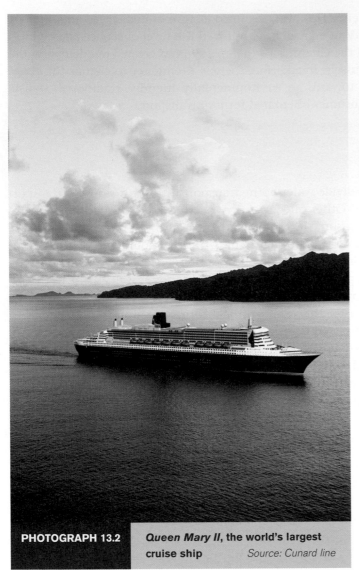

PHOTOGRAPH 13.2   *Queen Mary II*, **the world's largest cruise ship**   *Source: Cunard line*

Modern vessels, such as the wave-piercing catamaran and hydrofoils, have been introduced on some routes in recent decades. Their main aim is to offer a shorter crossing time than the traditional ferry service. Their speed is up to three times that of a conventional ferry, while they have a great maneuverability, fast turn-around in port and need minimum dock facilities. They therefore attract up-market tourists who appreciate the importance of their time and desire to reach the destination as soon as possible. However, these vessels are:

- much more expensive than the ferries;

- vulnerable in rough seas and strong winds; and

- noisy.

Air transport

Travelling by air is probably the most important transport innovation of the twentieth century. It has enabled the transportation of passengers in the shortest time and it has boosted the demand for long-haul trips. In fact no part of the world is now more than 24 hours' flying time from any other part.

Air transport has managed in the past few decades to gain a very significant share of the transport market, especially for movements over 500 kilometres. As new aircraft, such as the Boeing 747–400 series, have come online, the range for air travel has been extended to up to 15,000 kilometres for non-stop flights.

Scheduled airlines offer a safe, convenient, reliable, frequent and relatively consumer-orientated product; airlines attract business travellers, who appreciate the speed and flexibility between the various flights, especially on popular routes, as well as the leisure passengers who enjoy the ability to arrive at the destination quickly, and without spending time and money en route. Normally, ground services and the terminal facilities are much more advanced and sophisticated than for any other mode. The quality of services and the comforts offered on board have introduced new industry standards for the other modes of transport. Finally, airlines offer a number of incentives for their loyal customers through various 'frequent flyer' programmes. However, air transport is the most expensive mode of transportation, especially for the short-haul routes, say in Europe, where an economic cruising speed cannot be achieved.

Promotional fares try to offer cheaper prices by minimising the opportunities for alterations on the travel arrangements and by securing the passenger as early as possible. These fares include **advanced purchase excursion fare (APEX)**; previously standby and other forms of **instant purchase fare (IPEX)** were experimented with. Yield management enables the airlines to alter their fares in order to achieve maximum yield by taking account of potential demand and supply factors, historical data, time lost before the flight and current load factors. Thus appropriate prices are suggested for the current market environment in order to maximise the airline yield. Following on from developments in the USA, in Europe we have seen the emergence of low-cost, no-frills airlines, but frequencies and schedule times cannot compare with the established operators (see Mini case study 13.2).

The term 'low cost' is often associated with budget airlines or no-frills carriers. The concept developed in the USA following deregulation of air services in 1978 as was pioneered by Southwest Airlines. The concept transferred to Europe in the early 1990s with the emergence of several carriers copying the Southwest Airlines approach between 1995 and 1998. Outside Europe and the USA, adoption of the low-cost model has been slow. However, since 1999 there has been the emergence of carriers in Australia, Canada (albeit with very low market share), South Africa and Latin America. Southwest Airlines was set up in 1971 to operate services within Texas. Its home base was the subsidiary airport in Dallas (Love Field) which was much closer to downtown Dallas than the main airport Dallas Fort Worth, an irony considering the subsequent criticism levelled at low-cost carriers, particularly in Europe, over the use of airports up to 100 kms from the town centres. Its strategy from day one was to offer low fares, high point-to-point frequencies and good reliability. Following deregulation of the US domestic market in 1978 it cautiously expanded into services between states, predominantly of two- to four-hours' flight duration which it could serve with a single type of airplane, and on routes where there were no other operators. Today it is the USA's fifth largest airline (passengers carried) and has been profitable year on year in marked contrast to other US airlines. The driving force behind this success is a very low-cost base. Doganis (2001) indicates that low-cost carriers can achieve costs per seat km at around 40% of the costs of full service airlines on short- to medium-haul routes (two–four hours). Such carriers will attempt to reduce costs as detailed under the following subheadings.

AIRPORTS

- By operating from subsidiary airports of a major destination or from regional airports where landing charges and operating costs are lower (airports may be some distance from the city centre).

- By seeking discounts, and even subsidies from the new airport to which services are being offered. The EC have ruled such subsidies as anti-competitive and unlawful with regard to Ryanair's agreement with Charleroi Airport in Belgium.

- By effecting very rapid turn-around times at all airports and to arrange for staff to work more productive shifts and timings. The use of uncongested airports enables the airline maximise in-flight or revenue-earning hours per aircraft per day.

- By multiskilling of ground staff.

OPERATIONAL

- By operating at the highest load or seat factor possible.

- By purchasing modern fuel-efficient aircraft according to the needs of the route network operated.

- By standardising the fleet, initially on one aircraft type but, as the airline expands and operates routes of varying length and different characteristics, standardisation on two or three types. This reduces maintenance costs, training costs and the storage costs of spares.

- By operating a single class of seating with a relative low seat pitch (29°–31°) to maximise capacity.

- By operating with the minimum number of cabin crew allowed by safety regulations.

- By offering only point-to-point services as opposed to multiple stop operations and not to engage in interline activities at airports or with other carriers.

- By operating effective yield management systems resulting in ticket prices varying according to how far in advance the purchase is made.

- By not offering free food and beverages on board but by charging for extra services provided on board.

- By offering as an extra revenue earning activity additional services such as car hire and hotel booking at the time of issuing of tickets.

- By encouraging the use of Internet booking mechanisms and direct payment online, the non-use of agents and payments of commission and where possible the issuance of e-tickets or paperless tickets.

- By avoiding paying commission to travel agents.

- By not offering pre-assigned seating at check-in and adhering to very strict baggage limits.

- By making full use of special offers and even free tickets so as to gain market share against established competitors.

- By minimising ex gratia payments to customers in carriage and issuing of tickets so that no change is permitted to existing bookings or, if permitted, then only after the customer pays a substantial administration charge; in the event of delay or cancellation, the airline will, at best, offer a refund of the fare paid or a place on the next available flight which might be some days away.

- By operating a policy that lost baggage when found may not be delivered to the customer's home but should be collected and by generally offering low levels of customer service.

- By keeping administration costs low.

Mini case study 13.2 now explores in greater depth the expansion of the low-cost concept across Europe, Australasia and the possibility of developing the concept to long-haul routes.

MINI CASE STUDY 13.2
The expansion of the low-cost concept in airlines

EUROPE

In Europe deregulation of air transport came later and in three phases the third of which became operational in 1997. Essentially, this allowed carriers from one member state to offer services to another and to operate as a carrier within another member state and to fix fares without reference to regulatory authorities.

Ryanair began in 1985 on the route Waterford Ireland to London Gatwick at a time when the regulatory regime between the UK and Ireland was liberal. However, while the fares undercut Aer Lingus the airline made substantial losses and following a visit to Southwest Airlines in the early 1990s it decided it had to reduce its cost base along the lines pioneered by them. Although this saw the company move into profit from 1992, it did not expand to non-UK–Irish routes until 1997, since when it has displayed phenomenal growth. By 2004 it had 146 routes and served 90 destinations in 16 countries.

easyJet, the second largest low-cost airline in the UK in 2004, began operations in 1995 based at Luton and in 2004 operated 125 routes from 39 airports. Debonair commenced operation in 1996 but went into receivership in 1999 to illustrate that not all such ventures were a success. Some argue that Debonair was more of a hybrid and included a business class cabin and some frills which affected its cost base. Another low-cost operator, Virgin Express, based in Brussels (launched in 1996) has also adapted the Southwest model to allow interchange, which again impacts on the cost base.

An interesting development was the establishment of low-cost subsidiaries by established scheduled airlines. Go was set up in 1998 by BA and Buzz (2000) by KLM. These were short-lived experiments and the former is now part of easyJet and the latter Ryanair.

Although the low-cost industry has seen concentration into two main groupings following takeovers and business failures there have also been new low-cost carriers entering the market. Flybe is the UK's number three low-cost airline and developed from British European Airways and is based in regional locations in the UK including Southampton and Exeter. Bmibaby is an offshoot of the scheduled carrier British Midland International and operates mainly from a location in central England and in 2004 operated 40 routes to 10 countries.

The evidence from both the USA and Europe is that the very low fares of low-cost carriers has meant that although low-cost carriers will attract passengers from the higher cost full-service airlines, they also generate significant new traffic. Contrary to popular belief, they also carry business passengers, although this varies significantly from route to route, as well as leisure passengers, attracted in part by the high frequency on some routes.

AUSTRALASIA

As stated earlier, adoption by the rest of the world has been slow. One essential requirement is at least a very liberal if not deregulated operational environment. Two low-cost airlines were launched in Australia in 2000 following the earlier failure of a start-up carrier, Compass. Technically, the Australian domestic market has been deregulated since 1990, but following the failure of Compass has operated as a duopoly with Ansett and Qantas. Some commentators suggest that predatory behaviour by the two incumbents significantly contributed to Compass failing (Lawton, 2002).

Virgin Blue is a wholly owned subsidiary of the Virgin Group. Its emergence was dependent on the Australian government removing restrictions on the foreign ownership of domestic airlines. While the companies growth strategy is focused on under-served markets away from the busiest and most crowded airports where they believe there is route growth potential, very much along the lines of the Southwest model, but in 2001 they also entered Australia's busiest business route (Sydney–Melbourne). In the opening year of operation Virgin Blue carried around 650,000 passengers at an impressive average load factor of 74%. While early results are considered satisfactory it is envisaged that it will take three to four years to achieve profitability. In 2003 it operated 37 domestic routes capturing a 30% market share. Its costs were 40% less than Ansett before its collapse.

The second Australian low-cost carrier, Impulse, ceased operations on trunk routes in May 2001. It used Boeing 717–200 jets with a capacity of 117 seats rather that the low-cost airlines normal choice (Boeing 737s) and as a result incurred higher unit cost. It also chose routes in the Brisbane–Melbourne–Sydney triangle, which meant it was in direct competition with Qantas and Ansett on virtually all routes, rather than trying to develop new markets. Following the demise of Ansett in 2001 the Australian market is a duopoly again, albeit one of the incumbents is a low-cost carrier.

Other low-cost carriers to emerge include WestJet (Canada), Kulula.com (South Africa), Gol Transportes Aerosand (Brazil) and Air Asia (Malaysia). There are two trends to monitor and these are the emergence of low-cost carriers operating between different sovereign territories or countries and scheduled carriers developing their own low-cost operations such as United Airlines with Ted in United States and Thai Airways with Nok in Thailand. Many scheduled carriers have considered starting up a low-cost carrier and some are doing so (Air Canada and Tango) either to counter the possible competition from others or because it might be profitable. The cycle of airline development following deregulation in the United States may not be repeated in Europe and the European experiences may not be repeated elsewhere in the world.

LONG HAUL

There has been increasing debate as to whether the low-cost no-frills principles of operation can be applied to long-haul services. Following increased competition from new low-cost carriers in the USA, Southwest has extended its operations to routes of over 1,000 kms. However, the cost savings achievable over full-service airlines on long-haul services will be lower, perhaps 20% to 25%. Full-service airlines already achieve high vehicle utilisation, there are limits as to the minimum acceptable seat pitch for longer flights and it is unlikely an airline can offer no refreshments. Nevertheless it appears there will be attempts to start such services between the UK and Canada from the summer of 2004.

DISCUSSION QUESTIONS

1 Why do low-cost airlines use secondary and regional airports?

2 Why don't low-cost airlines use the main CRS systems used by the world's major airlines?

3 How might so-called 'full-fare' or scheduled carriers respond to the competition from low-cost airlines?

Charter flights are utilised widely to facilitate the movement of holidaymakers on package tours although up to 20% of passengers are carried on 'seat-only' arrangements. Most charter airlines belong to tour operators who attempt to integrate their operations vertically such as Britannia Airways and Thomson Holidays in the UK (see Chapter 12). Charter airlines offer *ad hoc* transportation services; they normally fly directly to the final destination and therefore passengers do not need to change aircraft at a hub. This can be achieved by:

- minimising the flexibility in altering flights;
- flying at inconvenient and therefore not busy hours for the terminal;
- reducing the space within the aircraft; and
- offering elementary luxuries and services.

The higher **load factor** achieved on **charter services** (of 90% or more) compared with **scheduled services** (averaging 70%) is the final factor explaining the substantial difference in the unit cost of production and the price at which the product can be sold. (For a more detailed analysis of charter airline costs see Doganis, 2002.)

The bulk of air travel is orientated towards either business or leisure travellers. In the first case people travel for their economic activities and therefore their fares are paid by their employers. Maximum flexibility is required in order to be able to alter their travelling arrangements at short notice; as a result business travellers tend to prefer scheduled airlines. Services, terminals and aircraft have to be designed to facilitate the function of the busy business traveller. It is estimated that business travellers account for about 30% of all international air traffic.

Leisure travellers' share of air transportation has increased rapidly during recent decades. Leisure travellers have much more time and they do not necessarily require very high-quality services. They are free to make their holiday arrangements well in advance and thus they do not need flexibility. However, unlike the business traveller they do pay their own fares and, therefore, they are price conscious. The

485

development of specific leisure fares by scheduled airlines as well as the charter airlines in Europe has catered for the needs of this market adequately. Overall it is estimated that around 15% of international tourism uses air transportation while 86% of Europeans use planes for trips outside of Europe.

POLITICAL INFLUENCES ON TRANSPORT FOR TOURISM

International tourist movements have always been affected by the activities of governments and transport for tourism has also been influenced by such factors. Barriers to communication, apart from distance, have been border controls, the need for visas or transit visas and customs controls. For rail and road the boundary between nations is the place of border control, and for sea transport the land/sea interface or the port is the point of control; however, for air transport the airport terminal, wherever located, is the processing point.

The concept of sovereignty of airspace versus the freedom of the high seas has always been a factor limiting and influencing provision of transport for tourism by air. Rail transport across and between nations, apart from gauge differences, has always been relatively smooth compared with quota regulations for coaches in transit or entering other countries. The motorist has been affected by the insurance requirements for a 'green card' and international driving licences, but in Europe such barriers and restraints have all but disappeared.

Because of its very nature, transport for tourism by air has developed as a complex political issue and the key factors need to be highlighted. Airlines are important within the national economy for foreign exchange and for fare payments from foreign travellers. Generally airlines have been owned by the state, have been subsidised by governments and have been seen to be prestige elements flying the colours of the national flag. Scandinavian Airline System (SAS) and Air Afrique are exceptions to the rule that most countries possess their own national airline. Equally, the size of an airline is not necessarily related to the size of traffic potential of that country; the examples of KLM and Swissair illustrate this point.

Transport for tourism operates within a competitive political and economic environment, especially in the international context, because it represents the means to transfer across borders and to cross other territories to reach the intended destination. This competitive environment is illustrated by the extent to which transport for tourism has been regulated and controlled by governments.

REGULATION OF COMPETITION

Since their inception, transport media have been subject to regulation by governments for safety and technical reasons. In addition, legal and economic forms of regulation have applied to specific transport modes. In many countries transport operation has been subject to legislation to protect so-called 'pioneer operators' who incur costs, set up routes and pick-up points, but are then vulnerable to another operator moving in without those costs to recoup. This was the basis of coaching legislation in the UK which was heavily regulated from 1930 up until deregulation in 1980 followed by the deregulation of the larger bus industry in 1985. The USA (1982), Scandinavia, Portugal and Greece have all followed. A new period of fierce competition on long-distance coach services in the UK appears imminent with the emergence of Megabus.com. Railways tend to be natural national monopolies and to be state owned and subsidised, but in Europe there have been attempts to privatise and to introduce competition following the European Commission Directive 91/440/EEC.

Regulation policies

Policies on regulation have tended to focus on air transport to a greater degree than other modes; international air law is a factor that controls the extent to which national airlines may operate. In the United States the so-called anti-trust provisions have always existed to prevent the development of price fixing, cartels and collusion between competitors. In Europe under the Treaty of Rome, transport has been deemed to be subject to competition rules and the European Commission has outlawed agreements between pairs of national carriers who pool their capacity and revenues and still judges whether potential mergers of airlines are anti-competitive or not.

The need for regulation of transport has hinged on the relative ease of entry into operation of a service; the barriers to entry are relatively low compared with other industries. Given that the evils of cut-throat competition can lead to both the demise of a regular reliable schedule and lead to social disadvantages to travellers, regulation policies have specified procedures for entry into and exit from operation. The arguments for and against regulation are many, but basically in the short term, customers benefit from increased competition and efficiency through lower fares; but in the long term, they may suffer disadvantages from the lack of an organised and reliable schedule of services as competitors go out of business.

The Airline Deregulation Act 1978 was introduced in President Carter's era in the United States and led to the development of an open-skies policy. This Act is often cited as the extreme of what deregulation can do in practice. The Civil Aeronautics Board as a regulatory body devising policy was phased out. Its role had been to devise regulations on conditions of service such as frequency and capacity, on exit and entry into operation and on fares and prices. Such matters then became the subject of free competition within the US domestic environment. Up until the late 1970s the International Airline Transport Association (IATA) was the *de facto* controlling body worldwide, being a trade association for airlines, though in reality it represented governments as well. However, ever since the famous Show Cause Order where IATA had to show good cause why it should be exempt from the provisions of US anti-trust provisions, this body has lost its stature and strength to implement fare structures to protect its high-cost member airlines. IATA's influence varies from continent to continent and it is still strong in parts of Europe, Africa and Latin America.

Following the Chicago Convention of 1944 where a truly multilateral agreement between countries was not reached, a series of bilateral arrangements between governments emerged. National governments approve and license carriers nominated to fly between the home, country and an overseas destination; fares are fixed by reference to IATA conference machinery or between respective governments. Even in a truly deregulated environment fares are fixed by mutual agreement between

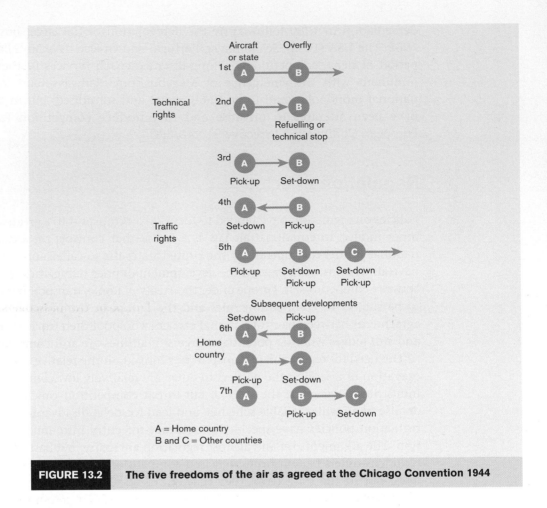

FIGURE 13.2 **The five freedoms of the air as agreed at the Chicago Convention 1944**

partners or merely filed. The so-called 'five freedoms of movement' giving technical and traffic rights to airlines are still important for international movements. These are outlined in Figure 13.2. Subsequent to the Chicago Convention, sixth and seventh freedoms have been formulated.

The extent to which US domestic policies have been translated to overseas situations has been limited. Within the USA, as a result of fierce competition, instability was initiated where a great number of air carriers entered the market and the fares reached their lowest levels. However, in the following years only a few carriers could survive and most of the small or weak airlines were absorbed or merged with the stronger ones.

European skies have been quite reluctant to open up to complete deregulation. This is partly because of the public sector's role in the airline industry as well as the social role of the carriers to maintain uneconomic routes in the peripheral areas purely for national and social reasons. After three directives from the European Commission, the development of true cabotage arrangements for Europe, where it is seen as one domestic territory, finally happened on 1 April 1997. Europe, though, is still dominated by state-controlled and owned airlines, some of which have received substantial subsidies from the European Commission. There is another issue which involves the agreements made between United States and UK over air traffic between the two countries and the extent to which the EU has a right to be involved. Historically, bilateral agreements between USA and UK were the so-called Bermuda I agreement dated 1946 and the Bermuda II agreement that replaced it in 1977. In 2002 the European Court of Justice declared that the 1977 agreement meant that the UK had failed to fulfill its obligations under the European Treaty and in effect the EU has held that it sees itself as having the rights to govern and negotiate agreements with foreign countries such as the USA. It is expected that there will be protracted negotiations for modification of agreements between EU member states the European Commission and the USA for some time to come.

FUTURE TRENDS

Currently passenger transportation is probably at its most competitive since its existence; alternative forms and modes of travelling develop strong competitive advantages and they attempt to attract the bulk of the passengers. Each mode has, of course, distinctive characteristics and attributes as well as strengths and weaknesses for each market segment. In this section we provide an analysis of the external environment and the future trends of passenger transportation.

Efficiency

Great pressure has been placed upon all transportation media to reduce their prices and offer a better quality of service. This has forced all companies to identify new methods of increasing their efficiency; in particular this has been applied in the airline world where modern techniques such as yield management, hub and spoke operations and modern distribution channels such as CRSs have changed the way that business is operated.

Yield management maximises the airline's revenue by suggesting the maximum prices which can be achieved for every available seat. It has been defined as the maximisation of revenue through optimum seat mix, competitive buy-up pricing strategies, accurate overbooking, high-yield spill and spoilage controls and demand forecasting.

CRS has been used to control scheduled seats and fares in order to distribute products effectively and to maximise profits following the deregulation of air transportation in the USA. CRS enabled other efficiencies and competitive techniques (such as yield management and frequent flyer programmes) to be developed while becoming a source for strong competitive advantage and changing the balance of the airline world.

Development of hub and spoke systems increased the rationalisation of air transportation by using major airports as transit points. Short-haul flights (spokes) connect through a limited number of airports (hubs) and passengers are transferred to long-haul trips. This enabled the airlines to achieve higher load factors and keep prices down.

Air congestion is an emerging problem which will influence the airlines severely since the lack of terminal and air-corridor capacity is now becoming apparent. It is suggested that the growth in intra-Europe traffic by the year 2010 will lead to many of Europe's leading airports reaching their capacity; the result would damage air transportation and stimulate people to switch to alternative modes.

A number of improvements are therefore required at airports and, more specific-ally, on the control procedures, the design and construction of the terminals and the interconnectivity with other modes of travel. Furthermore, the efficiency of airlines should increase by extending hub operations, reorganising the schedule, utilising larger aircraft and by achieving higher load factors.

Some see the solution being larger aircraft, such as the Airbus A380, offering 555 seats, but there remains uncertainty over passenger acceptance of such large aircraft and the ability of route structures and infrastructure (air traffic control, airports, etc.) to sustain and support such large loads.

GLOBALISATION AND INTEGRATION

Globalisation is one of the major trends in the international tourism industry and involves a convergence in tastes, preferences and products. The global firm is one that capitalises on this trend and produces standardised products contributing to the homogenisation of the world tourism market. Essentially, this means an increase in worldwide business between multinational corporations irrespective of the geo-graphical location and can lead to the virtual firm as a transport operator. The truly global carrier as some have predicted has not really emerged in part due to wishes by governments and other trading blocs to retain national sovereignty as vested in their national carriers. However, there has been a further consolidation of strategic and marketing alliances and an integration of services and operations

Airlines, as they expand their services on a global basis, are forging strategic alliances because of:

- the maturity of domestic traffic;

- the competition for terminal space and slots;

- the need for extensive networks worldwide;

- the necessity for economies of scale in airline operation;

- the control of the new distribution channels (CRS); and

- the gradual deregulation in world transportation.

Many examples can illustrate the globalisation of airlines but perhaps the best is British Airways, which:

- has franchise operations such as that with British Mediterranean Airways;

- in 1992 bought a stake in US Air but decided to sell in 1996 but has plans for a transatlantic alliance with American Airlines;

- has shares in Qantas and plans for closer relationships with carriers such as Iberia;

- is a major player in the Oneworld Alliance and has codeshare agreements with alliance and some non-alliance carriers.

Other schemes include the Star Alliance programme which originally at its inception in 1997 comprised the founder members of Thai, Air Canada, United, Lufthansa, SAS and in 2004 had 14 members.

Some of its objectives were to:

- integrate products and connecting services;

- offer common check-in and reservation services;

- share airport lounge services; and

- share marketing, communications and rewards services.

As far as vertical integration is concerned, the transportation industry has always acknowledged that travellers need to use a combination of the various modes in order to complete their trip. Therefore, transportation companies are moving towards alternative modes which can be combined and offer integrated services. As a result, chauffeur services are offered by various airlines for their loyal and full-fare customers, while fly–drive programmes are very successful. Finally, the ambition of airlines such as Lufthansa to penetrate into rail transport, by offering private services primarily for their airline clients, demonstrates the point.

The trend towards globalisation has been seen in respect of numerous attempts to merge. To date, few attempts have been successful especially in the European context due to great pride in government ownership and national sovereignty. There have been notable examples of bankruptcy in the early 2000s in the form of Sabena, the Belgian flag carrier, and Swissair but which later re-emerged as Swiss International Airlines. In 2004 there was the merger of Air France and KLM, finally approved by the competition regulators in Brussels and Washington.

Post-deregulation in the United States saw great competition between established carriers and new start-ups some of whom were labelled as low-cost airlines. After merger, exit from the market, and consolidation only a small number of big players survived and of the new low cost start-ups only Southwest Airlines is still in operation. In 2003 it was the fourth largest domestic carrier in the USA.

A similar cycle of low-cost carriers has grown up in Europe, often termed budget airlines or no-frills carriers. Since the final deregulation of air transport in the EU in 1997 the emergence of a European open-skies policy has led to the emergence of a new phenomenon in air transport not only in Europe but in South East Asia and to a limited extent in Australia, Canada and South Africa. Whether the cycle which occurred in USA will follow in the rest of the world remains to be seen.

Environmental policies

There will be much greater emphasis on environmental issues over the coming decade. Concern has been expressed about the continued growth of both car traffic and air traffic and in particular their contribution to both greenhouse gasses and other noxious emissions. Already policies of restraint on car use are being explored and introduced by various governments and the introduction of congestion charging in London appears to show that policies of constraint can be both successful and, perhaps more importantly, politically popular. There are some concerns that for certain large department stores turnover has been reduced by up to 9%, but there are other factors in play (not least a reduction in North American visitors to the UK post-September 11, 2001) and the majority of businesses are reporting increased turnover. Other schemes of car restraint appear inevitable.

The position with regard to air travel is more mixed. It is estimated that air transport will account for 5% of CO_2 emissions by 2050 and yet most governments still retain a 'predict and build' approach. Such is the relative economic importance placed on air transport (it is estimated that London Heathrow alone accounts for 1% of the UK's GDP). Government policy is to attempt to meet demand for air services where and when it arises leading to the decision to expand airports. Environmental groups argue that there should be some form of pollution taxation and the view that aviation fuel should not be zero rated for VAT is gaining ground and the impact of air transport on the environment will emerge as a large-scale controversial topic over the coming years. Increases in environmental taxes or airport charges will disproportionately affect the cost structures of fast growing low-cost carriers and fares will have to rise.

CONCLUSION

As tourism demand grows, transportation – and indeed transportation infrastructure – will become increasingly important. New technology in respect of every aspect of transportation will be influential, and the transport industry of the future will supply visitors with ticketless travel, smart card technology for payment, and also perhaps for visa and passport purposes in certain country groups.

However, the transport industry for tourism has many issues confronting it as numbers of visitors worldwide increase. All forms of transport pollute the environment and some will never be able to develop totally green policies. Airlines will still burn kerosene and create noise. Trains can be electrically operated, but ultimately rely on nuclear or fossil fuels. Coaches and cars burn fossil fuels and sea-borne craft likewise, except leisure craft, which are wind driven. As other suppliers of the elements of the tourist product develop more environmentally friendly policies and practices, operators must be seen as natural polluters in the foreseeable future – whether curbs on transport operators that pollute will affect the price or availability of transport for tourism remains to be seen.

Self-check questions

1 What is the purpose of government regulation of transport? Is it desirable?

2 Compare and contrast the environmental impacts of different modes of transport.

3 List the components of a transport system and illustrate how the overall performance of a mode of transport is governed by the relative strengths and weaknesses of each.

4 Explore how transport demand in destination areas brings benefits to public transport operators. Does it also bring conflicts or problems?

5 What do airlines gain from membership of inter-airline alliances?

Essay questions

1 Critically evaluate the long-term prospects of the cruise industry. Can the growth rates of the last 20 years be sustained?

2 Transport for tourism is a derived demand. Using specific examples outline the operational difficulties this brings transport operators and review potential policies to serve uneven patterns of demand.

3 Examine the case for policies to reduce our dependency on cars for travel purposes. What will be the impact of such policies on the tourism industry?

4 Discuss the viewpoint that transport for tourism is a homogeneous product.

5 Critically assess the impact of deregulation of the aviation industry.

Annotated further reading

Books

Doganis, R. (2001) *The Airline Business in the 21st Century*, Routledge, London.
A key text from an acknowledged leading author on airline economics and planning. The book includes a detailed chapter on airline alliances and one on the emergence, strategies and economics of low-cost no-frills carriers.

Graham, A. (2003) *Managing Airports: An International Perspective*, 2nd edn, Butterworth Heinemann, Oxford.
A detailed text on the operation and management of airports. Very current and includes a chapter analysing the impact of September 11, 2001 as well as detailed data on many aspects of airport operation.

Lumsden, L. and Page, S. (2004) *Tourism and Transport*, Elsevier, Oxford.
An edited volume with contributions from 15 authors exploring the relationship between transport and tourism and their dependence upon each other. Includes chapters on cruise ships, airports, airlines, the role of transport in tourism development with case studies of Zimbabwe and North Queensland and transport requirements in tourist destinations.

Peisley, T. (2003) *Global Changes in the Cruise Industry 2003–2010*, Seatrade Communications Ltd, Colchester.
The latest in a series of detailed reports on the size and characteristics of the cruise ship industry. Includes up-to-date statistics on the size of the cruise market, capacity and trends at the main destinations, the number and value of new ship orders and an analysis of the main cruise lines. Very comprehensive and again very current with an analysis of the impact of September 11, 2001.

Web sites

http://www.cruising.org

The site of the CLIA and dubbed 'the official site of the cruise industry'. A good way to keep up to date with current developments in the cruise industry, although it does have a US bias (not a problem given the nature of the industry). The Press room/ Research menu gives access to the detailed news items, although access to the most detailed industry reports appears restricted to those with journalist accreditation.

http://www.dft.gov.uk

The site of the Department for Transport in the UK and therefore has an obvious UK bias. Nevertheless, one can download detailed policy documents from this site such as the 1998 White Paper on policies to manage road traffic growth or the 2003 White Paper on airport development, which include concepts and ideas that can be applied more widely. Some of the published statistics include international comparisons.

http://europa.eu.int/comm/dgs/energy_transport/index_index_en.html

The site for the Transport Directorate of the EU. Again full EU White Papers can be downloaded from the site and it also offers access to transport statistics for the whole of the EU area. Current policy documents prominent on the site are on rail development and on inter modal comparisons of the charges for transport infrastructure.

References cited

DETR (1997) *Air Traffic Forecasts for the United Kingdom 1997*, Stationery Office, London.

DETR (1998) *A New Deal for Transport: Better for Everyone*, Stationery Office, London.

DFT (2003a) *The Future of Air Transport*, Stationery Office, London.

DFT (2003b) *Transport Statistics Great Britain*, Stationery Office, London.

Doganis, R. (2001) *The Airline Business in the 21st Century*, Routledge, London.

Doganis, R. (2002) *Flying Off Course: The Economics of International Airlines*, 3rd edn, Routledge, London.

Graham, A. (2003) Managing *Airports: An International Perspective,* 2nd edn, Butterworth Heinemann, Oxford.

Kain, P. (1998) 'The reform of rail transport in Great Britain', *Journal of Transport Economics and Policy* **32**(2), 247–66.

Lawton, T. (2002) *Cleared for Take-Off: Structure and Strategy in the Low Fare Airline Business*, Ashgate, Aldershot.

RAC Foundation (2002) *Motoring Towards 2050*, RAC Foundation, London.

Robbins, D. (2003) 'Public transport as a visitor attraction', pp. 86–102 in Fyall, A., Garrod, B. and Leask, A. (eds), *Managing Visitor Attractions: New Directions*, Butterworth Heinemann, Oxford.

Royal Commission on Environmental Pollution (1994) *Transport and the Environment*, Eighteenth Report, Stationery Office, London.

Welsby, J. and Nichols, A. (1999) 'The privatisation of British Railways', *Journal of Transport Economics and Policy* **33**(1), 55–76.

MAJOR CASE STUDY 13.1
THE CRUISE SHIP INDUSTRY

The cruise ship industry has grown into a genuine form of mass tourism over the last 25 years. Measurement of cruise taking can be quite misleading as the usual figure quoted is the number of cruises taken. However, there is a very significant difference in terms of consumption and in terms of economic impact between a passenger on a short cruise of say three to four nights and a passenger cruising for 14 nights or longer. A measure of cruise nights would be more illuminating. Nevertheless, the growth over the last 20 years by any measure has been staggering. Annual growth rates between 1980 and 2002 are 8.4% per annum to produce 11.2 million passengers by 2002 (Table 13.3).

To accommodate the growth there has also been substantial investment in new vessels perhaps best illustrated by the delivery of Cunard's *Queen Mary II* which undertook its maiden voyage in January 2004. Growth rates in cruise capacity have averaged 8.3% between 1980 and 2002 so overall occupancy levels have been virtually unchanged. This represents huge levels of investment. Between 2001 and 2005 there are confirmed orders for between 50 and 60 vessels costing some £12 and £14 billion, although only three new vessels have been ordered in the two years since September 11, 2001.

PATTERNS OF DEMAND

The US market dominates cruise demand (Table 13.3). Around 65% of all cruise passengers are from North America. The 1990s saw very dramatic rates of growth from the UK market, which has seen it emerge as the most significant European market (ahead of Germany), but its significance is still dwarfed by North America.

Although there has been diversification of destinations by the cruise companies the Caribbean region still dominates (Table 13.4). While it is estimated that the Caribbean accounts for some 50% of all cruises, such has been the popularity of short cruises in the region it accounts for a slightly lower level of cruise night capacity (42%). However, the annual figures of capacity hide another significant pattern. There are many more cruise ships in the Caribbean between October and the following March than there are between April and September. CLIA statistics show that around 62% of annual Caribbean capacity is offered between October and the following March.

The Caribbean therefore takes on huge significance for the future growth and prosperity of the global cruise industry. Other important destination markets demonstrate seasonal demand. The Mediterranean has a season stretching from March to September, while other important destinations such as Alaska, the Baltic or the Norwegian fjords have even shorter peaks. Cruise lines have found it increasingly difficult to find alternative destinations to the Caribbean between October and March. There have been some successes (the Atlantic Islands) but overall progress has been slow. Vessels are therefore repositioned from seasonal markets back to the Caribbean to achieve high annual utilisation.

Following a decade of falling market share in 2002 cruise capacity in the Caribbean grew by a staggering 22% due to a significant re-positioning of ships away from Europe to the Caribbean by US cruise lines as a reaction to September 11, 2001. European destinations are now recovering lost ground in 2003 following this initial reaction.

TABLE 13.3	Total cruise passenger market ('000)				
YEAR	North America	UK	Rest of Europe	Rest of world	Total
1990	3 640	179	330	345	4 495
1991	3 979	187	354	414	4 980
1992	4 136	219	407	490	5 460
1993	4 480	254	420	467	5 940
1994	4 448	270	502	1 196	6 280
1995	4 378	340	694	1 481	6 440
1996	4 656	416	785	N/A	6 850
1997	5 051	522	928	N/A	7 580
1998	5 428	663	902	850	8 210
1999	5 894	746	994	1 160	9 067
2000	6 882	754	1 096	N/A	10 138
2001	6 906	776	1 205		10 267
2002	7 460	823	1 296		11 198

Source: CLIA, 2004

TABLE 13.4	Cruise capacity for selected destinations (CLIA members)				
	Bed nights				
Destination	1989 nights % '000	1995 nights % '000	2001 nights % '000	2002 nights % '000	% change 1989–2001
Alaska	1 598 6.5	3 008 8.4	4 698 7.9	5 053 8.0	194
Caribbean	10 982 44.5	15 245 42.8	21 833 36.6	26 741 42.1	98.8
Mediterranean	1 879 7.6	3 447 9.7	7 546 12.7	6 497 10.2	301.6
North Europe	774 3.1	1 582 4.4	4 837 8.1	6 932 10.9	525.0
Transatlantic	407 1.6	658 1.8	1 129 1.9	1 006 1.6	177.3
Total	24 699	35 661	53 862	59 581	118.1

497

TRENDS IN THE INDUSTRY

- Cruise passengers are attracted from an ever-increasing range of socio-economic, income and age groups. Penetration has been increased by a trend towards shorter cruises. Cruises of between two and five days have been by far the fastest-growing segment of the North American market (Table 13.5). The provision of cruises by tour operators pioneered by Airtours in 1995 and now accounting for 35% of all UK cruise passengers also widened the appeal and affordability of cruising. CLIA have reported that over one million children now take a cruise worldwide.

- Vessels are getting bigger bringing operational economies of scale to the cruise lines. Mega vessels such as the Royal Caribbean Lines 137,300 gwt *Voyager of the Seas* entered service in 1999 carrying 3,900 passengers. The *Queen Mary II* entering service in 2004 is larger, but carries 2,620 passengers. This development is changing the nature of the product with fewer ports of call as the vessel becomes more of the leisure experience (the experience economy). The vast majority of the megavessels are deployed in the Caribbean but in a strategy to enable the region to cope with this additional demand as many as six cruise lines own private uninhabited Caribbean islands.

- There has been the creation of an oligopoly following the take over of P&O cruises by Carnival. The largest three cruise companies Carnival, Royal Caribbean Cruises and Star Cruises now account for 70% of all cruise capacity.

TABLE 13.5	Market share of North American market by length of cruise, 2002	
Length of cruise	%	% growth 1980–2002
2–5 days	35.5	680.9
6–8 days	53.6	384.0
9–17 days	10.5	264.2
18 + days	0.4	76.4
	100	33.8

Average growth 1980–2002
8.4% per annum

Source: CLIA, 2004

FUTURE PROSPECTS FOR GROWTH

The cruise industry is bullish about its future prospects. The 2002 CLIA estimates that only 15% of the US population have ever cruised. There are similar figures for the UK market. Mintel (2003) estimate that 13% of the UK population have ever cruised and for the rest of the world the levels of penetration are even lower. Regular market research surveys by the CLIA indicate that 50% of their target market of US residents have indicated a strong interest in cruising within the next five years. With such a large untapped market they argue that the growth rates of the last 20 years can be sustained in the future. They further argue that a high percentage of cruise passengers cruise again and the 2002 Market Profile Study shows that 56% of those who have ever cruised (23 million people) have done so in the last five years. They expect a high percentage of this 'active' market to assist future growth by producing repeat business. The 'large potential untapped market' argument is convincing given past trends and clearly cruise companies have confidence in it, otherwise they would not be investing £12 to £14 billion in new vessels. However, such surveys do need treating with some caution bearing in mind they are asking hypothetical questions about future consumption.

Forecasts of future rates of growth have been adjusted downwards in the aftermath of September 11, 2001, with an expected 17 million cruises by 2010, down from the initial forecast of 20 million (Peisley, 2003).

BARRIERS TO GROWTH

Discounting

There is some evidence that the dramatic growth over recent years has been partially 'supply led' rather than demand led. Industry sources indicate that 75% of North American passengers and 45% of European passengers travel at a discount. The temptation for cruise lines to discount is obvious. Once substantial investment in new vessels is made, those vessels have to be filled. There is scope for significant on-board spend, the largest three areas being at the bar, on shore-based excursions and in the casino areas of vessels. Indeed, cruise lines will argue that passenger psychology is such that a low brochure price makes marketing sense. Passengers will put substantial energy into achieving relatively small savings in the brochure price and yet while actually on the cruise itself they are far less conscious of spending levels. However, as new capacity has come on stream discounting by the major cruise lines has been fierce reducing cruise line yields and affecting cruise line profitability. The concerns of the financial markets over falling profitability and the potential of future over capacity in the market led to falls in the share price of all the major cruise companies in 2000. The repercussions of September 11, 2001 added further impetus to the trend to cut prices in order to fill cruises, although some 12 months later the industry appeared to have partially recovered from this factor.

Industry sources believe that the current pattern of heavy discounting will continue perhaps to 2005, when they expect the growth in demand will exceed the growth in supply improving yields and profitability. The rationale for such a forecast is not entirely clear to the author.

SATURATION OF CRUISE DESTINATION AREAS

Around 24 cruise lines operate around 70 vessels in the Caribbean over the year. Berth capacity offered by cruise vessels is predicted to exceed the number of hotel beds by 2006 (Wood, 2000) and Caribbean governments are beginning to question the value of cruise activity continuing to grow at this level. The majority of the 30 megavessels coming on-stream between 2001 and 2005 are destined for the Caribbean market. The number of ports the largest vessels can call at are reduced but the socio-cultural or environmental impact of each call from such ships on small port destinations that can accommodate them are considerable. The cruise call does bring economic benefit for the destination. The ships may require fresh water, sewage disposal facilities, bunkerage, and fresh food all offering the potential for local jobs. Passenger spend can, however, remain relatively low, limited to shopping, light refreshments (perhaps lunch) and organised excursions which, if booked on board, may see much this spend retained by the cruise line.

The trend for cruise lines to purchase small, uninhabited Caribbean islands may overcome some of these problems but reduces the economic benefit to the region. Cruise lines also argue that the trend to larger vessels is helpful in accommodating growth without a comparable increase in ship calls. Nevertheless, local governments are giving consideration to limiting cruise calls to the region along the lines of the quotas introduced to the number of cruise calls to Bermuda in the mid-1980s. It is difficult to envisage the continued growth of cruising at current levels if the Caribbean does not accommodate a fair share of future growth. The most significant issue is alternative destinations to absorb global cruise growth between October and March.

ENVIRONMENTAL PRESSURES

Continued growth at the current levels may not represent sustainable development. A large cruise ship generates around 210,000 gallons of sewage, millions of gallons of grey water, 25,000 gallons of oily bilge water plus solid waste and hazardous waste every week. The disposal of ship waste and sewage, while more highly regulated than before, undoubtedly causes damage with such a high concentration of vessels in the Caribbean (Lester and Weeden, 2004; Wood, 2004). There is also increased pressure for additional dredging to deepen harbours to enable ports to accept the larger vessels.

CONCLUSION

The cruise industry is confident of future profitable growth. The former CEO of Princess Cruises, Peter Ratcliffe, sums up the industry view:

> Our industry has sustainable long-term growth characteristics despite the impact of recent events on short-term trading. The key indicators of demographics, penetration, high levels of customer satisfaction and trends in leisure spend point to significant growth over the long term and increasing globalisation of the industry.

Time will tell whether this optimistic view for continued growth is right.

Source: http://www.cruising.org

REFERENCES

CLIA (2004) '2003 fall overview', Cruise Line International Association, New York.

Lester, J. and Weeden, C. (2004) 'Stakeholders, the natural environment and the future of Caribbean cruise tourism', *International Journal of Tourism Research* **6**(1), 39–50.

Mintel (2003) 'Cruises', *Leisure Intelligence*, April 2003.

Peisley, T. (2003) *Global Changes in the Cruise Industry 2003–2010*, Seatrade Communications Ltd, Colchester.

Wood, R. (2000) 'Caribbean cruise tourism: globalization at sea', *Annals of Tourism Research* **27**(2), 345–70.

Wood, R. (2004) 'Cruise ships: deterritorialized destinations', pp. 133–45 in Lumsdon, L. and Page, S. (eds), *Tourism and Transport*, Elsevier, Oxford.

DISCUSSION QUESTIONS

1 How have cruise lines widened the age and socio-economic profile of passengers?

2 What are the main benefits and disbenefits of cruise calls to the Caribbean region?

3 What are the potential barriers to the continued growth of the cruise shipping industry?

CHAPTER FOURTEEN
PUBLIC SECTOR
AND POLICY

Governments are involved with tourist organisations at both the international and national level. In the latter case they are normally the instigators for the establishment of a **national tourist organisation** (NTO), while in the former instance, they are partners along with other member states in such bodies as the World Tourism Organization (WTO), the European Travel Commission (ETC), the Pacific Asia Travel Association (PATA) and so on. All these bodies can contribute to the formation of a country's tourism policy. In this chapter we look at the overall policy framework and consider the experience of different governments in order to illustrate the changes that occur in policy, noting the very many organisations that express an interest in tourism at the national level. As national tourist offices are commonly the executive agency for government policy, their administrative structure and functions are considered in some detail. The last part of the chapter examines intervention by the public sector in tourism. Particular consideration is given to the variety of instruments governments have at their disposal to manage the direction of tourism development in the interests of the host community.

LEARNING OUTCOMES

The focus of this chapter is on the role of the public sector, in the shape of governmental organisations, in tourism. Specifically, upon completion, you will have:

- a knowledge of the key organisations globally with an interest in and influence upon tourism;

- an understanding of the key functions of NTOs;

- an insight into how NTOs might be structured and how responsibilities are divided;

- an overview of the role of the public sector; and

- a knowledge of the instruments available to governments in order to manipulate demand for tourism and control the supply of it.

PUBLIC POLICY FRAMEWORK

With tourism set to be one of the main international economic drivers in the twenty-first century, together with increasing demands from the domestic population for leisure and recreation, the industry is a development option that few governments can afford to ignore. A critical difference between tourism and many other agents of development is that of inseparability, in that tourism is consumed at the place of production, thus involving itself with the host community, and requiring some **commodification** and sharing of traditions, value systems and culture. Since the tourist industry does not control all those factors that make up the attractiveness of a destination and the impact on the host population can be considerable, it is necessary for the options concerning the development of tourism to be considered at the highest level of government and the appropriate public administrative framework put in place. As a rule the greater the importance of tourism to a country's economy the greater is the involvement of the public sector, to the point of having a government ministry with sole responsibility for tourism.

Beyond this, governments are involved in supporting a variety of **multinational agencies**. The official flag carrier for international tourism is the WTO (see Mini case study 14.1), which is vested by the United Nations with a central and decisive role in promoting the development of responsible, sustainable and universally accessible tourism. Elsewhere there are a number of other international bodies whose activities impinge upon tourism: these include the World Bank (whose commercial arm is the International Finance Corporation (IFC), which takes on private sector projects, whereas its other arm, the International Bank for Reconstruction and Development (IBRD), provides government funding for **structural adjustment** and infrastructure developments), other United Nations' bodies (such as the International Civil Aviation Organisation (ICAO), the World Health Organisation (WHO) and UNESCO), the International Air Transport Association (IATA), and the Organisation for Economic Co-operation and Development (OECD).

At a lower level, there are a variety of regional bodies such as the Organisation of American States (OAS), Pacific Asia Travel Association (PATA) and the European Travel Commission (ETC). Most of their efforts are devoted to promotion and marketing, though they do provide technical assistance. For example, the ETC carries out its objective to promote Europe as an attractive destination through consumer advertising and travel trade promotions, public relations, market research and professional development for its members, and liaison with the principal international agencies. Its work is supported by the European Commission, which sees tourism as an activity of great economic and social significance within the European Union (EU), particularly for the peripheral and somewhat poorer regions of Europe. Although a wide variety of regional disparities exist across the EU, from early on it was realised that there is a distinct tendency for the poorest regions to be situated on the outer areas of the Union and, since the late 1980s, greater emphasis has been given to stimulating small tourism firms and **indigenous development** in areas to take advantage of their natural surroundings.

Apart from the World Bank, funds for developing tourism in low-income countries may be obtained from regional banks such as: the European Bank for Reconstruction and Development (EBRD) for Eastern Europe and the Commonwealth of Independent States; the Inter-American Development Bank; African Development

The WTO can trace its origins back to 1925 to a non-governmental body that after the Second World War became the International Union of Official Travel Organisations (IUOTO). IUOTO was made up of a mixture of private and public sector organisations dealing with the technical aspects of travel and tourism. However, by the 1960s, the growth of tourism, its international dimensions and the increasing activities of national governments in this field, necessitated the transformation of IUOTO into an intergovernmental body, the WTO. The latter was ratified in 1974 and was empowered to deal on a worldwide basis with all matters concerning tourism and to cooperate with other competent world agencies that came under the umbrella of the United Nations organisation.

The WTO is an operative rather than a deliberative body that pays particular attention to the interests of the developing countries in the field of tourism. Its functions include:

- helping member countries, tourist destinations and businesses maximise the positive economic, social and cultural effects of tourism;

- identifying markets;

- assisting in tourism planning as an executing agency of the United Nations Development Programme (UNDP);

- advising on the harmonisation of policies and practices;

- sponsoring education and training, and identifying funding sources;

- promoting the broader relationship of visitors to the physical and social environment, by defining sustainability as development which meets the needs of present tourists and host regions while protecting and enhancing opportunities for the future;

- encouraging the implementation of a Global Code of Ethics for Tourism for the observance of human rights and fundamental freedoms.

As an intergovernmental body the WTO's membership works largely in terms of political groupings that can bring pressure on the general formulation of tourism policy. In order to benefit from advances in operational practice, the WTO has an affiliate membership scheme for organisations working within the tourism sector. While the general assembly of the WTO is largely concerned with debates on policy, the meetings of affiliate members usually take up topical issues affecting tourism, for example taxation. A major success of the WTO has been the methodological design of the tourism satellite account, which has set the standard for measuring the economic importance of tourism within the framework of the United Nations system of national accounts.

DISCUSSION QUESTIONS

1 Consider the benefits of having a world body that has tourism as its sole sphere of interest.

2 What priorities would you attach to the range of functions covered by the WTO?

3 If your country is a member of the WTO, what benefits do the tourist authorities perceive they get from membership?

Bank; Asian Development Bank; Arab Bank for Economic Development in Africa; East African Development Bank; and the Caribbean Development Bank. Their principles of operation are mainly for the granting of medium or long-term loans (often with various grace periods and low rates of interest) to specific projects or to national development institutions, and providing technical assistance in project preparation. They are sometimes prepared to take a minority shareholding in investments, provided there is an option for onward selling, preferably to host country nationals.

Looking at the structure in Europe, officially, tourism in the EU comes under Directorate General Enterprise, but the development work of Directorate General Regional Policy also involves tourism projects as a means of overcoming regional disparities. With the adoption of the Single European Act (1987), there is a commitment by the EU to promote economic and **social cohesion** through actions to reduce **regional disparities**, and the Maastricht Treaty (1992) acknowledged, for the first time, the role of tourism in these actions. The resources for mitigating regional differences are drawn from the structural funds, which are made up of contributions from member states with the express purposes of: helping regions lagging behind, particularly rural and sparsely populated areas; assisting the economic conversion of regions facing industrial decline; combating long-term unemployment. Alongside public monies, commercial funding of tourism projects is obtainable from the European Investment Bank.

The direct role of the EU in tourism is seen as one of simplification, harmonisation and the easing of restrictions on trade. Specifically, strategy is developed around the following objectives:

- improving the quality of European tourism services through both product development and training to upgrade skill levels;

- stimulating the demand for European tourism outside common borders;

- improving the business environment in which tourist enterprises operate, particularly through the exchange and dissemination of information via the new technologies;

- managing the impacts of new technologies; and

- moving forward tourism developments in a sustainable manner, in order to guarantee that the activity continues on a regular basis.

It is important that, in developing its strategy for tourism, the European Commission does not duplicate the work of other organisations. Ultimately, the differing nature of the tourist product within Europe leaves the Commission with little option but to assign the primary role of tourism policy to member states and proceed with tourism projects only in close partnership with national and regional bodies. The principle applied is that of **subsidiarity**, which argues for decisions to be made at the lowest level of authority so as to best meet local needs. Tourism policy is therefore, to a large degree, the responsibility of member states but the provision of research and statistics, facilitation in terms of easing frontier formalities and improvements to transport infrastructure, together with general image promotion in association with the ETC, appear to be the most favoured policies for the Commission.

All European countries have NTOs: some are part of government as in France or Spain, or in Eastern Europe, while others are established independently of government but are supported by central grants and other income-generating activities, as in the UK. The case for public sector involvement in tourism rests on concepts of market failure, namely that those who argue for the market mechanism as the sole arbiter in the allocation of resources for tourism are ignoring the lessons of history and are grossly over-simplifying the complex and varied nature of the product. In an EU context, research among member states has indicated a number of sources of market failure that the respective governments are seeking to address:

- developing tourism as a common good that collectively benefits many businesses, with the NTO acting as a broker between suppliers and potential visitors;

- infant industry development as part of regional policy (including peripheral areas), where commercial viability requires public sector support through the provision of essential infrastructure and financial incentives;

- improving the tourism product, via the implementation of measures such as benchmarking good practice and training programmes for tourism workers;

- incorporating the concept of sustainable and balanced growth into tourism by giving due regard to the cultural and environmental dimensions of tourism.

By way of contrast, the US Congress took a much more market-orientated stance and closed down the United States Travel and Tourism Administration (USTTA) in 1996, some 15 years after its establishment. In place of USTTA, a Tourism Industries office was established within the Department of Commerce with the twin objectives of increasing the number of exporters by providing research and technical assistance to communities and businesses interested in tapping international markets, and coordinating tourism-related activities and policies within government itself. The major responsibility for tourism marketing and development rests with the individual states. Nevertheless, much of the tourist product in the USA is under federal control through the Department of the Interior, whose responsibilities include:

- preserving national scenic and historic areas;

- conserving, developing and utilising fish and wildlife resources;

- coordinating federal and state recreation programmes; and

- operating job corps **conservation** youth camps.

The Forest Service of the Department of Agriculture also takes an active role in promoting and sustaining the nation's landscape.

The US experience of changes in direction of tourism policy is not uncommon in other countries. In Britain, the 1969 Act was instigated by the recognition of tourism as an important earner of foreign exchange after the devaluation of 1967. Over the years since the Act's inception, the economic policy emphasis for tourism has shifted back and forth to the extent that there is little doubt that the frequent alterations in direction have been more of a handicap than a benefit to the development of public sector tourist organisations in Britain. There have been continual changes in tourism ministers followed by one tourism review after another, though

507

all falling short of repealing the Act, but rather confining themselves to using funding as a means to curtail or expand the activities of the national boards. The tourism policies of various UK governments were summed up by the Trade and Industry Committee of the House of Commons in the following manner:

> The truth is that the Government cannot quite decide what its own role is. Along with general policy on industry, the present Government does not want to interfere with the development of the tourism industry in the private sector. Indeed, we were told that 'the Government see their own main role in relation to tourism as promoting a general economic climate favourable to the industry's development'. Given that the Government cannot control the most important climatic factor in this context – the weather – more specific strategies are needed. The Government minimises the appearance of involvement by reducing policy aims to statements of the obvious but maintains the fact of involvement in the tourist boards and the grants provided through them. The trouble is that this actual financial commitment is then left without there being any clear specific strategy to guide its use.

On the question of financial commitment, the WTO has long used the rule that the minimum of 1% of a country's tourist receipts should be devoted to the NTO, but in Britain this has never been the case.

For political reasons there is always the temptation for governments to switch policy directions. This gives the impression of the dynamics of change, but can, in practice, generate chaos through conflicting objectives. It takes a long time to create tourist destinations and build up market positions. It is, therefore, rather simplistic to behave as if the factors influencing such developments can be turned on and off as with a tap. One of the principal difficulties is that tourism is a diverse and fragmented industry with many different economic agents acting in their own interests (often on the basis of imperfect information), which may not be to the long-term benefit of tourism as a whole. Uncoordinated market competition can, in these circumstances, produce cyclical growth patterns, with a consequent waste of resources. This places a premium on an overall planning body such as an NTO, which is able to give a sense of direction by marketing the destination and acting as a distribution channel by drawing the attention of potential tourists and the travel trade to the products that the numerous suppliers in a country have to offer.

ADMINISTRATIVE FRAMEWORK

There are considerable variations in the structure of public administration of tourism, which in turn depend on the size of the tourist industry and the importance the government attaches to the various reasons advanced for public sector involvement in tourism. A generalised hierarchical structure is presented in Figure 14.1: it demonstrates a chain of direction from the governing assembly, which could be a council of ministers, a congress or a parliament, downwards to the destinations, where tourism policy and plans are implemented.

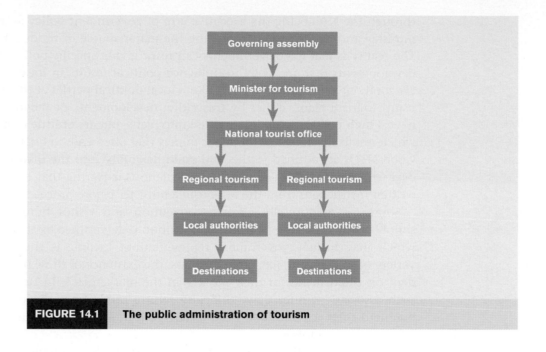

FIGURE 14.1   The public administration of tourism

Some of the most common arguments put forward for government participation in tourism include:

- foreign exchange earnings and their importance for the balance of payments;

- employment creation and the need to provide education and training;

- the fact that tourism is a large and fragmented industry which requires careful coordination of development and marketing;

- the need to maximise the net benefits to the host community;

- the need to spread the benefits and costs equitably;

- building the image of the country as a tourist destination;

- market regulation to protect consumers and prevent unfair competition;

- provision of public goods and infrastructure as part of the tourist product;

- the need to protect resources and the environment;

- the need to regulate aspects of social behaviour, for example gambling;

- the need to monitor the level of tourism activity through statistical surveys.

In most cases, where tourism is a significant element of economic activity, it is common practice to have a Ministry of Tourism. This is particularly true of island economies, which frequently form some of the world's most attractive tourist destinations. The position of the NTO within this framework may be inside or outside the ministry. In the latter case, the NTO becomes a government agency or semi-governmental body. It usually has a separate constitution, enacted by law, and a board of directors appointed from outside government which, in theory, gives independence from the political system. However, the link is maintained through the NTO being the executive arm of government policy as agreed by the ministry and public money providing the major source of funds for most NTOs. The reality is that few governments can resist giving specific policy directions for developments that are likely to influence political results in locations where the electoral outcomes are close. This allows local political parties at the destination to usurp tourism plans, either by frustrating developments or having projects that have a high political visibility inserted into plans, but are of little economic worth, which results in poor value for public money that often ends in financial insolvency. Good NTOs are attuned to this and build flexibility into the planning process to deal with barely concealed electoral calculations, ensuring that they receive prior written instructions from the responsible minister before proceeding.

Some NTOs, normally termed 'convention and visitor bureaux' (CVB), are simply private associations whose constitution is determined by their membership, which may include government representation. Income is thus raised from a variety of sources and, like other business, the existence of these bureaux is dependent on the demand for their services in the marketplace. In times of recession, such associations often have difficulty raising funds from the private sector to maintain their activities and need to have injections of public funds to continue with long-term projects.

Since the 1980s, the upsurge in market economics has seen more and more governments urging their NTOs to generate matching funds from the tourist industry. Methods to achieve this objective have included joint marketing initiatives and charging for a range of services, for example, market research reports and **brokerage fees** from arranging finance. However, the main obstacles to raising private sector revenue have always been the long-term and non-commercial nature of many of the tasks undertaken by NTOs. Added to this is the fact that when NTOs do embark on commercial activities they may be criticised by the private sector for unfair competition, because they are largely funded from taxation. Some countries, for example, many of the island tourist destinations such as Bermuda, have recognised these difficulties and have levied specific **tourist taxes** on the private sector to pay for the work of the NTO, although where such taxes are not separately set aside for tourism, it can also be argued that the tourist industry is just another source of tax revenue.

Structure of a national tourist office

A stylised organisational layout for an NTO, illustrating its principal divisions, is presented in Figure 14.2. This type of NTO is at 'arm's length' from the Ministry of Tourism by virtue of having its own chairman and board of directors. Where an NTO is a division of a ministry, which may have a wider portfolio of activities than just tourism, then it is usual for the director of tourism to report to the senior civil servant in the ministry rather than a board. Some NTOs only have marketing responsibilities and are designated as such, for example, the Singapore Tourism Board, which has overseas offices in 12 different countries. In these cases, Figure 14.2 should not have a development division and research activity is likely to be included under the marketing division.

Clearly, the exact structure of an NTO will depend upon the objectives laid down for it by government and the tasks the organisation has to undertake in order

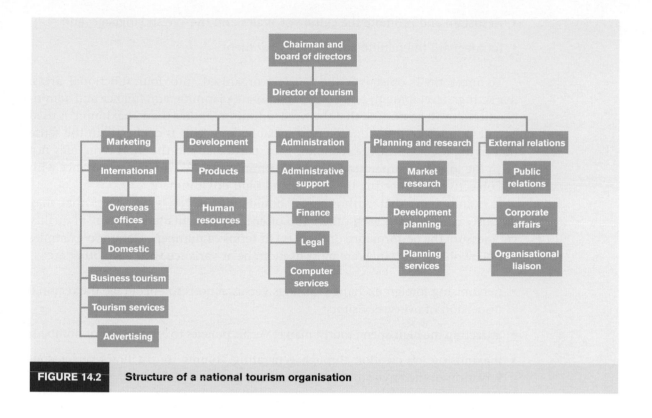

FIGURE 14.2 Structure of a national tourism organisation

to meet those same objectives. For example, the policy objectives of the Wales Tourist Board (WTB) are as follows:

- to encourage the development of tourism facilities and amenities in Wales, with a view to enhancing the quality, market appeal and competitiveness of the product;

- to conduct a cost-effective and targeted programme of strategic marketing aimed at presenting Wales as an alternative destination for holiday and day visits through the year;

- to encourage the provision of tourist information, quality controls and other means of securing visitor satisfaction within Wales;

- to encourage education and training facilities for employees in tourism, and to promote the industry as an effective and proper source of employment;

- to inspire and work with all other organisations whose activities can help to develop and market tourism in Wales;

- to assist developers and operators within the tourism industry in Wales through advisory services;

- to encourage greater community involvement and indigenous enterprise in tourism, and to seek to integrate tourism development more closely with other forms of economic, community and social development;

- to undertake research and provide policy advice, with a view to assisting decision making within the industry and helping to monitor the performance of the industry to the Board;

- to sustain and promote the culture of Wales and the Welsh language; and

- to safeguard the natural and built environment.

To meet these objectives the WTB is organised into four functional areas: marketing; development; research and corporate planning; and finance and administration. It will be noticed that the word 'optimum' rather than 'maximum' is used as a description of the economic and social benefit. This is deliberate in the sense that trying to maximise the economic gain, particularly in the short term, may not be in the long-term interests of the host community and could be at variance with the objective of protecting the natural and built environment.

It is important that governments should not set NTOs objectives that may seriously conflict with each other. Too often governments talk of tourism quality yet measure the performance of the NTO in terms of numbers. Common examples of policy objectives which are most likely to be at variance with each other are:

- maximising foreign exchange earnings versus actions to encourage the regional dispersion of overseas visitors;

- attracting the high-spend tourist market versus policies to expand visitor numbers;

- maximising job creation through generating volume tourist flows versus conservation of the environment and heritage; and

- community tourism development versus mass tourism.

MARKETING FUNCTION OF NTOS

Marketing is the principal responsibility of an NTO and therefore usually forms the largest functional area, especially when overseas offices are included. The marketing division formulates the NTO's marketing strategy and is given the task of producing the advertising campaign and publicity materials, and promoting sales through the media and the travel trade. The latter is achieved through the provision of 'familiarisation' visits to the destination, circulating a regular newsletter and press releases and attending a series of travel trade shows, of which the most significant are the International Travel Exchange, Berlin, and the World Travel Market, London. Overseas offices are responsible for exercising the functions of the marketing division in a manner which takes particular account of the preferences of the travel trade and the potential visitors in the countries or areas where they are located. They also act as 'shop windows' where potential visitors may obtain information and brochures about the host country. Many governments do not actively promote domestic tourism and so their NTOs have this section absent from their structure.

Business tourism often merits its own section within an NTO because of its importance in terms of tourist expenditure and the different servicing requirements of meetings, exhibitions and incentive travel groups when compared with leisure tourism. Likewise, advertising is such a key activity that it may command its own specialist group to plan campaigns and deal with outside advertising agencies. Tourism services include a multitude of tasks such as:

- operating a reservation system;

- handling tourist complaints;

- licensing and grading of hotels and other suppliers (which may include price controls);

- programming festivals, events and tours; and

- managing tourist facilities provided either solely or jointly by the NTO, for example, tourist information centres (TICs) or tourist beaches, as in Cyprus.

DEVELOPMENT FUNCTION OF NTOS

The development division can only have truly operational involvement if it is given funding to engage in projects with the private sector and implement training programmes and activities. If this is not the case then it can only take on a coordinating and strategic role. The former is achieved by acting as a 'one-stop shop' for prospective developers through intermediation to obtain planning permission, licences and any financial assistance or incentives from the relevant authorities. In a strategic role the development division will acquire the planning functions that have been allocated to the planning and research division in Figure 14.2. The reason for the separation in Figure 14.2 rests on the fact that an operational development division is likely to be too heavily involved in day-to-day project management to be able to incorporate long-term development planning. The latter is a research activity and therefore best located in the unit equipped for this task. The planning services section is an important addendum to the role of an NTO in that it seeks to capitalise on the expertise of the organisation to provide advice and even undertake studies for the private sector and other public bodies, for example, drawing up tourism plans for local communities.

The remaining divisions shown in Figure 14.2 are, to a large extent, self-explanatory. Administration is responsible for the internal smooth running of the NTO and will normally adjudicate on legal matters in respect of tourism legislation, including, in some countries, carrying out prosecutions. External relations is a functional area of considerable significance because the NTO is frequently the representative of the government, both at home and overseas, and has to deal with a mass of enquiries from the public, the media and commercial operators, as well as taking an active stance in public relations to support the advertising and sales promotion administered by the marketing division. It is for the latter reason that external relations may be allocated to marketing, although the tasks given to the division are usually much broader than those required by marketing, as is the case of liaison activities with a variety of public bodies and voluntary associations who have an interest in tourism.

Given the complexity of the tourist product, more recent emphasis on the liaison role of the NTO has focused on building partnerships in line with models of community tourism development, so as to bring the various stakeholders together. If the institutional framework is to function in a manner that is socially compatible, then there is a prerequisite for local involvement in the development process to encourage discussion about future directions. Cultural conflicts need to be resolved through, say, staging development and using marketing communication channels to prepare guests better for their holiday experience. From experience in **less developed countries** (LDCs), the greater the difference in lifestyles between hosts and guests and the less the former have been exposed to visitors, then the longer should be the period of adaptation.

IMPACT OF THE PUBLIC SECTOR

In the light of public sector involvement with tourism, either directly through a ministry with responsibility for tourism and the NTO, or indirectly through, say, foreign policy, legal controls or the provision of infrastructure, the government has at its disposal a series of instruments that can be used to manage tourism flows to meet its policy objectives. The manner in which actions by governments influence tourism may be classified in two ways:

- demand and revenue management; and
- supply and cost management.

Demand and revenue management

There are primarily five policy instruments used by governments to manage demand:

- marketing and promotion;
- information provision and network development;
- pricing;
- controlling access: and
- safety and security.

MARKETING AND PROMOTION

As has already been observed, marketing is the principal function of the NTO and its job is to create and protect the 'brand image' of the country/destination. The specific techniques are discussed in Part Four of this book, so it is sufficient here to point out that the key requirements for effective marketing are clear objectives, a thorough knowledge of markets and products, and the allocation of adequate resources. It would, however, be putting the 'cart before the horse' without the product, which is generally not under the control of the NTO, hence the importance of assigning the NTO some development powers. Typically, with many other calls on the government's budget, treasury officials are naturally parsimonious with regard to expenditure on marketing because of difficulties in measuring effectiveness. As a rule, the amounts spent by governments and other public organisations on destination promotion are only a fraction of what is spent in total by the private sector. One of the main reasons for this is that private enterprises are competing for market share *at the destination*, whereas governments are interested in expanding the total market *to the destination*.

INFORMATION PROVISION AND NETWORK DEVELOPMENT

The ability of tourists to express their demands depends upon their awareness of the facilities available, particularly attractions, which are a key component of leisure tourism. For a number of years there has been government interest in creating computer-based national reservation systems. NTOs in Europe have already been operating 'holiday hotlines' and out-of-hours telephone information. In many countries, local tourist information centres (TICs) offer a booking service to personal callers, though still very much a manual system requiring TIC staff to telephone accommodation establishments to check availability. For example, in Britain, the TIC network was used to develop the 'Book a Bed Ahead' scheme for the independent traveller touring different parts of the country. However, as more and more bookings are being made electronically, what is ideal is a fully networked **computerised reservation system** (CRS). The key to penetrating the source markets from the destinations lies in using the CRS to link suitable accommodation to a range of 'things to see and do', so what is being sold is a complete holiday, not just accommodation. Although desirable, this does not necessarily mean complete packaging of other products: it would be an improvement just to use complementary suppliers in marketing and to couple this with the provision of good information on site. Others would go further and recommend a complete destination management system that acts as a neutral facilitator to the tourist industry, which would put small businesses on the same footing as the major corporate suppliers.

Implementation of a **destination management system** via the NTO or regional tourist association is no easy task: in the past, proposals at the local level have foundered on the unwillingness of small enterprises to give commission, to make booking allocations available, competitive jealousies concerning the equity of how bookings will be distributed by TIC staff and arguments over classification and grading, an essential ingredient for the inclusion in such a scheme, as in all tourist bureau publications. Such experiences suggest that a computerised destination management system cannot be implemented or sustained without a great deal of public sector involvement, particularly if the ETC's ideal of Europe as a single destination is to be realised. Examples of such systems can be found in Austria, Denmark and Switzerland, but it appears that the most likely route is for NTOs to act as facilitators to bookings through provision of information on their web sites and links to agencies providing reservation services, so that end users and re-sellers can access the product of the destination, and search, book and pay in a single application, as well as building networks to connect businesses and consumers to TICs. Why people do not book online is to do with ease of booking, credit card security, trust in the supplier and lack of consistent information.

The evidence suggests that the creation of trails or tourist circuits will enhance the visitor experience as well as regulating tourist flows. The establishment of a network of TICs and tourist information points (TIPs) at transport terminals and prominent tourist spots will both help the visitor and assist in dispersion. It is often not appreciated that it is the poorly informed visitor who is likely to contribute to crowding and traffic congestion because of a lack of knowledge about where to go and what there is to see at the destination. Normally, visitors will first look for the main attractions and then move on to lesser attractions as their length of stay increases. Giving prominence to the variety of attractions available, restricting advertising and informing excursion operators of times when congestion can be avoided are examples of the way in which information management can be used to try to relieve pressure on sensitive tourist areas.

In some countries, NTOs use the provision of information to influence tourists' behaviour. This may come about through editing the information in the tour operator's brochure so that it does not generate unrealistic expectations about a destination and presents the tourist with an informed view of the culture of the host community. An alternative approach is a poster and leaflet campaign aimed directly at the tourist to explain the 'dos and don't's' of acceptable behaviour; for example, several island resorts offering beach holidays produce leaflets on standards of dress and the unacceptability of wearing only swimsuits in shops, banks and so on.

PRICING

There are several ways in which the public sector may affect the price the tourist pays for staying at a destination. The direct influence arises out of state ownership, notably in the case of attractions. Many of the most important attractions at a destination fall within the public domain, an issue that is examined in some detail in Chapter 10, which is specifically about attractions. The trend in market-orientated economies is for governments to introduce charges for publicly owned attractions. Many of the world's airlines are owned by governments, though the trend is increasingly towards privatisation or, if not, the liberalisation of air policy, particularly in response to the rise of low-cost airlines. It is not uncommon in less developed countries to find state ownership of hotels and souvenir shops. Thus in some countries, the key elements making up holiday expenditure are directly affected by the public sector, to the point of reaching total control in the situation that existed in the former centrally planned economies of Eastern Europe.

Indirect influences come from economic directives such as foreign exchange restrictions, differential rates of sales tax, special duty-free shops for tourists and price controls. Exchange restrictions are commonly employed in countries where foreign exchange is scarce and the tourist is usually compelled to change money at an overvalued exchange rate which serves to increase the real cost of the trip. Tourists are discouraged from changing money on the black market by threats of legal prosecution and severe penalties if caught. The case for price controls is advanced in terms of promoting the long-term growth of the tourist industry and preventing monopolistic exploitation of tourists through overcharging, a practice that can be damaging to the reputation of the destination.

The argument for price regulation is illustrated in Figure 14.3. Initially the destination is receiving V_1 visitors, paying an average package price of P_1 for their stay, with equilibrium being determined at the intersection of the demand schedule D_1D_1 and the short-run supply curve S_1S_1. Demand expands to D_2D_2, which gives the opportunity for suppliers to raise prices to P_2, at the market equilibrium point B. This arises because significant parts of the tourism sector, such as airlines and hotels, are open to revenue or yield management systems, whereby market adjustment is more likely to be through price than quantity. These systems are designed to improve performance in situations where the product is relatively homogeneous and perishable, demand is seasonal, capacity is fixed in the short run and suppliers have the ability to segment the market. In simple terms this is described as 'making money while you can', which can be counter-productive, because demand in the longer term is more sensitive to price than in the short run, as illustrated by the slope of D_{L2}. The reasons for this lie in the number of competing destinations and the holiday price consciousness of travellers. The price control argument says that by keeping price at P_2 existing suppliers will make excess profits, but

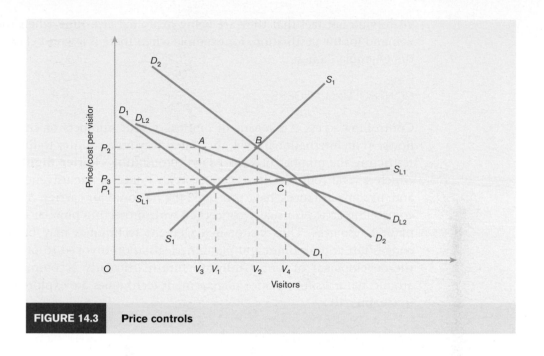

FIGURE 14.3   **Price controls**

this could be at the expense of the destination's market share. This is shown on Figure 14.3 as a new market equilibrium position at A, where visitor numbers have fallen back from V_2 to V_3. The destination is perceived as 'pricing itself out of the market'.

There is no doubt that destinations are aware of their price competitiveness and some NTOs compile a tourist price index for their own country as well as others, in order to assess their relative market position. Where governments regulate prices, the objective is to set their level at, say, P_3 which is sufficient to encourage the long-run growth in supply as shown by S_{L1} and commensurate with market expansion to an equilibrium point such as C, giving a growth in visitor numbers to V_4. Producers, on the other hand, are prevented from making short-term excess profits.

Where price controls are enforced, they are normally a further stage in an overall market regulation package, which commences with the registration and licensing of establishments. In the case of hotels this will include classification and possibly a quality grading system. Price regulation can be found in almost all instances where the government manages capacity and therefore restricts competition. Worldwide, the most common example is the licensing and metering of taxis. Where competition exists then the argument put forward in Figure 14.3 hinges upon whether supply adjusts more quickly than demand. There have been many examples of Mediterranean resorts where the growth of bed capacity has outstripped demand and so the problem for the authorities has been more an issue of controlling standards than prices, as well as trying to prevent ruinous competition among hoteliers. In market economics there is a basic ideology that is against regulating prices and where opportunities for suppliers to make excess profits in the short term do arise, control is often exercised informally through exhortation that it will not be in the long-term best interests of the destination. This has been termed 'maintaining rate integrity' through long-term pricing strategies, so that visitors do not feel that they are being exploited at a time when there is a high demand for the destination, for example when there is a world-class event such as the Olympic Games.

CONTROLLING ACCESS

Controlling access is a means of limiting visitor numbers or channelling visitor flows. At an international level, the easiest way for a country to limit demand is by restricting the number of visas issued. Prohibiting **charter flights** is a means by which several countries have conveyed an image of exclusiveness to the market and, in some instances, have protected the **national air carrier**. At the destination, controlling access is usually concerned with protecting popular cultural sites and natural resources. Thus visitor management techniques may be used to relieve congestion at peak times and planning legislation invoked to prohibit or control the development of tourist infrastructure (particularly accommodation) near or around natural sites. (Visitor management techniques are explored in more detail in Chapter 10.)

SAFETY AND SECURITY

There have always been issues of criminal activities targeted at tourists, particularly in countries where there are large disparities between 'the haves and have-nots'. Older age groups are perceived as being more vulnerable, which is compounded by the fact that many tourist environments are designed for open access and some are from the past when the security of guests was not high on the agenda. Increasingly, tourist enterprises have tightened security and visitors have been given advice to make them 'street-wise'. Governments have also instituted special tourist police, as in Egypt and Brazil, and tourism victim support services, for example, Ireland and Holland.

On the supply side, the cash-rich nature of tourism operations makes them a convenient channel for money laundering from organised criminal gangs, or simply from individuals evading taxes or trying to find a safe haven for their money abroad because they have no confidence in the domestic financial system due to corrupt practices. Casinos, real estate transactions and purchases of luxury items such as jewellery are distinct favourites for money-laundering activities.

Unfortunately, terrorism is much more difficult to deal with, because its causes have little to do with tourism. It is associated with political and religious fanaticism, civil wars, and rich–poor income gaps that result in political turbulence, giving rise to mass protests and riots. What is special about the destruction of the World Trade Center in New York in 2001 is that tourist destinations were largely caught unawares, as few had crisis management plans to deal with the consequences for international travel flows.

One additional issue of safety and security to consider is the growing tide of anti-globalisation protests around the world, particularly at highly sensitive political meetings such as those held by G8 and the World Economic Forum. Although not directly targeting tourism, the increasing global nature of much of the tourism industry may make it a future target for protesters. Irrespective of how real the threat is, or is likely to be, tourism needs to heed the viewpoints of all stakeholders when planning future developments.

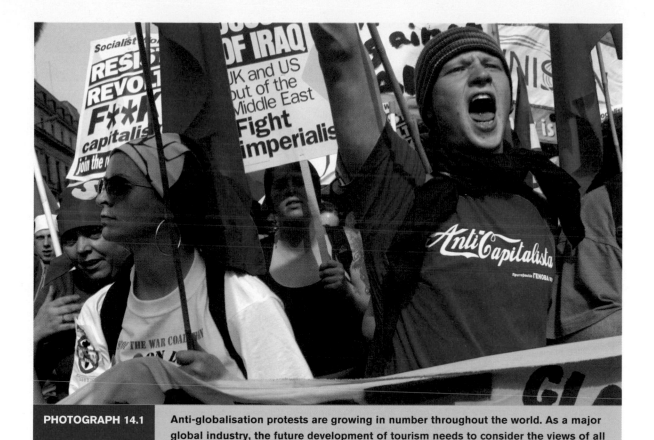

PHOTOGRAPH 14.1	**Anti-globalisation protests are growing in number throughout the world. As a major global industry, the future development of tourism needs to consider the views of all its stakeholders if it is to be compatible with economic, environmental and wider societal objectives**
	Source: In Visu/CORBIS

Supply and cost management

Government activity on the supply side is concerned with influencing the providers of tourist facilities and services, as opposed to demand management policies aimed at guiding the tourist's choice, controlling the costs of stay or stimulating/regulating visitor numbers. We have already stressed that the development of tourism should be regarded as a partnership between the private and public sectors. The extent of government involvement in this partnership depends upon the prevailing economic, political and social policies of a country. Where the government envisages a particular direction for tourism growth or wishes to speed up the process, it may intervene extensively in the marketplace by setting up a tourist development corporation (TDC) and assigning it the responsibility for building resorts. A well-known example of this process was the building of new resorts in Languedoc–Roussillon, France, but many countries have instituted TDCs at one time or another, for example, Egypt, India, Malaysia, Mexico (see Mini case study 14.2), New Zealand and a number of African countries. In theory, once the resort has been built, the development corporation's function ceases and the assets are transferred to the private sector (at a price) and the local authority. This is the general trend in market-orientated economies, but in countries where there is a strong degree of central planning, the TDC often maintains an operational role in

MINI CASE STUDY 14.2
FONATUR: Mexico

Tourism in Mexico began as a totally private sector activity. Its growth was limited in size (largely in the area of Acapulco), the product on offer was generally poor and developments were unplanned. To counteract this, the government of Mexico, in 1974, created FONATUR (Fundo Nacional de Fomento al Turismo) for the purpose of developing resorts and funded the organisation from oil revenues and World Bank loans. Apart from trying to regulate development, the principal reasons for state involvement were:

- to realise potential demand by increasing the number of resorts;
- to generate foreign exchange;
- to create employment; and
- for regional development, in particular moving the jobless from Mexico City to the new resorts and raising regional GDP.

FONATUR has developed and consolidated six regional resorts, attracting a wide range of international investors. The government gives FONATUR the development land it requires without charge, the resources to develop a master plan and the money to construct the necessary infrastructure, including hotel building. Once complete, the investment is sold to the private sector. The terms for private sector projects are generous: loans for up to 50% of the capital investment, over a period of 15 years. The 'flagship' project was Cancun on Mexico's Caribbean coast, but this is now mature and issues have arisen about spillover developments outside the original zone and adverse impacts on the environment.

The Mexican government's approach here has a long lineage in terms of development policy. Much of regional tourism development planning is underpinned by the 'growth pole' principle, with the aim of raising regional export values through tourism. The focus is the creation of a destination (growth pole) through an investment strategy that provides a balanced range of facilities to meet visitor requirements and at a level that gives the area 'tourism presence' in the marketplace. At a more local level the same principle can be found in the formation of partnerships to promote community tourism development.

Source: FONATUR

DISCUSSIONS QUESTIONS

1 Consider the strengths and weaknesses of public ownership of tourism facilities.

2 Is regional intervention an efficient policy in a market economy?

3 Suggest other methods FONATUR might use to stimulate regional development.

running hotels and tours. Beyond this, governments may also establish a development bank with duties to provide special credit facilities for tourist projects and on-lend funds made available by multinational aid agencies. This is common in LDCs where capital funds are short and local capital markets are weak.

The methods that are frequently used by governments to influence the supply side of the tourism industry are:

- land-use planning and environmental control;

- building regulations;

- market regulation;

- market research and planning;

- taxation;

- ownership;

- education and training; and

- investment incentives.

LAND-USE PLANNING AND ENVIRONMENTAL CONTROL

Control over land use is the most basic technique and arguably the one that has the greatest influence on the supply of tourist structures. All governments have a form of town and country planning legislation whereby permission is required to develop, extend or change the use of almost every piece of land. As a rule, the controls are designed to protect areas of high landscape and amenity value. The case is that the environment has an intrinsic value, which outweighs its value as a tourism asset. Its enjoyment by future generations and its long-term survival must not be prejudiced by short-term considerations.

Zoning of land and compulsory purchase are commonly used as a means of promoting tourism development. One of the key aspects of land control is that before any detailed site plans and future land requirements for tourism are published, the appropriate administrative organisation and legislation is in place in order to prevent speculation, land division or parcelling. Dealings or speculation in land prior to legislative control have been a common cause of failure in tourism master plans.

BUILDING REGULATIONS

Building regulations are used to supplement land-use control and typically cover the size of buildings, height, shape, colour and car-parking arrangements. The last is a matter that is not always given the attention it deserves in some resorts. To private sector operators, car parks are often considered unproductive space and so there is a tendency to avoid having to provide them, leaving visitors little alternative than to park their cars in nearby streets. This may only serve to add to traffic congestion and the annoyance of local residents. In addition to structural regulations, many countries also have protective legislation governing cultural resources such as historic buildings, archaeological remains, religious monuments, conservation areas and even whole towns.

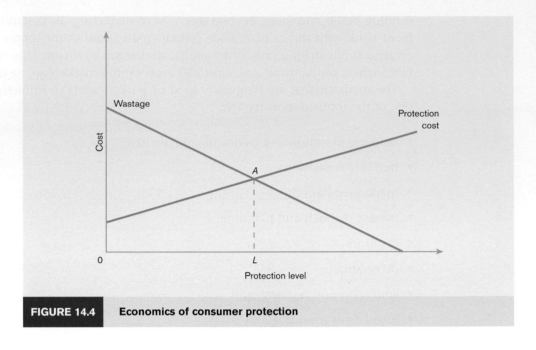

FIGURE 14.4   **Economics of consumer protection**

MARKET REGULATION

Governments pass legislation to regulate the market conduct of firms in matters of competitive practices and also to limit the degree of ownership in particular sectors of the industry to prevent the abuse of monopoly power. Governments may also regulate markets by imposing on suppliers obligations to consumers. This does not have to be legislation; it could be industry-enforced codes of conduct of the kind laid down as conditions for membership of national travel trade associations, though in Europe such codes have passed into the legislation of member states as a result of the EU Package Travel Directive.

One of the economic criteria dictating the optimal workings of markets is that consumers should have complete knowledge of the choices open to them. For if consumers do not have the right to safety, to be informed, to choose or of redress and firms are not behaving according to the accepted rules of conduct, then resources will be wasted, which may be seen to be inefficient. The economic aspects of a consumer policy are shown in Figure 14.4. As the level of protection increases, so wastage or compensation payments decline, while at the same time the costs of protection increase. The optimum amount of protection is where the two schedules intersect at point *A*, which defines level *L* on the axis below. This is the economic rationale: on social or political grounds the state may legislate to ensure nearly 100% protection. But the economic consequences of such an action could be to raise the supply price of the good or service to the point where the market is substantially diminished. At the consultation stage of the EU Package Travel Directive amendments were accepted to some of the proposals on the grounds that their compliance would significantly raise holiday prices.

MARKET RESEARCH AND PLANNING

The tourist industry usually expects the public sector to collect statistical information and carry out market surveys. The NTO is naturally concerned with understanding demographic and lifestyle changes in its source markets and how they affect the image of the country. For their own part, governments are interested in monitoring changes in the industry and carry out research to identify the social benefits and costs of tourism. The emerging research themes that suggest themselves from the new tourism trends discussed in this book are: changes in the demographic structure and lifestyles upon tourism demand; product management and innovations in distribution facing the industry; improving the attractiveness of destinations through product development and the strengthening of public/private sector partnerships.

When dealing with products that belong to the tourism sector, the transformation of invention to innovation cannot be compared to the processes seen in manufacturing. Manufacturing starts with product innovation (invention and introduction of the product), qualitative process innovation (the setting up of the manufacturing systems), and quantitative process innovation (improvements and rationalisation of the production system for mass supply). Tourism products start with the quantitative process innovation by taking established products and using them to increase the efficiency of current service production, which, in turn, leads to qualitative changes in the production system and then wholly transformed or entirely new service experiences, which are the output of the tourism industry. Thus some of the most successful visitor attractions are the result of brand extensions of products that are the output of another industrial process, as for example, LEGOLAND parks (see p. 378, Chapter 10).

TAXATION

There are two main reasons why governments levy specific taxes on the tourism sector. The first is the classic argument for a **tourist tax**, namely to allocate to the supply price the external costs imposed on the host community through providing public amenities for tourists. The second is for purposes of raising revenue; tourists are seen as part of the overall tax base and, from a political perspective, they are not voters in the destination country. With the growth of tourism worldwide, there has been an escalation in the number of countries levying tourist taxes and in the rates of taxation, drawing the inference that governments principally see such taxes as a source of revenue. It is not unreasonable that the tourist industry should pay taxes, but the World Travel and Tourism Council (WTTC) has argued that such payments should be made in accordance with the following guidelines:

- Equity: the fair and even-handed treatment of travel and tourism with respect to the other sectors of the economy.

- Efficiency: the development of tax policies that have a minimal effect on the demand for travel and tourism, unless specifically imposed for the purpose of regulating tourist flows, to, say, environmentally sensitive areas (see Chapter 10).

- Simplicity: taxes should be simple to pay and administer, so as not to disrupt the operation of the travel and tourism system.

The most common forms of raising public income from tourism are airport departure taxes, ticket taxes and taxes on hotel occupancy. When it comes to raising revenue, casinos can be a very profitable source: governments have been known to take as much as 50% of the 'drop', which is the amount of money taken in from the tables.

523

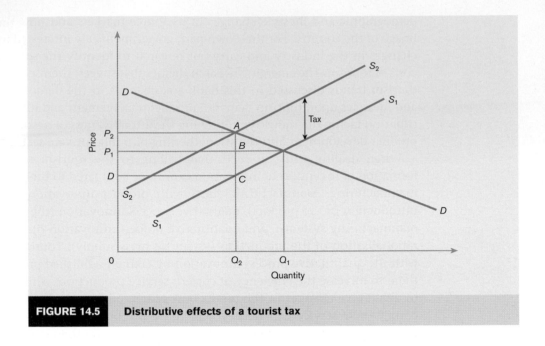

| FIGURE 14.5 | Distributive effects of a tourist tax |

Although a tourist tax may be paid by the guest at the hotel and collected from the hotelier, the incidence as to who bears the tax will depend on the responsiveness of demand and supply to a price change. In Figure 14.5, the imposition of a tax raises the supply price by moving the supply curve from S_1S_1 to S_2S_2, which in turn reduces the quantity of, say, room sales demanded from Q_1 to Q_2. However, the amount of tax income raised P_2ACD does not all fall on the tourists in the form of a higher price. Price rises from P_1 to P_2 only and the larger share of the incidence of the tax P_1BCD falls on the supplier in the form of reduced profits. Tourists contribute P_2ABP_1 of the tax revenue. The less sensitive tourists are to price, something that can be reflected in a much steeper demand schedule DD, the greater is the ability of suppliers to pass on the tax in the form of a higher price and therefore, the larger will be the share of the tax burden falling on the tourists.

OWNERSHIP

Mention has already been made of state ownership of attractions, natural amenities and some key revenue-earning activities such as hotels, modes of transport (especially airlines) and souvenir shops. It is possible to add to this list conference centres, exhibition halls, sports and leisure complexes (including casinos), and the provision of general infrastructure. The last may include: banks; hospitals; public utilities (water and energy supplies); telecommunications; road networks; transport terminals; and education and training establishments. The arguments for public ownership of these facilities rest on their importance as essential services for any economic development, the fact that outside investors would expect such provision and economies of scale in production. Traditionally, public infrastructure and transport networks have been regarded as natural monopolies; the minimum scale of production is such as to make it impossible for more than one firm to enjoy all the economies in the market, so that even if they were not publicly owned, these organisations would need to be publicly regulated.

EDUCATION AND TRAINING

The provision of an educated and trained labour force to meet the demands of a modern economy has been a task that has fallen to many governments. In common with other planning activities, this requires an assessment of the current occupational distribution of the tourism work force, which is then mapped onto the general educational level of each occupational group. Overall forecasts of economic activity for the tourist industry are then turned into manpower needs, which are compared to projections of supply from existing trends in the education system, enabling the estimation of surpluses and deficits. It is then possible to lay down a strategy for the implementation of projects in the education and training sector to bring demand and supply as close together as might be deemed practical, given the somewhat looseness of the linkage between education and the skills base of the labour force. Actions to augment this may be the provision of low-cost housing for key workers in resort areas, as well as immigration policies to add to the quality of the workforce.

INVESTMENT INCENTIVES

Governments around the world offer a wide range of investment incentives to developers. They may be grouped under three broad headings:

1 Reduction of **capital costs.** This includes capital grants or loans at preferential rates, interest rate relief, a moratorium on loan repayments for, say, x years, provision of infrastructure, provision of land on concessional terms, tariff exemption on construction materials and equity participation.

2 Reduction of **operating costs.** In order to improve operating viability governments may grant tax 'holidays' (5–10 years), give a labour or training subsidy, offer tariff exemption on imported materials and supplies, provide special depreciation allowances and ensure that there is double taxation or unilateral relief. The latter are government-to-government agreements that prevent an investor being taxed twice on the same profits.

3 **Investment security.** The object here is to win investors' confidence in an industry that is very sensitive to the political environment and economic climate. Action here would include guarantees against nationalisation, free availability of foreign exchange, repatriation of invested capital, profits, dividends and interest, loan guarantees, provision of work permits for 'key' personnel and the availability of technical advice.

The administration of grants or loans may be given to the NTO, a government-sponsored investment bank or the TDC. Tax matters will usually remain the responsibility of the treasury or the ministry in charge of finance. Less developed countries are often able to attract low-cost investment funds from multinational aid agencies, which they can use to augment their existing resources for the provision of development finance.

It may be taken that policies to ensure investment security are primary requirements for attracting tourism developers. The objective of financial incentives is to improve returns to capital so as to attract developers and investors. Where there is obvious market potential the government may only have to demonstrate its

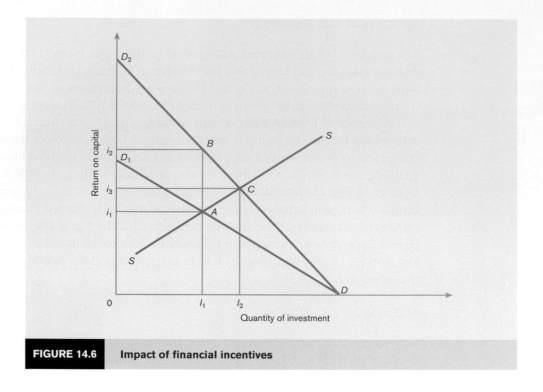

FIGURE 14.6   **Impact of financial incentives**

commitment to tourism by providing the necessary climate for investment security. Such a situation occurred in Bermuda during the early 1970s and so, in order to prevent over-exploitation of the tourism resources, the Bermuda government imposed a moratorium on large hotel building.

The impact of financial incentives on the amount of investment is illustrated in Figure 14.6. The schedule SS represents the supply of investible funds while D_1D is the scheduled of returns to capital employed. D_1D slopes downwards from left to right as more and more investment opportunities are taken up – the declining marginal efficiency of investment. In the initial situation, equilibrium is at A with the amount of investment being I_1 and the rate of return i_1.

Conditions of market failure imply that the community benefits from tourism investment are not entirely captured in the demand function D_1D. Optimal economic efficiency is where the demand function includes these external effects, as represented by D_2D. The government now implements a range of financial incentives that have the effect of raising the rate of return per unit of capital to i_2, moving the marginal efficiency of investment schedule to D_2D. The new return i_2 equals $(1 + s)i_1$, where s is the effective rate of subsidy. If the amount of investible funds available for tourism is limited at I_1, then the impact of incentives serves merely to raise the return to investors by raising the equilibrium point to B. The loss to the government treasury is the area $i_1 AB i_2$ which equals the gain to private investors.

There is no doubt that many countries have been forced by competitive pressures for foreign investment into situations that are similar to those above. Countries can become trapped in a bidding process to secure clients and as a result the variety of financial incentives multiplies together with an escalation of the rates of benefit, without evaluating their necessity or their true cost to the economy. Given that the supply of investment funds is responsive or elastic, the net effect of an incentives policy is to expand the amount of tourism projects to I_2 and the rate of return settles at i_3, the equilibrium point being C. The private opportunity cost of the investment funds is the area under the supply curve, $I_1\,AC\,I_2$, while the public willingness-to-pay for correcting for market failure is the area $I_1\,BC\,I_2$: subtracting the two areas gives a net gain represented by the area ABC.

It is important to note that there are frequent instances where it is gross uncertainty, as in times of recession, rather than limited potential that prevents the private sector investing. In such situations the principal role of government intervention is to act as a catalyst to give confidence to investors. Thus public funds are able to lever in private money by nature of the government's commitment to tourism and enable the market potential of an area to be realised.

In implementing a tourism investment policy the government has to decide to what extent incentives should be legislated as automatic entitlements, as against being discretionary awards. It has already been noted that automatic incentives may give too much money away, when what is required to ensure that the treasury receives maximum benefit from its funds is the application of the concept of 'project additionality'. The latter seeks to provide financial support or the equivalent benefits in kind to the point where the developer will just proceed with the project.

The implication of **additionality** is an ideal situation where all incentives are discretionary and therefore offered selectively. The legislation would be fairly general, empowering the ministry responsible for tourism to offer loans, grants, tax exemptions and equity investment as it sees fit. As an example, such legislation is embodied in the UK 1969 Development of Tourism Act. Section 4 of the 1969 Act states that:

4. (1) A Tourist Board shall have power –
  (a) in accordance with arrangements approved by the relevant Minister and the Treasury, to give financial assistance for the carrying out of any project which in the opinion of the Board will provide or improve tourist amenities and facilities in the country for which the Board is responsible;
  (b) with the approval of the relevant Minister and the Treasury, to carry out any such project as aforesaid.

  (2) Financial assistance under subsection (1) (a) of this section may be given by way of grant or loan or, if the project is being or is to be carried out by a company incorporated in Great Britain, by subscribing for or otherwise acquiring shares or stock in the company, or by any combination of those methods.

  (3) In making a grant or loan in accordance with arrangements approved under subsection (1) (a) of this section a Tourist Board may, subject to the arrangements, impose such terms and conditions as it thinks fit, including conditions for the repayment of a grant in specified circumstances; and Schedule 2 to this Act shall have effect for securing compliance with conditions subject to which any such grant is made.

  (4) A Tourist Board shall not dispose of any shares or stock acquired by it by virtue of this section except –
  (a) after consultation with the company in which the shares or stock are held; and
  (b) with the approval of the relevant Minister and the Treasury.

The granting of incentives to prospective developers is in accordance with ministerial guidelines, which are regularly reviewed in response to the level of tourism activity.

To have only **discretionary incentives**, however, is a counsel of perfection. Competition for tourism investment frequently requires countries to legislate for automatic financial help in order to attract investors in the first instance. Some countries may legislate for all the incentives discussed here; others for a subset of them. Several countries have been guilty of copying incentive legislation without any real grasp of its meaning.

The appropriateness of the various financial incentives available depends on understanding the nature of the business risk and the probable returns to the tourist industry, as well as the ability of the country to afford them. Thus developing countries may find themselves in no position to offer grants or cheap loans, which highlights the importance of contributions from aid agencies. One of the main sources of business risk in tourist enterprises is the tendency to have a high ratio of capital charges in relation to operating expenses. It is for this reason that incentives to reduce capital costs are the preferred form of assistance when the viability of the business is being considered.

INTERVENTION POLICY

The range of policy instruments available to governments is considerable and enables the public sector to exercise varying degrees of influence over the direction of tourism development. From the perspective of the NTO charged with implementing a national development strategy, it might be thought that once the objectives have been defined then it is simply a matter of packaging the appropriate instruments to achieve the desired results. However, this ignores the political dimension. We have already discussed earlier how outside political influences at the destination level may alter policy at the top, but in any representative political system there are a number of inside influences on the governing authority.

Political parties influence the government of the day through the preparation of the manifesto, which it is the task of the minister to steer through the governing assembly. The pressure groups on the assembly to form policy are many. They range from the governing party itself, various statutory bodies, trade associations, trade unions, individual industries, clubs and ordinary people. Typical activities undertaken include: holding receptions at the assembly; representations to government; meetings with senior civil servants; individual lobbying of elected representatives; and evidence to government committees. The latter are the 'workhorses' of government for policy purposes, as the floor of the assembly is largely a debating chamber where matters under discussion may be secondary to the objective of 'scoring a point' over the opposition.

The membership of a government committee is normally representative of all the major political parties, with a majority in favour of the governing party for voting purposes. A committee will normally conduct its enquiry in three ways:

- invite written memoranda;
- take oral evidence from expert witnesses; and
- undertake fact-finding tours.

All evidence given to a government committee has to be received formally, since it provides the basis on which recommendations are made. The reality is that in making recommendations a committee can only act within its sphere of influence, otherwise it can appear foolish. If a particular project does not appear in the report, it is because no supporting evidence was given. In the taking of oral evidence, the presence of the press can make the questioning combative, and while this may produce headlines for some politicians, it usually serves no useful purpose. With expectations raised, it becomes impossible to have a discussion of the issues without them appearing in the press as a major row.

Generally speaking, to be accepted the recommendations of government committees have to fit into a tourism strategy that is structured around tolerable political criteria rather than tourism needs. It should be remembered that the 'status quo' in politics is a powerful force to be reckoned with. The government is unlikely to accept recommendations that are politically contentious, in respect, say, of its manifesto or require significant legislative changes or are likely to upset the Ministry of Finance. It is not surprising therefore, that tourism professionals will often be frustrated by the direction of government policy, which may be described as 'the art of the possible' within the context of the various interest groups. At best the outcomes of government committees are improvements to policy and at worst they are a damage limitation exercise, filtering out 'bizarre' ideas.

CONCLUSION

Around the globe governments have intervened to assist and regulate the private sector; this is because the complex nature of the tourist product makes it unlikely that private markets will satisfy all the tourism policy objectives of a country. The role of governmental organisations in the influencing of tourism supply and the manipulation of tourism demand is critical in the shaping of the tourism system. We saw how governmental involvement may influence the demand for tourism in Part One of this book and, in this part, we demonstrated the function of public sector bodies in coordinating and funding the supply aspects of the tourism product. The trend towards pure market-led economics stemming from the 1980s has led to a clawback of state involvement and the questioning of intervention as mechanisms more likely to lead to market distortions than market corrections. This was in total contrast to the concept of sustainable development, which challenges the ability of private markets to improve the distribution of income and protect the environment. The spillover benefits of tourism are well known, and, more than any other industry, tourism deals with the use of natural and cultural resources. The lessons of the past indicate that it is unwise for governments to abandon their ability to influence the direction of tourism development. Tourism is a truly global business that has reduced the power of national governments to shield themselves from outside events, so what is required is a pragmatic approach to intervention and regulation, with an emphasis on collaboration between government agencies through international bodies. It would be convenient if there were a few instruments or levers, which could be considered optimal for the implementation of tourism policy. Certainly, the tourist industry responds strongly to legislation and the availability of finance, but the tourist product varies so much around the globe that it is customary for states to adopt a bundle of instruments and adjust them over time, in response to feedback information on their workings.

Self-check questions

1 Why are international tourism organisations important for tourism and tourism development?

2 Suggest some of the areas in a continent of your choice that might be classified as peripheral and the features that would make them attractive for tourism development.

3 Suggest some of the non-governmental organisations in your own country that have a significant influence on tourism policy.

4 Why are pan-regional organisations, such as the EU and PATA, concerned about regional inequalities?

5 How important is tourism in respect of its contribution to the GDP of member states and employment in a political union of your choice?

Essay questions

1 What are the strengths and weaknesses of positioning tourism projects within an overall strategy to guide their use as opposed to opportunistic development?

2 The nature of grant aid from the EU has been described as conditional matching funding. Other forms of grant mechanisms are lump-sum payments, which may be tied to specific projects (conditional) or just given to the overall programme (unconditional). Discuss the relative merits of these different systems.

3 Taking a country of your choice, define the roles and functions of its national tourism office. How might an NTO exercise its responsibilities for marketing a country?

4 Compare and contrast the complementary and conflicting roles of the public and private sector in the coordination and funding of tourism.

5 The new approach in the USA is to treat tourism in the same manner as any other traded good or service and withdraw from direct action – is this correct? What are the principal features of tourism in the USA that seem to dictate a policy that runs counter to that of most governments in the world?

Annotated further reading

Books

Hall, C.M. (2000) *Tourism Planning: Policies, Processes and Relationships*, Harlow, Prentice Hall.
Michael Hall provides a general text that draws together the various concepts and policies that can be found in the academic literature.

Inskeep, E. (1991) *Tourism Planning: An Integrated and Sustainable Development Approach*, Van Nostrand Reinhold, New York.

A first-class book that has been put together by someone who has worked both as teacher and practitioner. It is rich in experience and carries with it many lessons learnt from years of fieldwork. It is now in need of updating on some issues to reflect more recent thinking.

Mason, P. (2003) *Tourism Impacts, Planning and Management*, Butterworth Heinemann, Oxford.
As with Michael Hall's book, Peter Mason provides a sound overview and synthesis of accepted wisdom in this field, and is a very modern text.

Web sites

http://europa.eu.int/comm/regional_policy
The European Union's principal site for regional policy which encompasses issues pertaining to tourism development.

http://pata.org
A comprehensive web site from the Pacific Asia Travel Association which includes a mass of market data related to the region. PATA is the clear authority on travel and tourism in the area and this is reflected in its membership which includes nearly 100 government, state, and city tourism bodies, over 55 airlines and cruise lines, and hundreds of tourism companies.

http://www.world-tourism.org
An all-embracing web site providing the official view from the United Nations on tourism issues with a definitive set of tourism statistics and approaches to tourism development.

MAJOR CASE STUDY 14.1
TOURISM PROJECT ASSISTANCE FROM
THE EUROPEAN UNION

The purpose of this case study is to provide an understanding of the framework for the alloca-tion of structural funds by the European Union, to illustrate the range of criteria against which proposals are judged and funds allocated, and to offer an overview of the system in action.

INTRODUCTION

Above the investment help offered separately by the governments of the EU, there is the pan-European programme of regional aid made available to member states through the Union's structural funds. The objectives are to improve economic convergence; that is to eliminate major disparities of wealth, and ensure a better spread of economic activities throughout the territories located within the boundaries of the Union. Project assistance from the Union is given under four structural funds:

1 The European Regional Development Fund (ERDF), which is focused mainly on product-ive investment, infrastructure and SME development in less favoured regions, and is the principal vehicle for regional support.

2 The European Social Fund (ESF), which has the task of promoting jobs through investing in educational systems, vocational training and employment assistance.

3 The European Agricultural Guidance and Guarantee Fund Guidance System (EAGGF), which promotes the adjustment of agricultural businesses and rural development measures to help retain population in the countryside and preserve the landscape and rural heritage.

4 The Financial Instrument for Fisheries Guidance (FIFG), which was established in 1993 to promote structural measures in that sector to adjust and modernise fishing practices com-mensurate with preserving fish stocks and employment.

The European Commission recognises that the funds make a major contribution to the devel-opment of tourism in the EU and, in so doing, progress the objectives of economic and social cohesion as defined in Article 130a, Treaty of the European Union (the Maastricht Treaty), 1992. In essence, the Commission's policy for using tourism as an instrument of regional economic development is one of taking advantage of the many positive aspects of the industry, namely:

• the continuing growth in tourism worldwide;

• disadvantaged regions often have a comparative advantage in natural tourism resources;

• tourism attracts spending from outside the regions;

• tourism has important spillover benefits (multiplier effects) elsewhere in the regional economy; and

• job creation within a relatively short period of time is an important aspect of tourism development.

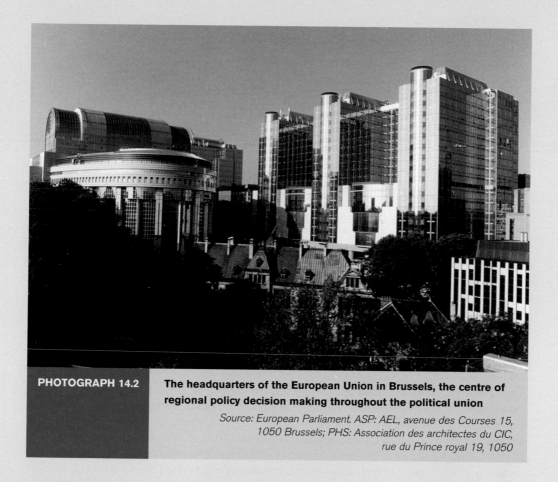

PHOTOGRAPH 14.2 — **The headquarters of the European Union in Brussels, the centre of regional policy decision making throughout the political union**

Source: European Parliament. ASP: AEL, avenue des Courses 15, 1050 Brussels; PHS: Association des architectes du CIC, rue du Prince royal 19, 1050

BACKGROUND

Prior to 1988, there was no coherent system for the disbursement of the structural funds, which resulted in the dissipation of funds over many areas, thus reducing their effectiveness. Therefore, in 1988, a new regulation on the uses of the funds was adopted in preparation for the first planning period 1989–93, with lesser changes for the next interval from 1994–99. The changes were based on three fundamental principles:

1 Transforming structural policy into an instrument with real economic impact by concentration on priority objectives.

2 Using a multi-annual programming approach for expenditure planning to assure member states of the stability and predictability of EU support.

3 Implementing a partnership with all the parties actively participating in structural policy, especially the regional authorities.

From 1989 onwards, member states were required to coordinate, for the first time, the use of the funds and draw together all forms of Union support, including lending by the European

TABLE 14.1	Structural funds' objectives, 2000–2006
Objective	**Aim**
Objective 1	Development and structural adjustment of regions whose development is lagging behind (those whose GDP per capita is 75% or less than the EU average).
Objective 2	Economic and social conversion of regions in structural difficulties.
Objective 3	Adaptation and modernisation of policies and systems of education, training and employment.

Investment Bank (EIB) and the European Coal and Steel Community (ECSC). This also allowed the EU to adopt a greater degree of control on the use of the funds within the sphere of integrated regional development plans put forward by member states.

In general terms member states put forward a development plan to the European Commission, which provides the basis for negotiation for community support frameworks (CSFs) where priorities are determined and agreed by the Commission, working in close association with member states and the competent regional or local authority designated by them, from which a series of operational programmes are derived. This is most appropriate for regions coming within the scope of the structural funds for the first time or where totally new priorities are being considered. For regions that already have an established track record of support from the structural funds, member states may submit single programming documents (SPDs), which combine priorities and programmes from the outset and become operational as soon as they have the Commission's approval. In contrast to the investment incentives discussed in this chapter, which may be applied in a piece-wise manner, project promoters are only eligible for assistance from the structural funds if their schemes are included within the planning process and meet one of the Community objectives shown in Table 14.1. In the 1994–1999 planning period there were six objectives, but at the Berlin Summit held in March 1999, the Council of Ministers agreed to amalgamate them into three.

The objectives shown in Table 14.1 are used to classify regions and allocate funds. Thus Objective 1 is supported by ERDF, ESF, EAGGF and FIFG, while Objective 2 relies on ERDF and ESF, and ESF is the sole fund for Objective 3.

FUNDING POLICY

The ERDF is the principal instrument for regional intervention and the sums available dwarf the other three structural funds. The method of subvention from the funds is grant aid that is conditional to the project and requires matching funding from the project promoter. The limit rate of grant is normally 50%, but can be up to 55% in the case of projects of particular importance to the development of the region or areas in which they are located. The majority of projects no longer receive support at the limit rate. For tourism investment, grants are unlikely to be in excess of 45% of the investment cost and may usually be less.

Tourism projects tend to be public sector led and the principal aspects that should be addressed when bidding for European assistance are:

- the use of the project should be 50% non-local;
- the project should result in an increase in overnight stays;
- the project should result in an increase in employment opportunities;
- the economic position of the project within the local area should be examined;
- the project should form part of a tourism strategy for the local area. Thus the project should sit within a CSF/SPD that forms the regional strategy approved by the member state and the Commission; and
- national/regional tourist organisation support will give weight to the application.

EVALUATION

Member states are given considerable flexibility as to how they present a proposal, which is consistent with the principle of *subsidiarity* outlined in this chapter. What follows is therefore representative of the criteria that are employed in evaluating a project proposal, namely:

- the project should be feasible in that the scheme has the capacity to generate revenues above operating costs so that it can support its own running arrangements;
- viability is assured after financial assistance in order that the project can service the capital investment costs out of its operating surplus;
- the need for structural funds support should be proved;
- displacement of visitors from other tourism businesses within the area of the CSF, or from any other European-assisted area, should be minimised; and
- multiplier effects in terms of job creation should be examined.

Impact assessment

A key political objective for public intervention lies in some loosely connected social welfare function that links tourist expenditure to local income generation and thence employment. These are the most significant factors affecting project acceptability, since the primary use of structural funds is to correct for regional imbalances. We may note that tourism and hospitality projects are usually well suited to European funding requirements because they are labour using and commonly have a high operating leverage; that is, a relatively low level of operating costs but a high level of fixed costs caused by prior capital spending. Once the financing of the capital has been adequately taken care of, the project usually runs into surplus after three years and can maintain itself thereafter.

Tourists come to a destination for many reasons, but if the requirement is to establish the economic worth of an investment that has been assisted through European funds, the first step is to draw up a model to reflect the impact visitors have on tourist expenditure in the area.

METHODOLOGY

Suppose that there exists a tourist destination with two attractions and a seaside. Visitors are surveyed at both attractions and on the beach to ascertain what motivated them to come to the destination. Total spending at the destination (T) amounts to expenditure at Attraction X (T_x) plus expenditure at Attraction Y (T_y) plus all remaining expenditure (R). Let the pull factor (reason for visit) for Attraction X be a, for Attraction Y, a value b, leaving $c = 1 - a - b$ as the significance of the beach. It follows therefore that attributable tourist expenditure by drawing power is:

Attraction X $= aT$

Attraction Y $= bT$

Seaside $= cT$

where $T = T_x + T_y + R$

It is proposed that European assistance should be given to Attraction X and so there is a requirement to evaluate its worth in terms of its contribution to tourist spending and employment in the area. The benefits of Attraction X (B) are the difference between with and without the project. The without situation is:

Attraction X $= 0$

Attraction Y $= b(T_y + R)$

Seaside $= c(T_y + R)$

$T_w = (b + c)(T_y + R)$

Hence:

$B = T - T_w$

$= T - (b + c)(T_y + R)$ (14.1)

Expanding T gives:

$B = T_x + a(T_y + R)$ (14.2)

EMPLOYMENT EFFECTS

The benefits shown in equation 14.2 are in two parts. The first term on the right-hand side is on-site expenditure and the second, off-site expenditure. The amount of off-site expenditure attributable to the attraction depends on its ability to generate visitors to Attraction Y and the area in general. This is termed the 'visitor additionality' factor. The application of employment multipliers per unit of tourist spending to equation 14.2, either on a full-time equivalent (FTE) or employment headcount basis, will give estimates of the gross employment (E) generated by Attraction X. These multipliers are calculated so as to measure the direct employment effects of the attraction, the indirect effects arising out of intermediate purchases made by the attraction and the induced effects on the local economy as a result of the re-spending of local incomes derived from the attraction, and similarly for off-site expenditure. Thus:

$$E = T_x e_x + aOe_o \qquad (14.3)$$

Where e_x is the employment multiplier appropriate to the attraction, O is the sum of off-site expenditure $(T_y + R)$ and e_o the required employment multiplier.

However, equation 14.3 ignores any demand diversion from competitors elsewhere in the area: this is the displacement effect and in this respect it is important to define the boundary of the attraction, since the larger the area the more likely it is that the attraction could divert expenditure and employment from elsewhere. National finance ministries sometimes argue that in the case of the economy as a whole, all expenditure, and consequently employment, is displacement and there is in effect a zero-sum game being played out in which there are only regional distribution benefits.

At a national level, the above argument assumes that market forces are moving the economy towards full employment equilibrium so that public investment expenditure, whether raised through taxation or borrowing, is simply displacing private funds in the capital market. Similarly, the operation of the attraction is displacing demand in the same or related product markets and likewise in the labour and property markets. In reality, economies do get stuck at a level of Keynesian unemployment disequilibria and one of the major objectives of regional policy is to 'kick-start' a demand deficient economy so as to raise the level of output through the multiplier process. This discussion does not imply that displacement should be neglected so that policy decisions are made in terms of the gross effect only, but merely raises the issue that the logic of the crowding-out effect ends up with a 'do nothing' policy. Modern growth theory places emphasis on the importance of embodied technical progress so that intervention policies designed to help product improvement will affect development through raising efficiency on the supply side.

If d is the proportion of locally diverted demand (or demand diverted from other assisted firms) in equation 14.2, then, from equation 14.3, net employment is:

$$N = E - dE$$
$$= (1 - d)(T_x e_x + aOe_o) \qquad (14.4)$$

Equation 14.4 forms the core of the basic evaluation model that can be used to judge in employment terms the return to public funds given to a business by way of a range of incentives.

CASE EXAMPLE

In Table 14.2 we present data that have been drawn from case study material on attractions, to show how the employment effects of a tourism project may be measured. The workings of Table 14.2 are along the following lines: using visitor expenditure surveys, the total expected on-site and off-site spending arising from the project is estimated at €25,050,000.

It is at this point that the concept of visitor additionality is invoked: clearly, on-site expenditure by visitors is attributable absolutely to the attraction as the customers have demonstrated their preferences through their willingness to pay, but this is not the case with off-site spending. The extent to which off-site spending may be attributed to the attraction depends on the

TABLE 14.2	Assessing the impact of a tourist attraction	
Item	On-site expenditure (euros)	Off-site expenditure (euros)
Visitor markets		
Stay	2 210 000	12 920 000
Day	2 465 000	2 200 000
Local residents	3 825 000	1 430 000
Total	8 500 000	16 550 000
Visitor additionality		
Stay	Not applicable	12%
Day	Not applicable	90%
Local residents	Not applicable	100%
Displacement		
Stay	0%	0%
Day	30%	30%
Local residents	100%	100%
FTE multipliers per €10 000		
Direct	0.0765	0.0628
Indirect	0.0412	0.0391
Induced	0.0059	0.0059
Total	**0.1236**	**0.1078**

importance of the attraction in the customer's decision to visit the location. This can only be ascertained by surveying visitors and asking about their motivations for coming to the destination. As expected, a much higher percentage is recorded for day visitors and local residents, because they normally make a specific decision to go to a place, an event or an attraction. Using the visitor additionality factors in Table 14.2 to account for attributable off-site expenditure, the gross expenditure benefits (B) from the attraction are:

$B = €8,500,000 + (0.12 \times €12,920,000) + (0.9 \times €2,200,000) + (1.0 \times €1,430,000)$

$= €13,460,400$ (14.5)

It is anticipated that the attraction will create 74.5 FTE jobs directly on-site, and so the required additions to this number will be the expected indirect and induced employment generated from on-site spending. The direct multiplier is not used here as it refers to the average attraction, so it is better to use the direct estimate of employment in these circumstances. Using the appropriate FTE multipliers shown in Table 14.2 and calculated as a decimal fraction of a given amount of tourist expenditure, this figure comes to $(0.0412 + 0.0059) \times €8,500,000/€10,000 = 40.0$ FTE jobs. Off-site jobs amount to $0.1078 \times €4,960,400/€10,000 = 53.5$ FTE jobs, where €4,960,400 is the total of attributable off-site benefits. Hence, the gross employment generated (E), in terms of FTEs, is expected to be:

$E = 74.5 \text{ FTEs} + 40.0 \text{ FTEs} + 53.5 \text{ FTEs}$

$= 181.0 \text{ FTEs}$ (14.6)

So far the analysis has only measured gross FTEs likely to be generated by the attraction. The net figures have to account for what is termed displacement, which is factored into Table 14.2. Displacement has to do with the extent to which an attraction may capture tourist spending from competitors in the local area. It is estimated that 0% of staying visitors will be taken from competitors; the attraction is providing more to 'see and do' at the destination and the tourists' budgets have sufficient margin of flexibility. For day visitors, it is probable that 30% will be displaced from other attractions, while for local residents a conservative assumption is made that all expenditure will be displaced from elsewhere in the local economy. The latter assumption is overly pessimistic in practice, for household budgets are not that inflexible.

Weighting the displacement factors in Table 14.2 by the different categories of visitor spending gives an overall displacement expenditure of €6,588,500. Hence the value of d is €6,588,500/€13,460,400, which is equal to 0.4895. Thus, the net employment (N) that can be expected to result from the attraction is:

$N = 181.0 - 0.4895 \times 181.0$

$= 113.6 \text{ FTEs}$ (14.7)

It is this number of FTEs that should be used to evaluate the project's worth in public policy decision making when applications for European support or comparisons with alternative projects are being are being made.

PROJECT MONITORING

Once the bundle of projects has been agreed upon for assistance, the principle of subsidiarity devolves the monitoring function to the local level through programme monitoring committees. The latter are made up of representatives from central and local government, public agencies and any other interested parties, and they will be responsible for all projects within a CSF/SPD. For every project, targets are set at the approval stage and returns must be submitted quarterly, showing the progress of each scheme against its targets.

It is a member state's responsibility to make site visits and evaluate project performance: these tasks usually fall to the government department responsible for administering the CSF/SPD that contains the project. Member states have the responsibility to ensure that European funds are correctly spent and yield good value for money in terms of the project evaluation criteria. This responsibility is regulated by the European Court of Auditors, who have powers of examination and verification to establish that projects are:

- eligible for European funds as specified;

- managed in accordance with European Commission's rules with regard to technical and financial controls; and

- claiming grant against justifiable expenditure.

The above verifications are undertaken by making one or two visits every year and subjecting a group of pre-selected projects to detailed checking.

CONCLUSION

Since about 1975, the entry of the EU into regional policy, in order to create a greater convergence between the economies of the Union, has ended member states' monopoly of regional policy within their borders. Inside the Union, there is a distinct tendency for the poorest regions to be situated on the geographical periphery and the more prosperous regions, with the benefit of market access, to be centrally located. With the adoption of the Single European Act (1987), with the intention to create one market in Europe and a single currency, there is a commitment by the EU to promote economic and social cohesion through actions to reduce regional disparities and the Maastricht Treaty (1992) acknowledged, for the first time, the role of tourism in these actions.

The resources for mitigating regional differences are drawn from the structural funds, which are continually being increased, in real terms, from one planning period to another. The funds have specific objectives, as shown in Table 14.1, and support for tourism development particularly manifests itself in the Objective 1 regions, which already have an established tourist industry; also, in Objective 2 regions, where tourism has contributed to the diversification of economic activities in areas of industrial decline. Tourism programmes are seen as key activities in reducing of regional imbalances. In support of this, the case study discusses the principles of structural assistance and the methodology for project evaluation, with particular emphasis on job creation, though we should be mindful of the clear intention of the European Commission to propagate tourism developments in a sustainable manner, in order to guarantee that the activity continues on a regular basis.

The division of intervention in the tourist industry between member states and the EU is always likely to remain contentious, but given the diversity of the tourist product, the Union has to work in close partnership with national and regional authorities. At the political level, this issue has been technically put to one side by Article 3b of the Maastricht Treaty which states that:

> The Community shall take action, in accordance with the principle of subsidiarity, only if and in so far as the objectives of the proposed action cannot be sufficiently achieved by the Member States and can therefore, by reason of the scale or effects of the proposed action, be better achieved by the Community.

DISCUSSION QUESTIONS

1 How would you go about preparing a local area tourism strategy?

2 What are the concepts that lie behind the measurement of direct, indirect and induced income and employment multipliers?

3 The capital investment for the attraction project illustrated in Table 14.2 is €7,600,000. The European Commission decides to grant aid the scheme at 30% of the capital cost. What is the grant cost per direct FTE job created on-site for the gross employment generated and net jobs created by the project?

PART FOUR
MARKETING FOR TOURISM

CHAPTER FIFTEEN
MARKETING FOR TOURISM – THE
HISTORICAL ROOTS 548

CHAPTER SIXTEEN
MANAGING MARKETING FOR TOURISM 572

CHAPTER SEVENTEEN
MARKETING PLANNING 606

CHAPTER EIGHTEEN
MARKETING MIX APPLICATIONS 640

INTRODUCTION

Marketing is assuming an ever more important role given the lack of stability of world markets. The tourism market will never be the same again given the new realisation that terrorism and health-related problems can affect generating countries and tourist demand behaviour. Terrorist attacks affected the overall economy of the United States and subsequently led to changes in the consumption patterns of travel around the world. However, it would be wrong to highlight the foregoing as the turning point for a downturn in tourism demand. Even before September 11, 2001, there were the signs of a recession where many international hotels and destination markets were experiencing a softening of demand and reduction in average daily expenditure. The reasons include factors such as over forecasting, investing in expansion of supply which in turn created risk and excessive debt. In addition other events have compounded the problems of tourism companies whereby the risk of illness, such as SARS, ongoing terrorist activity and subsequent conflict has occurred.

All tourism activity is changing from a relaxed thrill of the trip to some apprehension of what may be the downside risk. Given the need for steady demand the role of marketing will become increasingly important for tourism organisations, operating in both public and private sectors, as they continue to strive to protect and improve their market share.

The process of marketing and its management provides companies and organisations with the many complex tools to affect demand in target markets. It is a complex area that, as this section highlights, requires expertise and experience for success. In this section, we provide a comprehensive evaluation of all aspects of the management of tourism marketing including the strategies and tools that may be applied to deliver the tourism product effectively and efficiently to satisfy the tourism consumer.

In Chapter Fifteen, Marketing for Tourism – the Historical Roots, we begin by looking at the historical development of marketing in general and how its roots have influenced the application of marketing theory to the tourism product in particular. While marketing in one form or another has been in existence for centuries, the relative recency of sophisticated techniques and an awareness of services marketing requirements have meant that current marketing is evolving rapidly to suit the needs of the tourism industry.

In Chapter Sixteen, Managing Marketing for Tourism, we introduce and discuss the characteristics of the service product such as intangibility, perishability and inseparability which, it is argued, differentiate the tourism product from others. In addition, we outline other characteristics related to the notion of risk which also distinguish the tourism product from manufactured goods. To combat the risk brought about by the characteristics of the product, the concept of quality – and its management – has become a prevailing force in tourism marketing: the lack of control over the service process, which is essentially an unpredictable human encounter, has become a prime target for the application of quality techniques to standardise the delivery of the product. We present key models in respect of the service delivery system appropriate to the tourism industry and outline some of the criticisms that have been levelled at tourism marketing.

Chapter Seventeen, Marketing Planning, is concerned with the introduction of tactical and strategic marketing planning procedures in respect of the tourism product. We define marketing planning and emphasise its role and application to the diverse sectors which, when amalgamated, form the tourism industry. We review the benefits and purposes of marketing planning, consider the structure of a marketing plan and explore the implications of neglecting tourism marketing planning.

The final chapter in this part, Chapter Eighteen, Marketing Mix Applications, relates to the **marketing mix**. This is a key strategic tool which is integral to the effective manipulation of the tourism product and the successful implementation of marketing planning procedures. However, the fundamental starting point for the creation of a successful marketing mix strategy is the definition of target markets since this will dictate the direction of the elements of the marketing mix and provide a focus for all marketing mix decisions and activity.

Thus, Part Four presents a complete approach to the marketing of tourism, together with a comprehensive review of key issues and considerations. However, the application of marketing management techniques in the tourism industry can be found to be hampered by a number of factors that are inherent in the nature of tourism itself:

- First, it has been suggested that while the tourism product is sufficiently distinctive to demand a unique marketing approach, the result of this has been that marketing strategies, tools and techniques in tourism are less evolved and advanced than in other industries (including manufacturing).

- Second, the relative immaturity and diversity of the tourism industry has also impaired the development of marketing procedures designed specifically to take into account the unique characteristics of the product.

- Third, the predominant practice in tourism is developing managers from grass roots. The implications of this are that while they may be good generalists few have the marketing training and expertise necessary to maximise marketing potential.

- Fourth, many enterprises in tourism are small operations which have neither the expertise, nor the resources, to devote to a fully fledged marketing management approach.

- Finally, the late development and application of technology in tourism has also handicapped the tourism industry, especially in relation to product formulation and distribution.

While some of these criticisms are accurate, some do not take into account more recent changes in the tourism industry. Although it is important that the unique nature of the tourism product is recognised by marketers, there is now a body of knowledge and series of techniques for marketing in the service industries and these are outlined throughout the next four chapters. The tourism industry does, however, create its own handicaps to effective marketing:

- Data relating to the market and to the actions of competitors are weak or scarce.

- A short-term outlook prevails, denying a carefully structured and strategic marketing planning approach.

- Managers in tourism tend to have risen through the ranks and to be generalists. The organisation of the industry thus mitigates against the development of specialists in marketing, and indeed some managers neither respect nor value marketing-related skills.

In addition, it is important to make the point that the tourism industry is subject to governmental regulation of its activities, and consumer protection is well developed in tourism. These factors may be instrumental in restricting the marketing options of a tourism company.

Public sector organisations in tourism are also somewhat handicapped in adopting a true marketing orientation. It is, for example, not uncommon to find visitor and convention bureaux with the following problems:

- They may be hidebound by government personnel operating guidelines in terms of working hours and remuneration of staff.

- They may possess insufficient resources to build a presence in the marketplace, particularly in respect of the international arena.

- They may lack sufficient marketing expertise.

- They may have to be even-handed in their support of products and enterprises at the destination.

- They may have little or no control over the quality of the product they are marketing.

- They may be driven by 12-monthly budgeting cycles which preclude the long-term planning framework essential to enhance and improve the tourism product or image.

This section clearly emphasises the interlinkages that characterise the tourism industry. For example, the nature of tourism demand is inextricably linked to marketing of the product and the manipulation of the marketing mix to attract pre-identified **segments**. Moreover, marketing is also linked to the supply of tourism at the destination being marketed: it is crucial, if the destination is to sustain its market share, that the range and quality of the attractions and facilities on offer live up to those promises as communicated to target market(s) via the marketing process.

Marketing is, therefore, an important tool in an industry where loyalty in both the distribution chain and to the company is low; indeed, many companies have promotional campaigns targeted at other sectors of the industry (such as retail travel agents) as well as the consumer to encourage more loyalty in the distribution chain. Similarly, governmental organisations often find it more cost effective to market to intermediaries and carriers rather than to potential travellers.

Due to the pressures of over-supply of capacity in many sectors of the tourism industry marketing is becoming a more important function and we would contend that improving training and education among the tourism workforce, coupled with the realities of increasingly intense competition, are encouraging a new emphasis on marketing management and a greater marketing orientation within the industry.

CHAPTER FIFTEEN
MARKETING FOR TOURISM – THE HISTORICAL ROOTS

INTRODUCTION

In this chapter we introduce the evolution and concept of marketing as it applies to tourism. We demonstrate that tourism marketing has emerged as a result of business and social changes which have occurred throughout the past decades as a reaction to the conditions that impinge on business operations. However, while we are able to identify different business philosophies that have influenced the adoption of a marketing orientation and the application of the marketing concept, a fuller understanding of marketing lies in the way marketing management functions in attempting to create and maximise consumer value and satisfactions.

LEARNING OUTCOMES

This chapter provides the reader with a comprehensive introduction to marketing as it relates to the tourism industry. By the end of this chapter, therefore, you will:

- understand the concept of marketing, what it is and how it has developed into its current form;

- be able to differentiate between selling and marketing;

- recognise that companies may have different business philosophies and be able to identify the implications of these differences for marketing; and

- appreciate the importance of value creation as part of the process of marketing management.

WHAT IS MARKETING?

Tourism can be traced back for centuries but because the elements of the product and conditions of the marketplace have changed so enormously in the last few decades, there has been a corresponding requirement for a change in business methods. This has led to the adoption and use of tourism marketing. Historically marketing has been carried out in tourism for many years as illustrated by the photograph below. We have all experienced 'marketing' in some form and given it affects us all in different ways, everyone has their own idea of what marketing is. We are all involved in, or influenced by, marketing in one way or another. As such, it will not have been long since you last saw a promotion for an airline, hotel group, holiday, leisure centre or overseas country.

We are continually bombarded with promotional material. Each day Internet pages will offer links to one type of offer or another. There are thousands of general advertisements on television and radio stations and all shops have numerous promotional messages. We are surrounded by invasive messages and communication that have been paid for out of marketing budgets. However, this is a very narrow interpretation of the activity of marketing and, as we shall see, marketing is far more than the promotion of a product. This forms only *one* aspect of marketing.

It is often stated that we live in an era of marketing, but what does this actually mean? One possible method of understanding marketing is to treat it as the development of ideas. If this is the case all we have to do is to trace what has been written of marketing in the past. Unfortunately, this is not straightforward because while historical accounts show that trade has always existed, the term 'marketing' was only used as a noun in the first part of the twentieth century. Thus, marketing as defined and described in this chapter is a relatively new phenomenon. The use of the word marketing in the early stages was associated with a number of actions that were loosely related to the activity of achieving a sale rather than marketing. Therefore, the evolution of marketing as we know it today is a relatively recent development.

One way of attempting to answer the question 'what is marketing?' is to examine accepted definitions. Although it is very easy to describe what the term marketing means, it is far more difficult to describe the practice of marketing. This is because a central tenet of marketing is the body of underlying concepts that form the general guide for organisational and managerial

PHOTOGRAPH 15.1

Tourism marketing has been carried out over many years

Source: Advertising Archive

thinking, planning and action. Consequently, for a comprehensive understanding of marketing it is necessary to master the underlying concepts.

THE EVOLUTION OF MARKETING

Marketing has evolved against a background of economic and business pressures. These pressures have required an increased focus on the adoption of a series of managerial measures based upon satisfying consumer needs. The key to the importance of marketing within tourism has been the level of economic growth in the past 60 years which has led to subsequent improvements in living standards, an enlargement of the population, and increases in discretionary time. Such changes led Disney management in 1955 to launch the Disneyland theme park concept and in the same year McDonald's to open its first fast-food restaurant.

In a short period of time the tourism industry has become one of the most important industries in the world in economic terms. Occurring simultaneously with this growth has been the continuing concentration of the tourism industry into fewer and larger organisations. Such organisations need to reduce the widening gulf between managers of the business and the consumer which is developing as a result of a lack of first-hand knowledge of the consumer's tastes and needs.

Where marketing has been adopted, the emphasis is on developing a full understanding of the dynamics of consumer behaviour (see Chapter Two). We should be aware that those organisations that use marketing are not limited to commercial companies. Marketing techniques are being used by tourist boards, museums and charities organising free or subsidised holidays for the elderly or handicapped. However, within the marketplace those organisations that have adapted most successfully to contemporary changes have done so by directing management resources to obtaining research on market and consumer trends, and by improving channels of distribution and communication campaigns.

The nature of the tourism industry is one where custom and tradition have been particularly strong. The interpersonal service delivery aspects of the industry have created styles of interaction where the service provider remains distanced from the act of service provision. As with many other industries in the service sector this has preserved the customary, well-established ways of doing business.

Often the need for change has been forced upon the industry because of the changes that have occurred in relation to consumer and market forces. Modern tourism marketing has emerged as a business reaction to changes in the social and economic environment, with the most successful companies or tourist bodies having demonstrated a keen sense of providing the right organisation structure and product offering for the consumer or visitor. This relies as much upon an approach or attitude to business or the market, as it does to specific management expertise. Marketing is therefore initially a philosophy that relies on the art and science of different managerial approaches.

The development of marketing is fashioned as the outcome of social and business pressures. The most widely accepted account of the development of marketing is that proposed by Keith (1981) who discerned an evolution of production, to sales, and finally to marketing in the Pillsbury company in the USA. In 1960 Keith (1981) argued that the growing recognition of consumer orientation 'will have far reaching implications for business, achieving a virtual revolution in economic thinking'. He inferred that, in the late 1950s, consumer orientation was only just beginning to be accepted as a business concept. A survey of the literature reveals an account of the history of marketing and modern business practice as having developed in three distinct stages (adapted from Gilbert and Bailey, 1990):

1 **The production era.** This occurred when there was a belief that if products were priced cheaply enough they would be purchased. Therefore, it was important to supply products to the marketplace with the emphasis on consistently reducing costs. The focus of management was on increasing efficiency of production which involved an *inward, product-orientated* emphasis rather than an outward, market-orientated emphasis. The main focus for managers at the time was a concern for improving production capacity, financing expansion, having quality and cost control and meeting the rise in demand. The overriding objective for management was the development of a standardised product which could be offered at the lowest price to the market. The market was characterised by a lack of problems with demand and as such managers focused on process and systems and not the customer. Nowadays, in destinations that have high demand this approach on process, which ignores the importance of the customer, can be recognised in many aspects of the delivery of the tourism product.

2 **The sales era.** This is an evolutionary phase where companies attempted *to sell the products they had formulated without assessing the acceptability of the product or offer*. The problem is often one of a market with declining demand and surplus capacity, which in turn leads to a search for more effective means of selling. We can recognise this today in destinations where hotels or restaurants face greater competition, as there is often a shift to increase promotional and sales efforts to improve demand. However, there is little analysis as to the reasons for the problems as the belief is that the product is acceptable. Given the product was basically unaltered and as competition increased companies became better at improving their sales and promotion techniques with the use of increased advertising, use of price discounts or improving distribution, therefore, in the sales era companies attempted to influence demand and tailor it *to meet their supply* but primarily through simple sales techniques.

3 **The marketing era.** This era is characterised by a reversal of the preceding philosophy as organisations started to provide the products they could sell, *rather* than trying to sell what they had produced or formulated. Organisations adopted a consumer-led approach and concentrated on improving the marketing mix. This era was effectively based upon the recognition that meeting **customer needs** and providing **consumer satisfaction** were the most *effective basis* for planning and that an organisation has to be *outward looking* to be successful. The philosophy of this era is that tourism business activity has to recognise the customer as the central driving force of an activity that realises survival and prosperity is based upon meeting individual customer needs.

There are continuing arguments as to the dates of the above eras leading up to marketing as we understand it today. Moreover, some question whether they can be treated as discrete periods at all. For our purposes, in the majority of texts, the marketing era is identified to have been established from the 1950s onward. For a full discussion see Gilbert and Bailey (1990) or Baker (1999). The interesting aspect of living in today's marketing era is that we can still find tourism companies which act as if in a preceding era. The important factors that have ushered in marketing during the past half a century are as follows:

- The increases in demand were at a lower rate than the rises in productivity. In tourism, this culminated in an oversupply of accommodation in specific locations, and of aircraft seats on important routes and too many inefficient companies in the marketplace. The increase in competition and the risks associated with the tourism marketplace led to more reliance on the use of marketing. The business system can be viewed as an organism that is concerned with survival and proliferation. Following this argument, when a business system is threatened it will take functional steps to improve the situation. As marketing can provide for tactical change and modification of the system, in times of risk where there is over-supply and market saturation, marketing assumes a much more important role.

- The consumer was becoming more affluent and therefore it was possible to develop products that could be sold using a range of non-price attributes. This required the development of methods designed to create or change consumer attitudes and beliefs.

- The distance between the tourism product provider and tourist has been continually increasing. This led to a need for marketing research related to the gathering of information on market trends, evaluating levels of satisfaction and understanding consumer behaviour.

- New tourism and hospitality products were being launched which required more emphasis on marketing. For example, in the 1970s the new wide-bodied aircraft coming into service and more recently easyJet, required high levels of demand to make them viable.

- As society developed, the mass market splintered into a number of submarkets, while at the same time the mass market became increasingly difficult to reach. This was due to the increase in specialist media and the potential for a whole range of alternative leisure pursuits. The changes required improved expertise in the **segmentation** of markets and the provision of different marketing mix strategies which would maximise demand for individual segments.

DEFINITIONS AND CONCEPTS OF MARKETING

Any conceptual definition of a business discipline is, by nature of its condensed form, a limited abstraction of values, techniques and practices which are the focus of its activity. Therefore, no single definition can be comprehensive enough to describe the true essence or complexity of marketing. Various definitions of marketing have been offered based upon the values prevalent at the time. A popular early definition utilised for many years stressed marketing as being a managerial process of providing the right product, in the right place, at the right time and at the right price. This definition is mechanistic and stresses the provision of the product offer without due regard to any of the actors or functions involved in the process.

No definition of marketing can ever disregard the importance of Philip Kotler. He has established himself as the most widely referenced proponent of general marketing theory. Kotler (2003) defines marketing as: 'a societal process by which individuals and groups obtain what they need and want through creating, offering and freely exchanging products and services of value with others'. Kotler argues the definition has a social basis and is built on the main concepts of wants, needs, demands, satisfactions of marketing and marketers because they are central to the study of marketing. For him marketing management is the art and science of choosing target markets and getting, keeping, and growing customers through creating, delivering and communicating superior customer value.

MINI CASE STUDY 15.1
The risks of tourism have affected the operation of cruise ships

Ships are now potential targets especially given the fact that a US warship was successfully bombed in Aden. Many of the island governments which rely on the cruise-line business have taken US concerns over terrorism seriously in the way they have acted promptly to try and make US citizens, who represent 78% of the world consumer market for cruising, feel less at risk on their trips. However, some ships are carrying around 3,000 passengers and the cruise companies find it difficult to assure security as their ships utilise many of the hundreds of ports worldwide and can be crewed by individuals from many different nationalities. Destinations are now more aware of the needs of the current tourist for safety given Port of Spain, Trinidad, and Scarborough, Tobago, were ignored by the P&O Princess group in 2003 on the basis of a British Foreign and Commonwealth Office report which indicated the risk to British cruise passengers becoming terrorist targets while in port was high. Ports around the world are installing passenger luggage X-ray machines because of the heightened safety risk to cruise ships. More recently with some cruise companies there has been the introduction of plastic identity cards with the passenger photograph so that all passengers can be checked when reboarding. In addition ports and cruise ships are more likely to utilise surveillance cameras and be more careful about the access individuals have to ships when in port areas whereby passenger guests are not allowed onboard. Given cruise ships are docked in busy cargo areas where loading and unloading takes place the security situation is of some concern.

DISCUSSION QUESTIONS

1 Do you think the measures taken by cruise lines will alleviate the level of risk associated with modern travel? If not what else can be done?

2 How much delay and disruption to travel do you think security measures can take before travellers become highly dissatisfied and affected by the lack of a positive experience? How can these measures be less intrusive or personal?

3 How is the launch of bigger ships such as *Queen Mary II* going to affect the future management of risk?

In 1984 the British Chartered Institute of Marketing defined marketing as: 'the management process responsible for identifying, anticipating and satisfying customers' requirements profitably.'

An examination of both definitions reveals significant core similarities. On comparison it is found that both stress marketing as a process. Such approaches provide a concept as one where the process is established by way of a marketing channel connecting the (tourism) organisation with its market. This is based upon management to convert customer purchasing power into effective demand. In addition the British Chartered Institute clarifies the management responsibility to be one of assessment of consumer demand through the identification and anticipation of customer requirements. This denotes the importance of research and analysis as part of this process.

One important difference is that Kotler's definition is more appropriate to non-profit organisations where there is free entrance or subsidisation toward the cost of a service. It is also more fitting when facilitators of tourism such as tourist boards are considered.

However, the most important aspect and one that should be at the heart of any definition of marketing, is the emphasis placed on the consumer's needs as the origin of all of the organisation's effort. The **marketing concept** has been expressed in many succinct ways from the: 'Have it your way' from Burger King, to 'You're the boss' of United Airlines. This is the basis of the modern marketing concept whereby the principal means of success is based not only on identifying different consumer needs but also on delivering a tourist product whose experiences provide sets of satisfactions that are preferable to those of the competitors. In addition these satisfactions have to be delivered with attention to their cost effectiveness, since marketing has to be evaluated on the basis of its efficiency of expenditure.

We have seen how the definitions of marketing lead to the marketing concept, whereby the consumer is the driving force for all business activities. Prior to the introduction and discussion about the notion of the marketing concept we will spend some time with aspects of delivering value prior to differentiating the principles and activities associated with marketing and selling.

The concept of value within tourism

As mentioned above the aspect of delivering superior value is an important aspect of the marketing management approach. This means companies have to find ways to ensure they optimise the delivery of value. As such there is a requirement for a way of uncovering the value sought by the customer, the development of that within the company and then the delivery of optimum value to the end customer (see Table 15.1).

Value of a tourism product includes a number of different aspects which include the perception of price, quality, and image as well as the economic and social aspects of the consumer. Consumers of today have far more information with which to make comparisons between alternative offers. As we are dealing with perceptions these will differ as they are based upon the available time individuals have to carry out comparisons. Also, some individuals have a wide network of acquaintances and may consult alternative information sources in making a decision about what offer delivers more value than another. No one company projects a single image as this is a multi-attribute concept. This means perceptions of value will fluctuate within the population.

TABLE 15.1	A system for delivering value		
Approaches	**Uncovering value needs**	**Developing value**	**Delivering value**
Gathering/ analytical	Data/feedback of company representatives, surveys, etc.	Operations/customer interfaces and touch points	Logistics/product quality, service
Organisational	Interpretation of customer requirements and resultant expected organisational competencies	Training/motivation of staff and working with suppliers who also add quality	Improved attitudes and behaviour of employee interfaces

Product perceived value is based upon:

- Actual price asked and the relativity to prices for the same or similar product offered elsewhere.
- Perceived quality, service and image associated with the brand/product.
- Convenience of purchasing method or channel, and its congruence to the needs of the customer.
- Consumer difficulty in ability to assess the benefits/relative price of the product.
- Experience associated with the purchase or consumption process.

It will be seen from the last point in the list above that the focus on any judgement of value for money will include intrinsic aspects, so that either the purchase itself as a pre-trip activity or the actual tourism experience can be treated as of value for its own sake. For example, an experiential perspective may include the symbolic, hedonic and aesthetic aspects of the consumption process. This means that practical consumer judgement has to include hedonic criteria, based on an appreciation of the good or service for its own sake. As such value can be based upon the thinking and feeling dimensions of purchase and consumption behaviour. Consumption by value criteria is based upon a multiplicity of inputs which contribute in varying ways to consumer judgement in different choice situations. In fact tourism can be thought of as producing a **total tourist experience** that will include everything from the pre-planning, the purchase, the journey, the visit/and perhaps stay, the return journey and overall reflection on the activity. This total tourist experience involves all aspects of the offering and experience which provide sets of satisfaction and dissatisfactions related to the whole episode. Marketing has to consider all these aspects to ensure value and satisfaction is judged to be above the tourist's expectation. A good overall experience will culminate in the tourist being an advocate for a company or destination and lead to the telling of others of their experience in a positive way.

If we consider the early success of McDonald's the value is not simply the hamburger or fries it is the way the service, cleanliness, and speed of food production has provided an added value to the food. McDonald's customers are made up of a whole series of segments who value a fast, light and reasonable cost meal. This is all achieved by means of a great deal of planning and understanding. The company sets itself a series of high standards to achieve, which is known internally as 'QSCV'. QSCV is Quality, Service, Cleanliness and Value and provides a defined target area of value delivery for its operations. This is only one aspect that is important in the running of the company. The marketplace is dynamic and therefore McDonald's has had to renew itself on a constant basis by introducing new menu items, which fit with the values of health and nutrition in order to react to the changing market environment.

In order to deliver value through lower prices the low-cost airlines need to keep operating costs significantly lower than the 'traditional' flag-carrying airlines in order to be successful in the niche they have selected. This is achieved through specific marketing measures such as direct booking by use of the Internet and lower cost by means of ticketless travel (easyJet passengers receive an email containing their travel details and confirmation number when they book online); high utilisation of aircraft whereby time on the ground is reduced; use of cheaper secondary airports; reduction in variable costs by not offering free meals on board.

Understanding the overall experience from a marketing perspective is extremely important. However, the marketing concept – where the consumer is the driving force for all business activities – must not be confused with a sales approach. The next section ensures that difference is understood and then we will introduce you to the notion of marketing orientation.

THE DIFFERENCES BETWEEN MARKETING AND SELLING

By now it should be obvious to the reader that marketing and selling are not the same. Levitt (1960) described the differences as follows:

> Selling focuses on the need of the seller; marketing on the needs of the buyer. Selling is preoccupied with the seller's need to convert his product into cash; marketing with the idea of satisfying the needs of the customer by means of the product and the whole cluster of things associated with creating, delivering and finally consuming it. (p. 45)

Drucker (1973) points out:

> Selling and marketing are antithetical rather than synonymous or even complementary. There will always, one can assume, be a need for some selling, but the aim of marketing is to make selling superfluous. (p. 64)

The contrast between the sales and marketing approach highlights the importance of marketing planning and analysis related to customers and the marketplace.

	Focus		**Means**		**End**	
Sales concept	→	Selling/products	→	Promotion	→	Profits through sales volume
Marketing concept	→	Customer needs	→	Integrated marketing to specific segments	→	Profits through customer satisfaction

FIGURE 15.1   **The sales and marketing concepts compared**

The sales concept focuses on products and uses selling and promotion to achieve profits through sales volume. The underlying weakness is that the sales concept does not necessarily satisfy the consumer and may only culminate in short-term, rather than long-term, company success. The marketing concept focuses on customer needs and utilises integrated marketing to achieve profits through customer satisfaction (Figure 15.1).

DIFFERENT BUSINESS PHILOSOPHIES

As we have seen, marketing is a business philosophy that places the consumer, and his or her needs, at the forefront of all activities. For example, it is known that business travellers want frequent and reliable transport systems with sensible timings of departure and arrival. They favour priority check-in and check-out facilities and efficient, good-quality staff. Business travellers need to feel they can make their trips and have their meetings without any worry of delay or discomfort. Therefore, knowledge of business travellers' needs occurs only when someone takes care to identify those needs.

While it is important to recognise the importance of structuring any organisation so that its focus is upon the customer, a number of alternative philosophies can be identified (see Figure 15.2). Each of these philosophies acts as a guiding orientation and system of approaching the market, and while a product-led company may be less effective, it is still possible to identify such companies within the tourism sector.

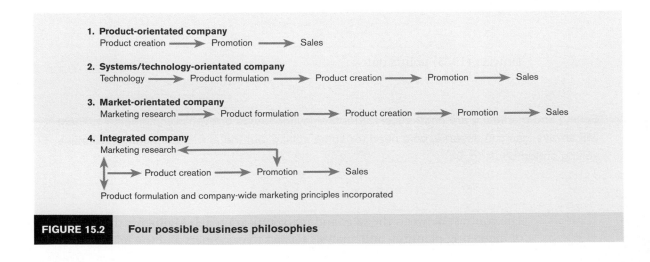

1. **Product-orientated company**
   Product creation → Promotion → Sales

2. **Systems/technology-orientated company**
   Technology → Product formulation → Product creation → Promotion → Sales

3. **Market-orientated company**
   Marketing research → Product formulation → Product creation → Promotion → Sales

4. **Integrated company**
   Marketing research ←
   → Product creation → Promotion → Sales
   Product formulation and company-wide marketing principles incorporated

FIGURE 15.2   **Four possible business philosophies**

It is important to understand the initial starting place within the chains of the individual systems in Figure 15.2, since this is the first stage in the sequence of events which clearly demonstrates the focus of the organisation's approach to effecting exchange relationships. Examples (1) and (2) can be ineffective because of problems encountered in having the wrong product for the market, and as a consequence, having to waste more resources on promotion and selling in order to achieve a sale. In these examples it is normal to find that organisations believe their products are acceptable, and that all that is required for sales to occur is the identification of prime markets and methods of selling. Such an approach to the marketplace by destination, hotel or airline marketing department is characterised by an emphasis on pictures of empty bedrooms, bleak looking buildings or the exterior of an aircraft. An emphasis on the product rather than the benefits the consumer is seeking is still at the heart of a great deal of today's marketing. Quite often tourist promotional literature is devoid of scenes of tourists enjoying rest, enjoyment or good service. A product-focused philosophy is more acceptable when there is shortage or boom times, which are characterised by little competition. However, both the first two philosophies provide for inward-looking management, which concentrates on improvement within the company, rather than on outward-looking management which concentrates on the consumer and emerging tourist needs.

PHOTOGRAPH 15.2   **Promotion of channels of distribution take precedence over aesthetics for low-cost operations**

Source: easyJet

MINI CASE STUDY 15.2
A new departure for the easyJet business model

With the departure of flight EZS923 from Geneva to Nice last week, easyJet entered a new era. For the first time passengers of the fast-growing UK no-frills airline boarded an Airbus rather than a Boeing aircraft. The group's bold experiment in moving to a mixed fleet (see Photograph 15.2 for the company's 737 aircraft) appears to break one of the cardinal rules of the low-cost airline business model, where maintaining simplicity is the holy grail. Ryanair, easyJet's Dublin-based rival, which to date has beaten it hands down in the business of making money, is firmly on its way to an all-Boeing 737-800 fleet and is accelerating the decommissioning of its 737-200s, which are more than 20 years old. Dallas-based Southwest Airlines, the pioneer low-cost carrier and role model for all subsequent start-ups, has also stuck with iron discipline to a single-manufacturer fleet of Boeing 737s, albeit by now spanning three generations of aircraft.

When Airbus defeated Boeing a year ago to win the fiercely contested easyJet order for 120 aircraft plus 120 options to power the group's growth, the airline made clear that the offer from the European aircraft maker could not be refused. 'It surprised all of us to see just how aggressive Airbus was in the final round of sealed bids,' says Ray Webster, easyJet chief executive. Stelios Haji-Ioannou, son of a Greek Cypriot shipowner and the flamboyant founder of easyJet, who was in the final days of his chairmanship when the decision was made, said the price difference between the Airbus and Boeing offers was 'so substantial we would have been in breach of our fiduciary duty – it would have been an offence – to buy Boeing as offered'. According to sources close to the negotiations, Airbus granted a discount to easyJet of about 50% off the $5.3 bn (£3.2 bn) list price in one of the best aircraft deals ever. The price reflected both Airbus's determination to capture one of the big two European low-cost airlines as a customer and the severely depressed state of the aircraft market.

For easyJet the hard work starts now, as it sets out to make the mixed fleet strategy work in practice. The first Airbus A319s are arriving following nearly a year of preparations – with five to be delivered to the airline's Geneva base from the Airbus line in Hamburg by the end of the month. easyJet, like its Irish rival Ryanair, is committed to heroic growth. Its fleet of 75 aircraft (one A319 and 74 737s) at the end of September [2003] is due to more than double to 164 (120 A319s and 44 737s) by September 2007. By late in the decade both no-frills operators expect to have overtaken all the traditional flag-carriers including the big three, Lufthansa, Air France and British Airways, to become the biggest short-haul airlines in Europe. As part of its latest order easyJet has also already taken an option on a further 120 Airbus aircraft for delivery up to 2012.

easyJet hopes to avoid some of the complexity of operating both the Boeing and Airbus aircraft types by separating them between its various bases. By the end of 2005 it will have 44 Boeing 737s (12 older-generation 300s and 32 new-generation 700s), which will be 'quarantined' to a relatively static part of the network. The group is highly dependent on the UK market serving 12 airports including 10 that are linked to at least one destination in continental Europe; but Mr Webster says its future growth will increasingly come from continental Europe. It currently has seven bases in the UK, where aircraft stay overnight and crew are domiciled, and only Geneva on the continent, but that is about to change. Paris Orly is already emerging as a base with local pilots and cabin crew being recruited, and both Barcelona and Nice are close to having the necessary scale of operations to become bases. With the liquidation of Air Lib in France early this year and the recent bankruptcy of Aris, easyJet hopes that it can become the second force in the French aviation market, allowing it in particular to pick up more take-off and landing slots at Orly.

Chris Avery, aviation analyst at JP Morgan, says that easyJet has just about digested the big strategic moves, including the integration of Go, and is about to resume the standard low-fare airline business model. Investor concerns about the mixed fleet issue have been overplayed, he says, and in any case Airbus is carrying much of the cost of duplication in the early stages, with support for crew training and the supply of spares as well as guaranteed maintenance costs. 'It is a complication; but when you have that sort of dollar saving through a well negotiated tender, you can live with it. There is a chance now that 20% top line growth can also become 20% bottom line growth.'

Source: Kevin Done, Financial Times, *8 October 2003*

DISCUSSION QUESTIONS

1 Is the change in business model to that of the use of a mixed fleet of aircraft going to affect the easyJet revenue and profits?

2 Are no-frills operators such as easyJet going to have continued growth or are the traditional scheduled carriers improving their own cost base and prices to compete; and therefore will this make it harder for the existing no-frills operators?

3 Are takeovers of other airlines such as Go the best way for easyJet to expand its business base?

Examples (3) and (4) in Figure 15.2 offer the ideal approach to organising business in the modern tourism marketplace. They are driven by research that creates an understanding of the consumer, the business and the marketplace. Research will be both secondary and primary. Information has to be collected from within and outside the company in order to establish a clear picture of the marketing environment. The integrated approach provides a sequence of events that commences with an understanding of the consumer, the competitors, the types of product that the company is capable of providing and a system that sensitises the whole organisation to a marketing orientation. The integrated system helps to ensure that methods of improving the satisfaction levels of the consumer are incorporated into each department's objectives.

Within the final two examples of company philosophy, it can be seen that the feedback process allows the marketing department to develop products as well as different forms of promotion that are right for the consumer. This establishes a more effective means of ensuring products are successful and that marketing budgets are used efficiently.

The tourism industry is spending vast sums of money on developing new attractions, improving products, building hotels and investing in technology. The only way for the risk level to be kept to a minimum is through the adoption of a marketing philosophy that provides products related to the needs of consumers.

However, all companies operate in a fiercely competitive environment that impinges upon the flexibility of management and company action. Marketing starts with the consumer and the market. This reflects the sovereignty of the consumer in the process. Such an approach has to be the correct strategy because it is the consumer who ultimately supports, through personal expenditure, tomorrow's tourism marketplace.

MARKETING ORIENTATION

The dynamic nature of business activity has led to many different sales and marketing opportunities in the tourism industry. The industry has thrown off many of its traditional attitudes toward the customer. This has come about through the realisation of the importance of a marketing orientation. As such, five main areas can be identified as follows.

1 **It is a management orientation or philosophy**. The focus of the organisation's effort is placed on the consumer as a set of guiding values, and this then leads to the customer being the centre of attention. These ideals should lead to a proactive approach in ensuring marketing efforts optimise exchange transactions within which consumers feel they have been rewarded with value and satisfaction. When customer's needs are met they are more likely to return to the cruise line, tour operator, hotel or restaurant; and more importantly to let others know of their satisfaction. There is the recognition that the conduct of the organisation's business must revolve around the long-term interests and satisfactions of the customers it serves. This is an outward-looking orientation which requires responsive action in relation to external political, economic, social or technological events, and competitive actions.

2 **It encourages exchange to take place**. These involve the attitudes and decisions of consumers in relation to the willingness to buy from producers or distributors. As the marketplace becomes more competitive strategies to strengthen an existing customer base have become increasingly important in tourism as it has been recognised that long-term relationships with existing customers are less expensive to maintain than forever attempting to attract new customers. If a close long-term relationship can be achieved, the possibility is that customers are more likely to provide higher purchase patterns and lower marketing costs per customer. While the objective of marketing is to achieve enduring relationships with the customer it should also be recognised that, in some situations, short-term sales (i.e. transaction marketing) may be just as important when there is little likelihood that the customer will be a repeat purchaser. As such marketers have to develop innovative methods to encourage both exchange transactions as well as retention.

There is the need to ensure the service offers value for money which may mean there is a requirement for creating a range of benefits over time. This has led to loyalty schemes and what is known as 'relationship marketing' (RM). Relationship marketing is an approach whereby marketers attempt to retain the customer over longer periods of time through club or loyalty programmes such as hotel, car rental

TABLE 15.2	The difference between transaction and relationship marketing
Transaction marketing	**Relationship marketing**
Short-term orientation: sale as end result	Long-term orientation: the sale is only the beginning
'Me' orientated	'We' orientated
Focus on achieving a sale	Focus on retention and repeat sales
Emphasis on persuasion to buy	Stress on creating positive relationships
Need to win, manipulation	Providing trust and service
Stress of conflict of achieving a transaction	Partnership and cooperation to minimise defection and provide longer term relationships (with customers or strategic alliances, joint ventures, vendor partnering, etc.)
Anonymous customer won by conquest in a carefully planned event	Individual profile of customer known so that a continuing process can emerge

or airline frequent flyer programmes. This is based upon the organisation becoming more involved with the customer as part of relationship marketing as opposed to the idea of concentrating on only a single sale or transaction (Table 15.2).

As part of the analogy, the RM process is available to advance relationships to higher levels of loyalty until a status is achieved whereby the customer is not only loyal but also champions the company, the employees and service to others. RM should not be confused with brand loyalty based upon simple commitment to the product, as RM is a far more complex and wider alliance and association (see Gilbert, 1996, for a full discussion of relationship marketing and airlines).

The rationale for RM is that it makes business sense to focus on long-term financial benefits that can accrue once a customer has been won for the first time. This is because it has been estimated to be five to ten times more expensive to recruit a new customer than to retain an existing one. Therefore, there is importance placed upon the retention of a customer with commercial consideration of the lifetime value of customers based upon quantity of repeat purchases. Such an approach enables the costs of acquisition and conversion of the prospect to be set against the revenues earned over the longer term. In an effective scheme sales and profits improve in direct proportion to the length of the relationship.

In relationship marketing customers will represent a diverse set of purchasing and spending patterns. However, it is important to be able to make marketing decisions which reflect the worth and potential of any one customer over a period of time. The analysis which allows this is known as **lifetime value** (LTV). Lifetime value, related to a frequent flier programme or similar tourism loyalty scheme, allows for the measurement of the total worth to the organisation of its relationship with a particular identified customer over a period of time. This is based upon the time-related income and costs of that individual adjusted so that the future amounts are discounted in order to provide a net present value worth of the individual. Therefore, in order to make a calculation of LTV the company has to capture or estimate the costs and revenues of each relationship. The costs will be related to the acquisition, communication and any rewards or incentives given during any one year. The period of time that the relationship is expected to last is discounted for inflation to provide a realistic real value of each customer. This is to compare it to an alternative investment that could have been made in an interest-bearing deposit account. The analysis of a frequent hotel guest or frequent flier will reveal the profile of customers who provide high returns as well as those who are costly for the company to service. The LTV information will allow for improved decision making regarding:

- The assigning of appropriate acquisition allowances to attract high-spending customers will be a reflection of the longer term benefit of certain individuals. The profile of these individuals is utilised to identify and segment the targeting strategy.

- Improving media strategies in order to acquire higher LTV individuals. Database analysis will provide information as to the optimal allocation of marketing communications budgets to alternative media in recruitment campaigns.

- Providing selection policies for customer marketing programmes. LTV analysis will allow a division of customers into graded levels of worth to the company. This allows for different rewards and privileges to be given to the different levels or categories of customer. It also allows for the cutback in communication for those individuals who represent only breakeven or loss when marketing costs are taken into consideration.

- Which individuals to contact and reactivate from the lapsed category. The database can identify the timing and worth of purchases made by individuals. If a previously higher spending individual indicates lapsed behaviour a 'winback' policy may be triggered. As such a reactivation allowance can be agreed based upon the likely return of the individual and their future revenue potential.

3   **It involves long- and short-term planning**. This requires the systematic organisation of strategic planning and tactical activity. In the short term an organisation does not normally have the flexibility to change rapidly even if the marketplace warrants this. The physical infrastructure of a hotel building, the skills of the workforce and other production capabilities can often only be changed marginally. Therefore, in the short term the constraints of earlier planning will restrict the choice a company or resort area may have. Because of the short-run constraints one aspect of planning which increases in importance to capacity risks is the control mechanisms for the monitoring of performance against targets. The long-term success of an organisation requires the efficient use of resources and assets, while tactical action will be required to keep plans on course. IT systems offer the opportunity to

model demand and take tactical action at the earliest opportunity to sell unsold inventory or expand supply. This approach includes the balance between long- and short-term aims for the renewal and development of the organisation's efforts for its products and other aspects of its marketing mix.

4   It requires efficient, cost-effective methods. Marketing's principal concern within any organisation has to be the delivery of maximum satisfaction and value to the customer at acceptable or minimum cost to the company, so as to ensure long-term profit. The use of resources within marketing has to be both efficient and effective. The trend in the use of relationship marketing to build closer bonds and better retention with valued customers who provide repeat business is more effective than treating all customers as equal. However, in many organisations, the dilemma is that management is often judged by short-term success in relation to sales and profit performance.

5   It requires the development of an integrated company environment. The organisation's efforts and structure must be matched with the needs of the target customers. Everybody working for the organisation must participate in a total corporate, marketing environment with each division maximising the satisfaction level of consumers. Integration is not just a smile or politeness. Barriers to serving the customer have to be destroyed. The onus is on the organisation to provide organisational structures that are responsive and will undergo change to suit customer needs. Such an environment has to be based upon a culture of adaptation of each and every company department in line with customer and market requirements.

CONCLUSION

We have demonstrated that the concept of marketing and its practical application have evolved as a result of changing business and social conditions that have emerged throughout the last century. The differences between sales and marketing were covered so that the reader will be more aware of why marketing planning and understanding the consumer is an important component of tourism marketing. In the course of this chapter we have identified different business philosophies that currently exist, the benefits of a marketing orientation and the basis of the marketing concept – including that of building relationships and delivering superior value.

Self-check questions

1 Name the three eras which have characterised the lead up to the use of a fully integrated marketing approach.

2 Whose needs underpin the main definitions of marketing?

3 Name three ways that value can be added to the tourism product.

4 Provide five ways in which a no-frills airline achieves cost savings which can be passed on as value – by means of lower prices.

5 What are the economic benefits of adopting a relationship marketing approach to business?

Essay questions

1 Examine the business philosophy and marketing concepts of both a no-frills airline and also a full service airline. Discuss whether there are any significant differences between them; and whether one of the business models is better than the other.

2 Read the following abstract from the article 'A history and market analysis of tourism in Tanzania', from *Tourism Management*, Vol. 22, No. 1, February 2001, pages 93–101. Then describe how you would go about applying tourism marketing principles to Tanzania in order to improve its products and demand for the country.

Tanzania contains some of the world's greatest natural wonders. Following major reforms in its foreign tourism policies in the mid-1980s, tourism has increased to become the nation's second leading foreign exchange earner. Tanzania is a less developed nation than its East African neighbours, and seeks to offer a low-density, high-quality, and high-priced tourism experience. Numerous deficiencies, however, are present in its tourism product. A lack of infrastructure, trained staff, and legal and regulatory framework offer severe challenges for the delivery of world-class service quality. In addition to a lack of marketing and promotion, the tourism industry has failed to diversify into areas beyond wildlife, such as culture and beach tourism. Consequently, most visitors treat Tanzania as an add-on to their Kenyan safari. Tanzania however, is moving towards developing the infrastructure necessary to occupy its market niche. With careful planning and management, Tanzania has the tremendous potential to develop a diverse and sustainable tourism industry.

3 United Airlines has offered the following changes. Indicate how important such services are and what value they add to the overall air flight product.

Flight status alerts. Customers can sign up for a free service to be informed of flight delays, cancellations, gate information and upgrade requests. Messages can be automatically sent in a voice or data format to a customer's personal computer, cellular phone or pager, enabling travellers with wireless capabilities to stay abreast of schedule changes even when they are on the road. United was the first airline to offer customers with hand-held wireless devices the ability to retrieve current-day arrival and departure information via a direct connection to United's reservations system. The automated flight information system can be accessed by calling a toll-free number, and then customers can obtain a wide variety of automated flight information through a voice-prompted menu.

4 List the reasons relationship marketing may or may not be a better business model than transaction marketing. Now discuss whether the airline, hotel and

car hire sector is predominately one approach or the other and if you think changes need to be made.

5 List the aspects of value that were important to you the last time you went on a major journey or holiday. Also, discuss how the service providers could have added more value to your experience.

Annotated further reading

Books

Kotler, P. Bowen, J. and Makens, J. (2002) *Marketing for Hospitality and Tourism*, 3rd edn, Pearson, Upper Saddle River, NJ.
The book draws upon the marketing material of Philip Kotler's other books and as such is based upon his pedigree which has been developed over a number of years of writing marketing textbooks. However, the examples are often not very good and other specialist books need to be read in conjunction with this one. This latest edition now covers electronic marketing, has case studies and lets students understand the role of marketing in hospitality and tourism. Specialist areas covered are customer quality management and destination marketing.

Middleton, V. and Clarke, J. (2001) *Marketing in Travel and Tourism*, 3rd edn, Butterworth Heinemann, Oxford.
Marketing in Travel and Tourism explains the basic principles and practice of marketing in the contemporary setting of the new pressures affecting tourism including areas not normally included in such texts such as NTOs. In addition, international case studies are included.

Shaw, S. (2004) *Airline Marketing and Management*, 5th edn, Aldershot, Ashgate.
This fifth edition text offers a comprehensive overview of the needs of the current airline industry to utilise and formulate marketing approaches within their sector. It includes new material on terrorism, economic and regulatory pressures, as well as airline alliances. Its strength is that the book examines the structure of the airline marketplace against the major principles of marketing.

Web sites

britishairways.com: www.britishairways.com/press/

easyJet Web site for news:
http://www.easyjet.com/en/about/investorrelations_financialnews.html

References cited and bibliography

Ang, S.H., Leong, S.M. and Kotler, P. (2000): 'The Asian apocalypse: crisis marketing for consumers and businesses', *Long Range Planning* 33(1), 97–119.

Baker, M. (1999) The *Marketing Book*, Butterworth Heinemann, Oxford.

Chartered Institute of Marketing (1984) Cookham, Berkshire.

Drucker, P. (1973) *Management Tasks, Responsibilities, Practices*, Harper & Row, New York.

Economist (2001) 'Ready for take off', *Economist* **361**(8247), 52.

Economist (2002) 'So many planes, so few passengers' and 'Signs of life', *Economist* **364**(8290), 51–52, 57.

Gilbert, D.C. (1996) 'Relationship marketing and airline loyalty schemes', *Tourism Management* **17**(8), 575–82.

Gilbert, D.C. and Bailey, N. (1990) 'The development of marketing – a compendium of historical approaches', *Quarterly Review of Marketing* **15**(2), 6–13.

Keith, R.J. (1981) 'The marketing revolution', pp. 44–9 in Enis, B.M. and Cox K.K. (eds), *Marketing Classics*, 4th edn, Allyn and Bacon, London.

Kotler, P. (2003) *Marketing Management*, Prentice Hall, Englewood Cliffs, NJ.

Levitt, T. (1960) 'Marketing myopia', *Harvard Business Review* July/August, 45–56.

MAJOR CASE STUDY 15.1
AIRLINE STRATEGIES IN TIMES OF ADVERSITY

The events of September 11, 2001, the war in Iraq, health worries of travelling and continued terrorist attacks have triggered problems of the economies of major world countries. Particularly, these events have caused a major downturn in the demand for tourism which in turn has affected the overall industry. One serious outcome is that some countries have suffered a recession. A recession can be defined as a decline in economic activity lasting two consecutive quarters. During a recession sales decrease and in order to safeguard profits companies may reduce capacity, investment, labour and other costs in line with falling revenues. In order to survive a recession it is normal for companies to be more cost efficient with their resources. Depending on the length and severity of the recession this may affect the wider economy through increased unemployment, asset deflation and slower growth. A major problem is that this scenario erodes consumer confidence. This both psychologically and financially affects consumer behaviours of spending on products and services. There is lower participation in leisure–recreation activities, more price comparisons, and more postponement of purchasing expensive durables, more do-it-yourself activity, and greater desire on obtaining value for money. After September 11, the airline industry was greatly affected by a considerable fall in the number of people who were willing to fly. In the USA, US Airways filed for bankruptcy, while United Airlines cut wages and capacity in an effort to secure a federal loan to stave off bankruptcy. In Europe, Swissair and Sabena were previously struggling carriers that could not cope with the new business conditions. British Airways and other European carriers all suffered a drop in overall traffic especially in the lucrative business travel sector. The decline in business travel can also be attributed to many companies reassessing their travel budget and opting to use other forms of travel or methods of contact.

LOW-COST CARRIERS

Despite the hardships faced by the airline industry after 2001 the no-frills low-cost carriers, such as Southwest Airlines, Blue Jet, easyJet and Ryanair did not have a similar level of problems. They reacted with value for money price offers and could survive due to their business models of having had a cost leadership strategy for a number of years.

British Airways has been forced to tighten its finances and deal with the competition with a number of cost-cutting strategies aimed at reducing their high cost base. First, the workforce was gradually reduced, a reduction in capacity was achieved by decreasing the number of flights and efficiency was achieved on long-haul routes by means of using smaller 777 aircraft. British Airways also cut commission fees to travel agents and offered lower priced tickets directly on their web site. BA also examined the ways of cutting meal costs and reducing in-flight services in an attempt to reduce the prices in order to win back price conscious customers. To tackle downturns in demand and survive in the recession, companies commonly utilise the strategies of BA. However, planning changes such as those of BA could lower the reputation of the brand and lead to a price war.

DISCUSSION QUESTION

With the threat of deep vein thrombosis litigation and possible terrorist attacks directed at airlines or cruise ships what key marketing strategies can a major scheduled airline such as British Airways or Air France employ to build their business in a time of adversity? You are to assume the role of the marketing director and provide a plan for the next five years of what needs to be achieved.

The following ideas may help your analysis.

Marketing actions

In general, the following can be adjusted in order to deal with problems of weak demand.

1 Market mix: concentrate on growing and developing the most profitable market segments and dispense with the weaker ones.

2 Customer mix: concentrate on attracting the most profitable customers and retaining them through valued relationships.

3 Product mix: ensure that there is a sufficiently broad product line at different price levels so that the overall company offer can withstand changes in customer spending patterns.

4 Marketing mix: increased competition means that either market share or margins will suffer. Price reduction may be necessary but should be done in a way that can be reversed after the downturn/recession (e.g. special offers or packaged deals).

5 Overheads and costs: internal cost reduction measures should be adopted but not those that risk losing customers through unacceptable reductions in quality or value.

Strategy development for airlines in times of adversity

PRODUCTS	
Existing	**New**
A PROTECT/BUILD • Consolidation and defence of key markets • Selective market penetration of safe markets • Form alliances	**B** PRODUCT DEVELOPMENT • Look beyond the current problem and plan renewal • Develop new markets based upon competences (training, engineering, consultancy) • Think outside the box
C MARKET DEVELOPMENT • New routes/territories • New uses such as chartering or private jets • Benchmark and improve on capabilities • Utilise the database to identify key segments and try to grow their business • Work closer with corporates, agents, tour operators, etc.	**D** DIVERSIFICATION • Assess the possibility of acquiring other businesses due to the lower cost in times of adversity • Examine setting up new businesses based upon existing competencies (such as yield management systems)

CHAPTER SIXTEEN
MANAGING MARKETING FOR TOURISM

INTRODUCTION

In this chapter we show that marketing management related to tourism cannot ignore the principal characteristics that set tourism apart from other products. Tourism, as a specialised service product, creates a number of important considerations which need to be fully understood if a tourism enterprise or organisation is to maximise its potential and be successful. The management of tourism cannot be divorced from the management of service and quality. In addition, the need to undertake the tasks of research, analysis, product formulation, recommending price policies, promotion and distribution are of paramount significance for those involved in tourism marketing management.

We demonstrate that a great deal of management involves decisions based upon judgement, information and experience. All these areas rely on an understanding of the characteristics and issues that apply specifically to the market conditions for a product. When marketing any one of the different tourism products we find in the marketplace, there are a number of tasks and characteristics of which we need to be aware. In this chapter we stress that the first factor that managers of tourism have to understand is the service management aspects related to the purchase of the tourism product.

LEARNING OUTCOMES

The objective of this chapter is to furnish the reader with a comprehensive understanding of the main aspects of marketing management for tourism. After reading this chapter you should:

- appreciate the importance of the characteristics of the service product and the implications of these differentiating characteristics for the approach an organisation might adopt for its marketing effort;

- recognise that the purchase of tourism products is associated with the need for quality management and the reduction of perceived risk;

- understand the importance of quality management in the tourism industry and the methods that may be employed to establish an integrated approach; and

- be familiar with the key criticisms targeted at tourism marketing and the problems of properly utilising tourism marketing techniques.

THE SERVICE PRODUCT

With tourism, hospitality and leisure products we are dealing with a **service product** that has specific characteristics that set the product apart from the more general goods sold in the marketplace. The concept of service is very complex since service varies from personal service to service as a product. However, an understanding of the complexity of the service product concept is an essential prerequisite for successful tourism marketing. This is because the emphasis is increasingly placed on the service provider to develop a deeper understanding of the linkages that correspond to consumer benefits sought and the nature of the service delivery system itself.

A starting point is an examination of the dimensions and characteristics of the service product concept. Products can be placed along a continuum of services and goods, with most products being a combination of the two. A pure service would be consultancy or teaching whereas a pure good would be a can of beans or clothing. Some products will have more service content than others, and if they are able to be placed to the left-hand side of the continuum shown in Figure 16.1, they may be termed service products.

The characteristics of the service product

INTANGIBILITY

The service product has the characteristic of **intangibility** which means it cannot be easily evaluated or demonstrated in advance of its purchase. For example, a travel agent cannot allow the testing or sampling of the tourism product and a sales representative for a hotel cannot take anything but secondary material to a sales call meeting. On the other hand, an automobile or computer game can be tested prior to purchase, and clothing can be tried on. Much of the selling of tourism and hospitality is related to the promise of safe and timely delivery of the individual by transport companies, or comfort and good service by accommodation companies. Only a ticket, voucher or Internet reservation number is exchanged at the time of purchase. The marketers of tourism and hospitality products, therefore, face greater difficulty. Because of fixed time and space constraints they cannot easily demonstrate the benefits of the products they are selling. The problem for the tourism service marketer is overcome by the production of a range of printed literature, videos or other means of providing clues as to the type of product on offer in an attempt to increase tangibility. In addition, there is a need to ensure marketing provides

Products	
Service	**Good**
Intangibility	More tangible
Perishability	Often storable
Inseparability	Standardisable

FIGURE 16.1   **Services and goods continuum**

clear and well-managed branding of accommodation, transport and distribution organisations. This positions the brand name more tangibly in the mind of the consumer. In addition ensuring that the tangible aspects related to uniforms, décor and physical evidence give cues as to the quality of the service. These final points are important as marketers need to realise that there is a distinction which should be made between the degree of intangibility of the actual service and the intangibility, or lack of physical evidence, surrounding the process of service delivery. The airline industry is an example of this where the physical evidence represents a major component of the service because the performance characteristics are supported largely by means of tangible elements such as food and drink, the cabin configuration and comfort of the seat, inflight entertainment system, etc.

PERISHABILITY

The characteristic of **perishability** means that service products such as tourism, unlike goods, cannot be stored for a sale on a future occasion. For example, a hotel bed or an airline seat unsold or a convention centre left empty is revenue that can never be recouped. This leads to the high-risk nature of the tourism industry. Perishability is also linked to the seasonality of demand whereby some companies or destinations have high and low periods of demand and in low periods the problem of perishability is exacerbated. Marketers in the tourism and hospitality sector have to devise complex pricing and promotion policies in an attempt to sell 'off-season' periods and create greater synchronisation of staffing levels and supply to match demand patterns. Weak demand is not the only problem as the sector is characterised by hotels, airlines, attractions, museums, galleries, etc., all of which have fixed capacity with a maximum upper level demand constraint. In peak periods the industry often has difficulty in coping with demand and therefore charges premium prices or uses queuing as a control mechanism, but in the low periods there is a need for greater marketing activity. The reaction to perishability is for marketers to try to smooth out demand curves by careful use of the marketing mix, for example, cheaper tickets for matinée shows. There is also a concentration on the use of computerised reservation systems in order to forecast the need for tactical action if demand is believed to be below expected levels; and of specialist web sites to sell off last minute availability.

INSEPARABILITY

Service products are often referred to as being **inseparable** which means the product is often consumed and produced simultaneously. This means that both the service provider and customer are present when the service function occurs. (See Photograph 16.1 which shows the richness of a tourist service experience.) Because there is less opportunity to manage and pre-check a tourism or hospitality product, it can vary in the standard of its service delivery. This is sometimes characterised by authors as *heterogeneity* or *variability*. The tourism sector offers an amalgam of services which make up the delivery of the product. This occurs in a fragmented system where different organisations may have responsibility for the level of service delivery. Even for a single service such as air travel there will be the travel agent, airport checking-in agent and staff, airline staff, catering company, baggage handling staff, cabin cleaning staff; all of whom provide the single continuous

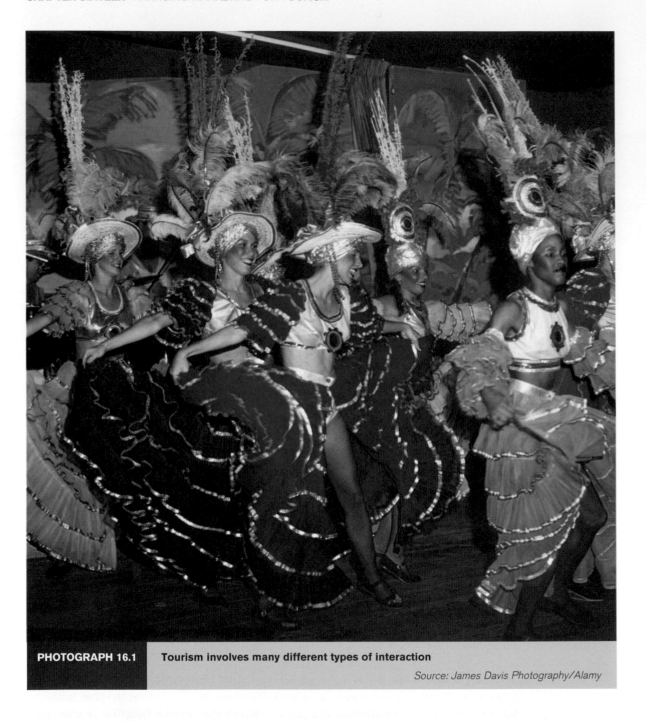

PHOTOGRAPH 16.1   **Tourism involves many different types of interaction**

Source: James Davis Photography/Alamy

flight experience. Variance occurs because of the inseparable nature of the product's delivery when the customer is part of the production system. The simultaneous process of production and consumption can lead to situations where it is difficult to ensure the overall satisfaction of consumers. For example, peak demand load cannot always be forecast and may create dissatisfaction by way of secondary problems of lack of staffing. There is also the potential problem of having groups or types of clients with conflicting needs that may result in disharmony. A couple wanting a quiet romantic anniversary dinner in a restaurant could find the evening unacceptable if a group of the local football club supporters decide to eat at the same time. Whether on the aircraft, in the hotel, or in the restaurant there could be the clash of social values, noisiness, drunkenness, high spirits or a child crying. Staff may also have had personal problems or be feeling ill or tired, and this can affect their level of commitment to their performance of giving good service or resolving problems.

As the nature of the tourism service product is largely one of interpersonal relationships, where the performance level of staff is directly related to the satisfaction and overall experience of the consumer, there is a need for quality assurance programmes. Staff are emotional and changeable and if a high content of the product is based upon interpersonal relationships between 'strangers', as guest and service provider, it is important to ensure standardised service levels are adhered to. Quality assurance is important as a basis of planning for competitive advantage and controlling the standards of staff interactions. To reduce the problems that can be associated with inseparability there is a need for investment in company training programmes for all service staff.

Other aspects of tourism as a service product

1 **Shorter exposure to service delivery.** The customer's exposure to the delivery of the service is normally of short duration. This allows only a limited time during which company personnel can build a relationship and affect repeat business.

2 **More personal.** The self is very much involved emotionally in the service encounter and as such the personal feelings created by contact service personnel are an important determinant of future demand. Therefore, it is important to recruit staff for personal qualities and then train for skills.

3 **Growing use of self-service.** To reduce costs and provide more timely service companies are more likely to introduce self-service buffet meals, Internet reservation technology etc. rather than interpersonal service alternatives. This requires the customer to handle the self-service process or technology appropriately and for the service not to be so complicated that there is any danger of negative consequences. An important consideration for companies using self-service processes and technology is the potential lack of personal interaction between the service employee and the customer which allows the opportunity to exceed customer service expectations.

4 **Greater significance on managing evidence.** Due to the intangible nature of the tourism product it is important to plan to deliver cues as to the positioning and quality of the offer by means of aspects of cleanliness, décor, uniforms, signage, etc.

5 **Complementarity is greater.** The overall tourism product is often made up of an amalgam of many different services each of which has to add up to an overall positive experience. Destinations are aware that they have to control service quality to ensure a satisfactory experience and therefore attempt to regulate tourism providers.

6 **Easier copying of services.** Services can be easily benchmarked and copied by other organisations due to their visibility.

577

TOURISM PRODUCTS AND RISK

Tourism products are important in relation to the type of marketing they require. Tourism has developed rapidly over the past few decades, led by a marketing thrust which has created diversity of supply, focused on important consumer segments and stimulated high levels of demand. Within this development marketing has often concentrated more on improving the product than on understanding the consumer, and the complexity of his or her decision processes. As uncertainty is part of the process of purchase and consumption this is often associated with personal reservations and a judgement of **perceived risk**.

A major aspect of consumer behaviour, linked to the purchase of tourism products, is the notion of risk and a consumer's judgement about the likelihood of a problem occurring. Tourism products often involve a complex decision-making process because the purchase is of relatively high risk and high involvement. However, the concept is complex given that throughout the population the threshold at which an individual perceives *economic*, *physical*, *performance* and *psychological* risk differs by age, income and experience. The concept is also related to individual feelings of uncertainty based upon the subjective possibility of any occurrence of the following types of risk.

Economic risk

Economic risk is associated with the decision for potential tourists as to whether the product offer is of good value or not. Given the range of prices offered for short-haul flights from both no-frills and scheduled carriers there is frequently some uncertainty as to which airline to book with and which price to pay. All consumers face economic or financial risk when they purchase tourism products given they cannot be sure whether their choice will deliver the benefits they desire. Tourism often involves the purchase of an expensive product that cannot easily be seen or sampled prior to consumption such as that of the annual holiday. This type of risk is heightened for those with low levels of disposable income, for whom the purchase represents a major expenditure.

Physical risk

Some overseas destinations may be perceived to be dangerous owing to disease or crime, and some transport companies such as ferry or airline operators are thought to be safer than others. The fear of an illness such as SARS or travelling at the time of war or civil unrest is a clear indication of this concept. Some people fear flying no matter what airline they fly with, while others may reduce the perception of physical risks by selecting certain 'safer' airlines. A study by Lepp and Gibson (2003) based upon a random sample of US-born young adults found that there are seven important risk factors which are: health, political instability, terrorism, strange food, cultural barriers, a nation's political and religious dogma, and crime. Analysis revealed the more experienced tourist was less likely to be concerned about terrorism. It was also found there is a difference by gender in that women perceived a greater degree of risk regarding health and food. However, tourist role was the most significant variable, with familiarity seekers being the most risk adverse.

Performance risk

The quality of different destinations or unknown hotel brands cannot be assessed in advance. This type of risk is associated with feelings that the product may not deliver the desired benefits. It is rarely possible for those who have had a bad holiday to make up for it by attempting to have another better holiday in the same year. Most consumers do not have the additional money or holiday entitlement to make good the holiday that went wrong. This heightens their awareness of the risk factors involved. One important performance risk for UK travellers is weather. The risk of poor weather while holidaying in the UK is one reason why many people travel abroad.

Psychological risk

Status can be lost through visiting the 'wrong' country because it has no status in the minds of others, or travelling with a company that has a poor image. This risk occurs when the potential customer feels the purchase may not reflect the self-image he or she wishes to portray. This may be connected to social risk, which suggests there could be a loss of social status due to the act of purchasing from a company that has a poor image.

From a marketing point of view, the above perceptions of risks need to be minimised through product and promotion strategies. Creating and delivering information in brochures and leaflets that helps to convince the potential traveller of the reliability of the company will lessen the perception of risk. However, it is important to realise that communications 'by word-of-mouth' whereby a friend reassures another about a purchase is a more powerful source than company-controlled literature. By acquiring information the consumer builds up mental pictures and attitudes that create the expectation of positive benefits from the travel or destination experience.

It is also important for the quality of the product to be controlled especially in relation to the process of service delivery.

PLANNING THE SERVICE ENCOUNTER

If we examine a systems perspective that identifies the linkage between the consumer's needs and the service delivery, we can be more aware of the management principles associated with service products. This can also be utilised in the establishment of benchmark points against which the service can be positioned.

A well-positioned service enables the organisation to achieve the following two important objectives:

- to differentiate its position so as to distinguish itself from competitors; and

- to deliver service superior to that accepted as the norm.

The above objectives allow the organisation to plan and build competitive advantage by establishing leadership principles of service standards and delivery. Once the standards are established there should be a policy to communicate and reinforce the service provision philosophy at every possible opportunity: meetings, training and internal marketing programmes, induction programmes and appraisal systems. The human resource function needs to be organised so as to ensure the different levels in Figure 16.2 are always clearly understood and reinforced through organisational culture and reward. Often services are managed on the subjective opinions of managers, when they should be based upon objective designs to ensure there is no confusion as to what needs to be achieved. Without good internal organisational procedures and relationships it is unlikely that even the most well conceived of quality programmes will be successful.

The levels shown in Figure 16.2 illustrate the linkages for designing a successful service delivery process. For the model to be successful there is the need for the implementation process to consider the need for the following:

- Leadership and commitment by senior management based upon clear goals and a policy on quality being established and communicated to employees. There is also the need to release the appropriate resources to create changes and achieve the required results.

- All changes and objectives to be defined by the customer. All the approaches related to quality delivery and standards have to be delineated in all of the dimensions of the service delivery with reference to what customers' value. What customer's expect and value should consequently be incorporated into the company induction and training programmes.

- The organisation having the flexibility to change and improve service. This requires a process and systems approach to match or exceed customer expectations. Such a system may incorporate a quality audit system which applies measurement and inspection to ensure defects are corrected and the system delivers optimum quality results.

- Effective human resource management to hire those with service competencies and inclinations and then to motivate, train and educate staff to deliver the concepts of quality. This is reinforced through teamwork values and a culture that champions quality product delivery as a prerequisite for competitive advantage.

- An assessment to be made of the added value and benefit of any change rather than there being a simple cost-cutting and price-leadership strategy. The long-term benefits of any change need to be the focus of service encounter decision making.

- Quality audits and control to ensure the service meets or exceeds customer expectations.

It is crucial that an organisation creates its own quality management culture and does not simply attempt to clone a system used by a competitor. A successful service

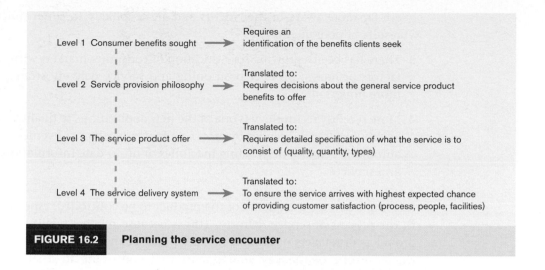

FIGURE 16.2   **Planning the service encounter**

encounter approach requires honest two-way communication between management and staff which will build confidence in the implementation process. This means the staff has to be allowed to own up to weaknesses and problems of poor quality in a supportive atmosphere where the organisation attempts to learn from weaknesses rather than to punish staff. Such methods create teamwork, confidence and commitment. However, there is also the need for competence to deliver the changes. This may require further training and seminars for staff and follow-up sessions. The recognition that there is a need to treat other members of staff as internal customers will assist the transition to a **total quality management** (TQM) system.

It is obvious that organisations have customers from within as well as without. With this in mind, if employees visualise the relationships between each other based upon supplier and customer links as a quality chain, then the question is always, 'am I meeting the full requirements of my role?' For example, the secretary is a supplier to the boss with the need to provide timely error-free work in order to aid him or her as supplier to his or her internal customer, who may be a director. An organisation, therefore, is a web of internal suppliers and customers. Such chains are easily weakened or broken by faulty equipment or by fallible people. The important issue is that an internal quality chain failure will ultimately have some effect on the external customer.

QUALITY MANAGEMENT

We cannot adequately describe the management of tourism without touching on the importance of the growing emphasis on quality management. There are four main reasons that can account for the growing relevance of quality management:

1 Organisations need to find ways of creating differential advantage by having better service levels than their competitors.

2 The increased level of consumerism and the greater media attention on quality has meant organisations have to be more responsive to quality issues. Consumers

are far more aware of their rights and are less likely to suffer quietly from the results of poor quality.

3 There has been a growing sophistication of consumer markets with the non-price factors of image, product positioning and service delivery strategies becoming more important.

4 More recently technology is one of the new applications to quality enhancement. Technology can aid service by providing higher levels of convenience, for example automatic vending or ticketing machines or up-to-date information for products and services.

It is important for the quality of the product to be controlled, especially in relation to the process of service delivery. This is because relative quality between service providers or retailers has implications for market share and profitability. Quality is therefore one of the key components that contribute to a successful strategy. Quality has emerged as a major competitive component of a service organisation's strategy. However, when we examine the employment of the term 'quality', there is almost a super-abundance of the use of this word in relation to the way management operates. There is a crusade for quality management and improvement within industry worldwide and the campaign for improved quality was rooted in the manufacturing industry prior to the expansion into the service industry. However, many individuals in the industry are still unaware of the theoretical grounding of quality management. Such management has to consider core and peripheral services which need to be developed and delivered after a careful diagnosis of customer expectations and perceptions.

What are the key terms for quality?

There are several key concepts related to quality. Quality is the totality of relationships between service providers (functional aspects) and the features of the product (technical aspects) which are related to the delivery of satisfaction. It is therefore important to create systems of **quality control** which are checks and monitoring to ensure measurement of service delivery is taking place. To this end TQM is a holistic organisational approach which systematically attempts to enhance customer satisfaction by focusing on continuous improvements without incurring unacceptable cost increases. These improvements are part of an unending quest for excellence in all aspects of quality service delivery. Therefore, TQM has to form the values and mind set for all employees, which leads to quality being an integrated element of corporate culture. For success, quality must be the concern of all employees and the culture, therefore, should not be based upon a departmental or technical understanding of quality. Instead, the notion of quality must be disseminated to employees throughout the organisational structure and implemented as a systematic process extending throughout the organisation. The focus of any change in quality must be based upon external customer expectations and not internal organisational ideas.

TQM is managed by **quality assurance** arrangements whereby a system is instituted to allocate responsibility for planned and systematic activities that will ensure the product will provide the right levels of satisfaction to all concerned. A service guarantee system can provide more quality control and data capture in an organisation.

This facilitates a better understanding of potential for improvement by capturing information on what is going wrong. Following this the information gathered on what goes wrong allows for a reaction in improvement of service. Some companies are now guaranteeing their service or paying out compensation with schemes such as flight delay insurance. A good service guarantee is identified as unconditional, easy to understand and communicate, meaningful, and easy to invoke in order to obtain recompense. But there is a need:

- not to promise something your customers already expect;

- not to shroud a guarantee in so many conditions that it is meaningless; or

- to offer a guarantee so mild that it is never invoked.

A guarantee can set clear standards and allow the company personnel to be clear about what the organisation stands for. If customers can complain easily, there is the benefit of collecting data on common problems that subsequently need to be addressed and eradicated. This is because a guarantee system forces the focus on why the failure occurred and what needs to be done about it to improve service quality. Moreover, a guarantee adds credibility and weight to the marketing effort of the organisation. It allows for a communication of the presence of the guarantee which may lead to a reduction in the perception of risk associated with purchase and can lead to higher levels of demand.

As a measure of whether the quality delivery complies to the planned delivery of the service a quality audit needs to take place to judge the effectiveness of the total service delivery arrangements. For a system to be audited correctly there is a need for a method of creating unbiased feedback. While a range of aspects of quality can be assessed, a number of categories exist. These may include the following, which are based upon various research that attempted to establish categories of service quality determinants:

- **Tangibles.** This will include physical evidence of the service, such as physical aspects of airline cabins, hotel bedrooms and facilities or material the customer can see, touch, use etc., like equipment, merchandise, personnel, e.g.:
  - physical facilities such as extra legroom on the aircraft or size of hotel room;
  - appearance of personnel and condition of the surroundings;
  - technology or equipment used to provide the service;
  - physical representation of the service, e.g. airline loyalty card;
  - other customers in the service facility.

- **Reliability.** This involves consistency of performance and dependability. Gaining the customer's confidence is vital in service organisations. The ability of the service provider to establish a relationship of trust and faith greatly influences perceived service quality. A company should perform the service right the *first time* in order to achieve a good reputation. In many circumstances reliability is an expected dimension, as an airline should deliver this as a core service. It means the firm should honour its promises and have the ability to trust employees with the responsibility to deliver service consistently and accurately which meets policy standards, such as:

- accuracy in a bill or charging;
- collecting and keeping the correct records;
- assuring confidentiality and security of any personal data held;
- performing the service at designated time, e.g. delivery of opening or departure time promise.

- **Responsiveness.** This refers to the willingness or readiness of employees to provide service, their reaction and willingness to help customers and give timely service, such as:
  - serving complimentary drinks on a delayed flight;
  - mailing a transaction slip or sending an email immediately;
  - calling a customer back quickly after a query or problem;
  - giving prompt service (e.g. arranging a change of itinerary; or reacting to the hotel guest's request).

- **Competence.** This concerns knowledge and courtesy of employees as well as the peace of mind that the company is to be trusted. This then delivers the assurance that employees will have the knowledge, skills and courtesy to create trust and confidence in the customer base, e.g.:
  - knowledge and skill of the contact personnel;
  - explaining the actual and wider service available;
  - the reputation of the organisation;
  - personal characteristics of the contact personnel;
  - confidentiality, financial and personal security.

- **Empathy.** This relates to the individualised attention to customers; the caring, individual concern and attention for others and their emotions, such as:
  - recognising and relating to regular customers;
  - learning the customer-specific requirements;
  - providing individualised service (customisation or personalisation is regarded as an essential attribute of service offerings due to the ability to tailor offers to customer specific requirements).

The elements that could be assessed in the above could also include: availability of items the customer demands; after-sales service and contact; the way telephone orders and queries are handled by contact centres; the reliability and safety of the product being sold; availability of sales literature and brochures; the number and type of items that can be demonstrated; technical knowledge of staff; the way an employee deals with a complaint, etc. In addition the organisation can use the above list as a means to assess the way it could develop its positioning strategy in order to distinguish itself from its competitors.

Table 16.1 indicates some of the ways that quality can be assessed. It is important to realise that whatever system is used to audit quality at the end of the day, that which is not measured cannot be controlled.

Is quality a cost or a long-term benefit?

Although there are benefits for firms adopting TQM approaches it is found that some organisations embarking upon service quality programmes perceive them to

TABLE 16.1	Auditing systems	
Internal inspection		**Auditing**
• Statistical process control based upon quality failure information and objective measures		• Internal auditors of quality
• Visual inspections to check against standards and consistency		• External bodies
• Management by walking about		• Consultants, regular users, non-user surveys and feedback
• Quality control group feedback		• Cross-department audits
• Inspection of competitors' offer and assessment of own company offer		• Mystery shoppers
		• Content analysis of complaint and praise letters and documented problems
		• Free telephone line feedback

be costly; to need a lot of management time; to create difficulty in measuring the intangible benefits; and to be difficult to implement. Tourism is characterised by a high number of front-line service workers who are expected to deliver quality individualised service while at the same time be productive and efficient in what they do. This produces a tension between being both effective and efficient and leads to questions about what is the best means to achieve high levels of quality while achieving productivity. Of course, there is always going to be a trade-off between the two.

Given the nature of tourism as a people-based industry with employee performance and interaction being of paramount importance, then we are dealing with a human medium where errors are inevitable. There is therefore a need to judge the benefit of increased usage and repeat business in relation to the loss of custom. The moment of truth or impact on the bottom line of any organisation is therefore the judgement by customers of the quality of its service. Figure 16.3 is based upon Hart, Heskett and Sasser (1990) who argue for the linkages of service encounters as creating a self-reinforcing mechanism. It indicates the relationship between the customer on the left and the service provider to the right. This overcomes the notion that improvement in quality is associated with increased costs. The model indicates that in the long-term true quality improvement leads to an improved trading position.

The above proposition that a continuous improvement in service is not a cost but an investment in a customer who will return more profit in the long term is becoming more widely supported. The premise is based upon research which indicates the cost of acquiring a new customer is five times as high as retaining an existing customer through providing quality service. Such argument is based upon non-traditional accounting practices which stress: satisfied customers will be willing to pay higher prices owing to the service quality they have experienced and liked; there is a free advertising benefit due to the positive word-of-mouth recommendation; there is a different cost in acquiring new customers as opposed to retaining existing customers over longer time periods. Thus, in general, following

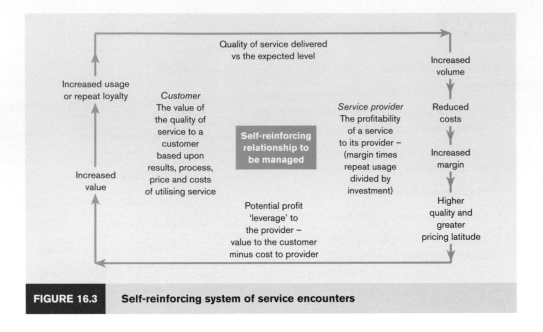

| **FIGURE 16.3** | **Self-reinforcing system of service encounters** |

the ideas of relationship marketing, it is suggested that to keep a customer over the long term provides important savings. On a cost–benefit basis good service quality is thought to increase revenue and reduce long-term costs.

Given that the cost of finding a new customer is far greater than that of retaining an existing one, there is growing emphasis on customer retention and relationship marketing as discussed in Chapter Fifteen whereby long-term revenue can be enhanced by service recovery strategies. These include the following:

- **Training.** As service is an interpersonal performance activity then the provision of communication and customer relation skills will enhance the ability of staff to deal with the most difficult of situations. Perhaps, more importantly, training will allow staff to feel confident in the service encounter transaction and allow them to deal professionally with all situations.

- **Watching for sign language.** Allowing those customers who are reticent or mute when it comes to complaints to break their silence. Organisations need the opportunity to prove their commitment to the customer through service quality measures. However, the silent customer who is not satisfied will escape company notice but may tell many acquaintances of the problem. Some organisations provide free telephone lines for complainants or employee training to enable staff to test for the weak signals of a customer's dissatisfaction. Many organisations empower staff to provide remedial action if they suspect poor service has been experienced. Alternatively service may be tested with the use of mystery customers or staff listening to customers' reactions to the service provision.

- **Preplanning.** There is the need to analyse the service delivery process so as to anticipate those aspects of service that may exceed the tolerance level of customers. Times of peak demand or low levels of staffing may affect the judgement of the customer as to the overall level of service quality delivery. Staff can be asked to describe situations which if improved would lead to a more error-free service standard.

- **Empowerment.** A great deal of staff service delivery goes unsupervised. The front-line staff therefore need to react quickly to service problem situations without the input of supervisors. The policy of identifying problems quickly and correcting them at the local level is far more effective than relying on official complaint systems. A staff member who provides some extra means of satisfying a customer may allay a more difficult or serious situation. A long wait to be seated in a restaurant may be acknowledged by a reduction in the bill or free coffee. Empowerment provides an obligation to act in order to recover the situation which relies on trust of the front-line staff. This is in contrast to a system where the focus is on blame for a poor service encounter rather than resolution.

Good service recovery procedures allow a customer to refocus on the satisfactions received from the service delivery process rather than to question why corrective action was not taken. A problem tests the system and if a customer complaint is dealt with appropriately, the customer is likely to become more loyal. If a formal complaint is made it should be treated *individually* according to the *urgency* of the complaint and customer's *value* to the organisation.

A complaint system must be in place for prompt and personal customers' communication:

- to acknowledge the receipt of written/verbal complaints and to inform customers about the resolution;

- to keep customers fully informed with progress reports;

- to encourage customers to appeal to a higher authority within the company in case of a dissatisfactory initial resolution;

- to assign and authorise one department to be accessible at all times during office hours for complaint processing and review;

- to have a complaint system which is both user and staff friendly.

We can classify the different approaches to quality management into two categories: the product-attribute approach and the consumer-orientated approach (Gilbert and Joshi, 1992).

THE PRODUCT-ATTRIBUTE APPROACH

The product-attribute approach is based upon trying to match the product's conformance to standardised requirements which have been set by reference to what organisational managers think the failure point to be. Product-attribute approaches rely on trying to control the organisation's products using an internal product perspective. This relies on an inward-looking product-led approach.

THE CONSUMER-ORIENTATED APPROACH

It is therefore more appropriate to adopt a consumer-orientated approach which recognises the holistic process of service delivery has to be controlled by taking into consideration the expectations and attitudes of tourism and hospitality clients.

In tourism, an assessment of quality is made during the process of service delivery and this can be treated as an encounter between the customer, the service provider and the physical aspects of the place of delivery. More recently this encounter has involved the interface of technology as depicted in Photograph 16.2. The customer will judge the outcome of this encounter in terms of levels of satisfaction. If the starting point for management is the understanding of how quality is judged by clients then the perception processes of this judgement, as to whether a service is good or bad, can be managed. Gronroos is a leading author who has clarified this concept.

The Gronroos model

Gronroos (1982) developed a model to explain what he called the 'missing service quality concept'. The model shown in Figure 16.4 focuses mainly on the construct of image, which represents the point at which a gap can occur between expected service and perceived service. Gronroos makes us more aware of the ways image is created from the aggregation of different aspects of technical and functional variables. By following his model of different inputs, we are alerted to the fact that we should not reduce quality to a simplistic description, but should try to understand the full range of inputs. This is because to speak just of quality gives the manager no indication of what aspects of the product should be controlled.

PHOTOGRAPH 16.2 **New tourism is increasingly about interactions with technology**
Source: Scream.co.uk

Gronroos argued that the function and range of resources and activities include what customers are looking for, what they are evaluating, how service quality is perceived and in what way service quality is influenced. He defined the 'perceived quality' of the service as dependent on two variables. These are 'experienced service' and 'perceived service' which collectively provide the outcome of the evaluation.

As part of his analysis, Gronroos distinguished between 'technical quality' and 'functional quality' as the components of the service image delivery:

- Technical quality refers to what the customer is actually receiving from the service. This is capable of objective measurement, as with tangible goods.

- Functional quality refers to how the technical elements of the service are transferred. We know that a customer in a restaurant will not only evaluate the quality of the food consumed but also the way in which it was delivered (the style, manner and appearance of the staff, or the ambience of the place itself). Figure 16.4 shows that the attitudes, behaviour and general service-mindedness of personnel can be influenced by management.

FIGURE 16.4	Managing the perceived service quality	Source: Gronroos, 1982

MINI CASE STUDY 16.1
The SAS experience

The Scandinavian Airline System (SAS) is an example of a company which recovered its position through properly planned market-orientated leadership. SAS was losing money when, in 1980, Jan Carlzon took over as its new president. Carlzon introduced a consumer orientation into the organisation, which led to an emphasis on research, improvements of service and new values which provided the organisation with a new direction. The repositioning of the company involved sending 10,000 front-line staff on an SAS course entitled 'The human factor' in order to improve service to the business traveller. Carlzon also ensured his managers would create the right environment for staff to take responsibility for improvements in service. The changes produced an improved reputation for SAS which contributed to its gradual recovery. The impact of Carlzon's vision and leadership, in redefining the focus of the organisation as the satisfaction of the consumer, led to a series of changes which, at the time, culminated in higher profits.

SAS in 1997 was active in the formation of Star Alliance. Within the Star Alliance network, members of a frequent flyer programme of one of the member airlines can earn and redeem miles with others. Star Alliance offered one of the first truly global airline networks with members of Star Alliance in 2004 being SAS, Air Canada, Air New Zealand, All Nippon Airways, Asiana Airlines, Austrian Airlines Group (Austrian Airlines, Lauda Air, Tyrolean Airways), British Midland, LOT Polish Airlines, Lufthansa, Mexicana, Singapore Airlines, Spanair, Thai Airways International, United Airlines and Varig. The company has a good domestic reputation having won the Grand Travel

Award by Norwegian travel agents each year from 1999 to 2001 and in 1999 SAS Cargo received the European Cargo Airline of the Year award. However, in the wake of terrorist attacks on New York's World Trade Center and Washington's Pentagon and their immediate consequences on international civil aviation, in 2001 SAS announced capacity cuts (12%), staff reductions and the grounding of 16 of its 200 aircraft. More recently SAS announced that it would introduce a new distribution concept in Scandinavia in 2003. The airline planned to apply net prices, while reducing prices by an amount equivalent to the previous commission. This means that the price of travelling with SAS will vary according to the customer's choice of sales channel – like a travel agency or via the Internet – and level of service required.

BACKGROUND TO SAS AND THE CHANGES IN ALLIANCES

1992 Air Canada and United Airlines unveil an Alliance agreement.

1993 United Airlines and Lufthansa announced marketing agreement and code sharing. The US Department of Transportation (DOT) grants anti-trust immunity to the Northwest Airlines and KLM Royal Dutch Airlines, creating the first unified transatlantic alliance.

1996 United, Lufthansa and SAS are awarded trilateral antitrust immunity by the US Department of Transportation. This allows the carriers to coordinate schedules, expand code sharing and share revenue on their transatlantic routes. Also, American Airlines and British Airways announce a proposed transatlantic alliance that includes a comprehensive marketing agreement and code sharing.

1997 Star Alliance, the first multi-airline alliance (comprising United Airlines, Lufthansa German Airlines, Air Canada, SAS and Thai International Airways) is announced.

1999 Opening of a Star Alliance city office in Paris. US DOT rejects the petition by American Airlines–British Airways to establish an alliance on the grounds that no agreement regarding UK open skies or more access to London's Heathrow International Airport could be achieved.

2000 Delta Airlines and Air France serve as the core of the SkyTeam alliance. Though they do not yet have anti-trust immunity, both airlines are permitted to implement extensive code sharing. Star Alliance is joined by British Midland and launches Starnet, IT solutions that links computer system of the members.

2001 Star Alliance is the first to launch a global e-service initiative to the public – official opening of the first Star Alliance lounge in Zurich. American and British Airways apply to US DOT for approval of a fully immunised transatlantic alliance to compete with Star Alliance, Wings and SkyTeam.

2002 US DOT grants anti-trust immunity to Delta and its SkyTeam partners, Air France, Alitalia and Czech Airlines. US DOT also issues a preliminary order conditioning approval for an AA/BA alliance or forfeiture of 16 daily slot pairs at Heathrow – equivalent to American's entire slot portfolio. US Airways announces it will join Star Alliance.

2003 LOT Polish Airlines and Spanair joins the Star alliance network

DISCUSSION QUESTIONS

1 Do you think the changes brought about by SAS are enough to sustain an airline company in today's competitive marketplace. If not what else is required?

2 How important are airline alliances for the future success of an airline like SAS?

3 Can any alliance allow a no-frills airline to join it given the type of service these airlines offer? Justify your arguments given the size and route networks of some of the no-frills carriers.

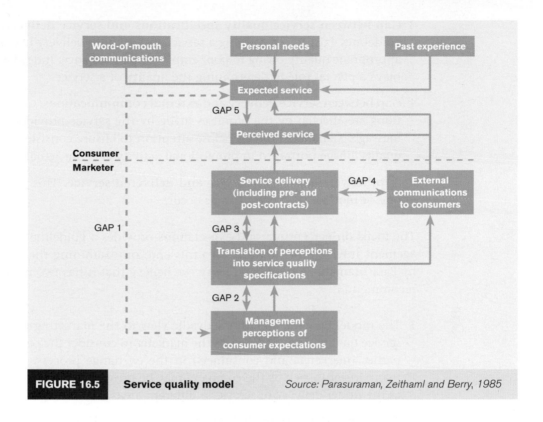

| FIGURE 16.5 | Service quality model | Source: Parasuraman, Zeithaml and Berry, 1985 |

The Parasuraman, Zeithaml and Berry model

Parasuraman, Zeithaml and Berry (1985) also developed a model of service quality which claimed the consumer evaluates the quality of a service experience as the outcome of the difference (gap) between expected and perceived service (Figure 16.5). The model highlighted the main requirements for a service provider delivering the expected service quality. By understanding the flow of this model we believe it is possible to provide greater management control over tourist service relationships. This should lead to an improved realisation of the key points of influence on the satisfactions of the consumer.

From the model we can identify five gaps that may lead to unsuccessful service delivery.

1 **Gap between consumer expectation and management perception.** This may result from a lack of understanding of what consumers expect from a service. An extensive study by Nightingale (1983) confirms this disparity, by revealing that what providers perceive as being important to consumers is often different from what consumers themselves actually expect.

2 **Gap between management perception and service quality specification.** This gap results when there is a discrepancy between what management perceives to be consumer expectations and the actual service quality specifications established. Management might not set quality standards or very clear ones, or they may be clear but unrealistic. Alternatively, the standards might be clear and realistic, but management may quite simply not be committed to enforcing them.

3 **Gap between service quality specifications and service delivery.** Even where guidelines exist for performing a service well, service delivery may not be of the appropriate quality owing to poor employee performance. Indeed, the employee plays a pivotal role in determining the quality of a service.

4 **Gap between service delivery and external communications.** Consumer expectations are affected by the promises made by the service provider's promotional message. Marketers must pay close attention to ensure consistency between the quality image portrayed in promotional activity and the actual quality offered.

5 **Gap between perceived service and delivered service.** This gap results when one or more of the previous gaps occur.

The focus on perceptions and expectations provides a guideline for quality management intervention strategies. To this end, on examining the model proposed by Parasuraman, Zeithaml and Berry, we believe that it has two main strengths to recommend it:

1 The model presents an entirely dyadic view to the marketing task of delivering service quality. The model alerts the marketer to consider the perceptions of both parties (marketers and consumers) in the exchange process. This can lead to many insights such as the company may be providing the over-delivery as well as the under-delivery of service in different areas.

2 Addressing the gaps in the model can serve as a logical basis for formulating strategies and tactics to ensure consistent experiences and expectations.

Employee performance is crucial to improving the quality of service delivery and perceived service quality. Internal marketing is a means by which companies can influence the interpersonal performance of staff. Providing promotional communications that lead staff to achieve high levels of customer care and service quality is becoming increasingly important. One poster targeted to staff read, 'Good enough is not good enough' which sets the standards and aims of the company personnel above the average. This type of inward marketing provides a means to change the general attitudes of staff toward quality.

Zone of tolerance

The **zone of tolerance** concept assumes that customers do not have expectations of a service attribute on one given level. Rather, they can tolerate a variation in their experiences and still consider them acceptable or not according to their preconceived expectations. This concept implies that customers' expectations exist on two levels, a desired level and an adequate level. The desired level reflects what level the service should be, whereas the adequate level is what customers believe it could be. The latter level is the least acceptable level of the service experience. Expectations of service delivery will obviously alter on the basis of each customer as within the delivery of services consumers will have different levels of tolerance. There is a parameter for service zone of tolerance whereby the majority of customers will fall within a zone between the upper and lower desired and adequate levels of performance. This is not fixed as the area of the zone of tolerance can increase or decrease for individual customers depending on other variables such as alternatives provided by the competition, how much was paid and whether it represented value for money, or other differences in the company's service. It is also important to realise that there are differences between individual customers' perceptions; similarly each customer may have different expectations of one brand in comparison with another. For example, if Airline A has delivered more consistent service over time than Airline B then the expectations for the Airline A brand are higher. If Airline A service were to decline to the level consistently offered by Airline B, the customer may be more disappointed by the service received from Airline A – even though the service standards are similar.

MANAGEMENT TASKS

A marketing orientation relies on a series of management responsibilities. To clarify the situation, marketing can be seen to provide for a business-to-customer or business-to-business interface with responsibility for specific management tasks. These tasks are more clearly explained in Chapter Eighteen on the marketing mix. However, it should be quite clear that tourism organisations without a proper commitment to a marketing orientation have little likelihood of effectively executing the marketing function.

The marketing function requires the combination of a number of related activities. Whether they are those involving staff, intermediaries or customers they are all focused on expediting transactions and relationships. The tasks itemised in Table 16.2 ensure that marketing will provide the functional inputs to deliver a sound basis for company activity. In addition this can be treated as a system which is designed to be an interface with the customer. This system is outlined in Figure 16.6.

TABLE 16.2	The business-to-customer interface
Task	**Marketing function**
1 Identifying the customers' needs for a tourism-related product	→ Marketing research and database analysis
2 Analysing marketing opportunities	→ Analysis and selection of target markets (segments) and understanding buyer/supplier relationships
3 Translating needs into products	→ Product planning and formulation
4 Determining the product's value to the customer at different seasonal periods	→ Pricing policy and creation of value delivery
5 Making the product available	→ Distribution policy
6 Informing and motivating the customer	→ Promotion (communicating, advertising, sales effort and relationship scheme)

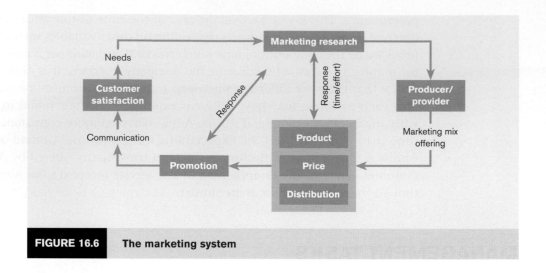

FIGURE 16.6 The marketing system

THE ADOPTION OF A MARKETING ORIENTATION

The tourist industry, owing to the high service-based content of the product, has been characterised by a history of custom and tradition. There has been a lack of vision in the industry which has meant the demise of many organisations throughout the past 20 years. The airline sector has probably been the most at risk. An acknowledgement of the degree of competition between airlines brought about the tourism industry's earliest transformation to a marketing orientation (see Mini case studies 16.1 and 16.2).

From the previous description of marketing and the examples presented, you should now be aware that tourism marketing involves a number of special characteristics:

- Marketing is a philosophy with the overriding value that the decision-making process of any organisation has to be led by the consumers' needs, the market-place and the company's assets and resources.

- Successful marketing requires a special organisation structure that believes in integrating the principles of consumer orientation throughout the organisation.

- Marketing requires innovative methods of thinking and planning so that new ideas are generated to take advantage of opportunities or to improve existing methods of marketing.

However, it is important to remember that while the use of marketing is expanding, as a practice, it is not without its critics.

CRITICISMS OF THE MARKETING CONCEPT

The twenty-first century will be characterised by increasing concerns regarding the impact of tourism. There is a growing concern for protection of the environment and the adoption of business policies that will enable the earth's resources to be sustained. The new values emerging are placing pressure on the underlying concepts of marketing. This is creating a great deal of debate regarding the ethical standpoint of marketing. Some of the most significant criticisms are considered in this section. Governments are aware of this and will judge if changes in the marketplace are detrimental to the consumer. The Office of Fair Trading in the UK examined the proposed merger between easyJet and Go and concluded that the merger would not substantially lessen competition. The judgement not to recommend the competition commission to look at the case was given on the basis that leisure and business travellers would continue to have choice among destinations and among rival carriers and that increased competition may be a good thing. It was also judged that entry barriers are not high given the past history of the entry and growth of the low-cost carriers.

Disregard of the environment and non-consumers

The marketing concept can lead to a tunnel vision, focusing on the potential consumers of the product and not the wider society. Other groups, such as the host population of a country, can be adversely affected by insensitive tourism marketing policies. In addition, pollution and damage, as by-products of tourism activities, create environmental and social costs carried by the whole of society and not simply the organisation's consumers. Tour operators/wholesalers have continuously developed new areas, expanded successful resorts and created promotional campaigns without due regard to the cost of impacts on the area and local population (see Part Two). Another type of marketing pollution is the over-abundance of different types of promotional material, which makes a home or overseas destination less attractive. There are roadside poster sites, advertisements on taxi cabs, messages painted on buildings, and leaflets given away and then discarded, all of which create invasive pollution. There is a trend to produce advertisements that aim to shock, and there are others that offend, such as sexually unacceptable posters or advertisements. The overall effect of these trends is to lead the general public to mistrust marketing.

Over-emphasis on profitable products

The marketing concept dictates that products can only be offered to the marketplace when they are profitable. This has culminated in the axing of bus and train transport routes and the disregard of low-spending individuals. Where a want exists and the marketing opportunity cannot deliver the required profit return, then the product is seldom developed. The market-based system is guided by self-interest and profit motivation. Therefore, consumer preferences are only accounted for if there is an ability to pay. These values are represented by a lack of concern for those who cannot afford a holiday, or for the supply of amenities to cater for those who are disadvantaged or handicapped. Facilities for blind, infirm and handicapped people are of low priority in resort and accommodation planning.

595

MINI CASE STUDY 16.2
Pollution problems of aircraft

FT

In 2003 a cross-party committee of UK MPs called for a sharp increase in the price of flying whereby every airline passenger should pay an 'emissions charge' to compensate for the pollution caused by their journey. In a highly critical report, the environmental audit committee attacked the government's public consultation on the creation of new runways by accusing ministers of showing an 'overt bias' towards the aviation industry. The MPs argued that transport secretary Alistair Darling had 'significantly distorted and overstated' the economic benefits of flying, while playing down the environmental havoc wreaked by aircraft. They reported the cost of aircraft emissions are £18 bn annually. A suggestion was that VAT should be levied on airline tickets in addition to an emissions charge, which would replace the existing air passenger duty charges. The committee chairman said: 'We need air fares which reflect the true cost of pollution. If the government's figures are correct, by the middle of the century aviation will account for 90% of all our carbon emissions.' He said growth in aviation could destroy the government's commitment to a 60% cut in carbon dioxide emissions by 2050.

Air quality is a continuing issue around Heathrow and BAA is introducing new ways of managing aircraft at Heathrow's fifth terminal which is due to open in 2008, aimed at reducing emissions. It is planning to use fixed electrical ground units to provide power on the aircraft stands instead of the aircraft using their own engines to charge electrical systems and run air-conditioning. In addition, BAA is considering a mandatory scheme for the use of less polluting road vehicles on the airport. There may also be a congestion charging scheme to reduce the number of private vehicles coming to Heathrow and to encourage greater use of public transport.

Based upon: Kevin Done, 'Heathrow pricing scheme aims to cut aircraft pollution', *Financial Times*, 8 November 2003 and Andrew Clark, 'Make passengers pay for aircraft pollution, say MPs', *The Guardian*, 30 July 2003

DISCUSSION QUESTIONS

1 Should the passenger pay for the pollution or is the economy so reliant on tourists and business travel that these costs should be covered from other sources?

2 Is this example limited to the UK? What are the implications in differences or similarities between the approaches to airline pollution of the UK and European countries or America?

3 Are politicians the people who are best suited to make decisions over the future policies of air transport and airport development? If not how should these decisions be made?

Invasion of privacy

The power of IT allows organisations to capture a complete range of personal inform-ation for use in targeting direct mail campaigns. The more recent use of database and micro-marketing places the emphasis on using mailing lists with or without the full consent of individuals. As organisations begin to spend more on research there is also the problem of a greater use of telephone, and high street interviews. If this is for a reputable survey there is no problem but a number of companies are simply collecting information under the disguise of research to be used in further sales efforts. In addition research is not confined to the business world as there is an increasing amount of research and projects carried out in schools and colleges. A consequence of the amount of interview requests is the growing refusal by many members of the public to take part in any form of research.

A personal computer is not that personal when emails can be sent which are unsolicited. It is estimated that hundreds of millions of emails are sent each day. Of these around 30% are unsolicited and form what is known as 'Spam'. Spam emails are those which are not welcome and therefore should not have been sent. Therefore, companies should be considering permission marketing as a means to decide that a recipient is happy to receive information and messages. Good per-mission marketing is where the individual 'opts in' to receive the messages rather than has to tick an 'opt out' box in order not to get the mailings. The concern to com-panies and individuals is that Spam is a cost to the company. This is based upon: the cost of time taken up in deleting or dealing with the mailings; the waste of resources due to the cost of the email being carried through third-party systems; and, the annoyance factor of having to check unwanted mail and finding it irrelevant.

Waste of resources on tourism marketing

Marketing is perceived as wasteful owing to the high amounts of money spent on promoting products. The money given over to tourism promotion is often associ-ated with enticing consumers to buy products that they may not want. In addition, competitive advertising is argued to be responsible for higher costs and subse-quently higher prices. It is therefore argued that if advertising were reduced, or did not exist, there would be more competition based upon price and service. The consumerist standpoint is that it would be better to spend the money on inform-ative advertising rather than competitive advertising. It is believed the most disad-vantaged tourist consumers are the ones most likely to be influenced by high expenditure on tourism marketing. The levels of marketing expenditure are quite often blamed for changing consumer attitudes and bringing about a materialistic society where status is derived from the number and type of destinations we visit, or leisure and activities we undertake, rather than how good we are as caring members of society. There is little doubt that marketing panders to materialistic values. However, the question is does marketing create these values or simply appeal to the values already imbedded within society? It is found that the most simplistic of societies have members who want to accumulate possessions. In many tribal societies status comes from the number of animals or possessions an individual owns. On the other hand, marketing may well enhance or reinforce the appeal of materialism.

A SOCIETAL MARKETING APPROACH

It has been argued that the pressures affecting the image of marketing need to be more carefully considered. This has culminated in the movement toward a societal concept of marketing which stresses the enhancement of the needs of society as well as the consumer. We believe that this is an academic exercise, as definitions have to evolve out of business practice rather than from academic debate. Some organisations such as brewers and distillers are creating campaigns to warn people of the excesses of drinking, but it is questionable whether they are worried as much about the customer as about the legislation that could affect their operations.

While some organisations may pay lip service to a societal concept for PR purposes, in a competitive situation many of the problems related to tourism, and its marketing, will continue. It is also important to recognise that consumers are now better educated and are competent to select products that are not creating undue problems to society. Moreover, if organisations or their products do create problems, there are articulate pressure groups and government legislation available for consumer and environmental protection.

While there is a great deal of concern about marketing practice we should be aware that companies are made up of people similar to us and the problems may not be divorced from what we all do. Some studies have highlighted that up to one-third of middle managers have submitted deceptive reports to their supervisors and that even more would bend the rules to gain personal advancement. There is growing recognition that companies need to discover approaches to the marketplace that will build a socially responsible and ethical company culture. There is a need to understand the following three basic issues:

- **Consumerism.** This is organised group pressure, by all consumers, to protect and benefit consumer groups and the environment. This means it is not solely those consumers buying from a company, it is a broad movement to bring about improved exchange relationships.

- **Corporate social responsibility.** This is the decision of a firm to conduct its business in the interest of society as a whole as well as its own interests.

- **Ethics.** This involves personal decisions on the moral principles of what would be the right or wrong activity for individual employees. These decisions will be linked to the values and culture of the organisation. Ethical values are the core beliefs and standards that will dictate the stance a company takes in relation to its marketing; such as honesty and fairness.

A truly societal marketing approach is problematic due to the need to resolve multifaceted decisions over profit, pollution, social and environmental impact concerns. However, some companies perform their marketing activities better than others and are judged in positive terms by the public. Some companies are quite good at giving something back to the industry that supports them. Since the early 1990s, United Airlines has donated some of its Boeing 727s and 737s to museums and universities in the USA. The universities turn the aircraft into hands-on classrooms for students pursuing careers in aircraft maintenance, flight or aviation administration. United's initiative on this will bring it longer term benefits as the disposition of the public to a brand is an important aspect of contemporary marketing.

If managers are going to achieve change it is argued they need to put themselves in the consumer's position with regard to how they or their family would feel others should treat them. The following points are relevant in this context:

1 Good business managers should be socially responsible to all stakeholders (customers, employees, suppliers, shareholders, society, etc.) related to the company or tourism offer so as to minimise social costs. They should also have regard for laws or regulations and be ethical in management decisions.

2 Managers should be honest in claims and promotions, not be deceptive or agree to misleading advertising. They should show fairness to third parties. In addition, there should not be any hidden costs – or should identify extra costs which may be applicable. For example, hoteliers should display the prices of rooms, and supplements in a prominent public position and always make their cancellation policy clear at the time of booking and have it written into their communication literature.

3 The products offered should not cause harm or unacceptable tourism impact and managers should communicate any risks which are known to be associated with any product.

4 Marketers should undertake not to adopt sales techniques under the guise of it being research (such as that associated with time-share selling). Also, it is unfair and unethical to use promotions as research when adequate stock is unavailable because the research is being used as a method of deciding on the supply requirements.

CONCLUSION

The tourism product is predominately a service product with the main characteristics of intangibility, perishability and inseparability. The tourism purchase involves complex decisions related to perceptions of risk and the expectation of high levels of quality. As such there is a need for a deeper understanding of the process of TQM and consumer's expectation of service delivery standards. The use of marketing should take into account the issues surrounding the criticism of its application and as such an understanding of consumerism, social responsibility and ethics is important.

Self-check questions

1 Name three main aspects which characterises the service product.

2 Provide a list of the four main types of risk which a tourist may experience.

3 What are the reasons that quality management is now more important than in the past?

4   Name five areas that quality management should assess when dealing with TQM.

5   What aspects may be included in any invasion of privacy?

Essay questions

1   Describe the differences between the service product's main characteristics of intangibility, perishability and inseparability and discuss whether all tourism or leisure products need to treat them of equal importance or not.

2   Examine skiing brochures, airline web sites and tour operator brochures to identify the strategies that are used by the tourism industry to alleviate the perception of risk in the purchase of the tourism product.

3   Taking two tourism companies or organisations with which you are familiar, consider how each delivers the quality dimensions of tangibles, reliability, responsiveness and empathy. Then compare and assess each approach to the pursuit of quality management.

4   Choose three Internet sites of international hotel groups and then look at the ways they utilise their sites to encourage the browser to go to the relevant pages, provide offers, incentives, target different groups, etc. Write a report indicating how hotel companies can improve the marketing aspects of the web site.

5   List what you believe to be intrusive marketing and then discuss what impact the different types of marketing will have on a family, an older person and a group of young people.

Annotated further reading

Books

Kotler, P., Bowen, J. and Makens, J. (2002) *Marketing for Hospitality and Tourism*, 3rd edn, Pearson, Upper Saddle River, NJ.
The book draws upon the marketing material of Philip Kotler's other books and as such is based upon his pedigree which has been developed over a number of years of writing marketing textbooks. However, the examples are often not very good and other specialist books need to be read in conjunction with this one. This latest edition covers electronic marketing, has case studies and lets students understand the role of marketing in hospitality and tourism. Specialist areas covered are customer quality management and destination marketing.

Lovelock, C. and Wirtz, J. (2004) *Service Marketing: People, Technology and Strategy*, 5th edn, Pearson, Upper Saddle River, NJ.
This book offers insight into the challenges facing the service sector by offering a well-researched and, at the same time, practical text. Coverage is given to service processes and systems, service positioning and service management. The text questions other approaches and allows the reader to experience new material not to be found in other textbooks dealing with a similar subject area.

Martin, W. (2002) *Quality Service: What Every Hospitality Manager Needs to Know*, Prentice Hall, Harlow.

This book has many applications to the hospitality and tourism sector including not only tourism, hotels and restaurants but also theme parks and clubs. The book has a number of figures and clear explanation of some of the main concepts.

References cited and bibliography

Dann, G.M.S. (1981) 'Tourist motivation: an appraisal', *Annals of Tourism Research* **8**(2), 187–219.

Gilbert, D.C. (1989) 'Tourism marketing – its emergence and establishment', pp. 77–90 in Cooper, C. (ed.), *Progress in Tourism, Recreation and Hospitality Management*, Vol. 1, Belhaven Press, London.

Gilbert, D.C. (1991) 'An examination of the consumer behaviour process related to tourism', pp. 78–105 in Cooper, C. (ed.), *Progress in Tourism, Recreation and Hospitality Management*, Vol. 3, Belhaven Press, London.

Gilbert, D.C. and Joshi, I. (1992) 'Quality management and the tourism and hospitality industry', pp. 149–68 in Cooper, C. and Lockwood, A. (eds), *Progress in Tourism, Recreation and Hospitality Management*, Vol. 4, Belhaven Press, London.

Gronroos, C. (1982) *Strategic Management and Marketing in the Service Sector*, Swedish School of Economics and Business Administration, Helsinki.

Hart, C.W.L., Heskett, J.L. and Sasser, W.E. (1990) 'The profitable part of service recovery', *Harvard Business Review* July/August, 148–56.

Lepp, A. and Gibson, H. (2003) 'Tourist roles, perceived risk and international tourism', *Annals of Tourism Research* **30**(3), 606–624.

Nightingale, M. (1983) Determination and control of quality standards in hospitality services, MPhil. thesis, University of Surrey.

Parasuraman, A., Zeithaml, V.A. and Berry, L.L. (1985) 'A conceptual model of service quality and its implications for future research', *Journal of Marketing* **49**(4), 41–50.

Zeithaml, V.A. and Bitner, M.J. (2000) *Services Marketing*, 2nd edn, Irwin McGraw-Hill, New York.

MAJOR CASE STUDY 16.1
SCOTTISH TOURISM: EXCERPTS FROM
THE PROGRESS REPORT 2003/4

The *Tourism Framework for Action* published in 2002 set out a vision for Scottish tourism, and described three priority areas for action: these were Scotland's tourism market position, its tourism consumer focus and the need to enhance the status of tourism in Scotland. Papers from the Steering Group and Implementation Group can be viewed at www.scotex-change.net.

MARKET POSITION – SELLING SCOTLAND IN THE TOURISM MARKET

Within the market position priority area, the Framework set out three objectives. The first, to achieve high brand awareness among target market groups, which is being measured. Within the Scottish tourism brand as a whole, the Framework set out the need to identify key products: the VisitScotland marketing strategy now includes a portfolio of such theme and niche products which capitalise on Scotland's strengths. The Framework objective of attracting major cultural and sporting events to Scotland is also on track with the announcement by the Executive of EventScotland. The third objective within the market position priority area was to increase direct access opportunities into Scotland. That is now being taken forward by means of the Executive's new Interim Route Development Fund, which has already stimulated a number of new low-cost air links between Scotland and European markets.

Better marketing

After its restructuring, the top priority of VisitScotland was the creation of a marketing strategy that established a clear brand for Scotland rather than the individual regions within it. Important research on the basis of a comparative study against competitor destinations indicated that Scotland needed to be marketed aggressively, at the expense of regions within it, in order to grow tourism and avoid mixed messages to key markets. Clearly there is still a place for local destination marketing where that fits in with the overall brand strategy. VisitScotland has developed a portfolio of product themes which apply across Scotland, recognising that, increasingly, people are much more interested in deciding when booking their visit what they can do when they come to Scotland, rather than just where they will stay. In addition, new work is being done to improve the method by which VisitScotland's return on marketing investment can be measured, with a target of improving the return on marketing investment from 12:1 to 14.5:1 over the next year. Also, the re-organisation of the British Tourist Authority (BTA) presents a new opportunity to ensure that BTA better delivers VisitScotland's marketing strategy overseas. Importantly, BTA is strengthening its overseas marketing of Britain and Scotland by moving staff and resources from London to seven new hub offices in key markets abroad and VisitScotland is considering how best to use BTA's overseas presence in the promotion of Scotland abroad.

Technology – converting market awareness to sales

E-tourism is growing extremely quickly, and with potential visitors from all over the world now able to book a holiday at the touch of a button, Scotland must exceed other countries in the use of technology. Much has been achieved in the past year and several actions under the Framework discharged. VisitScotland, the area tourist boards and the private sector have set up visitscotland.com in 2002. Over £1.3m worth of new business has flowed to Scottish tourism enterprises since then and the telephone call to sales conversion ratio for Edinburgh and Lothian has shown a twentyfold increase over the same period. The Executive's target is that, by 2005, 75% of all of Scotland's tourism accommodation will be e-bookable and the Executive has encouraged local authorities, which own and operate a major part of the tourism infrastructure, to register their facilities with visitscotland.com.

Marketing Scotland as an easy-to-reach destination

There are other aspects of the changing face of global tourism. The continued growth of low-cost airlines has opened up hundreds of new destinations for potential visitors. In November 2002, the First Minister announced £6.8m for an Interim Route Development Fund designed to promote more direct air access routes into Scotland. However, not only air routes bring more visitors to Scotland. The Rosyth–Zeebrugge ferry has been successful in bringing many more visitors directly to Scotland from the Continent over the last year. VisitScotland, Scottish Enterprise and Highlands & Islands Enterprise will, as a priority, continue to work closely with all transport operators to build more direct links to Scotland.

Business tourism

On average, business tourists spend half as much again as leisure tourists, with a wide seasonal spread. A high proportion of visits take place between October and March so encouraging business tourism is a good way of using spare capacity off season. The performance of the main cities in business tourism has been very strong, with Glasgow especially having had a very successful year. VisitScotland is putting more emphasis on business tourism in 2003, increasing its business tourism budget by over 50%. It will also restructure its Scottish Convention Bureau into a new Business Tourism Unit which will work very closely with the existing players in this field and with EventScotland.

CONSUMER FOCUS – EXCEEDING OUR VISITORS' EXPECTATIONS

Good quality sells. The statistics for 2002 show that, in general, the higher the quality grading of tourism accommodation, the higher the occupancy rates achieved. It is clear that our visitors expect quality and it is the quality of the overall experience, including that of the people they meet, which will bring them back again and again. That is why the Steering Group decided to accord consumer focus the highest priority for action under the Framework. Although skills and training issues are primarily an issue for the enterprise networks, their importance was emphasised in strategic guidance VisitScotland received from the Tourism Minister which highlighted product quality and employee skills and training as the key strategic priorities for further development.

In June 2002 an industry-driven partnership of business leaders and public agencies formed the Tourism Innovation Group. This is an industry response to the challenges of the Framework, accepting responsibility for an industry innovation agenda. The companies and entrepreneurs in the group believe that only by innovating can businesses in Scotland arrest tourism's decline and make it grow again. This means new ways of operating as well as new business opportunities including:

* a planned ambassador programme within the industry to communicate the tourism brand and support businesses to re-engineer themselves;

* promoting to businesses the values behind the Scottish brand so they can respond better to customer expectations;

* benchmarking and web-linking initiatives;

* sharing good practice and a key alliances project using webcams to promote Scotland and individual businesses in Scotland.

Scottish Enterprise have also championed the innovation agenda, introducing a range of support to help tourism businesses, including an innovation tool kit, innovation seminars and the Tourism Innovation Development Award that will provide match funding for individual and collaborative tourism projects that are genuinely cutting edge.

Product quality

Scotland will never be a low-cost destination, so we have to aim for the very highest standards of quality. But there are still too many instances of visitors being disappointed by the inconsistent quality of their experience, and this is hampering progress towards that aim. Consideration is being given to the eventual introduction of statutory quality registration of all tourism establishments as a way of ensuring consistency of basic quality standards right across the sector. Over the past year, local authorities have been working more closely with VisitScotland on the quality grading of their facilities and registering them with visitscotland.com. This will allow them to become a more integrated part of the tourism infrastructure of Scotland and information on them will be more easily available to visitors. An increasingly important element of product quality is sustainable tourism, although the Framework did not adequately spell out that importance. The sustainable development of Scottish tourism is vital to its long-term success and the Executive is committed to it. Scotland is well placed in this area. The concept of sustainable tourism has in the past tended to focus on eco-tourism opportunities like watching wildlife, but the challenge now is to change attitudes across the sector as a whole towards issues such as energy use and waste disposal. Local authorities have always played a major role in Scottish tourism.

Skills and training

It is clear that, more than anything else, the skills and attitudes of those who work in tourism at every level are key to the overall quality of the experience provided to our guests. A recent Futureskills Scotland survey of employers in Scotland showed that employees in the hospitality, retail and business industries, which make up a large part of the tourism sector, are lacking in 'soft' skills such as customer handling and team working. Worryingly, 57% of those employers that did not train their staff (off the job) said that no training was necessary in their business. There is no shortage of training availability, but rather there is a shortage of demand; declining training uptake sometimes means that tourism or hospitality courses are taken off the curriculum by colleges because of low demand. That is why it is important for businesses to appreciate the commercial benefits of valuing their staff, enabling them not just to attain qualifications but to master the kind of skills described above. Doing so will also have the effect of reducing the high staff turnover which much of the sector experiences. Work is being planned to change the way in which tourism careers are presented to youngsters at school and to change the way in which tourism businesses come across to potential recruits.

Source: www.scotexchange.net

DISCUSSION QUESTIONS

1 Provide assessment of the case and indicate the strengths, weaknesses and missing opportunities it reveals.

2 How would you improve the ways in which the need to work closely with the local business in tourism could be achieved? Provide a plan of your approach.

3 What methods and approaches are available to improve the quality of the accommodation product for tourists – in a country of your choice?

CHAPTER
SEVENTEEN
MARKETING
PLANNING

INTRODUCTION

In this chapter, we outline an approach to marketing planning in tourism and suggest that the marketing plan represents a structured guide to action. As such, it acts as a systematic method of data collection, logical analysis and objective setting of the most appropriate direction for an organisation, distributor or destination product. If a marketing plan is to be accepted by all concerned then the compilation of the plan has to involve all levels of personnel. This is because marketing plans require organisation-wide commitment if they are to be successful.

The plan must reflect the dynamic nature of the marketplace and as such the plan needs to be thought of as a loose-leaf binder rather than as a tablet of stone. This means the plan acts as a working document which can be updated or modified to take into account new opportunities, challenges or unanticipated problem situations.

LEARNING OUTCOMES

Marketing planning is crucial to organisational survival in an environment that is increasingly unpredictable and volatile. In this chapter, therefore, we consider all aspects of marketing planning to ensure that, by the end of the chapter, the reader is able:

- to recognise the importance of marketing planning in respect of tourism and the implications of inefficient planning procedures;

- to understand the purposes of marketing planning in protecting the organisation and enhancing its market position;

- to appreciate the key stages of marketing planning and thus be in a better position to develop and implement a marketing plan successfully; and

- to identify the structure and content of an effective marketing plan.

WHAT IS MARKETING PLANNING?

We all need to plan to some extent if we are to make a success of our lives. Very few Olympic medalists could be successful without a planned programme of training and events leading up to their Olympic finals and achievements. Whether it is for examinations, sports events, going on holiday or organising a party, the use of planning leads to a greater certainty that the event will be a success. Without the right approach, and a sensible plan, alternative courses of action may not have been considered and, consequently, there is the likelihood that individuals, companies or organisations may not function to their maximum potential.

Planning is the most important activity of marketing management. It should provide a common structure and focus for all of the organisation's management activities. It is therefore essential for us to understand planning in its context as the key function of management.

The tourism sector provides a combination of different products and activities, which range from the small taxi firm and guest house to the largest airline or hotel group. The concepts of change and survival are as important to the small business as they are to a destination, major international hotel chain or airline. The fact that change will occur, and with increasing speed, is the most predictable aspect of contemporary business life. It would therefore seem sensible to become familiar with the underlying trends and forces of change that impinge on tourism business activities. This enables the management of change towards desired objectives rather than being driven blindly before the tide of market forces.

The long-term survival of any organisation is dependent on how well the business relates to its environment. This relies on devising forward plans of where an organisation, destination or product would be best placed for the future. Some of the key points relating to marketing planning may be identified as follows:

- The plan requires control over the changes that have to be made.

- It needs to allow for the exploitation of any short-term advantages and improvement on weaknesses.

- It has to promote the use of analysis, reason and evaluation as an integral part of planning procedure.

A lack of marketing planning will result in a wide range of possible consequences. For a destination, this could involve one or more of the following:

- failure to take advantage of potential growth markets and new marketing opportunities – such as increasing use of the Internet;

- lack of maintenance of demand from a spread of markets and erosion of market share due to the actions of competitors;

- demand problems in low-season periods;

- low level of awareness of the destination's product offering;

- poor image of the destination;

- lack of support for cooperative marketing initiatives;

- poor or inadequate tourism information services;

- decline in quality levels below acceptable limits;

- difficulty in attracting intermediaries to market or package holidays;

- disillusionment and lack of motivation of tourism service employees.

Thus, the implementation of marketing planning procedures can be instrumental in alleviating many of the difficulties which tourism organisations may face. This is reflected in Mini case study 17.1 which focuses on Disneyland® Resort Paris, and some of the weaknesses in the marketing planning procedures in respect of this venture.

However, although planning cannot guarantee success it can make the organisation less vulnerable to market forces and unpredictable events. Perhaps the first casualties of tourism with the demise of Laker Airways, Braniff Airways, Courtline and ILG could have been avoided if more attention had been given to planning activities by their respective managements, especially in relation to cash flow, fixed cost and expansion attributes. The early lower price advantage of Sir Freddie Laker's operation or the image of Braniff with Gucci-designed uniforms and the cheap price policy of ILG provided excellent market positions for the products, yet the weakness of financial planning played a major part in each company's downfall.

Organisations or destinations that rely on *ad hoc* initiatives or fail to manage their future will find their future has been managed for them. Each organisation will adopt a different approach to the task of planning based upon the way senior executives see the purpose of a **marketing plan**. The values of any organisation fall along a continuum which begins at *wait and see*, moves through the next set of values to *prepare and predict* and finally ends with organisations that want to *make it happen*. An organisation will benefit more from a future that is made to happen because of the clear direction provided which provides fewer surprises for the workforce and less pressure on the requirements of company resources.

THE MARKETING ENVIRONMENT OF THE ORGANISATION

Each and every organisation has to operate within a market environment. This environment is made up of different levels of influence that will affect the opportunities and marketing decisions that need to be made. The historical conditions affecting competition and rivalry in company markets, the values of stakeholder groups and the political, economic, social and technological changes of the wider environment, all affect the likely performance of the organisation and its brands.

The organisational setting, or environment of operation, is related to the four levels identified in Table 17.1. It should be noted that the influences and pressures of the different levels shown are only taken into account by those organisations following a market-led business philosophy. At level 1 the organisation needs to be adequately resourced to be successful. As companies grow they have to be more aware of level 2 as the marketplace they operate in may become more difficult; and at level 3 there is the emphasis on creating a 'value chain' from the stakeholder participants whereby different relationships have to be fostered and reinforced in positive ways. The wider macro-environment (level 4) places pressures on

TABLE 17.1	Four levels of marketing environment affecting the organisation	
Level 1	The organisation	Marketing sub-functions need to be well organised and integrated with other organisational functions. Marketing has to communicate the needs of the market environment as described in the subsequent levels and marketing thinking has to dominate any strategy formulation.
Level 2	Company markets	Identification of domestic and international consumer markets for products/services, or industrial, intermediary or institutional markets. The degree of rivalry and competitive activity as well as extent of consumer behaviour will affect market activity choice.
Level 3	Organisational stakeholders	Interest groups will affect the context of decision making, e.g. shareholders, competitors, customers, employees, unions, government, suppliers, debtors, local community or banks, all of whom may have conflicting values but have some stake in the organisation.
Level 4	The wider environment	Analysis is required of social, technological, economic and political aspects of the marketplace (STEP). Interrelations of the different forces and changes in the foregoing are powerful market environment determinants.

management that are outside the control of the organisation. The broad categories of STEP involve a series of different levels of aggregation: regional, national and international, which are related to business constraints as well as opportunities.

THE PURPOSE OF THE MARKETING PLAN

The marketing plan is normally a short-term plan that will direct the organisation from one to three years. Typically, a five-year plan will be a strategic plan which is more general and less detailed than a marketing plan. **Strategic planning** involves developing and maintaining a fit between the environment, the competencies and resources of the organisation and its changing marketing opportunities. The strategic plan will concern itself more with external environmental influences and opportunities and less with the detail of the organisation's marketing activities. Strategic plans are normally either medium or long term and marketing plans are short or medium term.

The marketing plan and its compilation is able to provide a number of benefits for an organisation. The creation of a marketing plan will result in a wide range of management benefits as indicated in the following:

- Provide clear direction to the marketing operation based upon a systematic, written approach to planning and action. The planning system allows direction by virtue of requiring a written mission statement and set of objectives to be established, both of which can be transmitted to the workforce. This provides clear leadership principles and allows the workforce to know how their own efforts are essential to the achievement of desired results.

- To coordinate the resources of the organisation. This eliminates confusion and misunderstanding in order to achieve maximum cooperation. Tasks and responsibilities need to be set which clarify the direction and objectives of the organisation. To ensure there is a united effort, recommendations have to be presented in such a way that they can be fully understood at all organisational levels. The plan then acts as a master guide which will underpin all endeavours and decision making. The plan should lead to greater employee cohesion and make everyone feel part of a team in which each individual believes he or she can make a valuable contribution.

- To set targets against which progress can be measured. Quantified targets for volume or revenue provide the focus for individual, departmental or company performance. Some organisations will set targets at achievable levels whereas others will set artificially high targets to encourage enhanced employee effort. The targets, once set, act as the benchmark against which all marketing programmes are monitored.

- To minimise risk through analysis of the internal and external environment. The planning procedure allows managers to identify areas of strength and weakness so that the first can be exploited and the second surmounted. In addition, threats and opportunities can be assessed.

- To examine the various ways of targeting to different market segments. This allows for different marketing mix strategies to be appraised prior to their implementation. As such estimates can be made of the likely impacts in relation to sales and revenue targets to the marketing budget. For example, targeting more segments could require an increase in sales literature which may increase cost rather than profit.

- To provide a record of the organisation's marketing policies and plans. This allows managers to check on what has been attempted in the past and to evaluate the effectiveness of previous programmes. It also provides continuity and a source of reference for new managers joining the organisation.

- To focus on longer term business objectives. This allows the organisation to plan to be in the best position to achieve its longer term future aims. This allows management to develop continuity of thought and action from one year to the next.

Given you have understood the previous information on marketing then it will be agreed organisational objectives should be based upon relevant market-centred

MINI CASE STUDY 17.1
Tourism in a postenchanted world

A paradox in tourism marketing is that while travel and adventure are inherently motivated by enchantment (the seeking of the unique or the fun of travel) and hunger for the romantic, tourism lives today in a world in which travel is anything but romantic and often not enjoyable. We still see beautiful advertisements in travel magazines and sense the allure of the romantic in the press, and the promise of an unforgettable experience. Most travellers, nevertheless, have experienced a different reality. Today's travel involves long lines, transportation hassles and poor service at many restaurants and hotels. The fact that tourism magazines now offer advice for surviving one's trip and that business people who travel a great deal are called 'road warriors' tells both the student and tourism professional that there is a wide gap between the promise and the reality of travel and tourism.

Too many in the industry still live in a time warp in which travel marketing still assumes an industrial version of mass travel that may soon no longer exist in the developed world. Indeed it can be hypothesised that as travel is sold on a more massive scale, its allure decreases and the enchantment of travel fades. While land tours of the 'if it's Monday, it must be . . .' variety, with the exception of bus tours, are now passé, the advent of the mass cruise industry and the all-inclusive is still very much a current tourism success story. As the postenchanted age of tourism continues to dawn tourism specialists will need to consider new and innovative ways to recover something of tourism's past. An early example of the attempt to recreate enchantment in a postenchanted age is the 'fly-drive' tour. These 'tours' permit travellers ways to personalise their trips and search for unique experiences rather than the common experience.

Despite tourism's claims to the contrary, our industry often develops its facilities, and uses the assumptions of mass marketing to judge itself. One only has to ask for some small variation at a convention meal to learn that kitchens are developed to sell a uniform product without addressing individual tastes, preferences, and/or health or religious needs. A simple survey of brochures provides us with an example of how much tourism is tied to a mass marketing design. A perusal of travel brochures demonstrates the uniformity of these brochures and it is not uncommon to see the same photo adorning the brochure of two different communities! In mass-produced tourism, the differentiated becomes undifferentiated, and reality merges with the imagination of the brochures' writers. This new world of travel has brought about all or some of the following factors which tourism professionals will need to consider:

- In a world in which no one is safe from the threat of terrorism or new illnesses such as SARS, the thrill of tourism has been tempered by the fear of travel.

- Destinations must become less dependent on brochures and other mass-produced and orientated forms of marketing. Instead, word-of-mouth advertising in which genuine emotions are displayed will act as the most effective market developer.

- Our resource of time is so limited that the pleasure traveller is now forced into a stressful search-for-fun vacation.

- Vacation groups are no longer stable. The industry must prepare itself and offer alternatives for cultural and social individualisation.

- Service is of greater importance in this postenchanted high tech age: business people often no longer wish to travel.

- Originality is now essential. Locales that have truly original activities that can be protected and refined will have greater tourism pull than locales seeking to replicate that which already exists elsewhere.

- Being genuine is essential. No matter what the destination offers, the postenchanted tourist will shun the ersatz for the genuine. Locations that are 'real' and touch our emotions will have the potential of becoming major destinations.

Source: Abridged version of Tarlow, 2003

DISCUSSION QUESTIONS

1 To what extent do you agree or disagree with Tarlow's assessment of current tourism and its marketing and are there other areas he could also have included?

2 How can marketing planning for tourism marketing have a positive impact on the future development of tourism given the points made by Tarlow?

3 Discuss what new forms of tourism are required for the new post-enchantment period and how your recommendations could become reality through a planning approach.

opportunities. It is the responsibility of tourism marketers to identify these opportunities and to devise a system of planning that may lead to their exploitation. However, planning can be fraught with problems as the next section explains.

SUCCESSFUL PLANNING

Most textbooks suggest planning is simply the following of a series of simple steps. However, the true art of planning is to understand both the human aspects and procedural necessities involved. A poor planning experience may be a function of one or more of the following issues or problems:

- **Lack of senior management support.** A lack of support, from the chief executive and other senior people, is a major problem and one that is difficult to resolve. Any planning approach requires senior management support if it is to be treated seriously by employees.

- **Inappropriate planning procedures.** The system of planning which is adopted may not suit the organisation. There is often the separation of different planning functions from each other that leads to a lack of integration. Therefore, the planning system often has to be designed to match the organisation and to achieve a harmony of approach between employee groups.

- **Poor planning and management.** The system of planning is often blamed when the weakness is actually poor planning and management. Sometimes there is confusion over available data or even planning terms. The requirement is for a plan to be compiled which clarifies times and responsibilities for different actions and meetings which will lead to the appropriate information and people being utilised.

- **Unpredictable external events.** Unexpected environmental changes may create adverse affects on the organisation's performance. Planning is then often blamed for not having incorporated such a scenario. Plans need to be flexible and updated when necessary.

- **Organisational and managerial acceptance.** The values of the management team will imply different acceptance levels of the plan and may ultimately determine its success or failure. There is often hostility toward plans because of the feeling of a lack of involvement in the planning process. This often occurs when the planning is left solely to a planner or it becomes a once-a-year ritual.

- **Level of detail.** Problems occur when there is an over-abundance of information which has to be filtered for its relevance. Too much detail in the early stages can produce what is sometimes termed 'paralysis analysis' which means there is a need to decide what is important and what is not at an early stage of planning.

It is distressing that those travel companies that have recognised the need for a more structured approach to planning, and subsequently adopted the formalised procedures found in the literature, seldom enjoy the advantages claimed when embarking on planning. In fact, it is often planning itself which is brought into disrepute when it fails to bring about the desired changes within an organisation.

The problems faced in marketing planning have led to a growing body of literature which indicates organisations should do what they are good at, rather than embarking upon higher level planning exercises. We believe this is a retrograde step because organisations should attempt to take the most logical direction and not be hampered by internal failings of the human resource aspects of implementation, lack of planning expertise or disregard of the involvement of others in the planning process. An understanding of the social aspects of the organisation is a prerequisite for successful planning. It is necessary for those involved in planning to recognise the need for involvement of all departments in the organisation in the formulation of the plan. This means that personnel are more likely to be motivated toward its successful implementation. Moreover, key personnel bring valuable knowledge and expertise to marketing plan formulation. It is also important to understand that most accomplishments in service industries, such as tourism, are made through people. The control of schedules, budgets, monitoring performance or corrective decisions can take place only through the medium of people. Each employee, who has responsibility, requires clear objectives against which he or she can judge if any necessary tactical action needs to be carried out.

It is important to ensure plans are not prepared within the vacuum of one department or by a marketing team that believes it is an élite. Structured management meetings can offer a setting where deliberation, responsibility and authority are shared and taken by all. This precludes dogmatic assertions about the particular methods of preparing and organising marketing planning.

The marketing planning system offers a structured approach to organising and coordinating the efforts and activities of those involved in deciding on the future of an organisation. However, there is no one right system for any particular tourism organisation, since organisations differ in size and diversity of operations, the values of the senior management and the expertise of those involved in the planning exercise.

STRUCTURE OF THE MARKETING PLAN

The construction of the marketing plan is characterised by a range of headings developed by different theorists. Some authors offer a list of sections with the first headed 'SWOT issues' or 'situational analysis', the second headed 'statement of objectives and goals' or 'setting objectives', the third is 'strategy' or 'marketing programming' and the last is 'monitoring' or 'control'. We prefer to use different stages which are more easily understood by managers and students. The stages are:

1 What is it we want?

2 Where are we now?

3 Where do we want to go?

4 How do we get there?

5 Where did we get to?

These are represented in Figure 17.1. In reading the structure of the marketing planning model it is important to realise the system is not always the linear progression it appears. Quite often the process needs to involve an interplay between the various stages with the flexibility to move backwards as well as forwards. We should also understand that refinement of the plan takes place as understanding of the interconnections improves. We should not presume that perfection will be achieved until a number of drafts have been completed.

Linked to the simplistic stages above, the model of marketing planning can be described as involving:

1 Ensuring the humanistic consideration for successful planning.

2 Corporate mission and goals.

3 External and internal audit.

4 Business situation analysis.

5 Creating the objectives.

6 Providing an effective marketing mix strategy.

7 Monitoring the plan.

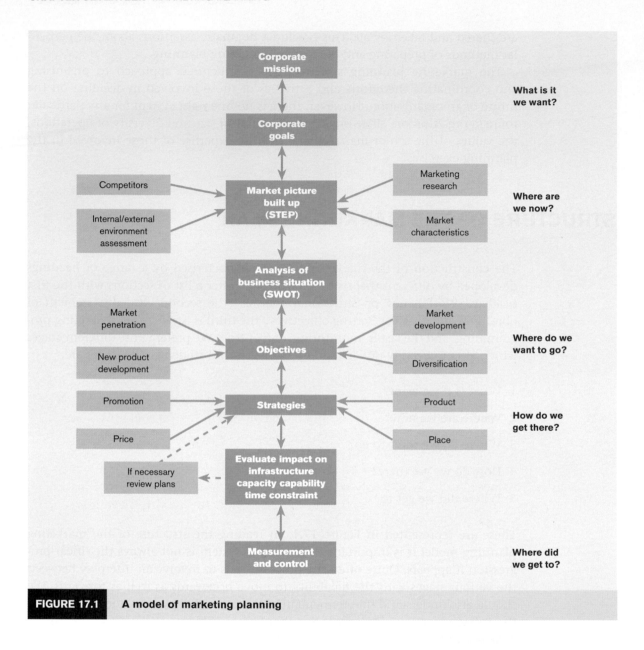

FIGURE 17.1   A model of marketing planning

The humanistic consideration for successful planning

The involvement of different departments will help reduce resistance to future changes or tasks. Continuous concern about the human aspects of planning can provide a greater possibility of the plan's success. The planner or planning team should be aware that they are only a technical service to a wider team. However, we have to be careful not to make the system too open as to be in danger of creating anarchy and loss of focus. On the other hand, the system should not be too closed, as this leads to problems of bureaucracy and apathy.

Good planning is a combination of qualitative and quantitative factors based upon creative, as well as analytical and logical thinking. As Albert Einstein once remarked: 'When I examined myself, and my methods of thought, I came to the conclusion that the gift of fantasy has meant more to me than my talent for absorbing positive knowledge.' Creative thinkers are able to bring specific benefits to the planning process such as:

- challenges to norms and assumptions and the ability to question what others automatically accept as true;

- the focus on chance and the unexpected rather than safe answers;

- the development of new ways of thinking which transform familiar ideas into more unconventional approaches and so provide new ways and means of thinking of 'taken-for-granted' situations;

- allow individuals to make associations and so combine seemingly unrelated events, topics and ideas;

- product, service and promotion ideas to be updated and revised; and

- keep the planning function from becoming too boring and so retain its excitement and innovation by bringing humanistic values to the whole process.

One vital behavioural consideration of any plan which affects all aspects of the company is that it should not clash with the organisational culture. Such a clash can be overcome by ensuring staff values are incorporated into various stages of the planning cycle. The involvement of the full range of staff leads to a situation where the organisational culture values of staff are reflected in the 'bottom-up' comments. This helps to ensure the plan is created as part of a process which makes it compatible with the corporate culture.

Again, we stress that organisations have to plan for the involvement level of staff. This needs to be as seriously considered as planning for the company's markets. Figure 17.2 provides one approach in dealing with the need to have marketing planning involvement at all levels.

FIGURE 17.2   Involvement levels for marketing planning

One other important aspect of influence when including a cross-section of people in planning is their ability to hinder or help the plan. Within any company or organisation, managers' competence to plan will be based upon how busy they are, their preoccupation with other business matters, their career goals, their experience and their ability to think analytically. These attributes are linked to other managers' values and the cultural climate within the organisation, which may be more or less responsive to change and adaptation through adherence to the planning system.

A plan when completed should be read by far more people than actually do read it. This is often due to the lack of time by busy executives and the complexity of the plan. To overcome the problem all plans require the addition of a good management summary, written in clear, concise language, which will ensure the dominant points and themes are communicated. The summary should concentrate on objectives, main target markets, opportunities and threats, key strategies and timings.

Corporate mission and goals

It is important to understand what is expected of the plan from the long-term goals set at corporate level. The goals may be based upon the values and objectives of the key shareholders, board directors or senior managers. In some situations goals are set only after the establishment and evaluation of the marketing programmes. This is a parochial, programme-led method of planning, where management does not attempt to meet higher level corporate goals within the planning process because managers are more prepared to settle for what they believe will work. An organisation with this approach will not investigate as broad a range of strategies as the organisation that is driven to ensure consistency with the overall corporate strategy and goals.

The most effective form of planning creates a balance between corporate direction and ensuring different levels of employee involvement (see Figure 17.2). If goals are dictated to employees, there is very little sense of ownership of the plan and a corresponding lack of motivation. Goals can be set in a functional, top-down approach or as a negotiation of goals through the combination of bottom-up and top-down processes.

The **mission statement** is a guide for employees to know what the purpose of the organisation is. The mission statement acts as a confirmation of what business the organisation is in from a consumer viewpoint. It then represents the overriding goal of the organisation. In the 1991/92 British Tourist Authority marketing plan the mission statement was: 'to strengthen the performance of Britain's tourist industry in international markets by encouraging the improvement and provision of tourist amenities and facilities in Britain'.

External and internal audit

It is necessary to gather enough relevant information about the external and internal organisational environment to be able to construct a business and market picture of current and future pressure and trends. One important part of marketing planning is knowing what to analyse. Executives have to be careful that they do not have too limited a view of the environment. Understanding the different needs

PHOTOGRAPH 17.1	Tourism marketing has to consider the different needs of the tourist

Source: Photograph (left) Richard Young/Rex Features; photograph (right)
© JFPI Studios, Inc/CORBIS

of the tourist, as illustrated by Photograph 17.1, is only one aspect which requires investigation. Market knowledge requirements are so complex these days that having checklists of necessary information is one way to prevent organisations scanning the environment based upon what they intend to do, rather than in relation to what they could or should do.

The information collected should, at the very least, form the basis of a STEP investigation. STEP analysis is an examination of the social, technological, economic and political changes that may affect the market, the organisation and ultimately the plan. Information gathering is part of an internal and external audit which should collect a range of information, as detailed below. In addition to incorporating these factors in the marketing plan this information should be gathered on the basis of how it affects the organisation, especially in relation to its key competitors.

STEP ANALYSIS AND MARKET ENVIRONMENT

This includes the following:

- **Social:** demographics, holiday/leisure time entitlement, values (consumerism), lifestyle, male/female role changes, delay of first child, education, workforce changes.

- **Technological:** innovations, new systems (reservations, yield management), Internet, broadband technology, mobile technology such as 3G, electronic fund transfer.

- **Economic:** inflation, unemployment, fuel costs, exchange rates, average salaries (plus see market environment list below).

- **Political:** taxation, duty, regulation, tourism policies, constraints on local authorities.

OTHER IMPORTANT ENVIRONMENTAL FACTORS

- **Total market:** size, growth, trends, value, industry structure, identify the competitors, barriers to entry, extent of under- or over-capacity of supply, marketing methods.

- **Companies:** level of investment, takeovers, promotional expenditure, redundancies, revenue, profits.

- **Product development:** trends, new product types, service enhancements, competitiveness of other companies' products.

- **Price:** levels, range, terms, practices.

- **Distribution:** patterns, trade structure, policies.

- **Promotion:** expenditure, types, communication messages, brand strengths, effectiveness of own current promotion methods.

UNDERSTANDING COMPETITION – PORTER'S MODEL

The plan has to be formulated in relation to those forces which impinge on the likelihood of success. Prime among such forces is competition. The plan cannot exist in isolation of other factors. As Porter has argued (1980), it is easy to view the competition too narrowly and too pessimistically. Porter views intense competition as natural, with the state of competition depending on the relationship between five basic forces (see Figure 17.3). Porter argues that it is the collective strength of these forces that determines the ultimate profit potential of any industry. The model has become widely known as the 'five forces' model of competition.

The focuses of rivalry among existing competitors are (1) the outcome of rivalry; (2) the bargaining power of suppliers; (3) the bargaining power of buyers; (4) the threat of new entrants; and (5) the threat of substitute products or services. Each of these forces, in turn, can be broken down into its constituent elements. The following discussion of these forces helps with our understanding of the tourism industry and clarifies the considerations we must take into account.

1 Rivalry among existing competitors

Factors which might affect the nature of competitiveness or 'the jockeying for position' by the use of tactics in the industry include the following:

- the degree of concentration in the industry and the number and relative size of the competitors;

- if industry growth is slow there will be increased struggle for market share;

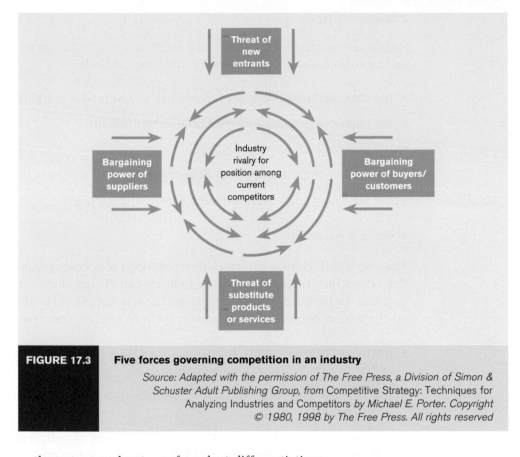

FIGURE 17.3 **Five forces governing competition in an industry**

Source: Adapted with the permission of The Free Press, a Division of Simon & Schuster Adult Publishing Group, from Competitive Strategy: Techniques for Analyzing Industries and Competitors *by Michael E. Porter. Copyright*

- the extent and nature of product differentiation;
- when fixed costs are high or the product perishable as is the case with much of the tourism industry offerings;
- capacity in relation to demand and characteristics of demand;
- high exit barriers will keep companies competing even though they may be earning low or negative returns.

2 Bargaining power of buyers

The bargaining power of the buyers (that is, demand for the products or services whether it is the company acting as buyer from suppliers or whether it is the final customer) is related to the following features:

- the degree of concentration relating to the relative importance of levels of demand on the customer side by comparison with that of the competing suppliers;
- the relative significance of the produce or service to customers in terms of quality, expenditure and service;
- relative ease and cost of changing to new suppliers (switching costs);
- the amount of information possessed by buyers;
- the ability of buyers to integrate backwards;
- profit levels of buyers;
- the extent to which buyers want differentiated products.

3 Bargaining power of suppliers

Factors relevant to the supply side of the industry will be similar to those mentioned on the customer side of the industry and, thus, include:

- the structure of the supplier side relative to the producer industry;
- the degree of product differentiation/substitutability;
- the potential for forward integration;
- the relative importance of the industry demand to suppliers;
- the feasibility and cost of producers switching suppliers.

4 Threat of new entrants

The ease, or difficulty, with which new producers may enter the industry affects the degree to which the structure of the industry can change due to the extra competition and the desire to gain market share. The seriousness of the threat is dependent on the type of barriers to entry and on the way existing competitors will react:

- the extent to which there are economies of scale (note that airline alliances such as Star or One World can provide these);
- the amount of capital required to capture customer loyalty and create brand identification;
- the capital required for inventories and absorbing start-up costs (for example, the cost of leasing new aircraft as a no-frills airline start-up);
- existing companies may have experienced learning curve benefits which lower costs (lower costs may be important to an airline when wanting to enter a new route on a large enough scale to compete with rivals);
- the level of customer switching costs (for example, for an airline are there frequent flyer benefits or loyalty considerations?);
- the existence of government regulation and legal limitations and barriers (for example, can an airline obtain desired take-off and landing slots or obtain an air operator's licence?).

5 Threat of substitutes

These include:

- the availability of substitutes and willingness of buyers to utilise substitute products which have the same functional capability (for example, video conferencing rather than business travel);
- the impact on profits of close substitutes;
- the impact of the comparative price and quality of substitutes.

The above approach to industry analysis can allow a company to understand the pressures on the industry and the likely effect on the prospects for short- and longer term success. More specifically, a company is able to take into consideration its true competitive position with regard to its opponents and can identify the possible strengths and weaknesses due to the current state of rivalry in the industry. It may then proceed to consider what level of importance should be attached to the marketing planning process in order to provide a competitive advantage and a position from which to achieve its financial objectives.

PORTFOLIO ANALYSIS

A portfolio approach allows for the analysis of an organisation's current position in relation to the marketplace, its own companies or products. A commonly used technique for consideration of the growth and share of an organisation is the Boston Consulting Group matrix (BCG). Portfolio analysis has been described as a family of techniques with BCG as the most famous (Abell and Hammond, 1979). The BCG approach has been used by a large number of planners in different marketing settings. This approach allows an organisation to classify the position of each of its strategic business units (SBUs) on one axis in terms of their market share relative to competitors and on the opposite axis to position annual industry growth. By creating a measurement based upon the scales of each of these axes, a spatial plot is derived which by the use of the creation of quadrants places each plot in a specific category. As part of the analysis, a company may identify which SBUs are dominant when compared to competitors, and whether the areas in which the company operates are growing, stable or declining. The two-by-two matrix (see Figure 17.4) describes four types of position labelled as: star, question mark, cash cow and dog.

Stars

These are SBUs or products with a high market share in a fast growing market and, importantly, offering good prospects for growth. As such, the objective would be

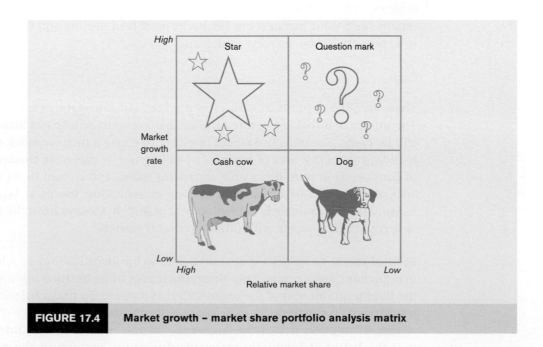

FIGURE 17.4   Market growth – market share portfolio analysis matrix

for an investment or protection for any SBU or product to be identified when it falls into this quadrant. The objective is to build on the strength of the position and/or to hold on to it in the face of any competition. If the organisation has a balanced portfolio, the transferring of money from a cash cow to the star SBU could be contemplated if this would create higher returns in the long run. This could be the airline route which offered the most return to the company or the destination to which a tour operator could obtain the highest demand.

Question marks

These are SBUs or products where there is some question about their position. Spatially, there is the potential for high market growth, but there is also low market share. The objectives would be to investigate further the possibility of any future movement in the market or from the competition, creating a new position of either a star or a dog. If the question mark has the possibility of becoming a star and if the organisation has a cash cow then money should be transferred to build the question mark position with the objective of creating a star. Alternatively, a poor outcome for the analysis may mean the objective has to be one of becoming a niche operator – or even divestment. If the unit of consideration were an overseas destination for a tour operator and a certain destination such as Florida fell into this quadrant, there may need to be an expansion of brochure space for the area and the use of increased promotion to increase demand.

Cash cows

This categtory is where the SBU or product is enjoying the benefit of a high market share but in a low- or zero-growth market. The objective would be to exploit the strong, positive cash flow situation but not to devote any investment into the SBU or product apart from to ensure its maintenance. The objective is normally to hold the position and harvest money so that it can be used to grow other parts of the business. This can be the case in some seaside resort areas where a good hotel retains high-value business but the resort itself is in decline and there is no reason to expect any future increase in demand.

Dogs

These are SBUs or products with a low market share and static or no market growth. The inference is that any future earnings are bound to be low and little or no profit will be made. The objective would be either to create a niche area for activity or to withdraw from this area of business by selling out or planning closure. If the unit of consideration were items on a restaurant menu and certain items fell into this area, there would be a case for reducing or removing the meal types from the menu. Another example is the withdrawal of British Airways from the Dublin route as it could not compete with other lower cost carriers.

Each of the BCG model's spatial areas allows an identification of what strategies may be most appropriate. This allows objectives to be decided upon which are in the long-term interests of the organisation as a whole, so that a balanced approach is taken which considers all aspects of an operation.

The assumption is that the higher the market share of any strategic business unit the better its long-term marketplace position, because of the probability of economies of scale, lower costs and higher profitability. In Figure 17.4 the vertical axis identifies the annual growth rate percentage of the operating market for the SBUs, companies or products being assessed. The logic of its inclusion is related to the notion that any organisation in a situation where there is high market growth will have derived benefit from the situation of buoyant development in the marketplace.

Relative market share is the horizontal axis and is used because of its ability to provide the unit of measurement as an indicator of the ability to generate cash based upon the relative position to the market leader. The measure of market share is expressed as a comparison to that of the largest competitor. This is important because it reflects market share relative to the leader and shows the degree of power the market leader has over others in the market. For example, if company 'A' had 25% share of the market and its competitor 'B' also had 25%, there is little advantage. However, the market situation is dramatically different and more favourable to 'A' if it is the market leader with a 25% share and its closest competitor has a 12.5% market share. The horizontal axis provides a relative ratio to the market leader and, therefore, the example given would create a 1:1 ratio in the first case and 1:0.5 in the second. These ratios are plotted on the horizontal axis against the market leader's share to reflect the individual positions of dominance for different units of measurement. The axis can be divided on any scale which makes sense for the market being considered but should enable the relative positions, across the range of the axis, to be plotted. As there is the use of a market leader share figure, the left-hand end of the scale will be no larger than 1 as no other SBU, product or company can exceed the size of the leader's share.

A certain amount of caution has to be applied to the indiscriminate use of portfolio analysis. At the outset it should be realised that portfolio analysis has more dimensions than simply market and market growth. In fact, one of the difficulties is to decide upon the scales for the axes. Once these are agreed, it may be difficult to obtain competitive data. With a BCG approach the spatial positioning outcome of any analysis is not necessarily related to profitability, as a high market share could be based upon low profitability if prices are lower than the competition; or vice versa. In addition, a higher market share for a company or a product may reflect a disproportionate amount of promotional expenditure which in turn could be creating unacceptable cost implications. There are conceptual and practical problems in defining both products and markets when using the matrix. While international flights to America or Asia may be a star, the main business for the airline could be suffering due to the impact of no-frills operators on European routes. Finally, a market which is growing may not be a good environmental fit, or suit the business strengths of the SBU or company. None of these weaknesses indicates there is a major problem with the BCG matrix or its principles but simply that it has to be utilised with some degree of caution. Its strength is that it allows for a more detailed analysis of the business.

COMPETITIVE ADVANTAGE

When tourism companies decide upon strategies that may offer them a higher likelihood of achieving market success they need to consider different generic routes to obtain competitive advantage. Porter (1980) describes the three generic strategies of *cost leadership* (a company that seeks, finds and exploits all sources of cost advantage – providing for a standard, no-frills package such as that successfully pioneered by Southwest Airlines in America and adopted a few years later by easyJet in the UK

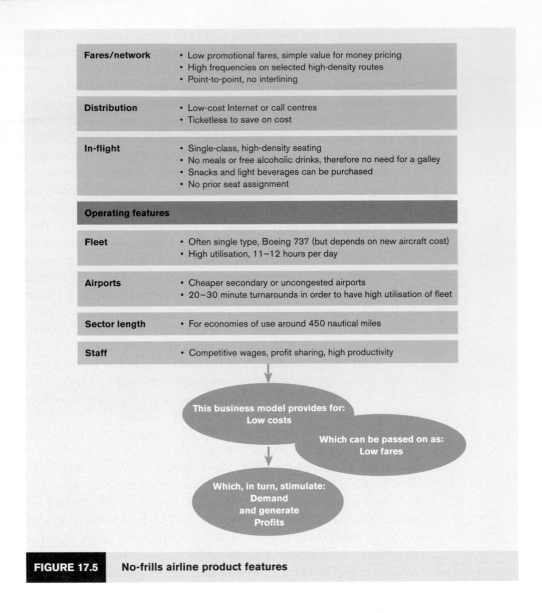

Fares/network	• Low promotional fares, simple value for money pricing • High frequencies on selected high-density routes • Point-to-point, no interlining
Distribution	• Low-cost Internet or call centres • Ticketless to save on cost
In-flight	• Single-class, high-density seating • No meals or free alcoholic drinks, therefore no need for a galley • Snacks and light beverages can be purchased • No prior seat assignment
Operating features	
Fleet	• Often single type, Boeing 737 (but depends on new aircraft cost) • High utilisation, 11–12 hours per day
Airports	• Cheaper secondary or uncongested airports • 20–30 minute turnarounds in order to have high utilisation of fleet
Sector length	• For economies of use around 450 nautical miles
Staff	• Competitive wages, profit sharing, high productivity

This business model provides for: Low costs

Which can be passed on as: Low fares

Which, in turn, stimulate: Demand and generate Profits

FIGURE 17.5 No-frills airline product features

(see Figure 17.5); *differentiation* (a company seeks something distinctive to set it apart from others that can bring in good profit returns – typically having attributes that are different to the competition such as the quality added value of the tour operator Kuoni); and a *focus* strategy (a company selects a segment of the market and targets that to the extent of excluding other segments whereby a tour company will specialise in a single type of product, such as walking holidays).

Business situation analysis

Once sufficient information has been collected, there is the need to carry out an analysis of the business situation and this is best done by identifying the major strengths, weaknesses, opportunities and threats facing an organisation. This is the so-called 'SWOT analysis'. There is also the need to check the results of the SWOT analysis against information provided from STEP analysis.

The systematic analysis carried out at this stage provides the formulation of a number of assumptions about the past performance, future conditions, product opportunities, resources and service priorities which all lead to the possibility of a range of strategic options for an organisation in the tourism sector.

At this stage of planning, it is possible to circulate the assumptions and forecasts to different company divisions. These should be offered as a range of alternatives. For example, if you have assumed the market will grow at x% and this will create £Y with a specific strategy, then it is also wise to create alternative scenarios. You should estimate sales at lower and higher rates than expected so that the impact on profits can be assessed. For example a rate of growth of $x + 2$% may create a profit of $1.3 \times$ £Y, or alternatively $x - 2$% gives $0.5 \times$ £Y. Managers can then involve their team in discussions about the relevance of the material created from the foregoing environmental scanning stage.

Creating the objectives

Objectives are a combination of what is expected of the organisation by its shareholders or directors, and an evaluation of the options emerging out of the first stages of the planning process. The objectives should emerge as the most logical course of action for the organisation to embark upon given the detailed analysis in the preceding stages.

We also have to ensure the objectives are not only related to volume of sales and financial objectives, but also involve broader marketing objectives. One danger in planning is that large organisations often set financial objectives in terms of growth rate in earnings per share, return on equity or investment and so on, and ignore marketing objectives such as the selection of specific segments as target markets and the improvement of products, brand image or consumer awareness. Objectives should also include the expected market share achievements because this performance may only be realistic if certain budgets are made available.

Objectives need to be a balance of the aspirational and realistic so that the organisation attempts to improve its market position within acceptable risk limits. The basic criteria for setting objectives based upon the SMART acronym is that they need to be:

- **Specific** by being focused on the results required.
- **Measurable** for each objective set.
- **Achievable** set against trends and market position constraints and assessed fully.
- **Realistic** given resource constraints of time and money, etc.; and set against
- **Time limits** of when the objective(s) should be reached.

The objective stage inputs of Figure 17.1 are based upon growth strategies whereby a company is attempting to expand. Organisations will normally want to attack the market share of others by penetrating the market to increase their own share of the market. This takes place in the current markets and is normally based upon a more aggressive use of the marketing mix. The organisation may attempt to increase existing customer usage rates or attract competitors' customers. For example, Visa combined with the Singapore Tourist Board and Singapore Airlines in 2004 to offer price discounts to platinum and gold card members; and the company has utilised promotional techniques such as being able to earn extra bonus points in relation to car hire in an attempt to get their cardholders to use their card while on holiday in preference to competitors' cards. Larger organisations or companies will try to increase sales through market development by attempting to sell current products in new markets. This may involve the addition of new locations such as McDonald's outlet openings to compete at airports, at tourist attractions and even within office buildings. Market development may also be based upon convincing the customer to find new uses for existing products. Larger organisations or companies will try to develop markets by selling the benefits of, say, self-catering holidays to those who take hotel holidays. Organisations may also develop their markets by expanding internationally such as Holiday Inn and the Accor group.

Objectives may also include **new product development** or diversification. The Eurostar Channel Tunnel service in 2003 improved the rail network and reduced the travelling time to Paris by 20 minutes. The objective for this investment required intensive product research and assessment. Tour operators/wholesalers develop new destinations and airlines embark upon new air routes. Diversification has occurred where companies such as Virgin developed a new business from its retail base into an airline operation in several different countries. Hotel organisations have developed contract catering operations and vice versa. There has also been the diversification of airlines into the hotel business.

Providing an effective marketing mix strategy

The success of the plan relies on creating the right marketing mix strategies for achieving the objectives (see Chapter Eighteen for a clear explanation of the different aspects of the marketing mix). The use of the marketing mix involves balancing the elements of the marketing mix to achieve the highest expected probability of meeting the plan's objectives. However, mix strategies have to be checked to ensure they are acceptable. For example, if the strategy is for expansion of a destination say by means of price benefits, an impact or environmental analysis should be considered. Figure 17.6 shows a situation where there is no extra benefit in expanding tourist numbers, since the social costs (due to extra arrivals) increase at the same rate as the benefits. Note that Q_1 and Q_2 are in exactly the same position in both parts (a) and (b) of Figure 17.6.

FIGURE 17.6 **Tourism demand problems**

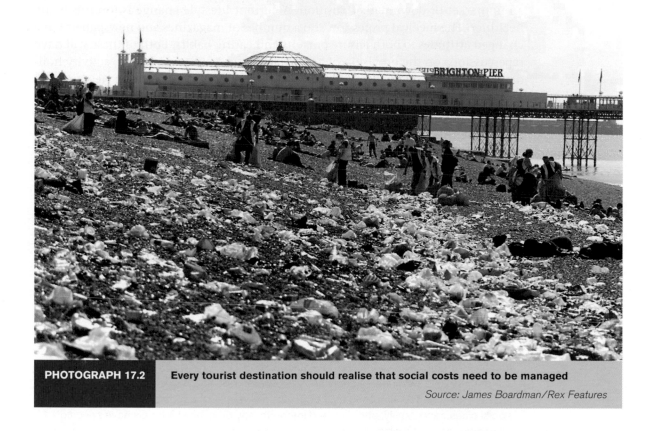

PHOTOGRAPH 17.2   **Every tourist destination should realise that social costs need to be managed**

Source: James Boardman/Rex Features

Figure 17.6(a) shows the relationship between demand and price for a tourism destination. If price is reduced from P_1 to P_2 then the resultant demand for the area increases from Q_1 to Q_2. Tourism destinations can reduce the average price of visits through government policies such as allowing more charter arrivals or reducing tourist taxes. If the positions of Figure 17.6(a) are examined against the social cost and benefit curves of Figure 17.6(b) it will be seen that position Q_2 is no better than position Q_1 as the social costs (such as those depicted in Photograph 17.2) have increased at a rate that cancels out the increase in social benefits. The result is that the destination is no better off socially from an increase in arrivals and may have to check other criteria and bring in policy changes before it agrees to expansion policies.

MARKET SEGMENTATION

Emanating out of the SWOT analysis will be the objective to target specific sub-markets or what are known as segments. Market segmentation is the process of dividing the total perceived market into subsets, in each of which the potential customers have characteristics in common, which lead to similar demand needs for a product or service. The marketer has to decide upon the coverage of the target market. This can be any one of a selection from a broad mass market, a selective market segment strategy or aiming at two or more multiple segments.

Mass tourism operators selling undifferentiated European and long-haul destinations will target a very broad subset of consumers. This is because their success lies in offering a wide range of popular countries at value for money prices. In contrast, a specialist tour operator/wholesaler can attempt to identify a new segment or adopt an upmarket or downmarket position. A current lifestyle change is towards being healthier. The medical profession and a number of magazines and newspapers have changed attitudes to both leisure pursuits and eating habits. Both of these will have repercussions on the provision of leisure centres in hotels and resorts, activity holiday supply, spa and health products as well as be an opportunity for new product development.

MINI CASE STUDY 17.2
Targeting different segments

The city of Manchester in England, along with other old industrial urban places, has endeavoured to attract different tourist segments as part of its programme of regeneration. One of its strategies is to target the gay men's market as a source of tourists. Why should this be? Several market research studies such as Mintel (2000) indicate the high travel propensity and high spend of the gay market. Gay men are characterised as 'high education, high income', with few family commitments, more free time and as being individualistic. In addition US gays are regarded as particularly frequent travellers and high spenders. British Tourist Authority (BTA) research also identified a high level of interest in Britain among US gays and their perception of the country as a gay-friendly destination. However, defining a market segment by its sexuality may be too simplistic as it conceals a diversity of age, income, occupation, social class, race, family, attitudes and interests, any or all of which may have specific influences on purchasing patterns.

DISCUSSION QUESTIONS

1 Search the web for gay holiday and travel sites and assess the potential which is related to this market segment.

2 Provide arguments for and against defining a market segment by its sexuality rather than as a combination with other consumer behaviour factors.

3 What are the important product offers which you believe would need to be available in order to attract a gay segment to visit an international destination?

Achieving strength of positioning

To be successful in positioning, a company or destination has to understand how to modify the perception of the consumer by improving, reinforcing or defending its position in the marketplace. Ries and Trout (1986) argue that positioning has to be correctly addressed, as it is the only way to counteract the confusion created by the communication jungle. Accordingly, Ries and Trout recommend 'the best approach in our over communicated society is the over-simplified message'. This has to happen at the right time and as such the secret of positioning becomes the organised system for finding the window in the mind. Ries and Trout contend that: 'Positioning starts with a product. A piece of merchandise, a service, a company, an institution or even a person . . . But positioning is not what you do to a product. Positioning is what you do to the mind of the prospect. That is, you position the product in the mind of the prospect.' To achieve success at positioning the tourism product or brand there is a need to ensure the position has clarity, is credible, has consistency over time and will remain competitive in relation to the needs of the company's chosen target groups. This is explained as follows:

- **Clarity.** It is important to realise that positioning is about communicating a message to the consumer so as to spatially place the tourism service offered in their mind. This has to be based upon a clear message with no confusion. If the message is not clear the consumer will not understand what the brand or offer is about. A positioning strategy requires a clear message that most people will understand.

- **Credibility.** A positioning message has to be believable. If we claim that our travel agency offers better service than it delivers in reality, consumers may well utilise it a first time but never again. They may well feel cynical about the company claims if they find the delivery does not match the promise. This is particularly vital in the case of services where it is not possible for customers to sample an offering very easily. Also, customers have a preconceived set of relative positions already in their mind as expectations and therefore they have learnt what is possible in terms of any claim to a specific position.

- **Consistency.** It has been pointed out that positioning is all about creating an image in the mind of the consumer. Clearly for this to be achieved the message has to be consistent. If a company changes its communications policy there will be no clear messages and the public will not be able to visualise the positioning the company is attempting to occupy. Of course, it is possible to change positioning but this takes time to achieve.

- **Competitiveness.** In any decision over position there needs to be a strategic decision which positions the company relative to that of the competition (we are friendlier, larger, offer more value, have better service, more modern, safer etc.) and this has to be accepted by the customer. Positioning the brand with a set of attributes that the customer does not care about is never going to be effective.

Selecting the segments to target

The identification and selection of segments will require judgement based on the analysis of different data. The purpose of segmentation is to select a segment (target market) with the best potential on a range of criteria. The objective set is then to create product benefits, features and promotional messages which will appeal to the needs of the selected segment(s). A number of characteristics are examined when deciding upon target groups (see Chapter Two on consumer behaviour for further discussion of some of these characteristics) as shown in Table 17.2.

In order for segmentation to be successful there is a need to apply intellectual rigour to the segmentation procedure. When a target group is identified it is prudent to use a checklist to ensure the segment offers a viable opportunity for the organisation, such as:

TABLE 17.2	Some general characteristics of segmentation strategies
Characteristic	**Typical classification**
Geographic	Region of world, country, area of country, urban, suburban, rural areas city, town, post code, type of house or by climate type
Demographic	Age group, gender, education, family life cycle, ethnic group. Socio-economic classification of household based upon A, B, C1, C2, DE classifications
Psychographic	Lifestyle. Personality type – introvert, extrovert, high/low ego drive, independent, compulsive, gregarious, group worker
Usership	Non-user, current user, past user, potential user, loyalty type, heavy user, medium user, light user
Kind of purchase	Special occasion (honeymoon, anniversary), annual holiday trip, business travel, method of purchase (agent, direct, etc.)
Attitudes	Towards product area, towards brand, towards usership and use situations
Benefits sought	Status, convenience, luxury, economy, etc.

- **Is the segment measurable?** Progress at various stages of the segmentation activity needs to be measured. Segment composition, size, purchasing power etc. in order for assessment need to be measurable.

- **Is the segment accessible?** The targeting decision requires that individual buyers can easily be contacted through promotional messages as well be accessible to be offered a purchase opportunity or service.

- **Is the segment substantial?** The segment must be large enough to provide a viable level of business.

- **Is the segment sustainable?** The choice of segment has to take into account whether the demand will last. Fashion and 'lifestyle' market segments are prone to change and fall into demise.

- **Is the segment actionable?** Are there any impediments in putting together a marketing mix so that the target market can be reached with a clear product positioning strategy and message which will fit the needs, aspirational ideals and behaviour of the segment?

- **Is the segment defendable?** Can the target market be defended against competitor activity if they also select the same target group, and will rivalry cause any viability problems?

British Tourist Authority's lifestyle segmentation for American visitors to Britain

In 1994 the British Tourist Authority decided that the following lifestyle segments were important target groups:

- **First-time visitor:** stays in London and visits traditional and well-known attractions and sights around London, e.g. Windsor.

- **The traditionalist:** divide, time between London and more established regional locations such as Oxford, Cambridge, Chester, utilising trains and occasionally B&B accommodation. The type seeks an enriching vacation.

- **The explorer:** wants to know the country better. Stays outside London and utilises cities as a base for further touring of areas such as Wales and Scotland.

- **The Britophile:** has a lot of knowledge about Britain, returns on a regular basis, stays in upmarket accommodation and may have friends or relatives in Britain.

Segmentation leads to positioning of the service or product offer so that it is right for the target audience. This is reliant on adherence to the initial objectives and results in the final choice of the marketing mix. Once the segments have emerged from the consideration process the objectives need to be reconsidered. If it is found that there are no problems with the objectives, and the plan is to be adopted, there has to be some assessment of whether the objectives can be achieved within specific time constraints. Competitors may be able to develop more quickly or the organisation may find it too difficult to change in a short period of time. The ability to change is often related to the availability of resources. It is necessary to question whether the resources available are sufficient to achieve the objectives (budgets, personnel, technology, existing hotels, aircraft or built facilities). If, after evaluation, it is decided the strategy is unacceptable, there is a need to review and revise the plan's objectives.

Agreeing the marketing mix strategy has to be linked to laying down task-related programmes which allocate budgets and create responsibilities and timings for the plan's implementation. There is always a need to link planning with budgeting which will allow for the adoption and execution of an effective marketing mix strategy to achieve the objectives of the plan.

Monitoring the plan

There should be a means of monitoring the achievements of the plan so that tactical action can be taken either to get the plan back on course or to take advantage of new opportunities. There is therefore the need for the provision of assessment and measurement methods that will monitor progress towards the achievement of the plan's overall objectives. There is also the need to know what deviations from the initial objectives are acceptable. This will allow for the review and amendment of the plan on a continuous basis.

The tourism and hospitality industry has invested in reservation systems that allow a continuous flow of financial and booking pattern data. This has enabled the modelling of different performance indicators. These can include forecasts of probable load factors or occupancy levels as well as assessment of the effectiveness of regional or national sales promotion, price changes and sales representative campaigns. Nowadays, the airline and hotel sectors are applying these systems to yield management systems as a means to monitor demand and maximise the revenue from consumers.

CONCLUSION

Marketing planning is probably the most important activity for any tourism organisation. The long-term survival of organisations is related to the way that an organisation understands how to assess its environment, set sensible objectives and choose logical strategies for achieving success. Utilisation of different models such as SWOT, STEP, Porter's five force model and the BCG model all allow for a more informed approach to the planning analysis. The conditions for maximising the advantages from planning are based upon the need to understand the human aspects of the process as well as the formalised procedures of a structured approach.

Self-check questions

1 Name the four levels of marketing environment affecting the company.

2 What do the acronyms STEP and SWOT stand for?

3 List the main sections you would expect to see in a marketing plan.

4 What do you understand the term 'portfolio analysis' to mean?

5 Explain the concept of positioning and its relationship to target groups.

Essay questions

1 Examine the following changes that have taken place in the operation of cruise ships. What factors have contributed to these changes? You should consider the cruise line company's needs as well as the changes related to the consumer as part of this analysis.

Early cruise products

- long distance
- long duration
- most time at sea
- larger liners used
- departure from home-generating area ports

Modern cruise products

- short distance
- shorter 7–14 night duration
- majority of daytime in ports
- specially designed for smaller ports and activity
- fly–cruise arrangements or warm water port departures

2   Taking a tourism-related organisation of your choice, analyse the current per-
    formance of its business and then develop a marketing plan based upon the
    content of this chapter.

3   One of the demographic trends in many countries is the increasing proportion
    of older adults. Is this important enough to warrant changes in approaches to
    the marketing of tourism products? Examine through a planning approach how
    either the hotel, cruise, airline or attractions markets may need to plan for such
    changes.

4   Describe the methods and approaches to the segmentation of markets for a com-
    pany that offers adventure holidays.

5   Think about the last time you organised a party and then, by examining the
    structure of a marketing plan, identify the similarities or otherwise between the
    two.

Annotated further reading

Books

Evans, N., Campbell, D. and Stonehouse, G. (2003) *Strategic Management for Travel and Tourism*, Butterworth Heinemann, Oxford.
The text provides a comprehensive insight into strategic planning for tourism organisations. It offers approaches to the selection, evaluation and implementation of strategic planning. It is specifically written in relation to the travel and tourism industry with an explanation of strategic management applications and theory. In addition it has case studies from Southwest Airlines, Airtours, Marriott and Thomas Cook.

Kotler, P., Bowen, S. and Makens, J. (2002) *Marketing for Hospitality and Tourism*, 3rd edn, Prentice Hall, Upper Saddle River, NJ.
The book draws upon the marketing material of Philip Kotler's other books and as such is based upon his pedigree which has been developed over a number of years of writing marketing textbooks. However, the examples are often not very good and other specialist books need to be read in conjunction with this one. This latest edition covers electronic marketing, has case studies and lets students under-stand the role of marketing in hospitality and tourism. Specialist areas covered are marketing planning, customer quality management and destination marketing.

McDonald, M. and Keegan, W. (2001) *Marketing Plans That Work*, Butterworth Heinemann, Oxford.
This text provides the reader with a comprehensive coverage of all the aspects of producing a successful marketing plan. The book concentrates upon the logical development of a marketing plan and only deals with the marketing concepts in a perfunctory manner so is recommended solely for understanding the marketing planning process and approach.

References cited and bibliography

Abell, D.F. and Hammond, J.S. (1979) *Strategic Market Planning Problems and Analytical Approaches*, Prentice Hall, Englewood Cliffs, NJ.

Gilbert, D., Child, D. and Bennett, M. (2001) 'A qualitative study of the current practice of "no-frills" airlines operating in the UK', *Journal of Vacation Marketing* 7(4), 302–315.

Gilbert, C. (2003) *Retail Marketing Management*, 2nd Edn, Financial Times/Prentice Hall.

Kotler, P. (2000) *Marketing Management – The Millennium Edition*, Prentice Hall, Upper Saddle River, NJ.

McArdle, J. (1989) 'Product branding – the way forward', *Tourism Management* **10**, 201.

McDonald, M. (1989) *Marketing Plans*, Heinemann, Oxford.

Mintel (2000) 'The gay holiday market', Mintel International Group, London.

Porter, M.E. (1980) *Competitive Strategy: Techniques for Analysing Industries and Competitors*, Free Press, New York.

Ries, A. and Trout, J. (1986) *Positioning: The Battle for Your Mind*, McGraw-Hill, London.

Tarlow, P. (2003) *e-Review of Tourism Research*, John Wiley & Sons, New York.

Urry, J. (1992) *The Tourist Gaze*, Sage, London.

MAJOR CASE STUDY 17.1
DISNEYLAND® RESORT PARIS

Disneyland® Resort Paris, formerly Euro Disney, became a huge embarrassment to the Walt Disney Corporation after it plunged into the red shortly after its opening in France in 1992. The initial cost of the theme park, at US$4.4 billion for the development of a 5000-acre site, represented the largest single piece of construction in Europe's history apart from the Channel Tunnel project linking England and France.

Cumulative losses at the end of 1993 exceeded US$1 billion. The loss is all the more significant when it is revealed that the then Euro Disney had achieved target attendance objectives of 11 million 'guests' in slightly over one year of operation. The situation did not improve in 1994 when Euro Disney reported a loss for the year to the end of September of US$317 million and attendance was 10% down on levels achieved in 1993. Share prices fell from a peak of FFr68 just before the park opened to only FFr6 in October 1994.

The main problem for Euro Disney can be found to lie with the planning assumptions and forecasts which did not reflect the European economy or the willingness of consumers to pay high entrance fees. There was also a mistaken belief in a flatter seasonal demand curve, which characterises demand in the USA, as a result of mid-semester or off-peak visits by parents with their children. As a result, the levels and patterns of demand never reached those anticipated by planners.

An additional problem is related to the homogeneity of European markets. Disney planners in the USA initially treated Europe as a single country, underestimating the inherent differences between the existing markets in respect of demand and importing marketing methods which had succeeded in America but which did not successfully transplant to the European context. Consequently, the American parent company was forced to accept that tourists' habits vary a great deal throughout the European context and that its prices were too high for French visitors.

As an integral part of the financial subsidisation for the development of the park, the plan had assumed that well-appointed, high-priced hotels and other property could be constructed and then sold on to entrepreneurs for considerable profits. Disney planners did not want to be faced with either the land-use problems they had experienced in the USA where extra land has had to be purchased for expansion or the financial limitations imposed in Tokyo where Japanese investors took huge profits while Disney earnt 10% of gross earnings on rides and 5% on food and beverage. Consequently, the planners were concerned with attempting to maximise profit opportunities from the outset.

Disney planners overlooked the worsening economic conditions prevailing in Europe in the early 1990s which led to a severe slump in the property market for accommodation. Euro Disney had embarked on a vast property development – including hotels, shops, offices and residential housing – ignoring the severe handicap this posed of potentially unrealistic financial obligations to its American parent. The hotels were not sold as originally planned and, in addition, currency devaluation in Great Britain and Italy further depressed purchasing power, driving down demand for foreign travel.

Other planning problems materialised. The design of the hotel restaurants, for example, did not take into consideration the different tastes of the guests and were often too small, because of the belief that few Europeans would eat a full breakfast. Consequently, long waiting times and queuing problems ensued, culminating in guest dissatisfaction and complaints. The park's outlets were designed for snacking but the pattern was that at one o'clock, there was a major demand for a reasonably substantial meal. Moreover, Disney outlets were restricted by a 'no alcohol' policy which meant the French custom of taking wine with a meal was not permissible.

The problems were further compounded by pre-opening reports by Disney that employees would have to comply with the written Disney code of dress which consisted, for women, of short fingernails, appropriate undergarments and strict policies on hairstyles. The global code was considered an insult by the French people who believed it attacked the underlying principles in French culture of individualism and privacy. Thus, unforeseen cultural issues emerged with newspapers, such as *Le Figaro*, stating: 'Euro Disney is the very symbol of the process by which people's cultural standards are lowered and money becomes all-conquering.'

French intellectuals accused Disney of stifling the imagination of young people, of turning children into consumers, even of creating a 'cultural Chernobyl'. In addition, Disney characters were attacked as likely to pollute the nation's culture. Euro Disney's image was further damaged by PR blunders by senior Disney officials who dismissed the criticism as fatuous. Nevertheless, concessions were made: emphasis was placed on European fairy-tale characters such as Snow White and Pinocchio rather than Bambi and Dumbo. Also, in order to echo French culture, the turret which the company's 'imagineers' built was modelled not on Neuschwanstein, the Bavarian castle reconstructed at Disney's other theme parks, but on a drawing from a fifteenth-century French manuscript.

RECENT CHANGES

Following the embarrassment of heavy losses and low levels of demand in 1993 and 1994, Disney brought in French senior management who orchestrated key developments at Euro Disney. The theme park was renamed Disneyland® Resort Paris and in 1994 a complete product reassessment and reduction programme was implemented. The number of souvenir lines was cut in half from 30,000 and restaurant menu items were also reduced from 5400 to 2000.

Marketing strategies were reappraised and advertising messages modified. The advertising was designed to make parents and grandparents sympathetic to their children's emotional pleasure while emphasising the adventure element for adults. Potential customers are targeted with special offers during off-peak winter months, a strategy which evolved in response to market research activity which demonstrated that levels of repeat visits were high. In addition, the promotional links with Eurostar have helped to increase the number of UK visitors.

Pricing policies were also adjusted to offer reduced entrance admission charges in the evening, for example. Job flexibility arrangements, customer care programmes and other efficiency drives were also instigated, leading to the first ever surplus for Disneyland® Resort Paris for 1995. This was related to improvements in hotel occupancy which rose steadily from 55% in 1993 to 68% in 1995, compared with an average of roughly 60% for hotels in and around the Paris area.

The current situation is linked closely to the need to pay off the park's debts and net loss in 2002 of 56m euros, but this is not easy given the problems of lower tourist visitors to France. For example, the American visitor market in 2003 was down 30% on the previous year due to fear of travel and the negative image created by France's opposition to the Iraq war. In fact, in America there has been a general boycott of French products based upon the anger of Americans. The company blames its poor performance on a reduction in European travel and tourism, strikes in France and the poor economic conditions of its key markets. However, given that the vast majority of its visitors are French (40%), British (21%), and German (7%) then the theme park probably requires other changes. The hope was that the Walt Disney Studios, which was modelled on the success of Universal Studios in Florida and opened in 2002, would attract higher numbers but this has not been the case.

Therefore, it is crucial that financial and marketing planning are implemented professionally if the park is to maintain its profitability and prosper in the European marketplace. This is especially important given increasing competition from other European theme parks such as Port Aventura in Spain and Parc Asterix in France.

Source: Based on information from various newspaper articles including 'Tourist drought hits Disneyland Paris: Iraq fallout, strikes and forest fires have kept Americans and Europeans away', by Amelia Gentleman in Paris, The Guardian, *a August 2003.* See also: http://www.telegraph.co.uk/arts/main.jhtml?xml=/arts/2003/08/25/ftdis25.xml&sSheet=/arts/2003/08/25/ixartleft.html

DISCUSSION QUESTIONS

Provide some analysis and marketing solutions for Disneyland® Resort Paris. For example is there:

1 A need to cater better for the German market and if so how can this be achieved?

2 Does the park need to have an improved communication programme targeted to potential visitors or past visitors?

3 Is it important to focus on the heritage of the well-loved Disney characters and if so is the target group the under-tens or other segments?

639

CHAPTER EIGHTEEN
MARKETING MIX APPLICATIONS

INTRODUCTION

Anyone who purchases a tourism product has probably been influenced by a promotional campaign, assessed the product offer, considered whether he or she is willing to pay the price and, finally, thought about how easy it would be to buy it. Each of these aspects of purchase is carefully planned by tourism marketers in an attempt to convince potential tourists to buy their products. They are the basic ingredients of the marketing mix, the aspect of marketing that we consider in detail in this chapter.

In actual fact a great deal of this book could have been written on the marketing mix, as it involves a whole range of different topic areas. Each of the areas that make up the marketing mix involves a complex set of management decisions which have to take into account both the individual mix strategy as well as the combined effect of the whole mix on the target market groups. This chapter will therefore provide some of the most important considerations for the planning of the marketing mix.

LEARNING OUTCOMES

The marketing mix offers management a set of tools that may be manipulated to meet specific objectives and attract predefined target markets. The marketing mix is the focus of this chapter and, by the end of this chapter, you will be able to:

- identify the elements that make up the marketing mix and understand how this may be applied to a tourism product;

- recognise that the manipulation of the marketing mix generally, and the promotion and pricing in particular, will be beneficial in meeting specific predetermined objectives;

- appreciate that distribution and product formulation are linked to, and influenced by, technological and structural changes in the tourism industry; and

- understand the centrality of the concept of the target market to the marketing mix.

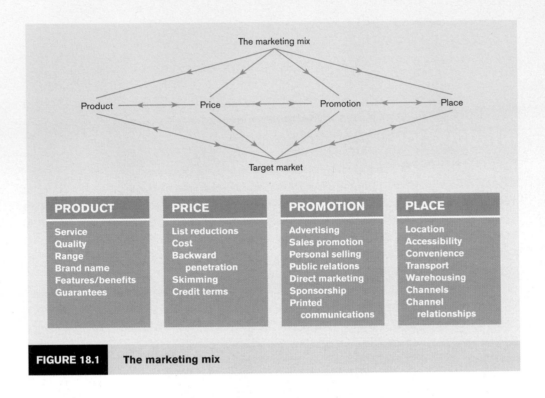

WHAT IS THE MARKETING MIX?

It is customary to accept that the marketing mix (Figure 18.1) is within the control of management and refers to decisions made in relation to the four Ps. These may be defined as:

- Product.

- Price.

- Promotion.

- Place (distribution).

There are, however, alternative approaches where authors stress the need for an expansion of these four. This is an interesting development because the four Ps were conceived by McCarthy (1978) as an abridged version of a much wider range of what were termed 'marketing ingredients'. McCarthy based the classification of his four Ps upon a whole collection of marketing ingredients offered much earlier by Borden (1965). We will discuss this later in this chapter.

Kotler and Armstrong (1996) indicate that the marketing mix is one of the key concepts in modern marketing theory. They define the marketing mix as 'the set of marketing tools that work together to affect the marketplace'.

Target market

The fundamental starting point for the creation of a successful marketing mix strategy is to ensure the **target market** is clearly defined. Although the target market is not part of the marketing mix, its role in dictating the different ways the mix is used makes it indistinguishable from the concept and of paramount importance. The target market is the focus for all marketing mix activity and is linked to the final selection of segments that we discussed in the previous chapter.

The market for a product is made up of actual and potential consumers. This total available group of consumers will be analysed and a decision will be made as to segments or subgroups to be targeted. The segments would probably have been identified as part of the marketing planning process (see Chapter Seventeen for an explanation of choosing segments) and would have emerged or been specified at the time of the setting of objectives. The specification of the target market has a number of important benefits which are discussed below.

BENEFITS OF TARGETING

Targeting facilitates the following:

- A fuller understanding of the unique characteristics and needs of the group to be satisfied is reached. The target market acts as a reference point for marketing decisions, especially as to how the marketing mix should be planned. This should lead to greater effectiveness for the mix which in turn provides for the success of the programme.

- A better understanding of a company's competitors is gained because it is possible to detect those who have made a similar selection of target markets. If an organisation does not clarify the markets it wishes to target, it may treat every other organisation in its sector as an equal competitor. Once a main competitor is identified their marketing efforts can be more closely followed – or benchmarked and then reacted to.

- An improvement is possible in an understanding of the changes and developments in the needs of the target market. Awareness is heightened due to the scrutiny focused upon the target group's actions, and reactions to slightly different forms of the marketing mix.

As we have seen with the section on segmentation in Chapter Seventeen, target markets can be based upon a number of factors such as:

- socio-economic groups;
- geographic location;
- age;
- sex;
- income levels;
- visitor type;

- benefits sought; and

- purchase behaviour and attitudes for both the international and domestic business, holiday visitor and recreationalist.

The target market acts as the focus for tailoring the mix so that target customers will judge the overall product to be superior to that of the competition. Segmentation and target marketing are central to efficient and effective marketing activity because they are instrumental in ensuring the marketing mix strategy is tailored to meet the specific needs of different customer groups.

PRODUCT

The effectiveness of planning the marketing mix depends as much on the ability to select the right target market as on the skill in devising a product offer which will generate high levels of satisfaction. We have to realise that the customer is looking for the right product to solve their problem of satisfying a need. Club Méditerranée is treated as having a singular product to offer yet it has more than 100 different holiday villages in over 40 countries, as well as expanding into boats and cruise ships, small 'villa' hotels and an escorted tour business. The service product (see Figure 18.2) is quite complex and can be thought of as being a combination of different levels with four important areas – *the core product*; *the facilitating product*; *the supporting product*; and *the augmented product*.

Core product

Every **product** is a package of problem-solving services and tangible attributes that will be successful if the package is valued enough to satisfy a need or want. A product includes everything that the customer receives and this includes the central level of the *core product* which is made up of the delivery of benefits and features. A holiday consumer in a travel agency is looking for the benefit of relaxing in the sun and having no hassle in the journey or stay. They leave the detail of how to arrange this to the travel agent. To put it another way, buyers 'do not buy quarter inch drills; they buy quarter inch holes'. Marketing staff have to uncover the subtle benefits that the consumer seeks when utilising a retail distribution channel or purchasing a product. We know that consumers buy products for the benefits they are expected to deliver. It therefore makes sense to incorporate different additions into the product that will help to differentiate it from the comparable product offered by competitors. Adding in the right features creates a higher probability that a purchase will occur. There are the different features which are added as the tangible aspects of the product which help to differentiate it from competitors. The tangible features may be the size of the hotel entrance, the physical aspects of a destination or the comfort of the airline seat. In order to understand a product it must be understood that service products are different and as such should not be confused with other general marketing literature concepts which are less complex in their approach.

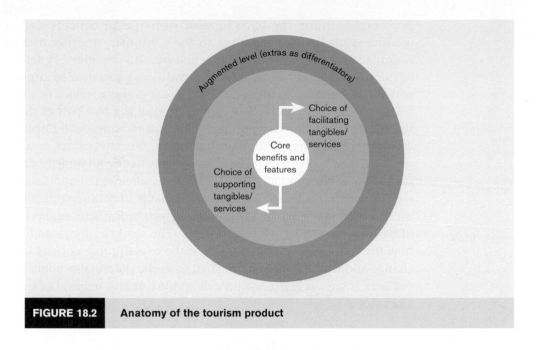

Core
benefits and
features

Choice of
facilitating
tangibles/
services

Choice of
supporting
tangibles/
services

Augmented level (extras as differentiators)

| FIGURE 18.2 | Anatomy of the tourism product |

Facilitating, supporting and augmented product

The *facilitating product* aspects must be present for the customer to utilise the services of the core product. This will be the service and goods such as lift service in a high-rise hotel, receptionist and telephone operator, credit card payment facilities, signage and easy access around the destination. *Core products* require *facilitating products* but do not necessarily have to include *supporting products* (see Figure 18.2). In fact the no-frills airlines need the facilitating products of check in and baggage handling but only provide a minimum of supporting products in order to adhere to their cost-leadership strategy. The supporting product for a scheduled full service airline may include such extras as separate lounge area, higher employee numbers providing superior service, service to deal with children travelling, and so on as these are all supporting products which may be planned into the product offer.

The *augmented* product level is the added aspects of the product which form the extras and which can help the product compete more favourably in the marketplace. This could be achieved through sensory marketing by creating a special atmosphere in an airline lounge area through creating garden setting spaces with bird song and different lighting as well as having sanctuary areas of peace and quiet such as those areas and lounges at places such as Singapore's Changi airport. In fact, Changi also has a nature trail to follow. Companies should take the opportunity to consider factors such as the use of materials and the décor of public areas which will provide the atmosphere within which the customer interacts. A feature could be the inclusion of flight-delay cover. Tourism is normally associated with the risk of delayed flights, exchange rate fluctuations on little snow on skiing holidays. The potential risk of flight delay or inadequate snow cover on ski slopes can be insured against by the operator who passes on only a small premium to its clients as part of the price of the trip. A further example is a contract agreement to hotel rates, the early buying forward of currency or advance purchase of aircraft fuel will allow a company to offer the guarantee of no increase in a quoted price.

By complementing the basic product with special benefits that add value, the product is made more appealing to the consumer. Another method could be to negotiate on behalf of the customer and pass on the added benefits as is discussed in the following. Arranging a contract with car parks near to airports in off-season periods can allow a company to offer the car-parking service free to its clients. The cost is passed on to each client as a fraction of the true cost of the service because the arrangement allows the car park to acquire business at a difficult time. Features such as free car hire, pick up at the airport, fast check-outs, study bedrooms and free tickets to tourism attractions or the theatre are all added benefits that can be planned into the product offer. Utilising the augmented approach the company is able to add extras which are more memorable and can act as differentiators over the competition when other aspects of facilitating and supporting products are likely to be similar between companies. The marketer needs to look constantly at how the different component parts of the overall product need improvement and change and this is sometimes referred to as the potential product in other contexts but here is seen as being within a development and renewal of existing levels, not a new level.

Service

This is concerned with creating the level of services to be offered. For a hotel, a tour operator/wholesaler, a restaurant or an airline, this poses the questions of how much of the service should the client be expected to perform and how much should be provided by staff. For example, self-service buffet-style food operations or the personal carrying of hand luggage is now thought of as acceptable and, at times, desirable by clients. Likewise, tea- and coffee-making facilities in hotel bedrooms where the guest helps him/herself is now seen to be integral to the accommodation product offering, especially if the provision of room service is limited to certain hours. Service provision for air travellers now satisfies communication needs, with some airlines offering an improved business product with in-flight telephone, telex or access to a personal computer. These developments are indicative of the relentless quest for cost-effective improvements to the service content of the tourism product. Any tourism operation is predominately service based and has to be able to deliver high levels of service.

Quality

Quality involves deciding on quality standards for the product and implementing a method of assurance on the performance level of staff and facilities. The management of quality is becoming an increasingly important management function (as discussed in Chapter Six) since it is crucial to create a good reputation for the quality of the product and service offered. This encourages a positive image for the company or organisation and a reputation for good quality is a major advantage in reducing the perception of risk in the minds of consumers. Tourism service providers are more likely to be successful if they can be depended upon to deliver higher quality service levels than their competitors. Success through quality is often associated with the outcome of the relationship between a customer's prior expectations of service delivery and the perception of the actual service. With this in mind, Swissair aims for at least 96% of its passengers to rate the quality of its service as good or superior, otherwise it will take remedial action.

Range

It is necessary to decide how different individual products will fit into the overall range of the organisation's products offered to the marketplace. A tour operator/ wholesaler has to decide whether to include five-star or two-star hotels in their range of offering, or whether they should operate to traditional or newly emerging destinations. More recently the cruise market has expanded and many tour operators/ wholesalers have altered their product range to include cruise ships to accommodate the resurgence of demand. In fact, the introduction of Cunard's *Queen Mary II* as the longest, tallest and heaviest passenger ship ever, bears witness to the investment in this sector.

Tourism enterprises have to decide on the range of offers and how each product fits into the product mix. Such decisions will produce change over time, as is illuminated by some of the milestones in the development and change of Thomas Cook in Table 18.1. The essence of the early success of Thomas Cook in providing unique experiences is reflected in the seeking out of new experiences as shown in Photograph 18.1.

Brand name

A **brand** is a name, a symbol, term or design or a combination of these that marketers attempt to promote so that the brand is well known and provides added value to a product. This can lead to consumers insisting on the product by brand name and, as a consequence of the delivery of satisfaction the achievement of brand loyalty or less price sensitivity.

The benefit of developing a strong brand is important as consumers are often prepared to pay a price premium for perceived added values related to buying well-marketed brands. The price premium, also known as *brand equity*, is the price customers are prepared to pay above the commodity value of a product or service. This being the case, well-respected brands – if well positioned and managed – can give a better return to the company. Brands with a strong personality are attractive to companies who own them and predator companies wishing to buy into their potency. A successful brand is a flag bearer as it provides visible signals of positional strength in the marketplace. There are also distribution benefits whereby a strong brand will obtain channel leverage due to customers wanting to purchase and travel agents or travel web sites wanting to have inventory. In this way successful brands provide their parent companies with a competitive advantage.

Figure 18.3 illustrates the benefit of creating a strong brand which is able to add value to the company offer. A differentiated position from that of the competition with a clear identity allows the brand to achieve higher prices and achieve higher levels of demand in periods of recession. A secondary consideration is that strong domestic brands provide a good base on which to build an international or global presence.

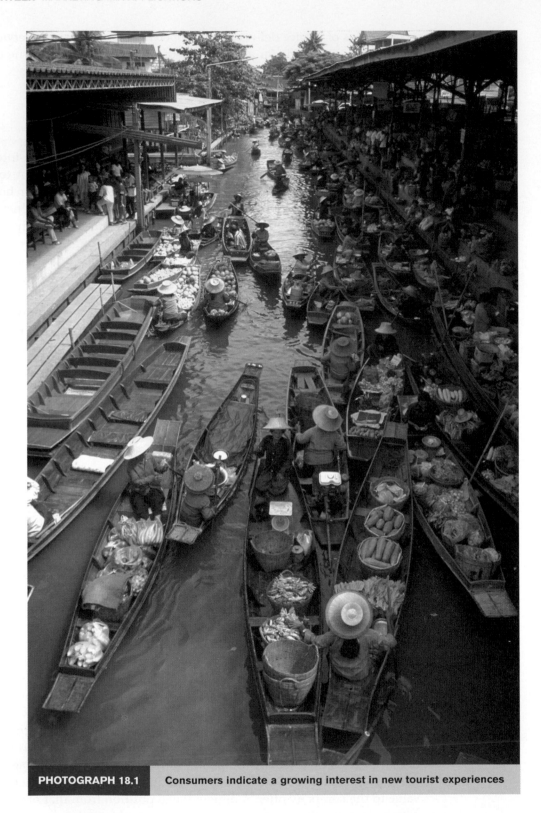

PHOTOGRAPH 18.1 Consumers indicate a growing interest in new tourist experiences

TABLE 18.1	Example of the historical changes to the product range for Thomas Cook
1841	First excursion from Leicester to Loughborough
1845	Trip to Liverpool and excursions to Wales
1846	First tours to Scotland
1851	Trips for 165,000 people to the Great Exhibition
1855	First continental tours
1863	Tours organised to Switzerland
1866	First tours to North America
1869	First tours to the Holy Land
1872	Pioneers of round-the-world tours
1874	Traveller's cheques introduced
1902	First winter sports brochures and motor car tours
1919	The company advertises air tours
1927	First air charter, New York to Chicago for Dempsey fight
1939	First package tour to south of France
1972	Thomas Cook becomes part of the Midland Bank Group
1981	Agreement to launch euro traveller's cheques
1988	Cessation of operation in the short-haul market

TABLE 18.1	(continued)
1989	Reinvestment in retail outlets to upgrade them
1989	Direct sales operation set up
1992	Thomas Cook sold by Midland Bank to Westdeutsche Landesbank (WestLB) and the LTU Group
1992	21.6% shareholding acquired from Owners Abroad in order to form an alliance (now First Choice)
1994	Thomas Cook corporate travel business and USA franchised travel offices sold to American Express
1994	Travel Kiosks set up to sell direct by the use of advanced technology
1999	The company rationalises and reduces the number of its sub-brands and also launches the new JMC brand
2000	The company became wholly owned by Thomas Cook AG (formerly C&N Touristic AG – which itself was formed as a merger of Condor and Neckermann)
2001	Thomas Cook UK was rationalised as part of a transformation programme to save costs and integrate the UK operation and JMC into the new parent group
2002	JMC brand abandoned three years after its introduction
2003	Thomscook.com adopted a customised system for customers to personalise their travel with a build-your-own (BYO) self-packaging technology linking flights, hotels, car hire and insurance
2003	Announcement of the merger of its two charter airlines, Condor Flugdienst and Condor Berlin, the sale of some of its hotels and other assets and a large reduction in staff, in order to reduce costs

In 2004 Thomas Cook AG was the second largest travel group in Europe and the third largest in the world.

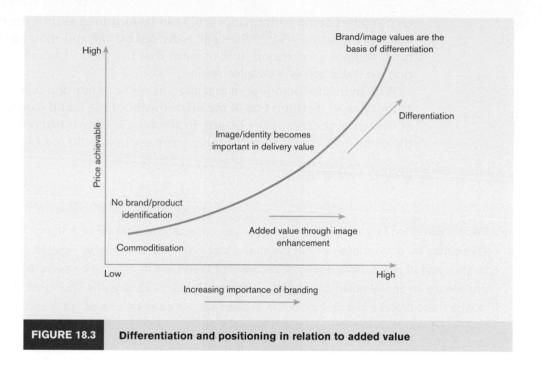

FIGURE 18.3   **Differentiation and positioning in relation to added value**

Brands, and ranges of brands, may fall into a number of different categories:

- **Family brands.** This is where each of the company's products adopts the same brand name. Examples include many of the leading hotel companies which have a family name, such as Holiday Inn with its different branded chains which are designed to attract different market segments due to a portfolio of product positioning. Similarly, Accor as a leading international accommodation provider emphasises brands such as Sofitel, Novotel, Ibis, etc.

- **Individual brands.** Alternatively, products offered by the same company may be branded very differently. For example, a tour operator or airline can have individual brand names within its businesses, with its long-haul, medium and budget-priced product offerings, each having individual brand names unrelated to the others. In America, Hilton hotels has the Hampton Court, Homewood studio and Embassy suite brands, which are individual brands.

- **Own-brands.** Finally, organisations can have own-brand products. For example, some travel agents will offer the leading tour operator products but may also have their own specialist brochures with the agency brand name which is used to sell their own product.

There are strengths and weaknesses associated with each strategy. The individual brand name approach, for example, allows a company to search for the most appropriate brand name. Its weakness is that the promotional budget for each brand has to be sufficiently large to support that brand. With family brands there is a spin-off effect for each of the brands from the expenditure on any one brand. Conversely, if one of the family brands obtains poor publicity, because of association, there will be damage to the other brands. For family branding, careful attention has to be given to the quality control of the products. One other benefit of family branding is that each product brand performance (PBP) can be measured against the overall family brand performance (FBP). When FBP is divided by PBP and shows an increase over time, without good reason, it may mean that the product brand needs modification, revitalisation or a detailed review.

With individual branding an organisation is able to position brands and products at the cheaper (bottom) end of the market without the brand damaging the image of the rest of the company's brands. In addition, if there is bad publicity for one of the company's brands then the other company brands do not necessarily suffer.

BRAND AWARENESS

People will often buy a familiar brand because they are comfortable with things familiar. There may be an assumption that the brand that is familiar is probably reliable, in business to stay, and of reasonable quality. A recognised brand will thus often be selected in preference to an unknown-brand. The awareness factor is particularly important in contexts in which the brand must first enter the evoked set – it must be one of the brands that are evaluated. An unknown-brand usually has little chance. (Aaker, 1991, p. 19)

Creating awareness of a brand is one of the biggest challenges for marketers as they need to ensure their product/brand is thought of (enters the evoked set) by customer's as one of any of the available brand options. In Figure 18.4 a customer's evoked set is shown by 'top of the mind' recall; this is the optimal awareness of a brand. This pyramid is only representative as there are no established scales or measurements connected with it, but it does serve as a conceptual framework.

Marketing strategy should take the 'evoked set' into consideration because the actual choices of individual customers depend crucially upon which brands are considered and evaluated by consumers and which are not. According to research it is found that consumers generally carry only a limited number of brands in their 'evoked set' – often no more than three to five brands. However, consumers do not necessarily select brands only from their 'evoked set' nor is their selection process logical, but if buyers recall a company's brand first the likelihood of them

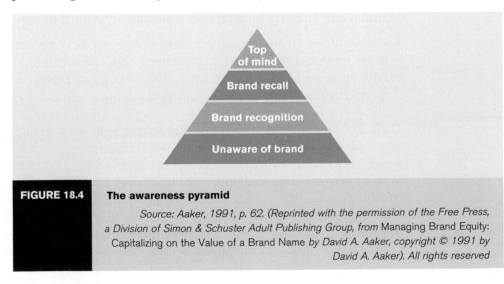

FIGURE 18.4   **The awareness pyramid**

Source: Aaker, 1991, p. 62. (Reprinted with the permission of the Free Press, a Division of Simon & Schuster Adult Publishing Group, from Managing Brand Equity: Capitalizing on the Value of a Brand Name *by David A. Aaker, copyright © 1991 by David A. Aaker). All rights reserved*

purchasing it increases. This concept accounts for the enormous amounts of money companies spend in buying out a well-branded competitor, to erase the visibility and reinforcement of alternative brands in the marketplace. Therefore, advertising is often aimed at facilitating the growth of brand awareness. Furthermore, it can develop an image and manipulate consumers' perception, which is fundamental to building values over and above the price–value relationship.

In addition, many consumers will also select a brand with which they are familiar and which, it has been proved, is capable of providing satisfaction and quality. A recognised destination will thus often be selected over an unknown destination: 'People will often buy a familiar brand because they are comfortable with the familiar' (Aaker, 1991). The awareness factor here is particularly important so a destination featured in a recent film or the coverage of an Olympics will increase customer awareness. The establishment of a strong brand image makes it more likely that the destination will be remembered and evaluated against other brands. A weak destination brand usually has little chance of entering any assessment and consequently will not be as successful.

PRICE

The pricing policy selected for a tourism product is often directly related to the performance of its future demand. Setting the right **price** is also crucial to the profitability of the tourism enterprise. We believe that, of all the marketing mix, pricing decisions are the hardest to make. This is because prices for tourism products have to take into account the complexity created by seasonality of demand and the inherent perishability of the product. Also, within tourism there are major differences in segments such as business travellers and those taking a vacation. The relative elasticities of demand for these segments are dissimilar and price sensitivity is affected by different factors.

Figure 18.5 shows demand curves that indicate different market reactions to price change, i.e. where demand is highly responsive (or price elastic) and where demand is not price responsive (or price inelastic). Tourism industry products related to vacations are associated with an elastic demand curve, where a small increase in price creates a large fall in demand. Leisure travel is price elastic because of the following:

- The ratio of tourism prices to income is normally high. This is the case not only for overseas travel but also for leisure centres, cinemas and attractions, especially in times of recession. However, the different types of tourism demand from business travel to deciding on a secondary holiday will be associated with different elasticities. These may be as shown in Figure 18.6.

- The consumer can choose a substitute or forgo the purchase if the overall value is considered to be unacceptable.

- It is relatively easy to judge the offer of alternative brands and products, and therefore easy to switch demand to cheaper alternatives. Although price may be an indicator of quality, the consumer is able to choose between several offers, by referring, for example, to the type of aircraft they may fly on or the star rating or brand of accommodation.

FIGURE 18.5 **Price elasticity of demand**

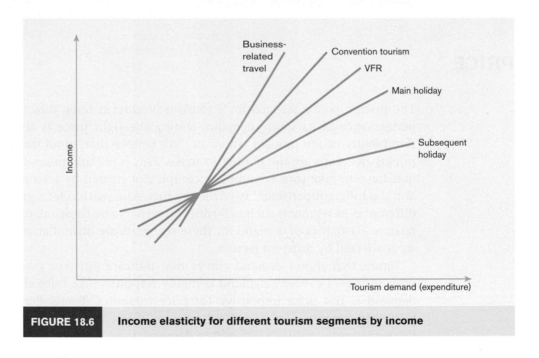

FIGURE 18.6 **Income elasticity for different tourism segments by income**

Elasticity is a key element in the understanding of the demand process. It is defined as the ratio of the percentage response in the quantity sold to a percentage change in price or one of the other marketing mix elements, such as the expenditure on advertising. It therefore measures the sensitivity in quantity demanded to a change in the demand determinant. Mathematically, elasticity can be calculated as follows:

$$\text{Elasticity} = \frac{\text{Percentage change in quantity demanded}}{\text{Percentage change in any demand determinant}}$$

For price elasticity the denominator is simply changed to a percentage change in price. The coefficient of price elasticity is nearly always negative because the price and quantity are inversely related. This means that when the price falls, the quantity demanded tends to rise; and when price rises, the demand tends to fall. Thus the tourism marketer would be interested in the size of the coefficient as a coefficient of more than one indicates that demand is elastic (if price rises, demand falls significantly) and less than one that it is inelastic (if price rises, demand falls but only slightly).

From this it follows that the mark-up on highly competitive products such as package holidays to Spain tend to be low because the demand for such items is price elastic. In general, mark-ups should vary inversely with price elasticity of demand if profits are to be maximised.

Factors affecting price sensitivity

A number of factors will affect the price sensitivity of products. From a marketing viewpoint a deeper understanding of price sensitivity assists with an understanding of the different target segments and the development of strategic planning. The main factors to consider are listed under the following headings.

PERCEIVED SUBSTITUTES EFFECT

Buyers are more sensitive the higher the product's price is in relation to another product or substitute they could purchase. Therefore, the consumer may choose a substitute or forgo the purchase if they believe the overall value is unacceptable. For example, local residents may avoid an area with higher priced shops frequented by tourists who are unaware of the alternatives.

UNIQUE VALUE EFFECT

Buyers are less sensitive to a product's price the more they value any of its attributes that differentiate it from competing products. For example, many customers are loyal to a national airline such as Thai or Singapore airlines because they perceive the airline to offer superior benefits.

IMPORTANCE OF PURCHASE EFFECT

If the risk of the purchase increases then the price will not be the most important aspect of the purchase. This occurs when the item is an important purchase such as a honeymoon or anniversary. The greater the importance of the product, the less price sensitive (more inelastic) the purchase will be.

DIFFICULT COMPARISON EFFECT

Buyers are less sensitive to price when they find it more difficult to compare alternatives. This may lead to a demand for the more established brands, or greater destination or brand loyalty, in order to reduce the perception of risk.

PRICE QUALITY EFFECT

A higher price may signal that the product is of superior quality. The result may be less sensitivity to price. This is not a conclusive effect as it applies to some products, while others may generate different reactions. For example, a restaurant menu at a higher price may signal improved quality but very few people would think higher priced fast-food items offered any real quality advantage.

EXPENDITURE EFFECT

Buyers become more price sensitive when the expenditure is larger, either in absolute money amounts or as a percentage of their income. This may curb demand for long-haul holidays and is most prevalent in low-income households in which all expenditure is carefully controlled. This effect is also stronger and more likely to occur in times of recession.

FAIRNESS EFFECT

If the buyer believes the price falls outside a band of what would be judged reasonable and fair then they become more price sensitive. With some types of products it is relatively easy to judge the offer of alternative brands and products and therefore easy to switch demand to cheaper alternatives. Consumers will perceive retailers, or the brands they stock, to be 'ripping off' customers if they exploit situations of shortage by being greedy. For example, street vendors are often seen to be selling drinks or ice creams at highly inflated prices when the temperature is extremely high.

Problems related to price cutting

The setting of price cannot be solely concerned with the consumer. Care and attention have to be given to both the reaction of the consumer, as well as that of the competition. Owing to the high-risk nature of the tourism industry, a price advantage which takes market share from a competitor will often provoke a hostile re-pricing reaction. If Company A, in Figure 18.7(a), attempts to increase its market share by price cutting, it will need to take market share from Companies B and C. This is a situation in which C and B are likely to react by cutting their own prices. The outcome is that the market shares remain similar and can, as in the second example, lead the market to grow in volume, as in Figure 18.7(b), although not necessarily in overall revenue. The long-term result is that the market remains extremely unstable because smaller margins are being applied. In this situation an organisation has to ensure it has a high volume of business in order to exceed its break-even point. Price-cutting policies have been a feature of the tour-operating business in the UK and the example provided above helps us understand what has led to the collapse of a whole range of different companies. The following list shows the various influences on pricing in the tourism industry.

- The perishable nature of the product, which is unable to be stored until a future occasion, leads to various forms of last-minute tactical pricing.

- The high price elasticity of demand exhibited by holiday and leisure markets places emphasis on setting prices at the right levels.

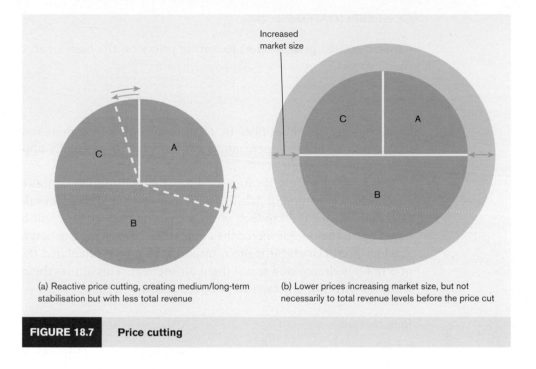

(a) Reactive price cutting, creating medium/long-term stabilisation but with less total revenue

(b) Lower prices increasing market size, but not necessarily to total revenue levels before the price cut

FIGURE 18.7   Price cutting

- Increased price transparency due to the ease of access to price comparisons by use of the Internet.

- The volatility of the market due to short-run fluctuations in international costs, exchange rates, oil prices and political events requires sophisticated forward planning.

- Many companies are reliant on high volumes to break even and will forgo short-run profit in order to create acceptable load factor or occupancy levels.

- Cost control is an important part of pricing policy. Many tourism enterprises have high fixed costs and price near to break-even positions. This can make them vulnerable to financial collapse or takeover if costs are not controlled.

- Some regions and countries have price controls for airline travel and hotel accommodation.

- Seasonal demand leads to peak and low-season periods, which require demand management pricing to cope with the short-run capacity problems.

- Price is associated with the psychological aspects of both quality and status. It is therefore always important to gauge the way prices or their change will be perceived by the different target segments.

- Cash flow is high due to much of the payment for tourism products being made in advance of consumption. Many tourism companies make profit on the investment of this money.

Pricing policy has to consider the above list and therefore the scope of choice is remarkably wide. The choice will probably be one or a combination of the following types of pricing.

COST-ORIENTATED PRICING

Cost-orientated pricing refers to setting prices on the basis of an understanding of their costs.

Cost-plus pricing

Cost-plus pricing sets prices in relation to either marginal costs or total costs including overheads. A percentage mark-up is then normally applied to reach the final price.

This form of pricing is often used for the retail outlets of tourist attractions. Its weakness as a method of pricing for tourism is that it does not take into consideration demand for the product, what prices the marketplace will bear and it is not based upon the price levels of the competitors. Knowing the cost breakdown of the product is crucial and it is often important to have calculated the operating price of a hotel bedroom or a sector flight airline seat. This allows the marketer to know what the effect of any tactical price reduction will be.

Rate of return

Rate of return pricing provides an organisation with an agreed rate of return on its investment. Whereas the cost-plus method concentrates on the costs associated with the running of the business, the rate of return method concentrates on the profits generated in relation to the capital invested. This approach is not appropriate for tourism enterprises as it ignores the need to link the pricing policy to the creation of a sales volume which is large enough to cover overheads and remains consistent over time.

To use either cost-plus or rate of return methods of pricing is generally not appropriate for tourism products that have to survive in a highly competitive marketplace.

DEMAND-ORIENTATED PRICING

Demand-orientated pricing takes into consideration the factors of demand rather than the level of costs in order to set the price. A conference centre, for example, may charge one price for admission to a rock concert and only half that price for admission to a classical concert.

Discrimination pricing

This is sometimes called flexible pricing and is often used in tourism where products are sold at two or more different prices. Quite often students and older people are charged lower prices at attractions, or events, than other segments. Discrimination pricing is often time related, with cheaper drink charges in 'happy hour' periods or cheaper meal prices in the early evening prior to high-demand periods as illustrated in Photograph 18.2. For price discrimination to be successful it is necessary to be able to identify those segments that, without the price differentials, would be unable to purchase the product.

To obtain a high flow of business, a hotel will have to discount for customers who offer significant volume. This means that, while business travellers may benefit

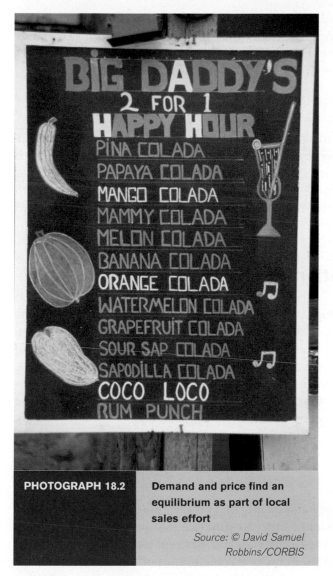

PHOTOGRAPH 18.2   **Demand and price find an equilibrium as part of local sales effort**

Source: © David Samuel Robbins/CORBIS

from corporate rates, those on vacation may be staying on tour operator/wholesaler rates.

Discrimination can also be based upon increasing the price of products that have higher potential demand. For example, if rooms in a hotel are all the same but some have good scenic views of the countryside or sea, then those rooms could be sold for a higher price.

Backward pricing

This is a market-based method of pricing that focuses on what the consumer is willing to pay. The price is worked backwards. First, an acceptable margin is agreed upon. Next, the costs are closely monitored so that the estimated final price is deemed to be acceptable to the target segment. The objective is to set a price that matches consumer preference. If necessary an adjustment is made to the quality of the product offer or service to meet the cost-led needs of this technique.

Tour operators/wholesalers selling on a price-led basis will often contract hotels one or two blocks back from the sea front, if this lowers the room rates making up the final price. Other methods include lowering the flight content of a holiday price by organising cheaper night flights which may also save on the first night's accommodation cost. To be successful with this method of pricing it is important to understand the psychological effects of creating products that may appeal to the price conscious. However, the holiday may not give satisfaction if the holiday experience and company are considered to be of poor quality.

Market penetration pricing

Market penetration pricing is adopted when an organisation wants to establish itself quickly in a market. Prices are set below those of the competition in order to create high growth for the company's products. Tour operators/wholesalers, when setting up an operation to a new destination, will use market penetration pricing for that destination in the first couple of years and then, once that destination becomes better established, will slowly increase the prices.

Psychological pricing

Companies will often price products below a round figure. This could be the changing of a menu price from say £10 to £9.95 or £9.99 to foster the perception of the price as being below that threshold at which the customer is willing to buy. Just as £9.95 may appear to be significantly less than £10, so a holiday price of £488 may seem to be more on a £400 level than a £500 level. However, there is no conclusive evidence that such pricing policies make any significant difference to profits.

Skimming pricing

This method is utilised when there is a shortage of supply of the product and where demand will not be dampened by charging a premium price. Luxury villas with pools, set in good locations, are normally priced with higher margins than other accommodation products because of their shortage. Market skimming policies can only occur where there is a healthy demand or strong destination image such as that of the south of France for the tourism product on offer.

Pricing and the relationship to value

Whatever pricing policy is adopted, a company has to take into consideration the potential consumer's perceptual assessment. In deciding to buy a product a consumer has to be willing to give up something in order to enjoy the satisfactions of the benefits the product will deliver. This concept is more complex than it seems. The majority of tourists are looking for value when they buy a product and value is derived from the functions of quality and price, as well as the added value of the image or brand. This may be expressed as:

$$\text{Value} = \frac{\text{Quality}}{\text{Price}} + \text{Image}$$

If a consumer believes the image and quality of a product is good, he or she will be willing to make greater sacrifices in order to purchase that product. This explains how first-class travel continues to be successful on different forms of transport such as trains, aircraft and cruise ships and why leading brands or destinations are able to attract higher prices. The interrelationship between price, quality and value plays a significant role in the buying behaviour of customers. Value was grouped into four categories by Zeithaml (1988):

- value as low price;

- value as whatever is wanted from a product;

- value as the quality one gets for the price paid;

- value as what one gets for what one gives.

Zeithaml describes value as a 'trade-off between salient benefit components and sacrifice components'. Benefit components according to Zeithaml include intrinsic attributes, extrinsic attributes, perceived quality and other relevant high abstractions. This means value is a judgement about superiority and benefits delivered. Therefore, having the lowest price may not be a sufficient strategy as the best route to marketplace success.

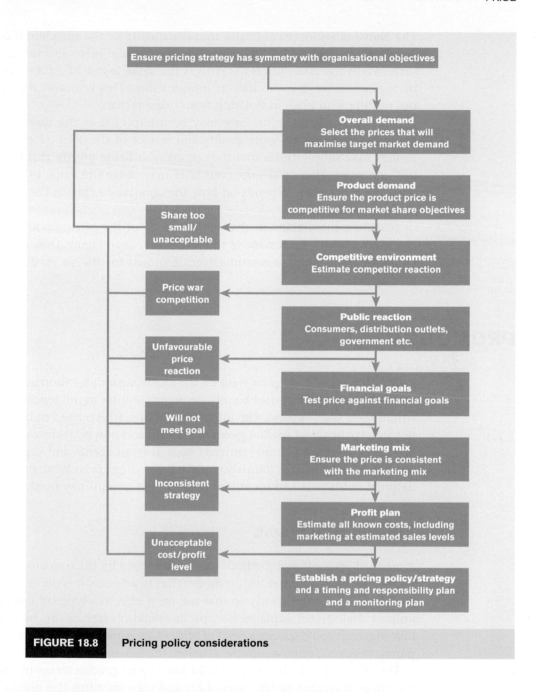

FIGURE 18.8   **Pricing policy considerations**

If prices change, this can affect the consumers' quality perception. A price reduction may be associated with a belief that the company is in financial trouble, that it will have to cut service and quality, or that prices are falling and if one waits, a price will come down even more. The value of the product is thought to have decreased because quality, by association with the changes, is observed to have fallen by a greater ratio than prices. The following shows the perception that the new value is at only half the level of its former position:

$$\text{Value} = \frac{\text{Quality}}{\text{Price}} \text{ with image constant, then if } V = \frac{Q/2x}{P/x} \text{ then } 1/2\,V = \frac{Q}{P}$$

The above relationship indicates that the quality of the merchandise or service is perceived to drop by half its former position while price and image remains the same. With the assumption that this is the same factor of x then value as judged by the consumer drops to half its former value. This indicates the importance of not dealing with price in isolation from other factors.

Alternatively, a price increase may be interpreted as the way the company is going to pay to improve the quality and service of the offer. However, some consumers may simply think that the company is being greedy and that quality has not improved. This means the consumer may judge the value to have fallen. The outcome quite often depends on how the company explains the increase in price to the consumer.

To ensure the maximum chance of success for the pricing policy adopted there is a need to check each stage of the procedure, as in Figure 18.8, p661. This figure identifies the important considerations required for the successful evolution of a pricing policy.

PROMOTION

Promotion is the descriptive term for the mix of communication activities that tourism organisations, or tourist boards, carry out in order to influence those publics on whom their sales depend. The important groups, which need to be influenced, are not simply the target market group of current, and potential customers. There is the need also to influence trade contacts such as retail agents and suppliers, as well as opinion formers such as journalists and travel writers. Even local, national and international politicians and important professional groups may need to be influenced.

Setting objectives

A range of promotional methods can be employed by the tourism marketer, so it is important to define what the promotion has to achieve. It is necessary to define the marketing objectives clearly so that the most effective types of promotion can be utilised. Figure 18.9 explains how promotional objectives can be developed. The mix strategies could specify a need to achieve awareness; to inform; to educate; create purchase action; improve loyalty; change the perception of the customer, etc.

The promotional objectives should have some precise terms in order to clarify the entire intention of the promotion and then monitor the results. This can be achieved by means of SMART objectives. SMART objectives will provide **S**pecific, **M**easurable, **A**ctionable, **R**ealistic/**R**elevant and **T**argeted/**T**imed results along the following lines:

1 The target audience or market has to be identified (by segment, geographical area, and for what products). For example, identifying grandparents of school age children living in London who would possibly take the children to Disneyland® Resort Paris.

2 The specific product (goods and service) to be promoted has to be identified. For example, mini break holidays in or near to France.

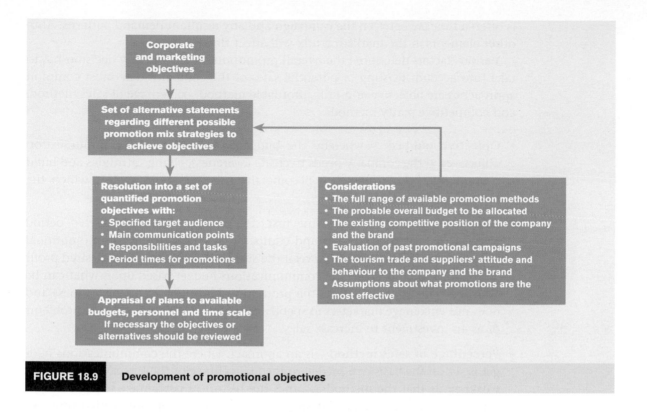

FIGURE 18.9   Development of promotional objectives

3 Specific goals should be set, perhaps that sales will increase by £*x*, or that attitudes to the product or brand will become more positive for the 40-plus age group. To fit with the SMART objectives these goals have to be *achievable* in that the company has to deliver to the objectives; also *relevant* to the task required.

4 The time horizon of when the expected effect will have occurred should be stated. For example, targets should be achieved by end September of a specified year.

Taking up the example used in the list above, a SMART objective would therefore be:

To ensure that the grandparents of children between the ages of four and 16, within the Greater London area, are communicated with and receive information on the France and Disneyland offers. Subsequently, sales for these products will increase by £150,000 over the previous year by 31 September.

Promotional budget approaches

The second important step in any promotion campaign is to agree the budget. There are different approaches to agreeing budgets that may be based upon a number of criteria. It is important to realise there is no one best method to set budgets. This is because promotional campaign measurement is not straightforward given there is often a time lag between the campaign and any resultant demand patterns. Also, other elements in the marketing mix will affect the demand.

Various factors determine the overall promotion budget but any decision has to take into account existing or potential sales of the company. The most common approaches are objective-and-task, affordable method, percentage of sales method, and competitive parity method:

- **Objective-and-task** – whereby the budget is related to the communication objectives. If the company needs to create awareness, change attitudes and build a brand then these objectives become the necessary tasks against which the budget is determined.

- **Affordable method** – where the first step is to produce a budgeted period forecast of the expected sales and company costs, excluding the promotional expenditure. The difference between the surplus expected and the desired profit allows for a decision over the communications budget based upon what can be afforded. This approach treats the promotion budget as a cost of business and does not encourage marketers to spend against the likelihood of future problems or as an investment to increase sales.

- **Percentage of sales method** – is an approach where the communications budget is set on the basis of a predetermined percentage of the forecasted sales. The weakness is that the method assumes the historical percentage is still relevant for the current marketplace. It also relies on accurate forecasts which provides for the chance of unacceptable error. In addition, if a company wants to build preference for a new product launch then a system of budgeting based upon the percentage of sales method may not raise the necessary budget to achieve the short-term task of ensuring awareness and acceptability. The other problem is that the method will provide for lower budgets when there is a downturn in the market or due to loss of sales based upon increased competitor activity that takes away business. This may lead to further sales decline as less and less money is spent on the company's promotion effort.

- **Competitive parity method** – allows the setting of the budget based upon both the share of market of the product or company and also the estimated expenditure level of its competitors. This method does not allow for specific marketplace opportunities as the parity level of expenditure will be held and consequently a strategic penetration of the market may not be achieved.

Communication effects

There is always the need to plan to achieve the most effective response from the target market. An important part of the promotional effort is the building of brand and product awareness. Sometimes it will take a long time for the consumer to know about the brand and the type of products on offer.

A promotion campaign should aim to provide knowledge about the product, to ensure the consumer will feel favourable towards the product and build up preference for it. Any campaign has to sell the benefits that a customer would be seeking in a credible way so that the potential customer feels conviction and is more likely than not to make a purchase.

(a) Demand shift through better awareness

(b) Demand becomes more inelastic due to image improvement

FIGURE 18.10   **Promotional effect on demand**

Figure 18.10 shows how a promotional campaign could be utilised by a destination or organisation to create awareness of the benefits of the product offer. The development of a positive image will create a more price-elastic demand curve, which means the product is more resilient to price rises and does not have to rely on having lower prices than the competition. In Figure 18.10(a) P_1Q_1 is existing demand before a campaign has been developed to create more awareness in the target audience. At P_1Q_2 demand has increased because, owing to a promotional effect, more people are now aware of the product benefits which the brand or destination can deliver. At P_1Q_3 in Figure 18.10(b) the campaign has improved the image of the organisation or destination so that more status is derived in travelling with the brand or to a destination. This changes the shape of the demand whereby it becomes more inelastic.

Advertising and sales promotion are the most widely used forms of promotion. Because of the intrusive characteristic of these forms of promotion, most consumers relate ideas of marketing to the use of advertising or sales promotion. The other major forms include public relations and personal selling.

Advertising

Advertising includes any paid form of non-personal communication through the media which details a product that has an identified sponsor. The media may include travel guides, newspapers, magazines, radio, television, direct mail, web pages and billboards.

Advertising is used to achieve a whole range of objectives which may include changing attitudes or building image, as well as achieving sales. Advertising is often described as 'above-the-line' promotion (due to the commission for the promotional activity being paid by the media company direct to the advertising agency) with all other forms of promotion, such as sales promotion or direct marketing, being termed 'below-the-line'. The difference between above and below the line is simply academic now as the emphasis is on integrating both areas, for example sales promotion and advertising working together to achieve the greatest impact. The approach is also to raise budgets for overall integrated campaigns so that expenditure accounting differences become non-existent. In addition advertising has developed different ways of affecting the consumer. Direct mail is being used to build awareness and TV being used to sell products direct to the consumer, and therefore there is a great deal more flexibility in the use of different promotional media.

COMMUNICATION THEORIES

Communication theorists have proposed several models to explain the way advertising works and each have some similarity. The basic underlying approach is to theorise that the individual will first move to a *knowledge state* or *awareness state* on the basis of information gained through experience and methods of communication. *Attitudes* are then formed and the importance is to move the potential purchaser to a *behavioural action* phase of purchase through desire and *conviction*. One model known as the DAGMAR model (Defining Advertising Goals for Measured Advertising Results) describes the sequence of stages through which the prospective customer has to move:

- unawareness;

- awareness;

- comprehension of the offer;

- conviction;

- action or inaction.

Through advertising, the marketer will make the potential customer aware of the company or destination and its range of offers. As part of the advertising communication process, information has to be clearly transmitted so it can be decoded and comprehended properly. The process is then to make the offer credible so that the potential customer can be moved to a favourable attitude to the product. The act of purchase may then follow.

Advertising has the potential to affect a large number of people simultaneously with a single message. The secondary effect of advertising is personal communications among consumers. This is known as the *two-step flow of communication*. The first step in the process is the communications flow from media to opinion leaders – the individuals whose attitudes, opinions, preferences and actions affect others. The second step is word-of-mouth communications from opinion leaders to others (followers). This communication can occur through personal conversation between friends or with work colleagues based upon communication about the company or product. It can also occur through non-verbal communications when someone displays video or holiday photographs. One implication of the need to achieve as much benefit as possible from the two-step model is the requirement to reach and influence opinion leaders.

Sales promotion

Sales promotion involves any activity that offers an incentive to induce a desired result from potential customers, trade intermediaries or the sales force. Sales promotion campaigns will add value to the product because the incentives will ordinarily not accompany the product. For example, free wine or free accommodation offers are frequently used in sales promotion campaigns for hotel restaurants which need improved demand at certain periods. Most incentives are planned to be short term in nature.

An integral part of sales promotion is the aspect of merchandising. Merchandising includes materials used in travel agents or inhouse locations to stimulate sales. For a hotel, these would include tent cards which may attempt to sell cocktails or deserts, menus, in-room material, posters and displays. Merchandising is important as a means of creating impulse purchase or reminding the consumer of what is on offer.

Sales promotion is often used in combination with other promotional tools in order to supplement the overall effort. However, it has to be remembered that it is sometimes difficult to terminate or change special promotions without causing adverse affects. Airline frequent flyer loyalty programmes are an example of this. Also a sales promotion (or series of promotions) has to take account of the likely effect it may have on the image of the brand or outlet. For example, there may be an unanticipated surge of negative perception which may occur due to association with banal and frivolous promotions.

EVALUATION OF SALES PROMOTION

To evaluate a sales promotion there should be a consideration of:

* the cost of the promotion in employee time, as well as for the cost of any merchandise, giveaway items or promotional literature;

* the increase in sales and profit, or improvement in awareness, based upon the campaign;

* whether the campaign had secondary effects of switching demand from other company products which would have been sold;

* whether there were any additional sales outside of the promotion, due to customers being attracted to the company or tourism product offer.

It is not always easy to isolate the above effects from other marketing factors, but it is always important to make some assessment of the benefit of different types of promotion.

Personal selling

Personal selling is an attempt to gain benefit through face-to-face or telephone contact between the seller's representative and those people with whom the seller wants to communicate. This type of selling may be utilised by a non-profit-making tourist attraction as well as the conference manager of a large hotel.

A number of employees in travel agents or retail related to tourism are often viewed as order *takers* but they could possibly be order *procurers*. The intent of personal selling is:

* to obtain a sale – often customers enter the retail outlet after acquiring information and the salesperson needs to persuade potential customers to purchase;

* to stimulate sales of 'impulse buy' purchases by bringing attention to extra requirements such as travel insurance, car hire, excursions and airport transfers; or

695

- to complete a successful transaction with the customer utilising a range of sales skills.

This will leave the customer satisfied and well informed about the detail of the transaction.

The benefit of personal selling is that a salesperson can adapt the communication of benefits to be gained to the specific needs of the customer. The feedback process of listening to the customer's needs allows the salesperson to be flexible in his or her approach. This is made easier in a selling situation because the personal contact produces heightened awareness and attention by the customer. However, the sales functions of retailers have to be carefully handled because staff who lack empathy will be judged as 'pushy'.

If we take the following example of a travel agency the retail selling process is made up of a number of the steps outlined in Table 18.2: preparing, anticipating a prospective sale, approaching, presenting, dealing with concerns, gaining commitment and establishing relationships. All these are linked into the feedback process of active listening and response.

TABLE 18.2	An approach to selling tourism products in a travel agents
1 Preparing through skills and knowledge (of the travel products available and systems)	Feedback and learning from prior listening and retail agency training
2 Anticipating and identifying a prospective sale based upon interaction with the customer	Having knowledge and an understanding of the needs of customers
3 Method of dealing with the potential customer in order to make a recommendation	Feedback and learning from prior listening plus asking appropriate questions
4 Presenting the features and benefits of the recommendation	Active selling skills and listening in order to check on acceptability of offer
5 Dealing with customer concerns	Active listening in order to revise the argument or recommendation to overcome objections
6 Building obligation and commitment and selling in other products (e.g. insurance)	Active listening in order to ensure the offer is acceptable and the sale can be concluded
7 Establishing affinity and relationship	Reinforcement of the relationship through creating a satisfied customer

Public relations

Public relations (PR) is non-personal communication that changes opinion or achieves coverage in a mass medium and that is not paid for by the source. The coverage could include space given to a press release or favourable editorial comment. PR is important not only in obtaining editorial coverage, but also in suppressing potential bad coverage. An organisation that has good links with the media is more likely to have the opportunity to stop or moderate news that could be damaging to their organisation prior to its release.

The major benefit of PR is that it can provide and enhance an organisation's image. This is very important for service-based organisations which are reliant on a more tangible positive image in order to be successful. PR is a highly credible form of communication as people like to read 'news stories' and will believe them to be less biased than information provided in advertisements. However, editorial decisions over what is communicated will produce control over the message, its timing, placement and coverage.

Table 18.3 details the common activities undertaken as part of PR. The benefits of good PR effort and coverage emanating from this are:

- PR is perceived to be impartial and acts as a neutral endorsement of the company;

- it is credible and believable as it is not identified as a paid form of promotion;

- it helps to build image of a brand and develop favourable opinions by the drip effect of the information provided;

- good PR coverage can generate interest and increased sales;

- it allows for a cost-effective means to promote special offers and sales initiatives; and

- it can possibly limit or neutralise negative or hostile opinions.

PR activity can be either planned or unplanned. Planned activity means the company attempts to retain control over the activity and news release. With unplanned activity, the company simply reacts in the most beneficial way to the chance of some publicity or to suppress a negative news item. Larger organisations will have a public relations agency or inhouse department. These will attempt

699

TABLE 18.3	Activities of public relations
• Media information releases/contact/ speeches	• Advertorials (which require PR copy along with an advertisement)
• Production of PR materials (video, CDs, web information, press kits, corporate identity materials, etc.)	• Inhouse and customer magazines
	• Facility visits to an overseas area (especially for travel writers), etc.
• PR events, media conferences and newsworthy 'stunts'	• Sponsorship and donations
	• Lobbying

to influence the company's 'publics'. The 'publics' are made up of those important to the company – customers, shareholders, employees, suppliers, local community, the media and local and national government. Planned publicity will involve: sending press releases and photographs to the media (trade papers, local and national press, radio and television), organising press conferences for more newsworthy events, sending letters to editors of journals or local newspapers, organising different creative 'stunts' to acquire the right tone of media coverage and making speeches (or writing articles) on informed tourism issues in order to be perceived as a well-informed company.

Other promotional activity

There is a growing use of **sponsorship** and **direct marketing**. These do not comfortably fit into the other four promotion categories. Sponsorship is the material or financial support of a specific activity, normally but not exclusively sport, education or the arts, which does not form part of the sponsor organisation's normal business. Direct marketing is direct communication with pre-selected target groups in order to obtain an immediate response or build closer relationships. Direct marketing is used extensively by direct-sell tour operators/wholesalers such as Saga Holidays and Portland. The main method is direct mail, which is postal communication by an identified sponsor. This is being expanded into database marketing based upon relationship marketing practices.

In addition, because tourism is an intangible product, a great deal of promotion includes the production of printed communications such as brochures or sales leaflets. The design, compilation and printing of tourism brochures is one of the most important of promotion functions. Printed communications are often costly. In fact, the printing and distribution costs of brochures constitute the largest part of most marketing budgets within the tourism industry. This is a necessary expenditure as the brochure or leaflet is the major sales tool for tour operators/wholesalers and tourism organisations.

Characteristics of each promotional technique

Each of the above promotional elements has the capacity to achieve a different promotional objective. While personal selling has high potency for achieving communication objectives, only a relatively small number of people can be contacted. Therefore, advertising is a more effective method of reaching a high number of people at relatively low unit cost. Public relations is more credible than advertising but organisations lack the control they have over advertising messages which may also be repeated on a regular basis. Thus, when it is difficult to raise advertising budgets, public relations is a lower cost alternative, but it is difficult to control the timing and consistency of PR coverage. Sales promotion, such as leaflet drops that offer price discounts, may produce an initial trial for a product, such as the purchase of a leisure break in a hotel, but this type of promotion should only be used over a short-term period. Some promotions are permanent as they are related to known patterns of demand fluctuations and the happy hour promotion (as shown in Photograph 18.2) is widely utilised in resorts to increase sales in early off-peak hours.

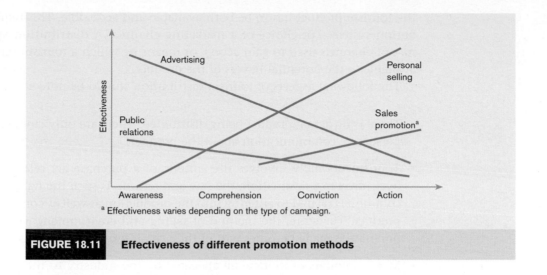

FIGURE 18.11   Effectiveness of different promotion methods

Each element of the promotions mix has its own strengths and weaknesses. While this may include the factors of cost, ability to target different groups and control, there are other important considerations. Figure 18.11 indicates the relative strengths of each of the four forms of promotion. They are compared on the basis of the level of awareness of the communication, its comprehension as well as whether it can build conviction and succeed in creating action.

Integrated marketing communications

It should be obvious that many of the activities of tourism promotion will occur in different areas of the company and with different activities taking place based upon the predilections of the individuals in control. Therefore, while it is obvious that coordination is required it is often not carried out in a systematic way. If it were all elements of marketing communications could work in unison so as to create a whole that is greater than the sum of the parts. To ensure such impact is achieved there is a requirement for an **integrated marketing communications** (IMC) approach throughout the business. Integrated marketing communications is the process a company adopts in order to integrate and coordinate its messages and media to deliver, clear reinforcing communication. However, this will only occur if the various components of the communication effort are coordinated. To achieve this the marketer has to provide policy planning guidelines which direct the efforts in every part of the organisation so that all aspects of communication will offer a reinforcement to each other.

PLACE (DISTRIBUTION)

The special characteristics of the tourism product have led to specific forms of distribution. The tourism product is one where no transfer of ownership takes place and service is simply rented or consumed. However, prior to consumption, the tourism product has to be both available and accessible. This requires a distribution system – or choice of a marketing channel. A **distribution system** is the mix of channels used to gain access, or means by which a tourism service is made available to the potential buyers of the product.

The following aspects of tourism distribution should be noted:

- There is no actual product being distributed. There are only clues given through persuasive communication about the product.

- Tourism normally involves the episode of a purchase act related to decisions over travel to a destination, the stay and return. As such the nature of travel distribution is related to entering into the production as well as consumption of the product. Therefore, the method of selling and environment within which the purchase is made becomes part of the overall tourism experience.

- Major amounts of money are allocated by the industry to the production and printing of literature as well as to its delivery direct to the customer or to the retail travel agent. Brochures and leaflets are produced in high quantity, and often the distribution cost involves an amount for warehousing and the planned despatch of packs of brochures via different modes of transport.

- Distribution of overseas holidays in the UK is dominated by travel agents who sell a homogeneous set of choices. These agents have a vast amount of power and control over the companies that sell the products (principals). Agents decide on the brochures to display on their racks and the companies they will recommend to consumers. However, airline bookings are progressively being switched to Internet-based direct systems (see Chapter Nineteen for more information).

There is continuing development of CRSs (computer reservation systems) or GDSs (global distribution systems). These offer an agent instant access to airline bookings as well as the major hotel groups, car hire and cruise lines. Such systems, utilising the Internet, allow both agents to tailor holidays to suit individual client requirements as well as the consumer to make their own arrangements, and this may lead to increases in direct bookings. The CRSs are led by developments from the principal airlines, with Galileo dominating the UK and being strong in both Europe and the USA, Amadeus being predominately strong in Europe, Sabre dominating in the USA, and, finally, Worldspan, which is a newer and in many ways very innovative company (see below).

The airline industry created the first booking systems in the 1960s in order to keep track of flight schedules, availability and prices. These GDSs were among the first e-commerce systems in the world as they facilitated B2B electronic commerce as early as the mid-1970s, when Sabre (owned by American Airlines) and Apollo (United) were successful in getting travel agencies to install their propriety internal reservations systems. Prior to this, travel agents spent an excessive amount of time manually entering reservations and using systems such as telex or fax to confirm reservations. The airlines realised that by automating the reservation process for travel agents, they could tie them into an extension of the airline's own sales effort. It is these original, legacy GDSs that today provide the backbone to the Internet-based travel distribution system.

There are currently four major GDS systems:

- **Amadeus** – founded in 1987 by Air France, Iberia, Lufthansa and SAS, Amadeus is one of the oldest of the four GDS companies. Its comprehensive data network and database are among the largest of their kind in Europe and serve more than 57,000 travel agency locations and more than 10,500 airline sales offices in some 200 markets worldwide.

- **Galileo** – founded in 1993 by 11 major North American and European airlines: Aer Lingus, Air Canada, Alitalia, Austrian Airlines, British Airways, KLM Royal Dutch Airlines, Olympic Airlines, Swissair, TAP Air Portugal, United Airlines, and US Airways. It is a major player in the GDS business throughout the world.

- **Sabre** – founded in the 1960s by American Airlines, in 1996 Sabre became a separate legal entity of AMR (parent company of American Airlines). It has been involved in a lot of Internet-led development of booking sites (Sabre owns Travelocity.com, which is now the world's leading online travel site) and is considered to be one of the most significant and competitive GDSs due to the fact that it anticipates and takes advantage of the changes in the information economy and develops innovative practices.

- **Worldspan** – founded 1990, Worldspan is currently owned by affiliates of Delta Air Lines, Inc., Northwest Airlines and American Airlines, Inc. Worldspan has successfully developed the strategies, solutions, and services for web-based distribution. Worldspan provides electronic distribution of travel information, Internet products and connectivity and e-commerce capabilities for travel agencies, travel service providers and corporations. Worldspan helped launch the Orbitz site in 2001, which is a US airline alliance-led Internet site set up to counteract the successful trends in disintermediation by companies such as Travelocity, which was taking increasing revenue in commission charges and kept valuable customer data for its own purposes. Prior to this Worldspan agreed to provide the booking engines in 1995 for Microsoft's Expedia.com and in 1998 for Priceline.com. Worldspan currently serves over 20,000 travel agencies around the world.

In addition, there are several minor GDSs, including SITA's Sahara, Infini (Japan), Axess (Japan), Tapas (Korea), Fantasia (South Pacific) and Abacus (Asia/Pacific) that serve smaller regional markets or countries.

The development of electronic distribution systems has strengthened the major players as the cost and adoption implications provide a barrier to entry. The current systems have standardised the channel for bookings to such an extent that small or medium-sized organisations will find it almost impossible to develop agency channel alternatives. This has implications for loss of control for smaller companies and therefore requires safeguards to ensure CRS owners do not manipulate the display or bookings procedure to favour their own brands.

Different tourism distribution needs

There are some forms of tourism such as museums, theme parks or physical attractions where no form of prior booking is required as there is almost always excess supply available and in peak periods queuing is the method of allocation. There are other types of tourism where excess demand and more complex product packaging and financial risk create the need for sophisticated advance booking systems. The booking system enables the organisation to spread demand as the consumer can often be persuaded to arrive or travel at a different time.

In order for a tourism organisation to sell in advance of consumption and to have a record of the reservation, the company has to sell its available capacity through an inventory system. Whether it is a small guest house or large hotel, a farmhouse or cruise ship, some method of allocating capacity and creating reservations, without creating overbooking is important. The timing of these bookings may range from minutes prior to departure for an aircraft or a reserved place on a train service to several years for a major conference. For these reasons, the use of a database booking system (CRS/GDS) is common in tourism. These systems combine the memory capacity of computers (to update and store information constantly) with the communication facility of telecommunications, which rapidly inform travel agents of the current capacity remaining. Such systems can then be programmed to maximise the 'yield' of the capacity as it is sold to the customer.

The next consideration is related to the location of the business. A well-located hotel, theatre or attraction will be able to pick up passing demand. In this case the consumers will find the product easily and there may be less need for a separate distribution channel. This is because the product is easily available for purchase.

In an increasingly competitive world, however, it has been necessary for most organisations to consider different forms of direct distribution. Companies are able to sell direct either from their place of location or through direct marketing methods. Many hotels organise weekend-break programmes to improve the weekend occupancy levels. These weekend packages are often promoted directly in newspapers and are booked directly with the hotel.

Development of travel agency distribution

In the UK there is the opportunity to have access to a wide network of around 7000 travel agency distribution outlets. The need for travel agents first arose in the 1950s due to the rapidly expanding operations of airline/ferry businesses. Transport providers required a means of distribution for their products that was more cost effective than establishing individual networks of booking offices around the country. Their subsequent development was a direct result of the increasing consumer demand for inclusive tours from holidaymakers who were largely uneducated and unsophisticated, and therefore looked to 'experts' to facilitate the process. These agents charge commission on the sales they make and they need to hold a stock of the companies' brochures or sales literature. The travel retail agent sells a product that is both intangible and perishable and this is very different from some of the more traditional types of retail. The bookings made for travel abroad, from the UK, are mostly organised through either high street travel agents for holidays or by specialist business travel agents for business travel. For many, a foreign holiday was an opportunity to emulate grand lifestyles through the services of a travel agent. However, changes in education, economic, social and experiential trends are leading to new ways of purchasing.

The UK has a different pattern of purchase from that of the rest of Europe where most bookings are made direct rather than through agents. In many European countries, twice as many bookings are made direct than in the UK. Figure 18.12

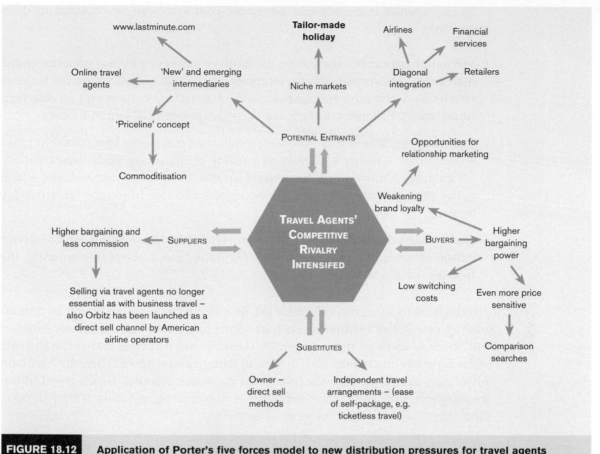

FIGURE 18.12   **Application of Porter's five forces model to new distribution pressures for travel agents**

Source: Adapted with the permission of The Free Press, a Division of Simon & Schuster Adult Publishing Group, from Competitive Strategy: Techniques for Analyzing Industries and Competitors *by Michael E. Porter. Copyright © 1980, 1998 by The Free Press. All rights reserved*

indicates the trends emanating from new distribution pressures which are now taking place in this once traditional retail arena.

The Internet has many implications for all areas of business and every sector of society. Its effect can be seen already in the precarious balance of travel distribution. Disintermediation does not appear to be lessening the travel industry's complicated distribution network, if anything it is adding to it.

Electronic retailing

Electronic retailing to consumers (or B2C) was first developed in the 1980s. The area is advancing at a rapid rate with retail and tourism organisations realising the growing importance of the sale of products through these new distribution channels. Electronic delivery systems do not necessarily require direct human interaction and, as such, they offer specific advantages. In principle, quality can be assured, the costs are lower, there is consumer convenience of access and distribution can be wider than normal retail channels. The key underlying reasons behind electronic retailing are: consumer time poverty, consumers wanting to have more control over time and place of transaction, the technology convergence allowing change to take place and growing experience of the benefits of the medium.

The companies that undertake electronic commerce can be classified in three main ways:

1 **Virtual distributors** – these have no shops or stores or physical presence in the high street, malls or out-of-town locations. They trade exclusively on the Internet or television and have to find new ways of attracting custom and serving consumer needs. Examples of these are Travelocity.com and lastminute.com.

2 **Two-channel distributors** – these are established companies that have developed an electronic retailing capability as a major or minor aspect of their business. For example Thomas Cook has also set up the thomascook.com web site which it has promoted by offering £50 discounted and free insurance for a holiday booking.

3 **Multi-channel distributors** – these are established companies which service customer needs in a number of ways, including shops, telephone ordering, the Internet, catalogues and TV.

Although many observers originally felt that electronic retailing would be dominated by new *virtual* distributors, it now seems likely that the e-commerce market will be made up of all three categories. However, what is clear is that the Internet offers suppliers much more benefit than utilising a travel agent. There are five main advantages associated with the Internet as a revenue channel, which travel industry suppliers, such as hoteliers and airlines, stand to benefit from if they develop more direct sales for their business. They are:

1 **Lower sales costs** – If a hotel were to sell its inventory via an online intermediary such as www.travelweb.com then the information need only be distributed via a switch to translate the data into a 'standard' language. However, selling with a travel agent involves a switch, a CRS and the travel agency commission of perhaps 10% of the total price, resulting in the hotel retaining substantially less revenue.

2 **Expanded market reach and presence** – The Internet does not recognise international borders, so tourism providers can potentially reach a world target audience. The site can be accessed 24 hours a day, which is also less restrictive. For example, an Asian customer in Hong Kong would be able to complete a transaction with an English company at a time that was convenient to them because the eight-hour time difference between the two destinations is immaterial. Also, many potential customers search the web site and then make an offline booking so it is important to have the web presence.

3 **Increased customer loyalty** – The decision by tourist providers to use travel agents to facilitate the sale of their products restricts the level of contact they have with the end customer, meaning that loyalty may be developed with the retailer rather than the actual provider. However, the Internet enables travel industry suppliers to address this and take a more active part in the transaction.

4 **Leverage for other sales channels** – Cost savings from this method of distribution can be used to have multi-channel strategies as lower costs in one channel can subsidise the more expensive channels, such as travel agents.

FIGURE 18.13   **The complexity of IT and tourism product distribution**

5 **Collection of databases** – Any system which is owned by the company has the benefit of collecting data on customers which can be used as part of a future relationship marketing exercise.

Given the above benefits of increased direct sales it is important that travel agents should anticipate further competition from existing businesses diversifying their portfolios to exploit a potentially lucrative market opportunity. Figure 18.13 indicates the changes taking place and the complexity of the distribution of tourism products.

PRICELINE.COM

Priceline.com has positioned itself as offering the cheapest prices on the Internet. Priceline receives requests based upon the 'name-your-own-price' system for airline tickets, rental cars, hotel rooms, long-distance calls and even new cars. Priceline then attempts to match each individual request with a supplier who is willing to fulfil the order at an agreed transaction price. Priceline creates revenue using the spread between the price at which airlines sell discounted tickets and consumers buy them. To achieve this Priceline monitors changing airline pricing and availability on a minute-by-minute basis. Consumers have the benefit of buying at a price which offers them value for money, while sellers may be able to move otherwise unsold capacity or to generate incremental revenue. The advantage of the Priceline e-commerce business model is they have no risk of inventory as they only facilitate transactions once they receive the customer's credit card details.

To date there is some sign that the sales of airline tickets are becoming more direct but not that the British package holidaymaker is buying direct. There is little doubt that for many, the convenience of using an agent to book the holiday is an important element in the buying process. This is because a travel agent may offer greater opportunities for advice on the parallel purchase of insurance, car hire, rail travel to the airport, traveller's cheques, and so on. The travel agent still offers a number of benefits which may have led to the reason more travellers have not booked direct (Gilbert, 1990a). (See the following summary of possible reasons for customers to continue to use travel agents.) However, with Expedia and Travelocity now widely known and accepted, the use of more direct systems of booking are expected to make inroads into traditional forms of distribution.

MINI CASE STUDY 18.1
An assessment of retail travel agents

This case study describes the experience a family may be confronted with when thinking of booking a tour across China and a visit to the Great Wall and the Terracotta Army at Xian. Read the following and keep in mind what you think the family may consider when selecting a method to make the booking.

TRAVEL AGENT BENEFITS

- **Easy accessibility**

  – to a full range and choice of brochures; to product components of visas, traveller's cheques, insurance, etc.;
  – to agent services in every main town and city, as well as to alternative agents, products and brands.

- **Convenience**

  – for obtaining independent information and advice (surfing the web can be very time consuming and may not provide for the best possible purchase; and the Internet often does not allow for further questions to be asked). Agents are more likely to take on an independent consultant's role, which is not offered through direct sell operations;
  – for making the purchase and payment for the holiday (with less perceived risk than would be the case with payment by credit card to an Internet site);
  – for making complaints and being represented by a third party if things go wrong.

- **Habit**

  – People can get into a pattern of behaviour which becomes habit forming. However, a major campaign by direct mail from Internet direct sell tour operators/ wholesalers could change this habit as well as the greater familiarity of use of the Internet for booking air tickets is now established.

- **Security/risk**

  – Consumers feel more secure when dealing with a reputable company or agent (Internet searches involve more personal individual responsibility of the outcome of payment and choice).

- **Environment/atmosphere**

  – Travel agents offer an environment that is part of the holiday experience. The travel agency environment is the perfect setting for personal selling methods which are a powerful means of generating bookings (the Internet is a much more impersonal medium).

- **Economic**

  – Because travel agents compete on price or added value, and tour operators/ wholesalers have the smallest of margins, there is little difference in the price between travel agent's products and those available through direct sell channels.

Source: Adapted from Gilbert, 1990b

Consumers are the ultimate decision makers in the usage of distribution channel, and therefore, it is worth considering the positive and negative aspects of using the Internet (as seen by an end user) over a 'bricks-and-mortar' travel agent. Also, of what benefit would it be for travel agents to develop Internet business? With these stakeholders specifically in mind the following summarises the key strengths and weaknesses associated with the Internet (as identified by the authors), which will then serve as the main basis of discussion. We now need to compare the above to the following tabulation indicating the benefits of the Internet as a sales medium.

The Internet as a sales medium

Travel agents	
Strengths	**Weaknesses**
• Ability to create a global presence • Opportunities exist for relationship marketing • Capital investment required is much less • Opportunity to maximise revenue generating potential • Opportunity to create large databases for direct marketing purposes • Can allow own-brand product to be provided	• Opened up the competitive playing field – 'new' intermediaries are emerging • Increased rivalry among travel intermediaries, which may worsen the competitive positions of some firms • Improves direct sell opportunities among tourist providers • Wider choice may detrimentally affect brand loyalty • The cost of web site design and implementation

Consumers	
Strengths	**Weaknesses**
• Lowers customers' search costs • Greater convenience • An opportunity to forge more effective supplier–customer relationships	• Successful surfing can be time consuming • A certain degree of inflexibility exists – what if consumers have further questions to ask? • Can value really be won? • Security issues given perception of risk • Greater individual responsibility • Impersonality

679

RECENT FIGURES ON BOOKING TRENDS

The latest trends on UK distribution of bookings indicates a growing independence of the purchaser and especially with the trend in purchases by means of the Internet.

Year	1996 %	2000 %	2001 %	2002 %	2003 %
Independent arrangement	21.5	23.8	24.5	21.9	20.2
Travel agent	63.8	57.7	53.3	52.2	49.3
Tour operator	14.7	18.5	18.9	19.3	19.9
Internet	N/A	N/A	3.3	6.6	10.6

Source: CIMtIG, 2004

DISCUSSION QUESTIONS

The preceding information should be considered in conjunction with the other information in this chapter and then you are required to answer:

1 Do travel agents offer enough benefits to be able to survive the changes taking place with regard to alternative channels of distribution?

2 Provide a future scenario of what you expect to happen in travel distribution in the next five, 10 and 20 years and justify your arguments.

3 Create a SWOT analysis of web sites such as Priceline.com and Travelocity.com and then compare and contrast it to the SWOT analysis above for travel agents.

THE MARKETING MIX REVISITED: ARE THE FOUR PS SUFFICIENT?

The adaptation of the marketing mix by authors such as Booms and Bitner (1981) has been based upon arguments that stress the original marketing mix is more appropriate to manufacturing rather than service companies. For example, Booms and Bitner added three extra Ps (see Figure 18.14):

- people;

- physical evidence; and

- process.

Product	Price	Place	Promotion	People	Physical evidence	Process
Range	Level	Location	Advertising	Personnel:	Environment:	Policies
Quality	Discounts:	Accessibility	Personal selling	training	furnishings	Procedures
Level	allowances	Distribution	Sales promotion	discretion	colour	Mechanisation
Brand name	commissions	channels	Publicity	commitment	layout	Employee
Service line	Payment terms	Distribution	Public relations	incentives	noise level	discretion
Warranty	Customer's	coverage		appearance	Facilitating	Customer
After-sales	perceived			interpersonal	goods	involvement
service	value			behaviour	Tangible clues	Customer
	Quality/price			attitudes		direction
	Differentiation			Other customers:		Flow of activities
				behaviour		
				degree of		
				involvement		
				customer/		
				customer		
				contact		

FIGURE 18.14   **The marketing mix for services**

Source: Reprinted by permission of the American Marketing Association from Booms and Bitner, 1981

Authors such as Booms and Bitner argue the marketing mix of four Ps is not comprehensive enough for the tourism and hospitality industry. The major difference is said to be the intangible element of human behaviour where quality and its control is of paramount importance.

We believe that there is a need for more research into the industry and its marketing before the four Ps require revision. For the present it is believed the four Ps offer an adequate framework into which the differences can be incorporated. The main task of marketers in tourism and hospitality is to understand the characteristics of the products they plan, control and manage. This will ensure that managers will attempt to control the aspects of the marketing mix which have most bearing on the satisfaction level of consumers. We provided the basis of this assessment in Chapters Sixteen and Seventeen on marketing management.

While it is obvious that there are differences between manufactured and service products, the framework of the four Ps is sufficient for planning purposes as physical evidence, people or process are part of the category of product or its implementation. The four categories do not presuppose the relegation of service product considerations to secondary importance. On the contrary, the four categories should ensure that within product formulation, greater focus will be placed on the integration of all the different service management considerations.

It should be apparent that marketing mix decisions must be geared to achieving the objectives of the company or organisation, and should be linked to acceptability throughout the organisation. While marketing departments often lead in setting the marketing mix strategy, they should not ignore input from others and should be sensitive to views on whether the strategy will be workable from an operational standpoint.

The marketing mix offers the range and spread of alternative strategies by which a marketer can influence demand. However, while the available range is very similar for all tourism marketers, the choice is not. For example, an NTO will not normally be involved in developing products or setting prices. The process of mix formulation and balancing is quite often unique to each organisation.

For an organisation to be successful with its marketing mix, it has to develop a differential advantage which will distinguish the organisation's product offering(s) from that of the competition. Only when an organisation has built an advantage will it find that customers seek it out, in which case it is easier to create higher profits. The advantage may be based upon quality, image, or product concept. Center Parcs in the UK has developed an advantage (through all-weather facilities, forest-like settings and many different activities) and the results can be seen in the high year-round demand for its product.

DESTINATION MARKETING

Destinations rely on tourism as a major tool in the creation of economic development and support for the indigenous population. Destinations can be local, regional or even national: we can speak of America, California or San Francisco with each, and all, capable of being a destination.

The understanding of destination image is important for any destination marketing plan. Destination image has two closely interrelated components: (1) the perceptive/cognitive evaluations, which refer to the individual's own knowledge and beliefs about the destination and (2) affective appraisals, which refer to the individual's feelings towards the destination. The two components together form a compound image from which an individual will draw upon to describe a destination to others; or in order to decide upon a visit. More specifically from a cognitive point of view, the tourist destination image comprises a set of attributes that match to the physical, social and built resources that a tourist destination has at its disposal. A destination offers a number of elements which allow individuals a choice of activities, and which culminate in experiences to remember on return.

Tourists form an image of a tourist destination after undergoing a process which, according to Gunn (1988) involves the following stages: (1) accumulating mental images of the destination, thus forming an organic image; (2) modifying the initial image after more information, thus forming an induced image; (3) deciding to visit the destination; (4) visiting the destination; (5) sharing the destination; (6) returning home; and (7) modifying the image on the experience in the destination. This led Gunn to distinguish between the two types of image – *organic* and *induced*. The organic image is based on non-commercial sources of information, such as news about the destination in the mass media, education at school, information received and opinions of friends and relatives. The induced image is based on commercial sources of information, such as different forms of advertising and information from travel agents and tour operators.

The marketing of destinations is complex as we are dealing not only with the tangible inventory of physical attributes such as the natural geography, built environment and attractions, accommodation and transport facilities but also intangible social and cultural factors. Although the destination is often the focus for all the marketing effort, it does not follow that there will be a local, regional or national agency that will take responsibility for its marketing. It is also often the case that where there is an organisation charged with destination marketing, its responsibility is based upon a fairly narrow set of powers and limited resources. Traditionally the public sector has been involved in destination marketing through NTOs, regional boards such as DMOs or local authorities, but increasingly, a trend is emerging where marketing agencies or conference and visitor bureau are established for cities. Such agencies are often funded by a mix of both private and public means.

The marketing of destinations

The marketing of destinations is a relatively new departure for many localities, particularly at the regional and local level. At these levels the lead agency tends to be the public sector and this in turn, has a number of implications for the marketing process which are rooted in the inability of the public sector to control the product. In addition, there is an issue here in terms of whether we should transform places where people live work and play into *products*. We are only beginning to understand how to translate generic marketing approaches to destinations. There are some key areas to consider here:

- The images of the destination which the marketing campaigns wish to communicate should take into account the views and sensitivities of local people.

- Public sector agencies have to be even handed in their support for businesses at the destination – it is difficult politically for them to back winners.

- The public sector controls neither the business plans of private sector companies at the destination nor the quality of service delivery.

- Tourist destinations often lack several key strategic business units and their limited resource base means that they are unable to redress this balance in their portfolio.

- Public sector marketing organisations seldom *close* a sale, rather they are instrumental in attracting the consumer to the point of sale – usually a private sector company. It is therefore difficult to evaluate the effectiveness of destination marketing.

- Finally, the critical issue of resources is a constant problem for public sector marketing budgets, especially for activities which may be perceived as dispensable – such as market research – but which in reality are crucial to success in the tourism marketplace.

The traditional role of many of these approaches has been elementary. The emphasis has been confined to promotional strategies which aim to improve the destination image or to produce more positive 'mental concepts' in relation to both potential as well as actual tourists. This is often related to the selection of desirable market segments that are targeted through the use of advertising, direct mail, print or PR campaigns (as discussed earlier in this chapter). There is further emphasis on providing information at the destination through information posters or tourist information centres.

Destinations need to identify those product attributes that will appeal to different tourist segments and then to ensure that the promotional campaign delivers a cohesive message. There is also the need to produce a distinctive identity or 'brand' which forms the basis of the 'positioning' of a destination area, providing it with a personality and differentiating it from competitors.

De Chernatony and McDonald (1992) describe the necessary attributes of a successful brand and these may also be applied to tourism destinations:

A successful brand is an identifiable product, service, person or place augmented in such a way that the buyer, or user, perceives relevant, unique added values which match their needs most closely. Its success results from being able to sustain these added values against competitors.

Such results may be achieved through the theming of an area by linking it to a famous personality who may have lived in the area, such as a painter (Constable country such as Dedham Vale, valley of the Stour river and East Bergholt), a writer or poet (Hemingway and Cuba or Wordsworth associated with the Peak District and Grasmere), a TV series or film, a historical era (Pompeii) or seasonal beauty (New England in the autumn). There are many other themes, of course, but all need to be developed with a creative flair for the tastes of the potential visitor as well as the acceptability of the theme to the media.

The involvement of tourist boards at the national and regional level is often one of facilitation. Facilitation is made up of a series of assistance schemes which support the constituent service sectors of the tourist industry forming the accommodation, transport and attraction provision of a country, region or locality. This may take the form of a set of objectives related to:

- the development of specific tourism areas or products;

- the targeting of specific segments from generating areas;

- the level of expenditure available;

- a range of promotional activities (PR, advertising, exhibitions, literature production); or

- the need for cooperative private initiatives or expenditure.

The industry is diverse and fragmented, comprising many small companies which require help in many areas such as:

- the collection and use of research data;

- the organisation of trade exhibitions and shows;

- representation through overseas offices;

- the production of trade manuals, catalogues and brochures (which can have space bought by smaller companies);

- the development of global reservation systems which can provide local information on a global basis; and

- research.

The facilitation process can help create an overall brand image of a destination through the total activity which takes place. However, the marketing, through all forms of promotion, will create a specific brand image. This is beneficial if a strong brand image is created.

An area that has a strong brand image is able:

- to achieve better margins and higher prices than commodity-positioned brands;

- to differentiate itself more easily from competitors;

- to provide a sense of added value and so more easily entice customers to purchase;

- to act as a sign and enticement to the potential traveller; which implies fulfilment of expectations;

- to build repeat visits and loyalty; and

- to improve the strength of its position as a status area rather than as a commodity.

MINI CASE STUDY 18.2
Tourism: culture tool to lift the neglect

The transformation of neglected, often run-down areas into vibrant new tourist attractions is one of the most powerful tools of urban regeneration available to environmental planners. The decay of areas blessed with solid, industrial buildings has led to a rapid increase in such projects. The trend began in the USA with developments such as Chicago's Waterfront district and has spread to Europe, most notably with the Guggenheim Museum in Bilbao and the ongoing redevelopment of London's Bankside area, home to the Tate Modern museum of art.

There are pitfalls involved in any attempt at regeneration. But the revitalisation of such areas can create new jobs and provide badly needed stimuli to ailing local economies if successful. The creation of cultural centres in run-down areas can often provide the first spark of regeneration, attracting new retail spaces and residential developments. In Newcastle and Gateshead, cities in the north-east of England which have launched a joint bid to be European Capital of Culture in 2008, the redevelopment of the Baltic flour mill on the bank of the River Tyne, has been followed by the opening of new hotels, shops and cafés.

The Baltic Gallery was built in an existing industrial building space and, like the Tate Modern, has an appeal which extends beyond art lovers because of its ingenious use of space. However, for successful regeneration projects, a wide-ranging strategy is needed. 'It has to be about more than the building,' says Andrew Hume, national director of Jones Lang La Salle, the real estate advisory group. 'An environment has to be created around the attraction, while planners would have to ensure there are spin-offs which also attract visitors and extend the time they spend there.' In Newcastle–Gateshead, the Baltic Gallery was accompanied by the opening of the Millennium Bridge, which allows pedestrians to cross the Tyne. Hotel developments have sprung up, new residential accommodation is being built and a state-of-the-art music centre will open shortly.

The two cities have already recorded an increase in the number of tourists visiting the region and expect many more if they succeed in their bid to be European Capital of Culture. More than £3 bn has been spent on transport, leisure, housing and commercial development during the past decade. £350 mn of this was spent on permanent cultural infrastructure and £100 mn on an events programme spanning five years from 2003. If the bid succeeds, the Newcastle and Gateshead local authorities are predicting an additional £1.2 bn will be spent in the region, creating 24,000 new jobs. 'What we are building is a creative city, so we can attract the artists, academics, entrepreneurs and innovators,' says Sir Ian Wrigglesworth, chairman of the Newcastle–Gateshead initiative.

In Liverpool, another favourite to win the European Capital of Culture contest, work has started on a £750 mn redevelopment of the city centre and a £225 mn tram system. The city is also proposing a £70 mn programme to redesign public squares and open spaces. The creation of new cultural centres with the aim of attracting tourists and boosting flagging local economies does not always work. The Armouries Museum in Leeds failed to bring in as many tourists as hoped, knocking regeneration plans. Similarly, the National Centre for Popular Music in Sheffield received £11.4 million of Lottery money but failed to attract sufficient numbers of visitors and folded. 'Extension of these cultural attractions to make these areas destinations for tourists takes time,' says Mr Hume. 'Events have to be put on which appeal to a broader range of people.'

Source: Matthew Garrahan, FT.com site, 27 May 2003
Note: Liverpool has subsequently been awarded City of Culture status.

DISCUSSION QUESTIONS

1 If an area is redeveloped, what segments do you think should be considered in the redevelopment programme and are these currently being considered?

2 What marketing planning would you use in conjunction with the relaunch of a redeveloped area? Explain the approach to the plan and provide a major section on the promotional strategy you would utilise.

3 Provide reasons as to why some of the initiatives related to redevelopment fail.

A destination has an image of place associated with it. This can be based upon differences related to what is normal in both a tourist-generating area and in the culture of the destination. The differences may be real or imagined. Promotion of a destination is based on an image selected by the tourism marketer and communicated to the generating markets, often providing stereotypical images of an exotic, carefree host culture. In reality this may mask a whole set of socio-cultural realities of what life is like for the average inhabitant of a destination.

The power to portray selective images of place relies on factors such as whether a tourist is a first-time visitor or a repeat visitor and also on the amount of information the tourist has gleaned from television, films, books or friends. A destination, once branded and having communicated a distinctive image, is in a far stronger position to influence demand if problems arise of price increases, excess demand and crowding or unfavourable currency exchange rates.

The Spanish Tourist Board, faced with the loss of a strong Spanish image for its resort areas, embarked upon an exercise to reposition and re-brand the country. The history, culture, traditions and inland areas had been under-promoted and weakly communicated. The campaign from 1992 emphasised the 'Spanishness' of the country within a campaign which stressed, 'Spain – Passion for life'. The painter, Miro, was commissioned to create a logo that would reflect the fundamental spirit of Spain. He created a vibrant logo reflecting the national flag colours of yellow and red and this was used on all communication messages.

Consumers' concept of 'self-image'

When consumers choose among brands, they rationally consider practical issues about the relative functional capabilities of all the brands on offer. At the same time, they evaluate different brand personalities, forming a view about the brand that most closely represents the image with which they wish to be associated.

Applying this to tourism, it is possible to suggest that when competing destinations are perceived as being equal and similar in terms of their physical capabilities, the brand that comes closest to enhancing the consumer's self-concept is more likely to be chosen. Consumers look to brands not only for what they can do, but also for the message they communicate about the purchaser to peer groups. Trips to Monte Carlo, for example, are chosen not just for their functional excellence, but also because they make an important statement about the traveller.

According to de Chernatony and McDonald (1992), the symbolic nature of brands increases the attraction for consumers as they:

- help set social scenes and enable people to mix with each other more easily;

- enable consumers to convey messages about themselves;

- provide a basis for better understanding of the way people act; and

- help consumers say something to themselves.

In effect, consumers are transmitting subtle messages to others by purchasing and displaying the use of particular brands in the hope that their reference groups decode the messages in a positive and acceptable way. Consumers hold what is called their own 'self-image' and buy brands that conform to that image. Consumers, therefore, could be said to admit brands and their 'personalities' into their social circle, in much the same way as consumers enjoy having like-minded people around them. When friends or colleagues admire a holiday destination choice, the traveller feels pleased that the destination brand reinforces his or her self-image and may therefore repeat the purchase.

The economic and social situation in which consumers find themselves will dictate, to some extent, the type of image they wish to project. Through anticipating and subsequently evaluating the people that they will meet at a particular event or destination, consumers then seek brands to reflect the situational self-image that they wish to display.

CONCLUSION

The marketing mix cannot be effective without a full understanding of the target market and the needs of each of the segments. The marketing mix is formulated and implemented to satisfy the target market. We take the marketing mix to be made up of the four Ps of product, price, promotion and place (distribution), but there are alternative approaches where authors argue for an expansion owing to the service characteristics of tourism and hospitality products. However, the additional ingredients can be included in the existing headings associated with the four Ps and, as long as the characteristics of the tourism and hospitality product are emphasised, there is little benefit in pre-dating McCarthy's late 1970s' simplification of approach.

Self-check questions

1 Name and describe the different product levels that may exist for a leading hotel.

2 Describe the benefits that a strong tourism brand may provide for the company.

3 Provide a list and understanding of at least five of the aspects which are related to price sensitivity.

4 Describe four ways of deciding upon the amount of money required when raising a promotion budget.

5 What are the five advantages related to use of the Internet as a channel?

Essay questions

1 Identify the elements of the marketing mix and explain how they may be used by each of the following organisations: easyJet, American Airlines, the Savoy Hotel and Travel Inn.

2 Consider the role and importance of the target market for a cruise ship and its implications for the manipulation of the various elements of the marketing mix.

3 For each of the following choose and *justify* a brand name, product formulation, product positioning and target segments: new health and beauty clinic for men, a company offering specialist adventure holidays. Also, discuss briefly what other marketing mix aspects you would adopt.

4 Visit the priceline.com web site and/or alternate travel-related web sites and discuss the trends and other impacts of the Internet on pricing policy for the tourism product.

5 Provide a list, and its justification, of the ways an exclusive hotel product could be augmented to differentiate it from its competitors (even if this increases costs to high levels).

Annotated further reading

Books

Kotler, P., Bowen J. and Makens, J. (2002) *Marketing for Hospitality and Tourism*, 3rd edn, Pearson, Upper Saddle River, NJ.
The book draws upon the marketing material of Philip Kotler's other books and as such is based upon his pedigree which has been developed over a number of years of writing marketing textbooks. However, the examples are often not very good and other specialist books need to be read in conjunction with this one. This latest edition now covers electronic marketing, has case studies and lets students understand the role of marketing in hospitality and tourism. Specialist areas covered are customer quality management and destination marketing.

Middleton, V. and Clarke. J. (2001) *Marketing in Travel and Tourism*, 3rd edn, Butterworth Heinemann, Oxford.
Marketing in Travel and Tourism explains the basic principles and practice of marketing in the contemporary setting of the new pressures affecting tourism including areas not normally included in such texts such as NTOs. In addition, international case studies are included.

Morgan, N. and Pritchard, A. (1998) *Tourism Promotion and Power: Creating Images, Creating Identities*, John Wiley & Sons, Chichester.
The book is underpinned by marketing theory and does not simply deal with the more general concepts related to tourism promotion. The book offers a different approach by taking a sociological and cultural approach to tourism marketing. It focuses on contentious issues of tourism imagery by discussing issues such as gender, sexuality and race as key determinants of tourism power dimensions. The book is underpinned by good case studies which are thought provoking.

References cited and bibliography

Aaker, D.A. (1991) *Managing Brand Equity: Capitalizing on the Value of a Brand Name*, Free Press, New York.

Aaker, D.A. and Biel, A.L. (1993) *Brand Equity and Advertising*, Lawrence Erlbaum Associates, Mahwah, NJ.

Bierman, D. (2003) *Restoring Tourism Destinations in Crisis: A Strategic Marketing Approach*, CABI, Cambridge, MA.

Booms, B.H. and Bitner, M.J. (1981) 'Marketing strategies and organization structures for service firms', pp. 47–51 in Donnelly, J. and George, W.R. (eds), *Marketing of Services*, American Marketing Association, Chicago, IL.

Borden, N.H. (1965) 'The concept of the marketing mix', pp. 386–97 in Schwartz, G., *Science in Marketing*, Wiley, Chichester.

CIMtIG (2004) D. Blastland (managing director, First Choice Holidays) 'Can tour operators and travel agents survive', January.

de Chernatony, L. and Daniels, K. (1994) 'Developing a more effective brand positioning', *Journal of Brand Management* 1(6), 373–9.

de Chernatony, L. and McDonald, M.H.B. (1992) *Creating Powerful Brands*, Butterworth Heinemann, Oxford.

de Chernatony, L. and McWilliam, G. (1989) 'The varying nature of brands as assets', *International Journal of Advertising* **8**, 339–49.

Gilbert, D.C. (1990a) 'European product purchase methods and systems', *The Service Industries Journal* **10**(4), 664–79.

Gilbert, D.C. (1990b) Strategic marketing planning for national tourism, *Tourism Analysis* **1**(90), 18–27.

Gunn, C. (1988) *Vacationscape: Designing Tourist Regions*, 2nd edn, Van Nostrand Reinhold, New York.

Hankinson, G. and Cowking, P. (1993) *Branding in Action: Cases and Strategies for Profitable Brand Management*, McGraw-Hill, London.

Kotler, P. and Armstrong, G. (1996) *Principles of Marketing*, Prentice Hall, Englewood Cliffs, NJ.

McArdle, J. (1989) 'Product branding – the way forward', *Tourism Management* **10**, 201.

McCarthy, E.J. (1978) *Basic Marketing: A Managerial Approach*, 6th edn, Irwin, Homewood, IL.

Zeithaml, V.A. (1988) 'Consumer perceptions of price, quality, and value: a means–end model and synthesis of evidence', *Journal of Marketing* 52, July, 2–22.

MAJOR CASE STUDY 18.1
NISBET PLANTATION HOTEL AND RELATIONSHIP MARKETING

Nisbet Plantation Hotel in Nevis has won accolades for employing *Integrated 1-to-1 Marketing*. The hotel's approach was based upon three objectives:

1 Build strong, personal relationships with affluent customers, prospects and the travel agents serving them. Nisbet wanted to exploit the fact that the most effective marketing in leisure travel continues to be 'recommendations from friends and relatives'.

2 Maximise productive use of the Internet – expand Nisbet's customer database to include email addresses and an expansion of data related to those prospects similar to current customers; develop an effective, instantaneous and cost-effective dialogue with its best customers and prospects.

3 Increase both immediate and long-term sales.

To meet Nisbet's objectives the resort has employed the following five key strategies (the major improvement to achieve these was based upon Nisbet's integrated database system):

1 Build a new web site capable of supporting an *Integrated 1-to-1 Marketing* program – add new features to maximise the visitor experience and encourage multiple repeat visits; build a data-capture mechanism for site visitors including name, address, email and travel preferences for future digital re-marketing efforts; add an online booking engine.

2 Develop company-wide systems to capture names and addresses at *all* points of contact (i.e. at guest registration, email communications, non-customers visiting for lunch or dinner, visitors to resort's boutique, etc.).

3 Focus *all* communications on delivering a strong brand message *and* directing individuals to the web site for data capture and follow-up relationship building.

4 Develop a permission-based email-marketing newsletter. Reduce the use of paper communications.

5 Develop ways to maximise the effectiveness of a highly constrained budget.

BUILD A NEW WEB SITE CAPABLE OF SUPPORTING AN INTEGRATED 1-TO-1 MARKETING PROGRAM

Nisbet's previous web site consisted of only five pages categorised as typical first-generation web brochure-ware. Immediate action included the development of a new site (http://www.thereefs.com/nisbet/) with significantly more content. Content throughout the site has been tailored to help ease visitors through the purchase process and to emphasise the resorts' positioning as an *Unhurried, Unspoiled and Uncommon* vacation.

Online sweepstakes

To encourage visitors to enter personal information into the database a sweepstake was developed. A banner promoting the sweepstakes is prominently displayed throughout the site.

To further encourage sweepstakes sign-up (data capture), the resort's privacy policy is prominently displayed on the contest entry form, assuring registrants personal information will be held in the strictest confidence. A contest winners' page was added to the site after the first sweepstakes winners were announced.

Online booking engine

To facilitate the booking process for online consumers, Nisbet Plantation employed the ASP services of WorldRes.com.

Photo contest

A photo contest was developed to serve three primary purposes:

- Generate more content for visitors.

- Get past visitors emotionally involved with the site and enhance the relationship.

- Have contest winners send friends and relatives to the site to see the photos and learn more about Nisbet and sign up for the sweepstakes (build the database).

Search engine marketing

Aware of the need for the web site to rank well in search engines, keywords and phrases were identified by examining server logs, customer comment cards, reservations staff and communications with customers. Emphasis was put on phrases *customers* used rather than words the hotel or marketing team would use to describe the resort. A plan was adopted for search engine marketing in order to achieve search engine optimisation; the linking of campaigns and to have paid placement.

STRATEGY TO DEVELOP SYSTEMS TO CAPTURE NAMES AND ADDRESSES AT ALL POINTS OF CONTACT

Consistent, high-quality brand messages are aligned to every form of communication, which wherever possible continue to direct individuals to the web site encouraging them to sign up for the sweepstakes and provide permission to receive more information from the resort. This strategy had its most significant impact on three areas:

1 Advertising.

2 Public relations.

3 Resort operations – training for effective email service/response.

Advertising

Several months before the new web site was operational an integrated marketing communications program designed to drive traffic to the site was developed. The communications included high-frequency schedules of small spaced advertising in a very few publications.

TARGETED NICHE MARKETING

Targeted niche marketing is concentrated in two areas: weddings and honeymoons and Sunday travel sections of major newspapers.

Sunday travel sections

Sunday travel sections of major metropolitan newspapers serve as the backbone of Nisbet's newspaper advertising. While size restrictions preclude the resort from promoting the sweepstakes, its web address is always featured prominently – continuing to address the primary marketing objective of driving traffic to the web site. Nisbet's headline includes the destination and web address while most other resorts feature the destination and the resort's name.

Public relations

Both the timing and message of public relations activity was coordinated with the advertising and promotional schedules to help maximise impact in the marketplace. Every press release included a mention of the resort's sweepstakes along with directions on where to go to sign-up.

Resort operations – training

It was not long before the volume of email messages received by Nisbet began to increase dramatically – more than tripling daily volumes. Responding to inquiries and comments in the past was part of the daily routine. However, the increased volume began creating staffing problems and causing response time and quality issues. As a result, training sessions and a manual were developed and instituted. The staff at Nisbet Plantation has an excellent reputation for taking special care of its customers. What was needed was to take the same customer care that transpires naturally face-to-face and translate it to a computer-to-computer interaction. Exercises in visualising the individual at the other end were undertaken – trying to decipher based on their email who they are, what their major concerns are, and what information they would need to make Nisbet the resort of choice. Responses were regularly reviewed by management through a web interface and later used in exercises to analyse and improve responses to:

- build more dialogue and a deeper relationship with the individual (almost like having a pen pal);

- induce individuals to select Nisbet and/or recommend the resort to a friend or relative.

In addition to being used to improve email responses, the monitoring systems allowed the marketing department to view consumer requests/issues and adjust the web site and provide greater clarity.

Email messages could be separated into two main categories:

- requests for information; and

- comments.

'Requests for information' were designated as the highest priority and receive a complete and proper response within a few hours of receipt. Nisbet receives numerous 'comments' from individuals that are not really requests for information. The resort now looks upon all correspondence as an opportunity to create a dialogue and build a relationship.

Rather than sending out two paper newsletters each year as it had in the past the resort was now sending out 12 email newsletters. Nisbet's email database (including customers, prospects and travel agents) is now seven times larger that the resort's customer database. Nisbet can deliver email messages personalised to the reader: messages to customers are written recognising them as customers – travel agents as travel agents, etc. Tracking and follow-up – through the email program, the resort monitors individual click-through activity on specific promotions. This allows for follow-up targeted marketing activities, i.e. people who click on Nisbet's honeymoon package receive a package in the mail with a brochure and a personal invitation from the resort's general manager to honeymoon at Nisbet.

Direct mail

One of the most effective and efficient vehicles has been direct mail promotional postcard mailings. To ensure Nisbet stays in contact with *all* past guests the resort uses a series of postcard mailings. This allows Nisbet to increase the frequency of contact with past guests and to invite them back. In addition to providing a strong promotional message, the postcards also encourage recipients to go to the web site and register for the sweepstakes.

RESULTS

This case study provides an overview of a few of the many different initiatives Nisbet took in order to develop its integrated relationship marketing program.

The following highlight the effectiveness of the program:

1 Occupancy – on a monthly basis, Nisbet consistently has either the highest or second highest occupancy of any resort in St Kitts and Nevis; well above average occupancy rates for all other island resorts and this occurs without discounting rates.

2 Relationship building – Nisbet's marketing program has generated a threefold increase in email communication between the resort and consumers and travel agents.

3 Database size – Nisbet has built a permission-based email database of customers, prospects and travel agents that is seven times larger than the total number of guests the resort has entertained over the past five years.

4 eNewsletter response – Nisbet's eNewsletter is a complete success with highly satisfactory (20%–40%) click-through rates and traffic driven to the web.

5 Online bookings – the online booking engine is now the number two producer for the resort.

6 Instantaneous dialogue capability – which can announce seat sales or other important news.

Source: http://www.thereefs.com/nisbet/

DISCUSSION QUESTIONS

1 Identify the main reasons for the success of the changes made by Nisbet Plantation hotel.

2 Create a model of the ways Nisbet have developed relationship marketing and compare this to the literature to find out if they have met or exceeded current theories.

3 Take a hotel that you know of and provide a plan of the project management implementation that would be required to develop its relationship marketing approaches.

PART FIVE
DEVELOPMENTS IN TOURISM

CHAPTER NINETEEN
INFORMATION TECHNOLOGY IN TOURISM   702

CHAPTER TWENTY
THE FUTURE OF TOURISM: TRENDS AND
ISSUES BEYOND OUR CONTROL   738

CHAPTER TWENTY-ONE
THE FUTURE OF TOURISM: TRENDS AND
ISSUES WITHIN OUR CONTROL   764

INTRODUCTION

This part provides you with a comprehensive coverage of tourism futures. It aims to provide you with five key knowledge areas:

1 A disciplined approach to analysing and viewing the future of the tourism system.

2 An understanding of the pace and scale of change in the world that impacts upon tourism.

3 An awareness of the importance of the linkage between products and markets in viewing future tourism scenarios.

4 An understanding of the key information and communications technologies (ICTs) available and their role in tourism.

5 A comprehension of the impact of the Internet and the tools of ICT on the structure and operation of the tourism system.

Part Five of this book has been organised to cover the three key areas that make up a consideration of tourism futures. In Chapter Nineteen we focus on technology; Chapter Twenty examines the changing world outside the influence of the tourism sector; and the final chapter analyses the impact of this changing world upon tourism futures. We have devoted a full section of this book to the analysis of tourism futures because we believe that an understanding of future trends will allow the tourism sector to manage the future more effectively, and be prepared for the pace of change which is now the rule, not the exception.

We have been careful not to 'over-hype' this part with breathless accounts of flying cars and a world where robots replace hotel workers. Instead, we have provided a disciplined approach to examining the future of tourism – this approach is in two parts:

1 First, we provide a systematic analysis of the driving forces of change in the world. These include not only the recent upsurge in terrorism and concerns for the safety of travellers, but also demographic, social, political and technological influences.

2 Chapter Twenty-one then sets out a framework, based upon Leiper's tourism system, which links markets and products and so allows us to create future tourism scenarios.

Of course, throughout the chapters it must be remembered that, while we isolate these drivers of change for explanatory purposes, in reality they are closely linked, combining to create a world where 'rapid and unexpected change' impacts upon tourism. For example, a clear demographic trend is the influence of the baby boomer generation in Europe and North America. But we must be careful to recognise that it is this generation that has become the 'new tourist'; it is from this generation that opinion leaders have emerged to champion the causes of sustainability and ethical consumption of tourism; and it is from this generation that the leaders of the new political world order are found. So, the trends are intricately linked and interwoven, a fact that can be usefully drawn out in the classroom through the use of case studies.

The first chapter in this part focuses on the role of technology in shaping the future of tourism. There is no doubt that technology has created a 'paradigm shift' across the tourism sector, impacting upon both the way that tourism is organised and operated and upon how consumers behave. We show how technology has become an essential tool of competitiveness of enterprises and destinations and demonstrate the competitive strategies that larger enterprises have adopted. This means that smaller enterprises are sometimes threatened and placed at a disadvantage by the growth of technology: but there is a paradox here as the Internet has allowed both small enterprises and small destinations to have an equally large Internet presence as multinational corporations. Consumers have adopted the new technology of global distribution systems and the Internet with enthusiasm as it allows them to create their own products and provides an array of information that was not previously available. At the leading edge of these developments we show how Internet portals are now embracing lifestyle segmentation to assist their customers to create the right tourism product to complement their lifestyles. The key to this approach is understanding the way that tourism distribution channels have evolved and the changing role of intermediaries, as we discussed in Chapter Twelve.

Despite the fact that tourism operations and markets are dominated by technology, it is only one driver of change in tourism (albeit an important one). In Chapters Twenty and Twenty-one we provide a systematic review of the other drivers of change in the world; change, which is not in the control of the tourism sector and yet has major implications for how tourism will develop in the future. We then go on to assess the response of tourism to these drivers. The key to this section is to take a long-term view of the future – for too long tourism has been concerned only with the short term. We know for example from forecasts, that volumes of international tourism will exceed one billion international tourist arrivals by 2010 and one-and-a-half billion by 2020. These are huge numbers and they will be accompanied by a change in the nature of the tourism market as other emerge countries to dominate the world's travellers (such as China). This begs the question as to whether the tourism sector is prepared for these Chinese travellers; are the hotel rooms designed with the principles of feng shui for example? Changes in the market will be also driven by demographic and social change in other generating markets. Not only will this be due to the ageing of some markets, but also new generations of consumers are emerging who are knowledgeable about technology and marketing and who will be experienced and empowered consumers of travel. To meet these challenges the tourism sector will recognise the importance of the 'new tourist' and develop new approaches to segmentation and research to understand and relate to them. Indeed as we show in this part, it can be argued that we are moving away from a 'services' economy to an 'experience' economy where 'tourism experiences', whether natural or artificially generated, will be sought.

These driving forces are all linked to the 'generating region' of Leiper's tourism system. Factors in the 'destination region' are equally significant and include political and sustainability issues. Destinations are set within political administrations and systems, which are themselves changing with the rise of economic trading blocs, such as the EU, the strengthening of city states where tourism plays a major 'promotional' role and, of course, the pervasive influence of globalisation where both the private and the public sector are affected. It is these very political developments that have led to one of the most significant trends to arise since the last edition of this book: that of terrorism. Since the attacks on the USA of September 11, 2001, tourism has had to learn to live with terrorism. The cost has been increased safety and security for all travellers and the development of risk management and crisis management planning for the sector. It is also since the last edition of this book that we have become increasingly aware of one factor that sits outside the tourism system and yet is proving to be very significant – that of climate change. Global warming in particular is having an impact upon consumer behaviour as beach resorts are shunned for fear of cancer and cataracts and on the destinations themselves as coral reefs are damaged and low-lying islands put at risk (the Maldives, for example). In order to respond to these challenges, destinations and the tourism sector are using concepts of sustainability as their organising framework. Notions of sustainability are evolving and now include community as well as environment. Here, destinations are involving their host communities in future planning as well as recognising the importance of being prepared for the demands of the new tourist through good visitor management and interpretation to satisfy the innate curiosity about these markets.

We conclude Part Five by looking at the shape of tourism products in the future in response to the combined demand- and supply-side trends identified above. Clearly, many tourism products of today will be around in the future, but there are emergent products – such as special interest tourism – which are catering for the increasingly fragmented market segments demanding niche products that range from gastronomic to 'dark' tourism. But for the more distant future it is technology that will take centre stage in delivering the tourist 'experience'. There is no doubt that space tourism will become a reality for increasing numbers of tourists and earthbound tourism may well become the preserve of virtual reality for a market 'cocooned' in their homes and safe from an increasingly dangerous world outside.

CHAPTER NINETEEN
INFORMATION TECHNOLOGY IN TOURISM

Inevitably, the tourism industry has been dramatically affected by **information communication technologies** (ICTs) and eBusiness developments leading to a wide range of opportunities and threats to both tourism organisations and destinations. These developments have changed the best operational and strategic practices for organisations on a global level and altered the competitiveness of enterprises and regions around the world. Innovative organisations, such as Marriott, Hilton, easyJet and British Airways, took advantage of the emerging technologies in order to improve their product and enhance their communication with consumers and stakeholders. The ability to expand the customer base to cover the global population was unprecedented. Large organisations, such as hotel chains, were able to access an international clientele and develop the tools to manage properties around the world at the touch of a button. Smaller companies could also for the first time develop their 'virtual size' and offer their services to global markets (O'Connor, 1999; Buhalis, 2003). However, several tourism organisations failed to meet the challenge that eBusiness introduced. Many of them failed to incorporate ICTs in their strategy and to appreciate the significant changes evident in the tourism industry structure caused by technology. Consequently, they found it increasingly difficult to maintain their position in the marketplace.

This chapter describes and explains the main ICTs' development in tourism and their strategic implications. It illuminates the complexity of the various types of systems and demonstrates how they fit together in the production, distribution and delivery of tourism products. The utilisation of ICTs and the Internet by different functions and sectors of the industry is examined and conclusions for the future impact of ICTs outlined.

LEARNING OUTCOMES

In this chapter we focus on the strategic and operational role of ICTs in tourism organisations. The chapter demonstrates a wide range of eTourism concepts to provide you with:

- an understanding of the key ICT and eTourism concepts;

- an appreciation of the generic ICTs' applications in the tourism industry;

- a knowledge of the basic concepts of computer reservation systems and global distribution channels;

- a comprehension of the impact of the Internet and ICTs' tools on the structure and components of the tourism system; and

- an appreciation of the strategic importance of ICTs and the Internet for the future of each stakeholder in the tourism industry.

INFORMATION COMMUNICATION TECHNOLOGIES AS A BUSINESS TOOL

Information communication technologies (ICTs) and the Internet ushered in a second industrial revolution in the late 1990s. The development and application of computerised systems accelerated rapidly and enabled their use for a wider range of business functions and activities. The enhancements in ICTs' capabilities, in combination with the decrease of the size of equipment and ICTs' costs, improved the reliability, compatibility and inter-connectivity of numerous terminals and applications (Gupta, 2000). The emergence of the Internet empowered the global networking of computers, enabling individuals and organisations to access a plethora of multimedia information and knowledge sources, regardless of their location or ownership, often free of charge. Thus, almost everybody with an Internet access (which is still only about 15% of the global population) can effectively access unprecedented levels of information and knowledge.

ICTs and eBusiness can be defined as:

The use of digital tools for business functions and processes.

They emerged as essential prerequisites for successful organisations in the new, Internet-ready business environment. Often a major business processes re-engineering was required to take advantage of the emerging technologies in order to transform their ability to operate and to compete in the emerging global marketplace (Laudon and Laudon, 2004). At the macro level, entire economies were empowered to communicate and trade through electronic tools, determining their ability to compete within the global economy. Consequently, economies and enterprises, regardless of their size, product and geographical coverage were affected.

The evolution of ICTs towards eBusiness

ICTs include not only the hardware and software required but also the groupware, netware and the intellectual capacity (humanware) to develop, program and maintain equipment (Table 19.1). Synergies emerging from the use of these systems effectively mean that information is widely available and accessible through a variety of media and locations. Users can use mobile devices such as portable computers, mobile phones as well as digital television and self-serviced terminals/kiosks to interact and perform several functions. This convergence of ICTs effectively integrates the entire range of hardware, software, groupware, netware and humanware and blurs the boundaries between equipment and software (Werthner and Klein, 1999).

The integration of information processing, multimedia and communications created the 'World Wide Web' (WWW), a multimedia protocol which is using the Internet (the network of all networks), to enable the near instant distribution of media-rich documents (such as textual data, graphics, pictures, video, and sounds)

TABLE 19.1	Information communication technologies

Hardware: Physical equipment such as mechanical, magnetic, electrical, electronic or optical devices (as opposed to computer programs or method of use).

Software: Prewritten detailed instructions that control the operation of a computer system or of an electronic device. Software coordinates the work of hardware components in an information system. Software may incorporate standard software such as operating systems or applications, software processes, artificial intelligence and intelligent agents and user interfaces.

Telecommunications: The transmission of signals over long distances, including not only data communications but also the transmission of images and voices using radio, television, telephony and other communication technologies.

Netware: Equipment and software required to develop and support a network or an interconnected system of computers, terminals and communication channels and devices.

Groupware: Communication tools, such as email, voice mail, fax, video-conferencing that foster electronic communication and collaboration among groups.

'Humanware': The intellect required for the development, programming, maintenance and operation of technological development. Humanware incorporates the knowledge and expertise pool of the society.

Source: Adapted from O'Brien, 1996; Gupta, 2000; Laudon and Laudon, 2004

and to revolutionise the interactivity between computer users and servers. This development instituted an innovative platform for the efficient, live and timely exchange of ideas and products, while providing unprecedented and unforeseen opportunities for interactive marketing to all service providers. It also enabled the development of 'intranets' ('closed', 'secured' or 'fire-walled' networks) within organisations, which use industry standard protocols that have been adopted by hardware and software to harness the needs of internal business users, by using a single controlled, user-friendly interface to demonstrate all company data. Increasingly, enterprises need to formulate close partnerships with other members of the value chain for the production of goods and services. As a result, 'extranets' utilise the same principle as computer networks to enhance the interactivity and transparency between organisations and their trusted partners. This is done by linking and sharing data and processes to format a low-cost and user-friendly electronic commerce arrangement, similar to the electronic data interchange (EDI) which was attempted in the previous eras of ICTs.

Hitherto, four main eras can be identified in ICTs' development, namely:

- *Data processing*, where the main objective was to improve operational efficiency by automating information-based processes. This era took place from the 1960s onwards and it mainly used mainframes and mini computers.

- *Management information system* (MIS), where the aim was to increase management effectiveness by satisfying the organisational information requirements. It began in the 1970s and it utilised local processing linked to information resources. Information systems were used primarily to address the needs of internal management and coordination, while emphasis was given on administrative and clerical functions, especially accounting or inventory.

- *Strategic information system* (SIS), in the early 1980s this era aimed to improve competitiveness by changing the nature or conduct of business. Integrated ICTs' networks were utilised to achieve organisations' strategic objectives; enhance performance; coordinate activities across functional and business unit lines as well as the interactions with external entities, in pursuit of competitive advantage.

- The introduction of the Internet in the early 1990s introduced a fourth and more profound era: *the network era*, where intra- and inter-organisational networking, is proliferated by using the local and wide area networks as well as the Internet and intranets, enabling efficient communication and multilevel integration. This era alters the competitiveness of firms in the global marketplace and reduces the significance of location and size in the product delivery processes (Robson, 1994).

Buhalis (2003) concluded that ICTs include 'the entire range of electronic tools, which facilitate the operational and strategic management of organisations by enabling them to manage their information, functions and processes as well as to communicate interactively with their stakeholders for achieving their mission and objectives.' Thus, ICTs emerge as an integrated system of networked equipment and software, which enables effective data processing and communication for organisational benefit towards transforming organisations into eBusinesses.

The pace of Internet adoption globally demonstrates that ICTs and the Internet in particular restructures the way we live, work, shop and play. Millions of people worldwide rely on the Internet for home shopping, tele-entertainment, tele-working, tele-learning, tele-medical support and tele-banking. The electronic/interactive/intelligent/virtual home and enterprise has emerged gradually, facilitating the entire range of communications with the external world and supporting all functions of everyday personal and professional life through interactive computer networks.

ICTs, competitiveness and strategy

The development of ICTs has a major effect on the operation, structure and strategy of organisations. Not only do they reduce both communication and operational costs, but they also enhance flexibility, interactivity, efficiency, productivity and competitiveness. ICTs are not a panacea and cannot guarantee financial success on their own. However, ignoring and under-utilising ICTs can be disastrous for the competitiveness of most tourism enterprises and destinations. This is because ICTs are instrumental in ensuring efficient internal organisation, effective communication with partners and interactivity with consumers. Certain 'prerequisites' are needed to be successful, namely:

- long-term planning and strategy;
- rational management and development of hardware and software;
- re-engineering of business processes;
- top management commitment; and
- training throughout the hierarchy.

These prerequisites facilitate the achievement of sustainable competitive advantage. Failure to address these issues can jeopardise the competitiveness, prosperity and even existence of tourism organisations.

Using ICTs as a stand-alone initiative is inadequate and has to be coupled with a redesign of processes, structures and management control systems. Provided that rational and innovative planning and management is exercised constantly and consistently, ICTs can support business success. As a consequence, 'business processes re-engineering' argues that yesterday's practices, traditional hierarchical and organisational structures and habitual procedures are almost irrelevant. In contrast, corporations should be able to respond to current and future shocks, by having the resources and expertise to design new processes from scratch, in a timely fashion. Corporations need to convert their operations from business functions to business processes, as well as re-conceive their distribution channels strategy and, even more importantly, their corporate values and culture (Tapscott, 1996). Perhaps the greatest challenge organisations face today is to identify and train managers who will be effective and innovative users of ICTs and would lead technology-based decision making. *Intellect* therefore becomes a critical asset, while continuous education and training are instrumental for the innovative use of ICTs and the competitiveness of tourism organisations.

As a result new best strategic and operational management practices have emerged to take advantage of the advanced ICTs. ICTs lead a shift from product-orientated organisations, to a flexible and responsive marketplace. Success will depend on sensing and responding to rapidly changing customer needs and using ICTs for delivering the right product, at the right time, at the right price, for the right customer. To the degree that ICTs can contribute to the value chain of products and services, by either improving their cost position or differentiation, they reshape competitiveness and thus have strategic implications for the prosperity of the organisation (Porter, 1985; 2001). The competitiveness of both tourism enterprises and destinations should be therefore reassessed according to the organisational needs for the utilisation, development and application of ICTs.

TOURISM AND INFORMATION COMMUNICATION TECHNOLOGIES

The ICTs' revolution has had already profound implications for the tourism sector. Poon (1993) predicted that:

> a whole system of ICTs is being rapidly diffused throughout the tourism industry and no player will escape ICTs' impacts.

Information is the life-blood of tourism and so technology is fundamental to the ability of the industry to operate. Unlike durable goods, intangible tourism services cannot be physically displayed or inspected at the point of sale before purchasing. They are normally bought before the time of their use and away from the place of consumption. They therefore rely almost exclusively upon representations and descriptions by the travel trade and other intermediaries, for their ability to attract consumers. Timely and accurate information, relevant to consumers' needs is often the key to successful satisfaction of tourism demand. As few other activities require the generation, gathering, processing, application and communication of information for operations, ICTs are pivotal for tourism. Consequently, the rapid development of both tourism supply and demand makes ICTs an imperative partner for the marketing, distribution, promotion and coordination of the tourism sector. ICTs have a dramatic impact on the travel industry because they force this sector as a whole to rethink the way in which it organises ICTs' business, ICTs' values or norms of behaviour and the way in which it educates the ICTs' workforce (Poon, 1993; Sheldon, 1997; Buhalis, 1998).

Hence, ICTs and the Internet enabled tourism organisations to develop their processes and adapt their management to take advantage of the emerging digital tools and mechanisms to:

- Increase their internal efficiency and manage their capacity and yields better. For example, an airline's reservations system allows the company to manage their inventory more efficiently and the managers to increase occupancy levels. They also incorporate sophisticated yield management systems that support organisations to adjust their pricing to demand fluctuations in order to maximise their profitability.

- Interact effectively with consumers and personalise the product. For example, British Airways has launched a strategy to enable passengers to undertake a number of processes, including booking, ticketing, check-in and seat and meal selection, from the convenience of their computer.

- Revolutionise tourism intermediation and increase the points of sale. For example, Expedia, Travelocity, Lastminute, Orbitz and Opodo have emerged as the most dominant electronic travel agencies, offering an one-stop shop for consumers.

- Empower consumers to communicate with other consumers. For example www.virtualtourists.com or www.igoyougo.com supports the exchange of destination information and tips, while www.untied.com or www.alitaliasacks.com enables dissatisfied customers to make their views available.

- Support efficient cooperation between partners in the value system. For example, Pegasus enables independent hotels to distribute their availability through their web sites and other partners online.

- Enhance the operational and geographic scope by offering strategic tools for global expansion.

Information communication technologies and tourism demand

The rapid growth of the volumes of travellers in the 1990s as well as the requirements for complex, specialised and quality products impose the need for ICTs' utilisation. Tourists have become increasingly demanding, requesting high-quality products and value for their money. New/experienced/sophisticated/demanding travellers rely heavily on the Internet to seek information about destinations and experiences, such as price and availability, as well as to be able to communicate their needs and wishes to tourism suppliers rapidly. The use of ICTs is therefore driven by the development of complex demand requests, as well as by the rapid expansion and sophistication of new products, which tend to address niche market segments. There is evidence that eTourism has already taken off in several countries. Marcussen (2003) demonstrates that the UK and Germany are the most mature travel markets and this is also demonstrated on the online markets where they represent 61% of the volume (see Figure 19.1). In the UK, for example, Continental Research demonstrates that in 2003:

- The buying of airline tickets was the most frequent transaction for online UK adults (5.8 million), followed by banking (5.2 million purchasers/users), holidays, supermarket shopping (3.1 million), music downloads (3 million) and insurance (2.9 million).

- Around 5.8 million UK adults or 22% of those with Internet access have used the web to buy airline tickets in the last year. A further 4.5 million (17%) have bought holidays online.

- The majority (27%) were in the 35–44 years' age range, slightly more than those between 25–34 (26%), while 12% were over 55 years.

- By social class, 73% of purchasers were ABC1s.

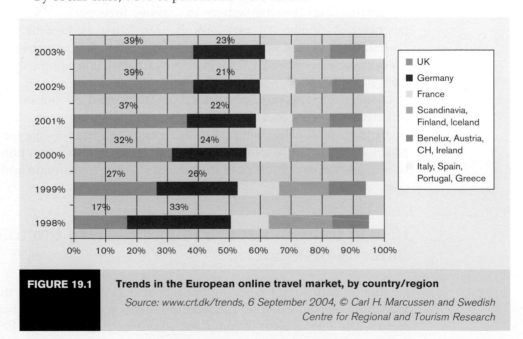

| FIGURE 19.1 | **Trends in the European online travel market, by country/region** |

Source: www.crt.dk/trends, 6 September 2004, © Carl H. Marcussen and Swedish Centre for Regional and Tourism Research

Similarly in the USA, PhoCusWright demonstrates that the American market is much more mature in eTourism as demonstrated by the following points:

- The number of Americans buying travel online increased to 35 million in 2003, a 17% increase on 2002.

- Some 45% of online travellers purchased all of their travel online.

- Over 75% of respondents who booked more than one part of their break online created their own package by putting together individual air, car or hotel elements.

- However, 59% also said they would be interested in purchasing traditional holiday packages online in the future.

- Some 33% of online travellers are not loyal to specific web sites.

- When booking airline seats, 93% of online travellers visited two or more web sites before making their decision, whereas just 69% tried multiple sites for hotel accommodation.

- Dynamic packaging tools will be the key to success as online travellers become more sophisticated.

ICTs enable travellers to access reliable and accurate information as well as to undertake reservations in a fraction of the time, cost and inconvenience required by conventional methods. Thus, they improve the service quality and contribute to a higher tourist satisfaction. The Internet provides access to transparent and easily comparable information on destinations, holiday packages, travel, lodging and leisure services, as well as about their real-time prices and availability. Increasingly, consumers utilise commercial and non-commercial Internet sites for planning, searching, reserving, purchasing and amending their tourism products. They can also get immediate confirmation and speedy travel documents, enabling them to book at the 'last minute'. Experienced travellers are empowered by ICTs and use information and booking systems to improve their personal efficiency and competencies. A number of new organisations, such as Expedia, Travelocity and Lastminute, emerged in the late 1990s online, empowering consumers to research their travel requirements. They gradually assumed a leading intermediation role on a global basis.

Looking forward, success will increasingly depend on the rapid identification of consumer needs and the interaction with prospective clients by using comprehensive, personalised and up-to-date communication media for the design of products which satisfy tourism demand. Thus, destinations and principals need to utilise innovative communication methods in order to maintain and increase their competitiveness.

ICTs in tourism supply: re-engineering the tourism industry distribution

On the tourism supply side, the impacts of ICTs are evident in the production, marketing, operational and distribution functions of both the private and public sectors. The development of computerised systems, until the early 1990s, facilitated the production and management of tourism enterprises by enabling them to handle their inventory and perform their business functions effectively and productively. Understandably, larger organisations took advantage of the emergent technologies earlier than smaller ones, as they had the resources to do so, and ICTs facilitated their further expansion. The ability of tourism enterprises to communicate and cooperate efficiently with remote branches, destinations, principals, agencies and to control their operational elements enabled them to expand their activities, while reducing costs and increasing their competitiveness. Both operational (schedule planning, pricing, inventory handling, and reservations) and support (payroll, accounting, marketing) functions were improved considerably and enabled several tourism enterprises to establish their business worldwide. In the networking era, the development of intranets enable organisations to improve their management at all levels, by sharing media-rich data and processes internally. In addition, extranets empower the cooperation between partners, by enabling a certain degree of transparency and interactivity and thus increasing efficiency and productivity, without compromising on security and confidentiality. This will also improve the interactivity between tourism production and distribution partners, supporting a closer cooperation towards the provision of seamless products. The Internet has also enabled organisations to communicate directly with consumers, enforcing a certain degree of disintermediation in the marketplace.

ICTs and the Internet have pivotal implications for tourism distribution. Since the early 1970s computerised networks and electronic distribution have been leading dramatic structural changes within the tourism industry, and becoming central to the distribution mix and strategy. A computer reservation system (CRS) is basically a database which enables a tourism organisation to manage its inventory and make it accessible to its partners. Principals utilise CRSs to manage their inventory and distribute their capacity as well as to manage the drastic expansion of global tourism. CRSs often charge competitive commission rates while enabling flexible pricing and capacity alterations, in order to adjust supply to demand fluctuations. Airlines pioneered this technology, although hotel chains and tour operators followed by developing centralised reservation systems. CRSs can therefore be characterised as the 'circulation system' of the tourism product.

Since the mid-1980s, airline CRSs developed into **global distribution systems** (GDSs) by gradually expanding their geographical coverage as well as by integrating both horizontally, with other airline systems, and vertically by incorporating the entire range of principals, such as accommodation, car rentals, train and ferry ticketing, entertainment and other provisions. Suppliers therefore realised that the key success factor was in systems integration through GDSs and the creation of standards that enable products to be displayed and purchased by consumers anywhere in the world. GDSs tend to have a stronger market share in the regions where their parent airlines operate, as commercial links with agencies have been exploited for the penetration of GDSs. Hitherto, GDSs concentrated on business travel, as this was the most demanding and profitable part of the business. However, increasingly they tend to offer more leisure products, by introducing theatre tickets, holiday packages and leisure destinations. This diversification responds to consumer demand, while enabling GDSs to use ICTs' developments and under-utilised capacity in order to diversify their portfolio to broader markets and therefore suffer less from their business market saturation. In the early 1990s GDSs emerged as the major driver of ICTs, as well as the backbone of the tourism industry and the single most important facilitator of ICTs' globalisation (Sheldon, 1993). However the emergence of the Internet has also revolutionised GDSs and recently airlines have been trying to disintermediate them to reduce their distribution costs. In essence, GDSs matured from their original development as airline CRSs to travel supermarkets. Four systems already dominate the global market, as demonstrated in Table 19.2.

TABLE 19.2	Key figures for leading global distribution systems, 2003				
	Galileo	**Amadeus**	**Sabre**	**Worldspan**	**Total**
Traditional	69%	93%	87%	54%	80%
Online	31%	7%	13%	46%	20%
Air	92%	84%	88%	91%	88%
Non-air	8%	16%	12%	9%	12%
USA	37%	9%	53%	76%	38%
Rest of world	63%	91%	47%	24%	62%
Air bookings (m)	245	356	323	180	1 105
Total bookings (m)	267	422	366	200	1 254
Relative share of air bookings	22%	32%	29%	16%	100%
Revenue 2003 $ (m)	1 659	2 195	2 045	929	6 828
Operating result $ (m)	459	365	166	90	1 080
Operating margin	27.7%	16.6%	8.1%	9.7%	15.8%
Net result	NA	182	83	49	NA
Net margin	NA	8.3%	4.1%	5.3%	6.1

Source: Adapted from Field and O'Toole, 2004

Since the late 1990s, GDSs have emerged as businesses in their own right, specialising in travel distribution. Many airlines have chosen to sell their shares on GDSs to improve their financial position following the cash crisis after '9/11'. Until their deregulation by the US Department of Transport in 2004, most GDSs represented the majority of principals, offering quite similar services. Their deregulation means that airlines and GDSs are free to negotiate individual deals, forcing both carriers and systems to change their relationships and their core business (Field and O'Toole, 2004).

The development of the Internet and the WWW in the late 1990s offered an unprecedented opportunity for distribution of multimedia information and interactivity between principals and consumers. The WWW's interlinking structure enables the provision and packaging of similarly themed information, products and services. Initially, the information available on the Internet was chaotic and loosely structured, mainly due to the immaturity of ICTs and the lack of any type of standardisation. Several issues prevented the full potential of the Internet, namely:

- security of transmissions;

- credibility and accountability of information;

- intellectual property and copyrights;

- bandwidth and speed limitations;

- slow take-up of technology by potential customers;

- user confusion and dissatisfaction;

- lack of adequately trained specialists;

- equal access for smaller and larger partners; and

- pricing structures for representation and distribution of information and reservations.

However, the WWW provided a globally distributed infrastructure for inexpensive delivery of multimedia information, promotion and distribution of tourism. It empowered the provision and marketing of tailor-made products to meet the needs of individual tourists and hence, it bridged tourism demand and supply in a flexible and interactive way. By the year 2004, only 10 years after the general public used the first browser, there was a certain degree of maturity evident in the marketplace. This was particularly evident for organisations in well-developed economies, such as North America, Europe, Australia and North Asia. This was demonstrated by a number of indicators, namely:

- Tourism was already one of the most successful areas of eCommerce and the sector that attracted the highest expenditure online.

- Most suppliers had established comprehensive and fully functional web sites.

- An estimated 18% of all airline bookings were made on the Internet, often reaching more than 90% for no-frills carriers.

- Most hotel chains and international car rental firms were reporting a significant increase in their direct sales through their web sites.

- Several key travel intermediaries emerged as global players.

- A large proportion of travellers search online before booking holidays.

- Most tourism destinations around the world had some sort of web site providing information for their region while advanced destinations had comprehensive systems supporting itinerary building and reservations (see, for example, www.australia.com, www.amsterdam.nl or www.tourist.reykjavik.is/).

Distribution is one of the few elements of the marketing mix which can still enable enterprises to improve their competitiveness and performance. ICTs enable the achievement of competitive advantage through product differentiation and/or cost advantage, by increasing both the unique characteristics of products, as well as efficiency throughout the production and distribution processes. ICTs increasingly transform distribution to an electronic marketplace, where access to information and ubiquity is achieved, while interactivity between principals and consumers provides major opportunities. Packaging tourism is becoming a much more individualistic activity and thus, a certain degree of disintermediation of the channel is inevitable, offering both opportunities and threats for partners. In addition, we can also observe a trend towards the re-intermediation of the tourism industry, as a plethora of online players emerge to bridge the gap between suppliers and customers, including hotel aggregators, electronic travel agencies and destination management organisations. The dramatic development of the Internet has instigated the re-engineering of the entire process of producing and delivering tourism products. It also enabled the design of specialised products and promotion in order to maximise the value-added provided to individual consumers, and to enhance the total quality of product (fitness to purpose).

MINI CASE STUDY 19.1
lastminute.com: from reservation system to lifestyle portal

In October 1998 Brent Hoberman and Martha Lane Fox launched lastminute.com in the UK. Using the Internet they match suppliers' distressed inventory with consumer last-minute demand. lastminute.com works with a range of suppliers in the travel, entertainment and gift industries and is dedicated to bringing its customers great value inspiration and solutions for all their travel and leisure needs.

SUPPLIER RELATIONSHIPS

lastminute.com has relationships with over 19,500 suppliers, including international scheduled airlines, hotels, package tour operators, theatre, sports and entertainment promoters, restaurants, speciality service providers, gift suppliers and car hire, both in the UK and internationally. Supplier relationships include Lufthansa, Air France, Alitalia, British Midland, United Airlines, Virgin Atlantic Airways, Starwood Hotels and Resorts Worldwide, The Savoy Group, Sol Melia, Kempinski Hotels, English National Ballet, The Royal Albert Hall and Conran Restaurants. lastminute.com carries almost no inventory risk, selling perishable inventory for its suppliers and, where appropriate, protects suppliers' brand names until after purchase. To achieve this it is of utmost importance to continually deepen the inventory sourced from high-quality suppliers across the entire range of goods and services.

TOWARDS A LIFESTYLE PORTAL

Their mission statement suggests: 'lastminute.com aims to maintain its position as Europe's number one independent travel and leisure website by delighting its customers with great-value inspiration and solutions'. This clearly defines their business as a lifestyle portal offering a wide range of products and services to people that impulse buy. Although tourism products dominate the site, many additional products are available including meals delivered at home, gifts including electronics and underwear and insurance. The company has developed a distinctive brand, which communicates spontaneity and a sense of adventure, attracting a loyal community of registered subscribers that use the lastminute.com's website and have submitted their email addresses and other data to receive weekly emails.

GLOBAL REACH

The company has over 9.6 million registered on-line subscribers to its weekly newsletter across the globe. lastminute.com aims to be the global marketplace for all last-minute services and transactions. Following the success of the UK site, localised versions have since been launched in France, Germany, Sweden, Italy, Spain, the Netherlands, Australia, New Zealand, South Africa and Japan.

This growing multinational presence will give the company the ability to develop and further strengthen the lastminute.com brand and product offering. lastminute.com seeks to differentiate itself by generating some of the lowest prices for many travel and entertainment deals and by packaging and delivering products and services, such as restaurant reservations, entertainment tickets and gifts, in convenient, novel and distinctive ways. It also aims to inspire its customers to try something different. Hence, lastminute.com aims at creating the one-stop shop for all last-minute needs.

REFERENCE

www.lastminute.com

DISCUSSION QUESTIONS

1 What is the unique selling point of the lastminute.com in comparison with other online intermediaries?

2 What do you think that lastminute.com should do in order to achieve strategic competitive advantage?

3 What factors of the external environment can influence the development of lastminute.com?

| PHOTOGRAPH 19.1 | **lastminute.com UK homepage** | *Source: lastminute.com* |

A conceptual synthesis of ICTs in tourism

A conceptual synthesis of the emergent ICTs in tourism yields a multidimensional communication and operational framework, which will determine the future competitiveness of principals and destinations. This framework shows the paradigm shift and the business process re-engineering experienced, which has already started to radically reshape the tourism industry. Table 19.3 illustrates several examples of the intra- and inter-organisational functions facilitated by ICTs. It also demonstrates how technologies advocate the multi-integration of the industry. Not only does this framework demonstrate the dependence of both demand and supply on ICTs, but it also illustrates that networking and interactivity will increasingly dominate the tourism production and consumption. This implies clearly that players who fail to participate in the electronic marketplace will be excluded from the production and consumption functions of the industry and jeopardise their future prosperity.

THE UTILISATION OF THE INTERNET AND ICTS BY THE TOURISM INDUSTRY SECTORS

The evolution of the Internet and ICTs has propelled a 'paradigm shift' where all practices and processes had to be changed dramatically affecting the industry structure. eTourism provides opportunities for business expansion in all geographical,

TABLE 19.3 **A multidimensional framework for tourism industry processes facilitated by ICTs**

Intra-organisational communications and functions

- Within a tourism organisation
    - Management and marketing
        strategic planning
        competition analysis
        financial planning and control
        marketing research
        marketing strategy and implementation
        pricing decision and tactics
        middle-term planning and feedback
        management statistics/reports
        operational control
        management functions

    - Communication between departments
        networking and information exchange
        coordination of staff
        operational planning
        accounting/billing
        payroll
        supplies management

- Communication and function with remote branches
        coordination of operations
        availability/prices/information
        orders from headquarters/administration
        share of common resource databases
        for customer and operational information

Inter-organisational communications and functions

- Tourist product suppliers and intermediaries
    - Pre-travel arrangements
        direct marketing
        general information
        availability/prices inquiries
        negotiations and bargaining
        contracting
        reservations and confirmations
        ancillary services

    - Travel-related documentation
        lists of groups/visitors
        receipts/documents
        vouchers and tickets production

    - Post-travel arrangements
        payments and commissions
        feedback and suggestions
        customer satisfaction survey
        complaint handling
        direct marketing

Consumer communication with tourism industry

- Travel advice/general information

- Request availability/prices/information

- Reservation and confirmation

- Amendments for a reservation

- Deposits and full settlements

- Electronic ticketing

- Special interest requests/inquiries

- Feedback/complaints

- Discussions groups/fun clubs

Tourism enterprise communication with non-tourism enterprises

- Other suppliers and ancillary services, vaccinations, travel formalities and visas

- Insurance companies and services

- Weather forecasting

- Banking/financial services/credit cards

- Remote Internet provision for travellers

- Other business services

717

marketing and operational senses. Several major factors make ICTs an integral part of the tourism industry, namely:

- economic necessity, as fierce global competition requires maximum efficiency;
- rapid advancements in technology which provide new marketing opportunities;
- low barriers to entry allowing many new entrants to the market;
- improvements in ICTs' price:performance ratios which yield better productivity for capital employed in ICTs and, finally;
- rising consumer expectations, as they become used to advanced products and expect better quality of presentation and service.

As a result of Internet developments a number of new players have come into the tourism marketplace. Perhaps the most significant change was the proliferation of no-frills airlines that use the Internet as a main distribution mechanism for direct sales. This development educated consumers that they can only find cheap fares if they go direct to the carrier online, threatening both traditional/flag carriers as well as their entire distribution system (GDSs and travel agencies). Equally the development of major eTravel agencies such as Expedia, Travelocity, Lastminute, Orbitz and Opodo has created powerful 'travel supermarkets' for consumers. They provide integrated travel solutions and a whole range of value-added services, such as destination guides, weather reports and insurance. By adopting dynamic packaging, i.e. the ability to package customised trips based on bundling individual components at a discounted total price, they effectively threaten the role of tour operators and other aggregators.

A thorough analysis of the various sectors of the tourism industry demonstrates the key developments and the influence of ICTs and the Internet for their internal organisation, their relationships with partners and the interaction with consumers and stakeholders.

Airlines

Airlines realised quite early the need for efficient, quick, inexpensive and accurate handling of their inventory and internal organisation, due to the complexity of their operations. Originally, reservations were made on manual display boards, where passengers were listed. Travel agencies had to locate the best routes and fares in manuals and then check availability and make reservation by phone, before issuing a ticket manually. In 1962, American Airlines introduced the SABRE CRS as an alternative to expand its Boeing 707 fleet by 50%. The growth of air traffic and air transportation deregulation stimulated the expansion of CRSs to gigantic computerised networks. As prices, schedules and routes were liberated, airlines could change them indefinitely, while new airlines entered the market. CRSs enabled airlines to compete by adapting their schedule and fares to demand. To increase competitiveness, airlines developed the 'hub and spoke' systems, while their pricing became very complex and flexible. 'Fare wars' multiplied the fare structures and increased the computing and communication needs, while most major CRSs installed terminals in agencies to facilitate distribution. In addition, vendor airlines biased their CRSs' screens in order to give higher display priority to their flights rather to their competitors. The remote printing of travel documents, such as tickets and boarding passes, itineraries and invoices, as well as the sale settlements between airlines and travel agencies, and the partnership marketing through frequent flyer programmes were invaluable benefits supported by the emerging ICTs. CRSs were developed to global distribution systems (GDSs) and re-engineered the entire marketing and distribution processes of airlines. They essentially became strategic business units (SBUs) in their own right due to their ability to generate income and to boost airlines' sales at the expense of their competitors. By 2004 many airlines sold their interests in GDSs enabling them to operate as independent distribution companies.

Distribution is a crucial element of airlines' strategy and competitiveness, as it determines the cost and the ability to access consumers. The cost of distribution is increasing considerably and airlines find it difficult to control. Nowadays ICTs and internal CRSs are used heavily to support the Internet distribution of airline seats. These systems are at the heart of airline operational and strategic agendas. This is particularly the case for smaller and regional carriers as well as no-frills airlines which cannot afford GDSs' fees and aim to sell their seats at competitive prices. This has forced even traditional/full-service/flag airlines, such as British Airways and Aer Lingus, to recognise the need for re-engineering the distribution processes, costs and pricing structures. Hence, they use the Internet for:

- enhancing interactivity and building relationships with consumers and partners;

- online reservations;

- electronic ticketing;

- yield management;

- electronic auctions for last-minute available seats;

- disintermediation and redesign of agency commission schemes; and

- maximising the productivity of the new electronic distribution media (Buhalis, 2004).

The Airline IT Survey 2003 demonstrates that the vast majority of airlines have a three-year IT strategy that aims to reduce costs and increase efficiency. On average airlines spend 2.4% of their revenue on ICTs investment and yet generate on average 15.8% of their bookings online, including 9.7% on their own web sites (O'Toole, 2004). Airlines are investing heavily in direct sales which coupled with 'customer relations management' and 'revenue management systems' will enable them to better control their distribution and strategic marketing.

Hotels

Hotels use ICTs in order to improve their operations, manage their inventory and maximise their profitability. Their systems facilitate both inhouse management and distribution through electronic media. '**Property management systems**' (PMSs) coordinate front office, sales, planning and operational functions by administrating reservations and managing the hotel inventory. Moreover, PMSs integrate the 'back' and 'front' of the house management and improve general administration functions such as accounting and finance; marketing research and planning; forecasting and yield management; payroll and personnel; and purchasing. Understandably, hotel chains gain more benefits from PMSs, as they can introduce a unified system for planning, budgeting and controlling and coordinating their properties centrally. Hotels also utilise ICTs for their distribution and marketing functions. Global presence is essential in order to enable both individual customers and the travel trade to access accurate information on availability and to provide easy, efficient, inexpensive and reliable ways of making and confirming reservations. Although central reservation offices (CROs) introduced central reservations in the 1970s, it was not until the expansion of airline CRSs and the recent IT developments that forced hotels to integrate their ICTs and develop hotel CRSs in order to expand their distribution, improve efficiency, facilitate control, empower yield management, reduce labour costs and enable rapid response time to both customers and management requests.

The development of the Internet has provided more benefits as it reduces the capital and operational costs required for the representation and promotion of hotels. For example, the cost per individual booking can be reduced from US$10–15 for voice-based reservations, to US$3.50–7.50 for reservations through GDSs, to US$0.25 through the WWW. Savings can also be achieved in printing, storing, administrating and posting promotional material. This trend illustrates that even small accommodation establishments can take advantage and promote themselves in the electronic marketplace. Although electronic bookings grew by 7750%, between 1981 and 1993 only 28% of all global reservations are booked electronically. This illustrates that there is a great potential for expansion in the future. Following the development of hotel CRSs by most chains, the issue of interconnectivity with other CRSs and the Internet emerged. As a result, 'switch companies', such as THISCO and WIZCOM, emerged to provide an interface between the various systems and enable a certain degree of transparency. This reduces both set-up and reservation costs, while facilitates reservations through several distribution channels (Emmer *et al.*, 1993; O'Connor, 2000). Table 19.4 demonstrates the growth of online bookings for Hilton Hotels.

However, as most hotels are small and medium sized, independent, seasonal and family enterprises, they find it extremely difficult to utilise ICTs. This is due to:

- lack of capital for purchasing hardware and software;

- lack of standardisation and professionalism;

- insufficient marketing and technology training and understanding;

- small size which multiplies the administration required by CRSs to deal with each property; and finally

- the unwillingness of proprietors to lose control over their property.

Hence, small hotels are increasingly placed at a major disadvantage as they cannot be represented in the electronic marketplace and jeopardise their future existence. However, they cannot afford to ignore the rapid developments of ICTs and therefore, should take advantage of the emergent ICTs' opportunities and decreasing cost, and enhance their competitiveness. The establishment of destination-based collaboration ventures would perhaps enable small firms to pool resources in order to share development and operation costs. Distributing their products through GDSs and the Internet would enable them to access their target markets at an affordable cost and gain benefits (Buhalis, 2003).

TABLE 19.4	Hilton Hotels online bookings

Hilton Hotels Corporation has announced that its family of hotels reported record-breaking gross online reservations and revenue from bookings on its brand web sites (including www.hilton.com, www.conradhotels.com, www.doubletree.com, www.embassysuites.com, www.hamptoninn.com, www.hiltongardeninn.com and www.homewoodsuites.com) in February 2004. These figures for the company and its major brand web sites included:

- More than 530,000 online reservations for Hilton International hotels – a 34% increase in online reservations over February 2003

- More than 18,500 daily online reservations on average during February – setting a new daily record of over 25,000 reservations

- A 41% increase in revenue from online reservations over February 2003

- A record 11.4% of overall net reservations through the brand web sites

- Some 83% of all online room nights for the month of February came directly through the own-brand web sites, providing a clear indication that their distribution strategy is working

Source: Adapted from Hilton Hotels Corporation News Release 13/4/2004
http://www.corporate-ir.net/ireye/ir_site.zhtml?ticker=HLT&script=412&layout=9&item_id=514223

One of the most promising developments in hospitality is 'application service providers' (ASPs). ASPs will be increasingly more involved in hosting a number of business applications for hospitality organisations. Hotels will 'rent' the same software for a fee and will use it across the Internet. For example, some hotel firms may 'rent' their PMS software application from supplier Micros/Fidelio. ASPs are ideal for hotels, especially smaller to mid-sized hotels, that want to leverage the best vertical and enterprise support applications on the market without having to deal with the technology or pay for more functionality than is necessary. As they do not have extensive ICT departments and expertise, they can easily access up-to-date applications and benefit from the collective knowledge accumulated by ASPs without having to invest extensively in technology or expertise building (Paraskevas and Buhalis, 2002).

Tour operators

Leisure travellers often purchase 'packages', consisting of charter flights and accommodation, arranged by tour operators. Tour operators tend to pre-book these products and distribute them through brochures displayed in travel agencies. Hence, until recently in northern European countries, where tour operators dominate the leisure market, airline and hotel CRSs were rarely utilised for leisure travel. In the early 1980s, tour operators realised the benefits of ICTs in organising, promoting, distributing and coordinating their packages. The Thomson Open-line Programme (TOP) was the first real-time computer-based central reservation office in 1976. It introduced direct communication with travel agencies in 1982, and announced that reservations for Thomson Holidays would only be accepted through TOP in 1986. This move was the

721

Fidelio was founded in 1987 and it emerged as one of the leading and most innovative international property management systems providers for the hospitality industries. Their software is adaptable to changing business requirements and it integrates both the ongoing technological developments and the organisational change experienced. Fidelio allows hotels and chains of any size and type, restaurants, cruise ships and catering and conference operations to computerise their operations and to integrate major industry software products through analysing individual requirements and appreciating their uniqueness. Different hotel chains and managers require special information to accommodate the dissimilar legal requirements, accounting systems, tax reporting and guest statistics of each country they operate in. Fidelio aims to meet these challenges and satisfies every type of information requested.

Fidelio incorporates four sets of functions:

- **The front-office function** which enables the management of reservations; guest histories and registration data; room itinerary management; pricing and yield management; billing per guest; group/allotment management; night auditing; cashiers function; maintenance; concierge programme; as well as production of operational and management reports.

- **The food and beverage management system** enables revenue and cost budget management; stock control; return on investment analysis for each menu; kitchen control systems; and bar management and control. A point-of-sales system integrates all revenue points with the central database facilitating the accounting and cashiering functions.

- **The sales and marketing programme** supports the entire sales and marketing functions of the hotel, such as group event management and reservation; account management; activity management; contract generation; and follow-up activities.

- In addition, Fidelio provides several **support functions** such as word processing; mail manager; calendars; and daily schedules. The system interfaces with most telephone and call accounting; point of sales; door locking; mini bar; energy management; voice mail; video; and paging systems enabling a multi-integrated management of all hotel processes. These functions are delivered through the development of a local area network which coordinates all processes and enables hotel departments to share a data-rich and constantly updated database.

REFERENCE

www.fidelio.com

DISCUSSION QUESTIONS

1 Explain the relationship between a property management system and the Internet distribution of a hotel chain.

2 How can Fidelio assist the strategic management of a hotel?

3 Discuss the suitability of Fidelio for a 20-room bed and breakfast operation and, if found unsuitable, design a system for their needs.

critical point for altering the communication processes between tour operators and travel agencies. Gradually, all major tour operators developed or acquired databases and established electronic links with travel agencies, aiming to reduce their information handling costs and increase the speed of information transfer and retrieval. This improved their productivity and capacity management whilst enhancing their services to agencies and consumers. Tour operators also utilised their CRSs for market intelligence, in order to adjust their supply to demand fluctuations, as well as to monitor the booking progress and productivity of travel agencies (Karcher, 1996).

Tour operators have been reluctant to focus on ICTs through their strategic planning. Few realise the major transformation of the marketplace, while the majority regard ICTs exclusively as a facilitator of their current operations, and as a tool to reduce their costs. However, several tour operators in Germany, Scandinavia and the UK are moving towards electronic brochures and will begin to distribute their products electronically. Successful operators report up to 25% of their packages are booked directly by consumers online. This enables them to concentrate on niche markets by:

- offering customised packages;
- updating their brochures regularly;
- saving the 10–20% commission and reducing the costs of incentives, bonus and educational trips for travel agencies; and
- saving the cost for developing, printing, storing, distributing conventional brochures – estimated to be approximately £20 per booking.

Strategically, Internet developments and dynamic packaging threaten the dominance of tour operators. Although a partial disintermediation seems inevitable, there will always be sufficient market share for tour operators who can add value to the tourism product and deliver innovative, personalised and competitive holiday packages. As ICTs will determine the future competitiveness of the industry, the distribution channel leadership and power of tour operators may be challenged, should other channel members or newcomers utilise ICTs effectively to package and distribute either unique or cheaper tourism products. However, many key players including TUI have started disintegrating their packages and selling individual components directly to the consumers. In this sense they will be able to re-intermediate, by offering their vast networks of suppliers through their channels.

Travel agencies

ICTs are irreplaceable tools for travel agencies as they provide information and reservation facilities and support the intermediation between consumers and principals. Travel agencies operate various reservation systems, which mainly enable them to check availability and make reservations for tourism products.

ICTs, and particularly GDSs, have been critical for business travel agencies to access information and make reservations on scheduled airlines, hotel chains, car rentals and a variety of ancillary services. GDSs help construct complicated itineraries, while they provide up-to-date schedules, prices and availability information, as well as an effective reservation method. In addition, they offered internal management modules integrating the 'back office' (accounting, commission monitor, personnel) and 'front office' (customers' history, itinerary construction, ticketing and communication with suppliers). Multiple travel agencies, in particular, experience more benefits by achieving better coordination and control between their remote branches and headquarters. Transactions can provide invaluable data for financial and operational control as well as for marketing research, which can analyse the market fluctuations and improve tactical decisions.

The vast majority of leisure travel agencies around the world utilise 'videotext networks' to access tour operator and the reservation systems of other suppliers – such as ferry operators, railways and insurance companies. On the plus side, videotext systems are relatively inexpensive to purchase and operate, require little training and expertise and are fairly reliable. However, on the minus side, they are slow; data have to be retyped for each individual database searched; they fail to integrate with the back office; cannot interface with multimedia applications; and are unable to take advantage of the emergent ICTs. Effectively, the type of agency and its clientele determine the type of ICTs utilised. Typically, business travel agencies are more GDSs dependent, while leisure agencies and holiday shops are more likely to use videotext systems (Inkpen, 1998).

The Internet has revolutionised the travel agency industry as, for the first time ever, agencies had the ability to reach travel inventory directly without having to invest in time and costs for acquiring GDSs. They are able to search and book suppliers such as airlines and hotels online, increasing their bookable inventory. They also have the tools to sell their own services and to promote their organisations. However, travel agencies have been reluctant to take full advantage of the ICTs, mainly due to:

- a limited strategic scope;
- deficient ICTs expertise and understanding;
- low profit margins which prevents investments; and
- focus on human interaction with consumers.

This has resulted in a low level of integration of ICTs and capitalisation on the Internet's potential. As a result many agencies lack access to the variety of information and reservation facilities readily available to consumers and therefore their credibility in the marketplace is severely reduced. This may jeopardise their ability to maintain their competitiveness and consequently, they may be threatened by disintermediation. Several forces intensify this threat:

- consumers increasingly search information and make reservations online;
- principals aim to control distribution costs by communicating directly with consumers and by developing customer relationship management;
- commission cuts; and
- travel agencies have limited expertise as they employ inadequately trained personnel.

In contrast, new players (such as Expedia, Travelocity, Orbitz, Lastminute and Opodo) have already achieved a high penetration the marketplace and grown spectacularly, as demonstrated in Table 19.5.

TABLE 19.5	Online majors travel bookings revenue (US$ million)		
Provider	**2001**	**2002**	**2003**
Expedia	3 600	5 300	8 200
Travelocity	3 100	3 500	3 890
Orbitz	818	2 566	3 440

Source: Clarke, 2004

As location becomes less significant electronic travel agents will dominate global travel retailing. Already in the USA more than 80% of online travel retailing is concentrated in the top five players. Therefore, the future of travel agencies will depend on their ability to utilise ICTs in order to increase the added value to the final tourism product and to serve their customer. Agencies which simply act as booking offices for tourism products will probably face severe financial difficulties in the future. In contrast, knowledgeable and innovative agencies which utilise the entire range of technologies in order to provide suitable integrated tourism solutions will add value to the tourist experience and increase their competitiveness.

Destinations

Destinations are amalgams of tourism products, facilities and services which compose the total tourism expertise under one brand name. Traditionally the planning, management and coordination functions of destinations have been undertaken by either the public sector (at national, regional or local level) or by partnerships between stakeholders of the local tourism industry. They usually:

- provide information and undertake some marketing activities through mass media advertising;
- provide advisory service for consumers and the travel trade;
- design and distribute brochures, leaflets and guides; and
- coordinate local initiatives.

Although ICTs were never regarded as a critical instrument for the development and management of destinations, increasingly 'destination management organisations' (DMOs) use ICTs in order to facilitate the tourist experience before, during and after the visit, as well as for coordinating all partners involved in the production and delivery of tourism. Thus, not only do DMOs attempt to provide information and accept reservations for local enterprises as well as coordinate their facilities, but they also utilise ICTs to promote their tourism policy, coordinate their operational functions, increase the expenditure of tourists and boost the multiplier effects in the local economy.

725

Despite the fact that studies on destination-orientated CRSs have been traced back to as early as 1968, it was not until the early 1990s that the concept of 'destination management systems' (DMSs) emerged. Even at this stage most DMSs are mere facilitators of the conventional activities of tourism boards, such as information dissemination or local bookings. Several planned DMSs have failed in their development phase, mainly due to:

- inadequate financial support;
- lack of long-term vision of the developers;
- lack of understanding of industry mechanisms and the interest groups;
- expensive and inappropriate technological solutions; and
- IT leading rather than following tourism marketing.

This has discouraged DMO managers to further invest in the development of suitable systems (Buhalis, 1997). However, by 2004 most destinations around the world had recognised the value of the DMS concept and had some type of system offering information about their region. Most importantly several DMS system providers – including Tiscover, World.net, Integra, and TouchVision – have emerged as the leading suppliers in the marketplace.

Using the emergent opportunities for multimedia distribution, DMSs increasingly utilise the Internet to provide interactive demonstrations of local amenities and attractions and to enable consumers to build their own itinerary based on their interests, requirements and constraints. In addition, DMSs are utilised to facilitate

PHOTOGRAPH 19.2 **Tiscover** *Source: tiscover.com*

the management of DMOs, as well as the coordination of the local suppliers at the destination level. DMSs are particularly significant for small and medium tourism enterprises which lack the capital and expertise to undertake a comprehensive marketing strategy and rely on destination authorities and intermediaries for the promotion and coordination of their products (Frew and O'Connor, 1999; WTO, 2001). Advanced DMSs would enable destinations to achieve differentiation by targeting niche markets, which would also improve the balance between the expectations and the perceived experiences for both tourists and locals, improving their interaction. This would enable destinations to integrate their offering and satisfy the needs of both indigenous people and visitors. In addition, DMSs will increase the bargaining power of local enterprises with tourism intermediaries and it will enable them to explore new and innovative distribution channels. The illustration of environmentally sensitive areas as well as the demonstration of socio-cultural rituals would enable a better understanding by locals and tourists and therefore would improve the tourism impacts in the area. DMOs should benefit by implementing advanced DMSs (or destination integrated computer information reservation management systems). These systems can rationalise destination management and marketing by supporting their promotion, distribution and operations and also by offering innovative tools for strategic management and amelioration of tourism impacts (Buhalis and Spada, 2000; WTO, 2001).

CONCLUSION – THE CONTRIBUTION OF ICTS TO THE FUTURE TOURISM INDUSTRY

The analysis of ICTs in tourism clearly demonstrates that ICTs represent a *paradigm shift* in the tourism industry. This has transformed best business practices and redefined the role and the competitiveness of all tourism enterprises and destinations. In particular, ICTs stimulate radical changes in the operation and distribution of the tourism sector, while empowering consumers to identify and access specialised products which satisfy their specific requirements. Moreover, ICTs provide innovative strategic tools for destinations to improve their tourism impacts by disseminating information and coordinating their offering. Hence, the visibility and therefore competitiveness of principals and destinations in the marketplace will increasingly be a function of the technologies and networks utilised to interact with individual and institutional customers. Therefore, principals and destinations need to understand and utilise innovative ICTs in order to enhance their long-term prosperity. Unless the current tourism sector utilises the emergent ICTs, and develops a multi-channel and multi-platform strategy they will be unable to take full advantage of the emerging opportunities (Buhalis and Licata, 2002). It is safe to assume that only creative and innovative principals and destinations which rationalise their utilisation of ICTs through their management vision and use intellect as a major asset will prosper in the future. It is evident that the 'only constant is change'. Organisations which compute will be able to compete in the future. Although ICTs can introduce great benefits, especially in efficiency, coordination, differentiation, and cost reduction, they are not a universal remedy and require a pervasive re-engineering of business processes, as well as strategic management vision and commitment in order to achieve their objectives.

Self-check questions

1 What are the key factors that influence the adoption of ICTs in the tourism industry?

2 What are disintermediation and re-intermediation in tourism?

3 Identify five innovative online players for each sector of the tourism industry and explain what makes them innovative.

4 How can tourism organisations maximise their online representation?

5 What are the Internet-related challenges for managing tourism brands?

Essay questions

1 What are the key strategic and operational functions supported by ICT for a tourism organisation of your choice?

2 What are the main opportunities and challenges of technology for small and medium-sized tourism enterprises?

3 How can tourism organisations be proactive and reactive online and how do ICTs assist this process?

4 Can ICT-related competitive advantages be sustainable? And what are the main conditions for achieving this?

5 Explain the main sources of ICT-related competitive advantages for tourism organisations.

Annotated further reading

Books

Buhalis, D. (2003) *eTourism: Information Technology for Strategic Tourism Management*, Pearson (Financial Times/Prentice Hall), London.
Comprehensive coverage of eTourism from a strategic perspective.

O'Connor, P. (1999) *Electronic Information Distribution in Tourism and Hospitality*, CAB, Oxford.
Focuses on the Internet and the emerging trends.

Poon, A. (1993) *Tourism, Technology and Competitive Strategies*, CAB International, Oxford.
Strategic thinking and vision towards the new tourism.

Sheldon, P. (1997) *Information Technologies for Tourism*, CAB, Oxford.
Overview of systems used in the tourism industry.

Werthner, H. and Klein, S. (1999) *Information Technology and Tourism – A Challenging Relationship*, Springer, New York.

Comprehensive coverage of eTourism from a technology and management techniques perspective.

Web sites

Organisations	URL	Description
IFITT	http://www.ifitt.org/	IFITT's web site
Eye for Travel	http://www.eyefortravel.com/	Commercial web sites with news and white papers
WebTravelNews	http://webtravelnews.com/	Newsletters and new developments
Travel Daily News	http://www.traveldailynews.com	Newsletters and new developments
Travelmole	http://www.travelmole.com	Newsletters and new developments
TIA	http://www.tia.org/	Information on travel developments in the USA
eTravelWorld	http://www.etravelworld.com/	Newsletters and new developments
Electronic Tourism	http://www.electronic-tourism.com	Newsletters and new developments and white papers
BTNonline	http://www.btnonline.com/	Newsletters and new developments
Infotec	http://www.infotec-travel.com/	Discussion group
Hotel Online	http://www.hotel-online.com	Newsletters and new developments on eHospitality
Nua Surveys	http://www.nua.ie/surveys/	Internet statistics
Jupiter	http://www.jup.com/	Internet statistics
Forrester	http://www.forrester.com/	Internet statistics
Genesys	http://www.genesys.net/	Information on tour operators and travel agencies
Phocuswright	http://www.phocuswright.com	Commercial web sites with news and white papers
Rene Waksburg's Wonderful Resources	http://www.waksberg.com/	Tourism research resources
World Tourism Organization	http://www.world-tourism.org/	World Tourism Organization
World Tourism Travel Council	http://www.wttc.org	World Tourism Travel Council
International Hotel Restaurant Associaton	http://www.ih-ra.com/	International Hotel Restaurant Associaton
StarUK	http://www.staruk.org.uk	Tourism statistics in the UK

References cited and bibliography

Beekman, G. (2001) *Computer Confluence: Exploring Tomorrow's Technology*, 4th edn, Prentice Hall, New Jersey.

Buhalis, D. (1993) 'Regional integrated computer information reservation management systems as a strategic tool for the small and medium tourism enterprises', *Tourism Management* **14**(5), 366–78.

Buhalis, D. (1994) 'Information and telecommunications technologies as a strategic tool for small and medium tourism enterprises in the contemporary business environment', pp. 254–75 in Seaton, A. *et al.* (eds), *Tourism – The State of the Art: the Strathclyde Symposium*, John Wiley & Sons, Chichester.

Buhalis, D. (1997) 'Information technologies as a strategic tool for economic, cultural and environmental benefits enhancement of tourism at destination regions', *Progress in Tourism and Hospitality Research* **3**(1), 71–93.

Buhalis, D. (1998) 'Strategic use of information technologies in the tourism industry', *Tourism Management* **19**(3), 409–423.

Buhalis, D. (2003) *eTourism: Information Technology for Strategic Tourism Management*, Pearson (Financial Times/Prentice Hall), London.

Buhalis, D. (2004) 'eAirlines: strategic and tactical use of ICTS in the airline industry', *Information and Management* **41**(7), 805–25.

Buhalis, D. and Licata, C. (2002) 'The eTourism intermediaries', *Tourism Management*. **23**(3), 207–220.

Buhalis, D. and Spada, A. (2000) 'Destination management systems: criteria for success', *Information Technology and Tourism* **3**(1), 41–58.

Clarke, R. (2004) 'Value proposition', *Airline Business* March, 44–5.

Connolly, D., Olsen, M. and Moore, R. (1998) 'The internet as a distribution channel', *Cornell Hotel and Restaurant Administration Quarterly* **39**(4), 42–54.

Emmer, R., Tauck, C., Wilkinson, S. and Moore, R. (1993) 'Marketing hotels using global distribution systems, *Cornell Hotel Restaurant Administration Quarterly* **34**(6), 80–89.

Feldman, J. (1988) 'CRS and fair airline competition', *Travel and Tourism Analyst* **2**, 5–22.

Field, D. and O'Toole, K. (2004) 'Where next for the GDS?', *Airline Business* March, 34–43.

Frew, A. and Horam, R. (1999) 'eCommerce in the UK hotel sector: a first look', *International Journal of Hospitality Information Technology*, **1**(1), 77–87.

Frew, A. and O'Connor, P. (1998) 'A comparative examination of the implementation of destination marketing system strategies: Scotland and Ireland', pp. 258–68 in Buhalis, D., Tjoa, A.M., Jafari, J. (eds), *Information and Communications Technologies in Tourism*, ENTER 1998 Proceedings, Springer-Verlag, Wien.

Frew, A. and O'Connor, P. (1999) 'Destination marketing system strategies: refining and extending an assessment framework', pp. 398–407 in Buhalis, D. and Scherlter, W. (eds), *Information and Communications Technologies in Tourism*, ENTER 1999 Proceedings, Springer-Verlag, Wien.

Gupta, U. (2000) *Information Systems: Success in the 21st Century*, Prentice Hall, New Jersey.

Hammer, M. and Champy, J. (1993) *Reengineering the Corporation: A Manifesto for Business Revolution*, Nicholas Brealey, London.

Inkpen, G. (1998) *Information Technology for Travel and Tourism*, 2nd edn, Addison Wesley Longman, London.

Karcher, K. (1996) 'Re-engineering the package holiday business', pp. 221–33 in Klein, S. *et al.* (eds), *Information and Communication Technologies in Tourism*, ENTER 1996 Proceedings, Springer-Verlag, Wien.

Laudon, K. and Laudon, J. (2004) *Management Information Systems: Managing the Digital Firm*, 8th edn, Prentice Hall, New Jersey.

Marcussen, C. (2003) 'Internet distribution of European travel and tourism services', Research Centre of Bornholm, Denmark. http://www.crt.dk/uk/staff/chm/trends.htm

O'Brien, J. (1996) *Management Information Systems: Managing Information Technology in the Networked Enterprise*, Irwin, Chicago.

O'Connor, P. (1999) *Electronic Information Distribution in Tourism and Hospitality*, CAB, Oxford.

O'Connor, P. (2000) *Using Computers in Hospitality*, 2nd edn, Cassell, London.

O'Connor, P. and Frew, A. (2000) 'Evaluating electronic channels of distribution in the hotel sector: a Delphi study', *Information Technology and Tourism* **3**(3/4), 177–93.

O'Connor, P. and Horan, P. (1999) 'An analysis of web reservations facilities in the top 50 international hotel chains', *International Journal of Hospitality Information Technology* **1**(1), 77–87.

O'Connor, P. and Rafferty, J. (1997) 'Gulliver – distributing Irish tourism electronically', *Electronic Markets* **7**(2), 40–45.

O'Toole, K. (2004) *IT Trends Survey 2003*, Airline Business/SITA, August.

Oz, E. (2000) *Management Information Systems*, 2nd edn, Thomson Learning, Boston.

Paraskevas, A. and Buhalis, D. (2002) 'Web-enabled ICT outsourcing for small hotels: opportunities and challenges', *Cornell Hotel and Restaurant Administration Quarterly* **43**(2), 27–39.

Peacock, M. (1995) *Information Technology in Hospitality*, Cassell, London.

Peppard, J. (ed.) (1993) *IT Strategy for Business*, Pitman, London.

Pollock, A. (1998) 'Creating intelligent destinations for wired customers', pp. 235–48 in Buhalis, D., Tjoa, A.M. and Jafari, J. (eds), *Information and Communications Technologies in Tourism*, ENTER 1998 Proceedings, Springer-Verlag, Wien.

Poon, A. (1993) *Tourism, Technology and Competitive Strategies*, CAB International, Oxford.

Porter, M. (1985) *Competitive Advantage*, Free Press, New York.

Porter, M. (1989) 'Building competitive advantage by extending information systems', *Computerworld* **23**(41), 19.

Porter, M. (2001) 'Strategy and the internet', *Harvard Business Review* **103D**, 63–78.

Porter, M. and Millar, V. (1985) 'How information gives you competitive advantage', *Harvard Business Review* **63**(4), 149–60.

Robson, W. (1994) *Strategic Management and Information Systems: An Integrated Approach*, Pitman, London.

Sheldon, P. (1993) 'Destination information systems', *Annals of Tourism Research* **20**(4), 633–49.

Sheldon, P. (1997) *Information Technologies for Tourism*, CAB, Oxford.

Smith, C. and Jenner, P. (1998) 'Tourism and the internet', *Travel and Tourism Analyst* **1**, 62–81.

Tapscott, D. (1996) *The Digital Economy: Promise and Peril in the Age of Networked Intelligence*, McGraw-Hill, New York.

Tapscott, D. and Caston, A. (1993) *Paradigm Shift: The New Promise of Information Technology*, McGraw-Hill Inc., New York.

Truitt, L., Teye, V. and Farris, M. (1991) 'The role of computer reservation systems: international implications for the tourism industry', *Tourism Management* **12**(1), 21–36.

Werthner, H. and Klein, S. (1999) *Information Technology and Tourism – A Challenging Relationship*, Springer, New York.

WTO (1995) *Global Distribution Systems in the Tourism Industry*, World Tourism Organization, Madrid.

WTO (2001) *eBusiness for Tourism: Practical Guidelines for Destinations and Businesses*, World Tourism Organization, Madrid.

MAJOR CASE STUDY 19.1
GLOBAL DISTRIBUTION SYSTEM:
AMADEUS

INTRODUCTION

Information communications technologies emerge as the backbone of the tourism industry as they revolutionise its intermediation, production and marketing functions. Global distribution systems (GDSs) which provide the 'circulation system' of the industry worldwide have been the most important facilitators of the tourism globalisation. GDSs enable the distribution of the entire range of tourism products globally and bridge the gap between principals and intermediaries. GDSs have also been instrumental in supporting eTravel agencies and Internet providers as they often support their inventory building, ticketing and commission settling functions. In addition, many GDSs have invested heavily in developing Internet interfaces (e.g. SABRE developed Travelocity) while others have invested in existing systems (e.g. Amadeus invested in OPODO). This case study analyses the development and operation of Amadeus, one of the four main GDSs and illustrates the range of offerings provided to ICTs' stakeholders as well as some organisational and strategic issues.

AMADEUS

Amadeus Global Travel Distribution, a neutral and global computerised distribution and reservation system for the travel industry, was founded in 1987 and began operations in January 1992. It emerged as a European response to the sophistication of US-based CRSs and their expansion plans in the mid-1980s. Although European national carriers had developed their own reservation systems which served their respective national markets, imminent air transportation deregulation in Europe made it imperative to create a distribution system able to serve both European and global markets.

The mission of Amadeus is to replace existing airline reservation systems in the markets of ICTs' owner and partner airlines with a system that provides a totally neutral distribution system with leading technology, to increase efficiency dramatically in airline bookings and to give equally comprehensive access to car rental and hotel services in order to create a global system.

The main shareholders in Amadeus are Air France (29.2%), Iberia (29.2%), Lufthansa (29.2%) and Continental Airlines (12.4%), while 36 national marketing companies, belonging to partner airlines are closely involved in the management and promotion of the system in 115 countries. With over one thousand employees, Amadeus is organised as a holding company based in Madrid, with three subsidiaries: Development (Sophia Antipolis), Marketing (Madrid/Sophia Antipolis) and Operations (Munich). In 1995 Amadeus acquired System One CRSs, a 100% subsidiary of Continental Airlines and expanded rapidly into the American markets. To meet the requirements of the European travel market, the Amadeus CRS is designed as a powerful international complement to the existing national distribution networks.

Amadeus has four primary goals, namely:

1 To offer travel service providers (airlines, railways, hotels, car rental firms, tour operators, ferry and cruise lines) a broad-based, efficient distribution network which gives access to the largest travel agency client base in Europe.

2 To offer Amadeus subscribers (travel agencies) products, booking facilities, and support services that make them competitive by being sensitive to local requirements and by integrating their front- and back-office needs.

3 To offer airlines neutral display of availability and the possibility of using Amadeus in their sales offices.

4 To provide global service through technical links and alliances with other systems, in order to enable principals to distribute their products globally and also to enable travellers to purchase all types of travel services anywhere.

THE AMADEUS SYSTEM

The Amadeus central system is located in Munich and connected to the world via its own reliable high-speed communication network (Amanet). It offers all the products and booking facilities that travel agencies need, namely: immediate guaranteed confirmation of airline, car hire and hotel reservations; integrated intelligent passenger name records (PNRs) which store all customers' travel data and integrate with customer profiles stored by agencies databases; online information on destinations, principals, airports, formalities, ski and sport events; online training for users; and customised procedures to save time. The central system (grouped in Amadeus Air, Cars, Hotels and Services) as well as the network operates 24 hours a day, 365 days of the year.

Amadeus Air incorporates most scheduled airlines, giving choice of thousands of city pairs and millions of routes and connections representing almost all scheduled flights worldwide. Booking details are transmitted to airlines which update their availability simultaneously and acknowledge the reservation by sending their own record locator to Amadeus and agencies. Amadeus Fare Quote system provides prices automatically for complex itineraries by incorporating the cost and restrictions for all segments and components. Negotiated fares between distribution channel partners can be incorporated into the fare quotation and ticketing process. Amadeus also provides access to live displays of aircraft seat maps and enables agencies to reserve a specific seat number.

Amadeus Cars provides access to 55 global car rental companies and enables the display of information on availability and pricing. Car companies are often displayed according to location or/and terminals of other modes of transportation, such as airports, train stations and ports. Last car availability enables transparency between car companies fleet stock and travel agencies. Reservations are confirmed instantly and incorporated in travellers' PNRs, while vouchers are printed automatically.

Amadeus Hotels provides accurate information on 30,000 hotel properties worldwide, covering hundreds of hotel chains. It shows location, last room availability, hotel features and rates. Access to major hotel chains gives up-to-date booking information so that agencies can check their availability data and get immediate guaranteed confirmation. Amadeus also offers the facility to access and sell special rates whether these are negotiated by travel agencies, the clients themselves, or they are promotional rates offered by the hotels. Amadeus hotels are also linked to the hotel switches THISCO and WIZCOM systems, achieving a higher transparency with hotel and other tourism-related CRSs.

Amadeus Service groups all the value-added functions and information features, which ease the reservation process and provide support for the use of system and products. Central profiles enable agents to secure and access travel related data for their private and corporate clients. Menu-driven and user-friendly displays include all possible information needed for a booking (traveller itinerary, contacts, history, payments, documents) and they are integrated with PNRs for future reference. Changes in clients' travel plans en route are easy to handle because all travel agencies connected to Amadeus have the option to authorise specified agencies using Amadeus to share central profiles.

Amadeus Leisure enables UK travel agencies to network with AT&T Istel and use their terminals as videotext links with tour operators and leisure travel suppliers. This provides an opportunity for travel agencies to use the same computer terminals and network for both leisure and business travel, covering the entire range of products.

The Amadeus Information System gives extensive, accurate information on travel products and destinations in a number of languages. In order to integrate the front and back office, Amadeus offers the 'Amadeus Pro' package, a PC/Windows-based travel agency management system which provides an interactive and integrated management and control system.

ADDING VALUE

Several benefits are introduced by GDSs and Amadeus in particular, namely:

- it saves time by providing single-screen access to all the travel, client and agency information that travellers need;

- it improves service by delivering up-to-date information around the clock in real time;

- it increases productivity by making on-screen information easy to find and understand;

- it saves money by maximising efficiency thanks to stable system performance and rapid response times;

- it improves control by integrating intelligent applications that cover the entire travel agency business processes; and

- it boosts profits by offering the ability to identify hidden opportunities, cross-sell products and provide clients with more of their travel service needs.

THE FUTURE

The future strategies of Amadeus include the improvement of their offering by increasing the range and length of principals represented; enhancing the interactivity between front and back office; and ensuring top-quality service to travel agencies and other clients. These can be achieved by reinforcing and extending Amadeus' market position through three parallel and complementary steps: expansion through partnership; expansion under own steam; and cooperation with other CRSs. The main competitive advantage of Amadeus is ICTs' structure between national marketing companies which provide a unique local knowledge as well as the constant improvement of their offering and their relationship with their partners and clients. This has resulted in its position as the number one in GDS billable air bookings in 2003, generating 356 million bookings and a revenue of US$2.2 billion. Amadeus is driven by a vision which aims to be the leading GDS in terms of customer satisfaction, product superiority and profitability.

CONCLUSIONS

Amadeus is seeking to increase ICTs market share around the world, especially where ICTs' shareholders have a strong commercial interest. Achieving greater penetration in more travel agencies is absolutely vital for the future of the system and therefore a range of add-ons are provided in order to offer an integrated solution package to ICTs' subscribers. In addition, recent investments in OPODO demonstrate that AMADEUS is looking into developing a closer interaction with consumers on the Internet and to take advantage of the direct sales trend. Although developments on the Internet are kept away from publicity, as they imply a certain degree of disintermediation and can create confrontation with travel agencies, Amadeus and all the other GDSs are looking into emerging developments and are identifying new opportunities. As the GDS industry is very volatile and it normally expands through mergers and acquisitions, Amadeus and other GDSs understand the fierce competition and therefore capitalise on their strength to expand their global position by serving niche markets. Constant innovation and change by using leading technology for the benefits of stakeholders are the only methods to meet the requirements of the marketplace and to ensure prosperity for the future.

Source: Compiled through Amadeus Corporate Communication material and www.amadeus.com

DISCUSSION QUESTIONS

1 What is the core business of Amadeus and GDSs in general?

2 What are the key factors that can potentially threaten the future of GDSs?

3 What are the reasons for the regulation and deregulation of GDSs?

CHAPTER TWENTY
THE FUTURE OF TOURISM: TRENDS AND ISSUES BEYOND OUR CONTROL

INTRODUCTION

Predicting the future in tourism is not an easy task. Tourism is increasingly faced with radical and unexpected change, underlining the need for a disciplined approach to the identification of future trends. At the same time, there is a need to utilise this understanding in order to manage the future in terms of policy making and strategies for the tourism sector. Indeed, futurists now accept that the one feature that will distinguish the new tourism from the old tourism is the fact that not only will rapid change be evident, but also that it will be accepted as inevitable – and therefore will need to be managed.

Outside the control of the tourism sector are a range of variables that will have a major impact upon the future of the tourism system. These include social, political and technological factors. There is a danger though, in isolating one trend from another. For example, consumer behaviour, political change, or globalisation are all dynamic and changes in any one of these variables will effect the others. What is also clear is that, while it is possible to identify a range of key variables whose influence is already evident (such as the Internet), others are still emerging. Cutting across each of these trends is a range of other agents of change such as human resources, technology, the search for an acceptable, sustainable tourism sector, the imperative to ensure that travel is safe, and changes in consumer behaviour. In combination, these will be instrumental in determining the future direction of tourism and accelerate the pace of change.

LEARNING OUTCOMES

In this chapter we focus on the drivers of change that will make an impact upon tourism in the future, and yet are largely outside the control of the sector. The chapter will provide you with:

- a disciplined approach to analysing and viewing the future of the tourism system;
- an understanding of the scale of social and political change, including the need for security measures in tourism;
- an awareness of the significance of climate change for tourism futures;
- a grasp of the implications of these variables for tourism; and
- an awareness of the importance of human resources for the future of tourism.

APPROACHING THE FUTURE

Although the history of tourism may be traced back many thousands of years to the Ancient Greeks and the Romans, it is only relatively recently, with the advent of mass tourism, that international activity has become so prevalent in the developed world. The rapid expansion of leisure travel from the 1960s onwards, precipitated by transportation developments, continues to influence all aspects of the tourism system today but it is the future of tourism to which we now turn our attention.

In this chapter we identify the variables that are the driving force of this change in the tourism system. We know that, in certain decades there have been predominant drivers of change. For example, in the mid-nineteenth century and the early decades of the twentieth century, transport developments were critical influences upon tourism. However, since the 1980s it is both technological developments and the maturing of the tourism marketplace that have come to the fore.

It is easy to 'hype up' the future of tourism and provide a sensationalist account of future scenarios from flying cars to virtual reality theme parks. However, this chapter takes a more disciplined approach to the issue by providing a framework within which to consider and analyse tourism futures. In the first chapter of this book we introduced Leiper's (1990) tourism system as a way of thinking about tourism. It is possible to recast this model to take into account the ideas and issues involved in the future of tourism and use this to act as a framework for the chapter (Figure 20.1).

The reason that we like Leiper's framework is that it is an all-encompassing approach to studying tourism. Tourism futurists commonly focus only on the tourism destination part of the system. But this fails to recognise the complexity of the tourism sector and the need to match up trends both on the demand side in terms of markets and consumer behaviour with trends in transportation and on the supply side, in terms of product developments and the destination. To consider any one of these in isolation would provide an unbalanced assessment of the future of tourism.

There are two important reports that cover both the demand and the supply side of tourism futures. On the supply side, the World Travel and Tourism Council's (2003) *Blueprint for New Tourism* lays out an agenda for the future of the tourism sector. As the world's peak tourism industry body, the World Travel and Tourism Council (WTTC) met in 2003 to discuss the state of tourism in the world at the beginning of the twenty-first century. This meeting was held against the background of unprecedented security issues and economic uncertainties for the sector. Indeed, it is these very events that are changing the way that consumers behave, the way that the industry does business, and the way that the public sector views tourism. The WTTC's supply-side agenda for the 'new tourism' has three dimensions:

1 Governments must recognise travel and tourism as a top priority.

2 Tourism business must balance economics with environment, people and cultures.

3 Tourism must develop partnerships to share in the pursuit of long-term growth and prosperity.

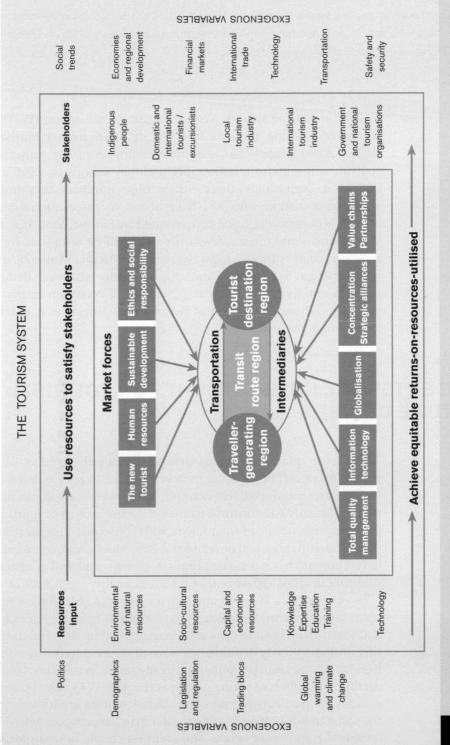

THE TOURISM SYSTEM

EXOGENOUS VARIABLES

Social trends

Economies and regional development

Financial markets

International trade

Technology

Transportation

Safety and security

Use resources to satisfy stakeholders

Stakeholders

Indigenous people

Domestic and international tourists / excursionists

Local tourism industry

International tourism industry

Government and national tourism organisations

Market forces

The new tourist

Human resources

Sustainable development

Ethics and social responsibility

Transportation

Tourist destination region

Transit route region

Traveller-generating region

Intermediaries

Total quality management

Information technology

Globalisation

Concentration Strategic alliances

Value chains Partnerships

Achieve equitable returns-on-resources-utilised

Resources input

Politics

Environmental and natural resources

Demographics

Socio-cultural resources

Legislation and regulation

Capital and economic resources

Trading blocs

Knowledge Expertise Education Training

Global warming and climate change

Technology

EXOGENOUS VARIABLES

741

FIGURE 20.1   A framework for tourism trends analysis: exogenous variables

To quote the WTTC (2003a, p. 3):

New Tourism looks beyond short-term considerations, it focuses on benefits not only for people who travel, but also for people in the communities they visit, and for their respective natural, social and cultural environments.

On the demand side the World Tourism Organization (WTO) has an honorable record of devising accurate forecasts of international tourism. These forecasts (WTO, 2001) suggest that, despite the setbacks of the early twenty-first century, tourism will grow to a billion international arrivals by 2010 and 1.56 billion by 2020. Yet, surprisingly, despite these huge numbers, they only represent 7% of world's population who will have access to international travel. International arrivals will continue to be concentrated in Europe, East Asia and the Pacific and the Americas and the major growth areas will be long-haul travel and newer destinations such as those in East Asia and the Pacific. Demand for domestic tourism will expand at a slower rate and some countries will reach demand-side ceilings of capacity and available leisure time which will constrain further growth. Similarly, on the supply side, problems of terrorism and disease may also discourage tourism growth in some areas.

THE EXTERNAL ENVIRONMENT FOR TOURISM: FUTURE DRIVERS

There are a number of trends that are outside the control of tourism itself and yet will have an impact upon its development. In reality, most of these trends and variables are interlinked, for example, while there is no doubt that the social trends that we identify will continue to encourage the growth of tourism, they will also act to change the nature of the tourism with consequent implications for the management of destinations and development of products. And, of course, the very economic development that has fuelled tourism growth, and will continue to do so, is contributing to climate change that threatens to alter the nature of many destinations.

In other words, these trends, when combined, will have a fundamental impact upon future tourism scenarios and so cannot be ignored. For example, demographic and social trends will be critical in shaping tourism demand in the twenty-first century and also clearly demonstrate how all of these trends are linked. Demographic trends such as ageing populations in the major generating countries, allied to the declining numbers of young people as the post-1945 baby bulge works through the decades are particularly important. Demographics are inextricably entangled with the social trends that are leading to later marriage, couples deferring having children, increased numbers of single- and childless-couple households, and the enhanced role of women in travel activity. Interwoven with these trends are the changing values of the population which effect consumer behaviour, in particular the adoption of family values and the search for safety and security, all wrapped into cocooning behaviour where the home becomes the basis for leisure activities. In the developing world a burgeoning workforce will lead to immigration to developed countries and the growth of knowledge and interest in other countries will see a convergence of lifestyles across the world. With increased media attention and levels of education, these trends will give people more time, resources and inclination to travel, fuelled by the growth and spread of discretionary incomes and the liberalisation of trade on an international scale.

SOCIAL DRIVERS OF CHANGE

Demographic trends

The world's population is growing by 80 million per year, placing pressure upon the world's resources. Indeed, in some countries tourism is, rightly, not seen as a priority. This may be due to issues of poverty and hunger, while elsewhere, shortages of resources such as water act to constrain tourism growth. However, for the majority of the key generators of both domestic and international tourism, population growth is either static or even negative. This means that, in the twenty-first century, declining birth rates will lead to a marked reduction of population in the developed world. In some developed countries, these downward pressures on population might be offset by increased immigration. Yet, although populations may fall, economies in most developed countries will keep growing. Higher productivity will mean higher per capita incomes and consumption of tourism products as discretionary income rises.

In the major generating markets for tourism, populations are ageing as birth rates fall and people live longer. Ageing populations tend to be associated with urbanisation and conservative politics and they are influencing patterns of public expenditure to reflect the needs of older people. Markets for the goods and services that older people need have clear implications for the tourism sector and it is the ageing baby boomer generations of the developed world that are one of the most important market segments. Their needs will change, as will tastes and preferences, towards travel for self-education, cultural and self-enhancing activities. They will be fitter, healthier and more demanding consumers than the previous generations. Equally, the younger generations – X and Y – will remain in the youth market longer as they marry later, but continue with the youth lifestyle. They will also influence future consumer behaviour as they will be both more technologically adept than the baby boomers, but they will also be more savvy when it comes to responding to marketing messages.

Social trends

Throughout much of society there is an increasing and conflicting concern for the environment and an emphasis on hedonic conspicuous consumption – both trends demanding a response from the tourism sector, and in part boosted by the September 11, 2001 attacks. In addition, tastes are polarising into comfort and adventure-orientated activities. Family structures in the developed world are changing with a trend to later marriage, more one-parent families and having children at a later age. Each of these trends has implications for the consumer behaviour of visitors and the consequent development of tourism products. Changing patterns of leisure time too are influential and predictions of a leisured society from the sociologists of the 1960s have never truly come about. This is because concern for job security means that leisure time is squeezed and workers do not take their full entitlement as the distinction between work and leisure time blurs. Also, ceilings on tourism growth are being reached in some countries, as growing numbers of people are time poor, but money rich. We can draw from these general social trends three that have specific implications for tourism:

1 Worldwide, more people will choose to live in cities. Urbanisation skews public expenditure towards urban services and infrastructure and changes patterns of private consumption. This trend also has important policy implications in terms of the growth of city states, as we note below, and the use of tourism to market cities. It also means that tourist resources will be increasingly located adjacent to the urban market, favouring artificial types of development such as theme parks as has occurred in Japan.

2 In many countries, both the status and influence of women are on the increase. More women will work in businesses or take paid jobs, achieving even greater economic and social autonomy. There will be strong growth in the market for the types of goods and services that affluent, autonomous women demand, including tourism, as women have an increasing say not only in purchasing decisions, but also in the types of products offered by the tourism sector.

3 Populations are also becoming more culturally diverse as improved communications, increasing wealth and mobility stimulate people to try to understand other cultures. Tourism products and their marketing will increasingly have to embrace cultural diversity and niche products – such as gay tourism – are emerging as a consequence.

POLITICAL DRIVERS OF CHANGE

The future of tourism cannot be divorced from political events and trends. Initiatives at different geographical scales are changing the world order and will impact upon tourism. For example, at the international level, tourism in the future will be influenced by three key trends – the development of trade liberalisation under the umbrella of the General Agreement on Trade in Services (GATS); the forging of international trading blocs; and globalisation.

GATS

The GATS is based on the principle that market forces are the best means of providing consumers with the best products at the best prices. In the GATS negotiations tourism is less of a controversial issue than other economic sectors and so has had a relatively low profile. While a business environment that is truly free of barriers is a good thing for tourism, the implementation of the principle needs to be done with an emphasis on sustainability – to quote the World Tourism Organization, this means 'liberalization with a human face', where vulnerable workers, environments and communities are protected. This will be a key challenge for the future of tourism. The GATS will have a number of major implications for the tourism sector:

- encouragement of open tourism markets to benefit economic development and poverty elimination in the developing world;

- elimination of barriers to tourism growth in the supply chain;

- fair competition for all countries and safety nets for developing markets;

- identifying and eliminating anti-competitive practices in tourism such as cartels and monopolies; and

- equal access to transport and distribution systems.

Trade blocs

An opposing trend to the GATS is the formation of a number of trading blocs across the globe as country groupings come together in economic alliances. Notable here are the North American Free Trade Agreement (NAFTA), the creation and expansion of the European Union (EU) and the Association of South East Asian Nations (ASEAN). In the EU, the adoption of the euro as a common currency is demonstrating the power of these blocs, as the currency is encouraging tourism across Europe; while the expansion of the EU itself will begin to change the balance of tourism flows within Europe.

However, a contradictory trend at the regional level is the rise of regionalism and a search for cultural identity – particularly among ethnic minorities. In the midst of this contradiction 'city states' are emerging as major visitor destinations where tourism plays a key role in 'boosting' the reputations, lifestyle and economies of cities. Examples here include the way that major events such as hosting the Olympic Games or the Football World Cup have benefited the image of cities (compare Sydney's approach to hosting the Olympics to that of Athens for example).

Globalisation

Underlying the changing world order is the globalisation of tourism businesses – a powerful force shaping national and regional economies, which are linked and interdependent as never before. Globalisation is a product of combining the revolution in information technology and telecommunications, a strengthening consensus among national governments in favour of free trade, the decline of communism and the democratisation of financial markets. The term applies to the increasing interdependence of markets and production in different countries. Key drivers of globalisation in tourism are:

- adoption of free trade agreements, removing barriers to international transactions;

- computer and communications technology encouraging 'ebusiness';

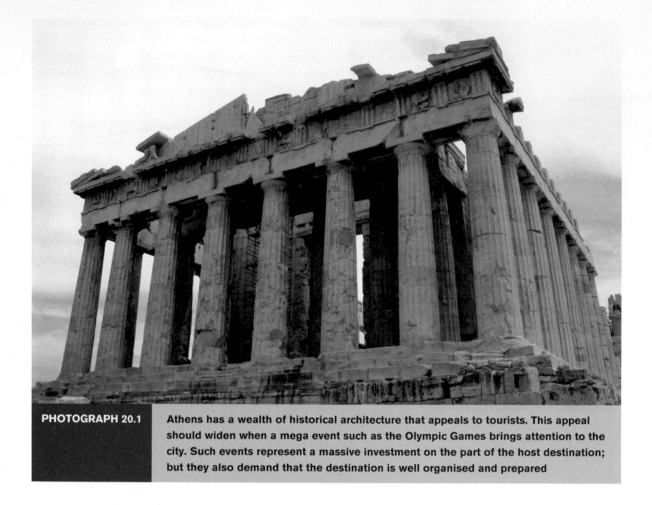

PHOTOGRAPH 20.1 Athens has a wealth of historical architecture that appeals to tourists. This appeal should widen when a mega event such as the Olympic Games brings attention to the city. Such events represent a massive investment on the part of the host destination; but they also demand that the destination is well organised and prepared

- worldwide acting suppliers utilising CRS and global distribution systems (GDS);
- decreasing costs of international travel allowing access to most markets in the world;
- increasing income and wealth in the generating countries; and
- newly emerging destinations and the increased demand for international travel.

In the future the consequences of globalisation for the tourism sector include:

- increasingly standardised procedures and quality control;
- increased competition;
- head office decisions on marketing and technology in the larger companies;
- forging of strategic alliances;
- increased concentration within the accommodation, transport and intermediaries sectors;
- adoption of global brands such as Disney, Hilton and American Express;
- changing management approaches;

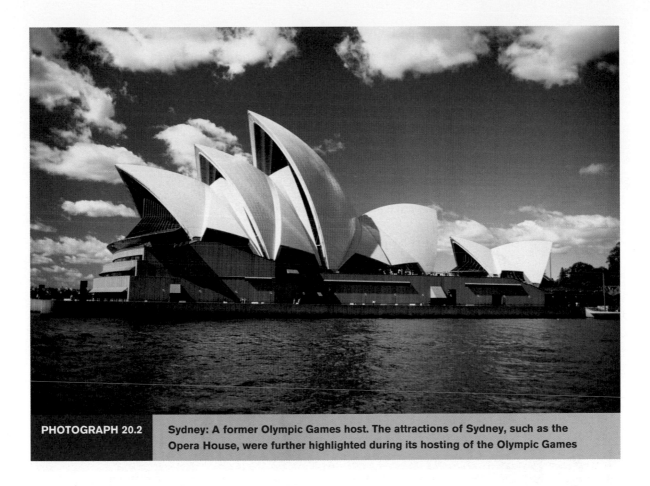

PHOTOGRAPH 20.2   Sydney: A former Olympic Games host. The attractions of Sydney, such as the Opera House, were further highlighted during its hosting of the Olympic Games

- adoption of new ways of doing business, such as use of email and the Internet;
- adoption of global distribution systems and yield management;
- changing human resource management practices; and
- more difficult trading conditions for small and medium-sized enterprises (SMEs).

As the last point above suggests, it is only the larger, international companies that can take advantage of these trends. Indeed, globalisation goes hand in hand with increased concentration in the tourism industry as major companies gain market share and market influence. At the same time we are seeing the concentration of capital in the hands of a few major players in the tourism sector; a trend that also drives tourism towards the performance indicators and business practices demanded by the finance industry. The pace of concentration being generated by both horizontal and vertical integration is such that for medium-sized companies in tourism the days ahead may be difficult. Quite simply for a tourism enterprise there are many advantages to increased size in a multinational market:

- ability to resource high-profile promotional campaigns;
- brand name benefits through standardisation and quality control;
- ability to spread the risk among various markets;

- implementation of advanced marketing techniques on an international basis;

- utilisation of technology (especially GDS and the Internet);

- optimisation of capacity/inventory usage and reduction of seasonality problems;

- access to the international labour market;

- advantages over other members of the distribution channel;

- improved political influence;

- managers who have more time to manage; and

- market prominence and stronger branding.

However, a particular problem associated with this trend is that most of the larger corporations do not have a relationship with a specific destination. They may therefore be less sensitive to the impact of their operations on host environments, economies and communities. In addition, small and medium-sized tourism enterprises and local destinations fear the 'neo-colonial' relationship which can emerge from dealing with large companies. This is an important consideration for tourism where, at the end of the day, the product is delivered locally; hence the conundrum of balancing the global forces upon an essentially 'local' product.

MINI CASE STUDY 20.1
Tourism SMEs fight back

THE ISSUE

Small and medium-sized enterprises (SMEs) form the backbone of most tourism destinations. In Europe for example, SMEs account for 90% of all tourism businesses and more than 94% of them are micro operators employing fewer than ten individuals. And they are a sector that should be encouraged – SMEs make a positive contribution to economic and social development at the destination, they encourage the entrepreneurial spirit, mobilise savings and boost regional development.

However, the globalisation trends identified above mean that tourism SMEs are an endangered species, as they struggle to compete with the larger companies. Smeral (1998), for example, confirms that globalisation is increasing the pressure on SMEs:

> The potential of SMEs for realising economies of scale is very low and the use of computer reservation systems (CRSs) has not spread significantly. Many restaurant and hotel businesses are sources of side income for people engaged in the agriculture sector. Furthermore, SMEs are disadvantaged because of their high unit average costs with respect to production.

THE RESPONSE

In response to this threat we can identify two key trends as follows.

1 Policy initiatives to assist SMEs to become competitive

There are a number of examples of policies that have been designed to protect SMEs from the worst excesses of global competition and to boost their competitiveness.

At the *international level*, the European Commission has formulated an enterprise policy to support SMEs and counter the advantages that the formation of the European Union has brought to the larger operators at the expense of the small one. For SMEs the policy aims to:

- create a favourable business environment by removing unnecessary and costly administrative, physical and legal burdens;

- encourage cross-border cooperation between enterprises;

- commit to providing business information and support; and

- encourage SMEs to set up joint transnational businesses in the European Union.

At the *national level* the Austrian government has implemented policies to support SMEs and family-owned tourism business to provide a favourable environment for tourism development. These policies include:

1 Subsidies to ensure that local capital is invested in the industry to counter the high share of foreign investment capital.

2 Promotion of cooperation to develop local networks to implement pilot projects such as multiple distribution channels, destination management schemes and joint marketing.

2 Response from the SME sector

Many destination-based tourism SMEs have realised that they are not necessarily competing against each other, but against SMEs in other destinations. This has given rise to a cooperative spirit by SMEs at the destination where they cooperate, but also compete – 'coop-etition'. Tourism lends itself well to this new business environment. Tourism services are consumed where they are produced, at the destination, and the fragmented and interdependent nature of the tourism product means that suppliers must coordinate their operations to provide the overall experience.

This cooperation is taking a number of forms but they coalesce around the idea of clusters. In tourism there are two main types of cluster: one based upon the destination where SMEs work together at the destination level; and one based upon a sector of tourism, such as say accommodation or restaurants. The benefits of SME clusters include:

- economies of scale by working together with others to boost buying power, marketing resources and research;

- information sharing about the latest techniques and technologies to keep SMEs up to date and competitive;

- more rational and efficient distribution of activities; and

- political cohesion among SMEs allowing them to lobby for their specific interests.

These clusters give individual SMEs competitive advantage, although this does depend on the strength of the other members of the cluster. In many tourism clusters leading enterprises play an important role. At a destination, the lead enterprise may be a large hotel which may support the costs of developing and running a public facility, sponsor local events or provide marketing actions for the area. Often, the public sector has a coordinating role to support these SME clusters.

THE RESULT

There is no doubt that SMEs are fighting back against globalisation and concentration in the tourism sector. As a result, a new breed of successful, smaller, niched, enterprises are emerging as influential in the future of tourism; enterprises that are cleverly networking and clustering together to compete with the larger organisations. Their competitive advantages include:

- a differentiated product which does not compete on price;

- a high level of personalised service;

- a high level of product knowledge;

- quality:price ratio; and

- a synergistic relationship with the destination.

However, it is also important to recognise that these SME initiatives are taking place within a public sector policy framework that is designed to protect tourism SMEs from globalisation, as both governments and consumers recognise the value of tourism products and services delivered at the local destination, by local enterprises, employing local people.

DISCUSSION QUESTIONS

1 Draft a list of the competitive disadvantages experienced by tourism SMEs in the face of globalisation.

2 What are the main benefits to an SME in joining a business cluster?

3 Why might an SME in tourism NOT want to cooperate with others?

Emergent patterns

The redrafting of the political map of the world has a number of continuing and future implications for tourism. The emergence of market economies in Eastern Europe has led to an increased demand to travel from the populations of those countries and also to the development of destinations and products in the region. Business and specialist leisure travel, particularly cultural tourism, has grown as travel restrictions have been eased, infrastructure improved and attitudes to service changed. Indeed, so successful has been the opening up of tourism in the region that Hungary, Poland, the Czech Republic and the Russian Federation have moved into the top 20 international destinations. In other parts of the world too, new destinations such as South Africa are developing as they have become politically acceptable, or emerge from conflict – as in Vietnam and the Lebanon.

SAFETY, SECURITY AND RISK

The events of the early years of the twenty-first century have tended to focus attention on security risks to travel associated with terrorism and acts of war. However, tourism is affected also by natural disasters such as earthquakes, floods and avalanches. The WTO therefore defines a crisis as:

Any unexpected event that affects traveler confidence in a destination and interferes with the ability to operate normally.

Recent events have changed the way that we travel as both acts of terrorism and war have brought both travellers and the tourism sector to the front line of the war against terrorism. Elsewhere in this book we have outlined the sector's response to September 11, 2001 and in this section we look to the future. Within a few weeks of the attacks of September 11 the tourism sector had adopted a new vocabulary including phrases such as 'risk management', 'destination recovery' and 'crisis management'. Bierman (2002) has coined a new scale for tourism to describe the magnitude of crisis that can have an impact upon a destination. He calls this the DESTCON scale with DESTCON 1 the most severe crisis that tourism can experience down to DESTCON 5, when normality resumes.

From the industry's point of view, the WTTC recommends a twin-track approach to security:

1 Promoting the virtues of a coordinated strategy and operational measures across all parts of the tourism sector.

2 Convincing the public and industry employees that the reality of tourism must be to co-exist with terrorism, providing that the risk is mitigated.

The essence of the WTTC's approach is the forging of partnerships between the private sector and governments and the fact that security *cannot* be an area for commercial rivalry. Their approach is based upon four principles:

1 Coordinate policy actions and communications. Here, for example, there is an ongoing debate as the role of 'travel advisories'.

2 Develop secure operating environments for travel including both equipment and personnel. Of course, this will be an inconvenience for travellers as evidenced by

the introduction of fingerprinting and photographs for all inbound travellers to the USA in 2004. In the future the introduction of biometric passports will occur with the inclusion of data such as retinal scans.

3 Access and work with the best intelligence to prevent future incidents and security breaches.

4 Deny terrorists freedom of action.

As a result largely of September 11, 2001 tourism enterprises, destinations and governments have begun to develop and implement crisis and risk management strategies. These strategies recognise the timetable of a crisis and document appropriate responses, as can be seen from the WTO's crisis guidelines for the tourism industry (Table 20.1).

Tourists' behaviour too, can be a bio-security threat to tourism as the spread of AIDS may render some otherwise attractive destinations no-go areas while increasingly vociferous campaigns against sex tourism may also alter tourism flows and motivations. Elsewhere, disease and decreasing levels of safety will constrain the uninhibited expansion of tourism. At the macro level, these factors are largely outside the control of tourism and their consequences may be severe, yet at the micro level, the tourism industry will increasingly have to manage issues such as safety and security at the destination.

TABLE 20.1	The WTO's crisis guidelines for the tourism industry
Before the crisis – be prepared	Prepare a crisis management plan Be prepared for promotional activity Review security systems Be research ready
During the crisis – minimise damage	Communicate from the front line Devise promotional messages Ensure security of the operation Do tactical research on the situation
After the crisis – recovering tourist confidence	Communicate confidence Use promotion imaginatively Evaluate security measures Use research effectively to build confidence

Source: WTO, 2003a

MINI CASE STUDY 20.2
Destination recovery: the Bali bombings

THE CRISIS

Bali is the largest holiday destination in Indonesia for both international and domestic tourists. Tourism is the major economic activity on Bali, employing 60,000 people in restaurants and hotels alone and estimates suggest that tourism represents around 50% of the island's economy. Arrivals to the island totalled 1.3 million in 2001, with a wide mix of visitors coming from the Americas (7%); Europe (32%); Asia (40%); and Australia/New Zealand (20%).

On Saturday 12 October 2002, almost 200 tourists and local people were killed by a series of terrorist bombings at a night club in Bali's most popular resort, Kuta. Many more people were injured.

The immediate impact of the bombings was devastating for the tourism sector in Bali with hotels recording occupancy levels below 10%, inbound air capacity was drastically reduced, many local businesses were forced to close and unemployment levels on the island rose significantly. Even where businesses were able to stay open, staff took voluntary pay cuts. In part this was due to the global publicity generated by the bombings, but also the impact of government 'travel advisories' advising against travel to Bali. Indeed, until the bombings, Bali was routinely excluded from travel advisories that applied to the rest of Indonesia. But from October 2002, Bali was branded as an equally 'risky' destination.

DESTINATION RECOVERY

There is no doubt that for tourism in Bali, the bombings represented a crisis on the scale of DESTCON 1 using Bierman's (2002) scale. To quote Bierman (p. 20):

> DESTCON 1: A crisis of this magnitude not only threatens the marketability of one destination but has widespread global or regional repercussions on tourism.

The task for the tourism sector in Bali was to reduce the destination from DESTCON 1 to almost normality – DESTCON 5, where there is a minimal precise threat to the destination and marketing conditions are back to normal. Needless to say both the Balinese and the Indonesian government received advice from many sources, but perhaps the most strategic recommendations came from the Pacific Asia Travel Association (2003a). They made eight recommendations to assist the destination recover from DESTCON 1:

1 Bring all the disparate elements of tourism together at the destination to follow the same agenda. This recommendation relates to the fact that so many different players are involved in a destination. The recommendation stresses the need for coordination and lobbying (of, say, governments re travel advisories) and that conflict and disagreements are counterproductive following a crisis of this magnitude.

2 Create an environment for careful planning within which issues of safety and security are addressed and if necessary become enforceable by law. Many destinations in Indonesia have been poorly managed in the past and this is an opportunity to look afresh at Bali and ensure that sound planning and management principles are applied as it recovers.

3 The government of Bali should establish, in coordination with the national government, an integrated crisis management plan in which procedures for crisis communication are included. The outline of a crisis management plan is shown in Table 20.1 and outlined in the PATA book on crises (PATA, 2003b). The lesson is that all destinations should be prepared for a DESTCON situation by putting a plan in place.

4 Recognise the importance of the aviation sector and work more closely with it. Islands are dependent upon their carriers, and this recommendation urges the island to work closely with them as recovery is underway.

5 Rebuild destination brand through the private/public/consumer sectors and work with a 'destination maker'. This recommendation urges the island not to enter a period of cost cutting, but rather to work with professional marketing organisations to rebuild the destination and its image.

6 Comprehensively broaden the Bali brand to encompass culture and heritage. In the past Bali has been known as a beach destination but has much more to offer in terms of tourism resources; resources that can deliver a competitive edge over other Asian beach destinations.

7 Introduce the Bali brand to contemporary market platforms. Effectively Bali can use this opportunity to look afresh at its source markets and begin to target new ones – such as China; India; Russia and Eastern Europe; and the Middle East.

8 Increase brand awareness through partnership marketing.

These recommendations are based upon sound professional judgement in tourism and emphasise the importance that image, branding and marketing play in the recovery of destinations. They also demonstrate that, tragic though the bombings were, a destination can use such an incident to re-evaluate its whole approach to planning, marketing and working with the international tourism industry.

Sources: Bierman (2002); Pacific Asia Travel Association (2003a)

DISCUSSION QUESTIONS

1 Using the Internet and print sources, identify some of the tourism products currently on offer in Bali. Do they suggest that the industry has taken on board PATA's sixth recommendation?

2 List the first things that come to your mind when you think about Bali – how can these perceptions be built into the 'brand' for Bali?

3 Crisis management plans are now essential for destinations. Looking at Table 20.1, draft a checklist of research that you feel would be useful in the plan.

CLIMATE CHANGE

The social, demographic and political drivers identified above have generally encouraged economic growth, and tourism. However, this growth over the last 150 years has also begun to have far-reaching consequences for the earth's climate. There is no doubt that one of the most significant environmental influences upon the future of tourism will be global climate change. This includes long-term factors such as **global warming** and the erosion of the ozone layer. In order to analyse the impact of climate change on tourism we need to consider the total tourism system, including transport. On the supply side, there is no doubt that the raising of the earth's temperature and the consequent rise in sea level will affect tourism destinations such as wetlands, islands and coastal areas. The major case study at the and of this chapter examines the impact of such change upon one of Australia's tourism icons, the Great Barrier Reef. Much of tourism investment is found in locations that fringe the coast, and global warming will irrevocably alter vital tourism resources such as the flora and fauna of destinations; as well as ski resorts as the snowline recedes. On the demand side, fear of skin cancer and cataracts may reduce the demand for products such as beach tourism which, in turn will impact upon destination and product development. Finally, we have to recognise that some transport modes used for tourism will contribute to climate change.

The seriousness of the problem has prompted policy and management intervention. At the international level, in 2003, the World Tourism Organization issued *The Djerba Declaration on Tourism and Climate Change* (WTO, 2003b), urging governments to:

- adopt the Kyoto protocol on greenhouse gas emissions;
- research and collaborate on climate change;
- move tourism up the agenda on climate change discussion;
- implement sustainable water use practices and the ecological management of sensitive areas; and
- raise consumer awareness of the issue.

HUMAN RESOURCES FOR TOURISM

Many of you reading this book will be looking towards the tourism industry for a career. Indeed, the challenges facing the tourism industry will only be met successfully by a well-educated, well-trained, bright, energetic, multilingual and entrepreneurial workforce who understand the nature of tourism and have a professional training. A high quality of professional human resources in tourism will allow enterprises to gain a competitive edge and deliver added value with their service. In this book, we have outlined a professional and analytical approach to tourism; an approach that demands high standards of professionalism and education. Achievement of many of the best practices that we outline will only be possible with a well-trained tourism workforce. We therefore conclude this chapter with an examination of future trends and issues in human resource management in the tourism industry.

Tourism is a high-touch, high-tech, high-involvement industry where it is the people that make the difference. Yet, in a number of countries, an acute shortage of trained manpower may prejudice the growth of tourism. There is no doubt that the tourism industry is under pressure. Changing markets, industry restructuring and more competitive domestic and international markets are placing great burdens on their expertise. The ability to succeed and the future performance of tourism and related activities will depend largely upon the skills, qualities and knowledge that managers will be able to bring to their business.

In the past, tourism has been characterised by a lack of sophistication in human resource policies and practices, imposed by outmoded styles of human resource management and approaches to operational circumstances. This leaves tourism vulnerable to ideas, takeovers and domination by management practices found in other economic sectors. Indeed, practices that are commonplace in other service industries – comprehensive induction, regular appraisal, effective employee communications – are underdeveloped in many tourism and leisure businesses. Educators and trainers have a role to play here by facilitating innovation, encouraging empowerment, motivating the workforce and, in partnership with industry, working to overcome the specific problems of tourism.

A high-quality tourism workforce can only be achieved through high standards of tourism education and training. Tourism education and training involves the communication of knowledge, concepts and techniques that are specific to the field of tourism, but which draw upon the core disciplines and themes of areas such as geography, finance and marketing. Traditionally, the domain of tourism education has been the encouragement of analytical thinking and the understanding of conceptual issues in order to contribute to the professional and intellectual development of a person. Tourism training, on the other hand, is more concerned with delivering practical knowledge, skills and techniques.

Tourism training has a long pedigree and emerged as the tourism industry grew both in size and complexity. Initially, training was linked to the operations of intermediaries, particularly in areas such as ticketing, or in the various craft operations for hospitality. In the developing world much of tourism training is still confined to these areas but in the developed world, tourism training has expanded to embrace many functions as the industry becomes more professional and technological and demands higher standards of its practitioners. Tourism education is a much more recent activity. Apart from a handful of institutions, most tourism education courses are a product of the 1980s and 1990s. This is because it is only in recent years that governments have recognised the value of tourism to their economies and, in particular, linked manpower planning and education/training for tourism with competitiveness and productivity.

The benefits of both education and training for tourism should be clear:

- They ensure a high quality of service is provided to the consumer.

- For the industry as a whole they add value, raise the quality of personnel and infuse a sense of professionalism and ownership.

- They also help to define the industry and point out the underlying similarities of the many differing sectors (transport, hospitality, attractions, etc.).

- Those working in the industry also understand the interrelationships of the sectors and begin to perceive business opportunities.

- Training, in particular, delivers skills and practical knowledge which boosts the performance and productivity of personnel across the industry and the linking of education and training with manpower planning allows a closer gearing of the needs of the sector with the output of hotel and tourism schools.

- They help to retain staff, provide a career path for employees and overall, achieve a better use of human resources in the tourism industry.

- They ensure that a destination's tourism product is delivered by local people and not by imported labour.

In the future, tourism education and training must be responsive to the changing needs of the sector and here, we can identify three key trends:

1 **Deepening within the subject area.** We are seeing an evolution of tourism education and training that recognises the need for a broad-based education system. In the past, the weight of provision tended to be confined to hospitality elements. The inclusion of tourism and travel into these programmes will ensure that not only will the accommodation sector be well managed, but also that the country's attractions, transportation and ground handling will be professionally organised with high standards of service, destination management and guiding.

2 **Broadening to other subject areas.** A second trend is the shifting balance between tourism and hospitality course content and core management and business areas such as finance or marketing. In the future, the tourism manager will need to be knowledgeable in, say, generic marketing approaches, but will also have to be able to apply that expertise within a tourism or hospitality context.

3 **Development of quality standards.** A third trend is the involvement of international bodies such as the World Tourism Organization to integrate quality standards into tourism education and training, through programmes such as the GTAT certification.

CONCLUSION

This chapter has attempted to identify the key trends that will influence the future of tourism and yet are largely outside the control of the tourism manager. The message is clear, tourism will only be an acceptable and successful industry in the future if a well-trained and professional workforce is in place and able to implement the very best practice in managing tourism. The tourism manager of the future will need to be aware of the trends in the tourism marketplace, external factors such as global climate change and not only the changing political order of the world, but also means by which this is being brought about. Here, the response of the tourism sector to the threats of terrorism and consumer reaction to these situations means that we must be more professional and disciplined in our management of tourism. No longer should tourism be the preserve of the amateur – as we have shown, small businesses have just as much to gain by adopting a professional approach.

Self-check questions

1 Draft a list of measurable characteristics that would allow a market researcher to identify a 'new tourist'.

2 Construct a list of the key dimensions of climate change and, for each, assess its potential impact on tourism.

3 Think back to your last tourism trip. List the security measures evident both on the journey and at the destination. Were there any gaps in the security that you noticed?

4 Make a list of the pros and cons of working in the hospitality industry as a waiter, kitchen assistant or hotel receptionist.

5 Think of one of the large multinational tourism companies such as a hotel group or airline. What are their major competitive advantages over a small business in the same sector?

Essay questions

1 Consider the implications of the emergence of the 'new tourist' for each part of Leiper's tourism system.

2 Taking a destination of your choice, assess the threat to the tourism sector posed by climate change.

3 Is the future of tourism a secure one?

4 Assess the role of women in future tourism consumer decision making in the developed world.

5 Write a critique of the WTTC's *Blueprint for New Tourism*.

Annotated further reading

Bierman, D. (2002) *Restoring Tourism Destinations in Crisis: A Strategic Marketing Approach*, CAB, Wallingford.
An excellent framework for approaching crises and a useful set of case studies.

Pacific Asia Travel Association (2003) *Crisis. It Won't happen to Us*, PATA, Bangkok.
A comprehensive hands-on guide to risk and crisis management for the tourism sector.

Wahab, S. and Cooper, C. (2001) *Tourism in the Age of Globalisation*, Routledge, London.
A systematic review of the impact of globalisation on all sectors of tourism.

WTO (2001) *Tourism 2020 Vision*, WTO, Madrid.
A thorough examination at both demand- and supply-side future scenarios for tourism.

WTO (2003) *Climate Change and Tourism*, WTO, Madrid.
The first comprehensive analysis of tourism and climate change.

WTTC (2003) *Blueprint for New Tourism*, WTTC, London.
A forward-looking document that accepts the realities of tourism in the twenty-first century and puts forward the agenda as viewed by the world's largest tourism companies.

References cited

Bierman, D. (2002) *Restoring Tourism Destinations in Crisis: A Strategic Marketing Approach*, CAB, Wallingford.

Leiper, N. (1990) *Tourism Systems*, Massey University Department of Management Systems Occasional Paper 2, Auckland, New Zealand.

Pacific Asia Travel Association (2003a) *The PATA Bali Recovery Task Force: Report and Recommendations*, PATA, Bangkok.

Pacific Asia Travel Association (2003b) *Crisis. It Won't Happen to Us*, PATA, Bangkok.

Smeral, E. (1998) 'The impact of globalisation on small and medium enterprises: new challenges for tourism policies in European countries', *Tourism Management* 9(4), 371–80.

WTO (2001) *Tourism 2020 Vision*, WTO, Madrid.

WTO (2003a) *Crisis Guidelines for the Tourism Industry*, WTO Madrid.

WTO (2003b) *The Djerba Declaration on Tourism and Climate Change*, WTO, Madrid.

WTTC (2003) *Blueprint for New Tourism*, WTTC, London.

MAJOR CASE STUDY 20.1
THE EFFECT OF CLIMATE CHANGE ON
AUSTRALIA'S GREAT BARRIER REEF

INTRODUCTION

Climate is altering the environment for tourism and has increasingly become the focus for policy and management initiatives. However, these initiatives must be based on sound, scientific
research. In this case study we outline the implications of scientific research on the Great
Barrier Reef off Australia's eastern coast. The Great Barrier Reef is one of Australia's tourism
icons and is worth over three-quarters of a billion US dollars to the economy through tourism
and fishing activity. However, global warming is increasing sea temperatures and impacting
upon coral reefs all around the world; so much so that reefs have been termed 'canaries'
of environmental change due to their sensitivity. Estimates suggest that sea temperatures
will rise between 1.5 and 4.5 °C in the twenty-first century. The rise in sea temperatures is
primarily caused by greenhouse gas emissions as a result of human activity such as the burning of oil and coal. Even if greenhouse gas emissions keep this sea level rise to the lower end
of the estimates, coral reefs around the world will suffer considerable episodes of coral
bleaching and death.

In 2004, scientific research by the World Wildlife Fund (WWF) on the impact of climate
change upon the Great Barrier Reef was published – and the news was not good. As a result
the report was greeted with sensational media headlines:

- **'Great Barrier Reef to be decimated by 2005'**
  Australia's Great Barrier Reef will lose 95% of its living coral by 2050 – predicts a new
  report. And this devastating situation will occur if the best case scenario for global warming unfolds.

  However, the damning predictions have sparked debate with some researchers saying
  the claims are exaggerated. They do not reflect the current level of uncertainty about either
  the impact of warmer waters on the reef, or likely climate change, say critics. (*New Scientist*,
  23/2/04)

- **Australia's reef day's 'numbered'**
  The Great Barrier Reef off the east coast of Australia will be largely destroyed by 2050
  because of rising sea temperatures . . .

  The new study predicts that within about 15 years the Great Barrier Reef tourist and
  fishing industries will lose thousands of millions of dollars and many thousands of people
  will be forced out of work. (*BBC News 21/2/04*)

The report also sparked a fierce debate about the accuracy of the estimates of rises in sea
temperatures with some scientists saying they may be as low as 0.4 °C. What is clear though
is that global warming will have an impact upon this tourism icon of Australia; indeed some
suggest that much of the damage had already been done in the twentieth century and the
damage is irreversible.

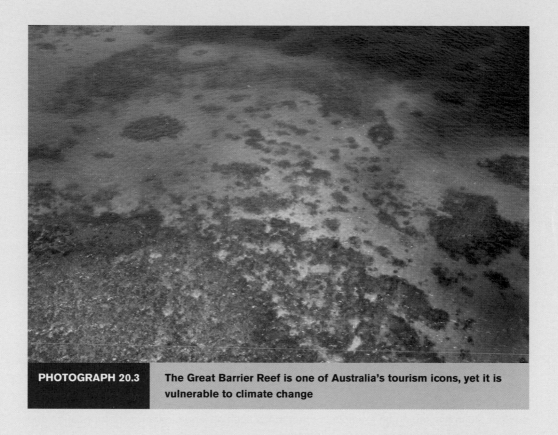

PHOTOGRAPH 20.3   The Great Barrier Reef is one of Australia's tourism icons, yet it is vulnerable to climate change

THE SCIENTIFIC EVIDENCE

The continued warming of the seas around the Great Barrier Reef is the most significant threat to its existence. The WWF report estimates rises in sea level in the region to be anything from 2 °C to 6 °C by the end of the century. As early as 2050 sea temperatures will be such that coral will become rare over much of the reef, with only 5% of existing coral remaining. Of course, this does not mean that the reef will disappear, but it will be much less attractive and lose the colourful fish and corals that attract tourism every year.

Quite simply, corals cannot adapt to rises in sea temperature quickly enough. The report says that over geological time scales the reef will recover, but few tourism forecasts work in geological time and any damage to the reef will impact heavily upon the tourism industry of northern Queensland.

THE ECONOMIC AND SOCIAL IMPACT

It is difficult to measure the true value of an economic resource such as the Great Barrier Reef. The major economic benefit from the reef comes from international and domestic tourism, with major gateways on the mainland such as Cairns, and many island resorts (such as the Whitsundays), and boat operators dependent upon the reef for income and employment. Indeed, without the attraction of the reef, thriving tourism destinations such as Cairns would lose a significant element of their tourism industry (some estimate 80–90% of tourism activity in Cairns is based upon the reef). While we know that tourism is a resilient industry and can recover from crises, this is a crisis of a different kind, effectively taking away the icon tourism attraction of a region and removing its competitive edge. Other economic activity such as fishing, mining and agriculture would also be heavily affected.

Social impacts will also be felt, for example, by the coastal communities along the reef where tourism delivers social well-being, and also for the indigenous peoples who will lose much of the natural and cultural heritage if the reef changes in composition.

FUTURE SCENARIOS

The Great Barrier Reef is probably one of the best managed reef systems in the world, overseen by the Great Barrier Reef Marine Park Authority (GBRMPA). Yet this cannot save it from climate change; an influence outside the control of the reef system. Greenhouse gas emissions determine climate change and rises in sea temperature. The worst case scenario is for economic growth to continue with expansion of greenhouse gas emissions up until 2050, followed by a decline in emissions due to alternative energy sources and increasing environmental considerations. A better case scenario is for environmental policy to be strengthened from local to international levels which will gradually reduce emissions, though it will depend upon global cooperation. Other scenarios stress the importance of strong local involvement and this has been evident in the communities on and around the reef. However, realistically, much of the damage to the reef is caused by factors outside the control of the local community.

This issue can only be seriously tackled at the international level. This will involve governments committing to the Kyoto Protocol of greenhouse gas emission targets and governments such as Australia setting an example in other areas such as land clearance, deforestation and the sustainable use and generation of energy.

For the reef itself it is clear that some damage has already been done. However, with wise resource management future damage can be minimised. GBRMPA are instigating a new zoning plan for activities on the reef with large reductions in fishing quotas. This should strengthen the reef's resilience to change. At the same time there are policies in place to reduce the level of water pollution affecting the reef.

But there is little that the tourism sector can do to save the reef. In this case study, tourism is a victim of wider social and economic activity that is impacting negatively upon one of the world's tourism cons. Of course, international action is needed to reverse these trends, but we must also ensure that the development of scientific research, as done here by the World Wildlife Fund, continues to inform the tourism sector and is effectively communicated to the world.

REFERENCE

World Wildlife Fund (2004) *The Implications of Climate Change for Australia's Great Barrier Reef*, WWF, Australia.

DISCUSSION QUESTIONS

1 How do you think tourists' perceptions of the Great Barrier Reef will be affected by the death of the coral?

2 Using the Internet and travel brochures, draw up a list of tourist products and activities on the Great Barrier Reef and along the coastal areas such as Cairns. Estimate how much of this tourism activity is dependent upon a healthy reef environment.

3 As a tourism accommodation enterprise in Cairns, how would you diversify your source of business ahead of a decline in visitors to your property caused by deterioration in the reef environment?

CHAPTER TWENTY-ONE

THE FUTURE OF TOURISM: TRENDS AND ISSUES WITHIN OUR CONTROL

INTRODUCTION

The turbulent environment within which tourism finds itself will not get any easier in the future. We have therefore advocated a disciplined and structured approach to understanding this environment and its implications for tourism. In the previous two chapters we have outlined both the role of technology and the range of external influences upon the future of tourism. In this chapter we turn to the tourism system itself and analyse the future of its various components. Within the tourism system there are a range of trends that can be identified. However, as stressed in the previous chapter it is dangerous to isolate one trend from another – consumer behaviour, destination development, markets, products, distribution and transportation are all dynamic and changes in any one of these variables will impact upon the others.

LEARNING OUTCOMES

In this chapter we focus on the future of the tourism system outlining trends and possible scenarios to provide you with:

- a disciplined approach to analysing and viewing the future of the tourism system;

- an awareness of the importance of the linkage between products and markets in viewing future tourism scenarios;

- a grasp of the key variables influencing the growth and development of tourism that can be controlled by the sector;

- an awareness of the key elements of changing tourism consumer behaviour; and

- an approach to understanding future products in tourism.

FUTURE DRIVERS OF THE TOURISM SYSTEM

This chapter focuses upon the tourism elements of Leiper's (1990) system (Figure 21.1). As mentioned in Chapter Twenty, the advantage of Leiper's tourism system is that it is an all-encompassing approach to tourism futures. It recognises the complexity of tourism and the need to match up trends both on the demand side in terms of markets and consumer behaviour with trends in transportation and on the supply side, in terms of product developments and the destination. To consider any one of these in isolation would provide an unbalanced assessment of the future of tourism.

Future markets for tourism

The demographic and social trends identified above have combined to change both the scale and nature of tourism markets. Many tourism futurists have suggested that the maturing of the tourism market is creating a new tourist who can be characterised as experienced, sophisticated and demanding. This means that the traditional annual family holiday mostly spent in a beach resort may be gradually superseded by multi-interest travel and a range of creative and innovative travel experiences (such as activity, adventure, learning and nature-based tourism). These trends will see the relative importance of conventional packaged tours decline in favour of independently organised tourism, or at least a more bespoke form of tourism.

The new tourist

The new consumer of tourism is knowledgeable, discerning, seeks quality and participation and, in the developed world, is increasingly drawn from an older age group. Motivations for travel are moving away from passive sunlust towards educational and curiosity motives. At the same time, travel will be facilitated by flexible working practices. To an extent, the new sophisticated traveller has emerged as a result of experience. Tourists from the major generating regions of the world have become frequent travellers, are linguistically and technologically skilled and can function in multicultural and demanding environments overseas. Add to this media and Internet exposure of tourism destinations and the reduction of perceived distance to reach such places and the stage is set for a reappraisal of holiday formulae. Education too has played a part, together with enhanced communications, and has led to more sophisticated requirements from holidaymakers who are now looking for new experiences combined with rewarding activities to fill their leisure time and satisfy their cultural, intellectual and sporting interests. Here, the emergence of the knowledge-based society is significant for tourism as travel products are merged with education and entertainment. This creates 'info-tainment' or 'edu-tainment' at destinations and specifically at commercial attractions through interpretation and education programmes. Pine and Gilmore (1999) have taken this one step further by suggesting that in the future consumption will be driven by 'experiences'. Tourism is perfect for this approach. For the **new tourist** travel is not just about *being at the destination*, but *experiencing being there* as travel becomes the medium for personal fulfillment and identity.

THE TOURISM SYSTEM

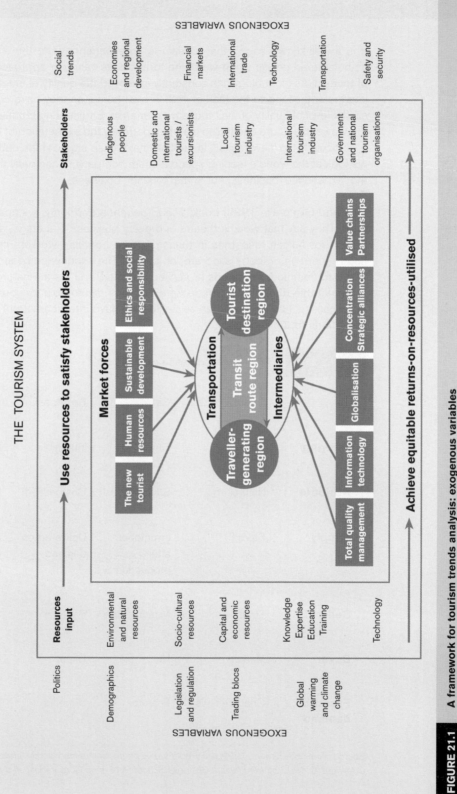

FIGURE 21.1 A framework for tourism trends analysis: exogenous variables

MINI CASE STUDY 21.1
The experience economy

It is a well-known saying that tourism is an experience, and therefore differs from manufactured goods when we come to asses its value, or approach the marketing of tourism. As technology has constantly improved the quality of entertainment, visual images and sound to the market in their own home, so they have come to expect a similar level of quality of their tourism experience. Engineering tourism experiences is the way of the future and it also matches perfectly the expectation of the marketplace – particularly the 'new tourist'. In the final major case study, at the end of this chapter, we look at the world's leading space tourism company, a company that sees itself in the 'experience' business, not in the 'tourism' business.

Pine and Gilmore's (1999) book, *The Experience Economy*, encapsulates this concept. They say that work is theatre and every business is a stage, a critical consideration for human resources in tourism where front-line workers in the restaurant, hotel reception or lobby shop are 'on stage'. The experience-based product is different to commodities, goods or services (Table 21.1), as the nature of the offering is memorable (the Disney parade for example is memorable for young children, it is personalised (the children can relate to their favourite characters); and it delivers sensations to the audience).

TABLE 21.1	From commodities to experiences			
	Commodities	**Goods**	**Services**	**Experiences**
Offering	Fungible	Tangible	Intangible	Memorable
Attribute	Natural	Standardised	Customised	Personal
Supply	Stored	Inventories after production	Delivered on demand	Revealed over a duration
Seller	Trader	Manufacturer	Provider	Stager
Buyer	Market	User	Client	Guest
Factor of demand	Characteristics	Features	Benefits	Sensations

Source: Pine and Gilmore, 1999, p. 6. Reprinted by permission of Harvard Business School Publishing. Copyright © 1999 by the Harvard Business School Publishing Corporation; all rights reserved

Pine and Gilmore ague that there are four types of experience that can be engineered:

1 **Entertainment** – here entertainment can be added to existing products, such as the old-fashioned aquarium that now has dolphin and seal shows. This 'engages' the visitor, but does not normally 'involve' all but one or two visitors in the entertainment.

2 **Education** – again the visitor is the passive recipient of the experience, but is more actively engaged than with an entertaining experience, because the very nature of an educational experience will change their levels of knowledge or awareness about a topic. Here the concepts of info-attainment or edu-tainment have been used to describe the process.

3 **Escapist** – this type of experience is much more about involving the visitor actively by immersing them in the experience. Here theme parks and virtual reality are examples.

4 **Aesthetic** – with this experience, the visitor is again immersed but does not impact upon the environment of the experience – gazing at the Taj Mahal or the Sphinx is an example here.

As we go down this list the visitor is increasingly immersed in the experience and participates. Pine and Gilmore argue that the nature of the experience should be engineered to 'transform' the visitor. It is here that the ideas of the experience economy can be of great benefit for tourism. By transforming the nature of the visitor to say, sensitive natural sites, managers can change their behaviour such that the visitor understands the nature of the site, and therefore is more inclined to protect it and behave in an appropriate way. Here marketing and visitor management come together to deliver the experiences that the 'new tourist' desires, while also beginning to change the way the visitors behave.

There is no doubt that the experience economy has many important insights for tourism, not only in how products are formulated and engineered into experiences, but also for the workforce that has to deliver these experiences, and for the next stage of the process – transformation – which may begin to change the behaviour of the 'new tourist' themselves.

DISCUSSION QUESTIONS

1 There are many critics of the experience approach who condemn it as an artificial and sterile world, where every worker is smiling. Do you agree with the critics or support Pine and Gilmore's view that the experience economy is the way of the future?

2 Taking each of Pine and Gilmore's types of experience (educational, aesthetic, etc.) draft a list of up to half a dozen tourism experiences for each category.

3 What are some of the issues that the workforce may face when creating 'experiences' for tourists?

769

Of course, the sophistication of the customer will have an impact upon product development throughout the industry; not only will there be an increased requirement for high standards of product design, efficiency and safety, but also the tourist will be more critical of the product and have the experience to compare offerings. At the same time, as the new tourist is conscious of value for money rather than simply price, other elements of the marketing mix will become important. In particular, this will mean that 'quality' will remain a key attribute in tourism product development and customer convenience in all its forms will be demanded by the new travellers, a trend fuelled by consumer legislation in tourism and the 'empowered' consumer. The issue of quality is increasingly important because the consumer is time poor and will increasingly demand that the products they purchase will be quality controlled and reliable. Determinants of quality will also link to their values of safeguarding the environment, authenticity and communities at the destination and include safety/security, hygiene, accessibility and tourism products that are designed to be in harmony with the human and environmental dimensions of the destination.

Market segments

Every tourist is different, bringing a unique blend of experiences, motivations and desires. Tourism is increasingly following the trend of other industries towards customising. Here technology enables products to be tailored to meet individual tastes. The old tourism products did not adopt this approach. Instead they were general and unspecialised with very similar characteristics traded as commodities rather than services under the mass tourism philosophy. This philosophy said that tourism products should appeal to all tastes and be sold at a low price in order to attract as wide a range of customers as possible.

This discussion points to the need for effective segmentation of the tourism market. Traditionally, tourism marketers have been using geographic and demographic criteria in order to describe their markets, but psychographics and behavioural criteria will be increasingly used in order to:

- provide detailed customer profiles;
- identify motivations, needs and determinants; and
- offer an appropriate marketing mix and service delivery strategy.

For the future, tourism market segments will be less stable and more fragmented. Tourism markets may be segmented in many different ways and there are no 'correct' segmentation criteria only those that are more efficient in differentiating between market segments and providing insights into the marketplace. Increasingly, segmentation approaches primarily based on product usage (comfort versus adventure) will be used, relying on the analysis of market research data. Indeed, one of the imperatives for understanding the tourist of the future will be deep and meaningful market research.

The destination

As the tourism system responds to the trends identified above, tourism flows will change as new generators of both domestic and international tourists, and new destinations, emerge. There is no doubt that these destinations of the future will need to be better planned and managed and show more concern and respect for their environment and host community than did their earlier counterparts. Indeed, all tourism-visioning exercises suggest that everyone involved in tourism will have to take increased responsibility for social and environmental issues. In the future, the focus of tourism will be on the destination as new management techniques are adopted and the attention to volume will give way to concepts of visitor experience and value. These concerns will be addressed by enhanced tourism planning and visitor management techniques and a clear agenda to involve local communities in the futures of their destinations. In this way, the imperative will be for the sustainable management of tourism destinations and the conservation of their unique characteristics.

Future destinations: sustainability

While many bemoan the fact that the tourism sector is not recognised by governments and the media, it is to be regretted that when such recognition does emerge, it often sees tourism as a despoiler of environments, exploiter of indigenous peoples and a sector focused on the short-term profit imperative. In part, these trends are a reflection of the growing maturity of both the tourist as consumer and the tourism industry itself. Mass tourism began with short-term perspectives as the industry and public agencies attempted to handle growing demand. In the 1980s and 1990s growth rates slowed and consumers questioned some of the excesses of tourism development. In response, longer planning horizons are being considered and alternative forms of tourism advocated. As we have seen throughout this book, sustainable tourism development has become the organising concept for all aspects of tourism and there is no reason to see a dilution of this trend. The future for destinations will see the translation of the concept of sustainability into practical measures that can be implemented at the local scale. These include:

- Increasing concern for the well-being of the local community and a consideration for all stakeholders to be involved in the tourism business. This is not as easy as it sounds as it is important to ensure that not only are all voices heard, but also that for communities to understand the complex nature of tourism. There are a range of planning techniques that can be used to achieve this, with perhaps the best known the 'limits to acceptable change' (LAC) approach.

- Adoption of the principles of sustainability across all forms of tourism and the translation of these principles into practical measures at the local destination level. These measures will include codes of conduct for visitors and certification for enterprises.

- Adoption of professional approaches to the management of visitors, traffic and resources at destinations, including the use of marketing and information management to influence the behaviour of visitors at destination, as shown in the second Mini case study in this chapter.

- Development of 'endemic tourism' that recognises the each destination has its own special character and that this is the attraction to visitors. This approach demands that good design utilises local materials and architecture at the destination, as well as the encouragement of local cuisine, crafts and festivals. It is important that these approaches stress a destination's 'point of difference'.

We can see that the central issue here is the gradual shift from short-term to longer term thinking and planning in tourism. It is no longer acceptable for the industry to exploit and use up destinations and then move on; indeed we are already seeing the results of this in the demise of some of the mass-tourism resorts built in the 1960s and 1970s – Acapulco in Mexico or Benidorm in Spain are examples here. The concepts of the tourism area life cycle and strategic planning provide a much needed long-term perspective in this respect. By this we mean that destinations can decide to remain at a particular point on the life cycle by using marketing and planning approaches, rather than being inexorably driven to grow – or decline. On the demand side there are also drivers of sustainability as consumers will place pressure upon the industry and destination managers to behave in a responsible manner; if they do not then their destination may be shunned as *environmentally unacceptable* to visit.

Future destinations: planning and management

Destinations are responding to these demands in a variety of ways. Resource-based destinations are adopting sophisticated planning, management and interpretive techniques to provide both a welcome and a rich experience for the tourist while at the same time ensuring protection of the resource itself. It is felt that once tourists understand why a destination is significant they will want to protect it. Good planning and management of the destination lies at the heart of providing the new tourist with a high-quality experience and it may be that tourists will have to accept increasingly restricted viewing times at popular sites, higher prices and even replicas of the real thing. The set of planning and management techniques involved here is known as visitor management, imported from recreation and parks management practice. This approach forms the basis of Mini case study 21.2.

MINI CASE STUDY 21.2
Visitor management

INTRODUCTION

Visitor management recognises that tourists will have to forgo an element of freedom if the characteristics and values of destinations are to be protected. Effectively this represents a trade-off for the visitor of 'freedom against quality of experience'. For example, in 2004, the Chinese government announced that is was going to restrict the numbers of visitors to the Great Wall of China and close off much of the 3000 kilometres of the Great Wall to allow it to be repaired. This foreshadows the future management style of destinations, a style that is designed to deliver a quality experience while at the same time safeguarding the integrity of the destination. The objectives of visitor management are twofold, as follows.

For the visitor it:

1 enhances the visit experience;

2 increases the chance of repeat visits;

3 encourages higher spending; and

4 encourages understanding of the destination and its special values such as, say, nature conservation.

For the destination it:

1 allows visits to be spread in space and time;

2 encourages a longer length of stay;

3 reduces the environmental and social impacts of visitation;

4 fosters a sense of pride in the local community.

THE VISITOR MANAGEMENT PROCESS

There are many examples of visitor management strategies for particular destinations, although many of UNESCO's designated World Heritage Sites still require such an approach and are suffering at the hands of increased visitation. The Great Wall of China is a good example of such a site. Although 3000 kilometres of the Great Wall still remain, only small sections have been restored and the management of visitors is minimal.

For this Mini case study we have provided a five-stage recipe for visitor management. This will allow you to learn about visitor management first hand by applying the recipe to a destination that you know well, or to the example of the Great Wall of China that we use throughout the case. If you choose to apply the recipe to a destination of your own choice, it could be a nature park, museum, historic house, monument, nature reserve or even a theme park.

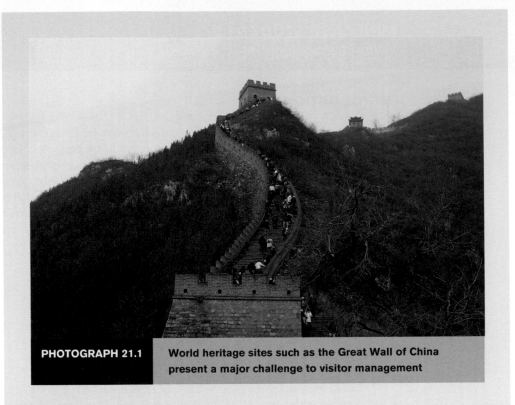

PHOTOGRAPH 21.1 **World heritage sites such as the Great Wall of China present a major challenge to visitor management**

1 **Determine your management objective** – The determination of objectives is critical for the management of any destination. The key question to answer is 'why are we encouraging people to visit?' The answer to this question drives the management process and can range from the simple economic objective of profit, to the more complex objectives of conservation.

For the Great Wall of China, what are the objectives: propaganda? pride in the Great Wall and a desire for the world to see it? education? conservation? or the generation of foreign currency? Depending upon which objective you feel is dominant, the approach to the visitor management of the Great Wall will be determined.

2 **Make an estimate of your market** – Who visits the destination? Are they predominantly families, children, school groups, or groups with a special interest in, say, nature conservation? Or is the market a more general unsegmented one? Again this is an important ingredient in the management mix as the wrong type of visitor will be problematic and the market will determine your approach to the type of information provided.

For the Great Wall, what will be the split between domestic and international visitors? Will these two markets need a different management approach?

3 **What is the capacity of your destination?** Make estimates of how many visitors can be comfortably accommodated at each part of the destination. For example, if you are considering a museum, then how many visitors can comfortably view objects in each room, and for how long?

Much of the Great Wall is in ruins but there are a few kilometres of restored wall where visitors can access it by cable car and on foot. Using Internet and other sources, calculate the length and width of the Great Wall that is open and estimate how many visitors per 100 metres would be acceptable at any one hour. Then multiply this figure by the length of the Great Wall and the number of hours that it is open to get a rough idea of capacity.

4 **Determine the main routes around the destination** – Once you know how many visitors can be accommodated at different parts of the destination, the next stage is to determine how to influence their movement around the destination. This is done to ensure that capacity levels are not exceeded at each part of the destination. This is critical and is done in two ways:

(a) **Hard visitor management** uses negative signage, fencing or security staff. Here the visitor knows they are being managed. For a linear feature such as the Great Wall, it may be necessary to have a 'one-way' visitor flow in place, and protection of valuable buildings and features may require 'hard management'. It may also be necessary to take the ultimate 'hard' decision and close of sections of the Great Wall to protect it, as is, in fact, being done.

(b) **Soft visitor management** uses more subtle techniques such as information levels and interpretation, landscaping, and location of facilities to influence movement. For the Great Wall an example here is the use of cable cars to access sections of the wall on high peaks. Effectively the numbers and timing of visitors can be closely controlled and matched to carrying capacity by the frequency of the cable car. In this way, the visitor does not realise that they are being managed. Soft management is the preferred approach, but must be linked to the market (stage 2 above).

5 **Monitor your plan** – Once you have decided on your visitor management plan, it should be monitored using perhaps a questionnaire to visitors asking them about their experiences, or simply by debriefing staff as to their observations on how well the plan is working.

This should be done for the Great Wall by monitoring the response of different markets to the experience and by ensuring that staff are well trained and continually debriefed.

Visitor management is the technique of the future – it caters to the new tourists by ensuring that levels of information and quality of experience are high, yet it also recognises that visitation will change a destination unless management is put into place.

DISCUSSION QUESTIONS

1 How well did this approach work for your destination or the Great Wall of China? In what ways might you improve on your plan?

2 Visitor management has been criticised as making tourism too scientific and organised and taking away the fun of discovery – do you agree with this criticism?

3 Taking a heritage destination that you know well, look at it with the eyes of a visitor manager – how well does it work, is there congestion for example? Are the facilities of high quality? Is the information provided to the visitor too simple – or too complicated?

Future destinations: sustainable enterprises and destination value chains

Enterprises at the destination are also responding to the drive for sustainable destinations. This is occurring in two ways:

1 Increasingly the techniques and approaches for sustainable tourism practices are being published as guidelines and manuals for sustainable enterprises. The tourism industry is anxious to demonstrate that it is both responsible and acting to curb some of the excesses of past development. The WTTC, for example, has been active in researching the impacts of tourism and communicating the benefits of a sustainable approach, whilst individual companies have initiated awards, such as *Tourism for Tomorrow* by British Airways. One approach is the certification and eco-labelling of products and companies. This

   • serves to encourage tourism enterprises to 'raise their game'' in terms of sustainability; and
   • allows the consumer to discern those enterprises that are attempting to be sustainable in their practices.

   The problem, of course, is that unless these systems are well policed, and therefore resourced, there is a danger that they will be abused by enterprises using them for 'green-washing' purposes – in other words they do not always practice what they preach. This is particularly the case if the systems are voluntary rather than mandatory. The other problem is that there is an increasing proliferation of these certification schemes and there is no common standard for the indicators used. There is also an element of self-preservation here as green products will become increasingly popular and a sector that is seen to be responsible will not attract regulation by government. It also raises the issue of the *ethical* consumption and development of tourism, where organisations recognise their long-term responsibilities and their relationship with a variety of stakeholders. This is becoming evident in the brochures of tour operator/wholesalers where the consumer is urged to 'respect, re-use, recycle *and* rescue' consumption.

2 Destinations will benefit from future trends in the tourism value chain. In the past, the tourism value chain was a combat zone with each member feeling they had to compete. For destinations this resulted in exploitation by tour operators who failed to recognise that the resort was, in fact, their product. In the future, tourism businesses will begin to recognise the importance of working with other members of the value chain and this will include tour operators investing in the destination.

   Networks or alliances of businesses and consumers along value chains will increase business efficiencies and improve communication. This trend is critical for the tourism sector and is leading to a shift in thinking away from management of individual sectors of the industry – such as transport, destinations, intermediaries and accommodation – to the concept of *integrated management*. For destinations, integrated management across all sectors of the tourism industry will be coordinated by NTOs or by strongly integrated companies. This allows the evolution of complementary products such as the merger of the business market with add-on leisure products. A further extension of the concept is that of destination-based marketing/cooperation. This is now recognised as a cooperative effective way to increase visitation.

Future destinations: the international agenda

The implementation plan arising from the 2002 Johannesburg World Summit on Sustainable Development is a clear indication of the future agenda for tourism destinations in terms of sustainability (paragraph number 43):

...in order to increase the benefits from tourism resources for the population in host communities while maintaining the cultural and environmental integrity of the host communities and enhancing the protection of ecologically sensitive areas and natural heritages...promote sustainable tourism development and capacity building in order to contribute to the strengthening of rural and local communities. This would include actions at all levels to:

(a) Enhance international cooperation, foreign direct investment and partnerships with both private and public sectors, at all levels;

(b) Develop programmes, including education and training programmes, that encourage people to participate in eco-tourism, enable indigenous and local communities to develop and benefit from eco-tourism, and enhance stakeholder cooperation in tourism development and heritage preservation, in order to improve the protection of the environment, natural resources and cultural heritage;

(c) Provide technical assistance to developing countries and countries with economies in transition to support sustainable tourism business development and investment and tourism awareness programmes, to improve domestic tourism, and to stimulate entrepreneurial development;

(d) Assist host communities in managing visits to their tourism attractions for their maximum benefit, while ensuring the least negative impacts on and risks for their traditions, culture and environment;

(e) Promote the diversification of economic activities, including through the facilitation of access to markets and commercial information, and participation of emerging local enterprises, especially small and medium sized enterprises.

So what of the future for tourism destinations? We can discern two clear trends:

1 The first is the trend towards the use of artificially, technologically enhanced destinations such as theme parks, cruises and resorts. Examples here include Las Vegas, the Disney theme parks and Carnival Cruise Line. The product is unashamedly artificial, creating a fantasy world that will be increasingly part of the 'experience' economy.

2 The second trend is for authentic, well-managed contact with nature and indigenous communities. Here eco-tourism and heritage tourism are the obvious examples with sympathetic encounters with wildlife (orang-utan encounters in Rwanda) or native peoples (a Masai campfire experience in Kenya). This type of destination demands a different type of management to the artificial fantasy destination as here it is the resource that is paramount in delivering the experience.

Transport

Historically, change in tourism has been closely linked to transport innovations. In the future, the influence of transport will be diluted by the emergence of other new drivers of change. Nonetheless, the influence of transport as a driver of tourism futures should not be underestimated. Tourism remains dependent upon transport technology and the consequent improvements in efficiency, range and safety of travel. This applies especially to new developments such as tourism in space. Equally, tourism may also be constrained by transportation in the future as old systems fail to accommodate increased levels of demand, or travellers perceive the security risks of travel as too great.

The inadequate capacity of transport infrastructure will act as a real constraint upon tourism growth in the future. The WTTC's (2002) infrastructure task force is concerned that this will particularly be the case in Europe and the USA. The WTTC's future agenda to address this issue includes:

- expansion of existing infrastructure and diversion of air traffic to secondary airports;

- development of alternative surface transport systems such as high-speed rail to take pressure from the air traffic system;

- planning legislation to protect land use and residents from the impacts of transport; and

- improved air traffic control. Here, for example, the inadequate capacity of the American and European air traffic control systems are cases in point, as are the many examples of inadequate airport capacity and aircraft noise restrictions which constrain tourism volume.

The future will also see a change in the management and approach of transport enterprises with an emphasis on both marketing and the building of strategic alliances to gain market share. The airline sector, for example, was very heavily affected by the downturn in travel following '911', and has seriously rethought its response to future markets and patterns of travel. Here there are two schools of thought. Boeing sees the future in medium-sized aircraft that can operate flexibly between hubs and also secondary regional airports. Airbus, on the other hand, sees the future in larger aircraft, with a longer range that will dominantly ply long-haul routes.

Environmental factors too will be a concern for all transport modes in the future, particularly as for air transport, emissions are unlikely to be reduced in the medium term. However, where the environmental factors may bite is in the consumer's concern for energy consumption and this may well lead to a gradual modal shift in transport away from air and towards surface modes, especially for shorter journeys. After '911' there is a concern that, on the one hand, the investment required to equip airlines with new aircraft will not be forthcoming, while, on the other hand, competition from surface transport is sharpening. In the future this will be characterised by improved rail services and products, the realisation of the environmental advantages of rail and continued technological developments in the area of high-speed train networks. A magnetically levitated (*maglev*) fast train service is already operating in Shanghai.

Forecasts of international transport predict that technological developments, increased airline efficiency and labour productivity savings will offset any rises in aviation fuel prices and thus, in real terms, fares will continue to fall. This is supported by the fact that on short-haul routes the 'no-frills' airlines are gaining market share from the traditional 'scheduled' carriers. An important cost consideration is the escalating price of security at airports and in the air. While it can be said that security systems are much more effective than they used to be for air travel, the Madrid railway terrorist bombing of March 2004 has focused attention on securing surface transport networks from attack. This will be a much more difficult and expensive task.

FUTURE TOURISM PRODUCT MARKETS

We can combine both the market and destination trends in the tourism system to identify a range of '**tourism product markets**' that will be available in the future. Each product is at a different stage of its life – beach tourism, for example, may not be seen as part of the future of tourism, but it will, in fact, remain a major part of the market, though its formula will change. Other products such as special interest tourism are developing rapidly in response to market demand and the consumer trends we have identified, while others are newly emerging – such as 'dark' tourism. Of course, there are also products of the future and here we include space tourism and virtual reality. We provide a commentary below on selected tourism products and look to their future.

Examples of existing product markets

BEACH TOURISM

Many suggest that the market is tiring of the traditional mass-tourism beach resort as new destinations and products are developed. However, the coast will remain a key focus of tourism in the future as resorts and enterprises reformulate their beach products to 'beach plus', while at the same time upgrading the quality of the infrastructure and superstructure. However, for many destinations, market diversification and product reformulation options are limited and can be copied by their competition. In the future, beach destinations will have to maintain a constant process of regeneration.

RURAL TOURISM

Rural tourism has been developed as a result of a wide range of influences, including improved access, the market's attraction for their rural roots, government policy to diversify the economy of rural areas and the increased trend for shorter and more frequent travel in urban hinterlands. In contrast to beach tourism, rural tourism is in a growth stage of its life cycle. In the future the key for rural tourism will be maintaining a sustainable balance between tourism development and the rural environment and communities and developing new products that go beyond the traditional 'farm stay'.

ECO-TOURISM

As eco-tourism has expanded away from its narrow concept of responsible travel that conserves environments and benefits the local community, it has grown not only in scale, but also broadened to include any tourism involving a natural component. Increasingly therefore there is a disillusionment with the very term 'eco-tourism' and some countries have ceased to use it in their promotion, preferring instead the term 'nature-based tourism'. For the future the key to eco-tourism will be the development of the educational component into a true tourism product and the engineering of experiences that closely mirror market needs while conserving environments and communities.

CULTURAL AND HERITAGE TOURISM

Rather like eco-tourism, cultural and heritage tourism has many different interpretations – from mass experiences in the world's leading attractions such as the Louvre, to individual, highly customised specialised educational tours of, say, Italian cuisine. For the future the key consideration will be the management and capacity limitations of the sites and resources; and as with eco-tourism, product development and theming will become important competitive tools.

Examples of emerging product markets

SPECIAL INTEREST TOURISM

With the increasingly fragmented market needs of the 'new tourist', the future for tourism product markets lies in developing specific niches that match the destination's strengths as well as the aspirations of developing market segments. These 'special interest products' range from culinary and wine tourism, through educational tours where skills are learned, to health and spa tourism, where it is less the 'cure' that is sought, but rather 'wellness' and preventative health and beauty treatments. One emerging area of special interest has been identified by Lennon and Foley (2000) as 'dark' tourism. This type of tourism involves visits to 'dark' sites such as battlegrounds, scenes of horrific crimes or acts of genocide such as the holocaust sites of Poland. Dark tourism poses severe challenges for the managers of these sites in terms of interpretation and for governments, deeper issues as to whether these sites should be available for visitation and, if so, the nature of the publicity involved. There are major ethical and moral questions for tourism posed by dark tourism, but while it remains a small niche market driven by varied motivations, such as mourning, remembrance, macabre curiosity or even entertainment, this is certainly a future tourism product – though one with early origins rooted in fairgrounds and medieval fairs.

Examples of future product markets

VIRTUAL REALITY TOURISM

Technological innovations such as virtual reality (VR) may one day replace the authentic travel experience all together; indeed the very nature of tourism as an 'experience' lends itself perfectly to VR. VR consists of three elements – visualisation of the destination through simulation; immersion in the destination; and interactivity with elements of the destination. In other words, VR is simply a further step along the road of 'engineering' tourist experiences and one that reinforces the trend of leisure activity based upon the home.

Simply strapping on a body suit and plugging into the virtual reality program could transport you to the sights, sounds and sensations of, say, a Pacific island. The tourist experiences the destination but without any risk of skin cancer, AIDS or the other side-effects of travel; while for the destination, negative impacts are removed, but so also are the positive effects of income, jobs and regional development. The debate as to the real impact of VR is still ongoing:

- *Proponents* say that as cocooning behaviour increasingly places the home as a central and secure base for leisure activities, VR may depress demand for the real thing.

- *Opponents* contend that VR will simply whet the appetite for more travel through enhanced exposure to, and awareness of, the product, as VR is used simply as an advanced form of tourist brochure.

SPACE TOURISM

Although space tourism can be thought of as an activity in the distant future, it is estimated that by 2020 space technology will be applied to intercontinental travel. Already two space tourists have gone into orbit and the company Space Adventures has a series of tourism products based upon space adventures and experiences – see the major case study in this chapter. As if this were not evidence enough of the fact that space tourism is set to become a reality, the US House of Representatives passed a bill in 2004 regulating commercial space flights.

Taking Leiper's system again, it is clear that space tourism should include not only the market for the product and the means of transport, but also the destination. For space tourism, the destination may indeed include the moon, but it can also be thought of as present-day theme parks on earth – such as the Kennedy Space Center at Cape Canaveral, Florida, or simulated rides such as Disney's Epcot ride 'Mission: SPACE'. Other earth-based simulations of weightlessness or driving moon buggies could also come under the label of space tourism. In the future, options will not only include the ability to travel to destinations in space, but also activities such as orbital flight or the ability to stay in space-based hotels or space stations.

Emergent patterns

In these three final chapters we have demonstrated that tourism is entering an age characterised by:

- moderating rates of growth;

- heightened concerns about security;

- intensified competition among destinations;

- greater deregulation and privatisation, encouraging market forces to operate;

- more awareness and attention paid to the growing impacts of tourism;

- a consumer who is more knowledgeable, experienced and empowered;

- a tourism sector increasingly dominated by a small number of large multinational enterprises;

- an increasing number of tourism product types competing for a fragmented market; and

- a technology-driven marketplace.

There is no doubt that Poon (1989), a leading commentator on future trends in tourism, was correct when she predicted the demise of the old tourism and the emergence of a new tourism (Figure 21.2). She saw the key trends leading to this new tourism as:

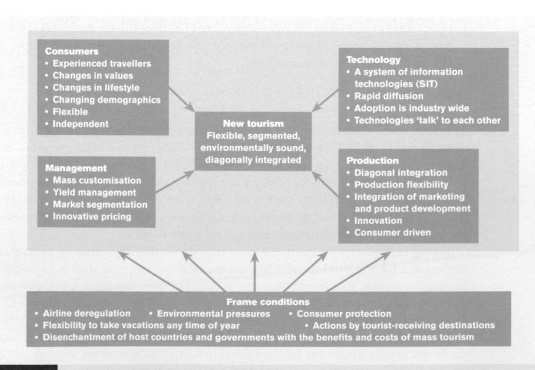

Consumers
- Experienced travellers
- Changes in values
- Changes in lifestyle
- Changing demographics
- Flexible
- Independent

Technology
- A system of information technologies (SIT)
- Rapid diffusion
- Adoption is industry wide
- Technologies 'talk' to each other

New tourism
Flexible, segmented, environmentally sound, diagonally integrated

Management
- Mass customisation
- Yield management
- Market segmentation
- Innovative pricing

Production
- Diagonal integration
- Production flexibility
- Integration of marketing and product development
- Innovation
- Consumer driven

Frame conditions
- Airline deregulation • Environmental pressures • Consumer protection
- Flexibility to take vacations any time of year • Actions by tourist-receiving destinations
- Disenchantment of host countries and governments with the benefits and costs of mass tourism

| **FIGURE 21.2** | **Poon's new tourism** | *Source: Poon, 1993* |

The diffusion of a system of new information technologies in the tourism industry; deregulation of the airline industry and financial services; the negative impact of mass tourism on host countries; the movement away from sun-lust to sun-plus tourism; environmental pressures; technology; competition; and changing consumer tastes. (p. 92)

We can see that change in tourism has become inevitable, just as we have come to accept long-term tourism growth as inevitable. This means that not only will more tourists be seeking authentic experiences in new destinations, but also most places will be seeking to take advantage of these heightened levels of demand to boost income and employment. This is the case for most regions of the world, even the ones that have not been traditionally regarded as potential destinations – urban centres, remote and hostile regions or industrial sites, for example. All of this means that it will be much more difficult for destinations to be successful. In particular, those destinations and enterprises in the decline stage of the life cycle will find it much more difficult to survive and may have to manage and even de-market their tourism in order to mitigate negative impacts.

CONCLUSION

The future of tourism is an exciting one with products being developed that are as diverse as adventures in space to sympathetic and managed encounters with endangered wildlife. The message of this book has been that, whatever the tourism product and its delivery, the future will only be successful if we take a scientific and disciplined approach to understanding and managing tourism. This chapter, for example, has resisted the temptation to 'hype' the future of tourism and instead, taken an analytical approach that matches markets and products. Of course, any book written in the early years of this century will be tested in a number of ways because tourism is faced with unexpected and rapid change in the modern world. However, we have tried to provide general principles and practices rather than specifics which will date. We offer you the challenges of tourism management and an exciting future – a future that we believe will become more legible if you follow the frameworks and approaches that we have provided.

Self-check questions

1 Draft a checklist of the factors that you think will be the most influential in shaping air travel in the next 20 years.

2 What are some of the problems involved with organising a host community to plan for their own tourism future?

3 Choose an emergent tourism product such as 'dark tourism' or 'space tourism' and identify the key elements of Leiper's tourism system for the product.

4 Outline your views on virtual reality tourism – hype or reality?

5 Can you find any examples of 'green washing' by tourism organisations in brochures or the media?

Essay questions

1 Critically review the contention that, in the developed world, tourists will begin to switch from air to surface transport in the future.

2 Identify and describe the major dimensions for market segmentation in tourism for future markets.

3 'In the future, sustainable tourism destinations will remain an illusion, not a reality.' Do you agree?

4 Review the challenges facing beach tourism destinations and their options to diversify their markets and change their products in the future.

5 Critically assess the market for space tourism in the next 20 years.

Annotated further reading

Books

Hall, M. and McArthur, S. (1996) *Integrated Heritage Management*, The Stationery Office, London.
The most comprehensive text on the 'new' management approaches for destinations.

Lennon, J. and Foley, M. (2000) *Dark Tourism: The Attraction of Death and Disaster*, Continuum, London.
A fascinating analysis of one of the future forms of tourism.

Pine, J.B. and Gilmore, J.H. (1999) *The Experience Economy*, Harvard Business School Press, Boston.
A visionary book, casting glimpses into the way that tourism products will be engineered and themed as 'experiences' in the future.

WTO (2001) *Tourism 2020 Vision*, WTO, Madrid.
A thorough analysis of future markets and products.

Web site

http//:www.spacetourismsociety.org
A comprehensive web site covering all aspects of space tourism.

References cited

Hall, M. and McArthur, S. (1996) *Integrated Heritage Management*, The Stationery Office, London.

Leiper, N. (1990) *Tourism Systems*, Massey University Department of Management Systems Occasional Paper 2, Auckland, New Zealand.

Lennon, J. and Foley, H. (2000) *Dark Tourism: The Attraction of Death and Disaster*, Continuum, London.

Pine, J.B. and Gilmore, J.H. (1999) *The Experience Economy*, Harvard Business School Press, Boston.

Poon, A. (1989) 'Competitive strategies for a new tourism', pp. 91–102 in Cooper, C. (ed.), *Progress in Tourism, Recreation and Hospitality Management*, Vol. 1, Belhaven, London.

Poon, A. (1993) *Tourism, Technology and Competitive Strategies*, CAB, Wallingford.

WTTC (2002) *Increasing Mobility, Expanding Infrastructure*, WTTC, London.

MAJOR CASE STUDY 21.1
SPACE ADVENTURES

THE COMPANY

The reality of space tourism is available in 2004, with the company Space Adventures providing genuine space tourism products. They also organise experiences based upon space adventures but not involving travelling into space (officially defined as 62 miles above the earth's atmosphere). The company was established in 1998 as a space tourism, entertainment and event production company that delivers and develops space experiences. It is based in Arlington, Virginia, USA and has a Russian office in Moscow.

To quote their web site (www.spaceadventures.com):

Company Purpose: Space Adventures will open space flight and the space frontier to private citizens. As the leading provider of space experiences to people on Earth, Space Adventures is in a unique position to... provide countless new opportunities for exploration and enterprise over the coming years.

Company Mission: Space Adventures will fly tens of thousands of people in space over the next 10–15 years and beyond, both orbital and suborbital, around the moon, and back, from spaceports both on Earth and in space, to and from private space stations, and aboard dozens of different vehicles; and by continually providing newly available space experiences.

The long-term vision of the company is to be in on the ground floor of space tourism believing that this is the century when tourists will travel into space. Their aim too is to enhance space exploration through the development and support of new technology such as re-usable launch vehicles to significantly cut the cost of getting tourists into space. In this way, profits from space tourism will be reinvested to benefit space exploration and improve the technology of space travel.

EXPERIENCE-BASED PRODUCTS

The company is the first serious player to offer genuine space tourism products. But these are also products that have been engineered to deliver real experiences – again the words of Space Adventures put it well:

Our programs and products are not about travel and tourism; the experiences that we offer provide people with an insurmountable feeling, an intense sensation, and an awe-inspiring encounter that only the exploration of an unknown frontier incites.

This is achieved through working with government agencies such as the US and Russian space agencies and accessing their facilities (such as the Gagarin Cosmonaut Training

PHOTOGRAPH 21.2   **Designing economical launch vehicles is the biggest challenge faced by space tourism enterprises**

Centre) to deliver the 'excitement and fantasy of popular science fiction'. In addition Space Adventures works with designers and aerospace companies to develop the technology of space tourism.

Space Adventures has four basic 'experience' products:

1 **Orbital flights** – The company is the only one in the world to have taken clients into space to the International Space Station using *Soyuz* 'taxi flights'. In 2005, the company has two seats available on a *Soyuz* spacecraft to the International Space Station 240 miles above the earth's atmosphere. Each seat costs US$20 million.

2 **Sub-orbital flights** – The company is developing a sub-orbital space program with the intention of offering passenger flights from 2006.

3 **Spaceflight training** – The company offers a range of training experiences which include products such as weightlessness training at Russian space centres. Here, the company is clearly positioning its experiences at the very top of the market and targeting the corporate sector. For example, Space Adventures' 'reach for the stars' team-building programme is aimed at large corporate clients. This programme has been cleverly engineered to act as a memorable team-building exercise, provide unique 'space' experiences and deliver 'celebrity' status to the participants. The outline programme, based in Russia, is as follows:

- zero-gravity training, including medical screening and a certificate;
- the group leader becomes an 'astronaut advisor';
- zero-gravity flight briefing with a cosmonaut followed by buffet of regional cuisine;
- zero-gravity flight;
- tour of Star City;
- DVD with photograph and video coverage of the event;
- celebrity dinner with cosmonaut; and
- a personalised web page showcasing the zero-gravity training.

4 **Space-related flight adventures** – The company offers a menu of different 'neo-space' type experiences which include flights in high-performance MIG-25 jets to the edge of space to see the curvature of the earth and 'zero-gravity' parabolic flights. Interestingly, the company also views the inner space of the oceans as part of their product portfolio. However, they again have engineered a memorable experience for clients by organising a visit to the wreck of the *Titanic*, 20,000 feet below the surface of the ocean using a MIR submersible.

SPACE ADVENTURES: THE MARKET

The company has been smart in its positioning in the marketplace. The products on offer are at the upper end of the tourism market, cleverly straddle the events sector, and target three segments of 'adventurers' – not 'tourists'. In addition, all of the products use VIP airport lounges, VIP customs and immigration processing, limousine transfers, five-star accommodation, VIP guided tours of the destinations, such as Moscow, and where relevant, contact with cosmonauts and those involved in the space business is arranged. The company has three key target markets:

1 **Individual and family adventurers** – Examples here include Dennis Tito, the first ever space tourist in 2001.

2 **Corporate buyers** – Corporate events, training days and team-building experiences have been designed to appeal to the corporate market. Clearly, this is the major market for the company's products.

3 **Media and celebrity clients** – The company works with the media to engineer experiences and with celebrities at their events.

Space Adventures represents the future of tourism. It is a professional, well-run organisation that is at the cutting edge of marketing, technology and tourism. It understands that it has to engineer experiences to create its products and in so doing has become a hybrid of tourism, entertainment, event management and technology.

REFERENCE

http//:www.spaceadventures.com

DISCUSSION QUESTIONS

1 Access the Space Adventures' web site (http//:www.spaceadventures.com) and find the resellers' inquiry form. As an independent retail travel agent in your country, draft a response to the two questions on the form:

- which Space Adventures' offerings do you feel you will be able to sell well?; and
- describe how you intend to market Space Adventures' offerings.

2 Draft an outline marketing plan for Space Adventures targeting the corporate market.

3 Why do you think Space Adventures think of themselves as being in the 'experience' business and not 'travel and tourism'?

9/11 or 911 The terrorist attacks in New York and Washington on September 11, 2001, *p462*.

A

ACIDIFICATION The process of increasing acidity or becoming acidic, *p206*.

ADDITIONALITY When new products or facilities are introduced if they add to the total value of tourist spend then they are said to provide additionality as opposed to **displacement**, *p527*.

ADVANCED PASSENGER TRAIN Introduced in the UK in 1979 to provide fast intercity rail transport, *p473*.

ADVANCED PURCHASE EXCURSION FARE Early booking of tickets often results in lower ticket prices also known as APEX fares, *p481*.

ADVERTISING Advertising includes any paid form of non-personal communication through the media which details a product that is identifiable, *p665*.

AGENDA 21 The programme action plan that came out of the 1992 Rio Summit. It was given the title Agenda 21 because of the 21 chapters dealing with a wide range of aspects relating to sustainable development, *p196*.

AIDS Acquired Immune Deficiency Syndrome, *p239*.

AIR TRAFFIC CONTROL The system that directs the movement of aircraft in time and space, *p469*.

AIR TRAFFIC MOVEMENTS Data on air traffic routes and runway utilisation, etc, *p471*.

ALTERNATIVE TOURISM Has a wide variety of meanings and was put forward as a response to the excesses associated with mass tourism, *p281*.

ANTHROPOLOGY OF TOURISM The study of tourism with respect to socio-cultural, linguistic and archaeological issues, *p227*.

AUTHENTICITY This term is generally used to show that something is original and honest, that it is what it appears to be, *p35*.

B

BACKPACKER HOSTELS Inexpensive accommodation facilities for backpackers, *p395*.

BALANCE OF PAYMENTS The balance of payments refers to the balance between foreign exchange spent and received in an economy, *p180*.

BARRIERS TO ENTRY Devices designed to prevent new companies from entering an industry. The barriers may be through production secrets, scarcity of resources or through the high price of inputs, *p310*.

BIOLOGICAL DIVERSITY The number, range and abundance of species living within a common environment, *p200*.

BOUTIQUE HOTELS Small unique hotels that are distinguished by their level of personalised service and individual style, *p407*.

BRAND A name, a symbol, term or design or a combination of these, *p647*.

BRAND EXTENSIONS OR STRETCHING The extension of product range under a single brand, *p363*.

BROKERAGE FEES Fees paid to brokers or **intermediaries** for their services, *p510*.

BUDGET HOTELS Value hotels for guests on a limited budget, *p407*.

C

CAPITALISM A social system based on individual rights where goods and services are produced and exchanged with minimal government interference, *p299*.

CHARTER FLIGHTS See **charter services**.

CHARTER SERVICES A system of conditions over a finite period that relates to levels of service and frequency of flights in order to secure capacity, *p485*.

CLICK AND MORTAR AGENCIES Established businesses with physical outlets engaging in e-commerce (internet trade), *p435*.

COMMERCIALISATION AND BASTARDISATION The change made to an event, skill, craft or ritual to make it more attractive to tourists, *p226*.

COMMODIFICATION The transformation of non-commercial relationships into commercial relationships, *p504*.

COMMUNISM A society where the people are responsible for resource allocation, production and distribution. Essentially classless and without a need for government, *p299*.

COMPARATIVE ADVANTAGE Where the opportunity cost of producing a specific good or service is less that it is in another country then the former is considered to have a comparative advantage in the production of that good or service. Is used as a justification for international trade, *p160*.

COMPUTERISED RESERVATION SYSTEM Software that handles inventory, prices and schedules, etc, *p515*.

CONSERVATION Managing environmental resources in a way that optimises their contribution to the quality of life, *p197*.

CONSORTIA A combination or group formed in order to undertake a venture that would be beyond the resources of a single individual/company, *p388*.

CONSUMER SATISFACTION The extent to which a company's business efforts matches or exceeds the expectations of the consumer, *p552*.

COST–BENEFIT ANALYSIS This type of analysis is used in project appraisal to determine the monetary value of costs and benefits (to a community) relating to a project (such as an airport extension, highway, new sewage treatment plant) to see if they are worthwhile, *p162*.

CUSTOMER NEEDS Customer-felt state of deprivation, *p552*.

D

DELPHI ANALYSES An iterative panel method of analysis where the panel members do not meet, *p248*.

DEMAND DETERMINANTS The factors that influence the scope and nature of travel, *p114*.

DEMONSTRATION EFFECT Influencing the behaviour, dress and attitudes of people through demonstration/imitation and interaction, *p233*.

DESTINATION IMAGE An individual's awareness of a destination made up of the cognitive evaluation of experiences, learning, emotions and perceptions, *p62*.

DESTINATION MANAGEMENT ORGANISATION A destination-based organisation tasked with the responsibility of coordinating and managing destination activity including planning and promotion, *p725*.

DESTINATION MANAGEMENT SYSTEM Also referred to as destination databases, destination marketing systems and visitor information systems. No clear definition exists but they are there to provide a comprehensive information system for a destination, *p515*.

DEVELOPING COUNTRIES Countries that are defined to be low- or middle-income countries by the World Bank, where living standards are thought to be low relative to high-income countries. Although there is no precise definition there are thought to be more than 125 countries with populations in excess of 1 million that have these characteristics, *p152*.

DEVELOPMENT STRATEGIES Approaches and plans designed to bring about the desired growth and development of tourism or an economy, *p196*.

DIRECT MARKETING Direct marketing is direct communication with pre-selected target groups in order to obtain an immediate response or build closer relationships, *p670*.

DIRECT SELL The absence of **intermediaries**. Therefore the product is sold directly from the supplier to the tourist, *p427*.

DISAGGREGATION The degree to which the various productive sectors of the economy are broken down (e.g. SIC 2, 3 or 4 digit levels of disaggregation), *p170*.

DISCRETIONARY INCENTIVES Incentives normally linked to conditions, such as job creation in depressed areas can also take the form of discretionary grants, *p528*.

DISINTERMEDIATION A reduction in the amount or value of transactions that are distributed through intermediaries, *p427*.

791

DISPLACEMENT Displacement refers to the amount of current revenue that is displaced by a new development. For instance, if a new five-star hotel is built in Quebec and 50% of its business is attracted from existing five-star hotels in the city then there is a 50% displacement rate, *p161*.

DISTRIBUTION (SYSTEM) Mix of channels used to gain access or means by which a tourism service is made available to the potential buyers of the product, *p672*.

DISTRIBUTIVE TRADE Distributive trade refers to all companies involved in the distribution of goods and services. The United Nations Standard Industrial Classification (SIC) incorporates distributive trade under heading 6 (i.e. 6.1 wholesale trade, 6.2 retail trade, 6.3 hotels and catering), *p164*.

DIVERSIFICATION The broadening of the economic base by the development of different industries, and/or A strategy to achieve company growth by means of starting up or acquiring new businesses outside the existing company products or markets, *p154*.

DOMESTIC TOURISM Domestic tourism is the activity of people visiting destinations within their own country's boundaries, *p5*.

E

EC European Community, *p478*.

ECOLOGICAL SYSTEM A collection of interconnected living beings (including humans) and the system in which they co-exist such as the earth's surface, *p200*.

ECONOMIC DEPENDENCE When the costs and revenues of one country, company or project depend upon that of another, *p157*.

ECONOMIC RECESSION A decline in economic activity (**GDP**) that persists for at least two quarters, *p154*.

ECO-TOURISM Nature-based tourism that attempts to minimise its environmental impact, *p281*.

E-INTERMEDIARIES e-intermediaries and emediaries are intermediaries that offer streamlined intermediation services across the Internet, *p437*.

ELASTICITIES OF SUPPLY AND DEMAND This is the responsiveness of supply and demand to changes in prices (price elasticity) or income (income elasticity), *p174*.

EMPIRICAL STUDIES Studies that are based on experience, experiment or observation, *p197*.

ENVIRONMENTAL ACTION PROGRAMMES Environmental policies and strategies, *p211*.

ENVIRONMENTAL AUDITING A management system designed to mitigate environmental impacts, *p209*.

EU PACKAGE TRAVEL DIRECTIVE A directive to protect consumers who purchase travel packages in the EU, *p446*.

EUTROPHICATION The process whereby water becomes enriched with plant nutrients and this replaces the oxygen, *p206*.

EXOGENOUS CHANGE IN DEMAND A change in final demand brought about by changes outside the economy in question, *p168*.

EXTERNALITIES The external economic effects that are not taken into account within the normal market place. Can be positive (benefits) or negative (costs) and are associated with the production or consumption of goods and services, *p476*.

F

FEUDALISM The social system that was prevalent in Europe in the eighth century onwards. Seen by some as control of a state by an entrenched minority for their own benefits, *p299*.

FIXED COSTS Those costs that do not vary with the volume of output, *p313*.

FLAGSHIP The chief or major one of a group, e.g. flagship attraction or hotel, *p347*.

FOCUS GROUPS A method of undertaking collective interviews that explicitly uses the group's interaction to generate results, *p248*.

'FOOTLOOSE' ATTRACTIONS Attractions that can be located almost anywhere where there is sufficient space, i.e. not dependent upon a specific natural resource or factor, *p359*.

G

GATS The General Agreement on Trade in Services. An attempt by the World Trade Organisation to liberate the trade in services in the same way that the GATT did for trade in goods, *p153*.

GDP Gross domestic product. GDP is a key indicator of an economy's performance and is based on the total value of goods and services produced by a country within its economy, *p152*.

GLOBAL DISTRIBUTION SYSTEM Computer databases used by intermediaries to book tourism products, *p711*.

GLOBAL WARMING The rise in the world's temperature due to the greenhouse effect, *p755*.

GLOBALISATION Globalisation is a term that refers to the process of increasing economic and communication connectiveness that has occurred over the past half century. Global markets replacing national and regional markets, e.g. capital markets, *p153*.

GNI Gross national income is the value of all income earned by residents of an economy whether it is earned within or outside of the national boundary (see **GNP**), *p157*.

GNP Gross national product. The value of all goods and serviced produced by a national economy. It differs from **GDP** by including the goods and services produced outside the national boundary, *p157*.

'GRAND INSPIRATION' ATTRACTIONS Attractions that are developed as a result of an individual's dream, *p360*.

H

HALLMARK EVENTS Hallmark is generally a sign of quality, authenticity or distinguishing feature therefore a hallmark event is intended to make the destination distinctive in some way, *p350*.

HEDGING A strategy that is implemented to reduce risk. An example would be for a business to take up a position in a futures market that is opposite to that held in the cash market so that risks are reduced, *p445*.

HORIZONTAL INTEGRATION The merging of two or more businesses that are operating at the same stage of the production process, *p340*.

I

IMAGESCAPE The medium or background in which people feel they live, *p357*.

INCLUSIVE TOURS The package tour, *p427*.

INDIGENOUS DEVELOPMENT Economic development that occurs as a result of changes within the country, *p504*.

INFLATION A persistent increase in the general price level over time resulting in a decrease in the purchasing power of a unit of currency, e.g. dollar, *p157*.

INFORMATION COMMUNICATION TECHNOLOGY (ICT) Digital tools used for business functions and processes, *p703*.

INFRASTRUCTURAL INVESTMENT Investment in infrastructure such as roads, airports, water supply and communications, *p248*.

INPUT–OUTPUT MODEL A general equilibrium approach to measuring the effects of a change in final demand on the rest of the economy, *p159*.

INSEPARABILITY The service product is often produced and consumed simultaneously, *p575*.

INSTANT PURCHASE PRICES Product is purchased at the time that the transaction takes place even though this may be well in advance of the dates of the trip, *p481*.

INSTITUTIONALISED OR MASS TOURISM A constant stream of large numbers of tourists to destinations., *p229*.

INTANGIBILITY The tourism product cannot be easily demonstrated, assessed or tested prior to purchase, *p574*.

INTEGRATED MARKETING COMMUNICATION Integrated marketing communications is the process a company adopts in order to integrate and coordinate its messages and media to deliver, clear reinforcing communication, *p671*.

INTEGRATION The combination businesses that are at the same or different stages of a process or distribution channel, *p427*.

INTERMEDIARIES Companies or individuals that act as brokers or middlemen between the tourists and the suppliers (travel agents, tour operators), *p422*.

INTERNATIONAL TOURISM International tourism is the activity of people visiting destinations outside their own country's boundaries, *p5*.

INTERSECTORAL LINKAGES The purchase and sale of goods and services between the various sectors of an economy – representing intermediate demand, *p152*.

INVISIBLE EXPORT The export of a service as opposed to a visible export which would be a tangible good. International tourist receipts are exports, *p152*.

K

KEY INFORMANTS People able to provide collective and important viewpoints and opinions, *p248*.

L

LEAKAGES Leakages refers to money that drops out of circulation within the local economy either by being saved or being spent on goods and services from outside the economy, *p161*.

LESS DEVELOPED COUNTRIES Countries defined to be so according to a variety of indicators such as income, literacy, life expectancy etc, *p513*.

LIFETIME VALUE The measurement of the total worth to the organisation of its relationship with a particular identified customer over a period of time, *p564*.

LIMITS OF ACCEPTABLE CHANGE The acceptable level of change that an environment can suffer without irreversible degradation, *p270*.

LINEAR HOMOGENEITY IN PRODUCTION This is the assumption that all companies within a single sector are making the same product/service in the same way and that there are no economies of large-scale production so that the next unit of output will require exactly the same proportion of inputs as the previous unit of output, *p173*.

LOAD FACTOR The measure of business and the indicator of efficiency for transport systems and is generally expressed as the percentage of available seats that are occupied on the journey, *p485*.

LOSS LEADER A good or service sold at less than market price in order to attract consumers, *p386*.

M

MARGINAL COST The incremental cost of producing one more unit of a good or service. Governments tend to intervene in the marketplace for market goods by providing subsidies or directly providing them so that the consumption of such goods and services is increased, *p368*.

MARGINAL PROPENSITY TO CONSUME The amount of each additional unit of income that an individual is likely to spend, *p170*.

MARKET FAILURE The inability of a market system to truly reflect the social costs and/or benefits associated with transactions. An example being the over-consumption of non-priced elements in the production process, such as the environment. In such cases, the market fails to find an efficient solution to the distribution, *p354*.

MARKET OR CATCHMENT AREA The area in which goods and services take place. Markets can also relate to the characteristics of potential purchasers and sellers such as specific segments of population, *p347*.

MARKETING CONCEPT The marketing management philosophy that places the satisfaction of the needs of the target market as a central guiding goal, *p555*.

MARKETING MIX The combination of product, price, place and promotion marketing tools that a company decides upon in order to affect consumer behaviour, *p545*.

MARKETING PLAN A detailed company approach to the selection of target groups and the formulation of a marketing mix to achieve marketing objectives and financial targets, *609*.

'ME TOO' ATTRACTION DEVELOPMENTS The development of an attraction on the basis of the evidence that it has worked before therefore it will work again, i.e. it ignores market saturation and displacement, *p359*.

MEGA-EVENTS Mega is a prefix that means one million. A mega-event is generally considered to be a large-scale event that has global publicity and or is associated with large-scale impacts, *p351*.

MERIT GOODS Goods that are deemed to have a greater value to society than is reflected in their market price, *p364*.

MISSION STATEMENT A short statement as to the main purpose or major goal of the organisation in relation to the wider environment, *p618*.

MONOPOLISTIC POWER The ability of a business to determine the price of the goods/services produced (to some extent), *p311*.

MULTINATIONAL AGENCIES Agencies that operate across national boundaries such as the United Nations Development Agency, *p504*.

MULTIPLIER ANALYSIS An economic technique for estimating the impact of tourism on the local economy, *p151*.

N

NATIONAL AIR CARRIER The airline that carries the national flag, the state airline, *p518*.

NATIONAL TOURIST ORGANISATION The tourist authority for a state/country, *p503*.

NEW PRODUCT DEVELOPMENT The introduction of a good, service or idea that is perceived by customers to be new, *p628*.

NEW TOURIST A tourist is experienced, aware of opportunities and empowered, *p766*.

'NEW VERSION' ATTRACTIONS Modern-day interpretations of classic attractions, e.g. from fairgrounds to theme parks, *p360*.

O

OECD Organisation for Economic Co-operation and Development. A collection of 30 member states that use the organisation as a discussion forum to further their aims for a free market system, *p196*.

OFF-PEAK The periods when travel and tourist activities are in less demand. Often associated with discounts to attract business, *p463*.

ONLINE TRAVEL The acquisition of information and the purchase of travel-related services from businesses selling on the Internet, *p434*.

OPERATING ACCOUNT An account for day-to-day operations of the business, *p439*.

OPPORTUNITY COSTS Opportunity cost is what a country, company or individual has to forego in order have something, *p160*.

OVERRIDES Extra commission paid by airlines, hotels and other suppliers for volume bookings, *p437*.

P

PAID HOLIDAY ENTITLEMENT The practice of employers providing employees with time off for pay, *p115*.

PEAK The prime period of demand, *p462*.

PERCEIVED RISK The interpretation of the seriousness of economic, physical, performance and pyschological aspects related to decision making, *p578*.

PERIPHERAL AREAS Areas away from the centre or the core, *p227*.

PERISHABILITY A characteristic of service products implies they cannot be easily stored for future sale, *p340*.

PERSONAL SELLING Personal selling is an attempt to gain benefit through face-to-face or telephone contact between the seller's representative and those people with whom the seller wants to communicate, *p667*.

POLLUTER SHOULD PAY Philosophy that supports the view that the costs of cleaning up pollution should be borne by those who create the pollution, *p372*.

PRESERVATION Not using or limiting the use of resources so as to preserve them for future generations, *p197*.

PRICE The amount of money charged for a product or service based upon what a consumer is willing to give up in return for the benefits delivered, *p653*.

PRICE COMPETITIVE Where small changes in the prices charged for a product may result in sales being won by a rival business, *p311*.

PRIMARY DATA New data gathered by the researcher for the purpose of the study, *p317*.

PRODUCT A package of problem solving services and tangible attributes formulated to satisfy a need or want, *p644*.

PRODUCT DIFFERENTIATION Making the output of a business distinctly different from the output of competitors, *p310*.

PRODUCT LIFE CYCLE A term borrowed from biological sciences that refers to the way that a product evolves over time, *p428*.

PROJECT APPRAISAL Project appraisal involves a collection of instruments that can be used to determine the financial viability (such as the internal rates of return) of a variety of projects, *p162*.

PROMOTION Descriptive term for the mix of communication activities that tourism organisations carry out in order to influence those publics on whom their sales depend, *p662*.

PROPERTY MANAGEMENT SYSTEM A computerised system for integrating all elements of hospitality information and management, *p719*.

PRO-POOR TOURISM Tourism strategies designed to alleviate poverty, *p26*.

PROTECTIONISM The opposite to trade liberalisation – the imposition of tariffs or quotas to stop imports, *p311*.

PSYCHOGRAPHIC ANALYSIS A way of categorising tourists according to their attitudes, values, behaviour and beliefs, *p230*.

PUBLIC OR COLLECTIVE GOOD A public good is one that everyone feels the benefits of and from which no one can practically be excluded and in non-rival in consumption. Collective goods have similar qualities but exclusion is possible, e.g. television broadcasts started as collective goods but have largely moved into the private sector domain – this movement does not detract from the 'collective' qualities they possess and there is no suggestion that the private market achieves an efficient allocation, *p354*.

PUBLIC RELATIONS Public relations is non-personal communication that changes opinion or achieves coverage in a mass medium and that is not paid for by the source, *p669*.

Q

QUALITY ASSURANCE The system which assures the end customers receive a level of service of which they will be satisfied, *p582*.

QUALITY CONTROL The checks against standards set to ensure the organisation achieves its quality objectives, *p582*.

R

REGIONAL DISPARITIES The differences between regions with respect to specified variables such as income, employment etc, *p506*.

REPATRIATED (INCOME) Repatriated income is that income sent home (out of the economy) by foreign workers or companies, *p176*.

RESOURCE ALLOCATION The way in which resources are allocated across different uses in an economy, *p181*.

S

SALES PROMOTION Sales promotion involves any activity that offers an incentive to induce a desired result from potential customers, trade intermediaries or the sales force, *p666*.

SAME-DAY VISITOR A person on a brief recreational trip, not exceeding 24 hours at the destination, *p13*.

SCHEDULED SERVICES Transport systems that operate according to strict conditions relating to frequency and scheduling, *p485*.

SEASONALITY The temporal fluctuations of tourism on a daily, weekly, monthly or annual basis, *p133*.

SECTORAL LINKAGES Sectoral linkages refer to the transactions (sales and purchases) that take place between companies in a single economy, *p169*.

SEGMENT A submarket of consumers who have been chosen as a target group and are marketed to differently to other subgroups, *p546*.

SEGMENTATION The process of identifying the most appropriate submarkets for the company's or destination's offer, *p553*.

SERVICE INDUSTRIES Companies that produce output in the form of services rather than goods, *p225*.

SERVICE PRODUCT The formulation of an activity or benefit which is essentially intangible in nature and does not lead to the ownership of anything, *p574*.

SEX TOURISM Defines the specific motivation of tourists to go on holiday for the purpose of engaging in short-term sexual relations, *p239*.

SIMULTANEITY OF PRODUCTION Where the production of a service and its consumption occur at the same instant, *p307*.

SMEs Small and medium-sized enterprises. (Medium – no more than 250 employees; small – no more than 50 employees and micro – no more than 10 employees.) Turnover or balance sheet restrictions also apply, *p214*.

SOCIAL COHESION The way in which society can work together as opposed to social divisions normally associated with gaps between the rich and the poor, *p506*.

SOCIAL NET BENEFITS The result of deducting social costs from social benefits. Adding the term social to benefits and costs means including a broader range of factors than purely financial ones, *p353*.

SOCIALISM A system of social organisation whereby the state government takes responsibility for resource allocation, production and distribution, *p299*.

SOCIO-ECONOMIC GROUPS Categorising people into groups by resorting to demographics (age, sex, occupation etc.), *p232*.

SPONSORSHIP Sponsorship is the material or financial support of a specific activity, normally but not exclusively sport, education or the arts, which does not form part of the sponsor organisation's normal business, *p670*.

STAGNATION A time period in which there is either little or no economic growth, *p152*.

STAKEHOLDERS The groups of businesses, residents, governments and tourists who have a stake in the development of tourism, *p259*.

STEP ANALYSIS An analysis of the environment based upon factors of society, technology, economics and politics, *p122*.

STRATEGIC PLANNING A planning approach to ensure a fit between the environment, the competencies and resources of the organisation and its changing marketing opportunities, *p610*.

STRATEGIC RAIL AUTHORITY The UK's public sector strategic specifier, providing industry leadership, *p470*.

STRUCTURAL ADJUSTMENT Policy of increasing privatisation and trade liberalisation intended to help countries generate greater wealth and reduce poverty. Has been criticised for inducing economic decline and endangering the welfare of the economically vulnerable, *p504*.

SUBSIDIARITY The assignment of political power to the smallest units of government, *p506*.

SUPPLY CONSTRAINTS When one sector reaches or comes close to full productive capacity it will not be able to respond fully to a further increase in demand for its output, *p172*.

SUSTAINABLE DEVELOPMENT Development that meets the needs of the people today without compromising the ability of future generations to meet their own needs, *p260*.

SUSTAINABLE TOURISM DEVELOPMENT As sustainable development but relating specifically to the tourism industry, *p264*.

T

TARGET MARKET A set of buyers selected as sharing similar needs or characteristics so that a company can organise a marketing mix to serve them, *p643*.

TARIFF STRUCTURE The nature of the tariffs associated with imports, *p319*.

TIED AGENCY A tied agent can only deal with the product or service of a single company, *p449*.

TIGER ECONOMIES The term within this book is used to refer to the East Asian tiger economies and includes Indonesia, Hong Kong, Malaysia, Singapore, South Korea, Taiwan and Thailand. The term 'tiger' relates to the aggressive policies of the countries towards achieving rapid growth, *p154*.

TIME-SHARE An ownership system that facilitates individuals 'owning' a specific period of time or percentage share of an holiday or vacation club, *p394*.

TOTAL QUALITY MANAGEMENT An organisation-wide process and system of ensuring that all activities carried out adhere to pre-agreed quality standards, *p581*.

TOTAL TOURIST EXPERIENCE The combined stages of preplanning, the purchase, the journey, the visit/ and perhaps stay, the return journey and overall reflection on the activity, *p556*.

TOURISM PRODUCT MARKET The combination of market trends and supply-side initiatives, *p779*.

TOURISM SATELLITE ACCOUNTS A set of accounts to show the total value to an economy of domestic and international tourism, *p151*.

TOURISM SYSTEM Leiper's (1979) description of a three-part system of tourist-generating region, transit region and tourism destination region set within social, economic and environmental contexts, *p9*.

TOURIST SATISFACTION The rating that tourists' give to their experience while on holiday, *p269*.

TOURIST TAX Taxes specifically levied on tourists generally through businesses that deal with tourists. Can be entry taxes, hotel taxes or other specific tourism industry-based tax, *p523*.

TRADE DEFICIT Trade deficit is where a country's expenditures on imports of goods and services are greater (in value terms) than the receipts from the export of goods and services, *p157*.

TRAIN DE GRANDE VITESSE TGV (literally, *high-speed train*) holds the highest speed record for a train on any national railroad, *p472*.

TRAVEL PROPENSITY The penetration of travel activity within a given population, *p41*.

TYPOLOGIES Classifications, *p227*.

U

UIP United International Pictures.

UNEP United Nations Environmental Programme, *p199*.

V

VALUE ADDED Value added is the amount of monetary value added to a good or service by a company before it is offered for sale, *p161*.

VERTICAL INTEGRATION When the same business owns establishments that are operating at more than one stage of the production, selling and delivery process, *p427*.

VFR Visiting friends and relatives (tourist motivation), *p242*.

VISITING FRIENDS AND RELATIVES **VFR** tourist motivation, *p242*.

W

'WONDER' ATTRACTIONS Attractions based upon some unique natural or artificial feature, *p360*.

Y

YIELD MANAGEMENT Management system that optimises the yield (returns) from a project, *p368*.

Z

ZONE OF TOLERANCE A customer will tolerate a range of standards in an area between desired and adequate rather than have one set standard of assessment, *p592*.

A

access
  control and NTOs 518
  visitor access function 355
Access to the Countryside Act
    1949 354
accommodation
  aircraft 396
  apartments 393–4
  bed and breakfast 389–93
  budget/economy sector 407–8
  camping and caravan sites 395
  campus accommodation 394
  classification 403–8
  commercial, management
    398–9
  consumer protection 403
  cottages 393–4
  cruise liners 395–6
  definition 387–96
  distinctive nature of 397–8
  environmental issues 408–9
  farmhouses 389–93
  ferries 395–6
  franchising 388
  gites 393–4
  grading of 402–8
  guest houses 389–93
  hotels 387–9
  human resources 410
  industry 387–96
  influence of USA 400–2
  information communications
    technology 409–10
  inns 389–93
  medical facility accommodation
    395
  quality issues 402–8
  sectoral origins 400–2
  sectoral overlap 399
  self-catering 393–4
  time-share 394
  tourism product 386–7
  trains 396
  visiting friends and relatives 396
  youth accommodation 394–5
Accor corporate structure 431
actual demand category,
    definition 39
ad hoc models, multiplier analysis
    169–70
additionality 527
administration
  governmental 508–13
  tour operation/wholesaling 447

Advance Purchase Excursion Fare
    481
Advanced Passenger Train (APT)
    473
Advanced Purchase Excursion Fare
    (APEX) 481
advertising promotion 665–6
affordable method of promotional
    budget 664
age
  as determinant of demand
    117–19
  sociological basis of
    development 232
Agenda 21 196, 261
AIDS 239
  case study 240–1
air seats, tour operation/
    wholesaling 451–2
air traffic control 469
air traffic movements 471
air transport 480–6
  airports 481
  charter flights 444–5, 485
  low-cost case study 483–5
  operation 482
  scheduled services 485
aircraft
  accommodation sector 396
  pollution problems 596
Airline Deregulation Act 1978
    487
airline(s)
  case study 568–70
  Deregulation Act 1978 487
  information communications
    technology 718–19
Airlines Reporting Corporation
    439
airports 481
alien cultural tourist experience
    246
allocentric types
  Plog typology 57
  psychological basis of tourism
    development 231
alternative tourism 281
Amadeus Global Travel
    Distribution Network 427,
    673
  global distribution system case
    study 733–6
American Society of Travel Agents
    438
anthropology of tourism 227
application service providers
    (ASPs) 721
Arctic tourism case study 222–3

artificial attractions/resources 351,
    356–7
Asian Development Bank 506
Association of British Travel
    Agents 438
Association of South East Asian
    Nations (ASEAN) 745
attractions
  artificial 351, 356–7
  authenticity 351, 374–5
  characteristics of 34752
  classification of 347–52
  commercial sector 366
  costs 367, 368
  developing 357–63
  development process 359
  economic aspects 364
  environment 371–4
  environmental regulation 372–4
  events 350–1
  flagship 347
  man-made resources/artificial
    resources 351, 356–7
  managing 363–75
  market failure and public
    provision 353–5
  market–imagescape mix 359–63
  natural 351, 352–6
  nature and purpose 346–7
  people management 368–9
  pricing policies 368
  product 358
  public ownership 364–5
  seasonality 369–70
  user-orientated attractions 349
  visitor management 370–1
  voluntary organisations 365–6
auditing systems and procedures
    585
augmented product 644, 645–6

B

backward pricing 659
balance of payments demand
    patterns 84
balanced growth 302
Bali bombings case study 753–4
base theory models,
    multiplier analysis 167–8
basic tourism development plan
    326
beach tourism 779
bed & breakfast accommodation
    389–93

behavioural effects, 237–9
Benidorm tourism development
  case study 305–6
Bermuda, investment policy and
  incentives 526
Boston Consulting Group (BCG)
  matrix 623–5
boutique hotels 406–7
brand
  awareness 652–3
  equity 647
  extensions 363
  stretching 363
branding
  brand name and image 647–53
  family brand performance 652
  product brand performance 652
British Chartered Institute of
  Marketing 555
British Tourist Authority 618
brochures 441–2, 446–7
Brundtland Report 260–1
budget/economy sector
  accommodation 407–8
building regulations, NTOs and
  521
business philosophies
  comparison 558–62
  integrated company 558, 561–2
  market-orientated company
    558, 561–2
  product-orientated company
    558–9
  systems/technology-orientated
    company 558, 559
business situational analysis
  marketing planning process
  626–7
business travel, transportation 486

C

Cabotage EC 488
camping 395
campus accommodation 394
capacity planning,
  tour operation/wholesaling
  442–5
Cape Canaveral Space Centre,
  Florida 781
capitalism 299
car, competitive analysis 475–6
caravan sites 395
Caribbean Development Bank 506
Caribbean Tourism Organisation
  314
carrying capacity 267–70
  alien factors 274–6
  determination 278–9
  dynamics 270

factors influencing 270–1
impacts 276–9, 280–1
local factors 271–4
measurement criteria 279
process of determining 271–9
carrying unit 472
Carter, President 487
causative models of tourist
  demand 127–8
characteristics
  attractions 347–52
  eco-tourism system 11–12
  segmentation strategies 629–33
  service product 574–7
  tourism distribution 670–1
charter
  flights 444–5, 485
  tourists 228
Chicago Convention (1944) 487,
  488
child prostitution 240
Civil Aeronautics Board 487
classical theory of economic
  stagnation 298–9
classification 15–22
  accommodation 403–8
  attractions 347–52
  internal visitors (WTO) 90
  international visitors (WTO) 86
  of tourists 17–22
climate change 755
  case study 760–2
coach transport 477
Cohen classification 60–1
commercial sector attractions
  366–7
commission, travel agent 437, 439
commodification, socio-cultural
  impacts 242, 243
communication theory of
  advertising 666
communism 299
comparative parity method of
  promotional budget 664
competitive advantage 625–6
competitive analysis
  (transportation)
  air 477–9
  car 475–6
  coach 477
  railway 477–9
  road 475–6
  sea 479–80
components of transportation
  motive power 472–5
  terminal 470–1
  vehicle 472
  way 469–70
computable general equilibrium
  models (CGE) 173–4
computer reservation systems
  (CRSs) 515, 672, 711–12
  hotels and 720

tour operators 721–3
travel agents 723–5
congestion, air transport and
  infrastructure 489–90
consumer behaviour
  buyer decision process 65–73
  concept of self-image 687
  decision-making framework 53
  demand 54–64
  determinants of 53
  effectors 53
  energisers 53
  extended problem-solving
    models 67–73
  family influence 62
  fundamentals of 52–3
  image 62–3
  individual decision-making
    process 53
  limited problem-solving models
    64
  model evolution 64–5
  models of 64–73
  motivation 54–60
  roles 53, 62
  travel-buying behaviour 69–71
  typologies 60–1
consumer protection
  accommodation classification
    403
  Package. Travel Directive 446
consumer-orientated approach to
  marketing 587–8
core product 644
corporate mission and goals 618
cost-benefit analysis 162
cost leadership 625–6
cost-orientated pricing 658
  cost-plus pricing 658
  rate of return pricing 658
Costa Rica sustainability
  accreditation case study
  283–4
costs
  attractions 367, 368
  fuel 473–5
  travel agents 439
crime 242
cruise liners
  accommodation 395–6
  transportation case study
    495–500
cultural heritage
  carrying capacity and 272
  tourism 780

D

DAGMAR model 666
dark tourism 780–1

data
  analysis 103
  collection procedures 247–50
  deficiencies and multiplier
    analysis 175–6
  multiplier models 167–74
  primary 248, 317, 318
  secondary 248
  socio-cultural impacts 249
  tourism planning process 317
data processing 706
decision-making process 53
DeKadt
  demonstration effect 232
  direct socio-cultural impacts 233
  indirect socio-cultural impacts 233
  induced socio-cultural impacts
    233
  negative socio-cultural impacts
    234–5
Delphi analyses 134–5, 248
demand
  actual demand category 39
  consumer behaviour 54–64
  curves 41, 43
  definitions 38, 39
  determinants 114–16
  domestic 89–94
  economic factors 124–6
  effectors 53
  energisers 53
  family influence 62
  forecasting 127–36
  growth forecast (WTO) 742
  image 62–3
  income elasticity 654–5
  indicators 41, 46–8
  individual demand curve 41
  information communications
    technology 709–10
  international 84–8
  macro-determinants 120–1
  market demand curve 43
  motivation 54–60
  no demand category 39
  political influences 126
  price elasticity 654–5
  promotional effect on 665
  and revenue management
    514–18
  roles 62
  schedules 41–3
  seasonality 133–4
  social factors 122–4
  suppressed 39, 120
  technological influences 124
  typologies 55–60
demand/supply and investment,
    vicious circles of 300
demand-orientated pricing
  backward pricing 659
  discrimination pricing 658–9
  market penetration pricing 659

skimming pricing 660
demographic trends 742–3
demonstration effect
  negative effects 237–9
  socio-cultural influences 233
dependency theory of
    development 302
destination management
    organisations 725–7
destination management systems
    515, 726–7
destinations
  eco-tourism and 11
  future developments 771–8
  information communications
    technology 725–7
  management organisations
    725–7
  marketing of 683–7
  psychographic position 230–1
  transport at 463–4
determinants of demand 53
  at individual scale 114
  lifestyle 114–16
  macro determinants 120–1
Development of Tourism Act 1969
    507, 527
development planning layers
  international tourism planning
    314
  national tourism planning 314
  regional/local tourism planning
    315
development theories 298–304
  role of tourism 302–3
differentiation strategy 625
difficult comparison effect on
    price sensitivity 655
diminishing returns, law of 299
direct effects
  economic impacts 162
  socio-cultural impacts 233
direct marketing promotion 670
Directorate General Enterprise
    506
discretionary incentives 528
discrimination pricing 658–9
Disneyland® Resort Paris case
    study 637–9
distribution and tourism
  characteristics of intermediation
    422–7
  different tourism distribution
    needs 673–4
  information communications
    technology 710–14
distribution channels structure of
    423
domestic age, tourism demand
    and 117–19
domestic tourism
  classification 90
  measurement methods 91–4

why measure 89–91
Doxey: tourist–host contact index
    235–6
drifter, Cohen's classification 61
drivers of change in tourism
    742–51
  future 742–3, 766–79
  political 744–51
  social 743–4

E

early empiricist phase,
    models of consumer behaviour
    64
Earth Summit (Rio Janeiro, 1992)
    261
easyJet airbus 560–1
economic aspects of attractions
    364–6
  commercial sector 366
  costs 367, 368
  pricing policy 368
  public ownership 364–5
  seasonality 369–70
  voluntary organisations 365–6
economic development theories
    298–304
economic impacts of tourism
  dependence on tourism 157–8
  direct, indirect and induced
    effects 162–3
  leakages 161
  measurement 162–3
  negative impacts 237
  tourism spending 161
economic significance 152–4
economic stagnation, English
    classical theory of 298–9
economics
  attractions 364–5
  carrying capacity and 273
  retail travel agents 439–41
  tour operation/wholesaling
    448–53
eco-tourism 281–3
  case study 11–12, 214–17
  characteristics 11–12
  future trend 778, 780
  in India, case study 291–4
ECPAT 240
education as determinant of
    demand 115–16
effective demand category
    definition 39
effectors of demand
  definition 53
  motivation 54–60
efficiency of transportation
    489–90

elasticity of demand
  income 654–5
  price 654–5
electronic retailing 675–8
elite, Smith's classification 228
employment
  as determinant of demand
    114–15
  multiplier 166
endemic tourism 772
energisers of demand 53
  Maslow's hierarchy 54–5
  motivation 54–60
energy use of accommodation
    sector 408–9
Engel
  extended problem solving
    models 67–73
  limited problem solving models
    66
Environmental Action
    Programmes (EAPs) 210–14
Environmental Auditing 209–10
environmental impact 196–201
  assessment 202–9, 212
  carrying capacity and 272–3
  case study 200–1
  checklist 204–5
  conservation and preservation
    197–8
  development strategies 196–7
  development planning process
    327–8
  empirical studies 197
  negative 198–200
  positive 197–8
  preservation programmes 196–7
  process 204–9
  regulation 372–4
environmental impact assessment
    212
  indicators 206–9
  process 206, 207
environmental indicators 206–9
environmental issues
  accommodation sector 408–9
  energy use 408–9
  fragility 409
  recycling 409
  transportation 491–2
  waste disposal 409
  water use 408
eras of marketing
  marketing era 552
  production era 552
  sales era 552
ERDF 532
European Agricultural Guidance
    and Guarantee Fund
    Guidance System (EAGGF)
    532
European Bank for Reconstruction
    and Development 504

European Commission 211,
    487–8, 506
  cabotage directive 488
European Court of Justice 488
European Environmental Bureau
    (EEB) 211
European Investment Bank 506
European Social Fund 532
European Travel Commission 504
European Union 213, 314
  role in tourism 506
  tourism project assistance case
    study 532–41
European Union Package Travel
    Directive, 1990 424, 446, 452,
    522
evolution
  information communications
    technology 704–5
  marketing 551–3
Expedia.com case study 434,
    435–6
expenditure
  measurement 163
  multiplier analysis 163–74
  effect on price sensitivity 656
experience economy 768–9
explorer
  Cohen's classification 61
  Smith's classification 228
extended problem-solving models
    67–73
external audit 618–26
extranets 705

facilitating product 644, 645–6
failure in tourism planning and
    development 324–8
fairness effect on price sensitivity
    656
family
  consumer behaviour 62
  brand name 651
  brand performance 651
farmhouse accommodation
    389–93
ferry services, accommodation
    395–6
feudalism 299
Fidelio 721
financial evaluation,
  tour operation/wholesaling
    445–6
Financial Instrument for Fisheries
    Guidance (FIFG) 532
five forces model of competition
    (Porter) 620–3, 675
fixed costs,

planning and development
    313–14
focus groups 248
focus strategy 626
forecasting methods 127–36
  qualitative 134–6
  quantitative 127–34
formative phase,
  models of consumer behaviour
    64
four Ps
  are four enough? 680–2
  place 671–7
  price 653–61
  product 644–53
  promotion 661–71
franchising, accommodation 388
Freedoms of the Air Chicago
    Convention 487
Fundo Nacional de Fomento al
    Turismo (Fonatur) case study
    520
future markets
  markets 766
  transportation 489–90

Galileo 427, 673
gender as determinant of demand
    116
General Agreement in Trade in
    Services (GATS) 153–4,
    744–5
General Agreement on Trade and
    Tariffs (GATT) 153–4
generating region ecotourism 11
Gibraltar case study 187–91
global distribution systems (GDSs)
    672–3, 713
  airline ownership 718–19
  Amadeus case study 733–6
  information communication
    technology 711–13
  travel agents 723, 724
global warming 755
globalisation 154
  transportation 490–2
government organisations
  administrative policy framework
    508–13
  impact 513–28
  intervention policy 528–9
  public policy framework 504–8
government revenue multiplier
    166
grading system, accommodation
    402–8
grand inspiration attractions 360
gravity model case study 40

Grenada sustainable development networks case study 277–8
Gronroos, C.: service quality model 588–9
gross domestic product 4, 152
gross national product 157
growth and development, theory of (Rostow) 300–1
guesthouse accommodation 389–93
Gulf War 473

H

hallmark events 350
health, socio-cultural impacts 242
hedging 445
heritage tourism 778
heterogeneity, service product 575
Hierarchy of Needs (Maslow) 54–5
historical perspective marketing 551–3
Holiday Inn 401
holidays
    image 63–4
    paid entitlement as determinant of demand 114–15
horizontal integration intermediaries 430–2
Hospitality Franchise Systems (HFS) 388
Hotel Property Management Systems 719–20
    Fidelio 721
hotels
    accommodation product 387–9
    information communications technology 719–21
    property management systems 719–20
hub and spoke systems transportation 489
human resources
    accommodation 410
    future trends 755–7

image
    consumer behaviour 62–3
    holiday 63–4
imagescape 357–8
    market–imagescape mix 359–63
impacts of tourism
    economic 152–83
    environmental 194–223
    socio-cultural 224–56

implementation
    plan failure 325–8
    tourism planning process 321
incipient mass,
    Smith's classification 228
income
    as determinant of demand 114–15
    elasticity of demand 654–5
    inequality, case study 238
    multiplier 166
    sociological basis of tourism development 232
independent tourists
    typology 228
India, eco-tourism case study 291–4
indicators of tourism demand 41, 46–8
indirect effects
    economic impacts 162
    socio-cultural impacts 233
individual brands 651
individual demand curve 41
individual mass tourist,
    Cohen's classification 61
induced effects
    economic impacts 163
    socio-cultural impacts 233
industry sector
    planning and development 309–10
    SMEs 309–10
information communication technologies (ICTs)
    accommodation 409–10
    airlines 718–19
    competitiveness and strategy 706–7
    conceptual synthesis of in tourism 716
    definition 704
    destination 725–7
    evolution 704–6
    future of tourism industry and 727
    global distribution systems 711–13
    hotels 719–21
    tour operation 721–3
    tourism and 707–16
    tourism demand 709–10
    tourism distribution 710–14
    travel agents 723–5
information management case study 107–10
information provision, NTOs and 514–16
infrastructural investment 248–50
Infrastructure, local 247
inns 389–93
input-output analysis models, multiplier analysis 170–3

inseparability,
    service product 575–7
Instant Purchase Excursion Fare 481
Instant Purchase Fares (IPEX) 481
institutionalised tourism 229
intangibility, service product 574–5
integrated planning and development 304–14
    labour intensive industry 308–9
    price competition 312
    price flexibility 311
    product characteristics 307
    protectionism 311
    structure of industry 309–10
    tourism and development 305–14
    training 309
    wealth redistribution 307–8
integration
    horizontal (intermediaries) 430–2
    vertical (intermediaries) 427–30
intermediation
    benefits 422–3
    integration, consolidation and concentration 427–34
    nature 422–37
    structure 422–7
internal audit 618–26
International Air Transport Association 504, 439, 487
International Civil Aviation Organisation 504
International Institute for Peace Through Tourism (IIPTT) 247
International Labour Organisation (ILO) 237
International Passenger Survey 163
international tourism 154–7
    classification 86
    development planning layers 314
    estimates 94
    forecasts 742
    receipts as percentage of exports 158
    tourism balance sheet 159
International Travel Exchange 512
Internet
    survey data collection 101
    utilisation by tourism industry sectors 716–27
intervention policy
    governmental organisations 528–9
interviews as data collection procedures 99, 100–1
intranets 705

investment and demand/supply, vicious circles of 3001
investment incentives, role of public sector 525–8
Iranian Crisis 473

Johannesburg Summit (2002) 261

key informants 248
Keynesian models, multiplier analysis 169–70
knowledge management 107–10

L

labour, negative effects on 237
Lastminute.com case study 714–16
law of diminishing returns 299
Le Meridien case study 390–2
leakages, economic impacts 161
Legoland case study 378–82
Leiper, N.: model of tourism system 8–10, 740, 766, 767, 781
leisure
  paradox 117
  price elasticity 654–5
  recreation and 17
lifetime value (LTV) 564
Limited of Acceptable Change (LAC) 270
limited problem-solving models 66
limits of acceptable change 771
local tourism planning 315

M

Maastricht Treaty 532
macro determinants of demand
  economic factors 124–6
  political factors 126
  social factors 122–4
  technological factors 124
management information systems (MIS) 706

Manila Declaration on World Tourism, 1980 36, 152
man-made (artificial) attractions/resources 351, 356–7
market failure 526
market segmentation
  future 770
  marketing planning process 629–33
market(s)
  demand curve 41, 43
  failure and public provision 353–5
  orientated company 558–9
  penetration pricing 659
  regulation and NTOs 522
  research, planning and NTOs 522–3
  segmentation and marketing planning process 629–33
  target 643–4
market–imagescape mix 359–63
marketing
  advertising 665–6
  business philosophies 558–62
  concept 553–7
  criticism of marketing concept 594–7
  definitions 550–1, 553–5
  destinations 682–7
  environment of an organisation 609–10
  eras of 552
  evolution 551–3
  historical roots and background 551–3
  management tasks 593
  mix strategy and marketing planning process 628–33
  NTOs 514
  orientation 562–5, 594
  selling vs. 557–8
  societal approach 598–9
  STEP analysis 619–20
  tour operation/wholesaling 446–7
  tourism organisations 512–13
  vs. selling 557–8
marketing concept 555
  criticisms 594–7
marketing mix 552
  are four Ps enough? 680–2
  definition 642
  marketing planning process 628–33
  market segmentation strategies 643–4
  place 671–7
  price 653–61
  product 644–53
  promotion 661–71
  services 681

target market 643–4
marketing orientation
  adoption of 594
  company 558, 561
marketing planning
  definition 608–9
  lack of 608–9
  model 616
  purposes 610–13
  reasons for failure 613–14
  structure of 615–34
  successful 613–15
marketing planning process
  business situational analysis 626–7
  corporate mission and goals 618
  creating objectives 627–8
  external and internal audit 618–26
  involvement levels diagram 617
  market segmentation 629–33
  marketing mix 628–33
  monitoring the plan 633–4
  STEP and market environment 626
Marx, Karl: historical approach to development 299–300
Maslow, A.: hierarchy of needs 54–5
mass tourist 229
  Cohen's classification 61
  Smith's classification 228
McDonald's, value concept of 556–7
me too attraction development 359
measurement
  carrying capacity 279
  demand 87–8
  domestic tourism 91–4
  economic impacts 162–3
  international tourism 87–8
  socio-cultural impacts 247–50
medical facility accommodation 395
mega-events 351
mid centric types, Plog typology 57
Ministry of Tourism 509
mobility
  case study 14–15
  as determinant of demand 115–16
models
  business philosophies 558–62
  carrying capacity 272
  characteristics for tourism analysis 19–22
  Cohen's classification 61
  consumer behaviour 64–73
  consumer decision-making framework 53, 65
  DAGMAR 666

models *(continued)*
  demand curves – individual 41
  demand curves – markets 43
  development of promotional
    objectives 661–3
  development plan 325
  distribution channels 423
  environmental impact
    assessment process 207
  interdisciplinary approach in
    tourism 8
  levels of cultural penetration 244
  managing service quality
    588–92
  marketing mix 642
  marketing planning 616
  marketing system 594
  Maslow hierarchy 54–5
  Mathieson and Wall model
    69–71
  Mayo and Jarvis model 69
  Moscardo model 71
  multiplier analysis 165
  planning process 316
  Plog typology 56–9, 230–1
  pricing policy 662
  psychographic position of
    destinations 230
  Schmoll model 67–9
  service encounter 586–7
  structure of an NTO 511
  tolerance levels 275
  tourism system 9, 10
  travel-buying behaviour 70
  Wahab, Crampon & Rothfield
    model 67
models of consumer behaviour
  64–73
  common characteristics 64–5
  evolution 64–5
modified basic development plan
  326
monitoring
  marketing planning process
    633–4
  reformulation 321
motivation
  consumer behaviour 54–60
  cultural 56
  Dann, G. M. S. 55–6
  Maslow, A. H. 54–5
  McIntosh, Goeldner & Ritchie 56
  physical 56
  Plog, S. 56–9
  status and prestige 56
  summary of concepts 60
  tourism demand 55–60
motivation research phase,
  models of consumer behaviour
    64
motivators
  cultural 56
  interpersonal 56

physical 56
  status and prestige 56
motive power 472–5
multiplier analysis
  ad hoc models 169–70
  base models 167–8
  computable general equilibrium
    models (CGE) 173–4
  concept 163–5
  employment multiplier 166
  government revenue multiplier
    166
  income multiplier 166
  input-output models 170–3
  Keynesian models 168–9
  methodological approaches
    167–74
  output multiplier 166
  size of value 177–80
  transaction/sales multiplier 166
  tourist multiplier 164
  types of 166–7
  policy implications 180–2
  weaknesses and limitations of
    multiplier models 174–80
MyTravel Group plc case study
  456–8

National Parks and Access to the
  Countryside Act 1949 354
national tourism offices
  access control 518
  administrative framework
    509–10
  building regulations 521
  demand and revenue
    management 514–18
  development function 513
  information provision 514–16
  investment incentives 525–8
  land use planning and control
    521
  marketing and promotion 514
  marketing function 512–13
  market regulation 522
  market research and planning
    522–3
  ownership 524
  policy objectives 510–13
  pricing 516–18
  public policy framework 507
  safety and security 518
  structure 510–13
  supply and cost management
    519–28
  taxation 523–4
natural resources 347–8, 352–6
natural wage rate 298

needs, Maslow's hierarchy of 54–5
network era 706
new tourism
  case study 14–15
  characteristics 766–70
  Poon model 782–3
  WTTC 740–2
new version attractions 360
New Zealand tourism strategy
  332–6
Nisbet Plantation Hotel case study
  691–4
no demand category 39
non-causative models of tourist
  demand 128–31
norms, tourist adaptation 228
North American Free Trade
  Agreement (NAFTA) 745

O

objective-and-task method of
  promotional budget 664
objectives
  marketing planning process
    627–8
  promotional 661–3
off-beat, Smith's classification 228
Olympics 232, 351, 608
online travel 434–7
operating cycle,
  tour operation/wholesaling 443
Organisation for Economic Cooperation & Development
  196, 206–8, 314, 504
Organisation of American States
  504
organised mass tourist
  Cohen's classification 61
output multiplier 166
ownership and NTOs 524
own-label brands 651

P

Pacific Asia Travel Association 504
package tourists typology 228
paid holiday entitlement 115
Parks Canada functional zoning
  case study 348
patterns of demand for tourism
  analysing 131–4
  principal generating countries
    155
  receipts 158
  seasonality 130
  world, case study 139–44

peace, socio-cultural awareness and 246–7
perceived substitutes effect on price sensitivity 655
percentage of sales method of promotional budget 664
performance risk factors 578, 579
personal selling promotion 667–8
physical risk factors 578–9
place
    different tourism distribution needs 673–4
    information communications technology 725–7
    marketing mix strategy 670–7
    reasons for use of retail travel agents 674–5
planning
    carrying capacity and 276
    development planning layers 314–15
    future destinations 772
    integrated approach 304–14
    international tourism planning 314
    national tourism planning 314
    planning team 321–4
    reasons for plan failure 324–8
    regional/local tourism planning 315
    service encounter 579–81
Plog, S. 56–9, 243
    allocentric 57, 230–1
    mid centric 57
    psychocentric 56–7, 230–1
    psychological basis of tourism development 230–1
policy
    formulation in tourism planning 319–20
    objectives of NTOs 510–12
    pricing considerations 662
    Wales Tourist Board 510–12
policy implications of multiplier analysis 180–2
political drivers of change 744–51
    emergent patterns 750–1
    GATS 744–5
    globalisation 745–8
    trade blocs 745
political influences
    demand for tourism 126
    transportation 486
political structure, carrying capacity and 273
Poon, A.: new tourism 782–3
portfolio analysis 623–5
postal surveys, data collection 99, 101
poverty alleviation case study 25–9
price
    backward pricing 659

competition in tourism 311, 312
controls 516–18
cost-orientated pricing 658
cost-plus pricing 658
cutting 656, 657
demand schedules 41–3
demand-orientated pricing 658–60
discrimination pricing 658–9
elasticity of demand 654–5
flexibility in tourism 311
four Ps 653–61
income elasticity 654–5
influences on 656–60
market penetration pricing 659
marketing mix strategy 653–61
NTOs and 517–18
policy 368, 660–1, 662
rate of return pricing 658
sensitivity, factors affecting 655–6
skimming pricing 660
Priceline.com 677
pride, local 246
principal stages of tour operating/wholesaling 442–8
    administration 447
    air seats 451–2
    capacity planning 442–5
    cycle of operation 443
    economics 448–53
    financial evaluation 445–6
    leverage 448–9
    marketing 446–7
    pricing 450–1
    research 442
    sales mix 449
    tour management 447–8
product
    attribute approach 587
    augmented 644, 645–6
    brand name 647–53
    core 644
    facilitating 644, 645–6
    family brand performance 652
    four Ps 644–53
    marketing mix strategy 644–53
    orientated company 558, 559
    product brand performance 652
    quality 646–7
    range 647
    service 646
    supporting 644, 645–6
production era 552
product-orientated company 558, 559
promotion
    advertising 665–6
    budget 663–4
    characteristics of promotional techniques 670–1
    communication effects 664–5

development of promotional objectives 662–3
effects of promotion on demand 665
four Ps 661–71
marketing mix strategy 661–71
other promotional activity 670
personal selling 667–8
public relations 669–70
sales promotion 666–7
protectionism 311
psychocentric types
    Plog typology 56–7
    psychological basis of tourism development 231
psychographic positions of destinations 230–1
psychological basis of tourism development 230–1
psychological risk factors 578, 579
public ownership, attractions 364–5
public policy framework 504–8
public provision
    attractions 364–5
    natural attractions 353–5
public relations 669–70
public sector involvement in tourism
    demand and revenue management 514–18
    framework for 504–8
    organisational structure of an NTO 510–12
    policy objectives of NTOs 510–12
    supply and cost management 519–28
purchase effect on price sensitivity 655
purpose of visit 18

quality
    accommodation 402–8
    assurance 582
    audit 583
    benefit/cost 584–8
    control 582
    management strategies 581–93
    tourism product 646–7
quality assurance 582
quality audit 583
quality management 581–93
    consumer-orientated approach 587–8
    cost or benefit 584–8
    key terms 582–4
    product-attribute approach 587

quality management (continued)
quality assurance 582
quality models 588–92
service recovery 586–7
questionnaires
data collection 99, 101
design 102

R

race as determinant of demand
116
railway transport 477–9
range, tourism product 647
rate of return pricing 658
receipts, percentage of export
earnings 156
recession, economic 154
recycling, accommodation sector
409
regional tourism planning 315
regulation of competition for
transport 486–7
relationship marketing
versus transaction marketing
563–4
repatriated income 176
research process
data analysis 103
designing questionnaires 102
methods of data collection
98–103
reporting of research 103–4
research design 98
sampling 102–3
setting objectives 97–8
value of 95–6
reserve army of unemployed 300
residual index of demand 132
resources
carrying capacity and 273–4
human 410, 755–7
man-made 351, 356–7
management 355–6
natural 347–8, 352–6
use factors, negative impact of
239
responsible consumption case
study 37–8
retail travel agents case study
678–80
risk 751–2
cruise ships and 554
economic 578
performance 578, 579
physical 578–9
psychological 578, 579
road transport 475–6
roles
decision-making process 61–4

family influence 62
Rostow: theory of growth and
development 300–1
rural tourism 780

S

Sabre 427, 673
safety 751–2
NTOs and 518
sales
era 552
multiplier 166
promotion 666–7
tour operation mix 449
sample surveys sampling 103
Scandinavian Airline System case
study 589–90
scenario writing 135–6
schedules of demand 41–3
Scotland
Commended Hotels case study
404–5
tourism case study 602–5
Scottish Tourism Co-ordinating
Group 203
Scottish Tourist Board 404
sea transport 479–80
seasonality
attractions 369–70
development planning 312–13
patterns of demand 133–4
security 751–2
NTOs and 518
self-catering accommodation
393–4
self-image, consumers 687
selling, definition 557
September 11, 2001 154, 751
impact on tourism case study
77–80
service
models 588–92
planning service encounters
579–81
product 574–7
recovery strategies 586–7
tourism product 646
sex, socio-cultural impacts
239–40
Shangri-La Hotels 414–18
Shih: VALS lifestyle categories
Show Cause Order 487
Single European Act 506
skimming pricing 660
small and medium-sized tourism
enterprises 214
case study 748–50
industry structure 309–10
Snoasis case study 361–2

social drivers of change 743–4
demographic trends 743
social trends 743–4
social structure, carrying capacity
and 271
socialism 299
societal marketing approach
598–9
socio-cultural awareness, peace
and 246–7
socio-cultural impacts of tourism
approaches to study 226–9
commodification 242, 243
crime 242
cultural experiences 246
demonstration effect 232
direct 232
health 239
host/guest differences 234–5
indirect 233
induced 233
measurement 247–50
nature 226
negative impacts 234–5, 236–46
positive impacts 246–7
psychological basis of tourism
development 230–1
role of socio-cultural
characteristics 234–6
sex 239–40
staged authenticity 242, 243–5
tourism development process
229–36
typology of tourists 227, 228–9
socio-cultural support 247
socio-economic characteristics for
tourism analysis 19–20
sociological basis of tourism
development 231–6
DeKadt 232–4
Doxey 235–6
Inskeep 234
Smith 233
sovereignty, transport and
political influences 486
space tourism case study 781,
786–9
special interest tourism 780–1
sponsorship 670
staged authenticity, socio-cultural
impacts 242, 243–5
stagnation 152
standardisation of socio-cultural
environment 245–6
standards, carrying capacity and
278
statistics
care in use of 94–5
destination surveys 92
en-route surveys 91
household surveys 91
interpretation 95
measurement methods used 88

statistics *(continued)*
  pace of growth (WTO forecasts)
    742
  supplier surveys 94
  value 87
  visitor profile 87, 88
  volume 87
STEP analysis 122–6
  marketing planning process
    626
  market environment 619–20
strategic alliances
  airlines 428, 490
strategic business units (SBUs)
    623–5
strategic information systems (SIS)
    706
strategic positioning
  tour operation/wholesaling
    452–3
Strategic Rail Authority (SRA) 470
structure
  distribution channels 423–7
  intermediaries 423–7
  marketing plan 615–34
  NTOs 510–13
study of tourism 6–7
subsidiarity 506
supply and cost management and
    NTOs 519–28
  building regulations 521
  investment incentives 525–8
  land-use planning and control
    521
  market regulation 522
  market research and planning
    522–3
  ownership 524
  taxation 523–4
supply/demand and investment,
    vicious circles of 301
supporting product 644, 645–6
suppressed demand category 39
surveys, data collection procedures
    98–9, 101
sustainability of tourism 264–84
sustainable development
  accreditation schemes case
    study 283–4
  capital stock 262–3
  definitions 261–3
  historical background 260–1
  networks case study 277–8
  strategy 284–5
sustainable enterprises, future
    destinations 776–7
sustainable tourism
  attractions 371
  carrying capacity 267–70
  concept diagram 371
  definitions 264
  destination 771–2, 776–8
  development 355

economic aspects 264–5
  environmental aspects 265
  products 281–3
  regulation or market solution
    372–4
  resource management 355–6
  socio-cultural aspects 265–7
  Ten 'R's 282–3
  Three 'R's 282
  thresholds 267–70
SWOT Analysis 626
systems orientated company 558,
    561–2

T

Taman Negara National Park
    (Malaysia) case study 238
target markets
  benefits of targeting 643
  definition 643
  marketing mix 643
  segmentation strategies 643–4
taxation
  effects of tourist tax 524
  NTOs 523–4
telephone survey, data collection
    100
terminals as element of
    transportation 470–1
terrorism 154, 518
  impact of, case study 77–80
Thailand travel time case study
    467–9
Thomas Cook case study 424–6
Thomson Open-Line Programme
    721
tiger economies 154
total quality management 581,
    582
  cost/benefit 584–8
total tourist experience 555
tour operating/wholesaling
  administration 447
  air seats 451–2
  brochures 441–2, 446–7
  capacity planning 442–5
  charter flights 444–5
  economics of 448–53
  finance 445–6
  financial structure 448
  information communications
    technology 721
  leverage 448–9
  market strategy 444
  operating cycle 443
  pricing 450–1
  principal stages 442–8
  research process 442
  sales mix 449, 450

strategic planning 452–3
  Thomson Open Line
    Programme 721
  tour management 447–8
Tourism Council for the South
    Pacific 314
tourism demand
  analysis 20–2
  concepts 38–41
  definitions 38
  demand schedules 41–3
  economic factors 124–6
  indicators 41, 46–8
  managing 36
  motivators 56
  patterns 131–4, 139–44
  political factors 126
  social factors 122–4
  technological factors 124
tourism development
  integrated approach 304–14
  planning layers 314–15
  psychological basis of 230–1
  sociological basis of 231–6
Tourism Development
    Corporation 519, 525
Tourism Development Planning
    Process 315–24
  basic development plan 325
  modified basic development
    plan 326
  reasons for failure of 324–8
  socio-cultural impacts 229–36
tourism multiplier concept 163–5
  methodological approaches
    167–74
  types 166–7
Tourism Penetration Index (TPI)
    269
tourism planning
  process 315–24
  reasons for 324–8
  tool kit 286
tourism planning process
  analyses 318–19
  diagram 316
  implementation 318, 321
  monitoring 321
  plan formulation 319–20
  planning team 321–4
  recommendations 320
  setting objectives 316–17
  study recognition and
    preparation 316
  survey existing data 317
tourism product
  accommodation 386–7
  characteristics and development
    planning 307
  composite 311
  markets 779–83
  risk 578–9
  transportation 462–4

tourism satellite accounts 15,
  158–61
tourism system 7–10
  eco-tourism system 11–12
  geographical elements 9
  tourism industry 9
  tourist destination region 9
  tourists 9
  transit route 9
  traveller-generating region 9
tourism trends analysis 740–2
tourism units 269
tourist
  contact index 235–6
  multiplier 164
  typologies 60–1, 227, 228–9
tourist activities, types of
  carrying capacity and 276
tourist attraction, transport as
  464
Tourist Authority of Thailand 214
tourist characteristics, carrying
  capacity and 274–6
tourist-generating countries
  155–6
Tourist–Host Contact Index
  (Doxey) 235–6
Tourist Information Centres 513,
  515, 424
Tourist Information Point 515
tourist project assistance (EU) case
  study 532–41
tourist satisfaction 269
tourist typologies
  socio-cultural impacts 60–1,
    227, 228–9
train
  accommodation 396
  transport 477–9
Train de Grande Vitesse (TGV)
  472
training
  future trends 756–7
  levels of 309
  on-the-job 309
transaction marketing
  vs relationship marketing 563
transaction/sales multiplier 166
transit
  transport as 462–3
  zone, eco-tourism 11
transportation for tourism
  air transport 480–6
  car 475–6
  coach 477
  competitive analysis 475–86
  components 469–75
  environmental policies 491–2
  factors influencing choice 465
  future trend 489–90, 778–9
  globalisation 490–2
  integration 490–2
  modes of 465–9

political influences upon 486
product types 466
railway transport 477–9
regulation of competition for
  486–7
road transport 475–6
sea transport 479–80
the motive power 472–5
the terminal 470–1
the way 469–70
tourism product 462–4
vertical integration 491
travel accounts 84
travel agents
  commission 437, 439
  developments and trends
    affecting 428
  dis-intermediation 427, 429,
    430
  distribution 674–5
  economics of 439–41
  information communications
    technology 723–5
  operating accounts 439, 440
  role of 437–41
  role of brochure 441–2, 446–7
travel propensity 41
Treaty of Rome 487
trip variables for tourism analysis
  20–2
Turkey, earthquake (1999) 322
two-step flow of communication
  666
typology of tourists 60–1, 227,
  228–9

UNSTAT 13
unusual, Smith's classification
  228
urban regeneration case study
  685–6
Uruguay Round of GATT 153–4

value
  concept of 555–7
  pricing and 660–1
variability, service product 575
vehicle, as component of
  transport system 472
vertical integration
  intermediaries 427–8
  transportation 491
vicious circles of demand/supply
  and investment 301
videotext systems 724
virtual reality tourism 781
visitor management
  attractions 370–1
  case study 773–5

Udaipur case study 254–6
unbalanced growth 302
unemployed, reserve army of
  (Marx) 300
unique value effect on price
  sensitivity 655
United Kingdom tourism survey
  92
United Nations Conference on
  the Environment, 1992 196,
  260
United Nations Development
  Programme 212
  code of conduct 213
United Nations Universal
  Declaration of Human
  Rights 36
United States, influence on
  accommodation sector
  400–2
United States Travel and Tourism
  Administration (USTTA) 507

Wales Tourist Board 511–12
waste disposal 409
water use 408
way, the, as element of
  transportation 469–70
weaknesses and limitations of
  multiplier analysis 174–80
  data deficiencies 175–6
  negative economic impacts
    176–7
  restrictive assumptions 174–5
  size of multiplier values
    177–80
wealth distribution case study
  160
wonder attractions 360–1
World Conservation Strategy
  (WCS) 260
World Heritage Sites 279
World Tourism Organization 14,
  36, 62, 314, 504, 508
  climate change 755
  case study 505
  classification
    internal visitors 90
    international visitors 86
  crisis guidelines 752
  on eco-tourism 281
  environmental codes 212, 213

World Tourism Organization
(continued)
estimates 94
forecasts for growth in tourism
742
index of receipts 156
international conference on
travel and tourism statistics
13
levels of tourism marketing 309
principal destinations (receipts)
156
principal generating countries
155
receipts as percentage of export
earnings 158

supply-side definition 15, 16
sustainability accreditation case
study 283–4
on sustainable tourism 264
tourism balance sheet 159
World Trade Organization 153–4
World Travel and Tourism
Council 4, 5, 776
environmental codes 213
new tourism 740–2
security 751–2
tourist industry taxes 523–4
world travel market 512
World Wide Web 704, 713
Worldspan 673

yield management transportation
489
youth accommodation 394–5

zones of tolerance 592–3
zoning, functional 348

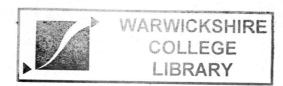